Innovation Masters
History's Best Examples of Business
Transformation

Innovation Masters
History's Best Examples of Business Transformation

GALE
CENGAGE Learning®

Detroit • New York • San Francisco • New Haven, Conn • Waterville, Maine • London

Innovation Masters: History's Best Examples of
Business Transformation

Project Editors: Miranda H. Ferrara, Michele P.
LaMeau

Production Technology Support: Luann Brennan,
Mike Weaver

Production Service: Anaxos, Inc.

Composition: Bookbright Media

Manufacturing: Rita Wimberley

Product Manager: Michele P. LaMeau

Publisher: David Forman

For product information and technology assistance, contact us at
Gale Customer Support, 1-800-877-4253.

For permission to use material from this text or product,
submit all requests online at www.cengage.com/permissions.

Further permissions questions can be emailed to
permissionrequest@cengage.com

Cover Images: Block of Post-it Notes ©Ed Phillips/Shutterstock.com, 2012; Close
Up of a Pacemaker in a Hospital ©Picsfive/Shutterstock.com, 2012; Computer Wafer
©Chang Hui-ju/Shutterstock.com, 2012; Edison Light Bulb with Looping Carbon
Filament ©Allison Achauer/Shutterstock.com, 2012; Set of Touchscreen Smartphones
©Oleksiy Mark/Shutterstock.com, 2012.

While every effort has been made to ensure the reliability of the information
presented in this publication, Gale, Cengage Learning, does not guarantee the accuracy
of the data contained herein. Gale accepts no payment for listing; and inclusion in the
publication of any organization, agency, institution, publication, service, or individual
does not imply endorsement of the editors or publisher. Error brought to the attention
of the publisher and verified to the satisfaction of the publisher will be corrected in
future editions.

EDITORIAL DATA PRIVACY POLICY: Does this product contain information about you
as an individual: If so, for more information about our editorial data privacy policies,
please see our Privacy Statement at www.gale.cengage.com.

LIBRARY OF CONGRESS CATALOGING-IN-PUBLICATION DATA

Innovation masters : history's best examples of business transformation.
  p. cm.
  Includes bibliographical references and index.
  ISBN 978-1-4144-9618-4 (hbk.)
  1. Diffusion of innovations--Case studies. 2. Technological innovations--Case
studies. 3. New products--Case studies. 4. Organizational change--Case studies.
  HC79.T4I5467 2012
  658.4'063--dc23

                                                                    2012005369

Gale
27500 Drake Rd.
Farmington Hills, MI 48331-3535

ISBN 13: 978-1-4144-9618-4
ISBN 10: 1-4144-9618-4

This title is also available as an e-book.
ISBN 13: 978-1-4144-9619-1   ISBN 10: 1-4144-9619-2
Contact your Gale, Cengage Learning, sales representative for ordering information.

Printed in Mexico
1 2 3 4 5 6 7 16 15 14 13 12

Contents

V

Contents

Preface

Business innovation takes many forms. It comes in the form of new products, processes, strategies, technologies and more. When innovations get to market, they can radically change industries in short spans of time, as evidenced by recent phenomena like online shopping and mobile telephony. In many cases, and with enough time to embed themselves in society, innovations can even alter the physical landscape around us (automobiles) or change the course of politics and current events (social media).

In fact, it is probably safe to assume that when Facebook, Twitter and other social media sites were launched, the last thing their founders were thinking of was fomenting peaceful revolution. And yet that is precisely how they were used in the Arab Spring uprisings of 2011.

One might say it is this larger impact that is the hallmark of true innovation. In an article in *The Industrial Physicist*, the director of physical sciences at IBM's T.J. Watson Research Center, Thomas Theis, and Hans J. Coufal, manager of science and technology at IBM's Almadin Research Center, summed it up neatly: "At IBM Research, we define innovation as more than mere discovery and invention. True innovation only occurs when new ideas enter the marketplace and make a difference for society."[1]

That's an amazing statement coming from a physicist. But it is emblematic of the people leading innovation today. Solving the technical problem, coming up with the creative marketing campaign, mapping out the disruptive business strategy—these are all great, but what really counts is bringing these concepts to market. Google's PageRank algorithm—the means whereby it prioritizes search results—would remain a mere invention, intellectually fascinating but ineffectual, without the innovation of the Google search engine itself and its millions of happy users. Success, in short, means impact.

These are the kinds of stories we have sought to capture in this volume. They illustrate innovation across industries, from the automotive assembly line to eBay, and seek to show not just what happened, but why. As such, they serve as useful examples of how to get it right—for students and teachers of business alike at the graduate and undergraduate level, and for advanced high school students.

---

1. Theis, Thomas N. and Hans J. Coufal. "How IBM Sustains the Leading Edge." *The Industrial Physicist*, April/May 2004 p. 18. Accessed February 1, 2012. http://www.aip.org/tip/INPHFA /vol-10/iss-2/p18.pdf.

Each essay is focused on the story of a particular innovation and was chosen for its ability to show, in a different time and context, how innovation takes place. An attempt was made to balance innovation across disciplines and to be as pluralistic as possible. However, these essays tend to focus on the twentieth and twenty-first centuries, if only because that time frame offers so much to work with in this field. And they tend to cluster around technical inventions that were commercialized as innovative products.

What mostly ties these essays together, however, is that each essay shows how an innovation made an impactful difference, disrupting industries, shifting economies, and changing lives. And, not incidentally, making a lot of money along the way. It is our hope that they serve not only to illustrate how innovation takes place, but also to inspire readers to engage in it.

Special thanks go to Product Manager Michele LaMeau for leading this initiative. This book is itself the product of some innovative publishing work, as Michele applied techniques gleaned from our agile software development practice to the production of content, the result being high quality production in record time. Thanks also to Miranda Ferrara, who served as hands-on mentor to Michele, to Mark Springer, Mike Huellmantel, and Keith Jones, who played pivotal roles in making this book a reality, and to numerous others who shared their talents to create this volume. I am grateful to all of them.

David Forman
Vice President and Publisher
Gale, Cengage Learning

SOURCES FOR *INNOVATION MASTERS*

Entries have been compiled from publicly accessible sources both in print and on the Internet. These sources include general and academic periodicals, books, and annual reports as well as company websites and blogs.

FULLY INDEXED

Innovation Masters has been fully indexed to allow researchers to locate innovations by key people, company, industry, and other avenues.

SUGGESTIONS WELCOME

Comments on this title and suggestions on how to make subsequent and similar titles better are always welcome. Please write:

The Editor
Innovation Masters
Gale, Cengage Learning
27500 Drake Road
Farmington Hills, MI 48331-3535

Gale, Cengage Learning, does not endorse any of the companies or products mentioned in this title. Companies, individuals and innovations appearing in *Innovation Masters* were selected without reference to their wishes and have in no way endorsed their entries.

Notes on Contributors

Agata Antonow
Writer and researcher based in Nova Scotia, Canada.

Dale Bowden
Freelance author/essayist, business and entertainment writer.

Lee Gjertsen
Writer and editor based in Cambridge, Massachusetts.

Bobby L. Hickman
Business journalist and technical writer based in Atlanta, Georgia.

Hilary Hylton
Journalist and writer based in Austin, Texas.

Paul Ingati
Business writer and researcher based in Nairobi, Kenya.

Atley Jonas
Canadian business writer and editor currently based in Japan; MBA specialized in global management and communications.

Christine Purfield
Writer and researcher based on Vancouver Island, Canada.

Lee Simmons
Writer and editor based in Austin, Texas.

Kelly Kagamas Tomkies
Writer, editor, and proofreader based in Columbus, Ohio.

3M Post-it Notes

Post-it Notes are the ubiquitous re-adherent pieces of paper found in most office settings. Sticky notes, as they are sometimes known, have a strip of repositionable adhesive in a thin strip on the back. This allows the small pieces of paper to be attached, detached, and reattached to computer screens, papers, and many other surfaces. Post-it Notes are used in a variety of ways, often to add notes and reminders to work surfaces and completed projects.

Originally, Post-it Notes were manufactured by 3M Company (originally known as Minnesota Mining and Manufacturing Company) as three-inch yellow squares. The patent for the notes expired in the 1990s, and in the early 2010s many manufacturers have their own lines of sticky notes, although the Post-it brand of notes is still manufactured by 3M and continues to be one of the most recognized brands of sticky notes. The trademark for the Post-it brand and the trademark for the distinctive yellow color of the original sticky notes is still registered and owned by 3M.

THE THREE MAIN CHARACTERS IN THE POST-IT STORY

Post-it Notes were made possible by the cooperation of two men working in a specific corporate culture. The two men most responsible for the development of the Post-it Note were Spencer Silver and Arthur Fry. Silver studied chemistry at Arizona State University and organic chemistry at the University of Colorado, graduating with a doctorate in 1966. Immediately after graduation, Silver joined a team of five people at 3M who were research-ing pressure-sensitive adhesives. By 2010 he was named on over 20 U.S. patents, although he was best known for developing the adhesive that allowed for the invention of Post-it Notes.

Fry was an inventor as a child growing up in the U.S. Midwest. As a young boy, he used scrap wood to design toboggans. He went on to study chemical engineering at the University of Minnesota, and while pursuing his degree, he joined 3M's new product development team. Fry retired from 3M in the 1990s, decades after inventing the Post-it Note using Silver's adhesive.

3M itself was also a key character in the Post-it Note story. According to Michael Gershman, in his book *Getting It Right the Second Time: How American Ingenuity Transformed Forty-Nine Marketing Failures into Some of Our Most Successful Products,* the company was founded on a failed concept. The original leaders of the company believed they had discovered a source of corundum, a mineral used in abrasives. When the discovery was found to be anorthosite (an igneous rock type) instead, the company decided to create sandpaper out of the find, eventually becoming successful with this venture. 3M also attempted to make a masking tape for the automobile industry. The company failed at this as well, according to Gershman, but instead developed Scotch tape, the best-selling adhesive in the world and, until Post-it Notes were created, 3M's biggest product.

According to Gershman, at the time Fry developed the sticky note, 3M had in place a culture that allowed inventors and workers to "bootleg" funds from one project to another to continue research. The company also actively encouraged idea sharing among departments and employees.

Other structures were in place at 3M to promote innovation and success, and it retained such practices in the 2010s. For example, the company gave the Golden Step award to employees who developed successful products. The company also had what was known as a "dual ladder" system of promotion. Employees were promoted for professional success or for management. Fry, for example, was promoted through this system until he reached the highest status in the technical area of the company: corporate scientist.

THE GLUE THAT LED TO THE STICKY NOTE

The Post-it Note was created almost as a response to a new adhesive. Silver developed a pressure-sensitive and low-track adhesive in 1968 while working for 3M. According to a 2010 *Financial Times* interview with Geoff Nicholson, the retired vice president of technical operations at 3M research and development, Silver's adhesive was in fact a happy accident. Silver had been tasked with making very strong adhesives for the airline industry. Silver said that as an experiment he added more of the chemical reactant that polymerised (joined together) molecules. The result was, in his words, "quite astonishing. Instead of dissolving, the small particles that were produced dispersed in solvents." Silver and his team were intrigued by this new reaction and decided to experiment further. His experiments eventually resulted in what Silver called a "high 'tack' but low 'peel'" adhesive that was also reusable.

In other words, while attempting to create a very strong adhesive Silver created one that was merely sticky. Indeed, according to William Lidwell and Gerry Manacsa, in their book *Deconstructing Product Design: Exploring the Form, Function, Usability, Sustainability, and Commercial Success of 100 Amazing Products,* Silver's initial discovery would have been considered a failure at the time, since adhesives were measured by their bonding strength.

The new adhesive was made from very sturdy but tiny acrylic spheres. The unique thing about them was that they would stick not only when they were flat up against a surface, the way other adhesives did, but also would stick when they were tangent to a surface. This meant that the adhesive was strong enough to bind papers to a surface but would allow the paper to be removed from the surface without tearing the paper. The adhesive could also be reused repeatedly.

Silver saw the potential of the idea but had trouble devising a profitable product from his invention. Initially, he considered selling the adhesive as a spray-on adhesive or as a surface on boards for posting and removing notices. In fact, one of the earliest uses of the adhesive was at 3M, where a bulletin board was covered with the adhesive so that notices could be posted and then removed easily.

THE POST-IT NOTE

For years, Silver gave seminars about his invention at 3M and tried to get others interested in the new adhesive by speaking about it at the company. In 1974 his colleague Art Fry attended one of his seminars. Fry told the *Financial Times* in 2010 that he heard about Silver's seminars during a golf game and decided to attend. At the time, Fry worked at the 3M tape division laboratory, where his job was to find new products and create businesses using those products.

Fry did not immediately think of a way to use Silver's adhesive. However, a practical use for the product soon presented itself. As a member of the church choir at St. Paul's North Presbyterian Church, Fry needed a way to mark pages in his hymn book without having bookmarks fall out. In June 1974 he realized he had a use for Silver's adhesive.

Fry got a sample of the adhesive from Silver to create a sticky bookmark for his hymn book. After trying it out, Fry noticed that the adhesive left some residue on the book's pages but otherwise solved his problem. Fry experimented until he developed a way of making the adhesive less sticky on the pages. He then developed some more sticky bookmarks.

Fry also created a report and placed one of his bookmarks on the front of the report with a question for his supervisor. The supervisor wrote a reply on the same sticky note and repositioned it on the front of the report. As Fry said in his *Financial Times* interview, "It was a eureka, head-flapping moment—I can still feel the excitement. I had my product: a sticky note."

Fry developed a proposal for his supervisors, who included Bob Malinda, product manager for the commercial tape division at 3M. He also began giving out samples of his new idea to colleagues at 3M. Supervisors at 3M were initially unsure about the effectiveness of the product, but when they saw the enthusiastic response, they gave Fry permission, a laboratory to develop his product, and the machines that would be needed to produce the sticky notes.

THE DEVELOPMENT OF STICKY NOTES

The original Post-it Notes were in their distinctive canary yellow because of another happy accident. While Fry and his team were experimenting with the adhesive, they needed some scrap paper to experiment with. According to the *Financial Times* interview with Nicholson, the team went to another 3M lab on the same floor and were given some scrap paper that happened to be yellow. Nicholson called it "another one of those incredible accidents," much like the invention of the adhesive itself.

According to Gershman, Fry ran into a few problems initially. One was that marketing professionals at 3M were not sure how to market his idea. Second, while Malinda was supportive of his idea, others were not as enthusiastic. As Gershman wrote, at 3M "No one said 'No'. . .but then, no one said 'Yes' either." Fry also had another, logistical, problem. For more than seven decades 3M had been selling its most successful adhesive products in the form of rolls. The company therefore had experience with adhesives on cellophane rather than paper. All the machinery was designed to create adhesives on rolls, whereas Fry imagined a pad of sticky notes.

Fry created the prototypes for what would become Post-it Notes in his basement. After months of work, he succeeded in creating a machine that could create the sticky note pads he envisioned. Malinda and Nicholson, as well as other 3M personnel, visited the house to observe the progress. They were impressed with the machine and wanted it moved to the 3M building, but the machine was so large that the company had to send construction workers to Fry's house to dismantle a wall, move the machine, and then repair the wall.

EARLY MARKETING EFFORTS

Fry initially called his sticky notes "Press 'n Peel" notes, and his first attempt at marketing was to hand out free samples of the notes to 3M employees. He kept track of who received samples and how long it took each person to request refills. Nicholson also handed out free samples to 3M employees and realized that people were visiting his office very frequently for refills. The success of the notes within the company led 3M to try to take the sticky notes to market.

In 1977 3M launched the sticky notes under the name "Press 'n Peel" in Denver, Colorado; Tampa, Florida; Tulsa, Oklahoma; and Richmond, Virginia, as part of a small-scale marketing effort. Before the test, 3M handed out samples of the products in standard sizes and in 8 1/2-by-11 inch format to retailers in the four cities. The company also ran advertisements in local trade magazines. In addition, 3M sent product samples and descriptive brochures to companies in the test cities.

The product did not elicit much interest from consumers, and the limited test launch was considered a failure at 3M. According to Gershman, the marketing test in the four cities was a "cool disaster." Response was lukewarm in Tulsa, Oklahoma and Denver, Colorado. In Richmond and Tampa, no one was interested in the new product.

Joe Ramey, the new general manager of the 3M division responsible for the product, traveled to Richmond, Virginia with Nicholson to find out why the test had not been a success. Nicholson and Ramey made cold calls in the test cities and even visited businesses in Richmond to find out what had gone wrong. They determined that no one knew how to use the new products. Nicholson

and Ramey gave personal demonstrations and found that they placed orders each time they did so. Ramey concluded that the communications package for the marketing test had not been enough. Although the concept seemed simple, and although 3M promoted the notes with the slogan "Press it on, peel it off" to help customers along, it was not enough without samples and demonstrations.

POST-IT SUCCESS AT LAST

The sticky notes were withdrawn from the test markets, and 3M launched another attempt. New merchandising materials were created and the company decided to try again with a seeding trial. The company sent free samples to CEOs across the country, asking the CEOs for input as to how the sticky notes could be used. According to Paul Marsden, in his essay "Seed to Spread: How Seeding Trials Ignite Epidemics of Demand," this was the turning point for the new product, as the seeding trial "generated goodwill and advocacy" from the CEOs, who were flattered to be included in the trial.

In 1978 3M also handed out free samples of the notes in Boise, Idaho, purchased eight advertisements in the *Boise Statesman*, and used promotional pricing, ceiling displays, counter displays, and window displays to promote the sticky notes. The company also hired temporary staff to visit companies in Boise to hand out free samples of the notes and to demonstrate their use. The Boise campaign was a success. Ninety-five percent of those who tried the free Post-it Notes in that city said that they liked the product and would buy it.

POST-IT NOTES EVERYWHERE

In 1980 3M launched the product, under the name Post-it Notes, across the United States. By 1981 Post-it Notes were being sold in Europe and Canada. They were 3M's most successful product by 1984. According to Anthony Rubino, Jr., in *Why Didn't I Think of That?: 101 Inventions That Changed the World by Hardly Trying*, Post-it Notes generated US$15 billion in sales for 3M by the 1990s and by 2010, the company had sold more than a trillion Post-it Notes. In 1995 3M was the recipient of the National Medal of Technology, in part because of the Post-it Note. The notes have been displayed in museums and have been recognized by historians as one of the most important office inventions since the paperclip. By 2009 Post-it Notes were generating US$1 billion in annual sales.

Post-it Notes have become a constant presence in homes, workplaces, and just about any setting where temporary notes, comments, or reminders need to be posted. The notes have also developed some unique uses. Artists routinely use them to develop Post-it Note art works, for example in 2000 designer Ilze Vitolina created 11 dress designs using Post-it Notes.

According to the 3M website, the Post-it brand had more than 4,000 different products as of 2011. Post-it flags, developed in 1987, are used for tagging places in books. In 1991 3M released pop-up Post-it Notes, which came in an easy-to-use dispenser. In 1994 3M released a Post-it easel pad, with adhesive-backed sheets that could stick to most walls. In 2003 Post-it Super Sticky notes were released, with a stronger adhesive that could stick to surfaces that normal sticky notes would not adhere to. In 2009 the company released a line of Post-it brand removable labels and Post-it Notes made from recycled paper. That same year, 3M launched Post-it Flag Highlighters, with a traditional highlighter tip, and Post-it book flags located near the top of the pen. Oprah Winfrey featured the pens on her talk show, creating an interest that paved the way for 3M to market ballpoints, permanent markers, gel pens, and combination pens and highlighters with the flags.

Post-it Sticky Boards were also invented by 3M. Post-it Sticky Boards are covered with the famous adhesive, so that notes can be attached and moved around on a board surface. Repositionable Post-it craft paper with an adhesive back is also available from the company, as well as Post-it Clear Pockets, which are were plastic pockets with an adhesive back.

Post-it Notes became available in electronic form. Microsoft's Windows 7 has a sticky note application that allows computer users to post an electronic version of the Post-it Note on their computer desktop. Post-it also has its own version of Digital Notes, which allows users to download the application to apply digital sticky notes to their desktop background. The Digital Notes, which are downloadable from the 3M website, include photo clipping and web-tagging options.

EVALUATING THE POST-IT NOTE

The Post-it Note story shows that a series of early failures does not necessarily preclude long-term success. Post-it Notes failed in some way at almost every step of their existence. Silver developed an adhesive that was the very opposite of the super adhesive he was trying to achieve. He then had trouble finding an application for his invention.

When the first sticky notes were developed by 3M, early marketing tests were not successful. Despite these failures, however, Post-it Notes became one of the most popular office products in the world.

BIBLIOGRAPHY

"Art Fry & Spencer Silver." Cambridge, MA: Massachusetts Institute of Technology, School of Engineering, 2011. Accessed December 6, 2011. http://web.mit.edu/invent/iow /frysilver.html.

Block, Ben. "Post-It Notes." *World Watch* 22, no. 5 (2009).

Fry, Art, Spencer Silver, and Sarah Duguid. "First Person: 'We Invented the Post-it Note.'" *Financial Times,* December 3, 2010. Accessed December 6, 2011. http://www.ft.com/cms /s/2/f08e8a9a-fcd7-11df-ae2d-00144feab49a.html#axzz18 hyDnyKX.

Gershman, Michael. *Getting It Right the Second Time: How American Ingenuity Transformed Forty-Nine Marketing Failures into Some of Our Most Successful Products.* Reading, MA: Addison Wesley, 1990.

Higgins, James M. "Innovate or Evaporate: Seven Secrets of Innovative Corporations." *The Futurist* 29, no. 5 (1995).

Kirby, Justin, and Paul Marsden, eds. *Connected Marketing: The Viral, Buzz and Word of Mouth Revolution.* Oxford, England: Butterworth-Heinemann, 2006.

Lidwell, William, and Gerry Manacsa. *Deconstructing Product Design: Exploring the Form, Function, Usability, Sustainability, and Commercial Success of 100 Amazing Products.* Minneapolis, MN: Rockport Publishers, 2009.

Marsden, Paul. "Seed to Spread: How Seeding Trials Ignite Epidemics of Demand." In *Connected Marketing: The Viral, Buzz and Word of Mouth Revolution,* edited by Justin Kirby and Paul Marsden. Oxford, England: Butterworth-Heinemann, 2006.

Obendorf, Hartmut. *Minimalism: Designing Simplicity.* London: Springer-Verlag, 2009.

Post-it. "About Post-it Brand." Maplewood, MN, 2011. Accessed December 6, 2011. http://www.post-it.com/wps/portal/3M /en_US/Post_It/Global/About/.

Rubino, Anthony, Jr. *Why Didn't I Think of That?: 101 Inventions That Changed the World by Hardly Trying.* Avon, MA: Adams Media, 2010.

"Sticking Around—the Post-it Note Is 20." *BBC News,* April 6, 2011. Accessed December 6, 2011. http://news.bbc.co.uk/2 /hi/uk_news/701661.stm.

Zambonini, Dan. "Why Are Post-it Notes Yellow?" *The Januarist,* February 25, 2010. Accessed December 6, 2011. http://www .thejanuarist.com/why-are-post-it-notes-yellow/.

3M's Use of Genesis Grants Encourages Innovation

Founded in 1902 as Minnesota Mining and Manufacturing, the 3M Company evolved from an unsuccessful mining enterprise to a producer of sandpaper and then to a global corporate enterprise with operations in over 65 countries, 80,000 employees, and worldwide sales in 2011 of US$29.6 billion. Some of the company's products and innovations are well known, such as Scotch tape, Post-It Notes, and scouring pads, but many are not. A September 2010 *CNNMoney* report by Marc Gunther noted that many of 3M's 55,000 products are embedded in items used around the home, in the car, in hospitals, factories, and offices. Gunther's interview subject, George Buckley, chairman and CEO of 3M, commented that his iPhone contained "lots of" 3M products.

In 2011 Thomson Reuters, a global business information service provider, named the 3M company as one of the year's "Top 100 Global Innovators." One of the reasons for its success, suggested Gunther, is the company's use of "a range of practices to promote out-of-the-box thinking." One such practice allows researchers to devote 15 percent of their time to pursue their own ideas. Another, wrote Michael Arndt in a May 2006 *Bloomberg Businessweek* article, is the formation of the Technical Forum. Established by the company's scientists in 1951, it invites all research and development scientists to an annual symposium to showcase projects on which everyone is working.

However, the empowering of creative ideas and encouraging collaboration are only one part of the process. Without funding, many ideas would not develop into profitable innovations. Recognizing that group or department managers, focused on core products and maintaining budgets, are not always receptive to financing the exploration or development of new ideas, 3M established an alternate source of internal seed or venture capital in 1984. A Genesis Grant is available to scientists on application and approval, and the company estimated that ideas funded by the program contributed over US$1 billion in annual sales.

THE GENESIS GRANT

Chris Holmes, vice president of 3M's abrasives division, suggested in Gunther's article that a Genesis Grant was a source of funds for projects for which "no sensible, conventional person in the company would give money." 3M, in its 2002 publication "A Century of Innovation," quoted Joe Abere, the corporate scientist who spearheaded the program, as saying that "Genesis is all about optimizing the innovative spirit at 3M."

A paper in May 2002, prepared for a Master of Business Administration (MBA) class discussion by Professor Vijay Govindarajan at Tuck School of Business at Dartmouth, described the application process. A corporate scientist would submit an application for funding under the program after all other avenues for normal budgetary funding had been exhausted. First, the employee should have approached their own group or division manager with the idea to seek funding approval. If deemed not appropriate for this group's area of specialization, then the employee could present the idea to any other group or division manager within the 3M global organization. If funding was not supported from within the traditional group or divisional budgets, an application could then be submitted to the Genesis Grant program.

A special report titled "The World's Most Innovative Companies," in *Bloomberg Businessweek* in April 2006, noted that awards were made annually by a panel of 20 senior scientists at 3M, and requests could be from US\$50,000 up to US\$100,000. The money could be used to conduct independent research, product development, or test marketing in any area of emerging technology. Approximately 15 to 20 grants were awarded each year. According to a report by the tax and advisory firm, Ernst & Young, the approving group specifically looked for creative ideas that might lead to a competitive advantage, particularly in areas where some experimental research had already been done.

GENESIS RESULTS

3M's publication, "A Century of Innovation," listed a few of the many successful innovations as a result of the Genesis Grant program, such as multilayer optical film, Trizact abrasives, and the Scotch Tape Pop-Up Dispenser, as well as the two first international 3M companies to receive Genesis Grants, 3M Canada and 3M Italy, for different innovations. The report detailed how in the 1990s, a team of 3M corporate scientists developed a new technology platform based on multilayer film. Research into multilayer film had begun at 3M in the 1970s when a division of 3M, the Central Research Process Technology Laboratory (CRPTL), explored the possibility of using a multilayer film as an inexpensive backing on tapes. Later, scientists found multilayer film was also useful in products that needed a resistance to punctures or tears, such as safety films for window glass.

Andy Ouderkirk and Jim Jonza, researchers at 3M, attended one of the company's technical forums and discussed with each other the possibility of the "flashlamp" treatment of film in order to prepare it for adhesion by applying a sudden burst of energy to the film surface. Ouderkirk had been experimenting with the technology and speculated that "if you could put together layer after layer of film, you could make a very interesting reflective polarizer." Jonza, a researcher in the Safety and Security Systems Division of 3M, quickly responded, "We can do that."

The two researchers joined forces with Mike Weber, a senior specialist in specialty materials at 3M, and applied for a Genesis Grant to continue the research further. The trio received two Genesis Grants to fund additional research and develop pilot projects. In the early 2010s the multilayer film technology was prevalent in computer technology, window reflector material, light piping products, and for reflective liners in light fixtures and signs. Scientists at 3M registered a number of patents to protect the company's investment in the technology, and 3M anticipated a continued significant return on investment from the product's commercialization.

In the 1980s two corporate scientists collaborated on a Genesis Grant application to research ways to link microreplication to abrasives. Microreplication was a manufacturing technology that applied precise, microscopic, three-dimensional patterns on various surfaces and was originally perfected by 3M for use in overhead projectors, traffic lights, and in making directional signs more visible, night or day. The initial research came as the result of an idea of a 3M scientist to increase the fuel efficiency of aircraft by sanding grooves into the wings. The Genesis Grants program created funds for personnel and equipment to develop a prototype, which they perfected on polishing golf clubs. The final product, the subject of a number of registered patents, was named Trizact Abrasives and was used in numerous applications including semiconductor wafer polishing. According to 3M, as the semiconductor industry looked to making wafers that could carry an increasing amount of information, Trizact Abrasives, along with subsequent innovations and products by 3M, could help reduce the number of steps and cost in the process.

In keeping with the approving panel's interest in considering innovative ideas where some research was already completed, the Scotch Pop-Up Dispenser would seem to be a natural candidate. However, the 3M report detailed how initially the idea met with resistance within the company. Scotch tape, the clear adhesive tape introduced in the 1960s, was considered "the crown jewel" of the company, said Casey Carlson, the 3M industrial designer who wanted to develop the dispenser. Its "legacy was so strong that it almost prevented innovation," according to Carlson.

However, Carlson was approved for a Genesis Grant and worked with his colleagues to develop a line of desktop and wristband dispensers that provided pre-cut, two-inch pieces of Scotch brand tape. The innovation was rewarded with awards both inside and outside the company, including being selected as a "Good Buy" winner by the magazine *Good Housekeeping* in 1997. The magazine described the dispenser as a "better than ever version of products we already loved."

Carlson also explained in the report that the dispenser opened the way for a new delivery system for various 3M products such as Post-It Notes and other stationary and office supply lines. Without the Genesis Grant, it was unlikely that the product would have received support from within the traditional group or divisional budgets.

GENESIS ABROAD

Noting that the United States accounted for less than 5 percent of the world's population at the dawn of the year 2000, 3M offered the Genesis Grant program to anyone working in any 3M group or division in the world to encourage and support entrepreneurial product development.

In the early 1980s 3M Canada registered a trademark for a product called Gen III. A Genesis Grant had been received by scientists in the company to research and develop a bone growth stimulator program that delivered an electric current across fractured bones to promote healing. In Italy's 3M Ferrania research laboratory, scientists received a Genesis Grant to work on an X-ray dosimeter program that measured radiation.

A TOLERANCE FOR TINKERERS

Gordon Engdahl, a retired human resources executive at 3M, was quoted in the firm's centennial publication as saying that part of 3M's innovative success was due to the fact that the company had "a tolerance for tinkerers." Vijay Govindarajan, in his July 2011 article in the *Harvard Business Review Blog Network* listed a "willingness to take risk and see the value in absurdity" as one of "Innovation's Nine Critical Success Factors." He quoted Albert Einstein, who once said, "If at first an idea doesn't seem totally absurd there's no hope for it."

In an April 2011 recorded webinar, the Conference Board of Canada, an independent not-for-profit research company, explained how the technological giant Google Inc. allowed or even encouraged all its employees to use 20 percent of their paid work time to pursue innovative ideas of their choosing. While 3M had a similar policy that allowed employees to use up to 15 percent of their paid work time to develop percolating ideas, it was the awarding of the Genesis Grant that illustrated the company's continued recognition and financial support of new ideas.

BIBLIOGRAPHY

3M Company. "3M Facts." St. Paul, MN, 2011. Accessed January 3, 2012. http://solutions.3m.com/wps/portal/3M /en_US/WW2/Country/Corp/Contact3M.

———. "A Century of Innovation." St Paul, MN, 2002. Accessed January 3, 2012. http://solutions.3m.com/wps/portal/3M /en_WW/History/3M/Company/century-innovation.

Arndt, Michael. "3M's Seven Pillars of Innovation." *Bloomberg Businessweek,* May 10, 2006. Accessed January 3, 2012. http://www.businessweek.com/innovate/content/may2006 /id20060510_682823.htm.

Conference Board of Canada. "Google's Innovative Approach to Innovation." April 2011. Recorded webinar. Accessed January 5, 2012. http://www.conferenceboard.ca/documents.aspx?did =4106.

Ernst & Young. "Igniting Innovation: How Hot Companies Fuel Growth from Within." London, UK, 2011. Accessed January 5, 2012. http://www.ey.com/GL/en/Services/Strategic -Growth-Markets/Igniting-innovation--how-hot-companies -fuel-growth-from-within---Set-up-a-formal-structure-for -intrapreneurship.

Garud, Raghu, Joel Gehman, and Arun Kumaraswamy. "Complexity Arrangements for Sustained Innovation: Lessons from 3M Corporation." *Organization Studies* 32, no. 6 (June 2011): 737–767.

Govindarajan, Vijay. "Innovation's Nine Critical Success Factors." *Harvard Business Review Blog Network,* July 5, 2011. Accessed January 5, 2012. http://blogs.hbr.org/govindarajan/2011/07 /innovations-9-critical-success.html.

Govindarajan, Vijay, and Julie B. Lang. "3M Corporation." Hanover, NH: Tuck School of Business, Dartmouth College, May 20, 2002. Accessed January 3, 2012. mba.tuck.dart mouth.edu/pdf/2002-2-0002.pdf.

Gunther, Marc. "3M's Innovation Revival." *CNNMoney,* September 24, 2010. Accessed January 3, 2012. http://money .cnn.com/2010/09/23/news/companies/3m_innovation _revival.fortune/index.htm.

Scanlon, Jessie. "How 3M Encourages Collaboration." *Bloomberg Businessweek,* September 2, 2009. Accessed January 3, 2012. www.businessweek.com/innovate/content/sep2009/id2009 092_680626.htm.

"Top 100 Global Innovators." *Thomson Reuters,* 2011. Accessed January 3, 2012. http://www.top100innovators.com/top100.

"The World's Most Innovative Companies." *Bloomberg Businessweek,* April 24, 2006. Accessed January 4, 2012. http://www.businessweek.com/magazine/content/06_17/b39 81401.htm.

Amazon Kindle:
Evolution of an E-book Reader

THE FIRST GENERATION

At a conference in 2004 online retailer and bookseller Amazon.com, Inc. CEO Jeff Bezos saw for the first time Sony Corporation's electronic book (e-book) reader LIBRIé. According to *Fast Company* blogger Adrian Slywotzky, in a 2011 article titled "The Real Secret of Kindle's Success," Bezos's immediate response was to realize, "This is a machine that could destroy my business." Bezos bought 30 of the devices and took them back to his staff at Amazon.com headquarters in Seattle, Washington. Subsequently, a development effort to create a similar device was started by Amazon.com at a facility called "Lab 126" in Silicon Valley, California's technology epicenter.

Just in time for Christmas 2007, Amazon.com launched its own device, a mobile wireless e-book reader named Kindle. Priced at US$399, the Kindle raised a few eyebrows with the high price, but there were compensations for the buyer. Kindle took advantage of a revolutionary new display technology described as electronic paper pared with E Ink font technology; together, they provided a clear, non-glare reading experience over its six-inch diagonal screen. Improvements over Sony's LIBRIé included a wireless connection, which was a big improvement in convenience over the USB-supported LIBRIé. Initially the Kindle was only available to U.S. buyers, due to the need to access Amazon.com's wireless delivery system, Whispernet, which would then automatically deliver purchased content to an individual device.

Amazon.com worked hard with publishers, with whom it already had extensive connections, so that buyers of the first edition of Kindle were able to choose from a library of over 88,000 book titles, as well as a number of newspapers, magazines, and blog content available by subscription service. This variety was also a major improvement over Sony's LIBRIé, which only had a fourth as many titles available at its launch three years earlier. Recent best-selling books were available on the Kindle for a fee of US$10.99, and users were typically allowed to read the first chapter of a book free before deciding to purchase. Older titles, such as classics, were available for a much smaller fee or occasionally even offered by Amazon.com for free. With its 250 megabytes of memory, the Kindle could hold approximately 200 unillustrated book titles. This first-generation device also featured an upgradable memory card for additional capacity. The Kindle was not simply just an e-book reader either. Users were able to venture out on to the Internet to view content or follow links from blogs.

Amazon.com immediately took advantage of its already large customer account system, which allowed any registered user to purchase a book with just one click. Within a little over five hours of the launch, the initial production run of the Kindle devices were sold out. Soon, shoppers at Sony's bookselling site Connect were far and few between, as Kindle sales outstripped LIBRIé three to one. The Kindle allowed Amazon.com to beat Sony at its own game: electronic device development and sales.

Not everyone was convinced, however. Well-known author Annie Proulx was quoted by Steven Levy in a 2007 *Newsweek* article as saying, "Nobody is going to sit down and read a novel on a twitchy little screen, ever." Even Jeff Bezos had his doubts and was quoted in the same article saying, in reference to the experience of reading a traditional book, "I love the smell of glue and ink. . .[because] I associate that smell with all the world I have been transported to." Another factor mentioned in the article was the lack of ability to resell a book once read, or to give it to a friend, things often cited as key advantages of conventional print books.

VERSION TWO

Hoping to keep the momentum won by the original Kindle, Amazon.com introduced an upgraded version, Kindle 2, only 15 months after the original, in February 2009. Kindle 2 included a number of updated features. While it dropped the bulky upgradable memory feature, allowing for a thinner device overall, the new Kindle was nonetheless able to store up to 1,500 titles, several times the original Kindle's capacity. Kindle 2 also featured a text-to-speech option that allowed access to content by the visually impaired, or those simply wishing to listen to a book rather than read it. In addition, Amazon.com reduced the price of the new version from US$359 to US$299, and then to US$259.

In October 2009 Amazon.com released a new international version of the Kindle 2. This undated model utilized an international web protocol called GSM, bringing downloadable service from Amazon.com to over 100 countries. In October 2010, locked in a competitive struggle with other debuting e-book devices, most notably the Barnes & Noble Inc. device Nook, Amazon.com lowered the Kindle's price to US$189. On Christmas day 2009, one-day e-book sales at Amazon.com exceeded print book sales for the first time ever.

VERSION THREE

In July 2010 Amazon.com launched the third version of the popular e-book reader. This version included a keyboard, was available in two colors, and featured an updated version of its display technology called E Ink Pearl, a higher resolution visual experience. Kindle 3 also allowed users the first opportunity to organize their purchases in folders, sorted by categories such as genre or author name. Price of the device continued to fall, with the most basic Kindle at just US$99 in 2011. The Kindle was now the e-book market leader, achieving an estimated 48 percent of worldwide e-book reader sales of 12.8 million units in 2010.

The era of the third-generation Kindle also witnessed a milestone in book sales. In July 2011 Amazon.com announced its e-book sales exceeded print book sales for the first half of the year. By then Amazon.com was making available over 765,000 different book titles for download. In December 2011 Amazon.com announced sales figures for the Kindle for the first time. Over one million of the devices were sold in each week during the peak Christmas season of December.

VERSION FOUR

Maintaining its rapid pace of upgrading the market-leading device, Amazon.com introduced the fourth version of the Kindle in September 2011. This version was split between three devices: a low-priced, advertising-supported version at US$79, or an advertising-free version of the same device at US$109; a touch screen version, called Kindle Touch, offering pricing variations from US$99 to a 3G device at US$189; and the new Kindle Fire. With the exception of the infrared touch screen and migration of the interface to only five keys instead of the full keyboard offered on Version 3, the fourth-generation version of the two lower-priced versions maintained very similar features to the Kindle 3, and was more of an upgrade to the existing model than a completely new version.

Kindle Fire, on the other hand, was an attempt to cross over into the tablet computer field, an all-new arena for Amazon.com electronic products. Utilizing Android, the operating system supported and backed by Google, Kindle Fire included a color touch screen, a larger seven-inch screen, eight gigabytes of memory, and an approximately eight-hour battery life. Once again Amazon.com timed the launch of the device just in time for the 2011 Christmas season and announced it expected to sell six million Fires by the end of the year.

THE APPLICATION MARKET

With e-books becoming a strong sales category for Amazon.com, the company decided in late 2009 to address the use of the Whispernet technology by other platforms. In late 2009 Amazon.com offered a Kindle for PC application, a free upload that allowed use of the e-reader technology and book-buying capability on conventional Windows-based home computers. Amazon.com followed up with a Macintosh-based version of the PC application a few months later. Over the course of 2010 and into 2011 Amazon.com offered other versions of the application for use on the iPad, the iPhone and various other cellphones, and a version for the Hewlett-Packard TouchPad.

THE NEXT VERSION OF KINDLE

The next steps for the Kindle during the 2010s were possibly hinted at by the domain registration names Amazon.com took out for the device. Besides the Kindle Fire, Amazon.com optioned the use of a number of names that included the Kindle brand, such as Kindle Air, Kindle Wave, and Kindle Scribe. Kindle Air suggested a lighter and thinner version of the current product. Kindle Wave might eventually evolve into a 4G version of the tablet device Kindle Fire. Kindle Scribe aroused speculation, in a 2011 article by *TIME* technology correspondent Jared Newman, that it might be a touch screen device that included a stylus, similar to Barnes & Noble's Nook. Such a device would allow users to write notes in the margins of a book without defacing and devaluing it, such as would occur with a printed book.

SUCCESS OF THE KINDLE

A number of analysts offered their opinions about why the Kindle has been such a successful product. Slywotzky, in *Fast Company*, attributed the popularity of the Kindle to a number of factors, including the successful employment of the E Ink technology, which made the e-reader not only easy to read but scalable, a key advantage for older users who might require larger type. Another factor was the device's ease of use and ordering capability. Amazon.com leveraged its powerful and popular website to make ordering content a one-step operation for already registered users. Significant in its success must also be the excellent support Amazon.com gave to the device by making so many more books available than any of its competition initially.

Analyst Florence Pichon of Editorsweblog.org, in her article "Kindle: Opportunities for Independent Publishers, Journalists, and Spammers Alike," cited the flexibility and new opportunities the device introduced, both to traditional publishing and independent authors. Amazon .com opened up the Kindle to the sale of original material by authors through the use of a self-publishing system. Authors could sell their material for as little as US$0.99, and some authors already sold as many as one million copies of their original work. Michael Angier of Success. net, in his 2011 article, "One of the Biggest Publishing Milestones since Gutenberg Invented the Printing Press," optimistically maintained that "Hundreds of thousands of people will become millionaires as a result of this technology and the publishing tsunami it's creating." Traditional media, such as *Propublica*, used the device as an avenue for selling timely news as well as selling stories and research considered too long for a traditional magazine article and too short for a long-form book.

Bezos has spoken about the success of the company and the Kindle in particular. He maintained in a *Newsweek* 2009 interview with Daniel Lyons titled "The Customer Is Always Right," that the company's customer-oriented process, which he characterized as "We start with the customer and we work backward," was most evident in the development of the Kindle. He also maintained that Amazon.com was willing to think and develop for the long term, something which was increasingly rare in the modern business environment. Bezos stated, "Kindle is a great example of that. It's been on the market for two years, but we worked on it for three years in earnest before that."

Amazon.com, Bezos maintained, noticed something that even technological guru Steve Jobs missed, when he predicted the Kindle would fail because people do not read anymore. For people who did read, reading was important to them, and electronic devices, while very useful for short-form reading such as e-mails, were not useful for long-form reading. Amazon.com's Kindle changed that and brought wireless technology to the long-form market.

Chief analyst of MobileTrax, J. Gerry Purdy, succinctly summed up the success of the Kindle when he reviewed the new Kindle Fire in October 2011. In an article titled, "Why Amazon Is So Successful with Kindle," Purdy stated: "These are good times for Amazon. As they continue to focus on providing excellent content, watch their sales continue to rise. This is a lesson for other tablet manufacturers: It's the content and services that win customers—not the hardware."

BIBLIOGRAPHY

Amazon.com, Inc. "Frequently Asked Questions about Kindle." Seattle, WA, 2012. Accessed February 9, 2012. http://www .amazon.com/gp/help/customer/display.html?nodeId =200127470#FAQs.

"Amazon Kindle's Timeline So Far." *Geekapolis*, September 29, 2011. Accessed February 3, 2012. http://geekapolis.fooyoh .com/geekapolis_gadgets_wishlist/6577509.

Angier, Michael. "One of the Biggest Publishing Milestones since Gutenberg Invented the Printing Press." *Success.net*, December 13, 2011. Accessed February 3, 2012. http:// successnet.org/blog/?p=460.

Levy, Steve. "The Future of Reading." *Newsweek*, November 7, 2011. Accessed February 3, 2012. http://www.thedailybeast .com/newsweek/2007/11/17/the-future-of-reading.html.

Lyons, Daniel. "The Customer Is Always Right." *Newsweek*, December 20, 2009. Accessed February 9, 2012. http://www .thedailybeast.com/newsweek/2009/12/20/the-customer-is -always-right.html.

McGlaun, Shane. "Report: Slew of Domain Name Registrations Hint Next Line Will Be Named After Elements." *Slash Gear*, August 25, 2011. Accessed February 3, 2012. http://www .slashgear.com/slew-of-domain-name-registrations-hint-next -kindle-line-will-be-named-after-elements-25174137/

Newman, Jared. "Report: 'Kindle Scribe' Could Be Amazon's Next E-reader." *TIME*, August 22, 2011. Accessed February 8, 2012. http://techland.time.com/2011/08/22/rumor-kindle -scribe-amazons-next-e-reader/.

Perenson, Melissa J. "Amazon Kindle Book Sales Soar." *PC World*, January 27, 2011. Accessed February 8, 2012. http:// www.pcworld.com/article/218039/amazon_kindle_book _sales_soar.html.

Pinchon, Florence. "Kindle: Opportunities for Independent Publishers, Journalists, and Spammers Alike." *Editorsweblog .org*, June 21, 2011. Accessed February 3, 2012. http://www .editorsweblog.org/multimedia/2011/06/kindle_opportunity _for_independent_publi.php.

Purdy, J. Gerry. "Why Amazon Is So Successful with Kindle." Wellington, FL: MobileTrax, October 19, 2011. Accessed February 3, 2012. http://www.mobiletrax.com/Newsletters /tabid/115/EntryId/130/Why-Amazon-is-so-Successful-with -Kindle.aspx.

Slywotzky, Adrian. "The Real Secret of Kindle's Success." *Fast Company*, September 26, 2011. Accessed February 3, 2012. http://www.fastcompany.com/1781303/kindles-success-a-look-behind-the-screen.

Analog Devices, Inc., and MEMS Sensors Research and Development

Microelectromechanical systems (MEMS) sensors are sensors that use tiny devices (from one micrometer to one millimeter in size) and electricity that are manufactured onto a semiconductor material. Many MEMS sensors are made from silicon. MEMS devices, including MEMS sensors, are often seen as the stepping stone to nanomachinery (microscopic machinery) due to their complexity and minute size. In addition to being used to make sensors, MEMS technology is also used to make switches, accelerators, light reflectors, and other devices across a range of industries. MEMS technology is also widely used in the medical field during heart surgery and to monitor blood pressure. MEMS technology is significant, as it can make sensors smaller, faster, more accurate, and less expensive. As of 2012 one of the biggest trends in MEMS technology was the increasingly small size of MEMS sensors. Scientists have already developed nanoelectromechanical systems (NEMS), which are even smaller than MEMS systems.

The term MEMS was first used during a microdynamics event held in 1987. By the early 1990s MEMS technology was commercialized. As of 2011 MEMS technology was a multibillion-dollar global business led by just a few companies including Analog Devices, Inc. (ADI); Hewlett-Packard Company, (HP); Robert Bosch, GmbH; and Texas Instruments, Inc. Of these organizations, Analog Devices is perhaps one of the best known for MEMS sensors. ADI is a publicly traded company based in Norwood, Massachusetts, known for producing signal conditioning (manipulation of analog signals), sensor, and data conversion devices. In 2010 the company held a 47.5 percent share in the global data converter market.

MEMS sensors from Analog Devices have been used in a variety of settings, such as ensuring stability in aircraft, submarines, and vehicles. MEMS sensors have also been used in health care settings for patient monitoring and medical imaging, among other uses. They have been used in simulation training for defense forces and in virtual reality applications. Some films have used MEMS sensors from Analog Devices to create special effects. Game makers have also used suits equipped with MEMS sensors to help create games and special effects in video games more effectively and more quickly. The Analog Devices ADXL001 is a vibration and shock sensor that is used to help industrial companies detect possible problems with equipment before a breakdown occurs.

THE HISTORY OF MEMS SENSORS

There are several components that go into creating a MEMS sensor, so it is no surprise that the history of MEMS sensors is quite complex. Although the first MEMS sensors were not developed until the early 21st century, the history of the sensors dates back to 1954, when C. S. Smith discovered the piezoresistive effects of germanium and silicon, two substances whose electrical resistivity changes when force or stress is applied to them. The discovery essentially meant that the two substances could sense water and air pressures more effectively than metals could. This is the effect used in silicon-based MEMS sensors.

In the late 1950s the first Integrated Circuits (ICs) were created. Prior to 1958 it was assumed that all transistors had to be connected to other electronics and wires, and this meant that all transistors had to be a certain size. In 1958, however, Jack Kilby created a circuit that contained three resistors, one transistor, and one capacitor, all on one germanium chip. The introduction of the first ICs in the early 1960s allowed for smaller transistors which eventually allowed for the tiny size of MEMS sensors.

In 1959 Richard Feynman delivered his famous "There's Always Room at the Bottom" presentation at the American Physical Society. Feynman discussed the importance of microtechnology and nanotechnology, and offered prizes to those who could build a tiny motor. By the dawn of the 21st century many organizations were offering prizes for nanotechnology innovations, encouraging scientists to think small and think nano.

In 1964 Westinghouse's Harvey Nathanson produced the first batch MEMS device, a resonant gate transistor (RGT), a device to switch or amplify an electrical signal. The RGT combined electronic elements and mechanical components and was only one millimeter long. It was not until the 1990s, however, that companies began using MEMS sensors for commercial use.

ANALOG DEVICES, INC.

Analog Devices was founded in 1965 in Cambridge, Massachusetts, by Matthew Lorber and Ray Stata. Both men were alumni of the Massachusetts Institute of Technology (MIT) with an interest in new technologies. The first product that Analog Devices launched was a small module used in measuring and testing equipment. Known as the model 101 op amp, the product was a few inches in diameter (about the size of a hockey puck), much larger than the eventual MEMS sensors Analog Devices would become known for. In their first year in business, Analog Devices had 46 employees and made US$574,000 in sales. By 1966 the company had expanded into the United Kingdom, helping to push sales up by 140 percent in the second year.

In 1967 the company began to publish its own magazine, *Analog Dialogue*, and two years later the organization went public. The year 1969 was also an important one for the company. During that year the organization became part of the semiconductor market by investing in Nova Devices, an analog start-up. Analog Devices would eventually acquire Nova Devices in 1971. That year also marked Analog Devices' move into the data conversion products market, a move that would lead to MEMS sensors.

In 1970 the company moved to Norwood, Massachusetts, and created a presence in Japan. By that time, Analog Devices had a sales presence in 17 countries and the share of sales taken up by non-U.S. buyers was steadily growing. This was an important part of Analog Devices' success. By marketing aggressively to overseas customers, Analog Devices was able to capture a large share of the global market for its product lines. In addition, once Asia became a dominant market in the electronics and computing market in the early 21st century, Analog Devices

had the long-established connections in Japan and other countries in Asia to capitalize on this development.

By 1974 a greater share of Analog Devices' business was coming from ICs. That year, IC sales accounted for 35 percent of the company's sales. By 1977 half of the company's sales would be from ICs and by 1979, Analog Devices was listed on the New York Stock Exchange. These developments in the 1970s were important to Analog Devices' MEMS success for a number of reasons. The initial public offering and the success with ICs gave Analog Devices the market position and the finances to aggressively research new technologies, including the MEMS process. In fact, Analog Devices' focus on research and development has been one of the reasons for the company's success. By 1998 the company had 500 active patents.

The company grew rapidly in the 1990s and into the first decade of the 21st century. In 1990 Analog Devices expanded by acquiring Precision Monolithics Inc. Just six years later the company was posting more than US$1 billion dollars in revenue. In 2000 Analog Devices bought five additional organizations, and sales ballooned to US$2.578 billion. Acquisitions made by the company in the 1990s and the first decade of the 21st century allowed it to further expand its product offerings and enter new markets.

ANALOG DEVICES AND MEMS TECHNOLOGY

It was in the 1990s that Analog Devices launched its first MEMS products, starting with the ADXL50, an accelerator for automobile air bags, in 1991. By 1994 the ADXL50 was used as a crash system sensor in air bag systems in some 1995 models of Pontiac, Buick, and Oldsmobile cars. By 1996, when ADI shifted its focus to the computer markets, it launched a second generation of the ADXL crash sensor. While the MEMS sensors used in air bags were the first MEMS technology devices created by Analog Devices, they also proved one of the most successful in the long run. In the mid-1990s, only the higher-end car models used air bag systems. By the 2010s, air bags were standard in most vehicles, and Analog Devices' sensors were used in many air bag sensor systems.

In 2002 Analog Devices launched the first integrated MEMS gyroscope, the iMEMS ADXRS. Analog Devices MEMS gyroscopes measure and detect the angular rate of objects, making them important in industrial applications. The product was one-100th the size of competing products due to the MEMS technology. In 2002 the company shipped its 100 millionth inertial iMEMS sensor. By 2005 the company had shipped 200 million inertial iMEMS sensors.

According to Hoover's, over 60,000 companies, including Royal Philips Electronics N.V., Telefonaktiebolaget

LM Ericsson, Sony Corporation, among others, use Analog Devices components. Analog Devices produced more than 10,000 products as of 2012, and only some of those products were related to MEMS sensors. Over 80 percent of the company's sales come from overseas customers.

ANALOG DEVICES FACES CHALLENGES

The 2008 recession affected Analog Devices negatively. According to an interview that Jerry Fishman, Analog Devices' CEO, gave to Junko Yoshida for a 2009 issue of *EE Times,* "Distributors, and in fact all the customers, just stopped, when the business went to hell. . .and the credit markets didn't allow people to borrow to buy inventories." By 2009, however, sales were slowly increasing.

Although the company has not been involved in many legal disputes, in 2010 Analog Devices was involved in a lawsuit against competitor Knowles Electronics, LLC, alleging that it violated Analog Devices' patent 7,364,942 for Wafer Anti-Stiction Application (WASA) by selling its version of a MEMS-based microphone. In late 2010 a judge ruled in favor of Analog Devices and the company sought to recover money lost through financial damages. Analog Devices had been selling its own version of MEMS microphones since 2008.

ANALOG DEVICES' MEMS PRODUCTS

As of 2012 ADI produced a number of products using MEMS technology, including MEMS accelerometers, MEMS gyroscopes, MEMS inertial measurement units, MEMS inertial sensors, MEMS microphones, analog and digital temperature sensors, and digital trip point sensors. Analog Devices MEMS accelerometers are designed to measure and perceive acceleration, shock, tilt, and vibration. Analog Devices MEMS Inertial Measurement Units (IMUs) detect and measure multiple degrees of freedom (DoF) motion. These sensors are used in navigation and in industrial stability applications. Analog Devices MEMS inertial sensors measure and sense tilt, acceleration, vibration, shock, rotation, and degrees-of-freedom, making them useful in automotive applications, including air bag systems.

Although Analog Devices is known for creating MEMS sensors that work primarily in important applications, such as health care settings and car air bag systems, the company has developed some MEMS sensors for use in more unique settings. For example, Analog Devices worked together with Xsens Technologies B.V. to create MEMS sensors attached to suits that were worn by the actors in the *Alice in Wonderland* and *Iron Man 2* movies. These ADI MEMS sensors were used to help filmmakers with the movies' special effects.

ANALOG DEVICES AND THE FUTURE

The growing market in the 2010s for mobile devices created new opportunities for Analog Devices' MEMS technology. Many of the newest devices in 2012 required a number of sensors and increasingly small and accurate machines. For example, MEMS microphones were a rapidly growing market due to the importance of mobile devices.

According to a 2012 article by Je're'mie Bouchaud in *ElectroIQ,* Analog Devices was the third-largest supplier of digital MEMS microphones in 2011, due in part to the company's microphone in the popular Apple iPad 2. According to Bouchaud, the digital MEMS microphone market was poised to explode, as mobile devices required smaller and more accurate microphones. In fact, sales for MEMS microphones were expected to increase 32 percent between 2011 and 2012 alone, up to US$493.5 million in 2012.

The use of MEMS in sports was also slated to grow. According to a 2012 article by R. Colin Johnson in the *EE Times,* Analog Devices was working on research in 2012 regarding the use of MEMS sensors in sports. Among the projects sponsored by the company was a project that would see MEMS gyroscope sensors and accelerometers in athletes' mouth guards and MEMS sensors in athletes' sports helmets. The aim of the sensors in these sports applications is to help detect injuries, especially brain injuries, which are challenging to evaluate using traditional methods. According to Johnson, the number of MEMS sensor applications in sports and health was expected to increase. In 2012 there were already MEMS sensors in sports equipment, including pedometers, but Johnson predicted a growing number of increasingly sophisticated MEMS sensors, which would allow athletes to gather fitness analytics and share them quickly through social media.

The MEMS sensor industry is expected to explode overall as well, which is promising for Analog Devices. According to a 2011 article by Melanie Martella in *Sensors* magazine, the compound annual growth rate for the MEMS sensor industry was 10 percent in 2011 and was expected to grow to 10.5 percent by 2015. The major areas of growth for the industry come from "MEMS pressure sensors, accelerometers, and gyroscopes," according to Martella, with more industries relying on MEMS sensors for business.

BIBLIOGRAPHY

Allen, James J. *Micro Electro Mechanical System Design.* Boca Raton, FL: CRC Press, 2005.

Analog Devices. "Investor Relations." Norwood, MA, 2012. Accessed February 5, 2012. http://investor.analog.com /phoenix.zhtml?c=95455&p=irol-irHome.

"Analog Devices, Inc." Austin, TX: Hoover's Inc., 2012. Accessed February 5, 2012. http://www.hoovers.com/company/Analog

_Devices_Inc/rfrrti-1-1njg4g.html.

"Analog Devices Receives MEMS Microphone Patent Case." *Entertainment Close-Up,* November 29, 2010. General OneFile. (GALE|A243009343). Accessed February 5, 2012. http://go.galegroup.com/ps/i.do?id=GALE%7CA243009343&v=2.1&u=itsbtrial&it=r&p=GPS&sw=w/.

Bouchaud, Jérémie. "MEMS Microphones Make Noise in 2012." *ElectroIQ,* January 2012. Accessed February 5, 2012. http://www.electroiq.com/articles/stm/2012/01/mems-microphones-make-noise-in-2012.html.

Conner, Margery. "MEMS Sensor Provides Early Detection of Motor-Bearing Irregularities." *EDN,* May 7, 2008. Accessed February 5, 2012. http://www.edn.com/article/472365-MEMS_sensor_provides_early_detection_of_motor_bearing_irregularities.php.

Hartwell, Peter G. "Rethinking MEMS Sensor Design for the Masses." *EE Times,* February 22, 2010. Accessed February 27, 2012. http://www.eetimes.com/design/analog-design/4006403/Rethinking-MEMS-sensor-design-for-the-masses.

"ITC Rules in Favour of Analog Devices in Patent Case." *Worldwide Computer Products News,* December 24, 2010. General OneFile. (GALE|A245154741). Accessed February 5, 2012. http://go.galegroup.com/ps/i.do?id=GALE%7CA245154741&v=2.1&u=itsbtrial&it=r&p=GPS&sw=w.

Johnson, R. Colin. "Slideshow: MEMS Conquering Sports." *EE Times,* January 20, 2012. Accessed February 5, 2012. http://www.embedded.com/electronics-news/4235003/Slideshow--MEMS-conquering-sports-.

———. "Xsens, Analog Devices Collaborate on 'Iron Man' MEMS Sensors." *EE Times,* May 19, 2010. Accessed February 5, 2012. http://www.eetimes.com/electronics-news/4199549/Xsens-Analog-Devices-collaborate-on-Iron-Man-MEMS-sensors.

Kempe, Volker. *Inertial MEMS: Principles and Practice.* New York: Cambridge University Press, 2011.

Martella, Melanie. "MEMS: The Future Looks Bright." *Sensors,* November 18, 2011. Accessed February 5, 2012. http://www.sensorsmag.com/sensors-mag/mems-the-future-looks-bright-9185.

Yoshida, Junko. "Analog Devices' CEO: 'Our Enemy Is Us.'" *EE Times,* December 3, 2009. Accessed February 5, 2012. http://www.eetimes.com/electronics-news/4086253/Analog-Devices-CEO-Our-enemy-is-us-.

Apple Inc.'s Ever Evolving Personal Technology Devices

In late 2011 Apple Inc. reached the pinnacle of business achievement by becoming the most valuable company in the world, based on a market capitalization of almost US$340 billion. It achieved this feat primarily by changing the way people perceived and used personal technology devices. In the first decade of the 21st century, Apple released a host of products and services, most with names that began with the letter *i,* and by doing so caused upheaval in such markets as music and cellular communications.

ORIGINS OF THE COMPANY

Steve Jobs, Ron Wayne, and Steve Wozniak founded Apple Computer in April 1976. Apple's first product was the Apple 1 computer, the brainchild of Wozniak, built when he could not afford to buy an Altair 8800. The Apple 1 personal computer was popular with computer enthusiasts. Despite his technical prowess Wozniak was not a salesman and his efforts to interest Hewlett-Packard Company and others in his machine, which utilized the BASIC program, proved fruitless.

With the help of Jobs and Wayne, Apple was able to secure the sale of 50 of the devices to an early computer sales chain. Wayne, who designed the company's famous logo and wrote the partnership agreement and operating manual for the Apple 1, left the company days later, receiving US$800 for his 10 percent share in the fledgling company. (In 2012 that 10 percent share of Apple would be worth approximately US$34 billion.) In later interviews, Wayne stated he left because he felt he was too old to keep up with his two partners (he was 41 years old at the time) and that he did not feel up to taking the risk the start-up would entail.

In January of the following year, with the help of Mike Markkula, who invested US$92,000 in the company, Apple Computer Inc. was officially created. In April, Wozniak's latest creation, the Apple II, was introduced and released for sale at US$1,295. With an appealing plastic case and the capability to display color graphics, it would seal Apple's early success. Through a succession of strategic partnerships, largely engineered by Jobs, the company grew, and in late 1980 it went public. At the time of the initial public offering Apple's shareholders, who included 40 employees, became instant millionaires.

In 1985, Jobs left Apple and went on to start his own computer company, NeXT, Inc. Over the course of the next few years Jobs and Apple went their separate ways, but neither found the success they desired. Apple faced increased competition from the rise of the IBM personal computer. Jobs' efforts at NeXT never produced a successful consumer product, despite a number of interesting products pioneered by Jobs and the company, including operating software.

THE IMAC

In late 1996, Apple bought NeXT for US$430 million and took Jobs back into the company in an advisory role. By late 1997 Jobs had the role of "interim CEO," a title he would hold until his death in 2011. Jobs moved quickly to return the company to profitability by introducing two new innovative and successful products, the iMac and the PowerBookG3. The iMac utilized Jobs' expertise in producing highly stylized and user-friendly products. It was sleek, easy to set up, and more compact than earlier versions. The PowerBookG3, also utilized Apple's evolving sleek lines, had a long battery life for a portable computer, and featured flexible docking bays for accessories.

These innovations, and the use of the "i" designation, would become hallmarks of Apple products for years to come, until by the early 2010s Apple was no longer exclusively known for its traditional computer products.

IPOD AND ITUNES

After the iMac, Apple took aim at the traditional business model of the music industry with its release of the iPod, a hand-sized music storage device managed through access to a conventional personal computer. Initial versions would only allow users to transfer music from their personal collections to the device. The device was an instant hit in 2001; just two years later, in June 2003, the one millionth iPod was sold. The iPod, though, was not the only music-based revenue stream, as in 2001 Apple also opened the iTunes Music Store with 200,000 songs for sale. Featuring high-quality versions of songs easily downloaded into an iPod, the iTunes store also became a major success. In February 2006, five years after its inception, iTunes reported that one billion songs had been downloaded from the site.

Successful as they were, the iPod and iTunes did not complete Apple's run of revolutionary products. In 2005 Jobs foresaw the inherent capabilities of a touch screen device and how this capability might revolutionize personal computing and consumer electronic products on a global scale. Furthermore, he realized that people did not want to carry around multiple devices to access the Internet, make calls, listen to music, or view their e-mail. He looked at ways to get those services from just one device. While the need was obvious, the obstacles were numerous: data networks were slow, operating software was not scaled down to work on the much slower processors available, and competition from other cell phone producers was increasing.

Undaunted, Jobs entered into a five-year exclusive development agreement with major phone carrier Cingular Wireless (now AT&T Mobility LLC) to share the costs of development and exclusively market a touch-screen-enabled device operating over Cingular's network. Early efforts of the 200 engineers assigned to the task were not encouraging. Early prototypes were disastrous and erratic. Jobs, viewing one prototype in a meeting, responded with an icy stare, an unusual reaction from the often temperamental chief, and one which had an unnerving effect on those present. Heated arguments ensued as efforts were redoubled to create a workable prototype.

THE IPHONE ARRIVES

In January 2007 Jobs unveiled the device, known as the iPhone, as the centerpiece of the company's presentation at the Macworld convention in San Francisco, California. In June of that year, the much-heralded device finally went on sale with much fanfare and, with what would subsequently become an Apple product launch trademark, long lines in front of stores. One of those faithfully standing in line was Apple founder and former chief product developer, Steve Wozniak. In spite of its high price at US$599, estimates for iPhone sales in that first weekend ranged from 500,000 to 1,000,000 units.

While initial activation proved problematic when the carrier's site was overwhelmed, and rival cell network carriers issued talking points to their employees to try to undermine the stampede of popularity, it made little difference. What some were now calling the "Jesus phone" was a major hit. Executives at rival phone makers like Motorola and Nokia were stunned by the apparent cultural impact of a mere handset, something that was fast becoming a valuable commodity before the iPhone launch. Additionally, Jobs had wrangled a deal with AT&T that gave it exclusive control over development of the device as well as a unique revenue-sharing arrangement with the carrier. Such concessions had previously been thought to be impossible to achieve with the major carriers, who were used to viewing handsets as just a means of giving customers access to their networks.

The iPhone reinvented the wireless carrier-centered market structure, bringing devices back to the forefront of consumer awareness. Consumers gravitated quickly to the easy-to-use handheld computers. In addition, Jobs released a developer's kit, which opened the device to third-party application development.

Cell phone carriers found themselves in an entirely different relationship with device makers. Seeing their business being captured by AT&T and Apple, they worked frantically to find a competitive device. Device makers and application developers found themselves in a much more competitive relationship with network companies. The wireless universe was developing some of the flexibility and multi-use capabilities previously available only to conventional computer users.

In November 2007 the iPhone was officially launched in Germany and the United Kingdom. In the next few months more European carriers would sign agreements with Apple. By the end of 2008, iPhone service was available in most European countries. Expansion to Asia followed shortly behind Europe where service became available in various regions between 2008 and 2011.

With another major success in its pocket, Apple did not rest on its laurels. In July 2008 Apple released the iPhone 3G, available through AT&T with a two-year contract. The iPhone 3G, as with all subsequent iPhone releases, coincided with the release of a new version of the iOS operating system. Besides a faster processor, the 3G had full cellular capabilities as well as an added video

GPS locator. The iPhone 3G also sported an option for increased memory capacity. As with all subsequent upgrades the 3G retained the 3.5-inch touch screen and color liquid crystal display.

The next two versions of the popular device were called the iPhone 3GS and iPhone 4, both technological upgrades to the same basic device. The 3GS, launched a year after the 3G, added a faster processor, higher resolution camera, video recorder, and compass. At that point Apple was facing some resistance to the high price of the device, with 42 percent of consumers saying that the US$199 price was a deterrent. Apple addressed the price issue when it released the iPhone 4 in June 2010 and made the iPhone 3GS available for US$99. By 2011 the 3GS was offered free with a service agreement with AT&T. The iPhone 4 debuted, much like its predecessor, as a basic upgrade. It featured more memory, a faster processor, and improved GPS capabilities.

By the end of 2010, the iPhone was a solid success, having sold 14.1 million handsets in the last quarter of 2010 alone, a 91 percent growth rate year-over-year. Total iPhones shipped since its introduction totaled 73.5 million units. In October 2011, Apple released another upgrade of its now iconic product, the iPhone 4S. The 4S continued the history of upgrades to existing features including a higher resolution and stabilized camera, a faster dual core processor, operability on most worldwide networks, and a natural language voice recognition system called Siri.

Siri, which allowed users to develop audio e-mails, notes, GPS searches, and other voice-to-text applications, received mixed reviews by the end of the year. Some found that the device, available only in English, had difficulty understanding many accents. Others faulted the device for unreliability. Many, accustomed to Apple releasing products that worked with few glitches, were upset that the company released Siri as a beta product. Others disagreed and found the application impressive where it worked. By December the application was so popular it was causing connection problems on networks due to the number of people using its voice-activated locating capability. Some analysts, such as Johnny Evans at *Computer World,* in a 2011 article titled "Apple, Siri and the New Search," predicted the application would become a game changer in search technology as well as a catalyst for up to 25 million new iPhone customers and upgrades in the months to come.

TABLET COMPUTING

In April 2010 Apple introduced the iPad to the U.S. consumer market. The iPad was a US$499, tablet-type computer device with a 9.7-inch diagonal screen. At its introduction, Jobs referred to the iPad, his pet project, as a "truly magical and revolutionary device," and suppos-

edly told others he expected it to be the most important thing he had ever done, according to Daniel Lyons' 2010 *Newsweek* article titled "Think Really Different." The iPad combined many of the features of a conventional computer and the iPhone. Users could carry the 1.5-pound device with them and wirelessly access email and browse the web as well as play video for up to 10 hours on a single battery charge.

Theoretically, an iPad could become a user's bookshelf, television, game station, music device, and newspaper. Within a year of the iPad's introduction, Apple had sold 15 million devices worldwide. In April 2011 Apple released the similarly priced iPad 2, a second-generation version of the tablet device. Improvements included a lighter, thinner case, faster processor, a video calling application called Face Time, and front and back cameras.

THE FUTURE OF THE IPHONE AND IPAD

In late 2011 a concept video of the iPhone 5 was available online and became one of the most widely viewed videos. This version of iPhone showed some truly revolutionary capabilities, including a laser device that projected a full-size useable keyboard onto a table, and a pop-up holographic projection. Jason O'Grady of *ZDNet,* believed the keyboard and holographic imaging were more likely to come later, perhaps in a iPhone 6 or 7.

In a 2011 *International Business Times* article titled "How Apple's Future Revolves Around Siri," Dave Smith predicted the future of the iPhone and the iPad were linked to the popularity of its voice recognition software Siri. By November 2011, Apple was holding meetings with several prominent media executives, outlining its plans for the two devices and a new television platform, presumably to be called iTV. According to the article, Apple explained that the future of the devices would be linked through Bluetooth technology, with Siri being the "brain" driving the devices. A *New York Times* report uncovered one quiet Apple project to build an iPod-like device that would wrap around the user's wrist and be communicated through Siri. Other wearable computers would surely follow, according to the 2011 article's author, Nick Bilton. Expectations were that Siri would become more useful through integration with databases that permitted a range of natural language questioning.

Other important evolving uses for the iPad devices with improved Siri capabilities may take place in schools, where the back and forth voice technology is expected to make the device an enormously useful tool. Already the iPad had demonstrated its remarkable abilities with children suffering from autism, as profiled in an October 2011 CBS *60 Minutes* television segment titled "Apps for Austism: Communicating on the iPad."

BIBLIOGRAPHY

"Apple History Timeline." The Apple Museum, 1998. Accessed February 9, 2012. http://applemuseum.bott.org/sections /history.html.

Apple Inc. "iPod + iTunes Timeline." Cupertino, CA, 2011. Accessed February 9, 2012. http://www.apple.com/pr /products/ipodhistory/.

"Apps for Autism: Communicating on the iPad." *CBS News – 60 Minutes,* October 23, 2011. Accessed February 9, 2012. http://www.cbsnews.com/8301-18560_162-20124225 /apps-for-autism-communicating-on-the-ipad/.

Bilton, Nick. "Disruptions: Wearing Your Computer on Your Sleeve." *Bits* (blog), *New York Times,* December 18, 2011. Accessed February 9, 2012. http://bits.blogs.nytimes.com /2011/12/18/wearing-your-computer-on-your-sleeve/.

Evans, John. "Apple, Siri and the New Search." *Computerworld,* October 16, 2011. Accessed February 9, 2012. http://blogs .computerworld.com/19105/apple_siri_and_life_after _google.

Lewis, Scott, and Jeffrey L. Covell. "Apple Computer Inc." In *International Directory of Company Histories,* edited by Jay P. Pederson. Vol. 77, 40–45. Detroit: St. James Press, 2006. Gale Virtual Reference Library (GALE|CX3483500017). Accessed February 9, 2012. http://go.galegroup.com/ps/i.do?id=GALE %7CCX3483500017&v=2.1&u=itsbtrial&it=r&p=GVRL& sw=w.

Lyons, Daniel. "Think Really Different." *Newsweek,* March 25, 2010. Accessed February 9, 2012. http://www.thedailybeast .com/newsweek/2010/03/25/think-really-different.html.

O'Grady, Jason. "Crazy iPhone 5 Concept Video Making the Rounds." *ZDnet,* August 30, 2011. Accessed February 9, 2012. http://www.zdnet.com/blog/apple/crazy-iphone-5 -concept-video-making-the-rounds/10968.

Satariano, Adam. "Apple Overtakes Exxon Becoming World's Most Valuable Company." *Bloomberg Businessweek,* August 10, 2011. Accessed February 9, 2012. http://www.business week.com/news/2011-08-10/apple-overtakes-exxon-becom ing-world-s-most-valuable-company.html.

Smith, Dave. "How Apple's Future Revolves Around Suri." *International Business Times,* December 19, 2011. Accessed February 9, 2012. http://www.ibtimes.com/articles/269509 /20111219/apple-future-siri-iphone-ipad-tv.htm.

Waugh, Rob. "Backlash Grows against iPhone's Siri Voice Control—and Tech Experts Question if Apple Has Lost Its Golden Touch." *Mail Online,* December 7, 2011. Accessed February 9, 2012. http://www.dailymail.co.uk/sciencetech /article-2071190/Backlash-grows-iPhones-Siri-voice-control --tech-experts-question-Apple-lost-golden-touch.html.

Arianna Huffington
and the Huffington Post

HUFFINGTON'S ETHOS

A controversial news source and aggregator, the *Huffington Post* successfully adapted journalism to Internet audiences, with 35.5 million unique visitors by June 2011, despite having been started only six years prior by Arianna Huffington. Punchy, alluring headlines ranged from celebrity gossip, such as "Lindsay Lohan Playboy: Hugh Hefner Says Issue Is 'Breaking Sales,'" to hard-hitting political stances, including "Boiling Discontent: Tea Party Fractures and What Mr. Potato Head Has to Do with It." In February 2011, AOL purchased the site for US$315 million, though a *New York* magazine profile by Vanessa Grigoriadis in November 2011 suggested, "The reality is that Huffington is subsuming AOL media into her personal brand." Largely due to the site, founder Arianna Huffington earned a number 12 slot on the *Forbes* list, "The Most Influential Women in Media" in 2009.

The most significant difference between *HuffPo,* as it is informally known, and traditional journalism has strong ties to its founder and her beliefs. Whereas traditional journalism prided itself on objectivity, Huffington had no such pretensions. The website consists of major tabs, including Politics, Business, Entertainment, Tech, Media, Life & Style, Culture, Comedy, Healthy Living, Women, and others. The site continued to increase its geographic range in 2011, from local coverage in Los Angeles, California; New York, New York; San Francisco, California; Denver, Colorado; Miami, Florida; and Chicago, Illinois, to Canada and Europe.

THE FOUNDER

Arianna Huffington (then Arianna Stanisopoulos) spent a significant portion of her early life in the United Kingdom. She attended Cambridge University and began her career as a writer. Influential in her development as a writer, thinker, and person was Bernard Levin, a columnist for the British newspaper, the *Times.* In an *AlterNet* article to memorialize Levin, Huffington wrote, "I had devoured his book *The Pendulum Years,* and I would meticulously cut his columns, underline them, and save them in a file (no, I did not put pressed flowers in the file, but might as well have)."

When they were thrown together, seemingly by fate on a *Face the Music* panel, Levin discovered a similar attraction. After this first meeting their relationship developed, and they spent years together as a couple. The relationship ended due to a pivotal disagreement: Huffington wanted children, but Levin did not. Eventually, Huffington moved to the United States. True to her intentions, Arianna Stanisopoulos married Michael Huffington and had two daughters, Christina and Isabella.

FOUNDING THE
HUFFINGTON POST

By the time the *Huffington Post* was founded in 2005, traditional news media was in flux. The year was a turning point in the transition from print to online media. According to a 2006 Pew *The State of the News Media* report on American Journalism, big metropolitan papers suffered quickly decreasing numbers of subscriptions, and innovations on the Internet were gaining popularity. Some networks anticipated the change, such as ABC, which began to broadcast its evening newscast online. At the same time, audience expectations regarding content changed as well. The principle of serving the public interest lost hold.

With it, emphasis on objectivity began to transition toward opinion, if only because biased news sold better to the online media consumer.

Arianna Huffington was well suited to the online media marketplace. After coming to the United States in 1980, she continued to publish her opinions with little mediation. After Monica Lewinsky came forward with evidence of her illicit relationship with U.S. President Bill Clinton, Huffington held nothing back. Responding to a question from a *Washington Post* subscriber about her stance regarding impeachment or resignation, the journalist opined: "I would definitely support resignation rather than a trial by the Senate. I feel there are many major social problems that are being overlooked, both foreign and domestic, and I really think there would be no greater gift to the nation than starting 1999 as a Monica-free zone."

Other examples of Huffington's candid statements abound from all of her endeavors. Her beliefs changed, as did her mediums of communication, as she searched for the right format where she could broadcast or convey her convictions. These formats included a column as a Comedy Central political commentator; the Detroit Project, which became infamous for its campaign against sport utility vehicles; Resignation.com; AriannaOnline; and a run in the 2003 California gubernatorial election. Regardless of her political orientation, which shifted from right to left during the 1990s, she continually proved her resourcefulness in communicating information provocatively and meaningfully.

HuffPo was a more successful attempt. In May 2005, it began as a group blog, featuring work from many of Huffington's connections. Actress Diane Keaton, Republican speechwriter David Frum, veteran newscaster Walter Cronkite, and Bill Clinton's former presidential advisor Vernon E. Jordan, Jr., were a few of the original contributors. However, many of these prominent and well-known people left or were replaced by a growing staff of editors, reporters, and unpaid contributors. In 2006 Huffington returned to her strength in reporting controversial political news. Melinda Henneberger, a former journalist for *Newsweek,* was hired when the site was claiming 2.3 million unique visitors per month. It added Entertainment and Business sections with plans to expand even further.

As a news aggregator, the site gained a significant advantage by utilizing search engine optimization (SEO). This came at a time when consumers were increasingly reading their news online. Print publications lost roughly 5 percent of their purchases, and online traffic grew by almost 30 percent in 2008, according to a Pew *The State of the News Media* report. Traditional news organizations dabbling in online markets frequently found that *HuffPo* received a superior position on the search engine results

page for summarized, aggregated content than their own, original work.

In 2007 Huffington brought on Betsy Morgan, previously a writer for *Newsweek,* as chief executive officer. Morgan immediately added even more focus to SEO efforts, looking to traffic statistics in order to guide the publication's attention toward trending topics. By 2008, with the presidential campaign starting to gain momentum, the website increased to 3.7 million unique visitors per month.

BUILDING THROUGH THE AOL MERGER

Recognizing that its competitive advantage lay in its willingness to learn the online playing field, the *Huffington Post* continued to bolster its technology staff. Paul Berry, chief technology officer in 2009, began using A/B testing on headlines. A/B testing was a valuable method of conducting user research. It was particularly useful for companies that wanted to know how presentation could change user perception. Berry wanted to know which kinds of headlines produced the most interest, so he presented half of users with one version of a headline (version A), and half of the users with a second version of a headline (version B). Over time, it became clear that some nomenclature tactics produced more interest than others, and those tactics were taught to writers in the organization.

Attracted by the *Post*'s exalted positions on search engine results pages and clickable headlines, users flocked to the website. President Barack Obama called on a *Huffington Post* reporter in a 2009 news conference, which solidified recognition of the *Post* as an official periodical. The same year marked Huffington's *Forbes* number 12 ranking in the "Most Influential Women in Media" list.

In June 2010 monthly site traffic reached 24.3 million visitors, moving ahead of the online presence of the prestigious publications, the *Washington Post* and *USA Today,* according to a July 2010 *Newsweek* article by Daniel Lyons. In addition to permanent staff members, Huffington generated free content by conscripting 6,000 bloggers. Thousands more sent content for review and publication. Reporters started to interview Arianna Huffington as a guru of online journalism. As reported by Harvard University's Laura McGann for the *Nieman Journalism Lab* on May 19, 2010, Huffington discussed how the traditional investigative process converged with technology on the Internet. "The traditional tenets of journalism. . .need to prevail and be supplemented by all the new technical tools and the new citizen engagement," she said.

By early 2011 after AOL bought the *Post,* Huffington had become an icon in the United States. A number of journalists wrote profiles of her, including the *New Yorker's*

Lauren Collins, *Vogue's* Elizabeth Rubin, and *New York* magazine's Vanessa Grigoriadis. The latter predicted the US$315 million AOL merger would spell the end of the AOL brand. She pointed out that even though the *Huffington Post* had moved into AOL's space, AOL office furniture was moving out. Although AOL had 1,000 journalists working on its news source, called Patch, the site was barely a footnote on *HuffPo.* Meanwhile, Huffington used the merger capital to expand. New sections developed, such as "HuffPo Gay Voices" and "HuffPo Weddings." Geographically, Canada became the first Huffington outpost in May.

WILL TRADITIONAL MEDIA FOLLOW SUIT?

HuffPo's greatest asset was also its largest source of criticism, at least initially. Intimate knowledge of the media's rules for the Internet kept audiences swelling, but content was derided for illogic, shoddy production standards, and lackluster journalistic integrity. Writing for *Science-Based Medicine,* on April 29, 2009, Steven Novella accused *HuffPo* writer, Kim Evans, of writing claims "right out of the pseudoscientific health claim play book, under 'how to distract from legitimate criticism with logical fallacies and misdirection'." He claimed that Evans resorted to nonsensical, provocative argumentation in order to defend her statement that cancer, as a whole, was caused by fungal infection.

Traditional news sources or, as Huffington labeled them, "legacy media," could barely retain their own journalistic integrity when writing about the *Post.* In a *New York Times* article on March 31, 2008, Brian Stelter wrote, "Ms. Huffington herself now spends less time on blog posts condemning the Bush administration (although there's still plenty of that) and more time reimagining the *Huffington Post* as what she calls an 'Internet newspaper'." Three years later, after a host of online periodicals were founded, the *New York Times* changed its tone, posting on its *Huffington Post* reference page: "The Huffington Post, like AOL, has faced criticism over its content, much of which is aggregated from other news sources. Yet it has started to invest more in original reporting and writing, hiring experienced journalists from the *New York Times, Newsweek,* and other traditional media outlets." While it was true that *HuffPo* continued to bring seasoned professionals onboard in 2011, this was the case in 2008, as well.

THE NEW RULES OF BIASED NEWS

HuffPo's success heralded a new era of subjective news production. Trendsetting required more than punchy headlines and unabashedly biased reporting. Other online pe-

riodicals competed in that realm. The strong, mysterious character of Huffington made the difference. Reporters and readers alike were fascinated by her paradoxically hard and soft natures. After the AOL merger, she quickly integrated AOL operations and content, accommodating the office to her voice and style, and even distributing mass quantities of baklava to spread her Greek influence, as reported by Grigoriadis.

Adaptability distinguished *HuffPo* from traditional papers, whereas the natural talents and determination of its leader set it apart from online media entrants. It constantly shifted its online strategies to suit online audiences. At times, this entailed different aggregation strategies. At other moments, it meant using hard data to guide headline production.

BIBLIOGRAPHY

Alexa Internet, Inc. "The Huffington Post." San Francisco, CA, 2011. Accessed December 21, 2011.http://www.alexa.com /siteinfo/huffingtonpost.com.

Byers, Dylan. "Huffington Post to Expand to France and Brazil and Where Else? The Audience Wants to Know." *AdWeek,* June 20, 2011. Accessed December 21, 2011. http://www .adweek.com/cannes-lions-2011/huffington-post-expand -france-and-brazil-132718.

Collins, Lauren. "The Oracle: The Many Lives of Arianna Huffington." *New Yorker,* October 13, 2008. Accessed December 21, 2011. http://www.newyorker.com/reporting /2008/10/13/081013fa_fact_collins?currentPage=all.

"Direct Access: Arianna Huffington." *Washington Post.* December 16, 1998. Accessed December 21, 2011. http://www.washing tonpost.com/wp-srv/politics/talk/zforum/huffington121698 .htm.

Estes, Adam Clark. "The Huffington Post Passes the New York Times in Traffic." *Atlantic Wire.* Accessed December 21, 2011. http://www.theatlanticwire.com/business/2011/06 /huffington-post-passes-new-york-times-traffic/38681.

Grigoriadis, Vanessa. "Maharishi Arianna." *New York,* November 20, 2011. Accessed December 21, 2011. http://nymag.com /news/media/arianna-huffington-2011-11.

Huffington, Arianna. "Bernard Levin Remembered." *AlterNet,* August 17, 2004. Accessed December 21, 2011. http://www .alternet.org/story/19579/bernard_levin_remembered?page=1.

"In Pictures: The Most Influential Women in Media." *Forbes,* July 14, 2009. Accessed December 21, 2011. http://www .forbes.com/2009/07/14/most-influential-women-in-media -forbes-woman-power-women-oprah-winfrey_slide_13.html.

Lyons, Daniel. "Arianna's Answer." *Newsweek,* July 25, 2010. Accessed December 21, 2011. http://www.thedailybeast.com /newsweek/2010/07/25/arianna-s-answer.html.

McGann, Laura. "Huffington Talks Convergence, and 'Monetizeable Free'." *Niemann Journalism Lab,* May 19, 2010. Accessed December 21, 2011. http://www.niemanlab .org/2010/05/huffington-talks-convergence-and-monetizeable -free.

Net Ratings, Inc. "Online Newspapers Enjoy Double Digit Year-Over-Year Growth, Reaching One out of Four Internet Users,

According to Nielsen/NetRatings." New York, November 15, 2005. Accessed December 21, 2011. http://www.nielsen-online.com/pr/pr_051115.pdf.

Novella, Steven. "The Huffington Post's War on Science." *Science-Based Medicine,* April 29, 2009. Accessed December 21, 2011. http://www.sciencebasedmedicine.org/index.php/the-huffington-posts-war-on-science.

Pew Research Center. "The State of the News Media." Washington, DC: Project for Excellence in Journalism, 2006. Accessed December 21, 2011. http://stateofthemedia.org/2006.

———. "The State of the News Media." Washington, DC: Project for Excellence in Journalism, 2008. Accessed December 21, 2011. http://stateofthemedia.org/2008.

———. "The State of the News Media." Washington, DC: Project for Excellence in Journalism, 2009. Accessed December 21, 2011. http://stateofthemedia.org/2009.

———. "The State of the News Media." Washington, DC: Project for Excellence in Journalism, 2010. Accessed December 21, 2011. http://stateofthemedia.org/2010.

———. "The State of the News Media." Washington, DC: Project for Excellence in Journalism, 2011. Accessed December 21, 2011.http://stateofthemedia.org/2011/overview-2/.

Rubin, Elizabeth. "Arianna Huffington: The Connector." *Vogue,* September 19, 2011. Accessed December 21, 2011. http://www.vogue.com/magazine/article/arianna-huffington-the-connector.

Seele, Katherine Q. "TV Ads Say S.U.V. Owners Support Terrorists." *New York Times,* January 8, 2003. Accessed December 21, 2011. http://www.nytimes.com/2003/01/08/business/media/08SUVS.html?pagewanted=1.

Stelter, Brian. "Citizen Huff." *New York Times,* March 31, 2008. Accessed December 21, 2011. http://www.nytimes.com/2008/03/31/business/media/31huffington.html.

"Topics: The Huffington Post." *New York Times,* February 7, 2011. Accessed December 21, 2011. http://topics.nytimes.com/top/reference/timestopics/organizations/h/the_huffington_post/index.html.

Aspirin: Painkiller, Analgesic, and Preventive Measure

Aspirin is the popular name for acetylsalicylic acid (ASA), a salicylate drug that is a popular remedy for aches, pains, fever, and, most commonly, headaches. The word "Aspirin" is also a registered trademark name and brand of Bayer AG. This trademark is recognized in more than 80 countries.

Aspirin is also an anti-inflammatory substance that has been linked to heart attack and stroke prevention. According to the Bayer website, Aspirin is the best-selling product made by Bayer and the most used drug in the world. According to Ken Flieger in "Aspirin: A New Look at an Old Drug" from *FDA Consumer* in 1994, there were more than 50 nonprescription drugs in the *Physicians' Desk Reference* that had aspirin as the main medicinal ingredient. Due to its ability to relieve pain and help prevent heart disease, aspirin is sometimes called a "wonder drug" because it is an affordable and accessible medication that helps with a variety of symptoms and conditions.

ASA works by inhibiting the production of prostaglandins in the body. Prostaglandins are naturally occurring substances that heighten the perception of fever, pain, swelling, and redness that can occur with injuries and illness. Since aspirin inhibits these substances, it relieves the symptoms of pain, inflammation, and fever.

THE DISCOVERY OF ASPIRIN

According to Flieger, Hippocrates reportedly used a powder from willow bark to treat fever and pain as early as the fifth century BCE. The bark contained salicin, a natural substance that would eventually be synthesized and used in pain treatment drugs such as aspirin.

According to Thijs J. Rinsema in "One Hundred Years of Aspirin" from *Medical History* in 1999, ASA was first made synthetically in 1853 but did not become popular until sometime later. In August 1897 Felix Hoffmann synthesized ASA while looking for a salicylic acid alternative for his father. Hoffman was a chemist with Bayer and hoped to create a rheumatoid remedy that was less troublesome than the treatment his father was taking. Sodium salicylate and salicylic acid were at the time used for rheumatic conditions, but they produced unpleasant side effects.

Hoffman synthesized acetylsalicylic acid, and Heinrich Dreser of Bayer ran extensive tests on the new discovery. In doing so, Dreser found some new properties of the medicine that could make the formula a rheumatism treatment and an analgesic (painkiller). In early 1899 the substance was named Aspirin, and in March of that year an attempt was made to register a patent for the invention.

BAYER

Farbenfabriken vormals Friedrich Bayer und Companie of Elberfeld, or Bayer, as it came to be commonly known, was originally a maker of synthetic dye products. By the middle of the 1880s Bayer began to make medicine as a profitable venture. From its work with dye products, Bayer had already learned to pursue intellectual property rights strongly. The company used this lesson in its production of Aspirin and other medicines.

By 1899 Bayer was already known for quality products and its scientific innovation, according to Jan McTavish's book, *Pain and Profits: The History of the Headache and Its Remedies in America*. The company did not advertise publicly because it wanted to maintain its reputation as ethical, and instead focused on marketing to physicians. At the time, drugs were not widely advertised, and the medicines that were advertised were seen as suspect by the medical establishment. From the outset, Bayer wanted to market its new product as an ethical drug of high quality, not one of the patent medicines sold at a lower cost and advertised garishly.

Bayer's first popular drug was in fact acetopheneti-din, an analgesic, but the company failed to move quickly enough in securing a German patent for the chemical product. In addition, strict German patent laws kept the company from becoming as profitable as it hoped, according to historian McTavish. Since the laws did not permit the company to patent its findings, competitors were able to create their own versions of drugs created by Bayer. Pricing agreements and sharing the market in this way kept profits low.

Bayer manufactured the drug under PhenacetinBayer, after its trade name Phenacetin. Competing firms that created their own versions of the drug advertised their own brands under Bayer's trade name, Phenacetin, using the trade name as the generic name of the product. Bayer was fearful that this history would eventually repeat itself with Aspirin.

EARLY ASPIRIN SALES

Bayer decided to turn to the U.S. market, in part because U.S. patent laws were quite different. The United States allowed parties to patent a product rather than a process, and the inventor who filed a patent could enjoy an effective monopoly for 17 years. In the United States, Bayer was able to get patents for its drugs and did not need to share profits the way it did in Germany.

By 1903 Bayer was producing its drugs in Rensselaer, New York, for the U.S. market. However, all was not well. Some pharmacists were effectively trying to boycott Bayer products because Bayer priced them much higher in the United States than it did in Canada and Europe. Some smuggling occurred to bring Phenacetin and other Bayer products from Canada into the United States. The company aggressively pursued litigation against anyone who tried to enter the United States with Bayer products from foreign countries and against anyone who tried to resell Bayer products bought abroad. Between 1895 and 1906 the company filed approximately 800 lawsuits against pharmacists and threatened an additional 7,000 lawsuits.

Initially, U.S. public sentiment was with the pharmacists, especially since Bayer was a foreign company that seemed to be charging unfairly high prices to U.S. companies. However, Bayer eventually got the upper hand, largely by publishing accounts of people harmed by fake Phenacetin sold by unscrupulous pharmacists. The Board

of Health in New York City inspected 375 Phenacetin samples from suspect pharmacists in 1902, and 315 of them were found to be contaminated or altered in some way.

By the time Bayer patented ASA in the United States in February 1900, the company had learned enough from its sales of Phenacetin to make the story of Aspirin more successful. As a brand name, Aspirin was already more successful, as it was easier to remember and pronounce. The name derived from the words spiraeic and acetyl, referring to the ingredients in Aspirin.

As in Germany, Bayer introduced Aspirin in the United States as a treatment for rheumatic ailments, and the drug was praised by the *American Journal of Pharmacy* in 1902 for its effectiveness. Within a few years, Aspirin's effectiveness as a general painkiller was established, and Bayer once again became concerned about smuggling. This time, Bayer priced Aspirin in the United States at US$0.43 per ounce, compared to US$0.65 for the same product in Canada, hoping that this would quash any potential profits for smugglers. However, generic ASA was available in Canada in 1902 for just US$0.18.

While Bayer pursued litigation against smugglers, a 1905 lawsuit in England created problems for the company. Bayer took Heyden Company to court, alleging that the Heyden Company was violating patent laws by importing ASA into England. However, in court, the Heyden Company argued that ASA had been present for many years before Bayer started selling it. The company also accused Bayer of obscuring the facts in its patent application. The judge in the case agreed, and Bayer's patent was voided in the United Kingdom. In the United States, however, a court case in 1909 established that Bayer's patent was valid, and so the company was able to maintain its monopoly in that country.

Between 1909 and 1910 Bayer sales in the United States jumped by US$185,000, although the company was spending less on advertisements. In 1909 alone Bayer sold about 686,000 ounces of Aspirin in the United States and was generating US$38,000 monthly for Bayer. By 1913 tests in New York City showed that only 28 of 200 Aspirin samples purchased from pharmacists were altered or counterfeit in some way, so it appeared that Bayer was winning the war on smugglers.

ASPIRIN AND BRANDING

The company needed to focus on branding, but one obstacle was the company name. Bayer was known as Farbenfabriken of Elberfeld, Continental Color, Bayer, and Elberfelder in the United States. In 1913 the company was renamed Bayer Company, Inc.

According to Karyn Synder in "Bayer's 'Wonder Drug' Still Going Strong after 100 Years" from *Drug Topics* in

1997, Aspirin no longer required a prescription by 1915. This meant that customers could ask for the product by name in a pharmacy. However, U.S. consumers preferred Aspirin in tablet form as opposed to powder, and Bayer felt that it could not produce ASA in this preferred form. Bayer sold powder forms of Aspirin to pill manufacturers (including Eli Lilly, Parke-Davis, Schieffelin, Sharp and Dohme, and J. Wyeth) and allowed them to make pills using the Aspirin name.

ASPIRIN AND WORLD WAR I

When World War I (WWI) commenced in 1914 it created immediate problems for Bayer, as sentiment against German products in the United States escalated and the supply of raw materials dwindled. However, the war also meant new opportunities. Since competitors and pill manufacturers were also having supply problems, Bayer could now produce its own Aspirin tablets, under the Bayer-Aspirin name, using its own small production of ASA.

The pills were packaged in yellow and brown packages and with the Bayer Cross on each tablet, which was similar to the appearance of Bayer's Aspirin throughout the 20th century. While Bayer was still cautious about marketing directly to pharmacists and doctors due to ethics considerations, the company did ensure that the product was known to consumers as well. At the same time, Bayer needed to make the Bayer brand recognizable without making Aspirin a public, general term, which would have jeopardized Bayer's claim to a trademarked name.

THE PATENT EXPIRES IN THE UNITED STATES

After February 27, 1917, the U.S. patent expired, and other manufacturers were able to make tablets with the same ingredients as Aspirin. Bayer made it clear that it would pursue litigation against any company that it perceived was infringing on the Aspirin name. In March 1917 Boston's United Drug Company petitioned for the trademarked name to be cancelled, and announced that it would sell its own version of ASA tablets as Aspirin. Bayer sued. By 1918 there were seven brands of ASA aspirin being sold.

However, Bayer also had to worry about the war as well as the Aspirin name. By April 1917 the United States was at war with Germany, and German products being sold in the United States were even more suspect. The U.S. office of the Alien Property Custodian (APC) was created to find and appropriate German property. The APC zeroed in on Bayer and seized Bayer assets and property in the United States. The APC assigned U.S. government employees to run the company and to continue to make a profit from Aspirin and other medicines. However,

pharmacists and U.S. residents were not completely sure of the APC-run company's loyalties, according to McTavish, especially since the appointees ran Bayer just as the previous employees had done, including aggressively protecting the trade name and pursuing the case against the United Drug Company. Advertisements for Aspirin promoting the Bayer brand as 100 percent American and contributing to war bonds did not do much to assuage the tide of negative publicity.

During the influenza epidemic of 1918 rumors circulated that Aspirin was poisoned or somehow contributing to the spread of the disease. There were also rumors that Aspirin advertisements contained secret messages to the enemy. Official investigations into the allegations showed that the rumors were unfounded. Bayer continued to do well, selling US$2.2 million worth of products in just one four-month period in 1918.

ASPIRIN UNDER NEW OWNERSHIP

Bayer Company, Inc. was purchased by Sterling Products in December 1918. Sterling sold a number of medicines, including Cascarets Candy Cathartic, Dr. James' Headache Powders, and other similar products. Sterling sold the Bayer dyestuff business to another company and used Bayer only to produce Aspirin. Also, Sterling employed a million-dollar budget to advertise Bayer tablets of Aspirin, once again running the same types of advertisements that stressed the dangers of buying other brands of ASA. In addition, Bayer-Sterling started offering new incentives to generate goodwill among medical professionals. The company provided free in-store displays and marketing ideas for pharmacists, paid cash for stock that did not sell, and used other incentives to make pharmacists and doctors enthusiastic about Aspirin.

While Bayer-Sterling continued to use conservative advertising techniques in newspapers such as the *New York Times,* by 1919 the company was advertising the uses of Aspirin in popular magazines, claiming that it could help "headache, neuralgia, toothache, aching gums, earache, rheumatism, sciatica, gout, neuritis, colds, grippe, influenzal colds, stiff neck, distress, lame back, lumbago, joint pains," according to McTavish. By 1919 millions of U.S. consumers were using Aspirin, especially for headaches, and the company made more than US$2 million from its products.

TRADEMARK HEADACHES

In 1919 the United Drug Company won its case against the Aspirin trademark. In England, the courts had ruled before the start of WWI that aspirin could be used as a generic term for ASA by any party. In France, aspirine had been used as a synonym for ASA, and Bayer had not been able to change that. Bayer-Sterling kept pursuing the case, but in 1921 another court deemed that aspirin was indeed a generic term.

By the 1920s and 1930s hundreds of aspirins were available, although Bayer-Sterling still sold one of the most recognizable forms. Although Bayer's Aspirin was more expensive, it remained popular. In 1937 there were 7,201,140,800 tablets of Aspirin sold in the United States. Although aspirin became a generic term, Aspirin and the unique Bayer aspirin cross and packaging remain a trademarked entity in the 2010s.

ASPIRIN EVOLVED

In the 20th century, aspirin achieved recognition for additional benefits. As noted by Jonathan Miner and Adam Hoffhines in *Texas Heart Institute Journal,* in 1950, Dr. Lawrence Craven reported that none of the 400 patients in his general practice in California who had been prescribed daily dose of aspirin over a two-year period beginning in 1948 had had heart attacks. Craven's work received little recognition at the time, but decades later other studies confirmed that aspirin could not only treat symptoms but could also be used as a preventive measure. By 1982 John R. Vane was awarded a Nobel Prize in Physiology or Medicine for his work concerning aspirin's mechanism of action. In 1980 the U.S. Food and Drug Administration (FDA) approved the use of aspirin to reduce the chance of stroke in some patients. By 1985 the agency approved aspirin labels that announced aspirin's ability to reduce the risk of heart attacks in some patients. By 2011 aspirin was widely recognized as a painkiller, analgesic, and a preventive measure for strokes and heart attacks.

As a result, in the 2010s aspirin remains a very popular drug worldwide. According to Snyder, people in the United States took 29 billion ASA or aspirin tablets annually, and 50 billion tablets are taken each year worldwide. Bayer continues to produce Aspirin as well as Aspirin brands of pills designed specifically for cardiac health. While Bayer lost control of the aspirin name, it succeeded over the long term in producing one of the most recognized products in the world.

BIBLIOGRAPHY

Bayer. "The History of Aspirin." Morristown, NJ, 2011. Accessed December 16, 2011. http://www.aspirin.com/scripts/pages/en/aspirin_history/index.php.

"Faster-Acting Aspirin Is Bayer's Rx for Flat Sales." *Daily Herald,* May 23, 2011.

Flieger, Ken. "Aspirin: A New Look at an Old Drug." *FDA Consumer* 28, no. 1 (1994).

Jeffreys, Diarmuid. *Aspirin: The Remarkable Story of a Wonder Drug.* New York: Bloomsbury Publishing, 2005.

McTavish, Jan R. *Pain and Profits: The History of the Headache and Its Remedies in America.* New Brunswick, NJ: Rutgers University Press, 2004.

Miner, Jonathan, and Adam Hoffhines. "The Discovery of Aspirin's Antithrombotic Effects." *Texas Heart Institute Journal* 34, no. 2 (2007): 179–186. Accessed January 15, 2012. http://www.ncbi.nlm.nih.gov/pmc/articles/PMC1894700/.

Rinsema, Thijs J. "One Hundred Years of Aspirin." *Medical History* 43, no. 4 (1999).

Sneader, Walter. "The Discovery of Aspirin: A Reappraisal." *British Medical Journal (BMJ)* 321, no. 40 (2000).

Synder, Karyn. "Bayer's 'Wonder Drug' Still Going Strong after 100 Years." *Drug Topics* 141, no. 18 (1997).

Ban Roll-On and Deodorant

WHAT IS THAT SMELL?

According to *Medical News Today,* "Body odor, or B.O. . . . is a perceived unpleasant smell our bodies can give off when bacteria that live on the skin break down sweat into acids." Human sweat itself is virtually odorless. It is the rapid multiplication of bacteria and the work they do in the presence of sweat that eventually causes an unpleasant smell. Body odor is most prevalent in the areas of the feet, armpits, belly button, behind the ears and, to a lesser extent, the rest of the skin.

The average human body has three to four million sweat glands, also called sudoriferous glands, that can be categorized into two types: eccrine glands and apocrine glands. Eccrine glands are found in any area where there is skin. The glands produce sweat that is directed to the skin via coiled ducts. The sweat evaporates and cools the skin. Eccrine glands control human body temperature and produce sweat with a high salt content that makes it harder for bacteria to break down into the aromatic fatty acids that produce the offending odor.

Apocrine glands are located in the breasts, genital area, eyelids, armpits, and ears. These glands have various functions, from secreting fat droplets into breast milk to helping in the formation of earwax and acting as scent glands. It is the apocrine glands that are mainly responsible for body odor due to their high protein content, which bacteria are able to easily break down.

Why people find body odor so offensive is a mystery, but the issue has plagued human beings for centuries and attempts to minimize, mask, or eliminate it have been around for just as long.

BEFORE COMMERCIAL DEODORANT

It is probable that our ancestors were not as smelly as may be supposed; evidence suggests that they continually took steps to eliminate offensive personal odors by either bathing (when and where possible) or by masking the scent with the sweet-smelling products of nature. The ancient Egyptians took great pride in their appearance and cleanliness, bathing daily in the local rivers or out of water basins in the home. As early as 10,000 BCE, Egyptian men and women used oils, herbs, and organic lotions to soften their skin and mask body odor. The ancient Greeks and Romans followed their example.

In medieval Europe, daily bathing was a popular practice until health fears (centering around the bubonic plague) and a reputation for bawdy behavior at bathing houses resulted in the shutting down of many such establishments in the 16th century. For the following couple of centuries, many people refused to immerse themselves in bath water, fearing that the warm water opened up their pores and made them more susceptible to disease. Disagreeable smells were kept at bay by ointments and lotions made from extracts of herbs and other plants; these were smeared about the body by those able to afford them. Presumably, the smell of the poorer classes was overshadowed by the constant stench of the open sewers and vermin.

It was not until the end of the 18th century in Western civilization that more frequent bathing and the resultant cleanliness returned. Europeans and Americans attempted to keep clean and smelling fresh by regularly changing the long linen shirts they wore closest to their skin. Native Americans and Africans, considered "uncivilized" by the explorers they met, simply went shirtless to reduce any odor.

FROM MUM TO BAN

It was not until the end of the 19th century that the first commercially produced deodorant became available, and the way people dealt with bodily odors changed forever. In 1888 an unknown inventor from Philadelphia created the first commercially available product to combat human body odor and named it "Mum" deodorant. History is vague on the origins of the name. It may have alluded to keeping silent about body odor or been named after the sweet-smelling plant. It might even be an acronym for "morning until midnight." Mum was sold to the public through the inventor's nurse. This initial deodorant was a waxy cream made from a zinc compound that was smeared under the arms to cover any offending smell. However, the cream left marks on clothes, and the chemical ingredient necessitated the washing of hands after applying.

In 1931 the small company then manufacturing Mum deodorant, Thomas Christy & Company, was sold to Bristol-Myers, and in 1940 a woman by the name of Helen Barnett Diserens joined the Mum's deodorant production team. In 1952, inspired by the recent invention of the ballpoint pen, Diserens designed a glass container based on the same principle. The container held the deodorizing ingredients, and the rolling ball allowed for an even spreading of the deodorant over the armpit area. Bristol-Myers named the product "Ban" and, with the help of renowned marketer Edward Gelsthorpe, it became one of the company's most successful toiletry products.

GROWTH OF AN INDUSTRY

The introduction and success of the Ban roll-on deodorant sparked an entire industry dedicated to eliminating body odor. In February 2011 Global Industry Analysts forecasted that the world market for deodorants would reach US$12.6 billion by 2015. with Europe and the United States accounting for a major portion. In the United States alone, sales of deodorant and antiperspirant grew from US$1.8 billion in 2004 to US$2.4 billion by 2008.

It was estimated that approximately 95 percent of U.S. consumers use either a deodorant, an antiperspirant, or both. A deodorant simply covers up the smell of body odor with fragrances. An antiperspirant uses an aluminum-based ingredient to temporarily clog the pores and reduce sweating. Many products on the market are a mixture of the two. The U.S. Food and Drug Administration (FDA) treats antiperspirants as an over-the-counter drug and regulates the products accordingly. Deodorants with no antiperspirant ingredients are treated as cosmetics.

Approximately 10 years after the introduction of Ban roll-on deodorant, the men's toiletry firm, the Gillette Company, marketed the first aerosol antiperspirant. Aerosols immediately became popular due to the convenience of application, and by 1967, 50 percent of antiperspirant sales were in an aerosol can. By the early 1970s that figure had grown to 82 percent. However, later in the same decade, the popular aerosol cans experienced some challenges.

First, in 1977 the FDA banned aluminum zirconium complexes due to concerns regarding the effects of possible long-term inhalation. Then shortly after, the U.S. Environmental Protection Agency (EPA) strictly limited the use of chlorofluorocarbons (CFCs), citing a growing concern that use of these chemicals could be connected to the deterioration of the planet's ozone layer. The cosmetic industry hastened to formulate a CFC-free version of the aerosol container for antiperspirants, but consumers had lost confidence in the product. In 1977 sales of the new CFC-free aerosols dropped to 50 percent of the deodorant market and plummeted to under 30 percent by the mid-1980s. Ban roll-on and similar products saw a resurgence in popularity as consumers perceived the solid stick antiperspirant to be a "cleaner" alternative.

HEALTH ISSUES

In the first decade of the 21st century, the deodorant industry came under attack for using toxic chemicals, particularly products containing antiperspirant ingredients such as aluminum. As discussed earlier, antiperspirants typically contained aluminum-based ingredients in order to temporarily block the skin's pores to reduce sweating. Rumors and some studies seemed to indicate that aluminum could be linked to Alzheimer's disease and dementia. While most researchers in 2011 no longer regarded aluminum as a risk factor for Alzheimer's disease, the Canadian Alzheimer's Association noted that researchers were still examining whether some people were at risk because their bodies had difficulty in dealing with foods containing the metals copper, iron, and aluminum. The association did not single out antiperspirants, however.

In 2009 studies appeared to indicate that cancerous tumors were most likely to appear in the parts of the female breast that were closest to where antiperspirants are applied. Of the women tested, studies noted, it was found that cysts in the armpit area of the breast had 25 times more aluminum than the amount usually found in blood. However, the U.S. National Cancer Institute responded that it was not aware "of any conclusive evidence linking the use of underarm antiperspirants or deodorants and the subsequent development of breast cancer." The FDA also stated that it did not have any evidence that ingredients in underarm antiperspirants or deodorants caused cancer.

THE FUTURE OF DEODORANTS

Selling deodorant is a finite market. There are only so many pairs of underarms and so many ways to mask odor or inhibit sweat. Manufacturers and marketers are therefore continually looking for new ways to target consumers or for different packaging methods to appeal to a younger market. Unilever's Dove brand, for example, which made its advertising mark by using a realistic view of women who were not supermodels in its "real beauty" commercials, targeted young consumers in the early 2010s with a partnership with MTV and a "Fresh Spin" campaign. Meanwhile, Ban deodorant, owned in the 2010s by the Japanese cosmetic giant KAO and using the catchphrase, "Don't Sweat the Small Stuff," offered more than 12 brands of its popular roll-on plus solid stick and gel products.

One 21st century industry trend has been to include antiperspirants in other products. Moisturizers for the body, dermal (skin) lightening agents, and some hair re-growth inhibitors, for example, include antiperspirant formulas to give multiple benefits. Other trends in the industry address market segmentation, particularly targeting teens (to try and establish early brand loyalty) as well as more specifically male teens (who often become more concerned with personal hygiene than they were previously).

There is no sign that U.S. consumers are going to give up their deodorant stick any time soon, but an October 2010 article in the *New York Times* noted that "some have concluded that deodorant is unnecessary after forgetting it once with no social repercussions." However, the article also noted that adults under the age of 24 admitted to using deodorant and antiperspirant more than nine times a week, and even older age groups did not drop their deodorant use to less than once a day.

BIBLIOGRAPHY

Byron, Ellen. 2011. "Unilever Tackles the Ugly Underarm." *Wall Street Journal*. Accessed January 9, 2012. http://online.wsj .com/article/SB1000142405274870369670457622311270 5412404.html.

"Diserens, Helen Barnett." *New York Times*. Accessed January 9, 2012. http://query.nytimes.com/gst/fullpage.html?res=9F05E 0D9103AF934A25757C0A96E9C8B63.

"Global Deodorants Market to Reach US$12.6 Billion by 2015, According to a New Report by Global Industry Analysts, Inc." *PRWeb*. Accessed January 9, 2012. prweb.com/releases /deodorants_spray/solid_stick_roll_on_cream/prweb8114939 .htm.

Jones, Renee. 2006. "Great Inventions: Deodorants." *New Zealand Herald*. Accessed January 9, 2012. http://www .nzherald.co.nz/health/news/article.cfm?c_id=204&objectid =10364004.

Olson, Elizabeth. 2011. "She Hopes to Help a Dove Campaign Become a Hit." *New York Times*. Accessed January 9, 2012. www.nytimes.com/2011/08/26/business/media/dove -campaign-includes-women-djs.html?_r=1&ref=deodorants.

Saint Louis, Catherine. 2010. "The Great Unwashed." *New York Times*. Accessed January 9, 2012. http://www.nytimes.com /2010/10/31/fashion/31Unwashed.html?adxnnl=1&pagewan ted=all&adxnnlx=1326128732-Nx1btWrIoZGQOkv /iKvRMg.

Soojung-Kim Pang, Alex. 2002. "Mighty Mouse." *Stanford Magazine*. Accessed January 9, 2012. http://www.stanfordalu mni.org/news/magazine/2002/marapr/features/mouse.html.

Stoyles, Pennie, and Peter Pentland. *The A to Z Inventions and Inventors. Volume 5: Q to S.* South Yarra, Australia: Macmillan Education Australia, 2006.

"Theme Park Bans Thrillseekers from Riding Rollercoasters with Arms in the Air. . .Because of Body Odour." *Mail Online*, Accessed January 9, 2012. http://www.dailymail.co.uk/news /article-1207324/Theme-park-bans-thrillseekers-riding -rollercoasters-arms-air--body-odour.html.

"What Is Body Odor? What Causes Body Odor?" *Medical News Today*. Accessed January 9, 2012. http://www.medicalnew stoday.com/articles/173478.php.

Willis, Garry. "Message in the Deodorant Bottle: Inventing Time." *Critical Inquiry* 15, no. 3 (Spring, 1989): 497–509.

Band-Aid Bandages:
A Brand Born out of Market Need

The term "Band-Aid" is often used to refer generally to any adhesive bandage, although in fact Band-Aid is a brand name for the line of adhesive bandages belonging to Johnson & Johnson. Band-Aids work on a very simple principle: they allow a piece of sterile gauze to adhere to the skin without sticking to the wound. Therefore users of the products are able to cover minor wounds which allows them to heal. Invented in 1920, Band-Aids have become ubiquitous in homes and in health care settings.

BEFORE BAND-AIDS: BANDAGES

To understand the history of the Band-Aid brand, it is important to understand the history of bandages. Dressings for wounds and bandages have been used since prehistoric times, with the early bindings likely made from animal hides or plants. Eventually, fabric was used to make bandages. By the middle of the 19th century, bandages saturated with a poultice or liniment oil were in widespread use. These were known as plasters or mustard plasters. Later in the 19th century sticking plasters were created. Also known as adhesive plasters, these used tapes to hold the bandage in place.

According to Henry Petroski in his book *Success through Failure: The Paradox of Design,* a new form of adhesive plaster was patented in 1845 by Horace Day and William Shecut. The new bandages were an improvement on traditional dressings because they allowed the wound to breathe while also being more comfortable than traditional plasters. Shecut and Day claimed that their invention always remained "soft, adhesive, and porous," according to Petroski.

The 19th century also yielded another bandage invention: the antiseptic surgical bandage. While in the 18th and early 19th centuries any fabric was used to make dressings, by the late 1880s Johnson & Johnson specialized in sterile bandages, much in demand in hospitals and in health care settings. Johnson & Johnson was founded in 1886 by three brothers in New Brunswick, New Jersey. The company's bandages were used largely for treating soldiers and patients in hospitals.

Fred B. Kilmer was the scientific director of Johnson & Johnson in the late 1880s. He noticed that many customers were complaining that the surgical bandages were not comfortable and could even cause skin irritation. As a result, Kilmer packaged the dressings with talcum powder, a popular product that was eventually sold separately as Johnson & Johnson Baby Powder.

THE INVENTION OF BAND-AIDS

Band-Aid Brand Adhesive Bandages were invented by Earle Dickson. In 1921 Dickson was working as a cotton buyer for Johnson & Johnson in New Jersey. That same year, Dickson also married, and a simple marital problem with his wife Josephine paved the way for the invention of the Band-Aid. Josephine frequently sustained minor injuries such as cuts while cooking and performing everyday household tasks.

At the time, large bandages were used to cover small and large wounds alike, but these were impractical and inconvenient for repeated small cuts. Josephine was especially prone to injuries on her hands and fingers and the large bandages of the day were especially clumsy for these small wounds. There were other problems with the regular bandages as well. According to Joel Levy's book, *Really Useful: The Origins of Everyday Things,* the bandages took some time to affix and were so clumsy that Josephine could not easily affix the bandages herself, in some cases waiting until her husband got home and was able to help her. The large cotton and gauze bandages had to be cut to size and then secured with a separate tape, a time-consuming process that was difficult to do without assistance as treating a wound required gauze, tape, and scissors.

To help his wife, Dickson came up with a simple idea: he unrolled the tape used with the bandages, folded small pieces of the bandages, and attached them in strips to rolls of surgical tape. He then used crinoline to prevent the tape from getting entangled and rerolled the tape to create a ready-to-use and self-adhesive bandage. He created, in effect, a large roll of surgical tape that contained a long strip of bandage in the center. Josephine could unroll the tape and cut off the pieces she needed with scissors.

The main advantage of the new invention was that Josephine could cut bandages for herself and did not need help dressing minor wounds. Moreover, the surgical tape allowed the sterile gauze to remain firmly in place as the wounds healed. Josephine could also cut pieces of the tape to size, easily treating smaller cuts on her hands and fingers without the clumsiness of the larger bandages.

BAND-AIDS ARE INTRODUCED TO THE MARKET

Dickson mentioned his idea to a colleague at Johnson & Johnson and was promptly encouraged to present the invention to management. In 1920 Dickson presented his idea to the company. Initially, the group was not too impressed, but then Dickson demonstrated how easy the new bandages were to use. Management was intrigued by the fact that Dickson's idea allowed people to attach a bandage to themselves, without assistance.

Johnson & Johnson decided to give Band-Aids a try in 1921 by selling the handmade bandages. The bandages were sold in larger sizes of 18 inches in length and 2.5 inches in width so that patients could cut off the sizes they needed. In the first year the company only sold US$3,000 worth of the new product. According to Levy and other historians, the inconvenient size of the bandages likely contributed to their less-than-stellar popularity. At the time, Johnson & Johnson worked with an advertising agency, Young & Rubicam, Inc. According to Nick Freeth, in his book *Made in America: From Levis to Barbie to Google,* one of the representatives at the advertising agency despaired that "not even a combination of sampling, advertising, and window display is sufficient to create a popular demand for Band-Aids."

BAND-AIDS BECOME POPULAR

In the 1920s Johnson & Johnson embarked on a new idea for promoting the new bandages. The company handed out vast quantities of what were called Band-Aids (named by W. Johnson Kenyon of Johnson & Johnson) to Boy Scouts and butchers across the United States. The rationale was that Boy Scouts and butchers frequently sustained just the types of small injuries and cuts for which Band-Aid bandages were designed. By showing these potential customers just how successful Band-Aids could be, customers would then seek out the product on their own.

The move proved successful and by 1924 the company was manufacturing Band-Aid products by machine, expanding its product line to a few different sizes. As success grew, Johnson & Johnson added improvements to the Band-Aid design. In 1928 for example, the company added aeration holes to the adhesive part of the bandage, allowing air to get in to help wounds heal. By 1939 the Band-Aid bandages were completely sterile. In 1940 Johnson & Johnson added a distinctive red pull string to Band-Aid packaging to make it even easier for people to open them.

During World War II, the war effort required many bandages. According to Johnson & Johnson, millions of Band-Aid bandages were shipped to Europe and beyond to help take care of U.S. soldiers. In the wartime hospitals and in the field, Band-Aid bandages were useful as they could be applied more quickly and easily than traditional gauze bandages. In addition, they kept out dirt and bacteria.

By 1951 Johnson & Johnson had introduced more modern and durable plastic bandages, and by 1956 the company had introduced its first decorative line. The following year saw the introduction of clear Band-Aid bandages, designed to be less noticeable. In 1958 Johnson & Johnson started making the bandages out of sheer vinyl. By 1961 the company was enjoying sales of US$30 million from the Band-Aid line of products annually.

The creation of the Band-Aid brand of bandages also helped Dickson in his career. Partly as a result of the success of Band-Aids, Dickson became vice president of Johnson & Johnson until 1957, when he retired. He remained on the board of directors at the company until he died in 1961.

THE BAND-AID MARKETING EFFORT

Johnson & Johnson used advertisements and commercials effectively to promote its Band-Aid bandages. Indeed, from the moment that the company distributed free bandages to Boy Scouts, Band-Aids were an example of savvy marketing. During World War II, advertisements for Band-Aids appeared in print, stressing the usefulness of Band-Aids in the war effort and on the home front. In one advertisement, the caption read "An Old Family Friend in a New Form: Sulfa-Thiazole Band-Aid." The images accompanying the advertisement showed a wounded soldier being taken for treatment on a stretcher and a mother placing a Band-Aid on a small boy's cut. The image clearly linked the dangers on the home front and the war front, with the accompanying text warning about "infection" and the importance of keeping dirt and other hazards out of a wound.

In the 1940s and 1950s Johnson & Johnson was also using television commercials, a relatively new medium at the time, to promote Band-Aids. One early commercial from 1948 showed a number of competing bandages unable to stick to an egg, while Band-Aid brand bandages stuck to the egg firmly enough to lift the small object. The advertisement then showed that Band-Aids continued to stick while the egg was boiled and then put in soapy dishwater.

In 1951 Johnson & Johnson introduced an even more intriguing marketing idea. That year, the book *Doctor Dan, the Bandage Man* was published. The children's book featured a small boy named Dan who was injured while playing with friends. When he ran to his mother for help, she washed the wound and put a Band-Aid brand bandage on it. Dan then proceeded to put Band-Aids on pets, toys, and others who were injured, earning him the nickname "Dan, the Bandage Man." The book, written by Helen Gasprad and published by Simon & Schuster, contained bright illustrations by Corinne Malvern. Six Band-Aids were included with each book, a move that according to Freeth ensured the popularity of Band-Aids. *Doctor Dan, the Bandage Man* was a runaway hit, with the first edition alone selling 1,600,000 copies, ensuring that Band-Aids made their way into millions of homes, six Band-Aids at a time.

Random House reported that *Doctor Dan, the Bandage Man* was one of the first times that product branding and book packaging were used together. Although the practice became quite common, it was not in the 1950s when the book was published. According to an introduction by Simon & Schuster in *Doctor Dan, the Bandage Man*, the publishing company got the idea for the book first, in part because Band-Aids were so popular. When the publishers approached Johnson & Johnson with the idea, Johnson & Johnson was intrigued but noted that Band-Aids were a trademarked item and asked the publishers to point this out in the book, a suggestion to which Simon & Schuster agreed. The book proved so popular that it became part of the Smithsonian permanent collection. It was republished in 2004 and remained in print as of 2012.

According to Debbie Millman's book, *Brand Bible: The Complete Guide to Building, Designing, and Sustaining Brands*, Johnson & Johnson used a variety of other marketing techniques to promote Band-Aids, including distinctive tin packages and collaborations with designers. Millman noted that the company has worked with fashion designer Cynthia Rowley and with Disney designers to create attractive and fashionable Band-Aids for adults.

THE LONG-TERM SUCCESS OF BAND-AIDS

Using marketing, Johnson & Johnson was able to take a promising idea and turn it into one of the most recognized products in a medicine cabinet. As the popularity of Band-Aids grew, Johnson & Johnson expanded its product line to address customer needs. In 1994 for example, Johnson & Johnson introduced Band-Aids for active lifestyles, including Sport Strip Bandages. Water Block Plus Bandages, Activ-Flex Bandages, and flexible fabric bandages followed. Many of these were waterproof and offered additional adhesiveness as well as cushioning and extra flexibility, ensuring that they would remain in place even during sports activities. In addition, the company offered Band-Aids with extra protection, including the breathable Ultra-Strips Bandages that were sealed on all sides to keep out bacteria and dirt.

The Band-Aid plus Antibiotic brand of bandages was introduced in 1997 and relaunched in 2006. These bandages included gauze saturated with antibiotic topical treatment, promising, according to Johnson & Johnson, faster healing and minimized scarring. The Advanced Healing Blister was made specifically for blisters and provided a cushioned surface to protect the blister.

By 2000 Johnson & Johnson had made more than 100 billion Band-Aids. By then, the ubiquitous bandages had become a part of virtually every emergency kit and medicine cabinet in the United States. In 2011 Johnson & Johnson had a wide range of Band-Aid brand products, including an antiseptic wash, plastic Band-Aid bandages, sheer Band-Aid bandages, clear Band-Aid bandages, and children's Band-Aid bandages with popular cartoon characters printed on them.

Band-Aids were created not by a company, but by one man with the motivation to conveniently solve a common household problem. Launched by a major company, Band-Aids did not succeed at first, but a judicious use of sampling, product placement, and advertising helped the company turn the Band-Aid brand of bandages into a multibillion-dollar business.

BIBLIOGRAPHY

"1950s–1970s Celebrity Commercials: Simonize to Max Factor." *YouTube*, June 19, 2010. Accessed December 31, 2011. http://www.youtube.com/watch?v=J428n7qFCV0.

"Band-Aid Adhesive Bandage." Cambridge, MA: Massachusetts Institute of Technology, November 2000. Accessed December 31, 2011. http://web.mit.edu/invent/iow/dickson.html.

"Band-Aid Commercial 1981." *YouTube,* June 17, 2010. Accessed December 31, 2011. http://www.youtube.com /watch?v=Jtm05pD6u-4&feature=related.

Freeth, Nick. *Made in America: From Levis to Barbie to Google.* St. Paul, MN: MBI Publishing Company, 2005, 20.

Gaspard, Helen. *Doctor Dan, the Bandage Man.* Racine, WI: Western Publishing Company, 1950. Accessed January 3, 2012. http://www.antiquebooks.net/readpage.html#golden.

Gurowitz, Margaret. "Doctor Dan, the Bandage Man." *Kilmer House,* July 22, 2008. Accessed December 31, 2011. http:// www.kilmerhouse.com/2008/07/doctor-dan-the-bandage -man/.

Johnson & Johnson. "Band-Aid Brand Heritage." New Brunswick, NJ, 2011. Accessed December 31, 2011. http:// www.band-aid.com/brand-heritage.

———. "Investor Relations." New Brunswick, NJ, 2011. Accessed December 31, 2011. http://www.investor.jnj.com /investor-relations.cfm.

Levy, Joel. *Really Useful: The Origins of Everyday Things.* Bufffalo, NY: Firefly Books, 2002.

Millman, Debbie, ed. *Brand Bible: The Complete Guide to Building, Designing, and Sustaining Brands.* Minneapolis, MN: Rockport Publishers, 2012.

Petroski, Henry. *Success Through Failure: The Paradox of Design.* Princeton, NJ: Princeton University Press, 2008, 74–75.

Bank of America and
the Evolution of U.S. Banking Industry

GIANNINI AND THE BANK OF ITALY

The origins of the modern banking giant Bank of America lie with the dreams of Amadeo Peter Giannini, one of the great financiers of U.S. history. Without Giannini and his persistent innovation in the finance sector, banking in the United States might have worn an entirely different face.

Amadeo Giannini was born in 1870, in San Jose, California. His parents were immigrants from Genoa, Italy. After his father died in a fight when Giannini was seven (in a dispute over the sum of one dollar), his step-father, Lorenzo Scatena, became an important influence in the young boy's life. Scatena was a businessman and teamster specializing in produce. Giannini only attended school until he was 14, after which he helped Scatena with his work; while doing so, Giannini quickly built a reputation for personal honesty and care for customers. The produce business became so successful that by the time Giannini had turned 31, he was prepared to sell all his shares in the business to the employees and retire.

However, retirement did not go as planned. One year later, Giannini joined the board of directors at the Columbus Savings & Loan Society of San Francisco, California. The society specialized in Italian financial services for other immigrants in the area, but with his experience in day-to-day trade Giannini soon noticed a discrepancy in the attitude of the banking organization. The other board members were principally interested in large-business clients, and when Giannini suggested a model closer to the original intent of the business, the board immediately rejected the idea. The experience provided Giannini with a valuable lesson in the banking practices of the time.

After a couple years of planning, Giannini began raising money for his own banking project. By 1904, he had amassed US$150,000 and proceeded to open the Bank of Italy in a converted saloon directly across from the Columbus Savings & Loan Society. Giannini had a dream for his new business, and it differed markedly from the habits of other U.S. banks at the time.

BANKING TRIALS AND RESPONSES

What Giannini had seen was the inevitable progression of the banking industry as a whole. Banking had become a much more universal service than it had been in the past. Tradition dictated that bank clientele were mostly businessmen with enough money to store in accounts or pay off loans based on private negotiations. Banking also was used by rich families, who fell under similar guidelines as businessmen. No other opportunities existed, because no other markets for banking had been created.

By 1904 Giannini realized that a new market had formed of its own accord. The Industrial Revolution, together with its effects on transportation and manufacturing, had created a flourishing middle class in the United States. These people were potential consumers, clients who might not be able to deal with the customary large business loans but who could pay off smaller individual loans and maintain personal savings accounts.

As a result, the Bank of Italy focused on small loans for Italian immigrants, capital for entrepreneurs bold enough to seek out loans for new business, and accounts for every worker who wanted a way to put money aside for later use. Many other Californian banks had been started by wealthy investors who had made their fortunes through silver mining, or by railroad barons who preferred California to the crowded East Coast and were interested in expansion. In a move that generated outcry among the banking leaders of the day, Giannini started actively marketing his banking services. Moving beyond word of mouth, he advertised his bank in local papers and created an aggressive sales strategy. In an era where financial services were considered a class above real business, Giannini went door-to-door and worked to make sales in the street, personally offering the services of his own bank.

It was not an easy sell. The average worker did not have enough experience with banks to immediately grasp the value in borrowing or depositing, but Giannini persisted in his explanations. He saw the potential of a vast, undersaturated market filled with small-time clients, with each new account adding up to overall success.

Giannini had been growing his business for two years when the Great San Francisco Earthquake occurred in 1906. The damage the earthquake caused to the buildings throughout the city was soon eclipsed by the fires that raged afterward, which ruined even more buildings and led to far greater fatalities than the earthquake alone. By the time the disaster had run its course, most business leaders were struggling to assess the damage, let alone resume operation of their companies. Giannini was not among them.

In a move that won acclaim lasting decades, Giannini had woken up during the earthquake and immediately rushed to the Bank of Italy. He managed to borrow a produce wagon and a team of horses on the way, so by the time he reached his bank he had both storage space and transportation, which were rarities in the middle of the disaster. While the bank building had been reduced to rubble, Giannini managed to salvage around US$2 million from his vault. He loaded the money into the borrowed wagon and took it back to his house, safely out of the epicenter of the disaster. When the fires swept through the area other bankers found their vaults inaccessible for days, while Giannini had access to a large portion of his own assets.

The legend continued as Giannini again defied the plans of nearby bankers to shut down banks until stability returned. Giannini reasoned that the days following the earthquake would be an ideal period to offer loans and withdrawals to those anxious to rebuild homes and businesses, or simply eager to obtain enough funds to live on until the disaster passed. While waiting for his building to be repaired, the entrepreneur reopened his bank in an impromptu shop in North Beach, California. He lowered his normally lax loan standards even further and offered deals based on what became known as "a face and a signature." These loans allowed families and low-end businesses the chance to rebuild, thereby hastening the reconstruction of San Francisco.

A year later, the Panic of 1907, a financial crisis exacerbated by the natural disaster of a year before, swept through California. Giannini benefited again as other banks folded under the pressure to produce funds as customers emptied their accounts. The Bank of Italy managed to stay solvent, thanks to the assets Giannini had rescued.

THE RISE OF BANK OF AMERICA

As San Francisco recovered and the West Coast of the United States grew, Giannini's dreams grew to match. He had revolutionized the concepts of lending and market specialization in the financial industry. The loans other banks had refused to make fueled much of the growth into the more agricultural parts of California, which bloomed rapidly as the population of the state increased. Next, Giannini turned his focus on the concept of banking expansion.

Tradition dictated that banks should stay centrally located around a single office or a single urban area. This made it easier to manage assets, and for most of history the transportation of funds between banking centers was both expensive and dangerous. However, the telegraph and railroad had been around for decades, and Giannini surmised it was time to rethink the old approach. He again treated his bank as though it was just another business, and started to plan an expansion throughout California. The strategy was unheard of at that time, but Giannini recognized an important lesson during the Earthquake of 1906 and Panic of 1907: a bank that spread out its assets and centers of operation could weather difficult times more easily than banks with only one location.

In 1909 Giannini started his long-term strategy by purchasing banks throughout California and combining them with his Bank of Italy. By 1918 he had created the first statewide banking network seen in the United States. As he worked, Giannini continued to expand his individual and small-business lending programs. Specialties developed, such as home mortgages, automotive loans, and installment plans for drawing on certain types of credit. A variety of Californian major industries owed their rise to his generous lending tactics. The wine industry in the Californian valleys began with help from his small-business loans. Without Giannini's support the movie industry would have struggled to find its footing, but the banker was willing to take a chance on the new technology. In 1923 he formed a division dedicated to financing Hollywood, California, and he was a backer of United Artists, which had such memorable founders as Charlie Chaplin and D. W. Griffith.

Both U.S. state and federal governments had instituted regulations to prevent bank branching, and especially interstate expansion, by financial companies. Giannini managed to work around these regulations by creating a series of holding companies, which owned different sections of his banking empire. In 1919 he began with the Bancitaly Corporation, which helped his expansion across California. By 1927 Giannini had acquired an additional line of banks, which he called the Bank of America California (the primary Bank of America being located in New York, New York). The following year he replaced Bancitaly with the new TransAmerica Corporation. In 1930 he merged his banking lines under TransAmerica into a single entity, renamed the Bank of America Natural Trust and Savings Association.

In 1930 Giannini retired once again and moved to Europe. Meanwhile, the Great Depression caused TransAmerica to refocus. Without Giannini and his vision, the company decided to pull back from small-time loans in order to manage liquidity more closely. However, Giannini saw this as a philosophy in direct contrast to his purpose in founding Bank of Italy. He immediately returned to the United States and began a proxy battle to retake control of the bank and restore its focus on individual accounts. With the help of willing employees and customers he managed to secure enough votes to become chairman once again, consolidating TransAmerica into Bank of America.

Giannini saw his vision maintained. Throughout the 1930s and for many years to come, Bank of America was the largest commercial bank in the world, offering a number of financial services to a broad market of entrepreneurs, families, and individuals. In the 1950s Bank of America had more than 500 branches spread out across the United States and more than US$6 billion in deposits.

CONTINUED SUCCESS

The battle between U.S. federal regulations and interstate banking would continue long after Giannini's death in 1949. Although TransAmerica was broken apart via U.S. federal action in the 1950s, the Bank of America name and approach to business continued until the 1990s. At this time new legislation permitted straightforward combination of banking companies across state lines and saw the emergence of the modern Bank of America, often abbreviated BoA.

Although eventual international expansion took decades, Bank of America kept the Giannini dream in mind. The business remained focused on the individual consumer and designed marketing tactics to appeal to the general U.S. population. When innovations were introduced in the commercial banking sector, Bank of America was ready to embrace them with the same enthusiasm on which the company had been founded. This was proven in the late 1950s when the first credit cards came to the market.

Store credit cards had been available to U.S. consumers for several decades, but universal credit cards had yet to be developed by banks. In 1958 Bank of America, in close competition with other banks, released one of the first universal credit cards, for use at a variety of California locations in place of money. Like offering consumer loans in the past, the idea was unique and had the potential to change the banking industry forever. The individual customer again came to the forefront as Bank of America targeted everyday workers.

The marketing for this new BankAmericard also mirrored Giannini's original designs. Customers in the United States showed hesitancy in accepting the idea that a credit card could be used for nontraditional, everyday expenses. Bank of America went directly to the U.S. customers themselves and created a promotional event centered on Ann Foley, a secretary who agreed to use the card for a full month in place of cash. Backed by Bank of America, Foley lived in a motel and spent the last part of the month on vacation across California, successfully proving that this innovation was also suitable for the individual U.S. consumer.

THE BANK OF AMERICA LEGACY

By 2000 Bank of America, now a multibranch, international corporation, had fallen behind Citigroup Inc., but it was still the second-largest commercial banking organization. Although the bank would go through a number of financial challenges caused by the housing market crash that began in 2006 and 2007 and resulting mortgage issues, Bank of America had proven its ability to provide services to the common U.S. worker. Without Giannini and his radical approach to the financing, banking in the United States and throughout the world would not look the same. The modern era of Internet banking, retirement accounts, investment services, and insurance management started when Bank of America dedicated itself to the individual U.S. consumer.

BIBLIOGRAPHY

"A. P. Giannini." Biography.com 2011. Accessed December 13, 2011. http://www.biography.com/people/a-p-giannini-38693.

Bank of America. "Think of It as Money." Charlotte, NC, 2011. Accessed December 13, 2011. http://message.bankofamerica.com/heritage/#/ourheritage/innovation/think-money.

"Bank of America History." *Real Estate Zing,* Accessed December 13, 2011. http://www.realestatezing.com/banks-in-usa/bank-of-america/history-bofa.html.

Doti, Lynne Pierson. "Banking in the Western U.S." *EH.net Encyclopedia,* edited by Robert Whaples, June 10, 2003. Accessed December 13, 2011. http://eh.net/encyclopedia/article/doti.banking.western.us.

Kadlec, Daniel. "America's Banker: A. P. Giannini." *TIME,* December 7, 1998. Accessed December 13, 2011. http://www.time.com/time/magazine/article/0,9171,989772-2,00.html.

Mehta, Stephanie N. "20 Business Decisions That Made History." *Fortune,* June 27, 2005.

Woosely, Ben, and Emily Starbuck Gerson. "The History of Credit Cards." *CreditCards.com,* May 11, 2009. Accessed December 13, 2011. http://www.creditcards.com/credit-card-news/credit-cards-history-1264.php.

BASF: Multinational Diversified Chemical Company

BASF AND THE BEGINNING OF *VERBUND*

BASF SE rose from humble origins in Germany to become the largest chemical company in the world in the early 2010s, with revenue greater than US$85 billion in 2010. The company entered a wide variety of industries, expanding from textiles into industrial chemicals and agricultural products. This diversity stemmed from the core values BASF began with, which were valuation of hard work, perfection of research techniques, and constant innovation. The corporation could claim a history of impressive survival through bold expansion into new, risky areas such as modern manufacturing techniques, fertilizers, and plastics.

COMPANY ORIGINS

BASF was an abbreviation for the German name Badische Anilin- und Soda-Fabrik (Baden Aniline and Soda Factory) AG. The company was founded in 1865 by Friedrich Engelhorn in the state of Baden-Württemberg, Germany. Engelhorn intended the company to be a fusion of the original coal gas company and a firm that explored new chemical products. By this time the Industrial Age had revolutionized manufacturing across Europe and through the world. Several important changes were altering the needs of old markets and creating entirely new market opportunities.

For Engelhorn, one of the most important changes had occurred in the field of textile dyes. Along with basic improvements in hygiene, factory workers began accepting new, factory-spun clothes with prices low enough for nearly anyone to afford. But textile firms had become accustomed to offering clothes in a variety of colors, and the burgeoning demand posed a problem. The textile industry could grow exponentially, but it needed access to more dyes. Previously used natural dyes were already in short supply and few replacements existed.

Engelhorn knew that European chemists had built an impressive inventory of synthetic dyes through recent experimentation, but no one was producing them in mass quantities for textile companies. Some of the dyes, including aniline purple and aniline yellow, could be derived from coal tars. Engelhorn analyzed the issue and realized he could open a chemical production facility that used his coal gas byproducts to make the needed dyes.

The business was an instant success, but rather than rest on one good idea Engelhorn began the BASF tradition of piling invention atop invention. The best-selling dyes were red and indigo, made from natural products that lasted longer than the coal tar colors. BASF set up a chemical research center, first headed by Heinrich Caro, to explore new sources of synthetic dyes as yet undiscovered by scientists.

The combination of research, chemical production, and partnership with the original coal tar company led to the development of what would be called the *Verbund* principle. A German term meaning "fully integrated," *Verbund*, defined how the company arranged its factories and linked together the many stages of production into a cohesive whole. *Verbund* created efficiency for the original firm and would prove invaluable as BASF continued to grow.

EARLY APPROACHES

The company started on basic, proven dyes, creating magenta with aniline by-products, then selling both the dye and the by-products to interested factories. In 1869 the company created alizarin, a new red dye derived from the madder plant. These two dyes proved invaluable for the growing business. As a readily available red dye, alizarin rose in popularity among eager textile manufacturers, both in Germany and throughout the Western world. By 1872 BASF had begun construction of a corporation mini-town called the Hemshof colony to house its workers and support necessary expansion.

While BASF had created the basic principles of *Verbund* to create a successful production business, the company lacked experience in marketing and sales. To solve the problem it acquired Knosp and Siegle, German dye merchants that could supply the sales front for the corporation. This represented another step in vertical integration for BASF, which already had a close partnership with the merchants and now held a trading network of more than 5,000 customers through their synergy.

The rest of the 19th century passed in a flurry of innovations. Not content with one profitable idea, the company built upon its first successes with even more activity. BASF created methylene blue, a dye for cotton that not only drew the interest of the vast cotton industry in the United States but also proved to be an ideal medical dye for bacterial and viral studies. New synthesis methods helped BASF produce old dyes more quickly at lower costs. In 1888 company chemists found a way to easily synthesize sulfuric acid (used for creating alizarin dyes) and became the largest sulfuric acid producer in the world. Advances in chlorine liquefaction and other vital industrial chemicals also occurred at the 18 primary laboratories BASF managed.

The company plants and employees also underwent changes. The plants modernized by installing a local telephone network in the early 1880s, and made human resources history by developing one of the first company health insurance plans around the same time. The chemical industry was still prone to serious, often fatal accidents, especially during experimentation phases, so the care BASF showed its employees was well appreciated.

BASF kept to its strategy of vertical expansion, moving into related fields drawn even closer through new technology. In 1890 it opened a patent department to manage its many chemical processes. In 1891 the first departmental version of BASF customer service was opened in a separate branch to deal with textile questions and technical advice. Again, the *Verbund* principle, on its way to becoming a codified part of company strategy, helped ensure all new departments and production methods fused with related businesses. By 1900 the company boasted more than 6,000 employees.

However, one of the most important innovations of the era proved to be synthetic indigo. After decades of struggling to find an effective way to synthesize the dye, BASF finally found a commercial version and marketed a synthetic indigo dye, which it reported to be one of its most important products to date. The announcement proved prophetic. In an era where durable worker clothes had become a necessity for factory labor, BASF encouraged development of trousers destined to have two immense growth spurts, one for practicality and one for style. These trousers despite using indigo dye, were called blue jeans.

THE FERTILIZER ERA: BASF AND THE WORLD

BASF continued its pattern of innovation and efficiency through *Verbund* and expanded its operations up and down the supply chain. Yet along with this expansion came participation in other industries. By 1910 BASF began operating not as a dye production company but as a full chemical plant, offering chemical solutions to all types of business.

The new company model of diversification came at a perfect moment for Great Britain and other nations with strong agricultural sectors. In the early 20th century, key harvests like wheat depended on natural nitrogen and ammonia fertilizers. Nearly the only source for the fertilizer was saltpeter from Chile, where supplies were running out. The need for synthetic versions of common fertilizers was immense, but chemists first needed to find a way to draw these chemicals from the air and fix them into a permanent state. BASF scientists led the way, and by 1913 the company had developed a synthetic ammonia fertilizer. Fertilizer chemicals quickly became a key facet of BASF expansion, almost overtaking the dye business.

The creation of new synthetic fertilizers required nearly constant innovation. BASF again proved its willingness to experiment, taking new steps in steel manufacturing, reactor development, and compressor engineering. This led to another production avenue, the area of high-pressure machinery. Application of high-pressure technologies promised to transform the manufacturing industry, and BASF entered the field well-positioned. Germany had become a world leader in chemical production and engineering (two fields becoming more inseparable) and BASF was at the epicenter.

Without the *Verbund* principle of interlocking departments, BASF might have struggled to hold itself together. Fortunately, the company kept strict control of its manufacturing facilities and the constant development of new machinery or processing steps. Guidelines and setup were transferred exactly from plant to plant so that no step was missing. The chain of management and structure of employee communication also remained strictly intact through each expansion project. Raw materials were used precisely with minimal waste. Infrastructures were designed to accomplish production tasks without superfluities. BASF also chose to conduct extensive trials on all new fertilizer products so safety parameters could be set and the business could give farmers complete instructions on how to properly use the synthetic chemicals. This led to the development of a separate agricultural research station and laid the groundwork for future safety protocols in the chemical industry.

Verbund also helped BASF survive World War I and the economic turmoil afterward. New national regulations created by the German republic in the 1920s made it more difficult for BASF to keep its existing employee model, but the company continued its policy of following innovation after innovation. While the war had brought out the dark side of chemistry in explosives and deadly gases, BASF pushed exploration in other areas as well, including modern surfactants used in laundry.

Although the dye market was fading, the corporation continued to produce breakthroughs, including the synthesis of methanol in 1923, the hydrogenation of coal, and the development of protective industrial coatings. By the mid-1920s BASF was one of the few successful major corporations left in Germany. Bowing to both internal and external pressures, company leaders agreed to streamline services and merge BASF with five other chemical producers to creation the megacorporation known as IG Farben. BASF continued making strides in the chemical industry within IG Farben, developing the first usable antifreeze solution for cars in the late 1920s and exploring the potential of styrene, one of the first plastics.

However, in the 1930s and 1940s the combination of the Great Depression and the increasingly national and socialistic nature of German politics forced continual reorganization of the company, until IG Farben and its subsidiaries were fully caught up in World War II.

POSTWAR GROWTH AND WORLDWIDE EXPANSION

Not many companies could have survived the chaos that World War II and its aftermath brought to Germany, especially companies so involved in war-related activities as BASF had been under IG Farben. For a number of war crimes, including the use of concentration camp labor, IG Farben was dissolved, but BASF was allowed to reclaim its old independence and attempt to succeed in a war-torn country marked by lack of resources, ruined industrial areas, and confiscated goods.

Beginning with a workforce of only 800, BASF attempted to rebuild its chemical empire. The goal might have not have been possible, but the company used patents

it had developed during World War II while rebuilding its concept of *Verbund* once again to maintain order and efficiency. Fortunately, BASF would be involved with another world-changing innovation: the creation of plastic materials. In the 1950s BASF moved into producing perlon, nylon, and the highly versatile polyethylene, all materials in high demand by the emerging manufacturing industry. BASF supplemented its plastics segment with new work in agriculture and dyes, too. From insulator foam to the sudden new demand for blue jeans and their indigo dye, BASF rebuilt itself with unprecedented speed.

BASF expansion in Germany swiftly turned to expansion throughout the world. Branches or close partnerships sprang up throughout Europe, then across the Atlantic Ocean in areas like Brazil and the United States. Plastics led to petrochemicals, advances in microbiology became new agricultural products, and BASF also expanded operations into rubber, oil, blood plasma substitutes, and a host of other products.

Verbund developed into a full business model for successful production. BASF split the original *Verbund* concept into several different facets. Energy *Verbund* governed the use of energy in BASF plants, leading to the creation of heat reclamation techniques and responsible use of chemicals with minimum waste, toxic or otherwise. Logistics *Verbund* governed material transportation. BASF linked its primary production plants with private pipelines that allowed sites to exchange resources and energy quickly and effectively. The company also continued to find ways to reuse or recycle by-products in the same way Engelhorn did when first deriving dyes from coal tars. Research *Verbund* worked to organize the dozens of research and development centers BASF managed in Europe, the Americas, and Asia, linking discoveries or information as quickly as possible. By the early 2010s BASF had more than 9,600 workers in research alone, all sharing data through proprietary networks.

BIBLIOGRAPHY

BASF. "BASF Historical Milestones." Ludwigshafen, Germany, 2011. Accessed December 16, 2011. http://www.basf.com /group/corporate/en/about-basf/history/index.

"BASF." *Chemistry Daily,* January 4, 2007. Accessed December 16, 2011. http://www.chemistrydaily.com/chemistry/BASF #BASF_history.

BASF. "Types of Verbund." Ludwigshafen, Germany, 2011. Accessed December 16, 2011. http://basf.com/group /corporate/en/about-basf/profile/verbund/types.

BASF Corporation North America. "What Is Verbund?" Florham Park, NJ, 2000. Accessed December 16, 2011. http://www2 .basf.us/about/verbund.html.

Braille System

The Braille system uses small raised dots to help the visually impaired read and write. The system makes use of a series of six dots known as cells. Each cell is made up two columns of six dots total, with two dots across and three down. To create a character in Braille, a specific pattern of dots is raised. For example, to create the letter *a,* the top upper left dot is raised. To create the letter *b,* the top upper left dot and the one immediately below it are raised. Each Braille character corresponds to a letter, punctuation mark, or number. When readers run their fingertips over the dots, they can distinguish the letters and numbers that the combination of cells represent.

Users of Braille can also create written text by punching holes in the appropriate formations on paper. A pointed stylus and slate can be used for this. The slate keeps the paper steady and also provides cells as a guide for the writing. Users of Braille can also use a machine known as a Braillewriter, which is similar to a typewriter, to create printed Braille. Braille has a number of uses. It is used in books, on currency, and even on elevator buttons. Since 2001, the European Union has required that all medication packages contain basic information about dosage and medication name in Braille.

A FLEXIBLE SYSTEM

Although the term "Braille" is generally used to describe the system of raised dots used for reading and writing, it is more accurate to say that Braille is a series of systems. For example, Braille is different in every language, as every language had unique characters. A different form of Braille is used for music notation and for mathematics. In addition to elementary Braille, a form of contracted Braille is also available. This form of Braille is like shorthand in that it saves space and allows advanced users to read and write more quickly. According to the National Federation of the Blind, Braille users can read 200 words a minute or even more, and contracted Braille makes higher speeds possible.

Although the Braille system is often seen as a fixed method of writing and reading, it has changed over time. The Braille Authority of North America (BANA), for example, advocated for changes to Braille, in part because of the increased visual and interactive nature of 21st century communication. Braille, however, has always been a changing medium. For example, as BANA notes, the Braille characters for mathematics were changed repeatedly until 1972, when the Nemeth Code for Science and Mathematics Notation became the standard. In the 1960s, when visually impaired students entered regular classrooms, BANA added new characters to Braille so that students could get Braille textbooks that more closely mimicked the books of their peers.

EVOLUTION OF BRAILLE

The Braille system was invented by Louis Braille, and it is helpful to understand Braille's life in order to understand his system. Braille was born in Coupvray, France, in 1809. At the age of three, he was playing in his father's harness shop with a sharp tool used to puncture holes in leather. His hand somehow slipped, and the tool injured his right eye. The young boy lost sight in both eyes by the age of five because of inflammation and infection.

At the time, visual impairment created serious impediments to a normal life. In Louis's village, there were two other blind men, and both were destitute. Louis's parents were literate, which was not common in Coupvray, and they were adamant that Louis would not become like the two impoverished men in the village. Louis's parents had the young boy take part in regular family activities as much as possible. According to biographer C. Michael Mellor, the Brailles taught Louis the alphabet by hammering upholstery nails into a wooden board. The nails created the shapes of letters, so that Louis could get familiar with the shapes of letters through touch and thus learn the alphabet and acquire basic literacy.

The village priest, Father Jacques Palluy, gave Louis lessons for a year. Palluy eventually requested that Louis be allowed to join the regular village school as a pupil, and Louis was led to the school every day by a local boy so that he could attend classes. Louis remained at the school for two years and was an excellent student. In 1818, however, the school was forced to adopt a new instructional style, one in which students taught each other, and Louis could no longer attend. Father Palluy asked the lord of the manor at Coupvray to write to Valentin Haüy of the Royal Institute for Blind Youth in Paris (now the National Institute for Blind Youth), and Louis was accepted at that school in 1819.

At the Royal Institution for Blind Youth, Louis Braille first encountered tactile writing. Valentin Haüy, the founder of the school, had developed his own version of tactile writing using raised print. The idea was that visually impaired students could run their hands over the print and learn to recognize the raised letters. However, as Louis and other students quickly realized, many letters (for example, *q, o,* and *c*) could feel very similar under the fingertips. In addition, the system of reading this form of raised print was slow, since each letter had to be individually identified.

CREATION OF BRAILLE

Charles Barbier de la Serre, a captain with the French Army, visited the Royal Institution for Blind Youth while Louis was a student there, hoping to introduce his own system for tactile reading. De la Serre had designed this system, called sonography, to allow soldiers to communicate through the written word at night and in other low-light conditions. Sonography used a 12-dot cell and allowed each character to represent a sound, so that words were sounded out rather than spelled out. Louis Braille studied the system and soon concluded that the 12 dots made the system difficult to use and hard to learn. Trying to guess a word by the sounds was also confusing, but Louis used the 12-dot cell system as the basis for his own system.

While still in school, at the age of 15, Louis developed his own tactile system for reading and writing. Louis Braille shared his new system with André Pignier, the di-

rector of the school, as well as with students and teachers in October 1824. At the same time, he showed the Royal Institution for Blind Youth new slates for writing what would become known as Braille, which were based on de la Serre's model. Biographers believe that Gabriel Gauthier, Louis's best friend at the school, was the first to learn to read Braille. Initially, the Braille system was received enthusiastically, and Pignier even ordered slates for the school. Students at the school could easily take notes, write letters to each other, and read easily and quickly.

Louis Braille continued to develop and perfect his system throughout his lifetime. A music lover, Louis went on to create a Braille representation of music in 1828 so that visually impaired people could read and write music. He also created a Braille system for mathematics. In 1829, Louis published the *Method of Writing Words, Music and Plain Song by Means of Dots, for Use by the Blind and Arranged by Them.* The book outlined the Braille system and described it at length. By 1837 the first Braille textbooks were printed by the Royal Institution for Blind Youth.

OPPOSITION TO THE BRAILLE SYSTEM

One early problem that Louis had to solve was that while students could use the Braille system to communicate with each other, writing to sighted parents and friends was still a challenge. In response, Louis invented a system called raphigraphy. This system involved creating traditional letters using raised dots. The letters were recognizable by sighted people but still tactile for the visually impaired. The system, however, required a lot of work, as each letter required many dots.

In 1841 inventor Pierre Foucault created a piston board. This machine punched out complete raised-dot letters, making raphigraphy writing much easier for sighted readers to understand. By 1847 Foucault had invented a typewriter known as a keyboard printer, which created black type for sighted people but which could easily be used by the visually impaired.

These technical problems were not the only early challenges that Louis faced. Some teachers at the Royal Institution for Blind Youth were worried about their jobs and resentful about having to learn Braille. Louis also faced serious opposition from P. Armand Dufau, a teacher at the school who eventually became assistant director and then director of the Royal Institution for Blind Youth. Dufau had published his own book about teaching the blind, and he had his own ideas about education for the visually impaired. When Dufau became director of the school, he removed subjects such as Latin, geography, and history from the curriculum. He also chose to teach students using a form of the tactile letter system known as Boston

Line Type rather than the Braille system. He took away the styluses that students used to write Braille and even burned Braille books and notes at the school, effectively banning the system.

In 1843 the National Institute for Blind Youth (Institut National des Jeunes Aveugles) was opened in a new building, and Louis Braille continued his teaching at this school for nine years, until his death in 1852. Around this time, Dufau may have started actively promoting the Braille system. His attempts at a Braille ban had failed as students continued to use the system, and some historians have theorized that he had to concede defeat. In addition, Joseph Guadet, Dufau's assistant, supported the Braille system. According to the American Foundation for the Blind, Guadet was instrumental in convincing Dufau about the effectiveness of the Braille system. Some biographers and historians have speculated that Dufau eventually supported Braille because the system was shown publicly to be effective, and Dufau stood to gain more recognition by supporting Louis Braille than by working against him.

In a sense, Dufau's opposition and apparent about-face was typical of the early challenges that Braille faced, and typical of the increasing acceptance of the system in the late 19th century and beyond. According to Louis Braille biographer Mellor and other historians, many people, including Dufau, had developed their own systems for teaching the blind to read and write. Most of these systems, including the popular Moon Type and New York Point, were variations on the raised letters that Louis Braille had encountered during his schooling. They were created by sighted teachers, who in many cases hoped for recognition and fame for their inventions. The inventors were not keen about being upstaged by a reading system developed by a child. Initial opposition also occurred because the cells did not look anything like the alphabet, and the system was challenging for sighted people to understand. Biographers like Mellor also noted that discrimination played a part in the early rejection of Braille, and that sighted people did not always want to make the visually impaired more independent.

SPREAD OF THE BRAILLE SYSTEM

In a way, the success of the Braille movement is the success of a grassroots movement. While sighted people may have had their reservations about the system, visually impaired students taught themselves the system and taught other students as well. Deprived of styluses when Dufau banned Braille, they used knitting needles and cutlery to write Braille. At the same time, a number of studies and reviews demonstrated what the students already knew: Braille was a more effective system for the visually impaired. For example, on February 22, 1844, the National Institute for Blind

Youth held a very public demonstration of the effectiveness of the Braille system. The widespread adoption of the system by the visually impaired as well as such public acknowledgement helped the system expand and become accepted.

Louis Braille died in 1852. At the time, the true value of his invention was recognized by some, but was ignored by most of the sighted world. Slowly, however, the system was adopted by the visually impaired and then by national governments. By 1854 Braille was adopted as the system for reading and writing for the visually impaired in France. By 1869 Braille had entered the United States. By the 1950s according to the National Federation of the Blind, more than half of young visually impaired children in the United States were learning Braille. Braille was adopted for visually impaired people as the Standard English Grade Two Braille code in 1932. By 1972 Braille was adopted in the United Kingdom.

TECHNOLOGY AND THE BRAILLE SYSTEM

In the 1960s visually impaired students were integrated into regular schools in the United States, especially after the passage of Public Law 94–142, which required students with visual impairments to be educated in less "restrictive environments." This move coincided with a decline in Braille literacy, a decline that deepened as technology such as tape recorders and computers became more widespread. By the mid-1980s audio books and computers were more widely available to visually impaired students across North America. By that time, screen readers were also available to help computer users read the words on a computer monitor.

New technology in the 1990s and first decade of the 21st century created even more options for the visually impaired. Audio texts were often less expensive and faster to produce than Braille books and allowed students to engage with content without the time-consuming process of learning Braille. Voice-recognition software allowed individuals to write using their voice, while accessibility features available on most computers after 2008 allowed written text to be read back to computer users. Job Access With Speech (JAWS), a computer program, was developed developed for Windows computers to allow the visually impaired to surf the Internet. Also, text-to-voice software was used to write and read electronic communications, including e-mail. For paper documents, character recognition scanners converted documents into a form that could be read out loud by a computer.

DECLINING BRAILLE LITERACY

According to statistics released by the National Federation of the Blind, fewer than 10 percent of the 1.3 million legally blind Americans in 2009 could read and write Braille. Only about 10 percent of legally blind children that year were being taught Braille. In 2010 the CNIB (formerly known as the Canadian National Institute for the Blind) reported that less than 10 percent of the 830,000 visually impaired individuals in Canada could read Braille, and statistics showed similar rates of Braille literacy in the United Kingdom.

Part of the reason for this decline, according to the National Federation of the Blind, is that many teachers find Braille to be outdated, and there are fewer programs available to teach the Braille system to the visually impaired. In her article, "With New Technology, Few Blind Canadians Read Braille," Angela Mulholland consulted Shawn Marsolais of Blind Beginnings, a Canadian organization for visually impaired children, who said that the problem also sometimes stems from parents, who want their visually impaired children to integrate as fully as possible.

A RENEWED INTEREST IN BRAILLE

According to the American Printing House for the Blind, Braille illiteracy was a considerable problem. Studies referred to by *MSNBC* in 2009 show that while legally blind U.S. adults faced an overall 70 percent unemployment rate, Braille readers and writers faced only a 44 percent unemployment rate, compared with a 77 percent rate for those who did not read Braille. The National Federation of the Blind believes that Braille literacy leads to greater independence, advanced degrees, and better work opportunities.

Mulholland also consulted John Rafferty, head of the CNIB, who said that learning Braille is especially crucial for younger students, as it can teach sentence structure, syntax, spelling, and other essential tools for literacy. Without this information, Rafferty noted, children cannot learn the basic function and structure of language, which can make it harder for them to master basic literacy skills needed for employment.

Although modern technology resulted in reduced use of Braille in some cases, such technology could also help to promote Braille literacy. In 2011 a New Mexico State University student, who was attending a Stanford University summer course for the development of innovative applications, developed a Braille writer program. The software worked similarly to much more expensive Braillewriters, in that it allowed users to type in Braille rather than trying to find specific buttons. Just like the Braillewriter, the software made use of eight buttons, so that anyone who was familiar with the Braillewriter could use the new software. The software was inexpensive and could be used with any device that had a touch screen. This type of invention, as well as increasing awareness about the benefits of Braille, could encourage parents of the visually impaired to seek out Braille programs.

BIBLIOGRAPHY

American Foundation for the Blind. 2009. "200 Years: The Life and Legacy of Louis Braille." New York. Accessed January 9, 2012. http://www.afb.org/louisbraillemuseum/braillegallery.asp?GalleryID=44.

Bickel, Lennard. *The Life of Louis Braille.* Leicester, UK: Ulverscroft Large Print, 1989.

Cavendish, Richard. "Death of Louis Braille: January 6th, 1852." *History Today* 52, no. 1 (2002).

"The Evolution of Braille: Can the Past Help Plan the Future?" 2011. *Braille Monitor.* Accessed January 11, 2012. http://www.nfb.org/images/nfb/Publications/bm/bm11/bm1105/bm110506.htm.

"Fewer Blind Americans Learning to Use Braille." 2009. *MSNBC.* Accessed January 9, 2012. http://www.msnbc.msn.com/id/29882719/ns/us_news-life/t/fewer-blind-americans-learning-use-braille/#.TsrifPKa-ZQ.

Frieman, Barry B., and Sharon Maneki. "Teaching Children with Sight about Braille." *Childhood Education* 71, no. 3 (1995).

Mellor, C. Michael. *Louis Braille: A Touch of Genius.* Boston, MA: National Braille Press, 2006.

Millar, Susanna. *Reading by Touch.* London: Routledge, 1997.

Mulholland, Angela. 2010. "With New Technology, Few Blind Canadians Read Braille." *CTV.* Accessed January 9, 2012. http://www.ctv.ca/CTVNews/TopStories/20100416/future_braille_100417/#ixzz1eOJENVBi.

Myers, Andrew. 2011. "Stanford Summer Course Yields Touchscreen Braille Writer." Stanford, CA: Stanford Engineering. Accessed January 9, 2012. http://engineering.stanford.edu/news/stanford-summer-course-yields-touchscreen-braille-writer.

Popov, Irina, and Arthur Durando. "Louis Braille Inventor, Teacher and Organist." *American Organist* 43, no. 12 (2009).

Tea-Mangkornpan, Pinnaree. 2011. "Tablets for the Blind." *Stanford Daily.* Accessed January 9, 2012. http://www.stanforddaily.com/2011/11/15/touchscreen-braille/.

Weygand, Zina. *The Blind in French Society from the Middle Ages to the Century of Louis Braille.* Translated by Emily-Jane Cohen. Stanford, CA: Stanford University Press, 2009.

Wills, Cheryl. 2011. "Braille on Canvases Creates New Type of 'Visual' Artwork." *NY1.* Accessed January 9, 2012. Available from http://brooklyn.ny1.com/content/ny1_living/arts/150689/braille-on-canvases-creates-new-type-of--visual--artwork.

British East India Company:
Company Rule in India

The British East India Company (EIC) had an enormous impact on the power and reach of the British Empire and the burgeoning global trading industry. With the blessing of Queen Elizabeth I the EIC grew to become a major trading company, dealing in everything from spices and textiles to land and agricultural goods. For nearly 300 years it was almost single-handedly responsible for spreading British interests throughout Asia, importing Asian goods, and effectively taking over the government of India.

FIRST VENTURES

The EIC began in 1599 as a stockholder company. One year later the queen granted it monopoly status to begin trading with Asia. Following the success of similar ventures by Dutch and Portuguese traders, the EIC sailed its fleet around the Horn of Africa to reach its various Asiatic destinations. Taking this maritime route allowed the company to surpass the slower traditional caravans once used to import goods from abroad.

Embarking on a trade voyage was no easy feat, however. Planning, support, and patience were necessary as even a single mission required roughly two years to complete. In addition to the time commitment, trade journeys were fraught with danger, including storms, barely navigable waters, pirates, and disease. Although the imports were extremely valuable to the traders, the journey required state backing and shareholders wealthy enough to wait for their goods.

As trading routes developed throughout the 17th and 18th centuries, so did the variety of goods traded. Within a century of its founding the EIC controlled the European market for Indian cloth, with annual imports coming close to one million pieces. As the company's business with India grew over the years, it became more closely involved in Indian government and politics. The EIC based its operations in that country in small trading stations that provided expatriate employees a place to live, work, and worship in accordance with English law and in agreement with local rulers. As its power and influence grew, the company became more engaged in India's politics. In just a few decades, India was witness to an unprecedented shift of power from local governments to the EIC.

EMULATING THE DUTCH

On December 31, 1600, Queen Elizabeth I signed a royal charter establishing the EIC as a trading concern aimed at improving Asian imports. With a capital infusion of £72,000 and some 125 shareholders, the company was governed by a court of directors and a governor. The impetus, noted Anthony Farrington in "The Beginnings of the English East India Company," was a burgeoning Dutch trade. "The company really began as a London reaction to what the Dutch had started to do," Farrington explained. "Most Asian goods coming into London, principally spices, were coming through the medium of the Levant Company, which had been in existence from the late Elizabethan period and was trading to a lot of the world of the eastern Mediterranean."

The England-based Levant Company regulated the country's trade with Turkey and the Levant, a region in the eastern Mediterranean. By the late 16th century Dutch traders began sailing around the Horn of Africa to bring their goods directly into Amsterdam, Rotterdam, and other ports in the Netherlands. The English naturally saw Dutch and Portuguese operations as a threat. Consequently, the queen granted monopoly status to the EIC in the hope of not only stemming such competitive pressures but also boosting important customs revenues in the Port of London.

The first voyage of the EIC departed England in 1601 and its progress was besieged by difficulty. The four ships were stopped by calm waters along the Equator, slowing their journey toward the Cape of Good Hope. When they finally rounded the tip of South Africa, one-fifth of the crew of 500 had died. Finally, in December 1602, the ships sailed into the port of Bantam on the northern coast of the Indonesian island of Java.

That important moment marked the beginning of the first trading post of a commercial enterprise that soon dominated trade between England and Asia. Spices were the traders' target, as they gave taste to the otherwise bland foods that populated English dining tables of the time. In addition to food enhancement, spices could be blended and distilled into medicines and perfumes and their rarity only added to their value.

Much of the company's initial success came from the fact that Asian trading was relatively peaceful. "The company were turning up in heavily armed ships that could hold their own against any Asian shipping that we know of. And, at the end of the day, they were prepared to enforce their concept of free trade with guns," wrote Farrington. "If they felt that they were not being allowed a fair crack of the whip, they could retaliate against the whole trade of a particular port by blockading it."

Before long, the enormous quantities of black pepper being shipped back from Asia led to an oversupply in England. As a result, the company diversified. Textiles from India had become prized in England and throughout Europe during the 18th century, and the EIC saw a clear market opportunity. In 1608 the company established a trading post in Surat, on the northwest coast of India. Three years later it built another factory in Masulipatam, located on India's eastern coast. Business boomed and the EIC was quickly engaged in brisk trade from busy factories such as those located in the walled forts of Saint George in Bengal, India, Fort William in Madras, India and Bombay Castle located in Bombay (now Mumbai), India.

DUTCH CLASHES

Dutch traders arrived in Asia six years before the EIC ships sailed into Bantam. As such, the Dutch United East India Company (VOC) had no inclination to share its newfound market with the English newcomers. By all accounts the Dutch were also much better suited to trade: the VOC started with 10 times the capital of the EIC and was able to tap the vast manpower of northern Germany and the Baltic region. In addition, the Dutch were not afraid to

resort to firepower, as evidenced by their 1601 victory over a Portuguese fleet in the Bay of Bantam.

The extremely high price of the spices cloves, nutmeg, and mace made Asian trading even more lucrative for the Dutch and their rivals. "It soon became clear that the newly formed VOC intended a complete takeover of the European trade in fine spices and that it would do whatever necessary to squeeze out the English company," wrote Farrington. To accomplish this, the Dutch moved to seize control of production. The VOC offered protection against enemies to the rulers of the Spice Islands (now known as the Moluccas, a part of Indonesia) in return for exclusive rights to their spice crops.

The EIC's own attempts at building its Asian trade were consistently hampered by Dutch traders. Much of the 17th century was marked by open hostilities between the English and Dutch, including frequent naval skirmishes off the Indonesian coast, torture, and executions. Despite some attempts at cooperation between the two companies, competition remained fierce for the bulk of the century.

Meanwhile, the EIC began to see its trade in pepper boom. Much of what it sold in London, England was exported to markets in Poland, Russia, and the Ottoman Empire. This trade was partly responsible for the shift in balance between the Dutch and English traders in the latter part of the century. While the fall of Dutch trade was chalked up to a number of factors, the VOC was especially hindered by its narrow focus on Indonesia. As the EIC soon discovered, even greater wealth lay in other parts of Asia.

INDIAN CONQUEST

As the EIC struggled for decades to obtain a foothold in the pepper and spice trade of Indonesia, it also began making inroads in India. Specifically, Indian textile products were prized by importers throughout Europe and the company aimed to capitalize on that development. An important moment in that progress came in 1615 when EIC representative Thomas Roe won an imperial order from Mughal Emperor Jehangir to set up trading posts throughout his empire. The construction and operation of factories across India enabled the EIC to engage in brisk trade of cotton textiles.

As the company continued growing its industrial base throughout the Indian region it also found itself inextricably tied to its politics. Although controversial, the company's effective entry into regional and local politics was perhaps its most important tool in paving the way toward economic dominance. Its political aspirations came in large part from concessions it received from local rulers. In Bengal, India, for instance, the company was able to freely import and export goods without having to pay a tax. In addition, the EIC could issue special permits to certify the movement of goods. By the 18th century the company had successfully subjugated Bengal, India, and in time the whole Indian subcontinent fell under the EIC's sway.

While much of the EIC's growth in India came as a result of skillful diplomacy, it also used force. Company expansion throughout the country shifted into high gear in 1757 at the Battle of Plassey. On June 23, Robert Clive and his EIC forces defeated the army of Siraj-ud-daulah, the nawab (or ruler) of Bengal, India. Clive's victory occurred in Plassey, a small village and mango grove located between Calcutta, India and Murshidabad, India. While the skirmish lasted only a few hours, its consequences were significant. The new ruler, Mir Jafar, allied himself with Clive and agreed (with the help of bribes) to surrender to the EIC and turn over his forces' weapons. The victory was suggestive of others to come: chiefly, the British would gain control of India primarily through the use of bribery, although promises made by the EIC were not always honored.

Other battles helped cement the EIC's regional dominance, including the Carnatic wars (which eliminated the French from south India) and the Battle of Buxar (a 1764 skirmish that gave the EIC control over financial administration of Bengal, Bihar, and Orissa). "It is debated whether conquest was intended from the start, or if it was the unintended consequence of interfering in Indian politics in favor of regional stability for the sake of company trade," wrote Martha Ebbesen in the *Berkshire Encyclopedia of World History*, "but once conquest started, the company rapidly gained control over parts of India as the ruling Mughal empire weakened."

As the first British empire ended with the loss of the American colonies, by the late 18th century a second empire was quickly growing in India. The Marathas, a major people located on India's west coast who wanted to expand their power over the weakened Mughals, rewarded the EIC with land, titles, and influence for the company's offers of armed aid. The company gradually gained more control and authority as local rulers looked to the EIC for assistance. "This process continued until its culmination in 1818, when most of India was under direct or indirect company control," wrote Ebbesen. "This is a prime example of 'reluctant empire,' imperial expansion run by private companies, not government policies."

EIC LEGACY

While force certainly had its place in EIC history, the company was not entirely dependent on armed conflict in its Indian conquest. With the EIC firmly in control of India following the battles of the mid-to-late 18th century, political decision making continued to impact the country's future. Lord Cornwallis' permanent settlement of land revenue in 1793, for example, created significant hard-

ship for the people of Bengal, India. On the other hand, Lord Bentinck, governor-general from 1828 to 1833, established social and infrastructure reforms that would set India well ahead of other emerging countries by the time it won its independence over a century later in 1947.

Conservative elements within India were unswayed by Bentinck's social reforms, however, leading to the Great Mutiny of 1857 and 1858. With the British barely emerging victorious from the mutiny, Queen Victoria effectively ended the EIC's political control in 1858 and established a British Raj that would rule over the country until 1947.

IMPACT OF THE EIC

The EIC's legacy continues to be widely debated. In the early 21st century, high-profile exhibitions and popular histories revived the company's somewhat tarnished reputation and its founders were frequently hailed as globe-trotting adventurers. Business leaders likewise looked to the company as an example of entrepreneurial shrewdness. Others were more critical of its impact. "The East India Company deserves to be looked at as it was, a profit-making company that generated great wealth, but one that also contributed to immense suffering," wrote Nick Robins in *openDemocracy*. "Just as corporations today should be judged by the impacts of their core business rather than their often peripheral donations to cultural events, so the East India Company has to be assessed on the basis of its underlying activities rather than the occasional philanthropy of its executives."

Meanwhile, in the 2010s the East India Company continued to thrive in its London, England, headquarters, trading in gourmet foods.

BIBLIOGRAPHY

"Battle of Plassey." *Manas.* Accessed February 7, 2012. http://www.sscnet.ucla.edu/southasia/History/British/Plassey.html .

Cook, Geoffrey. "British East India Company." *Encyclopedia of Modern Asia,* edited by Karen Christensen and David Levinson. Vol. 1, 317–319. New York: Charles Scribner's Sons, 2002. Gale Virtual Reference Library (GALE|CX3403700390). Accessed February 7, 2012. http://go.galegroup.com/ps/i.do?id=GALE%7CCX3403700390&v=2.1&u=itsbtrial&it=r&p=GVRL&sw=w.

The East India Company. "The Company Today." London, UK, 2012. Accessed February 7, 2012. http://www.theeastindiacompany.com.

Ebbesen, Martha A. "British East India Company." *Berkshire Encyclopedia of World History,* edited by William H. McNeill, Jerry H. Bentley, and David Christian. Vol. 1, 258–260. Barrington, MA: Berkshire Publishing, 2005. Gale Virtual Reference Library (GALE|CX3455000090). Accessed February 7, 2012. http://go.galegroup.com/ps/i.do?id=GALE%7CCX3455000090&v=2.1&u=itsbtrial&it=r&p=GVRL&sw=w.

Farrington, Anthony. "The Beginnings of the English East India Company," May 2002. Fathom Archive, Columbia University. Accessed February 7, 2012. http://www.fathom.com/course/21701760/session1.html.

Paban, Patit. "British East India Company." *Encyclopedia of Business in Today's World*, edited by Charles Wankel. Vol. 1, 190–191. Thousand Oaks, CA: Sage Publications, 2009. Gale Virtual Reference Library (GALE|CX3201500127). Accessed February 7, 2012. http://go.galegroup.com/ps/i.do?id=GALE%7CCX3201500127&v=2.1&u=itsbtrial&it=r&p=GVRL&sw=w.

Robins, Nick. "The East India Company." *openDemocracy*, September 12, 2006. Accessed February 7, 2012. http://www.opendemocracy.net/globalization-vision_reflections/east_india_company_3899.jsp.

Cisco Systems:
From Routers to Networking Systems

CISCO: THE FIRST INVENTIONS

Cisco Systems, Inc., started with a revolutionary idea at the right time, centered itself on core competencies, and grew into one of the most important corporations of the Information Age. There was no century-long development for Cisco and its networking focus. By the 15th year of its existence, in 1999, Cisco had become the most valued company in the world (in terms of U.S. stock market capitalization), before the dot-com bust imbalanced the technology industry. By the end of the first decade of the 21st century, the business had risen to the forefront of the technology industry, defining the Internet era on an international level. Its rapid story of success was based on hard work, a practical look at the future of technology, and a willingness to reinvent business models as needed.

The origins of Cisco have become a frequently cited start-up fable. According to the famous account, Len Bosack and his wife Sandy Lerner, both Stanford University workers, began work on the company in 1984 because of their desire to send each other e-mails when located in two different buildings. While that story is true, Cisco was founded through the joint efforts of many Stanford University computer researchers and support staff members, although the husband-and-wife team of Bosack and Lerner was indeed central to the project.

In the early 1980s, Stanford University began to attempt to link its locations. After an agreement to collaborate with Xerox's Palo Alto Research Center was reached, Stanford students and researchers found themselves with access to some of the most advanced computer and Ethernet research stations in the United States. The problem was the location of Palo Alto, California. There was no way to connect the research hub to the various Stanford departments

so data could be rapidly transferred. The director of computer facilities at the time, Ralph Gorin, requested a way to link computers more easily and at greater distances.

The problem Len Bosack and Sandy Lerner had to overcome was the protocol (specific system for digital communication) barrier. Technology was approaching the Internet age, but obliquely, since computers at the time were not designed to communicate with each other. Different companies from around the world had such disparate programming that even simple messages could not be effectively coded and transferred between systems. There was no widespread translation service available.

THE ROUTER

Overcoming the computer communication barrier led to the first major Cisco invention, a component that would change the world. It was a router that took in many different protocols and changed them to a uniform format so information could be shared in one of the first true networks.

The computer circuit board was designed by Andy Bechtolsheim, who eventually became the founder of Sun Microsystems, Inc. The internal networking boards were developed by a team that included Bosack. Research engineer William Yeager wrote the software. After initial development was completed, Stanford installed several versions of the router in various locations around its primary campus. Updates and enhancements soon followed as the workers, including Bosack and Kirk Lougheed, identified ways in which the original router idea could be improved to allow communication between terminals, entire subnetworks, printers, and other devices.

By 1985 Stanford had grown accustomed to the router system. The university started plans for a new version that would use only a single format but allow multiple computers to communicate at once through an expanded network operating system. Other protocols would eventually be added back into the router, now nicknamed the Blue Box, to increase its adaptability.

At the same time Bosack and Lougheed moved forward with ideas of their own, seeing the commercial value in the Blue Boxes. They started a business, called Cisco (after San Francisco, California), and asked Stanford for permission to sell the router system. They were refused. Even so, the groundbreaking work the computer engineers did for the university also gave them the skills to piece together routers of their own at home, on their own time. The research and development took place at Stanford, while the commercial production started in Bosack and Lerner's living room.

Bosack, Lerner, and Lougheed began selling both the software for the router and a computer-like hardware model to go with it, a device to make businesses more comfortable with the idea of linking their terminals up to a central hub. Despite the rough code, which was constantly updated with new ideas or improvements, Cisco had begun to commercialize the first stages of the Internet, and people began to notice.

Stanford also took note. It appeared that Cisco was making products, or at least creating value, on Stanford time while profiting by it through commercial enterprise. By 1986 several confrontations at Stanford led to Bosack and Lougheed resigning, shifting their focus entirely to Cisco. Lerner, Greg Satz, Richard Troiano, and others who had been involved in the creation of the router joined them, and Cisco severed its ties from Stanford. The university considered the possibility of a lawsuit but decided not to pursue a legal battle for two reasons. First, as Pete Carey pointed out in "A Start-Up's True Tale," Stanford was not very interested in manufacturing routers itself (especially since it was a nonprofit organization). Second, as Perry noted, it was debatable whether the router business would even be worth pursuing.

In 1987 Stanford licensed the router software to Cisco in exchange for a small cash payment, product discounts, and royalties of US$150,000. Cisco offered stock as well, but Stanford followed its customary procedure of denying any offered ownership in companies. Cisco was free to pursue its growth, and the world was ready for the Internet.

BUILDING A NEW ERA

The router sold well in the late 1980s, became widespread in the early 1990s, and by the mid-1990s was the foundation of most Internet communication. Cisco stayed at the forefront of development and sales. Its success was due to its original product and belief that a new device like the router and its software had the ability to revolutionize communication. Eventually businesses would find it difficult to function without such products.

Part of the company's success was also due to location. California proved to be the center of technological innovation for many years. Cisco was positioned to manufacture and deliver routers quickly to the companies that first needed them. This gave the business an edge in the market that endured for nearly two decades. Bosack and Lerner retained this market-leading position through clever packaging, too. The key to the router product was the software inside, the core formatting processes that underwent the most improvement and enabled the key router functions. However, so early into the Internet era, even California technology companies were nervous about investing in unfamiliar programs. Therefore, Cisco hid the revolutionary software inside hardware encased in a familiar, personal computer design. This familiarity eased businesses' anxieties when it came to their initial purchases. By the time later sales had boosted Cisco profits and made the company an international name, the value of the router had already been proven.

Despite the simplicity of its basic router and switch product offering, Cisco still focused on future needs and reinvention. (A switch enables network devices to communicate with each other.) This was partly due to its dependence on the router. It needed to stay ahead of any competition in order to hold onto the developing market. In addition, Cisco had been founded with the intention of supplying what companies would need in the future. This mentality stayed with the corporation as it grew, and the result was a router company unafraid to tackle new problems or expand into new areas of growth. When sales began outgrowing the abilities of the Cisco sales department to keep up, it created a new reseller partner program in order to help distribute its products. This created an independent group of consultants, distributors, and developers that Cisco leveraged for customer service without funding internal customer service efforts using its own sales force.

Fueled by the belief that the Internet could carry any type of communication, Cisco became the leading provider of area networks, especially what would become wide area networks (WANs), but with some specialization in local area networks (LANs) as well.According to Charles Waltner, in "Cisco's Silver Anniversary: A History of Reinvention," Cisco, with its typical foresight, understood the new dependence on information would prompt businesses into sharing data in even more complex ways. The company started to reinvent itself as needed, eventually reaching a research and development budget of more than US$3 billion per year.

EXPANSION AND NEW MODELS

A variety of router products were available by the mid-1990s. Data management and flexibility were growing concerns, and industry standards were coalescing on national and international levels. Multiprotocol devices were still important, but businesses had more specific needs. They needed not only local and wide area networks, but also ways to connect and protect those networks. Businesses dependent on the Internet required scalability, software packages that allowed for easy, and quick growth in response to demand. Network hardware and network software became increasingly separate products. Data consultations and remote data services rose in popularity.

Cisco looked at this shifting landscape and reinvented itself once more. The time had come to offer not only router products, but also a variety of communication and data services for new businesses. Some of the innovations Cisco could handle itself. It was a small step from the old routers to new, more customizable versions for growing companies. However, when it came to peripherals, additional data support, and new ways of using data, Cisco recognized that it had little experience. The solution was innovation through acquisition. Cisco began a large series of acquisitions in the 1990s to prepare itself for the coming Internet-dependent era. Its first acquisition, in 1993, was Crescendo Communications, a company that developed network switches. This was one year before Cisco"s annual revenue stream officially hit US$1 billion.

At several points Cisco made large technology deals, such as the acquisition in 1994 of Stratacom, a company that produced the first commercial cell switch, for more than US$4 billion and the 1999 purchase of the optical equipment maker Cerent Corporation for US$7 billion. In between were nearly one hundred smaller purchases, all strategically chosen to increase the product and service offerings Cisco could make available. Some businesses made software for routing telephone calls. Some developed fiber-optic networking equipment. Others worked on wireless network systems. All had an innovation Cisco believed worthwhile, as well as talented engineers the corporation was willing to pay high prices in order to keep.

The acquisition strategy worked well for Cisco, which boasted a 70 percent success rate for all its bought businesses. As the leader in its field, Cisco had the clout and buying power to afford nearly any business it wanted. This allowed it to remain at the top of the networking industry. At the height of Cisco's success, venture capital firms were even funding start-ups with the primary goal of being acquired by Cisco in order to generate investor profits. Before the dot-com bust of 2000 and 2001, Cisco was one of the most valued companies in the world. In March 2000, its market capitalization grew to US$555.4 billion, surpassing Microsoft Corporation.

By the start of the 21st century, the habit of predicting the future with unnerving accuracy remained with Cisco, although the original founders had left the company more than a decade prior, in 1990. In 2001 the leader of the company, John Chambers, predicted that phone calls would eventually be free due to the incorporation of telephony abilities in business networks. Telecommunications businesses considered the idea ridiculous at the time, but before the decade was finished voice over Internet protocol (VoIP) services were making free telephone calls in business a near possibility.

RUNNING WITH IDEAS

The dot-com bust dropped Cisco from its high valuation, and new competition in the first decade of the 21st century emerged to challenge the business. However, despite its lowered status and an array of failed ventures into the home-based networking market, Cisco continued to innovate and reinvent itself. In 2009 it entered the server market. In 2011 Cisco announced the latest version of its Cius tablet computer, designed with extra security and data management features for business use. It has continued to make acquisitions and has kept a consistent market adoption strategy.

Through its years of rapid success, Cisco proved that a venture business could become an international giant with only one trick, provided the trick was sold at the right place and at the right time. Small innovations and solutions can prove to be world-changing, provided that entrepreneurs keep an eye on the future. Cisco ignored the derision of market leaders who saw no need for the product, and by the time the market came around, Cisco had a sufficient head start, and its domination of networking systems followed.

Later in its growth, Cisco proved a different kind of point. As the needs of its customers diversified, Cisco diversified in order to meet those needs. The company became so effective at acquiring smaller firms to advance into new markets that it outgrew major consumer sellers like Microsoft. The change in focus from a single offering to multiple, adaptable services showed that even a business as large as Cisco could reimagine its core business model when needed. The key was choosing the right time and the right way to change.

BIBLIOGRAPHY

Anthony, Scott. "Cisco's Curious Week." *Harvard Business Review Blog Nertwork,* March 25, 2009. Accessed December 23, 2011. http://blogs.hbr.org/anthony/2009/03/ciscos_curious_week.html.

Carey, Pete. "A Start-Up's True Tale." *San Jose Mercury News,* December 1, 2001.

Cisco Systems, Inc. "Cisco Overview." San Jose, CA, 2011.

Accessed December 23, 2011. http://newsroom.cisco.com /overview.

"The History of Cisco." *WebHostingReport.com,* 2011. Accessed December 23, 2011. http://www.webhostingreport.com /learn/cisco.html.

Leske, Nicola. "Analysis: Cisco Set on Proving It Can Succeed in Tablet Market." *Reuters,* December 2, 2011. Accessed December 23, 2011. http://www.reuters.com/article/2011 /12/02/us-cisco-idUSTRE7B127I20111202?type=company News.

Morris, Langdon. "Creating the Innovation Culture." Walton Creek, CA: Innovation Labs, 2007. Accessed December 23, 2011. http://www.innovationlabs.com/publications/creating -the-innovation-culture/.

Rogers, James. "Cisco's Boom and Bust: A History Lesson." *The Street,* August 9, 2011. Accessed December 23, 2011. http:// www.thestreet.com/story/11212172/1/ciscos-boom-and-bust -a-history-lesson.html.

Tajnai, Carolyn. "Cisco Systems Spotlight." Stanford, CA: Stanford University. Accessed December 23, 2011. http:// www.stanford.edu/group/wellspring/cisco_spotlight.html.

Waltner, Charles. "Cisco's Silver Anniversary: A History of Reinvention." San Jose, CA: Cisco Systems, December 10, 2009. Accessed December 23, 2011. http://newsroom.cisco .com/dlls/2009/ts_121009.html.

Coca-Cola: The Best-Selling Nonalcoholic Beverage in the World

Coca-Cola is one of the best-known brands in the world, and marketing innovation has been one of the Coca-Cola Company's strong points throughout its history. It converted an alcohol-based medicine into a new product, a sugary soft drink. It introduced a new soft drink container and several bottle sizes, making its drinks available at multiple price points. It made its soda available throughout the United States and later, the world. It also introduced several well-known promotional campaigns, including its famous Santa Claus campaign.

COCAWINE

The original Coca-Cola formula contained alcohol, specifically wine, along with the leaf of the coca plant. The chemist Angelo Mariani had read a scientific paper that described the health benefits of the coca leaf, and started selling Vin Terroir, a wine and coca beverage in 1863, according to Ken Payton's entry on the wine at the website Reign of Terroir. This wine was copied by many American brewers, who produced their own wine and coca blends.

One of the drink makers who based a beverage on Vin Terroir was the pharmacist Dr. John Pemberton, who produced his own blend, Pemberton's Red Wine Coca. The drink was popular among the citizens of Atlanta, Georgia. However, the Prohibition movement was growing in popularity during the late 1880s, and the city of Atlanta, Georgia, passed legislation against alcoholic beverage sales. In response, Pemberton developed a coca soft drink formula without the wine, and started selling it at the soda fountain of a local pharmacy in 1886.

INTRODUCTION OF COCA-COLA

Pemberton marketed his carbonated sugar and coca beverage as a health product, claiming it cured headaches. According to *World of Coca-Cola,* a website covering the history of the cola, this fountain beverage originally sold for US$0.05 per glass, and Pemberton sold approximately nine glasses per day. Although this amount was small, the drink did attract the attention of investors, including Asa G. Candler. After Pemberton died in 1888, Candler bought out the other investors and took control of the Coca-Cola Company.

Candler promoted Coca-Cola aggressively. He established a wider geographic reach than other soft drink sellers by paying traveling representatives to hand out coupons for free Coca-Cola, which was not a common promotion method. Candler also conducted an aggressive branding campaign, displaying the Coca-Cola logo on many products that were not related to soft drinks, and offering these branded products to pharmacy shoppers.

Candler remained cautious about the presentation of the drink. The first bottles of Coca-Cola were sold in 1894 by Joseph Biedenham, but most pharmacies continued to sell Coca-Cola from soda fountains, according to *World of Coca-Cola.* In 1899, Benjamin Thomas, Joseph Whitehead, and John Lupton asked Candler for the right to sell bottles of Coca-Cola on a much larger scale. Candler believed that Coca-Cola could not retain its original taste if it was bottled with the technology available at the time, so he did not consider the bottling rights very valuable. Candler agreed to the deal in exchange for a single U.S. dollar, which he never collected, according to the article "Chattanooga Coca-Cola History." The three entrepreneurs returned to

Chattanooga and constructed the Coca-Cola Bottling Company.

THE COKE BOTTLE

Candler had not considered the effects of future bottling innovations when he granted the three entrepreneurs bottling rights. In the 20th century, bottle caps were invented, and it was now much easier for a beverage maker to bottle soft drinks without compromising a product's taste. The bottling company was successful, and the three entrepreneurs earned additional income by licensing the Coca-Cola bottling rights to other drink makers.

Coca-Cola's competitors also used the new bottle caps to preserve their own cola drinks. Coca-Cola needed an innovation that would distinguish its bottles from those of its competitors. According to Cantwell, a unique label design was not sufficient because label stickers did not adhere strongly to glass Coke bottles in the damp environment of an ice box, and a customer often grabbed a soda bottle out of the ice box without looking at the bottle first.

Coca-Cola chose to make the glass bottles that contained its drinks unique, which would help solve another branding issue for the company. The other drink makers who licensed the bottling rights from the three investors had each introduced their own bottles to store Coca-Cola, creating an inconsistent presentation for the bottled drink. Instead of designing the new glass Coca-Cola bottle themselves, the entrepreneurs launched a contest. A group of glass makers in Terre Haute, Indiana, worked together to come up with the famous Coca-Cola bottle design. Cantwell explained that the successful design was the result of a misunderstanding, as the glass makers based their design on the shape of a cocoa seed because they thought Coca-Cola was a cocoa beverage.

BOTTLE PACKS

Up to the early 1920s Coca-Cola still relied on selling individual bottles of its soft drink to shoppers. The company noticed that some customers enjoyed the drink so much that they purchased several bottles of Coke at the same time during a shopping trip. Bringing these individual bottles home was inconvenient for a shopper, so the company decided to introduce packs of Coke.

Phil Mooney, writing in the *Coca-Cola Conversations* blog, noted that Coke started selling packages that contained several bottles of Coca-Cola in 1923, when it introduced six-pack cartons. Coca-Cola developed a significant innovation with its six-pack cartons, as it was the first company to introduce the concept of selling several soft drinks in a single package. The cardboard cartons also provided extra insulation that ensured that the bottles of

Coca-Cola would stay ice cold while the shopper returned to his or her house.

MARKETING CHALLENGES

Coca-Cola faced strong competition. The physician Augustin Thompson had brewed up a drink he called Moxie, which he promoted as a general curative. Thomson launched an effective advertising campaign in which he hired Moxie Men to travel around the United States and show off the drink in their Moxiemobiles. Moxie was not as sweet as Coca-Cola, but Thompson used this quality as a selling point, suggesting that drinking Moxie made the drinker stronger. The Moxie advertising campaign was so successful that a new word, moxie, was added to dictionaries. In 1928 the Moxie Company decided to take an even more aggressive position in the market by building a new and modern factory, Moxieland, reported Michael Reskind for the Jamaica Plain Historical Society.

Carbonated soft drinks were considered a luxury product, and the Coca-Cola company feared that many of its customers would stop buying soft drinks to conserve their cash during the Great Depression that began in 1929. During the 1920s Coca-Cola had successfully advertised its drink as a status symbol that a businessman could drink in a high-end department store or a country club. The company needed to develop a new advertising strategy for the 1930s that appealed to customers who were fearful about the United States's economic future.

As a chilled beverage, Coca-Cola held a strong appeal for customers during the summer months. The company wanted to sell its drinks all year long and marketing ice cold Coca-Cola in winter was a tougher sell. The new marketing strategy needed to address the advertising campaigns of competitors like Moxie, distract customers from their economic concerns, and improve sales during the winter season.

SANTA CLAUS

Advertising professional Archie Lee decided to enlist Santa Claus in Coca-Cola's marketing campaign. In the 1920s although people knew the Santa Claus story, they did not have a single well-defined portrait of him in their minds. He was often visualized as a gnome, elf, or other mythological creature rather than as a jolly old man.

Santa appeared in a popular Coca-Cola advertisement in 1930, in which he drank a bottle of Coke at a Saint Louis, Missouri, department store. Lee hired artist Haddon Sundblom to further refine the Coca-Cola Santa, whom he envisioned as the jolly old Santa that modern audiences recognize. Sean Chase, for the *Daily Observer,* reported that Sundblom drew inspiration for the Coca-Cola Santa from his neighbor, Lou Prentice.

Coca-Cola was not alone in creating the modern concept of Santa Claus. Bill Shrum reported for the *Stuttgart Daily Leader* that Thomas Nast illustrated Santa Claus in a 19th-century drawing that appeared in *Harper's Weekly*, in which Santa appeared in his iconic red and white suit as a jolly old man, along with other familiar details such as his North Pole toy factory. However, Coca-Cola could claim a good deal of credit for popularizing this image, as Sundblom continued to draw his Coca-Cola Santa in advertisements for many years.

The Santa Claus campaign helped Coca-Cola maintain sales during the Great Depression in the United States. Coca-Cola associated its drink with customers' memories of past Christmases, when gifts and good cheer were plentiful. Nostalgia effectively distracted U.S. customers from their economic problems, and Santa helped the company sell bottles of Coke during the Christmas season.

DEPRESSION AND WAR

In the early 20th century PepsiCo Inc. gained a foothold in the soft drink market by offering a superior value proposition. Pepsi matched Coke's price of US$0.05 per bottle, while giving its customers double the soda, at 12 ounces, according to a report by Eleanor Jones and Florian Ritzmann at the University of Virginia. Pepsi challenged Coke directly by creating a radio advertisement that explained that a soft drink buyer could purchase more soda from Pepsi at the price Coke charged. The bargain pricing attracted new customers, and Pepsi grew rapidly during the late 1930s.

During the 1930s Moxie's competitive position weakened. The company reduced its advertising budget to cut costs during the Depression. Coca-Cola and Pepsi both spent heavily on advertisements during the 1930s, and soft drink buyers forgot about Moxie. Moxie remained in business as a small, local company, although it could no longer compete with Coke and Pepsi for the national U.S. market.

Nostalgia helped Coca-Cola continue producing soft drinks during World War II. The war limited sugar supplies, so Coca-Cola needed to convince military authorities to let it continue to produce its drinks. Coca-Cola decided to market nostalgia to military leaders. Soldiers, pilots, and sailors missed the simple pleasures of living in the United States, such as sitting at a drug store soda fountain and talking to the soda shop girls. Coca-Cola reminded soldiers about their lives before the war and promised that life would return to normal after World War II ended.

DIET SODA

After the war, Coca-Cola noticed that its female customers had grown more concerned about the calories that soft drinks contained. Typical soft drink bottle sizes had increased, and soft drinks were no longer viewed as medicinal products. In 1963 Coca-Cola decided to launch a diet cola that contained saccharine and aspartame instead of sugar, under a new brand, TaB, in case it was not popular with customers. TaB was not the first diet cola, but it had a large market share in the 1960s and 1970s. Almost two decades later, in 1982, Coca-Cola released Diet Coca-Cola, which displaced TaB and became the company's most popular diet drink.

NEW COKE

New Coke was widely known as Coca-Cola's most famous failed innovation. In the 1980s, Coke faced strong competition from Pepsi and other soft drink manufacturers, and its executives believed that its original drink formula was obsolete. They developed a new product, New Coke, and decided to manufacture it in place of standard Coca-Cola. Customers were very angry once they realized that the company had stopped making its original formula soft drink, and the company was forced to bring the original Coca-Cola formula back again as Classic Coca-Cola.

A WORLDWIDE POWER

Coca-Cola continued to show strong financial results in the early 2010s, although its domestic soft drink sales were limited by the weak U.S. economy. The company reported its best growth in India, where volume grew by 17 percent. Volume also rose in Argentina (11 percent) and China (7 percent). Sales figures in European markets also displayed a positive trend. The company earned additional income from foreign currency effects.

COKE INNOVATIONS

The innovations Coke developed created the modern soft drink market. Its early decision to switch from fountain sales to bottled drinks gave the company a great early advantage in the U.S. market. Soft drink cartons and stylized soft drink bottles were also important innovations. With the introduction of its Santa Claus advertisements, Coke demonstrated how to conduct an effective, worldwide advertising campaign. Coke realized that it had to change with the times, and launching a diet soda brand was an effective strategy, although its New Coke initiative was one of the company's rare failures. Coke crafted effective growth strategies that helped it survive for decades and remain the best-selling nonalcoholic beverage in the world.

BIBLIOGRAPHY

Chase, Sean. "How Coca-Cola Gave Us the Modern Santa Claus." *Daily Observer*, 2009. Accessed December 18, 2011.

http://www.thedailyobserver.ca/ArticleDisplay.aspx?e=221 5001&archive=true.

Coca-Cola Bottling Company of Chattanooga. "Chattanooga Coca-Cola History." Chattanooga, TN, 2006. Accessed December 18, 2011. http://www.chattanoogacocacola.com /history.asp.

The Coca-Cola Company. "The Coca-Cola Company Reports Third Quarter and Year-to-Date 2011 Results." Atlanta, GA, October 18, 2011. Accessed December 18, 2011. http://www .thecoca-colacompany.com/dynamic/press_center/2011/10 /2011-third-quarter-results.html.

"Coca-Cola History." *World of Coca-Cola.* Accessed December 18, 2011. http://www.worldofcoca-cola.com/coca-colahistory .htm.

Lukas, Paul. "Coke Is What?" *Fast Company,* September 1, 2005. Accessed December 18, 2011. http://www.fastcompany.com /magazine/98/lab-test.html.

Mooney, Phil. "Coke's Early Innovation – The Six-Pack."

Coca-Cola Conversations (blog), October 8, 2008. Accessed December 18, 2011. http://www.coca-colaconversations.com /my_weblog/2008/10/cokes-early-inn.html.

Payton, Ken. "Vin Mariani." *Reign of Terroir,* January 31, 2008. Accessed December 18, 2011. http://reignofterroir.com/2008 /01/31/vin-mariani/.

Reiskind, Michael. "Moxie Soda Outsold Coca-Cola." Jamaica Plain, MA: Jamaica Plain Historical Society, 1995. Accessed December 18, 2011. http://www.jphs.org/20thcentury/moxie -soda-outsold-coca-cola.html.

Sheils, Thomas. "Coke History." *Cola Fountain,* 2006. Accessed December 18, 2011. http://colafountain.topcities.com/history .htm.

Shrum, Bill. "The Story of Santa Claus." *Stuttgart Daily Leader,* December 24, 2009. Accessed December 18, 2011. http:// www.stuttgartdailyleader.com/homepage/x664191129/The -story-of-Santa-Claus.

Colt's Manufacturing Company: Pioneering Firearms

In the 19th century, the majority of the United States was still a vast, uninhabited frontier. This provided many U.S. citizens the freedom to help build the country and establish lasting legacies. Some individuals even had the opportunity to amass great wealth. One such man, Samuel Colt, died in 1862 as one of the richest men in the United States. Sam Colt has an interesting place in U.S. history as a man whose products were used by law-abiding men and outlaws alike. Anyone could purchase his firearms, and in many wars and battles both in the United States and abroad, both sides could have been equipped with armaments from Colt's Manufacturing Company (CMC). CMC helped bring law and order to the remote corners of the U.S. West, and the tenacity of the Colt brand has withstood 175 years of history and remains a recognized name well into the 2010s.

While the company's founder, Samuel Colt, was alive, most of the products for which his company would come to be known had not yet been invented. However, Samuel Colt engaged in ingenious marketing campaigns and strategic acquisitions that would rival the tactics of any modern corporation. From product placement advertising to receiving honorary titles in the United States in order to gain audiences with world leaders abroad, Colt had a way of realizing his goals and making his company an industry leader around the globe.

Even in the 2010s CMC products are found in many branches of the U.S. military, in law enforcement agencies, and in the homes of millions of enthusiasts and collectors. The Colt Single Action Army revolver, nicknamed the Peacemaker, has gained a reputation for accuracy and reliability that has remained virtually unchanged throughout its nearly 140-year history. As of 2012 the Peacemaker

boasts a proud spot in the CMC product catalog. Almost as iconic as the Single Action Army revolver is the Model 1911A1 semiautomatic pistol. Made in 1911, it enjoyed a 74-year history as an official sidearm of U.S. military personnel, and even in 2012, an entire century since its inception, the 1911A1 continues to be used by law enforcement agencies and military units worldwide, as well as by countless recreational shooters, professional competitive shooters, and gun enthusiasts.

Aside from its revolver and pistol production, Colt made significant contributions to the manufacture of modern rifles, specifically the AR-15, also commonly known by its U.S. military designation, the M16. When the United States entered the Vietnam conflict in 1963, Colt was contracted by the U.S. military to produce the M16 in large numbers and hundreds of thousands of these rifles were ordered and produced. Colt also produced the AR-15 for the civilian market.

A PATENTED MESS

Samuel Colt was born in 1814 in Hartford, Connecticut. He spent most of his life inventing, advertising and marketing the products his company produced. Before dying in 1862 after suffering from multiple medical issues at just 47 years of age, Samuel Colt's most important contribution to the history of the handgun was the invention of the revolving cylinder. When he was still in his teens, Colt was sent to work aboard a ship named the *Corvo* to learn to become a sailor. There, according to numerous biographers, he was inspired by the movement of the ship's wheel and how it could be aligned with a spoke to hold it in place at any position. William Edwards, in his 1957 book

The Story of Colt's Revolver; the Biography of Col. Samuel Colt, disputed this, arguing that it was more likely that Colt observed the action of a ratcheted windlass (a form of winch) used in loading and unloading the ship's cargo. While this particular anecdote regarding the ship' wheel may be apocryphal, the fact that he patented the idea of a "revolving gun" in 1836 is not. It was on the basis of this patent that Colt created the Paterson Colt, a single-action, black powder, cap-and-ball pistol that had a revolving cylinder. As there were no major conflicts being fought at the time and also no large orders for the firearm, Colt's fledgling Patent Fire Arms Manufacturing Company (the company Colt formed in May 1836 to sell the product) went out of business in just six years. It would be several more years before Sam Colt would pursue his next entrepreneurial venture.

The 19th century was a difficult time for gun makers, and production decisions were often made based on who held a particular patent and to what extent it would be defended. In some cases, companies would develop a new design to bypass a particular patent held by another gun maker; in other cases, they chose to cooperate with a competing company and simply paid them royalties. In yet other instances, they ignored the patent altogether, risking litigation and financial penalties. This was the environment that characterized the years immediately prior to the invention of the Colt Single Action Army revolver.

Rollin White was a gunsmith who worked for Colt in the 1850s. During his time there he developed the idea for a system where the barrel and cylinder would both be bored through, and self-contained cartridges containing primer, gunpowder, and a bullet would be inserted, fired, and then easily ejected. The cylinder could then be quickly reloaded. Unfortunately for both men, Sam Colt dismissed the idea as a novelty; in subsequent years he ended his contracts with White, who then patented his concept in 1855. White promptly entered into an agreement with Smith & Wesson the very next year to produce the new revolvers, and through very vigorous patent enforcement and lawsuits, made it exceedingly difficult for anyone outside of his own company or Smith & Wesson to create anything like it until 1872.

THE SAA DEBUTS

The year 1873 was a pivotal one in the firearms manufacturing history of the United States. When the Rollins patent expired, one of the first to capitalize on it was CMC. Having designed its own version of a cartridge-based revolver, the company released the Colt Single Action Army (SAA) revolver with the goal of selling it primarily to the U.S. military but also to the civilian market. Expansion into the sparsely inhabited, western U.S. territories was in full swing and everyone from settlers to lawmen to bandits were buying up rifles and handguns to help tame the new frontier.

The SAA revolver was not the first of its kind, but it arguably became the most popular. One interesting bit of trivia rarely mentioned is that the original name for the revolver was not the Single Action Army as it was not adopted by the U.S. Army until after the product was released and marketed. The gun was originally known as the "strap pistol," because of the cylinder having a strap over the top in order to strengthen the frame, according to history writer Mike Venturino in *American Handgunner.* Previous designs all had the gun barrel attached near the bottom rather than the top, a design that would sometimes cause the gun to bend when firing large, powerful charges. A number of other factors helped fuel its popularity and secure its position as a legendary firearm. The first was the fact that, upon its release, it was adopted by the military almost immediately for use with the cavalry. Venturino noted that just about any weapon used by the military became a huge hit in the civilian market. In the first 20 years of production, the U.S. army ordered 37,000 of the revolvers, but in the same time, Colt had sold over 144,000 to the general public.

The second factor aiding the revolver's popularity was that it was available in several calibers (a form of gun barrel diameter measurement). The most popular was CMC's trademark .45 (which contained 40 grains of powder and a 255-grain bullet). Another very popular format of the handgun was the "Model P" .44–40. This configuration made it compatible with the ammunition used in the Winchester Model 1873 rifle, another popular frontier weapon at the time. The ammunition was called ".44–40 WCF," (Winchester Center Fire) and it was the most readily available and most popular cartridge available at the time, according to writer Chuck Hawks. Any frontier general store, no matter how remote, would stock quantities of this ammunition, which made it much simpler and more convenient to buy something that was usable in both a rifle and handgun.

The SAA was also available in a number of barrel lengths, ranging from 4.75 inches to 7.5 inches. The U.S. cavalry generally used the longer configuration, and the handgun was typically equipped with walnut grips and a colored, case-hardened frame. When used in this military configuration, the weapon was commonly referred to as the SAA. Otherwise, the civilian .44–40 version was called the "Colt Frontier," and also nicknamed the Peacemaker. They were essentially the same weapon with different names. So popular was the SAA that Colt produced this weapon until the 1940s when, during World War II, it concentrated instead on other products to be used directly in the war effort.

By CMC's serial number records, the first generation of SAA revolvers produced 357,860 handguns. When production of the SAA resumed in 1956 by popular demand, an additional 73,319 weapons were produced until production stopped again in 1974. The third generation, starting in 1976, were still in production in 2012, with many of the original design features, options, length, and caliber configurations as their predecessors nearly 140 years ago. While the original Peacemaker cost only US$17 by mail order (US$315 when adjusted for inflation in 2011), brand new SAAs from CMC's 2012 catalog started at US$1,315.

MORE THAN JUST A ONE-TRICK PONY

Although the undying legacy of the SAA is indisputable, a second handgun also brought CMC unparalleled fame and success. The invention of an automatic, magazine-fed pistol by John M. Browning resulted in the creation of the M1911 (also called the M1911A1). This .45 caliber handgun was bought and produced by CMC, and very quickly became the mainstay of every U.S. army officer as the sidearm of choice for nearly a century. The attraction and advantages of this type of firearm were numerous. First, most semi-automatic pistols have a magazine that allows for a larger number of rounds to be loaded than a revolver, which generally holds only five or six. Second, the semi-automatic action means that the gun is reloaded quickly by using the gasses released when firing a round to eject the spent casing and load a new round into the chamber.

The M1911 was used by all branches of the U.S. military until 1985, when most changed to a 9mm format, for which the Beretta 92F (whose military use designation is the M9) became the new standard. However, well into the 2010s, the M1911 continues to be used by many law enforcement agencies and civilians alike. CMC's product catalog lists a number of handguns that are the successors of this design, named the "1991 Series." While remaining quite true to the original 1911 design, the "1991 Series" also have several enhanced features such as high-profile sights and an improved ejection port, according to Colt's catalog.

A third product that has become nearly synonymous with CMC has been the M16. The nonmilitary name for this semi-automatic rifle is the AR-15, and interestingly, it is not a CMC invention at all, though the two are frequently mentioned in the same sentence. The AR-15 was actually invented by the ArmaLite Corporation, which started as an offshoot of the Fairchild Engine and Airplane Corporation. In 1959 ArmaLite sold the AR-15 design to CMC, which then manufactured them in great numbers for the military, especially during the Vietnam War and well into the 1980s.

By 1988, however, CMC was having internal difficulties, which seemed to affect the quality of its products. Subsequently, the U.S. military did not renew CMC

and commissioned its M16s to be produced by Fabrique Nationale d'Herstal, a Belgian company. In all, the AR-15 has been produced by dozens of different manufacturers, of which CMC was just one.

COLT'S ROMANTIC LEGACY

In spite of its many successes and lucrative government contracts, CMC filed for Chapter 11 bankruptcy protection in 1992. A combination of internal labor issues and consumer boycotts, all coinciding with the end of the Cold War, pushed the company into insolvency. In spite of its Chapter 11 filing, however, CMC was able to continue operating, and eventually, in 2002, retired United States Marine Corps Lt. General William Keys took over as the company's CEO and turned the company's fortunes around once more. In 2011 CMC celebrated its 175th anniversary.

When people talk about CMC and some of the firearms the company has created in its long history, many names, both real and fictional, spring to mind. Legends of U.S. Wild West gunslingers like Jesse James, Doc Holiday, and Wyatt Earp still spark the imaginations of gun enthusiasts well into the 21st century. Even without the driving force of Hollywood, CMC's legendary Peacemaker has had famous owners like U.S. General George S. Patton, whose ivory-gripped revolver became a symbol of U.S. accomplishments in World War II. Worldwide, CMC continues to supply service rifles to other countries like Canada and the Netherlands, and provides service pistols to countless government agencies and military units around the world.

BIBLIOGRAPHY

"Colt Single Action Army Revolver." Fairfax, VA: National Firearms Museum. Accessed February 16, 2012. http://www.nramuseum.com/the-museum/the-galleries/the-american-west/case-42-the-guns-that-won-the-west-colt-winchester/colt-single-action-army-revolver.aspx.

"Colt Single Action Army (SAA) Revolver." Gunclassics.com. Accessed February 16, 2012. http://www.gunclassics.com/colt45saa.html.

Colt's Manufacturing Company LLC. "2012 Colt Catalog." West Hartford, CT. Accessed February 16, 2012. http://www.coltsmfg.com/Catalog.aspx.

———. "Colt 1991 Series." West Hartford, CT. Accessed February 16, 2012. http://www.coltsmfg.com/Catalog/ColtPistols/Colt1991Series.aspx.

———. "Colt Domestic Retail Price List 2012." West Hartford, CT. Accessed February 16, 2012. http://www.coltsmfg.com/Catalog.aspx.

———. "History." West Hartford, CT. Accessed February 16, 2012. http://www.coltsmfg.com/About/History.aspx.

Edwards, William B. *The Story of Colt's Revolver; the Biography of Col. Samuel Colt.* New York: Castle Books, 1957, 23.

Fadala, Sam. *The Complete Blackpowder Handbook.* 5th ed. Iola, WI: Krause Publications, 2006.

Schellinger, Paul. "Samuel Colt." *Inventors and Inventions.* Vol. 1. Tarrytown, NY: Marshall Cavendish, 2008. Gale Virtual Reference Library (GALE|CX4097100042). http://go.galegroup.com/ps/i.do?id=GALE%7CCX4097100042&v=2.1&u=itsbtrial&it=r&p=GVRL&sw=w

"Self-Loading Pistol 'Colt' M1911." EnemyForces.com, 2010. Accessed February 16, 2012. http://www.enemyforces.net/firearms/colt1911.htm.

Taffin, John. *Single Action Sixguns.* Iola, WI: Krause Publications, 2005, 33–53,77–95.

U.S. Department of Labor. Bureau of Labor Statistics. "CPI Inflation Calculator." Washington, DC. Accessed April 11, 2012. http://www.bls.gov/data/inflation_calculator.htm.

Venturino, Mike. "Genesis of the Colt Single Action: The First Generation Colt Single Action Army." *American Handgunner,* August 2, 2011. Accessed February 16, 2012. http://www.americanhandgunner.com/exclusive-web-extra-the-first-generation-colt-single-action-army/.

Walter, John. *The Guns That Won the West: The Firearms of the American Frontier, 1848–1898.* London: Greenhill Books, 2006.

The Wild West. "Colt Peacemaker of 1873." Accessed February 16, 2012. http://www.thewildwest.org/component/content/article/246.html.

Compact Discs:
From Music Recordings to Computers

In the late 1970s, Sony Corporation and Royal Philips Electronics N.V. worked together to create a new music format that would change not only the way people listened to music, but the way data was stored by both businesses and consumers. The two companies developed the compact disc (CD), and although it was at first belittled by the record industry and lampooned by the media, it would replace long-playing vinyl records (LPs) and cassette tapes as the dominant music format.

LASERS AND DATA

Since the development of lasers, researchers had been looking for ways to use them to encode optical data. Development of optical data storage was slow because of the high cost and low performance of the lasers available. In the early 1970s Dutch electronics firm Philips had developed the most advanced pulse-code laser to date, but it had a lifespan of only 100 hours and was considered unsuitable.

Philips engineers had discussed using optical data storage technology to create sound recordings since the early 1960s. However, company management dismissed the idea as too simple and did not consider it worth pursuing. Instead, the company focused its efforts on using laser technology for video and images. The result was LaserVision, a disc format that the company debuted in 1975. However, LaserVision was not a success. Nearly half of the 400 units sold were returned largely because consumers were under the mistaken impression that it would record as well as play. Writing in the *Journal of the Audio Engineering Society*, Kees A. Schouhamer Immink, an engineer at Philips Research Laboratories who contributed to the design and development of the CD, stated that he believed the failure of LaserVision helped to open the door for the development of the CD.

JAPANESE AND DUTCH COLLABORATION

In the years following the failure of LaserVision, Sony and Philips executives began meeting in both the Netherlands and Japan to discuss collaborating on audio laser technology. Sony was one of the world's leading names in electronics, second only to Panasonic Corporation, then known as Matsushita Electronic Corporation. Founded in the years after World War II, Sony had consistently introduced electronic products that changed the way consumers enjoyed their leisure time. Although Philips was unsuccessful with LaserVision, it had gained valuable expertise developing the technology. Sony wanted to work with the Dutch company and use this expertise to develop a digital audio format.

Teams of engineers from the two companies met to discuss their respective strengths and weaknesses. Philips engineer Jacques Heemskerk told the BBC (in the article "Compact Disc Hits 25th Birthday") that in the days before globalization, this openness and sharing of ideas was unusual and quite uncomfortable for the Dutch engineers. The mutual distrust, however, subsided after a number of meetings, and it became clear that the two teams would be able to work together. Outside pressure from other companies that were working to develop laser audio technology helped to cement this relationship. The Dutch and Japanese engineers would enter into a friendly competition in which both tried to develop the most practical solution to each problem that they encountered.

The size of the CD was originally 11.5 centimeters, to match the length of the popular compact cassette tape, but was extended to 12 centimeters to accommodate more data. According to Immink, the widely held rumor that it was extended in order to fit Beethoven's Ninth Symphony on one disc was untrue. The decision, he said, was made in order to strike the best balance possible between optimal length and readability.

In March 1979, while the CD was still in production, Philips and Sony held a press conference in the Netherlands to show the world, and their competitors, the superior sound quality of the new technology. A week after the press conference, Philips executives traveled to Tokyo, Japan to convene a conference on standardizing the digital audio disc. One of the reasons Sony chose Philips as a partner in developing the CD was to create a worldwide standard format so that any disc could be played on any player. Philips and Sony created the Red Book standard, named after a red binder in which the specification data was written. This standard was adopted worldwide for CD specifications.

WORKINGS OF THE COMPACT DISC

The finished product was a plastic disc on which miniscule depressions were made. When played, a low-intensity, continuous-wave diode laser was focused and circularized so that it scanned certain areas of the disc as it spun. The small depressions in the disc reflected the beam and a decoder read the intensity and polarization of the reflected light, translating it into an electric signal. This signal then caused the attached speaker diaphragm to vibrate.

The design was revolutionary, but it would require something just as revolutionary to package it. Sony and Philips knew that there would be challenges in gaining public acceptance of the new technology, and the case in which the disc came would be crucial. The case needed to be durable so that it protected the disc but also cheap to produce. It needed to be as thin as possible but thick enough to contain a booklet. Like the disc itself, it also had to present a state-of-the-art image.

Several names were considered for the new format, including the Mini Rack, MiniDisc, and Compact Rack. In the end, Sony chose "compact disc" because of its resemblance to a previous product, the compact cassette, the success of which it hoped to replicate.

THE RECORD INDUSTRY STRIKES BACK

The first CD player, the CDP-101, was introduced in March 1982. According to a BBC timeline on the development of the CD, Philips technical director Lou Ottens announced at the time, "From now on, the conventional record player is obsolete." The CDP-101 retailed for around US$1,000.

The first compact disc (commonly referred to as a "CD") went on sale in November 1982. The first release was Herbert von Karajan conducting Richard Strauss' Alpine Symphony. The first pop release was Swedish group Abba's "The Visitor." Conductor Karajan was a major advocate of digital audio, comparing the technology of LPs to old-fashioned gas lighting.

Major U.S. record companies CBS Corporation, Warner Music Group, and RCA Music Group wanted no part of the CD revolution. The response of CBS was to create its own high-definition system called the Compatible Expansion (CX) system. It was a small electronic device that could be attached to a record player to reduce noise and increase dynamic range. It was capable of increasing the dynamic range by 20 decibels (dB) and made LPs sound nearly as crystal-clear as CDs. Since the CX system was only an attachment to the record player that most consumers owned already and was priced much lower than that of the new plastic discs, CBS felt that it had effectively defused the threat.

German record company Telefunken-Decca Schallplatten GmbH also responded by developing its own new technology. It was a minidisc with sound quality that was comparable to that of CDs. The main difference was that Telefunken's minidisc was double-sided and read mechanically. The mechanical reading aspect meant that the discs could be produced in the same manufacturing plants as its LPs, cutting costs and making them more affordable for consumers. However, the minidisc failed to catch on, and Telefunken became the first German company to license the CBS CX decoder.

Record retailers also did not like the idea of CDs. While CDs were immediately popular in Japan, European record stores were much slower to stock the shelves with the new format. Retailers complained that they would have to double up on their inventory to offer both LPs and CDs. Many also worried about theft since the discs were so small and light.

For Sony and Philips, there was much at stake. Both companies had spent millions of dollars on research and development, and they would not recoup this money for many years. Only pennies on the sale of each CD would actually go to company profits. The general response of the music industry was to wait and see what would happen. Record companies assumed that CDs would replace cassettes and eight-track tapes, but they strongly believed that LPs would endure.

THE END OF VINYL

In 1983 CD sales went beyond even the most optimistic expectations, with over 800,000 discs sold. Philips increased the number of titles to 1,000 by the year's end. Most of the early CDs were classical releases. Assuming that rock and pop fans could not afford CDs and CD players, Philips focused on the classical music market.

Each year, sales increased exponentially. In 1985 over 100 million CDs were sold and every major electronics supplier was forced to move into the CD market. Sales for the next year were around 150 million, and the demand for CDs overshot supply. Disc manufacturers reported that they would have sold 30 percent more if they could have made more discs.

While the sound quality was a major improvement over analog LPs and cassette tapes, it was the durability and portability of CDs that largely caused their popularity among consumers. CDs were made of polycarbonate plastic, the same material used for bulletproof glass. It was estimated that a CD could last as long as 100 years. In contrast, when LPs were played, the needle physically touched the record's surface, causing it to wear down slightly with each playing. In contrast, a CD player's laser never actually touched the disc. It sounded the same regardless of how many times it was played. CDs and their cases were small, light, and easy to carry, unlike their vinyl counterparts. Due to the rising demand for CDs, Sony introduced the portable CD player in 1984, and this product made the format even more convenient.

CD sales in 1988 surpassed 400 million discs, outselling LPs for the first time. The next year, only 300 million LPs were sold, while CDs sold 650 million. German record company Deutsche Grammophon GmbH was the first company to announce that it would no longer make LPs. Other companies began to follow suit, usually starting with their classical divisions. LPs continued to decline in sales, sinking below 100 million in 1990.

CD player sales also grew exponentially each year. Sony began to offer newer models for casual music fans that were much more affordable than the CDP-101. CD player sales hit the 10 million mark in 1985 and increased by approximately 10 million each year. Turntable sales dropped slightly in 1983 and remained flat for the remainder of the decade. In 1989 it was reported that 32 percent of households had CD players. The next year, this increased to 45 percent.

COMPACT DISCS VS. DIGITAL DOWNLOADS

By the early 1990s CDs had largely replaced vinyl phonograph records and cassette tapes as the main format for recorded music. Over the course of 25 years, from 1983 to 2008, more than 200 billion CDs were sold. However, like its analog predecessors, the CD's days were numbered. CD sales peaked in 2000 and then began a steady decline. During the 1990s many music fans replaced their LP and cassette collections with CDs and by this time, their CD collections were complete. CD sales were also hurt by an economic recession that occurred in 2001.

The real coup de grâce for the CD was a new digital music format that enabled consumers to get the music they wanted through their personal computers. In 1999, Napster, an online service that offered free music downloads via the Internet, made its debut. Although Napster was quickly shut down by a lawsuit filed by the music industry, the age of the digital download had begun. New file-sharing networks similar to Napster quickly arose to replace it, offering free music to anyone with Internet access. In 2001 Apple Inc. offered the first digital download service, iTunes, but by that time the damage was done. Consumers who had downloaded free music for the last three years were largely unwilling to start paying for it again. Recorded music sales in the United States, 85 percent of which was represented by CDs, declined from US$14.6 billion in 1999 to US$6.3 billion in 2009.

In a *Wall Street Journal* article on the CD's 25th anniversary, Jason Fry stated that the CD helped to destroy the format it was meant to dominate. He wrote that while the CD offered improvements over the LP in terms of sound quality and portability, in many ways it ruined the album format. The tiny booklet that came with CDs could not faithfully reproduce album cover art. In order to fill the available 74 minutes, record companies and recording artists added extra recordings such as bonus tracks that often affected the album's musical integrity. Albums could no longer be listened to easily in one sitting, and the ability to choose the track listeners wanted to hear with the touch of a button, rather than physically moving a record player needle, also contributed to the LP's demise. In the age of digital music sharing, Fry noted, "CDs have gone from Jetsons to jetsam. They're an annoyance—the leftovers from ripped albums and burns made for trips in rental cars."

DATA STORAGE

CDs would create an even greater impact on the world of computers. CD-ROMs (Compact Disc Read-Only Memory) were developed by Philips and Sony using the same technology as the audio discs. CD-ROMs could hold a wide variety of multimedia data such as video, text, animation, graphics, and audio, and were readable by personal computers. A CD-ROM could hold more than 260,000 pages of text. At a 1986 conference on the new technology that was later nicknamed the "Woodstock of CD-ROM," Microsoft Corporation CEO Bill Gates accurately predicted that the CD-ROM would be the future of data storage and distribution due to its large data capacity, durability, and low cost.

Although the use of Sony CDs had waned by the 2010s, its impact on the information age was far-reaching.

It was the first successful attempt to use lasers to code optical data and it spawned the CD-ROM, which quickly became the standard for storing software and data.

BIBLIOGRAPHY

"Compact Disc Hits 25th Birthday." *BBC News,* August 17, 2007. Accessed February 10, 2012. http://news.bbc.co.uk/2/hi/technology/6950845.stm.

Fry, Jason. "The CD Turns 25." *Wall Street Journal,* August 27, 2007. Accessed February 10, 2012. http://online.wsj.com/article/SB118788874188106745.html.

Goldman, David. "Music's Lost Decade: Sales Cut in Half." *CNNMoney,* February 3, 2010. Accessed February 10, 2012. http://money.cnn.com/2010/02/02/news/companies/napster_music_industry/.

"How the CD Was Developed." *BBC News,* August 17, 2007. Accessed February 10, 2012. http://news.bbc.co.uk/2/hi/technology/6950933.stm.

Immink, Kees A. Schouhamer. "The Compact Disc Story." *Journal of the Audio Engineering Society* 46, no. 5 (May 1998): 458–465. Accessed February 10, 2012. http://www.exp-math.uni-essen.de/~immink/pdf/cdstoryoriginal.pdf.

"Optical Data Storage." In *The Gale Encyclopedia of Science,* edited by K. Lee Lerner and Brenda Wilmoth Lerner. 3rd ed. Vol. 4, 2874–2876. Detroit: Gale, 2004. Gale Virtual Reference Library (GALE|CX3418501627). Accessed February 10, 2012. http://go.galegroup.com/ps/i.do?id=GALE%7CCX3418501627&v=2.1&u=itsbtrial&it=r&p=GVRL&sw=w.

Philips. "The History of the CD." Amsterdam, The Netherlands, April 12, 2011. Accessed February 10, 2012. http://www.research.philips.com/technologies/projects/cd/.

Timmons, Rebecca J. "The Invention of Compact Discs." In *Science and Its Times,* edited by Neil Schlager and Josh Lauer. Vol. 7, 540–542. Detroit: Gale, 2001. Gale Virtual Reference Library (GALE|CX3408504661). Accessed February 10, 2012. http://go.galegroup.com/ps/i.do?id=GALE%7CCX3408504661&v=2.1&u=itsbtrial&it=r&p=GVRL&sw=w.

Troester, Maura, David E. Salamie, and Paul R. Greenland. "Sony Corporation." In *International Directory of Company Histories,* edited by Jay P. Pederson. Vol. 108, 460–469. Detroit: St. James Press, 2010. Gale Virtual Reference Library (GALE|CX1302600091). Accessed February 10, 2012. http://go.galegroup.com/ps/i.do?id=GALE%7CCX1302600091&v=2.1&u=gale&it=r&p=GVRL&sw=w.

Corning's Innovative
LCD Formation Technology

CHEMCOR

The process that led to the development of Corning Incorporated's liquid crystal display (LCD) substrate began in 1957. (In an LCD display, the liquid crystals are placed between two layers of glass known as substrates.) Bill Decker, the CEO of Corning, wondered if the company could develop glass that did not break easily. Decker assigned the project to Bill Armistead. The tough glass research project received an appropriate name, Project Muscle. Armistead's researchers worked on Project Muscle for five years, presenting the shatter-resistant glass to Decker in 1962, according to *TIME*. At the time, the glass was given the name Chemcor.

Corning heavily promoted Chemcor, sending out a film clip in which its researchers slammed, bent, and stretched the glass, showing manufacturers its resilience. Corning offered Chemcor to airplane manufacturers, automakers, and other industrial companies. In 1964 Corning further refined the Chemcor manufacturing process with the fusion draw method, according to Ben Dobbin in the *Los Angeles Times* in 2000. In the fusion draw process, or overflow downdraw method, the liquid glass overflowed from the sides of a container and pooled under it. As the glass formed from the two flows outside of the container, it did not absorb any impurities from the container. The fusion draw process provided better quality than the float glass process in which the glassmaker poured the glass over a layer of tin and the glass absorbed some of the tin particles, according to Eric Wesoff for *Green Tech Media.*

The fusion draw method produced high-quality automobile windshields, but Ford Motor Company and other automakers decided that Chemcor was too expensive. According to Dobbin, in his 2010 article "Gorilla from the 1960s Could Be Hit for Corning," the British glassmaker Pilkington Brothers offered less expensive windshields to U.S. automotive manufacturers as the float glass process efficiently produced large quantities of window glass.

ASIAN MARKETS

Corning marketed Chemcor to Asian manufacturers and gained a few customers. The hard and durable glass was useful for smaller products, such as watches and calculators, according to Jeffrey Hart in his book chapter "Flat Panel Displays." The glass sheets that protected the electronics inside these devices were extremely thin, so a tougher material provided significant benefits. The higher cost of Chemcor did not deter the manufacturers as calculators were very expensive in the 1970s and a small sheet of glass was enough to protect these devices.

During the 1970s Corning also negotiated a partnership with the Korean manufacturer Samsung. This partnership revolved around another technology for which Corning was famous, its cathode ray tubes (CRTs). Corning had introduced large-scale production of CRTs in the United States during the 1940s, and was interested in selling CRTs to the growing Asian consumer market. Corning and Samsung did not produce LCDs during the 1970s, but the managers of the two firms did learn to work together on manufacturing projects.

Corning produced a LCD substrate without using the Chemcor process during the 1970s. Older technologies, such as float glass, could meet manufacturers' production standards at the time. Corning continued to search for another use for its fusion draw glass, developing sunglasses that could automatically darken when they were exposed to sunlight. Although Corning introduced photochromic sunglasses much earlier than many competitors, its attempts to sell the glasses in the 1970s were not very successful.

THIN FILM TRANSISTORS

Japanese manufacturers planned to produce small television sets, camcorders, and other portable products in the early 1980s. A common type of LCD display, known as twisted nematic (TN) screens, lacked the performance characteristics that Japanese manufacturers wanted for the screens of these high-end devices. The technology known as thin film transistor (TFT) LCDs, on the other hand, allowed the electrical current that illuminates the display to be switched on and off much faster, which offered better picture quality. Most U.S. manufacturers were not interested in producing TFT displays because of high production costs.

Glass often contains large amounts of sodium. According to Mitch Funahashi for *Pioneer Magazine,* sodium ions can damage TFT LCDs, so the Japanese manufacturers wanted a type of glass that did not contain sodium and other alkali metals. Although glassmakers could produce glass without using alkali metals, many of these glasses suffered from low heat resistance and other weaknesses. Borosilicate glass, which contained boron, offered good heat resistance and contained few alkali contaminants, but it was expensive to manufacture.

Corning managers reported unusually high demand for borosilicate glass in the early 1980s. The company realized that Japanese manufacturers needed expensive borosilicate glass for TFT LCDs. As a result, the company increased research on borosilicate glass. In 1982 Corning developed 7059 borosilicate glass which rapidly gained popularity.

The early TFT LCD screens were very small, but a two-inch diagonal screen could still be useful to show the image that a camcorder recorded. By the late 1980s manufacturers of consumer electronics could produce larger screens and vendors could offer products such as a television with a 13-inch diagonal display. During this time, Corning was competing with an International Business Machines Corporation and Toshiba Corporation joint venture that also manufactured TFT screens. Corning developed borosilicate 1737 glass, which performed better than its 7059 borosilicate glass.

SAMSUNG AND CORNING

The partnership agreement between Samsung and Corning was relatively unusual for Samsung. Sam Jameson, for the *Los Angeles Times,* explained that Samsung typically preferred to license technology patents from other firms, instead of forming long-term partnerships. The decision to establish a partnership helped both companies and by 1990 Samsung Corning was making more CRTs for the world market than Corning produced in the United States.

The two manufacturers believed that the laptop computer market would expand in the future. LCD screens could produce high-quality pictures on a portable device while consuming much less power than CRTs. As a result LCD technology showed great potential for the laptop industry. Samsung and Corning built on their earlier relationship and set up a new partnership, Samsung Corning Precision Materials, to produce high-quality glass substrates.

Corning had a significant advantage over other U.S. manufacturers because it established relationships with Japanese and Korean manufacturers early. Some Asian firms preferred to handle production themselves and were skeptical about partnering with other companies in their own nations, let alone companies in the United States. The joint ventures helped Corning avoid import barriers. Corning built upon its advantage by setting up research laboratories in Japan and South Korea, in addition to its facilities in the United States.

EAGLE 2000

Corning continued to research new formulas for its borosilicate glasses. The company produced even thinner screens for laptops and portable devices, which remained damage resistant and displayed clear pictures. A laptop manufacturer could use the thin glass to reduce the weight of a laptop or they could construct a laptop with a larger screen that weighed the same as earlier models. This glass, Eagle 2000, replaced Corning's 1737 glass.

Eagle 2000 impressed Japanese manufacturers so much that it was awarded the Advanced Display Product of the Year at a Japanese product exhibition in 2001. The Fine Process Technology Japan Show gave awards for technologies that demonstrated innovation in the flat-screen industry. Before this show, no other active matrix liquid crystal display (AMLCD) had received this prize.

FLAT-SCREEN TELEVISIONS

Manufacturers had always wanted to produce truly flat-screen televisions, which appeared in many futuristic stories. Without the bulky CRT, a flat-screen television could be hung like a painting on a wall, conserving a great deal of space. By 2000 Corning believed that its AMLCD television technology was ready for the mass market. Dobbin, reporting for the *Los Angeles Times,* stated that Japanese shops offered 15-inch AMLCD televisions at a retail price of US$1,500 in 2000.

Corning's managers believed that the AMLCD project would greatly benefit the company. Laptops, televisions, cell phones, tablets, and future devices would all benefit from the LCD substrate. During the dot-com bubble, Corning had moved away from its roots as a glass manufacturing company, and had invested a great deal of its resources in a national telecommunication network in the United States. However, income projections for this project relied on the exuberant predictions that were common in the bubble, and after the U.S. economy weakened in 2000, Corning experienced economic difficulties.

Corning earned about US$250 million in 2000 from its LCD substrate, about 7 percent of its earnings, reported Dobbin. After 2000, LCD glass took on a much greater role for the company. Jeffrey Hart, in "Flat Panel Displays," reported that Corning earned more than five times as much income from its LCD glass in 2004, around US$1.3 billion. The decision to focus Corning's efforts on producing LCD glass had solved its economic problems.

EAGLE XG

Eagle glass originally attracted customers for its toughness and thinness, and Eagle XG improved on those qualities. Corning also introduced a new selling point, environmental friendliness. Regulators were especially concerned about electronic waste. Japan, Europe, and the United States had passed laws that banned toxic chemicals (which were common in electronic devices) and established new disposal regulations.

Eagle XG lacked many of the contaminants that concerned regulators. As a halide-free glass, it had no fluorine, chlorine, or bromine. Several heavy metals, including arsenic, barium, and antimony, were not present either, according to *MSNBC*. Since these metals were no longer needed for Eagle XG, mining for them was also unnecessary. Corning saved money because it needed to pay fewer mining-related expenses. Mining was also a source of environmental damage, so avoiding the need to mine for heavy metals enhanced Corning's ability to present itself as environmentally friendly.

Customers continued to use older LCD glass products after the release of Eagle XG in 2006, so Corning emphasized that Eagle XG had been designed to satisfy future environmental regulations. LCD substrate revenue continued to improve, reaching US$1.7 billion in 2006, which was now over one-third of Corning's total income, according to *MSNBC*. Like its predecessor Eagle 2000, Eagle XG won the Advanced Display Product of the Year award in 2007, this time taking the grand prize. The Society for Information Display gave Eagle XG the Display Component of the Year Award in 2007, according to Corning's "Display Technologies Timeline."

GORILLA GLASS

With the rise in popularity of smart phones, consumers began to report that the weak glass that protected their smartphones' components broke easily. Corning realized it could dominate the market with a stronger material. Corning reformulated its flow glass naming this glass Gorilla Glass. Although Gorilla Glass included elements of the Chemcor glass that Corning had developed in the 1960s, the 2006 blend was a new formulation that was designed primarily for use in smartphones. Corning also marketed Gorilla Glass for use in tablets, LCD televisions, and other portable devices.

Corning conducted a marketing campaign that was similar to the original marketing campaign for Chemcor to promote Gorilla Glass. It placed video advertisements on YouTube that showed its scientists scratching, throwing, and attempting to break the glass, and allowed attendees at technology conferences such as the Engadget Reader Meet Up in San Francisco in February 2011 to make their own attempts to damage the Gorilla Glass. As electronic readers and MP3 players gained popularity, Gorilla Glass also became an important component of these devices. Corning's Gorilla Glass campaign was so memorable that technology enthusiasts specifically looked for products that contained the durable glass.

By 2011 Corning depended heavily on Gorilla Glass. Many of the popular tablet manufacturers, including Acer, Asus, Dell, Lenovo, Motorola, and Samsung used Gorilla Glass, according to Corning. After tablet makers started cutting back on manufacturing because of weaker sales, Corning announced that it planned to produce less Gorilla Glass in 2012. Erica Ogg reported in *GigaOM* that Gorilla Glass was even more widespread than analysts realized, because some manufacturers, such as Apple Inc., preferred to promote their own technology instead of promoting the brands of third-party suppliers such as Corning. Corning planned to reduce its reliance on tablet sales by promoting Gorilla Glass as a substrate for other devices, such as widescreen high-definition televisions (HDTVs), which required much larger segments of glass.

THE INNOVATION

Corning gained little initial benefit from its Chemcor glass. The company made a strategic decision by keeping the rights to its flow glass process while it worked on other products and developed relationships with Asian manufacturers. Although the company could have sold the Chemcor technology, and it did sell off other glass products including its consumer glass line, its managers were observant enough to realize that flow glass could become much more useful in the future. The company was also willing to invest in LCD substrates during the 1980s, even though this placed it at a temporary competitive disadvantage to U.S. manufacturers who had decided not to implement the technology on a wide scale to reduce their costs.

Corning was willing to change its marketing strategy. It could have continued to focus on high-end windshields, spaceship windows, and other products that required large segments of expensive glass. Corning realized that it could sell a large order of glass to a manufacturer who only needed a small sheet of glass to protect a watch face or a camcorder. Working with small sheets also helped Corning perfect its technology so it was ready for larger products such as LCD flat-screen televisions in the future. Developing a product that exceeded current environmental standards, instead of waiting for regulators to force it to produce heavy-metal-free glass, also helped the company.

BIBLIOGRAPHY

Boorstin, Julia. "'Gorilla Glass' for Phones and Tables Drives Growth at Corning." *CNBC,* January 7, 2011. Accessed December 29, 2011. http://www.cnbc.com/id/40968536/Gorilla_Glass_for_Phones_and_Tablets_Drives_Growth_at_Corning.

Corning Incorporated. "Display Technologies Timeline." Corning, NY, 2008. Accessed December 29, 2011. http://media.corning.com/flash/displaytechnologies/2008/new_timeline/en/index.html.

———. "Glass Once Used in Windshields and Space Crafts Reborn into Cell Phones and Electronics." Corning, NY. Accessed December 29, 2011. http://www.corning.com/news_center/corning_stories/gorilla_glass.aspx.

———. "Samsung and Corning – Thirty-Five Years of Working Together." Corning, NY. Accessed December 29, 2011. http://www.corning.com/news_center/corning_stories/samsung_corning_case_study.aspx.

"Corning Says New Glass to Cut LCD Costs." *MSNBC,* March 21, 2006. Accessed December 29, 2011. http://www.msnbc.msn.com/id/11947652/ns/technology_and_science-innovation/t/corning-says-new-glass-cut-lcd-costs/#

.Tvxrn 9TOX40.

"Corning's EAGLE2000-TM- Glass Substrate Wins Advanced Display Product of the Year." *Business Wire,* July 17, 2001. Accessed December 29, 2011. http://www.thefreelibrary.com/Corning%27s+EAGLE2000-TM-+Glass+Substrate+Wins+Advanced+Display+Product. . .-a076567127.

"Corporations: Built on Glass." *TIME,* September 28, 1962. Accessed December 29, 2011. http://www.time.com/time/magazine/article/0,9171,940122,00.html.

Dobbin, Ben. "Abandoned Glass Process Yields Cutting-Edge Imagery." *Los Angeles Times,* April 24, 2000. Accessed December 29, 2011. http://articles.latimes.com/2000/apr/24/business/fi-22828.

———. "Gorilla from the 1960s Could Be Hit for Corning." *R&D Magazine,* August 3, 2010. Accessed December 29, 2011. http://www.rdmag.com/News/2010/08/Materials-Glass-Gorilla-from-the-1960s-could-be-hit-for-Corning/.

Funahashi, Mitch. "The Boron Behind Your Little Screen." *Pioneer Magazine,* January 1997. Accessed December 29, 2011. http://www.borax.com/pioneer17.html.

Hart, Jeffrey A. "Flat Panel Displays." In *Innovation in Global Industries: U.S. Firms Competing in a New World.* 141–162. Washington, DC: National Academies Press, 2008. Accessed December 29, 2011. http://www.nap.edu/catalog.php?record_id=12112#toc.

Jameson, Sam. "Corning's South Korean Venture Is a Big Success." *Los Angeles Times,* July 5, 1990. Accessed December 29, 2011. http://articles.latimes.com/1990-07-05/business/fi-449_1_samsung-corning.

Ogg, Erica. "Is Tablet Demand Slowing Down?" *GigaOM,* November 29, 2011. Accessed December 29, 2011. http://gigaom.com/2011/11/29/is-tablet-demand-slowing-down/.

"TFT." TechTerms.com. Accessed April 9, 2012. http://www.techterms.com/definition/tft.

Wesoff, Eric. "Glass Expert Corning Joins Fortune 500 in Rush to Solar." *Green Tech Media,* October 11, 2011. Accessed December 29, 2011. http://www.greentechmedia.com/articles/read/Glass-Expert-Corning-Joins-Fortune-500-in-Rush-to-Solar/.

Cotton Gin: Eli Whitney's Invention Impacts an Industry

Of all the inventions that changed the course of the textiles and apparel industries over the past 300 years, perhaps most crucial is the cotton gin (shortened form of cotton engine). Invented by U.S. citizen Eli Whitney in 1794, the cotton gin helped usher in the concept of mass production. Whereas cotton workers throughout the Southern United States were previously lucky to clean seed from a pound of cotton per day, the revolutionary cotton gin enabled up to 50 pounds of cotton to be cleaned each day.

Born in 1765 in Westboro, Massachusetts, Whitney was the son of a farmer. Throughout his early years, he spent much of his time helping his father on the farm and was particularly enamored of his workshop. The young Whitney exhibited a knack for invention; during the American Revolution (1775–17830, he started a side business manufacturing nails. By the end of the war, Whitney's business made hatpins.

After graduating from Yale University in 1792, Whitney decided to move south to Georgia, where he intended to take up a tutoring position while studying law. Upon discovering that the tutoring post had been filled by the time he arrived, Whitney accepted the invitation of the widow of General Nathaniel Greene to move into her plantation home where he could pursue his legal studies and tutor her children. While there, he befriended the plantation's manager, Phineas Miller, who explained to Whitney the complications of growing cotton. Their conversations helped plant the seeds of what eventually became the cotton gin.

EARLY COTTON GINS

Contrary to popular belief, Whitney's invention, while revolutionary, was not the first cotton gin. In fact, various forms of the device had been used to remove seeds from cotton fiber for centuries. "The earliest gin was made from a single roller and a hard, flat surface," wrote Angela Lakwete in *Inventing the Cotton Gin: Machine and Myth in Antebellum America*. "Ginners in Asia, Africa, and North America used it to batch process fuzzy-seed, short-staple cotton."

Between the 12th and 14th centuries, commercial Indian and Chinese markets began to use gins with two rollers. Even though several types of gins populated the Byzantine Muslim and Mongol empires, an Indian-style two-roller device began to dominate the Mediterranean cotton trade. When the 17th century arrived, British interest in cotton exploded owing to its blossoming trade with Asia. Before long, consumers in Great Britain and throughout Europe were keenly interested in acquiring colorful Indian cotton prints, a phenomenon that led to the production of cheaper substitutes.

Before the American Revolution, colonial farmers dedicated much of their acreage to cotton for the British trade. That trade came into sharp relief following the war, however, as the new country debated its own development policy. "If United States citizens continued to ship raw materials like cotton to Great Britain and import manufactured goods, then Great Britain would continue to benefit from a favorable balance of trade and the added value accrued to manufactured goods," wrote Lakwete. "Americans would remain economic dependents." Alternatively, the U.S. colonists could develop their own domestic textile industry that hinged on domestically grown cotton to produce yarn and cloth products for international markets. For this purpose, rudimentary gins that originated in Asia were either utilized or copied by U.S. cotton producers, yet most, if not all, of the devices were an insufficient answer to what farmers really needed.

COMPLICATIONS OF GROWING COTTON

By the 18th century cotton had long been a staple ingredient of apparel and textile manufacturing around the world. The commodity was introduced to Europeans by Arab traders around the first century but did not gain real popularity in Great Britain until the 15th century. Nonetheless, cotton imports began to flow steadily to Great Britain in the late 18th century: in 1783, the country imported 9 million pounds, and by 1790 it imported 28 million pounds. By 1825, Great Britain's cotton imports rose to 228 million pounds.

To meet this growing overseas demand, U.S. farmers in the South fervently grew and harvested cotton throughout the 18th century. At the time, farmers worked with three main types of cotton fiber: long staple, medium staple, and short staple. Long-staple cotton such as Sea Island Egyptian was considered superior because its seeds were smooth and easy to remove and the longer fibers were suitable for weaving fine cloth. However, the long-staple variety proved the most difficult to grow.

Medium-staple cotton was easier to grow. In fact, some 95 percent of the world's cotton was of the medium-staple variety. Short-staple cotton was also grown and used in products such as blankets, carpets, and fiber blends.

Cotton became an important crop during early colonial America. Southern plantations in the United States relied heavily on slave labor to grow, harvest, and prepare cotton for sale. Cleaning cotton was no easy business in the U.S. South during the 18th century. Green-seeded cotton grew in abundance throughout the inland regions, but it was difficult to clean. A worker would typically spend an entire day cleaning seed from one pound of green-seeded cotton. Other types of cotton were easier to clean, yet more difficult to access. Black-seeded cotton was particularly easy to clean, but grew only along coastal areas. Farmers needed a solution.

WHITNEY'S COTTON GIN

In the late 18th century, a cotton gin was already utilized for cleaning seeds from cotton. Unfortunately, it was not effective on all types of cotton. Instead of removing seeds from green-seeded cotton, it crushed them, resulting in a stained end product. Such were the challenges faced by Miller and other plantation managers with whom Whitney spoke. Utilizing his skills as an inventor, as well as what he learned from local slaves, he set about drawing up plans for a new device that would quickly and efficiently extract seed from cotton, thereby improving farmers's daily yields.

Whitney set up a shop in the basement of the plantation house and, with a workbench and a few common tools, began building his device.

"He learned from a local slave named Sam that a comb could be used to remove the sticky seeds from the cotton fiber," wrote Tim McNeese in *Revolutionary War.* "With that information, he hammered together a simple combing device in ten days. Called the 'Cotton Engine' (or 'cotton gin'), Whitney had designed an answer to the cotton dilemma."

The initial model of Whitney's cotton gin was mediocre at best. The device contained a screen through which cotton was forced while seeds were left behind. The most troubling parts of the device were its teeth. "His first idea was to use teeth like those of a circular saw," wrote Frank Bachman in *The Story of Inventions.* "But he did not have any thin iron plates available that were strong enough to make such teeth. Fortunately, a coil of heavy iron wire, purchased to make a bird cage for Mrs. Greene's daughter, arrived at just the right time."

The wire gave Whitney an idea. With his crude tools, he dove into the slow process of drawing out the large wire into smaller parts, incorporating various lengths into the device, and running it through countless trials. Finally, Whitney concluded that one-inch wire teeth that were curved slightly back from the direction in which the cylinder turned proved ideal for seed removal. Still, he was left with the challenge of teeth that would become clogged with cotton fiber once the seeds were removed. When he noticed Mrs. Greene using her hearth brush (a fireplace brush) to remove the clogged cotton one day, he was captured by yet another idea: a revolving brush that would sit just behind the toothed cylinder.

Whitney's ultimate invention was constructed of a rotating drum with wire hooks, or ratchet-like teeth, that could pull cotton fibers between the teeth of a comb. The teeth were spaced close enough so that seeds could not pass through. A second drum would rotate faster and carry the brushes to dislodge cotton fibers from the first drum. Rotating the drums would be a belt-and-pulley system. A worker would simply drop cotton bolls into a hopper, which then guided the bolls to the face of the comb. (A boll is the protective casing in which the cotton fiber grows.) When the bolls were pulled through the teeth of the cylinder, the separated cotton fibers would emerge on the left of the gin and the collected seeds would emerge on the right.

Whitney introduced his new cotton gin, to the amazement of local planters. "They were quick to see that, with this machine to take out the seeds, they could raise cotton at a good profit," wrote Bachman. The local planters "congratulated Whitney on his ingenuity. They urged him to get a patent at once, telling him that his invention was sure to bring him wealth and honor." As Whitney would soon learn, however, fortune would not come his way.

OTHER FORTUNES

The excitement that Whitney's invention generated among local farmers was palpable. For the first time, a device had been built that could actually do the work that previous gins had failed to do with any degree of efficiency. Such enthusiasm was hard to contain, and before long news of the cotton gin began to spread across Georgia. Whitney, who had partnered with Phineas Miller to patent the device, kept it out of view in a shed on the plantation, but thieves broke into the shed one night and carried the gin away.

Despite the loss, Whitney rebuilt the machine, and he and Miller finally earned a patent in 1794. Almost immediately, they were beset by challenges. "Slow to grasp the implications of what he had documented, Miller grappled with two contradictory phenomena: mechanics were building the toothed gins and merchant ginners were using them even as others shunned them in favor of roller gins," wrote Lakwete. An unintended consequence of Whitney's invention was "roller gin enthusiasm." Joseph Eve, a wealthy cotton gin maker inspired by Whitney's patent, sought a patent for his own device, for which he had unsuccessfully petitioned Bahamian officials on a previous occasion. While manufacturers opposed Eve's patent pursuits, he nonetheless began selling his device, which promised a yield of 500 pounds of clean cotton each day.

"Spurred by roller gin enthusiasm, men from the professional and artisanal classes of Augusta and environs published notices of their roller gins throughout 1796 and 1797," wrote Lakwete. Miller consequently began taking all suspected makers of cotton gins that utilized the toothed-gin principle to court. The frenzied litigation and continued development of cotton gin knockoffs failed to bring to Whitney and Miller the wealth they had expected, but it nonetheless brought great wealth to the U.S. South. The cotton gin arrived at a time when tobacco and rice were cheap and farmland was difficult to make profitable. Thanks in large part to the cotton gin, "king cotton" would reap millions of U.S, dollars for Southern plantations in the United States for years to come.

Disappointed that his invention did not bring him wealth, Whitney left the South and moved back to Connecticut. Before long, Whitney began searching for his next invention. "[H]e looked for a new project where he could use his genius for mechanics and invention, and where, by industry and economy, he might perhaps make the fortune that he once thought was all but in his hands," wrote Bachman. Whitney identified a burgeoning market opportunity for mass-produced rifles and established a factory in New Haven, Connecticut, in 1798.

Until then, no two receivers, stocks, or rifle barrels were alike. Rifle makers handcrafted each gun individually, which required considerable skill but made replacement parts impossible to implement. Whitney's idea was to build power machines that would cut, file, drill, and bore the previously handcrafted parts. Dividing rifle manufacturing into 100 different parts, and each part into a series of steps, little skill was required to mass produce rifles. "Whitney is credited with popularizing this system of manufacturing in America," wrote Bachman. "He will always be honored, of course, as the inventor of the cotton gin; but his right to fame rests no less on what he taught the world about the use of machines in the making of common things."

BIBLIOGRAPHY

Bachman, Frank P. *The Story of Inventions.* 2nd ed. Arlington Heights, IL: Christian Liberty Press, 2008, 74–80.

Benson, Sonia, Daniel E. Brannen, Jr., and Rebecca Valentine. "Cotton Gin." In *U*X*L Encyclopedia of U.S. History,* edited by Lawrence W. Baker and Sarah Hermsen. Vol. 2, 399–400. Detroit: UXL, 2009. Gale Virtual Reference Library (GALE|CX3048900154). Accessed February 17, 2012. http://go.galegroup.com/ps/i.do?id=GALE%7CCX30489001 54&v=2.1&u=itsbtrial&it=r&p=GVRL&sw=w.

———. "Whitney, Eli." *U*X*L Encyclopedia of U.S. History,* edited by Lawrence W. Baker and Sarah Hermsen. Vol. 8, 1690–1692. Gale Virtual Reference Library (GALE|CX3048900672). Accessed February 17, 2012. http://go.galegroup.com/ps/i.do?id=GALE%7CCX30489006 72&v=2.1&u=itsbtrial&it=r&p=GVRL&sw=w.

Lakwete, Angela. *Inventing the Cotton Gin: Machine and Myth in Antebellum America.* Baltimore: The Johns Hopkins University Press, 2003, 1–66.

McNeese, Tim. *Revolutionary War.* St. Louis, MO: Millikin Publishing Company, 2003, 38.

Meltzer, Milton. *The Cotton Gin.* New York: Marshall Cavendish, 2003.

Mirsky, Jeannette, and Allan Nevins. *The World of Eli Whitney.* New York: Macmillan, 1952.

Creative Marketing and Sanitation Showrooms: Thomas Crapper's Inventions

As a young man in mid-19th-century London, Thomas Crapper likely did not anticipate how popular and enduring his surname would eventually become. Despite being falsely credited with inventing the modern toilet, Crapper's innovative sanitary products nonetheless helped usher in the modern bathroom. The word "crapper" is sometimes used interchangeably with "toilet."

Thomas Crapper was born in 1836 to a family of modest means in Yorkshire, England. As a 14-year-old, Crapper became an apprentice to a master plumber in London, England and soon found himself working as a journeyman (the stage between apprentice and master). By 1861 he had established his own plumbing products shop in the Chelsea, London neighborhood. Over the years, Crapper would grow his business and expand his reputation as a quality source of sanitary fittings. In particular, he introduced the concept of a bathroom showroom and displayed his products in the windows of his Marlboro Works facility, a decision that initially created a stir among passersby.

As Crapper's name and reputation grew throughout England, so too did his patents. Crapper successfully earned nine patents: four for drain improvements, three for water closets (later known as toilets), one for manhole covers, and one for pipe joints. One of his most significant contributions actually came from one of his employees, Albert Giblin. Crapper purchased from Giblin a patent for a "valveless water waste preventer," a device that enabled effective flushing without wasting unnecessary amounts of water. Another famous Crapper patent was for a "disconnecting trap," an underground drain fitting that represented a significant advance in preventing disease from sanitary waste. Yet another contribution, the ball cock, became an important tool in conserving bathroom water. Crapper's sanitary inventions soon garnered the attention of the Prince of Wales (later King Edward VII), who invited him to supply products for Windsor Castle, Buckingham Palace, and Westminster Abbey. The invitation eventually led Crapper to earn the distinction of being named royal sanitary engineer.

DEVELOPING A SAFER LAVATORY

The mid-19th century British society was still largely skeptical toward the concept of an indoor toilet, then known as a "water closet." Until that time, sanitary waste was firmly an outdoor matter, and the general public viewed an indoor alternative as unseemly and unhygienic. However, Crapper recognized enormous, untapped potential in the development and promotion of indoor sanitary products.

Contrary to popular belief, Crapper did not invent the flush toilet. That invention actually appeared three centuries before him, when Sir John Harington introduced a revolutionary water closet that he illustrated in *A New Discourse upon a Stale Subject: The Metamorphosis of Ajax*. Harington's godmother, Queen Elizabeth I, had his commode installed in Richmond Palace. Prior to that innovation, one of the earliest sanitary relics dated to 1700 BCE at the Palace of Knossos in Crete. There, wooden toilet-like seats attached to piping were created. Following Harington's innovation, the flush toilet underwent a series of improvements, such as S-curved water piping to trap odors, a chain-operated flushing device, and a pressurized siphon flush system that transferred waste from the toilet bowl to sewage pipes in a more effective manner.

However, until Crapper, sanitary innovations had yet to address the continued problems of heavy water consumption and risk of disease. Crapper's sanitary developments were twofold. First, he recognized the growing problem of unnecessary water consumption and disease borne of sanitary waste. To that end, Crapper devised a number of products aimed at improving water use and reducing the risks of disease. These included Giblin's valveless water waste preventer and Crapper's ball cock, both of which worked to conserve water, as well as a disconnecting trap that funneled sanitary waste underground and thereby greatly reduced health risks.

Second, Crapper saw the potential appeal in marketing sanitary products to the mainstream public. At that time, bathroom suppliers and manufacturers were chiefly relegated to discrete side-street locations. "Mr. Crapper introduced the first bathroom showroom," wrote Simon Kirby, chief executive of Thomas Crapper & Company, in his preface to *Did Thomas Crapper Really Invent the Toilet?: The Inventions That Changed Our Homes and Our Lives.* "Imagine the fuss when Crapper & Co. opened in London's King's Road, opposite Royal Avenue, with W.C. bowls in the windows! Ladies fainted in the street."

CRAPPER'S INNOVATIONS

Perhaps the most important of Crapper's sanitary contributions was the valveless water waste preventer, the device invented by Albert Giblin. That device came about in large part from a British Parliamentary act requiring that lavatories conserve water. Up until the 1860s water closet valves typically leaked a significant amount of water, and many users simply let their lavatories perpetually flush in order to keep the bowls clean. Crapper's valveless system required only half a tank of water yet was as effective as perpetual flushing. The cistern (receptacle for water) itself was made of cast iron and was connected to the wall above the water closet with a drain running from its bottom into the lavatory. The system included a flush lever, a main water chamber, a siphon, and a displacement plate. When the flush lever was depressed, a spindle inside the cistern raised the displacement plate, causing water to flow upward and then down into the siphon. With the aid of air at the top of the cistern, that flushing action created a natural siphon effect whereby more water was pulled up and then down the siphon at great speed. Once the cistern emptied, an incoming drain refilled the tank until a ball cock rose to a level to block the inlet and cease the flow of water. No water would escape until the flush lever was depressed again.

Crapper's valveless water waste preventer, marketed as a "pull and let go" model, came in either painted or galvanized (coated with zinc) varieties. The two-gallon model sold for 20 shillings and six pence, plus an extra cost for

a lid. Another important Crapper innovation was the "Kenon Disconnecting Trap," a device that enabled the underground transport of waste and prevented backflow into the toilet. Again, his disconnecting trap was partly a response to the British government's request for sanitary devices that would improve water flow and help prevent disease.

The disconnecting trap was essentially a stoneware-made device that consisted of three arms that connected to make an imperfect triangle. While Crapper's traps ranged in size, typically each arm of the trap was a few inches in length. At one end of the trap was a semi-egg-shaped inlet that connected to the manhole beneath the toilet. Just above the inlet was a locking cap, and at the other end of the trap was an outlet that connected to a drainage pipe leading to the sewer. The lower angled section of the trap, also known as the disconnection chamber, ran from the inlet toward the outlet, and maintained a full egg shape similar to the inlet before becoming circular at the outlet. Above the inlet, a cleansing arm ran to the outlet. The cleansing arm was plugged with an airtight stopper to release water from the disconnection chamber in the event that the trap became blocked. The egg shape of the disconnection chamber was known to provide better scouring properties than a circular-shaped chamber. Once water and waste funneled through the trap, sewer air, and thus disease, could not re-enter the bathroom through the pipe system.

Another important advance owed to Crapper was the ball cock, sometimes referred to as the "ball tap." The ball cock was attached to the end of an arm located inside the water cistern, typically situated on the wall above the toilet. When the toilet was flushed, water would exit the cistern downward through a pipe to the toilet. As water from a secondary pipe refilled the cistern, the ball cock would rise on the surface of the water and prevent the cistern from becoming overfilled. Modern flushing systems incorporate the same basic technology as Crapper's ball cock.

Finally Crapper's invention of a sanitary products showroom was influential in making the toilet and all its accessories a household topic. Crapper displayed his toilets and sanitary fittings in large plate glass windows in his facility near Marlborough Road in London, England. While the public display of water closets was initially met with shock, it nonetheless ushered in a new approach to the sales and marketing of bathroom products that continued into the future.

ENSUING SANITARY DEVELOPMENT

As Jan Martin Bang showed in *Ecovillages: A Practical Guide to Sustainable Communities,* Crapper's sanitary innovations came at a time of extreme water pollution and its inherent health risks. "Many if not most Londoners were literally drinking raw sewage," Bang wrote. "There was no sewage collection or treatment, and the wastewater ran straight into the ground, mixed with the ground water, which was pumped up and used for drinking." While Crapper did not invent the toilet, his patented improvements made the device infinitely safer and less wasteful, leading to continued innovations that eventually led to to the modern toilet. The valveless water waste preventer, for instance, was the first of many toilets to use a relatively small amount of water to effectively flush waste. Toilet water conservation continued to be a priority among manufacturers throughout the 20th century and into the 21st, and the low-flow-water toilets they introduced owed some acknowledgement to Crapper's original offering.

In addition, variations of Crapper's original ball cock design remain a consistent feature on modern toilets worldwide. Capitalizing on the conservation potential of such products, countries began passing legislation requiring new toilets to drain a fraction of the water of their predecessors. By 2010 toilet manufacturers utilized computer modeling and design techniques such as critical fluid dynamic analysis to improve water performance. Whereas older toilets could take as long as 12 seconds to flush, their modern counterparts required as few as 3 seconds to flush fully.

Perhaps as important as Crapper's inventions are his contributions to the sales and marketing of sanitary products. "Thomas Crapper became widely associated with toilets not so much for innovation, but salesmanship," wrote Cristen Conger in *Discovery News*. "The British plumber and entrepreneur established sanitation showrooms and cleverly imprinted his memorable last name on his wares."

Thomas Crapper & Company continued on after its founder's death in 1910. In 1963 the company was acquired by a rival firm but was resurrected in the late 1990s by an British enthusiast with a passion for the firm's history. In the early 2010s the company was operating in Stratford-upon-Avon, England, William Shakespeare's home, and continued to sell a wide variety of sanitary products via brochure and website. Included among its wares were recreations of Crapper's original developments, retrofitted for modern bathrooms.

AFTER CRAPPER

Thomas Crapper's innovations led him to enjoy favorable reviews and the attention of the royal family. "Crapper received a royal warrant as a manufacturing sanitary engineer to royalty," wrote Stephen Van Dulken in *Inventing the 19th Century: 100 Inventions That Shaped the Victorian Age*. "This was proudly referred to in his copious trade literature where the many designs, all with their own names (mostly named after streets near the Works) were displayed." By the time Crapper retired in 1904 his company and inventions helped transform sanitary products from a taboo subject into a suitable item for public sales and marketing.

BIBLIOGRAPHY

Bang, Jan Martin. *Ecovillages: A Practical Guide to Sustainable Communities.* Gabriola Island, BC, Canada: New Society Publishers, 2005.

Baynes, Thomas Spencer. *The Encyclopaedia Britannica: A Dictionary of Arts, Sciences, and General Literature* Vol. 21, 9th ed. New York: Henry G. Allen, 1886.

Conger, Cristen. "Who Invented the Toilet?" *Discovery News*, June 21, 2010. Accessed January 11, 2012. http://news.discovery.com/tech/who-invented-the-toilet.html.

Herring-Shaw, A. *Domestic Sanitation and Plumbing: A Treatise of the Materials, Designs, and Methods Used in Sanitary Engineering Manufacture, Jointing and Fixing of Pipes, Sanitary Fittings, Etc.; Removal of Waste Water; Water Supply; Hot-Water Services; Ventilation, Etc.* London: Gurney and Jackson, 1909.

O'Reilly, Catherine. *Did Thomas Crapper Really Invent the Toilet?: The Inventions That Changed Our Homes and Our Lives.* New York: Skyhorse Publishing, 2008.

Perraudin, Frances. "Thomas Crapper's Toilet." *TIME*, September 7, 2010. Accessed December 8, 2011. http://www.time.com/time/specials/packages/article/0,28804,2016258_2016259_2016274,00.html.

Ransom, William. "A Defence of the Disconnecting Trap." *Journal of the Royal Sanitary Institute.* Vol. 24. London: Offices of the Sanitary Institute, 1903.

Thomas Crapper & Co. Ltd. "A Brief History of the Company." Stratford-upon-Avon, UK. Accessed December 8, 2011. http://www.thomas-crapper.com/history02.asp.

"Thomas Crapper Commemorated by National Trust." *Telegraph*, January 28, 2010. Accessed December 8, 2011. http://www.telegraph.co.uk/news/newstopics/howaboutthat/7084341/Thomas-Crapper-commemorated-by-National-Trust.html.

Van Dulken, Stephen. *Inventing the 19th Century: 100 Inventions That Shaped the Victorian Age.* New York: New York University Press, 2001.

Dyson Vacuums

Dyson Appliances Limited made a vacuum cleaner both more attractive to customers and better at performing its task. The Dyson vacuum cleaner did not clog easily, so it was more effective at picking up dirt. As it did not use a bag, its owner no longer needed to worry about purchasing replacement vacuum bags. The Dyson vacuum's bright colors improved the aesthetic qualities of an appliance that frequently had a plain, utilitarian appearance, and its translucent dust containment section allowed customers to see its effectiveness firsthand.

THE BALLBARROW

In the 1970s James Dyson lived with his wife on a farm in the British countryside. While his wife earned the majority of the money, Dyson worked on various inventions. One of his most prominent inventions was the Ballbarrow, a wheelbarrow that used a ball instead of a standard wheel. Dyson created the Ballbarrow because a standard wheelbarrow that carried heavy supplies left tracks in his lawn, and the wheel that it used for navigation did not provide sufficient support.

The Ballbarrow initially sold well in the United Kingdom, but Dyson lost control of his invention when one of his workers stole his design documents and took the Ballbarrow plans to a wheelbarrow manufacturer in the United States, according to the *New Yorker*. This experience made Dyson much more concerned about protecting his intellectual property and the products that he developed. The Ballbarrow manufacturing process did help lead Dyson to the creation of the product that eventually made him famous, the Dyson vacuum.

Dyson needed to paint the Ballbarrows, so he coated them with spray paint in an enclosed room. However, the paint vapor quickly clogged the screens that he was using to capture the paint particles. Dyson visited a sawmill to determine how it filtered out large amounts of air pollutants. The sawmill had constructed a cyclone tower that sucked up all the sawdust, wood chips, and other materials without using a screen that needed to be cleaned frequently. This cyclone design would be integral to Dyson's vacuum cleaner design.

VACUUM DESIGN

Since his youth, James Dyson had known that vacuum cleaners suffered from design problems. *Business 2.0* reported that when Dyson was growing up he could smell the odor of his dog emanating from the bag of the vacuum cleaner. There was no obvious solution to this problem. Every vacuum cleaner was constructed with similar parts, such as the vacuum bag and the suction device. Researchers at the Hoover Company had invented many of the main concepts of vacuum cleaner design in the 1920s. Although there had been minor improvements to upright vacuum cleaners, and some metal parts had been replaced with plastic throughout the years, the basic concept remained relatively unchanged. Manufacturers competed by including new cosmetic elements, such as adding a new finish to a vacuum cleaner's plastic shell.

Dyson found inspiration for his new vacuum cleaner design in the filtration system for his Ballbarrow project. A cyclone tower efficiently sucked up sawdust, paint chips, and other air pollutants, so it would be very effective at sucking dirt out of a carpet. However, the industrial cyclone tower Dyson viewed at the sawmill was gigantic and expensive, so Dyson needed to develop a smaller-scale tower that could fit inside the shell of a vacuum cleaner.

In 1978 he started work on his cyclone vacuum project. After more than 5,000 attempts, he completed a prototype cyclone vacuum in 1983.

Dyson decided to make the collection bin on his cyclone vacuums transparent to show off their superior dirt collection capabilities. With a standard vacuum, the dust inside the vacuum bag was not visible to the user. Dyson decided to make the dust container inside his G-Force vacuum cleaner clear, so the user could see the dirt it had picked up. This was a very aggressive design decision, because consumers could have been uninterested in seeing the debris that the vacuum collected. The Corporate Design Foundation reported that focus groups rejected this design element, but Dyson decided to implement it anyway. The clear bin turned out to be a hit with shoppers. A Dyson owner could proudly show his or her friends all the dirt that the cyclone vacuum cleaner collected.

SEARCH FOR A BRITISH PARTNER

Dyson showed his cyclone prototype to British manufacturers, but they were not interested in his vacuum cleaner. The vacuum cleaner market was considered mature, as many people already owned a bag vacuum cleaner. Manufacturers in other industries did not want to compete with established vacuum cleaner brands such as Hoover, Red Rover, Eureka, and Kirby. The Corporate Design Foundation reported that even the British manufacturer that had previously made Dyson's Ballbarrows, which he partially owned, was not interested in producing his new vacuum cleaners. The other shareholders believed that companies like Hoover, which employed many skilled designers and engineers, had already investigated most of the potential vacuum cleaner improvements.

Vacuum cleaner manufacturers also had an incentive to reject Dyson's vacuum because it introduced a disruptive breakthrough that would negatively impact their companies' income. A vacuum cleaner manufacturer earned money from the initial sale of the vacuum, the sale of replacement parts, and the sale of replacement bags. If a manufacturer sold Dyson vacuum cleaners, it would lose the steady revenue that it collected from the sale of replacement bags.

INTRODUCTION IN JAPAN

Dyson searched for a manufacturer for two years, and in 1985 he found a Japanese company, Kanaya, Kajwara, and Tomachita, that was interested in making and selling his vacuum cleaner. The first model, the G-Force, was colored bright pink and had a retail price of approximately US$2,000. Dyson offered his G-Force to Japanese housewives through catalog sales. The cyclone vacuum was expensive, stylish, and was not sold in regular department stores, so it was marketed as a status symbol.

The G-Force was slow to gain popular acceptance in Japan. Kanaya, Kajwara, and Tomachita did not earn profits for several years after it started selling the cyclone vacuum cleaners. However, after the G-Force earned a design prize in 1991, sales improved significantly.

Dyson's marketing strategy was common for high-end technology products and luxury items, but it was relatively unusual for a vacuum cleaner. As an established product with a long commercial history, the vacuum cleaner usually targeted the mass market and sold in high volume at major retail stores. To use the early adopter strategy, Dyson needed to set a very high price for his vacuum cleaners initially, and then gradually lower the price as more consumers bought them. For certain items, consumers might have been willing to pay a high price to own a prestigious, high-end product a year before their neighbors, but it seemed very unlikely that this would apply to vacuum cleaners, because most households already owned one.

INTRODUCTION IN BRITAIN

British manufacturers and financiers still refused to work with Dyson, even after learning about the successful launch of the G-Force in the Japanese market. Still, the G-Force acquired some fans in Britain. The famous designer Sir Paul Smith owned a chain of high-end department stores where he sold clothing and other consumer products to wealthy shoppers. The hot pink G-Force impressed Sir Paul, and he placed it in his High Street shop. *LoveStyle* reported that some shoppers thought that the vacuum cleaners were actually Smith's own products at the time, as they were unfamiliar with Dyson.

The cyclone vacuum's dirt collection bin had viral marketing qualities of its own. As the Dyson vacuum could collect dirt that other vacuums did not pick up, the collection bin could fill up with waste from a floor that appeared clean. If homeowners bought a Dyson vacuum and wanted to show it off to their friends, they could run it across the floor and easily display the volume of dirt that it had collected. Product demonstrations had always had a strong role in vacuum cleaner marketing, from Hoover's early door-to-door sales to the Kirby Company's modern marketing efforts. Effectively, the clear dirt collection bin produced the same effect as hiring door-to-door sales representatives. The *New York Times* reported that because of these customer demonstrations, Dyson stated that most of its customers decided to purchase a cyclone from the company because of a friend's recommendation.

By 1993 Dyson had completed the construction of his own factory in the Uinted Kingdom, and he started selling his vacuum cleaners to British customers. They were very popular, and Dyson quickly gained market share. The

DC01, with its Dual Cyclone design, was very successful, although it was introduced at a relatively high price during the early 1990s recession.

MARKET CHALLENGES

Throughout the 1990s Dyson successfully operated his company in Britain, and it made him a billionaire. The competitors who had refused to work with him in the past now realized the potential of his cyclone vacuums. Hoover released its own cyclone vacuum cleaner in 1999. Dyson claimed that this product violated his patent, and a British court agreed with him. The *Appliance Magazine* reported that Hoover settled the dispute by paying Dyson US$6.3 million as compensation and removing the infringing vacuum cleaner from retail stores.

Competitors continued to work on their own cyclone vacuums, and in the earliest years of the 21st century, vacuums that did not violate Dyson's patents appeared in British stores. As a consequence of its nearly US$400 price tag, the Dyson vacuum was vulnerable to price competition, and several of these competing vacuums were available at about the same cost as a standard bag vacuum. A 2003 BBC article reported that Morphy Richards Limited was selling a cyclone vacuum in Britain for less than half the price of a Dyson vacuum. Market saturation also became an issue. In 2002 the company had 38 percent market share in Britain. By that time, many shoppers in Western Europe and Japan owned a Dyson vacuum cleaner.

DYSON RESPONSE

James Dyson dealt with the cost pressures in 2002 by relocating his vacuum cleaner factory. He announced that he was moving production from Malmesbury to Malaysia, closing down the British factory and laying off several hundred production workers. Dyson argued that the move would benefit the company because he would have more money to hire designers, engineers, and support staff, and many of these jobs would remain in Britain. Dyson also told the BBC that he had hired more than 13,000 Britons, made sizable tax payments, and paid interest to British bankers, so he provided many benefits to his native nation.

With the British market nearing saturation and the profit margin on each vacuum falling, Dyson needed to sell many more vacuum cleaners to maintain his company's profits. The U.S. market was much larger than the British one, but it had several established mass market competitors, including Hoover, Eureka, and Dirt Devil. The Kirby Company also sold high-end vacuum cleaners to customers who were willing to pay for a more powerful product. Although Dyson had resisted entering the U.S. market for almost a decade, he decided to enter it in 2002 to remain competitive.

INTRODUCTION IN THE UNITED STATES

Dyson entered the U.S. market with the DC07 cyclone vacuum. The *Daily Beast* reported that the DC07 was launched at US$399, much less than the US$2,000 list price of the original G-Force, although it was still more than triple the price of the mass market vacuum cleaners that were available at department stores and home goods retailers in the United States.

The Dyson launch in the United States occurred during a recession, and Dyson needed to make some marketing strategy adjustments for the U.S. market. The *Daily Beast* explained that displaying the vacuum in High Street shops was effective in Britain because the population was concentrated around London, England. With the more diverse population of the United States, Dyson needed to show its vacuum to potential customers in many cities, and it would have to convince big-box retail stores to stock a high-end product during a recession.

Dyson introduced its vacuums in the United States through an aggressive television marketing campaign. *Slate* reported that the Dyson advertisements were memorable, in contrast to most vacuum cleaner television advertisements, and gave the Dyson vacuum the appearance of a stylish product. The Dyson advertisements showed off the design of the vacuum cleaner, instead of focusing on the image of the company itself. Apple could sell its computers for higher prices than its competitors because of their striking design and product features, and it had expanded this strategy to other technological gadgets such as smartphones and tablets, but this approach was unusual in the vacuum cleaner industry.

Dyson's marketing efforts were successful, and the vacuum started to gain market share in the United States. Dyson continued to produce more television commercials, and the vacuum appeared as a status symbol on television shows. *Forbes* reported that Dyson vacuums appeared in episodes of *Will and Grace* and *Friends*. The *New Yorker* reported that in 2011, Dyson controlled almost a quarter of the market, and Dyson vacuums were on the shelves at major home improvement and retail stores.

HOW DYSON SUCCEEDED

James Dyson was willing to alter his strategy so that he could reach the market and fund his product, while sticking to his original design vision even in the face of external pressure. Dyson decided to introduce his vacuum cleaners in Japan, although he had originally attempted to launch his product in the British market, because he had manufacturer support there. This compromise did not damage the brand that he was marketing, as he could still demonstrate a cyclone vacuum in Japan. Dyson was right to keep his original design concept for the vacuum cleaner, although it was not standard in the industry. He could have launched a cyclone vacuum with the drab gray color of a lower cost appliance, with the dust collection bin hidden. Deciding to use bright colors, such as hot pink, was an important decision because it made the Dyson vacuum cleaner stand out. Dyson predicted correctly that a home owner would be willing to pay more money for a vacuum cleaner if it looked stylish in comparison to other models.

BIBLIOGRAPHY

Carruthers, Claire. "Sir Paul Smith: The Interview." *LoveStyle,* October 17, 2011. Accessed January 10, 2012. http://www.lovestyle.com/english/fashion/news/Sir_Paul_Smith-25015.aspx.

Clarke, Carolyn. "James Dyson – Tycoon Profile." *Millionaire Magazine.* Accessed January 10, 2012. http://www.millionaire-magazine.co.uk/james-dyson-tycoon-profile/.

Clark, Emma. "Dyson's Domestic Dilemma." *BBC News,* October 2, 2003. Accessed January 10, 2012. http://news.bbc.co.uk/2/hi/business/3113002.stm.

Corporate Design Foundation. "Dyson Fills a Vacuum." Boston, MA. Accessed January 10, 2012. http://www.cdf.org/issue_journal/dyson_fills_a_vacuum.html.

Finch, Julia. "Dyson's Profits Rise to £190m." *Guardian,* May 26, 2010. Accessed January 10, 2012. http://www.guardian.co.uk/business/2010/may/26/dyson-profits-rise.

Hickman, Martin. "Master of Invention (or Does Dyson Suck?)." *Independent,* October 4, 2006. Accessed January 10, 2012. http://www.independent.co.uk/news/uk/this-britain/master-of-invention-or-does-dyson-suck-418626.html.

"How to Reinvent the Wheel." *Business 2.0,* December 1, 2003. Accessed January 10, 2012. http://money.cnn.com/magazines/business2/business2_archive/2003/12/01/354219/index.htm.

"James Dyson: Business Whirlwind." *BBC,* February 5, 2002. Accessed January 10, 2012. http://news.bbc.co.uk/2/hi/business/1802155.stm.

Kelley, Raina. "Mr. Clean." *Daily Beast,* January 13, 2011. Accessed January 10, 2012. http://www.thedailybeast.com/newsweek/2011/01/13/mr-clean.html.

Linnell, Paul. "Upright Vacuum Cleaners." *Simply Switch On.* Accessed January 10, 2012. http://homepage.ntlworld.com/paul.linnell/sso_01/vacuums%20upright.html.

Sanghera, Sathnam. "When James Met Paul." *Creative Business,* December 17, 2001. Accessed January 10, 2012. http://specials.ft.com/creativebusiness/dec182001/FT3VM9UBCVC.html.

Seabrook, John. "How to Make It." *New Yorker,* September 20, 2010. Accessed January 10, 2012. http://www.newyorker.com/reporting/2010/09/20/100920fa_fact_seabrook.

Serafin, Tatiana. "Neat Fortune." *Forbes,* March 27, 2006. Accessed January 10, 2012. http://www.forbes.com/free_forbes/2006/0327/138.html.

Stevenson, Seth. "Hoover Glam." *Slate,* December 15, 2003. Accessed January 10, 2012. http://www.slate.com/articles/business/ad_report_card/2003/12/hoover_glam.html.

"Vacuum Makers Hoover, Dyson Settle Lawsuit." *Appliance Magazine.com,* October 10, 2002. Accessed January 10, 2012. http://www.appliancemagazine.com/news.php?article=3691&zone=0&first=1.

Walker, Rob. "Dirt Appeal." *New York Times,* August 8, 2004. Accessed January 10, 2012. http://www.nytimes.com/2004/08/08/magazine/08CONSUMED.html.

eBay: The Most Used Online Auction Website in the World

The remarkable story of eBay, the world's largest and most frequently accessed online auction website, started with a simple idea. The brainchild of Pierre Omidyar, a 28-year-old computer programmer in Silicon Valley, California, eBay started as a simple auction mechanism meant to connect the seller of an item to interested buyers. Buyers would submit bids to purchase items and win them if they were the highest bid. This new, online version of a very traditional method of sales propelled Omidyar from virtual anonymity in 1995 to being the 145th richest man in the world, with a net worth of US$6.2 billion in 2011, according to Forbes.com. His creation, which started out as a weekend programming experiment, not only brought in US$9.2 billion in revenues in 2010, but according to Google's DoubleClick Ad Planner, was the 26th most visited site on the Internet, having had 88 million unique visitors per month and over 10 billion page views by July 2011. Far surpassing all other competitors globally, eBay became synonymous with online auction, and established itself as an e-commerce powerhouse, with the value of goods being sold through the site exceeding US$2,000 per second.

APOCRYPHAL PEZ

One of the most often repeated and publicized stories regarding eBay, especially in the news media, is that Omidyar started the project because his girlfriend was passionate about collecting Pez dispensers, and he wanted her to have a way to expand her network to trade in these items more effectively. Although eBay headquarters in San Jose, California, pays tribute to the story with a wall display of Pez dispensers, Omidyar said on numerous occasions that this story is not quite accurate, although it does contain an element of truth. In an interview with *USA Today*'s Kevin Maney, Omidyar explained that his wife, Pam, upon returning from a European trip where she bought a number of Pez dispensers, began to trade and sell them on her husband's fledgling online auction site. Omidyar noticed "the passion that collectors have about ordinary objects," which reinforced his belief that his auction site had enormous potential for creating an efficient marketplace for such collectors. When Omidyar told the story to Mary Lou Song, eBay's first public relations representative, she felt it made a wonderful anecdote about the creation of the company, and spun it into the yarn that news media helped turn into something of a legend.

The timely beginnings of eBay came at a point in the evolution of the Internet when companies were just discovering the power of e-commerce and learning about leveraging this global network to capitalize new markets. Online auctions placed an older business model into a new, interconnected market. Unlike live auctions where an auctioneer generated excitement by calling for bidders to make offers and raise the selling price of an item, an online auction resembles a silent auction where bidders submit their best offer visibly or privately, giving the seller the opportunity to select the highest one. Excitement in an online auction is generated through the auction mechanism itself. As the time to an auction's end draws to a close and bids from different people are updated live, the top bidder is displayed. If the display changes, it means someone has just been outbid, putting pressure on the previous high bidder to increase his/her top bid by entering the new price on the web page and clicking a submit button, sometimes with only minutes, or even mere seconds, to spare.

"A LITTLE BIT OF AN EXPERIMENT"

In a 2009 interview with Barry Hurd for *The Henry Ford,* Omidyar revealed in detail the beginnings of eBay and how something that began as "a little bit of an experiment," according to the company history appearing on eBay's website, turned into a multibillion-dollar powerhouse. Omidyar, admitting to always having been a tinkerer and "gadget freak," got his first computer in the early 1980s when he was a high school senior. Along the way he became interested in programming, and in the early 1990s, the first standard protocols that would make the World Wide Web interactive had been released. In 1995 two-way communication with websites was on the forefront of technology.

One of these protocols allowed for the use of scripts written in the Perl programming language to interact with a website. It was a Perl script that Omidyar was experimenting with during Labor Day weekend in 1995. Having an interest in efficient market theory, he decided to create a basic online auction mechanism. He was also looking for an excuse to test out new interactive web functionality. His idea for a simple auction mechanism would allow someone to list an item for sale along with an asking price. Also included would be the capacity to search for items that were up for sale, and a way for would-be buyers to bid on and purchase these items. Completing his weekend project, he uploaded his work to a server on the morning of September 4, establishing AuctionWeb. According to eBay's history page, the very first item posted for auction was Omidyar's own broken laser pointer, which a collector purchased for US$14.83. From there, things started to move rapidly. According to Omidyar, it took people about one month to find out about AuctionWeb, and as more and more people found the site and traffic grew, his Internet service provider upgraded Omidyar's US$30 per month plan to a US$250 per month plan because he was exceeding his allowed bandwidth due to the number of people visiting and using the site. Shortly after that, he was moved to a US$500 per month plan, which was when Omidyar realized that it was time to create a revenue model in order to pay for the rapidly escalating server fees. This all took place within the first six months of AuctionWeb going online.

In 1995 Omidyar hired the fledgling company's first employee, Chris Agarpao, to help run the website and keep up with day-to-day operations. Omidyar, who did not even set out to start a company, quickly found himself in the unusual situation of deciding whether or not to pursue what began as a hobby. He quit his day job as a programmer for a now defunct company, General Magic, in order to dedicate himself to a rapidly growing, increasingly popular commercial website.

Almost a year into the experiment, in August 1996, Omidyar brought on Jeff Skoll, AuctionWeb's second employee. Skoll was responsible for creating the company's first business plan, and years later, would also lead eBay's initial public offering (IPO). Before the year was out, AuctionWeb had exceeded US$10,000 of revenue in a single month and had over 41,000 registered users.

One important innovation critical to the company's many successes in 1996 arose from a need that Omidyar had not originally anticipated. Some transactions were going sour, and both buyers and sellers were unhappy either with items for which they paid but did not receive, or with the condition or quality of some products. Some members responded in the way that seemed most logical to them: they contacted Omidyar. He started receiving all kinds of e-mails from people complaining about business transactions gone awry. In response, in February 1996, Omidyar came up with the idea of having a rating system where members could give each other both positive and negative feedback to rate how well or badly their transaction went. This rating system would prove to be an invaluable asset to many sellers on eBay who would set up entire retail businesses on the auction model, and send out thousands of products on an industrial scale using Omidyar's framework.

By mid-1997 Benchmark Capital's Bob Kagle, a venture capitalist, was brought on board to provide much-needed strategic planning assistance regarding the future of the company. Although Benchmark invested money into AuctionWeb, Omidyar admitted that the company never actually used those funds. The funds were put in the bank, since the auction company was already generating sufficient revenue from the very beginning.

ICON STATUS

Two important milestones that marked 1997 were continued explosive, exponential growth in revenues, and a name change for the company that would give it the iconic recognition known around the world. The first milestone was the rapid, monthly expansion brought on by thousands of new members joining the site. By the end of the year, there were over 341,000 members, and gross merchandizing volume (GMV) was US$95 million. The second milestone, a name change to eBay.com, happened through a trip to a domain registry office. As Omidyar had done his original design and programming work under the auspices of his sole-proprietorship consulting firm, Echo Bay Technology Group, AuctionWeb was simply just a part of this site. When it became clear that the auction site needed its own domain name, Omidyar drove to a registry office with the intention of registering "echobay.com". New domain registrations were generally processed in person at this time, so when he discovered that the name echobay had already been taken, he simply registered an abbreviated form of echobay: ebay.

Around this time the Beanie Baby craze took hobbyist collectors by storm. These miniature stuffed animals were being bought and sold at unprecedented levels, with rare Beanie Babies fetching exorbitantly high prices on the open market. eBay's online marketplace was the first stop for many would-be traders, contributing approximately 6.6 percent (US$500,000) to eBay's total volume. In 1997 eBay also sold its one-millionth item, a *Sesame Street* Big Bird toy.

Omidyar's company continued its feverish rate of growth. Month after month, eBay was expanding anywhere between 20 and 50 percent, with some months spiking as high as 70 percent. By late 1997 it became clear that eBay needed a CEO who could ensure its continuing success, and the company started searching for the right person. The next major milestone occurred in 1998 when eBay hired Meg Whitman to be chief executive officer. Whitman was initially reluctant to accept the position. *USA Today*'s Maney wrote, "She'd never even heard of eBay. She hoped the recruiter would call another time with something that looked more promising." In her own words, she went to the interview "in order not to make the headhunter mad."

The other key event in 1998 was eBay's IPO on September 21. Listed on NASDAQ under the EBAY symbol, trading began at US$18, but by the end of the first day share prices had risen to US$53.50. Numerically speaking, eBay ended the year with US$700 million in gross merchandise value (GMV) and 2.1 million users. Under CEO Meg Whitman, eBay continued to do extremely well, and Omidyar transferred control of the company to her, which freed him to pursue other projects. By March 1999 Omidyar had almost completed the process, and not long after that he moved his family to France and started to focus on philanthropic works, among other interests.

GLOBAL E-COMMERCE POWERHOUSE

The year 1999 was when eBay went global. Starting its foray into international online auctions, sites opened in the United Kingdom, Germany, and Australia. Austria, Canada, France, and Taiwan would follow in 2000 and Ireland, Italy, Korea, New Zealand, Singapore, and Switzerland were next, in 2001. In 2004 eBay expanded into the Philippines and Malaysia, and into Poland in 2005. The company's moves into Latin America, and countries like China and India, however, were a little more complex, involving investments and buyouts of preexisting local companies such as China's EachNet in 2002, and India's Baazee in 2004. eBay entered into a partnership with Latin America's e-commerce powerhouse MercadoLibre in 2001. Other countries not specifically covered, such as Japan, were directed to eBay's global site,

which was essentially a language-localized version of the main U.S. site.

At the start of the new millennium, according to eBay's own estimation, the company was ranked the top e-commerce site in 2000. With over 22.5 million users worldwide, eBay made news headlines with some of the world's most exotic and expensive items being sold on its site. The most noted was the 2001 sale of a Gulfstream jet, selling for US$4.9 million, making it the most expensive item ever sold on eBay up to that point. In 2006 this record was broken by the US$168 million sale of a 405-foot yacht, which was purchased by Russian billionaire Roman Abramovich.

Paralleling the growth and success of eBay, another company, PayPal Inc., was capitalizing greatly from the desire of buyers to use their credit cards for making eBay purchases securely, and without revealing such information to third parties. Sellers also found a great boon in being able to accept credit card payments, which were often far more secure and faster than checks or money orders sent by post. So popular was this form of payment on online auctions that eBay purchased Paypal for US$1.5 billion in 2002. It was, perhaps, eBay's most important purchase. Since then, PayPal has become a standard payment method for all eBay users, arguably becoming the world's most popular and frequently used form of transaction and payment method for consumer goods and services purchased online.

With the incredible scope and reach of eBay, thousands of small-business owners began to flock to the site, using it as a storefront for their retail businesses. As a business model, eBay offered a number of significant advantages, such as low start-up costs and barriers to entry. One of the most attractive features was the introduction of online auction software that gives merchants unprecedented control over their sales, inventory, and supply chain, working seamlessly with the eBay website. Countless software applications exist, ranging in price from free to hundreds of dollars, depending on a company's size and specific needs.

EFFICIENT MARKETS

When Pierre Omidyar set out to try a new idea for a transparent and efficient market using an online auction mechanism, he may not have realized how truly efficient and successful it would someday become. As sellers competed and offered products at below-retail prices, buyers got the best bargains. For this reason, it was indeed an efficient market as goods were sold for their true worth. In the early 2010s eBay continued to record significant revenues and growing numbers of participating buyers and sellers. Meg Whitman resigned as eBay's CEO in 2008 and was succeeded by John Donahoe, a Stanford University MBA graduate. Donahoe took over a company of more than 15,000 employees, and US$59.7 billion GMV, a number that grew to US$62 billion in 2010.

BIBLIOGRAPHY

"The 10 Most Ridiculously Expensive Items Ever Sold on eBay." *Complex Magazine,* September 19, 2011. Accessed December 12, 2011. http://www.complex.com/tech/2011/09/the-10-most-ridiculously-expensive-items-ever-sold-on-ebay#11.

"The 1000 Most-Visited Sites on the Web." Mountain View, CA: Google DoubleClick Ad Planner, July 2011. Accessed December 12, 2011. http://www.google.com/adplanner/static/top1000/.

"eBay Inc." *Bloomberg Businessweek.* Accessed December 12, 2011. http://investing.businessweek.com/research/stocks/financials/financials.asp?ticker=EBAY:US (accessed December 11, 2011).

"eBay Inc." *Forbes.com,* Accessed December 12, 2011. http://finapps.forbes.com/finapps/jsp/finance/compinfo/CIAtAGlance.jsp?tkr=EBAY.

eBay Inc. "eBay History." San Jose, CA. Accessed December 12, 2011. http://www.ebayinc.com/history.

"The History of eBay." *Telegraph,* April 15, 2011. Accessed December 12, 2011. http://www.telegraph.co.uk/finance/personalfinance/8451898/The-history-of-eBay.html.

Kane, Margaret. "eBay Picks Up PayPal for $1.5 Billion." *CNET,* July 8, 2011. Accessed December 12, 2011. http://news.cnet.com/2100-1017-941964.html.

Lacy, Sarah. "Pierre Omidyar on eBay and Pez Dispensers, Leaving the Valley and the Most Important Thing He's Ever Done." *TechCrunch.com,* March 20, 2010. Accessed December 12, 2011. http://techcrunch.com/2010/03/20/pierre-omidyar-on-ebay-and-pez-dispensers-leaving-the-valley-and-the-most-important-thing-he%E2%80%99s-ever-done/.

Maney, Kevin. "10 Years Ago, eBay Changed the World." *USA Today,* March 21, 2005. Accessed December 12, 2011. http://www.usatoday.com/tech/news/2005-03-21-ebay-cover_x.htm.

Noon, Chris. "Abramovich Speculated to Be Buyer of Gigayacht." *Forbes.com,* February 8, 2006. Accessed December 12, 2011. http://www.forbes.com/2006/02/08/abramovich-yacht-ebay-cx_cn_0208autofacescan04.html.

"Profile: Pierre Omidyar." *Forbes.com,* September 2011. Accessed December 12, 2011. http://www.forbes.com/profile/pierre-omidyar/.

Skoll Foundation. "Jeff Skoll." Palo Alto, CA, 2010. Accessed December 12, 2011. http://www.skollfoundation.org/staff/jeff-skoll/.

"Transcript of a Video Oral History: Interview With Pierre Omidyar." Dearborn, MI: The Henry Ford, March 25, 2008. Accessed December 12, 2011. http://www.oninnovation.com/media/25928/transcript_full-length_omidyar.pdf.

Electrophoretic Ink:
From Signs to E-Readers

Electrophoretic ink, or e-ink, used in the vast majority of electronic book readers (e-readers), was developed at the Massachusetts Institute of Technology (MIT) Media Lab in 1997. E Ink Corporation was spun off from the Media Lab that same year to continue developing e-ink into a plastic film that could be laminated to circuitry to create a display. The first applications were digital signs for use by businesses. Once e-ink was combined with a high-resolution active matrix display module, it was the pivotal technology that led to the booming e-reader market.

The success of Amazon's Kindle e-reader, which was launched in 2007, led to improvements in E Ink Corporation's display that kept it at the forefront of the e-reader market. Although color e-ink is possible with an overlay, it lacks the vivid colors and video capability of LCD displays used in color e-readers. While the future of color e-ink is uncertain, e-ink technology continues to gain ground in a variety of commercial and other consumer applications.

THE INVENTION OF E-INK

The MIT Media Lab in Cambridge, Massachusetts, was founded in 1985 to focus on the study, invention, and creative use of digital technologies. More than 100 companies were spun off from inventions at the MIT Media Lab over the next 25 years. Besides e-ink, other notable inventions included *Guitar Hero* (music video games) and LEGO Mindstorms (kits to create small, programmable robots).

Joseph Jacobson, an associate professor of media arts and sciences, was the director of the Molecular Machines Group at MIT. (As of 2012, he remained in that position.)

He developed e-ink, more formally known as a microencapsulated electrophoretic display (EPD), with two undergraduate students, Barrett Comiskey and Jonathan Albert. The three men filed a patent for their display in March 1997. They cofounded E Ink Corporation that same year, with Jerome Rubin, who was also working at the MIT Media Lab, and Russell Wilcox. The patent was approved in October 1999.

MIT's EPD consisted of a vast number of tiny dipole spheres, having positively charged white particles on one side and negatively charged black particles on the other side. Each sphere was about the diameter of a human hair. The spheres' white particles, were made of titanium dioxide, suspended in a dark fluid. This suspension gave rise to the term microencapsulated. The spheres were contained within a plastic film with electrodes on either side. When a positive electrical charge was sent to the electrodes on the back side, it repelled the positively charged white particles in certain spheres, and they would rise to the surface to create a message.

The design was an improvement on reusable electronic paper, called Gyricon, which was first developed by Nick Sheridon at Xerox's Palo Alto Research Center (PARC) in California. (PARC is credited with revolutionizing the personal computer industry with the development of a graphical user interface controlled by a mouse as well as for developing the Ethernet system for networking computers.) Sheridon's invention used the tiny dipole spheres and suspended them in oil sandwiched between transparent, flexible plastic. Since each half of the sphere contained an opposing electrical charge, if an outside electrical charge were placed against either side, they would rotate, depending on polarity of the voltage being applied.

The key benefit of e-ink was that it reflected ambient light to create a contrast between the message and the background, similar to ink on paper. Compared to liquid-crystal displays (LCDs), EPDs offered superior readability at a wide angle and in bright light because there was no glare from backlighting. In addition, since power was only used to change an image, not to hold it, e-ink had much lower power consumption than LCD displays.

SIGNS ARE THE FIRST E-INK APPLICATION

Before e-ink technology was combined with active matrix, in which a thin-film transistor (TFT) controlled each pixel, the applications for a monochromatic display were limited. The E Ink Corporation's original focus was in developing advertising signage. In May 1999, the company revealed its first commercial application, called Immedia, which was a large indoor sign that could be changed using a two-way pager. The e-ink technology used white pigment encapsulated in a blue fluid, which limited the signs to display white text against a blue background.

J.C. Penney Company, Inc. was the first company to test the product in stores in several cities to advertise promotions during Mother's Day weekend in May 1999. During the December holiday season at the end of that year, Yahoo! Inc. had people wear the signs to promote its online shopping to harried shoppers in San Francisco, California; Chicago, Illinois; and New York, New York. According to a 2000 article in *The Economist,* Immedia boards could be leased monthly or purchased outright for US$1,000. The E Ink Corporation planned to develop fade-resistant Immedia displays for use in storefront windows and for outdoor displays such as sandwich boards.

In October 1999, E Ink Corporation partnered with Lucent Technologies to develop flexible e-paper. Lucent would develop plastic TFTs that would work like those made from silicon but without brittle glass substrates (base material to which something is added). The result would be a flexible, shatterproof display that was thinner and lighter than an LCD display. Since the plastic TFTs would be printed onto the substrate, rather than etched in glass, they would also be more cost effective to produce. By November 2000, E Ink Corporation and Lucent had developed a flexible, low-resolution prototype built on a plastic substrate. In a joint news release by both companies announcing the breakthrough, Jim Iuliano, president and CEO of E Ink, said, "With this combination of technologies we believe that we have found a very promising means for achieving paper-like electronic displays."

As the technology developed, PARC seemed to be a step behind the competition. It was not until 1999 that Xerox partnered with 3M Corporation. to produce Gyricon. The following year Gyricon LLC, based in Ann Arbor, Michigan, was spun off as a subsidiary of Xerox Corporation to commercialize the product, but 3M ended its partnership with Gyricon in December.

E-INK IN FIRST E-READER

Around that time, E Ink Corporation began to license its technology to other companies to produce retail advertising and promotional signage and switched its focus to displays for use in handheld devices for consumers. Handheld electronics would require a high-resolution, grayscale active matrix display, where the pixels resided on a grid and were controlled by drivers connected to the corresponding column and row. In March 2001, E Ink Corporation announced it had partnered with Philips Components, Inc., to produce the TFT backplane for the active matrix EPDs. In February 2002, E Ink Corporation partnered with Toppan Printing Co., Ltd., to fabricate the e-ink technology into a thin film called a frontplane laminate. Philips agreed to invest US$7.5 million in E Ink Corporation to help advance research and development. Toppan Printing invested another US$25 million.

E Ink Corporation and its partners set about developing a display for an e-reader that would be comparable in size, weight, and readability to a paperback book. E Ink Corporation's next-generation e-ink display changed the sphere contents to white and black particles suspended in clear fluid, rather than white particles in a colored fluid. When a negative electronic charge was applied, it attracted the positively charged white particles and repelled the negatively charged black particles. This new design could display black text against a light-colored background, which was essential to mimicking ink on paper.

The joint effort of E Ink Corporation, Philips, and Toppan yielded the display that was used in the first lightweight e-reader launched in Japan in March 2004. The Sony LIBRIé e-reader had a six-inch display with 170 ppi, 800-by-600 screen resolution, and four shades of gray. The text contrast quality was said to resemble newsprint. Due to the e-ink display's low power consumption, four AAA batteries would last for more than 10,000 pages.

Meanwhile, Gyricon did not announce the first commercial application of its SmartPaper technology until December 2003. The battery-powered SyncroSign Message Board, priced at US$1,295, used Gyricon's SignSync software to change the message on a sign remotely. In April 2005, SyncroSign Messager was announced as a smaller nine-inch display capable of producing images. The planned release was in June at a retail price of US$650. Unable to find a cost effective source for the backplane, Xerox decided to license the technology. Ultimately, it discontinued the Gyricon business in December 2005.

In May 2005, Taiwan-based Prime View International, Inc. (PVI) acquired the ePaper business unit from

LG.Philips LCD Co., Ltd. to become the sole producer of active matrix EPDs. Founded in 1992, PVI was the first producer of TFT-LCD displays in Taiwan. LG.Philips LCD's new focus was on manufacturing flexible EPDs by rolling TFTs onto metal foil. Five months later, LG.Philips LCD unveiled the world's first 10.1-inch flexible EPD using E Ink's technology. In May 2006 LG.Philips LCD followed it with its groundbreaking 14.1-inch model, equivalent in size to an A4 sheet of paper. Exactly a year later, the company announced the world's first 14.1-inch flexible color EPD. The ability to produce up to 4,096 colors was achieved with a color filter over the plastic display.

FIRST E-READERS IN THE UNITED STATES

In May 2007 E Ink Corporation made some enhancements to its technology and announced the release of the new Vizplex Film Display, which doubled the refresh rate (the rate at which the image changes) and improved brightness by 20 percent. The company also announced it was developing smaller display sizes for use in mobile devices as well as larger displays (up to 9.7 inches) for e-readers and tablets.

Jeff Bezos, founder and CEO of Amazon.com Inc., witnessed a demonstration of the LIBRIé in 2004 and recognized the potential threat to his online bookstore. He met with E Ink Corporation and began developing his own e-reader. Meanwhile, the Sony PRS-500, the first e-reader in the United States, was released in September 2006. It was upgraded with the Vizplex display and released as the Sony Reader PRS-505 in October 2007. The original Amazon Kindle, released on November 19, 2007, also had a six-inch Vizplex display. Weighing just 10.3 ounces, it was lighter and thinner than most paperbacks. The somewhat large price tag of US$400 did not deter consumers, and Amazon.com was sold out within hours.

Kindle's wireless connection was an improvement over the Sony's USB connection, but the real competitive advantage was in what Amazon offered after the purchase. According to Adrian Slywotzky in *Fast Company,* "Amazon had 88,000 e-books available for download—more than four times the number Sony offered. Anyone with an Amazon account could buy an e-book with one click. . . . Beyond this, Amazon already had a relationship with 65 million online shoppers."

E-INK ADVANCEMENTS

The Kindle 2 debuted in February 2009 for US$359 (the price was lowered over time until it hit US$139 in January 2012) with a redesigned keyboard and a noticeably thinner profile. Improvements had been made to the Vizplex display as well, which offered crisper text against a more pristine background that looked less like grainy newsprint. Another improvement was a faster refresh rate. The comparable Sony Reader, the PRS-700BC, offered a touch screen display, but still lacked a wireless connection, and the readability of the display did not compare to the Kindle, according to *CNET.* The more compact Sony Reader Pocket Edition PRS-300, featuring a five-inch Vizplex display, was released in August 2009.

In May 2009 E Ink Corporation announced it had developed a 9.7-inch display with 1200-by-824-pixel resolution and 150 ppi, which made it suitable for reading newspapers, textbooks, and other large-format documents. According to the company, the display was 27 percent lighter weight than comparably sized LCD displays in tablets. This technology debuted shortly thereafter in the Kindle DX. Priced at US$489, the Kindle DX also featured an accelerometer that allowed it to be rotated for a landscape orientation of text.

In December 2009 Barnes & Noble, Inc., released the Nook e-reader for US$259. It featured the same Vizplex display as the Kindle but replaced the keyboard with a color touch screen. The Nook quickly sold out, leaving Kindle as the better option for many holiday shoppers. In addition, critical reviews from *Consumer Reports, Engadget,* and others did not help sell the Nook to consumers. Testers said the software was not intuitive, the touch screen was nonresponsive at times, and the refresh rate when turning a page was noticeably slower than the Kindle.

At the end of 2009 PVI acquired E Ink Corporation for US$215 million. PVI was renamed to E Ink Holdings Inc. in June 2010, and the following month the next-generation e-ink display, Pearl Imaging Film was released. Pearl boasted 50 percent higher contrast that more closely resembled reading a paperback. Both the Kindle, renamed the Kindle Keyboard, and the Kindle DX were rereleased with Pearl displays.

Pearl moved E Ink Holdings further ahead of its only other e-ink competitor, SiPix Imaging Inc. SiPix was formed in Fremont, California, in 1999 to develop Microcup electronic paper. Like E Ink Holdings's original design, each honeycombed-shaped Microcup used white particles suspended in a dark fluid. The Pandigital Novel was the first e-reader available in the United States to incorporate a six-inch SiPix display. Compared to the Kindle Keyboard, however, the background was much darker, yielding a lower contrast to the text.

While developing active matrix displays for e-readers, E Ink Holdings's and SiPix's active matrix and segmented displays were also in high demand for an assortment of consumer and commercial applications requiring dynamic content, a flexible or ultrathin display, or readability in bright sunlight. Consumer applications included stylish watch dials, cell phone displays, and battery-life indicators. In April 2010 Seiko was the first watchmaker to incorporate a Vizplex active matrix display in a watch face.

In May 2010 E Ink Corporation partnered with Chi Lin Technology Corporation, a Taiwan-based manufacturer of display systems, to leverage small and medium EPDs in custom industrial applications such as medical devices, thermostats, and electronic shelf labels.

THE THREAT OF COLOR

While the Nook snapped up approximately 20 percent of the e-reader market in its first year, color e-readers were being developed with a seven-inch Android-based LCD display. Color e-readers offered a more attractive option for consumers wanting to read full-color magazines or textbooks and could better compete with the Apple iPad and other tablets. The 800-by-600 resolution Pandigital Novel Color, launched in August 2010 by Pandigital, was the first color e-reader in the United States. Although value-priced at US$179, *PCWorld* gave it an abysmal review for poor screen quality and an unresponsive touch screen. The Nook Color, launched three months later at a retail price of US$249, offered a higher 1024-by-600 resolution.

E-ink was being used in over 50 monochrome e-readers worldwide by the time E Ink released its color Triton Imaging Film in November 2010. Triton used a color filter array on top of the monochrome display to achieve color while retaining all the benefits of e-ink. The downside was the colors appeared muted compared to an LCD color display. Although e-reader makers in the United States had chosen LCD over e-ink for color e-readers, the ability to render color using a color filter array opened new opportunities for e-ink in other applications. However, neither the Kindle nor the Nook incorporated Triton into their next product release. Instead, these e-readers continued to use a six-inch Pearl display but added an infrared detector underneath that functioned as a touch screen.

Since color e-readers with an LCD display are heavier, have a much shorter battery life, and are harder to read in bright light, it is likely that monochrome e-readers will continue to be popular. Color e-ink may find a place in the e-reader market or possibly as a hybrid display in a tablet. In April 2011 the media discovered that Apple had submitted a patent in 2009 for a hybrid display that would use e-ink technology on top of a LCD display and switch from one to the other depending on the application, lighting, and other variables. A hybrid display could certainly help E Ink gain a foothold in the booming tablet market, but it remains to be seen what the future holds for flexible electronic paper and other e-ink innovations.

BIBLIOGRAPHY

"Barnes & Noble Nook Review: Glitches Make the Kindle a Better Choice." *Consumer Reports,* December 11, 2009. Accessed January 12, 2012. http://news.consumerreports.org/electronics/2009/12/barnes-and-noble-nook-vs-amazon-kindle-comparison-buying-advice-review-slow-speed-gift.html.

"Digital Ink Meets Electronic Paper." *The Economist,* December 7, 2000. Accessed January 12, 2012. http://www.economist.com/node/442911.

E Ink Corporation and Lucent Technologies. "E Ink and Lucent Technologies Demonstrate World's First Flexible Electronic Ink Display with Plastic Transistors." Cambridge, MA, and Murray Hill, NJ. News release, November 20, 2000. Accessed April 10, 2012. http://www.eink.com/press_releases/e_ink_lucent_plastic_transistors_112000.html.

E Ink Holdings Inc. "Display Products." Cambridge, MA. Accessed January 13, 2012. http://www.eink.com/display_products.html.

———. "E Ink Holdings Inc." Cambridge, MA, November 2010. Accessed January 13, 2012. http://www.eink.com/eih.html.

"Electronic Reusable Paper." Palo Alto, CA: Palo Alto Research Center. Accessed January 13, 2012. http://www2.parc.com/hsl/projects/gyricon.

"First-Generation Electronic Paper Display from Philips, Sony and E Ink to Be Use." *PhysOrg.com,* April 12, 2004. Accessed January 12, 2012. http://www.physorg.com/news34.html.

Fitzgerald, Michael. "Electric Dreams." *Boston Globe,* November 1, 2009. Accessed January 18, 2012. http://www.boston.com/bostonglobe/magazine/articles/2009/11/01/electric_dreams.

Foresman, Chris. "Apple Exploring Hybrid E-Ink/LCD Display for iDevices." *ARS Technica,* April 8, 2011. Accessed January 12, 2012. http://arstechnica.com/apple/news/2011/04/apple-exploring-hybrid-e-inklcd-display-for-idevices.ars.

Judge, Paul. "E Ink's Message: We're Creating a New Medium." *Businessweek,* November 16, 1999. Accessed January 12, 2012. http://www.businessweek.com/ebiz/9911/ec1116.htm.

Leo, Alan. "Startups Struggle in the E-paper Chase." *Technology Review,* March 6, 2001. Accessed January 12, 2012. http://www.technologyreview.com/Infotech/12318.

Love, Dylan. "The Amazon Kindle: Clunky to Sexy in Just 4 Years." *Business Insider,* September 28, 2011. Accessed January 12, 2012. http://www.businessinsider.com/kindle-evolution-2011-9?op=1.

Mayfield, Kendra. "E Ink: Your Hands Will Thank You." *Wired,* March 1, 2001. Accessed January 12, 2012. http://www.wired.com/science/discoveries/news/2001/03/42056.

Perenson, Melissa J. "Amazon Kindle 2 vs. Kindle Original: We Compare." *PCWorld,* February 24, 2009. Accessed January 12, 2012. http://www.pcworld.com/article/160165/amazon_kindle_2_vs_kindle_original_we_compare.html.

———. "Pandigital Novel: Tablet Hampered by Poor Display, Unresponsive Interface." *PCWorld,* August 19, 2010. Accessed January 12, 2012. http://www.pcworld.com/article/203081/pandigital_novel_tablet_hampered_by_poor_display_unresponsive_interface.html.

Pilato, Fabrizio. "Sony LIBRIe–The First Ever E-ink E-book Reader." *Mobile Magazine,* March 25, 2004. Accessed January 12, 2012. http://www.mobilemag.com/2004/03/25/sony-librie-the-first-ever-e-ink-e-book-reader/.

SiPix Imaging Inc. "Microcup® Electronic Paper." Fremont, CA. Accessed January 13, 2012. http://www.sipix.com/technology/epaper.html.

Slywotzky, Adrian. "The Real Secret of Kindle's Success." *Fast Company,* September 26, 2011. Accessed January 12, 2012. http://bx.businessweek.com/multimedia-technologies/view ?url=http%3A%2F%2Fwww.fastcompany.com%2F178 1303%2Fkindles-success-a-look-behind-the-screen%3F partner%3Dleadership_newsletter.

Tong, Brian. "Amazon Kindle 2 vs. Sony Reader PRS-700." *CNET,* March 17, 2009. Accessed January 18, 2012. http:// cnettv.cnet.com/amazon-kindle-2-vs-sony-reader-prs-700 /9742-1_53-50005506.htm.

Topolsky, Joshua. "Barnes & Noble Nook Review." *Engadget,* December 7, 2009. Accessed January 18, 2012. http://www .engadget.com/2009/12/07/barnes-and-noble-nook-review.

———. "Nook Color Review." *Engadget,* November 16, 2010. Accessed January 18, 2012. http://www.engadget.com/2010 /11/16/nook-color-review.

Etsy.com: Selling Handcrafted Items on the Internet

THE IDEA BEHIND ETSY

In 2005, Brooklyn, New York, resident Robert Kalin was a 25-year-old entrepreneur looking for a website where he could sell his woodworking products. Kalin was not expecting to make millions of dollars. He was simply hoping to make a good living doing what he enjoyed, carpentry work. He thought about selling his products, which included wood cases for computers, on the eBay website, but he found the site too impersonal and vast. Once Kalin realized that there was no place on the web devoted to selling homemade or craft items, he decided to create his own site for that purpose. He soon became quite excited by the idea that he could help other people realize their dream of owning and operating their own business.

Few people would have predicted that Kalin and his idea would become so successful so quickly. Kalin dropped out of high school and later attended five different colleges before receiving his Bachelor of Arts degree from New York University (NYU). He then decided to pursue his love of carpentry and woodworking, getting contracts from local clients and working from his apartment in Brooklyn, New York. After he decided to create and build Etsy, he was able to leverage a few of these business relationships and gain early financing.

First, Kalin spent several days mapping out the website by placing masking tape on the floor of his apartment and marking it with the proposed site map. His idea was to create a community for artisans and craftspeople, where they could set up their own stores, discuss ideas and issues with fellow sellers, and buy supplies. Once Kalin had fleshed out the idea, he contacted two savvy fellow NYU alumni, Haim Schoppik and Chris Maguire (and later Jared Tarbell), to serve as the company's first website

engineers. When it seemed like the site would not launch quickly enough for Kalin, he invited his cofounders to move into his apartment so they could work on it nearly 24 hours a day during the last six weeks leading up to its June 2005 launch.

He also began seeking financing and proved to be successful at it. His first angel investors were two former furniture customers who were local real estate developers. Kalin said that because he was able to build trust with these customers, the former clients were comfortable giving him start-up funds. Kalin was also successful in gaining funding from another client, a restaurant owner, who had hired him to set up an Internet café in his restaurant. Kalin received the first US$50,000 in start-up funds before the site launched, and he received an additional US$100,000 within six months of the launch. This feat was especially impressive considering that Kalin had not completed his business plan when he received the funds. His grandfather had encouraged him to spend most of his time initially developing the business plan, but when he realized this meant a delay in launching the site, he set the plan aside in order to launch Etsy.

Written or not, Kalin did have a plan. His initial business model was simple. Users would build their own storefronts on the site and Etsy would collect a small fee (US$0.20) for each product listed for sale. Then, for each product sold through Etsy, the company would receive a 3.5 percent commission. A third revenue stream for the company was its advertising program available for sellers called Showcase. Sellers could advertise their storefronts using this site-specific advertising channel. This basic model worked well, and as of 2012, was still in use. Since the more products that were sold through the site, the more revenue Etsy received, the Etsy team, which rapidly grew throughout its first seven years, focused most of its efforts on making its users successful.

The name *Etsy* actually has no meaning, which was intentional. Kalin said that he was watching an old Italian film, Federico Fellini's *8 1/2* and noticed that the Italians said "et si" (which means, "oh, yes" or "ah, yes") a lot. He liked the sound of it and used it as the name of the site.

EARLY ETSY

After Etsy's launch, it became successful very quickly. Kalin had discovered an unmet online need, a rare thing in the middle of the first decade of the 21st century. In general, people across the world, and especially in the United States, were ready for products that were not machine made or manufactured. With so many big-box retailers and large national chains, many people welcomed the alternative of handcrafted, unique items. The downturn in the economy also played a factor in the site's success. People were looking for less expensive items to buy, and there were more people looking to sell items as a way to gain additional income, especially if they had experienced a job layoff.

Etsy's success can also be attributed to the fact that Kalin believed that the site could make entrepreneurial dreams come true. The company marketed the site that way, using a campaign called "Quit Your Day Job." This campaign let sellers know that the site offered the potential to earn enough money to devote sellers full time to their Etsy business. Kalin also wanted to attract small businesses to the site, rather than people selling items they may have collected at a garage sale. (Still, people could sell vintage items on Etsy.)

Etsy grew rapidly during its first three years but it continued to need investors until it became profitable. By 2008, Etsy was a community with more than 650,000 members, and a marketplace with more than 120,000 sellers in 127 different countries. Just 50 employees were supporting the site. Kalin returned to some of his original investors and also approached potential new investors and succeeded again in receiving additional financing.

One of the first major investors to jump on the Etsy bandwagon was Caterina Fake. At the time, she was the founder of Flickr, a photo management and sharing site that was subsequently purchased by Yahoo! Inc. It did not take much persuasion to get Fake to invest in Etsy. Kalin simply contacted her, letting her know he was a fan of Flickr and telling her about Etsy. Then he asked her for advice. Kalin received both financing and advice from Fake.

In 2008, Kalin acquired US$27 million through two existing investors, Union Square Ventures and Hubert Burda Media, and from a new investor, Jim Breyer at Accel Partners. The addition of Breyer was considered controversial for many Etsy members, primarily because he sat on the board of directors for Wal-Mart Stores, Inc., considered by many to be the antithesis of everything Etsy represented. However, Kalin was positive and enthusiastic about the leadership that Breyer could provide. With this financing in place, the company was set to continue its phenomenal growth.

Two of the original founders of the company, Schoppik and Maguire, left the company in 2008. Kalin then hired Chad Dickerson to be chief technology officer. Dickerson was formerly with Yahoo! In 2009, Etsy increased its employees to 65, and there were 3.8 million listed items being sold to 2.3 million registered members. Feeling that the company was moving along on its own momentum, Kalin stepped away as CEO and hired former National Public Radio (NPR) executive Maria Thomas to take his place. Kalin became chairman of the board and creative director. However, Thomas left Etsy at the beginning of 2010 and Kalin returned as CEO of the company. Still, Kalin was interested in having someone else run the day-to-day operations of Etsy so he could pursue other business interests and ideas. In July 2011, Kalin announced the promotion of Dickerson to CEO, while he remained the chairman of the board.

THE ETSY WAY TO RUN A COMPANY

One of Etsy's strengths is its connection to its community. It is this connection that Kalin strives to maintain and that he feels is vital to the continued success of the company. In fact, Kalin believes that creating and maintaining this connection is the way all successful web-based businesses run and that non-web-based businesses should consider operating this way as well. Kalin maintains this personal connection with the Etsy community in several ways. First, he maintains a blog on the Etsy site where he is very open about the company, the site, and all of its ups and downs. He also participates in the online forums where site members send him conversation threads to keep him in touch with the overall opinion of the community.

He is careful never to call his members "users." In an interview with the *Wall Street Journal,* Kalin said, "If you can keep that direct connection to your community, that's vital to success. I actually dislike the word 'users.' I don't see people in the community as those who 'use' us, and we're not trying to 'use' them either."

Kalin also stayed in touch with the Etsy community by offering weekly craft nights where members who were local to Brooklyn, New York, could attend and learn how to make specific crafts. Kalin said that usually between 50 and 80 people attended these craft nights. Additionally, Kalin held employee craft nights as well as town hall meetings where he could communicate with Etsy's members and give them an opportunity to ask questions and voice concerns. He felt it was important for all members to feel that they were working with people, not electronic devices, when they did business with Etsy. Although the town hall meetings became less regular after 2009, they still occurred throughout the early 2010s.

Gender is another aspect of the company that is distinct. More than 90 percent of Etsy's sellers are women, a figure quite high when compared to sites such as eBay. This may be because more women handcraft items such as wearables, jewelry, and decorative items.

Throughout the first decade of the 21st century, Kalin and Etsy received multiple awards and recognition. For example, the World Economic Forum, a nonprofit organization founded to develop global socially responsible economies, nominated Etsy as one of its 2009 Technology Pioneers. In addition, Kalin was named one of Crain New York Business.com's Top Entrepreneurs of 2009.

MEETING CHALLENGES

Like any company on the web that becomes wildly successful, Etsy has had many critics as well as fans. There are several reasons that some people have either become disillusioned with the company or have complained about the site.

One of the biggest problems that Etsy had to deal with first, and rather quickly, was the issue of scalability. As the Etsy community expanded, the capacity to process the storefronts and transactions diminished. Etsy's online community grew so quickly that the company had trouble maintaining it, and members soon began to complain that the site was slow. Etsy engineers had to scale up the technical side, and Kalin dealt with the criticism about the site by being transparent with its members. He admitted the site was too slow and let members know the company was working on it.

Scalability was not the only technical issue the company had to manage. Etsy also had its share of member concerns over privacy. One example was the announcement that a class-action lawsuit was being filed against KISSmetrics, one of Etsy's vendors. One of KISSmetric's browser techniques was tracking and collecting private data. According to an Etsy administrator, the company promptly checked to see if that technique was part of the package Etsy was using, and it was not. Nevertheless, Etsy disabled the KISSmetric software and publicized this action in a blog to its community. Another complaint that sellers have had is that if they decided to change the name of their business on the site, there was no easy and simple way to do it. Instead, they had to start from scratch, creating a new storefront, profile, and all the other items that go with creating a business on the site.

Perhaps the more challenging complaint Etsy has had to overcome is the fact that many members have become disillusioned because their business has not generated enough income for them to "quit their day jobs," which Etsy told them was possible. Even though there were many websites, blogs, articles, and other information available to help Etsy users become successful, there have been a relatively small proportion of members who have been able to work their Etsy business on a full-time basis. In fact, some members have said they barely earn minimum wage. Still, Etsy marketers have held fast to this concept and have continued to try to help members increase their sales, even though they also acknowledge that most Etsy members use the site as secondary income.

The company also had early problems with customer service. There simply were not enough people to answer questions online, and as with other complaints, Kalin was honest in admitting this shortcoming in all of his communications with the community and the public. In 2009, Kalin and the Etsy team incorporated a phone center staffed by 15 customer service employees. This move also fit Kalin's goal of the company maintaining a more personal relationship with its community.

Despite some problems, there seemed to be as many loyal fans of the site as there were critics. The support of its many fans could stem from Kalin's unique philosophy for the site and its members. Rather than letting the economy influence the business, Kalin hoped that Etsy would influence the economies of its member's countries instead. In the *Wall Street Journal* article he said, "Instead of having an economy dictate the behavior of communities, [my vision is] to empower communities to influence the behavior of economies."

BIBLIOGRAPHY

Bruder, Jessica. "The Etsy Wars: Artisans's Backlash against Craft Site." *CNNMoney.* Accessed February 3, 2012. http://money .cnn.com/2009/07/13/smallbusiness/etsy_wars.fsb/.

"Crain's New York Business.com Top Entrepreneurs 2009." *Crain's New York Business.com.* Accessed February 3, 2012. http://www.crainsnewyork.com/gallery/20090501/SMALL BIZ/501009996/5.

"Davos Interviews: Robert Kalin." *TechCrunch,* February 1, 2009. Accessed February 3, 2012. http://techcrunch.com/2009/02 /01/davos-interviews-etsy-founder-robert-kalin/.

Evans, Teri. "Creating Etsy's Handmade Marketplace." *Wall Street Journal,* March 30, 2010. Accessed February 3, 2012. http:// craftandhobby.wordpress.com/2010/03/30/wall-street-journal -interview-with-etsy-ceo/.

Kalin, Robert. " Etsy's First Five Years." *The Etsy Blog,* January 30, 2006. Accessed February 3, 2012. http://www.etsy.com /blog/en/2008/etsys-first-five-years/.

Facebook: The World's Most Popular Social Network

A social networking company, Facebook, Inc., started as a way for its users, initially college students, to make connections, organize groups, share photos, and stay in touch. By 2012, the site was much more than that. Users could play games or use any number of applications that facilitated video games, surveys, networking, and other activities. Facebook was not traded publicly before 2012, but the company was readying itself for one of the largest initial public offerings (IPO) in history. According to Shayndi Raice, social media reporter for the *Wall Street Journal,* in her article "Facebook Targets Huge IPO," the company's prospectus was prepared by the company itself, rather than by outsourcing to bankers and lawyers, which was typical of Silicon Valley precociousness. This costly feat was most likely possible due to the inordinately large revenue streams already available to founder, chief executive officer and Harvard University dropout Mark Zuckerberg. Zuckerberg was still under age 30, but his company pulled in US$4 billion in advertising revenues annually and was expected to continue increasing. Although Zuckerberg and his company were criticized for their aggressive tactics, particularly regarding user privacy, these complaints did not keep hundreds of millions of people from visiting the site every day.

ABOUT THE FOUNDER

Zuckerberg grew up in Dobbs Ferry, New York. His father was a dentist and his mother discontinued her psychiatric practice to take care of her children. In a 2010 *New Yorker* profile of the young entrepreneur, Jose Antonio Vargas reported a moment of childhood reminiscence: "In all of our talks, the most animated Zuckerberg ever got—speaking with a big smile, almost tripping on his words, his eyes alert—was when he described his youthful adventures in coding. 'I had a bunch of friends who were artists. . .They'd come over, draw stuff, and I'd build a game out of it.'" Recognizing their son's potential, Zuckerberg's parents paid a tutor to help develop his computer coding abilities. The precocious boy could be found attending graduate-level computer science courses at Mercy College in Dobbs Ferry while he was still in high school.

The rest of his education barely kept pace with his budding programming talent. For his high school senior thesis at Exeter Academy, Zuckerberg wrote a piece of software that tried to learn and adapt to users' musical taste. When America Online, Inc., and Microsoft Corporation expressed interest in buying the program, he turned them down.

After matriculating at Harvard University in 2002, the prodigy started to make programs that would appeal to his new audience. One helped students select courses based on the choices of other students. The next was a more controversial program, which allowed users to rate student photographs. After the Harvard administration shut down that project, Zuckerberg met twins Cameron and Tyler Winklevoss. The Winklevoss twins and Divya Narenda needed help with their website, Harvard Connection. Zuckerberg worked on the site for a brief period. While still helping the twins, he registered the domain name, "Thefacebook.com." In February, he opened the site to Harvard students. Within a month, Thefacebook.com swept across Harvard. When the site became immensely successful, spreading across the Ivy League and beyond, Zuckerberg dropped out of school.

There has been a great deal of speculation, argumentation, and opinion regarding the originality of Facebook.

The Winklevoss twins claimed that Zuckerberg essentially stayed around long enough to steal the idea for Harvard Connection and then sabotage the project to give Facebook a competitive edge. Zuckerberg claimed the two sites were wholly different. Where the twins' site was designed as a dating service, Facebook underscored more general social networking. The Winklevosses took their intellectual property dispute to court. In 2011, roughly six years after the initial claim, it seemed that the matter would finally be closed. The twins settled for US$65 million from Facebook but then appealed their own settlement claiming to have been misled by Zuckerberg. The U.S. States District Court for the Northern District of California upheld the settlement and summarized the proceedings as follows: "The Winklevosses are not the first parties bested by a competitor who then seek to gain through litigation what they were unable to achieve in the marketplace. And the courts might have obliged, had the Winklevosses not settled their dispute and signed a release of all claims against Facebook."

BYPASSING MYSPACE DURING THE SOCIAL MEDIA EXPLOSION

The Winklevoss twins may have pocketed US$65 million from their claim, but they did not invent the concept of social media. MySpace, Inc., was founded in 2003 and was sold to News Corporation two years later. Even with its solid financial backing and head start, the company was forced to watch Zuckerberg's company surpass it. How Facebook achieved this is a matter of some debate.

Focus on a specific audience certainly played to Facebook's advantage in its first years. Starting on Harvard's campus was a boon for the website, as the Ivy League setting gave the site a sense of exclusivity. In addition, because the college campus was a tight-knit environment, social networks already abounded. Clubs, fraternities, student governments, and alumni associations could all use the platform to organize activities and disseminate information. Word of mouth brought droves of students to the website. According to *New York Times* reporter Jason Pontin in his article "Who Owns the Concept If No One Signs the Papers?", Thefacebook.com registered half of the undergraduate student population within the first month of going live. After the site had time to spread across the Ivy League and beyond, Zuckerberg opened access to high school students. This occurred in September 2005, one-and-a-half years after the site opened.

Expanding to high school registrants opened up a new tier of possibilities. Since the majority of users were undergraduates, Thefacebook.com became a resource for college-bound seniors. *New York Times* reporter Kate Stone Lombardi described the multiple uses of the site in her 2007 article "Make New Friends Online, and You Won't Start College Friendless". A group of students who were accepted at Tulane University arranged a physical meeting prior to attending the university. Students accepted at the University of Pennsylvania boasted to each other about their relief and letting their grades drop. The site was also useful for observers, such as Robert Alexander, assistant vice president of enrollment at Tulane, who noted that "reading discussions was a good way for the university to learn students' interests and concerns." Anyone affiliated with undergraduate education in the United States could find a use for the social media platform, thus increasing site traffic rapidly.

In 2006, Zuckerberg opened the doors to everyone and new visitors flocked to the site's registration page. Growth surged, but even so, MySpace was still much larger, with 67 million members in 2007 when Facebook only claimed 24 million, according to *New York Times* writer Brad Stone in his article "Facebook Expands into MySpace's Territory." Despite these numbers Stone reported a number of factors in Facebook's favor. For one, Facebook enjoyed a cleaner reputation, which the writer attributed to the social network's restrictions. On the other hand, reported Stone, "MySpace. . .has fostered an anarchic aura with few restrictions on creativity, while allowing users to integrate tools from other companies into their pages, like slide show displays."

With its brand established, Facebook lost little time in developing key features to add value for users. Rather than allowing members to customize their individual pages as MySpace did, Facebook invited companies and programmers to contribute features. Working closely with developers to integrate new features, Zuckerberg maintained firm control of his site's look and feel. Facebook Marketplace was added, a move that created a stir in a variety of markets. In his article titled, "Facebook to Offer Free Classifieds," Brad Stone surmised that craigslist, inc.; Monster Worldwide, Inc.; CareerBuilder, LLC; and even college newspapers might suffer from competition with the up-and-comer. He was right.

LESSONS LEARNED IN PRIVACY

Facebook's clean, streamlined interface belied a slightly tarnished reputation in 2012. This came after a number of instances in which the company was caught taking liberties with user privacy. Many of the applications that were developed for the social media site seemed harmless. Games, such as Zynga's Farmville, or Birthdays, added convenience and entertainment. However, behind these application software programs (apps), the website discovered that it was bursting with a new currency: consumer data. Beginning in late 2007 Zuckerberg's company struggled between its desire to capitalize on this new resource and the need to respect the privacy of its members. The first conflict was started by an app called Beacon.

November 2007 saw the site grow to 50 million users, according to *New York Times* columnist Louise Story in her article "Facebook Is Marketing Your Brand Preferences (with Your Permission)", and Zuckerberg started increasing his advertisement campaigns to bring in revenue. The Beacon app was the company's first attempt to produce user-targeted advertisements. It automatically monitored user activity and then reported that activity to friends, linking the users' profile photos to advertisements and messages. All Facebook users were automatically subscribed to the application, which then sold their information for a profit.

Within two months of the program's release, protests mounted. The political group Moveon.org circulated a petition requiring Facebook to make certain changes to the Beacon system. According to Story, over 50,000 users signed the petition and Facebook made the requested changes. According to the 2007 article "Apologetic, Facebook Changes Ad Program," some users felt uneasy, as though their trust was abused. Although the company responded quickly to the complaints, its aggressiveness tarnished its reputation.

It was also just one exchange that became a pattern in the years to come. An audit by the U.S. Federal Trade Commission resulted in an order dictating that the site adhere to rules regarding user privacy. By 2011, when the order was given, Facebook had changed many of its practices, thus, no fine was issued. However, the ruling was that violations of the regulations would result in a US$16,000 fine for each day that any given regulation was breached. As reported by Somini Sengupta in "F.T.C. Settles Privacy Issue at Facebook," the order stipulated that the site not allow advertisers to collect personal data. The audit found historical activity suggesting that the site had allowed advertisers to take private information when users clicked on an advertisement. Furthermore, the order found the site guilty of sharing user information with app developers. None of these practices were to be tolerated in the future. Essentially, members could choose to share their information, but they needed to approve the conditions.

The site adjusted quickly. By January 2012, a new advertising system, quite similar to Beacon but in accordance with new regulations, was in place. *Forbes* writer Kashmir Hill recorded three main differences between the new and the old Facebook, but the biggest difference was in social media users, rather than in social media. "The idea of 'frictionless sharing' in 2007 kind of freaked people out. Not so much in 2012...Facebook users don't mind broadcasting what articles they're reading (even when that can be awfully revealing)." If the years from 2007 to 2012 were a negotiation, then that negotiation was resolved, certainly in social media's favor.

INITIAL PUBLIC OFFERING

By January 2012, investors highly anticipated what promised to be one of the largest IPOs in history. In typical maverick Silicon Valley, California tradition, Zuckerberg had the prospectus drafted in-house, a move that was reminiscent of Google's auction-style IPO eight years prior. By all accounts, Facebook was in an even better position to dictate terms. According to a *Wall Street Journal* article by Shayndi Raice in November 2011, Facebook claimed 800 million members, 500 million of whom logged in daily. As the company was expected to rake in close to US$4 billion in revenue for 2011, valuations of the enterprise reached US$100 billion. It was expected that over US$10 billion would be raised on the day of the offering. Google's offering in 2004 had raised US$1.9 billion.

Even with the favorable comparison between IPOs, Google remained a potential competitor. The company unveiled its own social network, Google+, in 2011. Levying a significant home-court advantage, the search engine juggernaut tied its new social capacities to its other features, such as Google Mail, Google Finance, and Google Docs. By January 2012 the service claimed 90 million members. Of those, 50 million had joined from October 2011 to January 2012, according to Suzanne Choney of *MSNBC*. Continuing that rate of growth would pit Google against Facebook in one or two years.

Zuckerberg anticipated the threat well ahead of time by forging an alliance with Microsoft. In 2007, Facebook allowed the software giant to buy 1.6 percent of the company for US$240 million. As part of the deal, Microsoft acquired rights to sell Facebook banner advertisements that appear outside the United States and share in revenue from those sales. Brad Stone reported in his article "Microsoft Buys Stake in Facebook," that competition with Google was a factor, at least for Microsoft: "Fearing it might lose control over the next generation of computer users, Microsoft has been trying to keep up with and in some cases block Google's moves, even if that effort is costly." Although Zuckerberg's reasons for signing were uncertain, the deal was a major turning point in the relations between the world's most popular search engine and what became the world's most popular social networking platform. By jumping in with a long-time rival of Google, Zuckerberg sent a strong message of opposition.

FACEBOOK AND THE ASCENT OF SOCIAL MEDIA

Facebook's success was due to more than luck and circumstance. Among a number of keen business decisions, Zuckerberg demonstrated a willingness to interact with his client base and adjust to member demands, which represented a healthy approach to public relations. It worked to keep the company afloat despite customer dissatisfaction, and it also worked to change member expectations. Privacy concerns, which Facebook users stubbornly held in 2007, were largely bypassed by 2012.

BIBLIOGRAPHY

Choney, Suzanne. "Google+ Hits 90 Million Members: CEO." *MSNBC,* December 12, 2011. Accessed February 3, 2012. http://technolog.msnbc.msn.com/_news/2012/01/19/10193464-google-hits-90-million-members-ceo.

Hill, Kashmir. "How Is the New Facebook 'Open Graph' Different from the Privacy Disaster That Was Beacon?" *Forbes,* January 19, 2012. Accessed February 3, 2012. http://www.forbes.com/sites/kashmirhill/2012/01/19/how-is-the-new-facebook-open-graph-different-from-the-privacy-disaster-that-was-beacon/.

Lombardi, Kate Stone. "Make New Friends Online, and You Won't Start College Friendless." *New York Times,* March 21, 2007. Accessed December 12, 2011. http://www.nytimes.com/2007/03/21/education/21friends.html?ref=facebookinc.

Pontin, Jason. "Who Owns the Concept If No One Signs the Papers?" *New York Times,* August 12, 2007. Accessed December 12, 2011. http://www.nytimes.com/2007/08/12/business/yourmoney/12stream.html?ref=facebookinc.

Raice, Shayndi. "Facebook Targets Huge IPO." *Wall Street Journal,* November 29, 2011. Accessed December 12, 2011. http://online.wsj.com/article/SB10001424052970203935604577066773790883672.html.

Sengupta, Somini. " F.T.C. Settles Privacy Issue at Facebook." *New York Times,* November 29, 2011. Accessed December 12, 2011. http://www.nytimes.com/2011/11/30/technology/facebook-agrees-to-ftc-settlement-on-privacy.html?_r=1&scp=2&sq=Facebook&st=cse.

Stempel, Jonathan. "Winklevoss Twins End Appeal of Facebook Settlement." *Reuters,* June 23, 2011. Accessed December 12, 2011. http://www.reuters.com/article/2011/06/23/us-facebook-winklevoss-idUSTRE75L7NS20110623.

Stone, Brad. "Facebook Expands into MySpace's Territory." *New York Times,* May 25, 2007. Accessed December 12, 2011. http://www.nytimes.com/2007/05/25/technology/25social.html?pagewanted=1&ref=facebookinc.

———. "Facebook to Offer Free Classifieds." *New York Times,* May 11, 2007. Accessed December 12, 2011. http://www.nytimes.com/2007/05/11/technology/11facebook.html?ref=facebookinc.

———. "Microsoft Buys Stake in Facebook." *New York Times,* October 25, 2007. Accessed December 12, 2011. http://www.nytimes.com/2007/10/25/technology/25facebook.html?ref=facebookinc#.

Story, Louise. "Apologetic, Facebook Changes Ad Program." *New York Times,* December 6, 2007. Accessed December 12, 2011. http://www.nytimes.com/2007/12/06/technology/06facebook.html?ref=facebookinc#.

———. "Facebook Is Marketing Your Brand Preferences (with Your Permission)." *New York Times,* November 7, 2007. Accessed December 12, 2011. http://www.nytimes.com/2007/11/07/technology/07adco.html?ref=facebookinc.

United States Court of Appeals for the Ninth Circuit. "The Facebook, Inc., et al, v. ConnectU, Inc., and Cameron Winklevoss, Tyler Winklevoss and Divya Narendra." April 11, 2011. Accessed February 23, 2012. http://www.foxnews.com/projects/pdf/Winklevoss_Facebook_petition.pdf.

Vargas, Jose Antonio. "The Face of Facebook." *New Yorker,* September 20, 2010. Accessed December 12, 2011. http://www.newyorker.com/reporting/2010/09/20/100920fa_fact_vargas?.

FedEx Corporation:
Its Launch and Constant Innovation

Since the 1970s global delivery company FedEx Corporation contributed an astonishing number of ideas to the shipping and logistics industry. The company can trace its roots to C.J. Tower & Sons, a Niagara Falls, New York-based customs broker established in 1913. Since then, FedEx has overseen the birth of the modern air-and-ground express industry, established one of the first centralized computer systems to manage delivery services, and introduced handheld barcode scanners to capture detailed package information, among many other accomplishments. In that time, the company shipped everything from giant pandas and sea turtle eggs to the Spirit of Liberty Bell (a traveling full-scale replica of the original Liberty Bell) and relief supplies to disaster areas.

FedEx's rise to the top of the package delivery market began in earnest in 1971, when Frederick Smith acquired Arkansas Aviation Sales in Little Rock, Arkansas. As a student at Yale University, Smith had written a term paper about passenger route systems utilized by airfreight shippers, most of which he considered inefficient. Smith identified a need for systems that could accommodate shipments of medicines, computer parts, and electronics, among other time-sensitive items, within two days. His research led to the creation of Federal Express, and within two years of beginning operations the company marked its first profit and became a leading carrier of high-priority goods.

By 2011 FedEx boasted the world's largest air-cargo fleet with 690 aircraft and a total daily lift capacity of more than 30 million pounds to some 220 countries, as well as 500,000 miles covered every 24 hours. Such extensive reach came in large part from the company's decision to base itself in Memphis, Tennessee, a centrally located U.S.

city with excellent weather for air travel out of its international airport. FedEx additionally lobbied hard for the air-cargo deregulation that eventually allowed it to use much larger aircraft, such as Boeing's 777 and Airbus's A-310. Meanwhile, in the early 2010s its ground couriers travelled 2.5 million miles per day, equal to roughly 100 trips around the globe, in 50,000 motor vehicles and trailers. In all, the company generated nearly US$40 billion in 2011 alone.

FedEx owed much of its success to its founder's vision as well as the improvements that followed. "At FedEx, changes were taking place every week," wrote Madan Birla in *FedEx Delivers: How the World's Leading Shipping Company Keeps Innovating*. "The pace of life was fast. There was excitement in the air. There was a sense of urgency, and everyone was fully engaged in the enterprise." FedEx's path to success was forged by a few key components, namely, the involvement of its executive leaders and the involvement of all stakeholders. From Smith down through all positions at the organization, FedEx became a symbol of an innovative culture to corporate leaders across the industry spectrum.

A LIFE-CHANGING COLLEGE PAPER

The idea for FedEx started with a college paper at Yale University. As a Yale student in the mid-1960s, Fred Smith "was an avid reader with an interest in a wide variety of subjects, a student of military and aviation history, and a creative and imaginative thinker," wrote Roger Frock in *Changing How the World Does Business: FedEx's Incredible Journey to Success—The Inside Story.* The "Yale paper" was inspired by problems Smith saw involving moving airfreight on passenger planes. In it, Smith said that airfreight would be a more economical venture with a system designed specifically for that purpose, rather than relying on passenger airlines. Frock suggested that Smith's paper contained an early version of a commercial aviation system that utilized the hub-and-spoke concept similar to the one employed briefly by the Indian Postal Service in the 1940s. That system connected four major cities of India (Bombay, Calcutta, Delhi, and Madras) through a hub at Nagpur, India, offering overnight airmail service among them.

Meanwhile, by the 1960s, airlines were struggling to find a way to turn their unused cargo compartments into revenue streams. Despite their endeavors, no single solution presented itself. However, Smith envisioned a new system in his college paper, whereby airplanes specifically designated for airfreight would accomplish express delivery economically and efficiently.

Smith's idea evolved from paper to reality. In the early 1970s Smith purchased Arkansas Aviation Sales, a business that provided fuel and hangar services for aircraft. He initially envisioned providing a flight courier service for transporting bonds. However, when he could not obtain insurance to cover potential losses, he fine-tuned his idea for the U.S. Federal Reserve. At that time, the process for clearing checks between banks could be lengthy, sometimes taking as long as 10 days for banks located in remote areas. Smith identified an opportunity to utilize a hub-and-spoke system that could take care of such transfers with much greater expedience. His plan was fairly simple: pick up checks and documents from each U.S. Federal Reserve bank every night, fly them to a central hub to be processed by Federal Reserve workers, and then fly the sorted documents to member banks the next morning. "Because the Federal Reserve would be his only client, he proposed to call his fledgling company Federal Express," wrote Frock. "The system would need fast, reliable aircraft to cover the distances involved in a national network; in fact, the same type of corporate jets that Arkansas Aviation was successfully brokering would be ideal candidates for the service." Eventually, Smith expanded his U. S. Federal Reserve concept to include the larger needs of time-sensitive shippers. The path to becoming a full-fledged delivery service, however, was not without a few obstacles.

HUB-AND-SPOKE

Turning Smith's vision of a U.S. national delivery service, one that could accomplish overnight or two-day shipments, required no small amount of strategizing and financial resources. "I already knew most major airlines treated cargo as an afterthought, operated as a stepchild to the more lucrative passenger side of the airline," wrote Frock, who worked with Smith in the early days of the business.

"I was certain of one thing from our past consulting work: airplanes were expensive to buy, modify, and operate." In consulting with Smith, Frock and his team devised a proposal that would identify the prospective U.S. market potential by market segment; identify likely users by industry and geography; identify likely products; and would evaluate possible customer attitudes about service features.

Their research included more than 100 personal interviews, a questionnaire sent to 4,000 organizations that were known airfreight users, and data from the U.S. Civil Aeronautics Board, the Air Freight Forwarders Association, the U.S. Department of Commerce, and the Dun & Bradstreet Corporation. Their findings presented a promising conclusion: overnight delivery was a service still in its infancy. However, unknown factors such as the time required to break even and reach full system capacity were daunting, wrote Frock. As such, FedEx would be more appropriate for the risk-hungry investor. "As the study progressed, we grew to appreciate Fred's brilliance and open-mindedness," Frock added. "Moreover, Fred's enthusiasm was contagious. I was beginning to suspect he had the drive and leadership skills to pull this off and that his enterprise was worthy of such optimism."

The underlying foundation to FedEx was a hub-and-spoke air route system. As first suggested in Smith's Yale paper, the system would essentially load company planes throughout the day all over the United States. In the evening, all planes would then fly to a U.S. hub with packages for delivery to other cities in the system. The "spokes" were represented by lines connecting both points: origin or destination city and the U.S. national hub. Such a system boasted significant efficiency by allowing for the sorting and consolidation of packages by destination. Planes then arrived back at the city airport the next morning with packages from around the United States bound for that city. Smith and his team selected Memphis, Tennessee, as FedEx's U.S. national hub, due in large part to its central location and fair flying conditions.

"It may seem strange for a package going from Chicago, Illinois to Louisville, Kentucky to go through the U.S. national hub in Memphis, Tennessee instead of flying directly to the destination. But it makes financial sense," wrote Birla. The high cost of flying airplanes meant that the company had to fully utilize each aircraft to keep its service prices reasonable. Over the years, larger markets required multiple aircraft to handle package volumes. This opened up the need for regional hubs; Indianapolis, Indiana, was added to the system in 1987, and others have joined since then.

In addition to having a central location, FedEx's hub-and-spoke system helped solve another quandary: limited time. The company's promise to deliver by 10:30 A.M. the following morning for overnight packages could not be accomplished without a hub-and-spoke system, according to Birla. A hub became absolutely essential in timely de-livery of overnight packages, particularly if demand fluc-tuated. While the system boasted a wealth of efficiencies, it also presented certain unavoidable risks. As Birla ex-plained, every function occurred under a tight schedule, and aircraft had to depart and arrive on time, every time. Otherwise, an entire sort of items (to get them to their respective destinations) at the hub could be delayed. "A late sort at the hub adversely impacts the whole system the following morning," Birla wrote. "It was once estimated that a one-minute delay in the system costs FedEx US$1 million."

STRATEGIZING FOR
UNPLANNED EVENTS

Perhaps most critical to FedEx's recipe for success was Smith's insistence on well-defined processes for handling "what if" questions. In fact, an entire department was es-tablished to think about such topics. The process might start with a note from Smith asking the team whether the company might open a hub in Dallas, Texas to ac-commodate growth. FedEx's operations research depart-ment would then convene over the question in a spirit of open collaboration, with the objective of having a free flow of ideas to accomplish the task at hand. Agreeing on and instituting such changes also required the involve-ment of stakeholders across the organization. Therefore, the operations research department at FedEx conducted three monthly meetings that involved people at all orga-nizational levels, including a meeting for managers and directors, a meeting for directors and vice presidents, and a meeting for the CEO, senior officers, and planning di-rectors, according to Birla. The initial manager meeting allowed managers to share their "what if" scenarios and other ideas. The vice presidents's meeting then discussed those operational ideas, and the senior meeting allowed Smith and senior officers to share their own insights. "Smith and his team had the rare combination of being visionary strategists, generating idea after idea while un-derstanding the tactics that would be needed for imple-mentation throughout the operation," Birla wrote. "They took personal interest, provided support, and followed up regularly to guarantee successful execution of the ap-proved plans."

FedEx's approach to open collaboration led to the de-velopment of several key ideas that propelled the company to the top of its market:

- COSMOS. The Customers, Operations and Service Master Online System was introduced in 1979 to put all package information on a centralized com-puter system. This enabled customer service agents to answer customer questions about package status,

and provided historical as well as current data to managers.

- DADS. The Digitally Assisted Dispatch System was introduced in 1980 to enable couriers to receive on-call pickup requests via a display monitor in their vans. DADS provided for timely response to customer requests and eliminated missed pickups.
- PC-Based Automated Shipping. In 1984 FedEx introduced a PC-based automated shipping system to help speed up the shipping process by eliminating paperwork.
- SuperTracker. SuperTracker, a handheld barcode scanner system, was introduced in 1986 to scan a package at each step of the delivery process and provide its status on a real-time basis.
- Online Tracking. Unveiled in 1994 Fedex.com became the first Web-based application to offer real-time information on package status via the Internet.

It turned out that seeking efficiencies served FedEx well, particularly during economic downturns. The reces-sion of 2008–2009 was especially challenging, but the company managed to face it with aplomb, according to Juan Pablo Gonzalez, Debra Jacobs, and Garrett Sheridan, the authors of *Shockproof: How to Hardwire Your Business for Lasting Success.* "Importantly, FedEx went beyond just reducing costs; it took the opportunity to optimize its routes and equipment, consolidate facilities, and refocus aircraft purchases to better match demand," they wrote. Smith's expectation of continuous change was useful in weathering the economic storm.

The vision that sparked the creation of FedEx in the 1970s was a value that continued to be embraced well into the 21st century. The company established FedEx Innovation, a cross-disciplinary team devoted to identi-fying emerging customer needs and technologies through accelerated prototyping, incubation, and commercializa-tion. In addition, the company continued its longstanding run of developing new technologies. Among its develop-ments was SenseAware, a sensor-based logistics service that coupled a multisensor device with a web-based shipment monitoring application. Customers could track their ship-ments and monitor particular factors such as temperature, location, and light exposure.

While the company continued to foster innovation within its own walls, it also embraced the value of promot-ing such efforts in its community. The company conse-quently established the FedEx Institute of Technology, a high-technology facility for think-tank sessions, corporate retreats, training, and U.S. national conferences located at the University of Memphis. Teams at the institute work on such cutting-edge technologies as artificial intelligence, geospatial analysis, and multimedia arts. Some 150 faculty, researchers, and staff worked at the institute in 2011.

BIBLIOGRAPHY

Birla, Madan. *FedEx Delivers: How the World's Leading Shipping Company Keeps Innovating.* Hoboken, NJ: John Wiley & Sons, 2005, 21, 25, 28.

"FedEx Corporation." Austin, TX: Hoover's, 2012. Accessed January 6, 2012. http://www.hoovers.com.

FedEx Corporation. "FedEx History." Memphis, TN, 2012. Accessed January 1, 2012. http://about.van.fedex.com/our _company/company_information/fedex_history.

———. "FedEx Innovation." Memphis, TN, 2012. Accessed January 6, 2012. http://about.van.fedex.com/our_company /fedex_innovation.

Frock, Roger. *Changing How the World Does Business: FedEx's Incredible Journey to Success—The Inside Story.* San Francisco, CA: Berrett-Koehler, 2006, 9–10, 12, 16, 22.

Gonzalez, Juan Pablo, Debra Jacobs, and Garrett Sheridan. *Shockproof: How to Hardwire Your Business for Lasting Success.* Hoboken, NJ: John Wiley & Sons, 2011, 31.

Flash Memory: Fujio Masuoka's Invention Signals Shift in Storage Technology

Flash memory represented a significant technological advance in digital products and helped revolutionize the manufacture of semiconductors. Invented by Toshiba Corporation engineer Fujio Masuoka in the mid-1980s, flash was a type of nonvolatile (requiring no electrical power) computer memory that could be programmed and erased. Since its introduction, flash memory proliferated into dozens of different formats and could be found in an array of electronic products, from digital cameras and portable music players to smartphones and video game consoles.

ADVANTAGES OF FLASH

Upon its introduction, flash memory provided immediate benefits over older memory types such as random access memory (RAM). Essentially, flash enabled the continuous storage of digital information without the presence of a power source, a notion that was previously unheard of with other types of computer memory. Not only was the technology power-independent, but it also provided faster access to data than traditional hard drives. Furthermore, its lack of moving parts made it better able to tolerate bumps and shocks than devices that utilized spinning disk drives. With the introduction of flash memory, a computer user no longer had to rely on error-prone disks (from floppy to DVD disks). Instead, flash drives could be connected to any computer via a USB terminal and could additionally be written to thousands, and sometimes millions, of times.

Flash memory came in two primary varieties: NOR and NAND. NOR and NAND were essentially logic gates, the elementary building blocks of a digital circuit.

According to Toshiba Corporation, NAND flash was designed with a very small cell size to enable low cost-per-bit storage of data. NAND was used chiefly for high-density storage for consumer devices such as digital cameras and USB solid-state disk (SSD) drives. NOR flash was utilized for code storage and direct execution primarily in portable electronics devices, such as smartphones.

However, late in the first decade of the 21st century, the distinction between both types became less clear. For instance, some cell phones incorporated NAND flash as an alternative to or in addition to NOR flash. Furthermore, with the proliferation of mobile applications such as music, video, and gaming, more portable devices incorporated NAND flash for its speed and erase performance.

While the development of flash memory proved an enormous advance for digital technology, its beginnings were not without controversy.

THE BIRTH OF FLASH

Dr. Fujio Masuoka developed flash memory while working at Toshiba in Japan in 1984. The name came from Masuoka's colleague, Shoji Ariizumi, who noted that the technology's process of erasing data reminded him of a camera flash. When Masuoka took his invention to the Institute of Electrical & Electronics Engineers (IEEE) in San Jose, California, that same year, semiconductor company Intel Corporation saw a huge opportunity to capitalize on the new technology. In fact, the invention was almost universally regarded as one of the most important computer technology developments of the 1990s, according to Benjamin Fulford in *Forbes*. "Flash memory was the most important semiconductor innovation of the 1990s, and it should have made Masuoka very rich," wrote Fulford. "His employer, Toshiba, recognized his efforts by awarding him a bonus worth 'a few hundred dollars'—and promptly let its archrival Intel take control of the market for his invention."

Indeed, Toshiba's loss was Intel's gain. A short four years after Masuoka's presentation, Intel unveiled the first flash chip, ushering in a new era of semiconductor manufacturing. Toshiba initially contended that it was Intel that developed the technology. However, after the IEEE awarded Masuoka the Morris N. Liebman Memorial Award recognizing his invention of flash, the company conceded that it did indeed oversee development of the product but failed to take advantage of that initial momentum.

THE MEMORY CHALLENGE

Masuoka's inspiration to develop flash memory was born out of a significant challenge facing the semiconductor industry in the late 1970s and early 1980s: retaining memory even when a computer's power was turned off. Engineers had until that point attempted to develop non-volatile memory for each piece of memory information, but they soon discovered that the process proved entirely too cumbersome. Masuoka instead saw a potential solution in storing information in large batches rather than individual bits. By doing so, the data stored in such big batches could be retained more easily since the process required simpler, compact circuit designs. According to Fulford, Masuoka took on the challenge and, without Toshiba's permission, spent nights and weekends fleshing out his idea. In 1980 he applied for the first basic patents on a version of flash memory, but it was not until 1984 that a company promotion allowed him to actually produce the first flash technology.

"[T]he American semiconductor industry saw it as a threat," Fulford wrote of Masuoka's innovation. "Back home, his superiors at Toshiba were mildly surprised when a number of U.S. computer companies, including Intel and also some automobile manufacturers, asked for samples." Intel immediately put 300 engineers on full-time flash development, while Toshiba designated five part-time engineers to assist Masuoka. In short order, Intel dominated the new memory segment and was soon generating US$500 million annually in sales.

Losing competitive position to Intel did not deter Masuoka from his research, however. Instead, he began development of a new type of flash memory. His idea was to create a NAND version of flash that could replace traditional hard drives. Unlike his original invention, which was directly connected to the central processing unit of a computer, his NAND concept could be detached from the computer, much like a floppy disk; however, it could store double the amount of information and sell for a fraction

of the cost. The trade-off was that NAND was slower than other memory types.

Still, Masuoka pressed ahead with his idea and produced his first batches of NAND flash in 1987. "His aim was nothing less than to replace the $50 billion-a-year market for hard disk drives on computers," Fulford wrote. "Flash memory has many advantages. It has no mechanical moving parts, it uses less than a hundredth the power of a hard disk, and it can be made very small."

FLASH FUNCTIONALITY

Flash memory chips used floating-gate transistors that were wired onto chips to store an amount of electrical charge for extended periods of time. Each chip was composed of a large number of memory cells where information was stored. Each cell consisted of an array of transistors. "Data erasure is very rapid for entire blocks of cells, which makes this type of memory ideal for applications requiring frequent updates of large quantities of data," wrote William Callister and David Rethwisch in *Fundamentals of Materials Science and Engineering: An Integrated Approach.* "Erasure leads to a clearing of cell contents so that it can be rewritten; this occurs by a change in electronic charge at one of the gates, which takes place very rapidly—i.e., in a 'flash'—hence the name."

NOR and NAND represented the two primary types of flash memory available on the market. Both were among the seven basic logic gates, the elementary building blocks of a digital circuit. Most logic gates consisted of two inputs and one output. At any given time, each terminal was characterized by one of two binary conditions: low (represented by the number 0) and high (represented by the number 1). As such, the logic state of a terminal often changed as the circuit processed data.

In NOR flash, the individual memory cells were connected in parallel, enabling the device to obtain random access to digital information. This internal circuit configuration allowed for short read times that were required for the random access of microprocessor instructions. NOR flash was consequently ideal for low-density, high-speed read applications and random access interface. However, NOR was also characterized by a slow write and erase speed.

On the other hand, NAND flash was constructed of an array of eight memory transistors that were connected in a series. This alternative version to NOR flash traded the random access capability of NOR in favor of high-density storage and a smaller cell size. As a result, NAND flash enabled a lower cost-per-bit. NAND's characteristics additionally included medium read speed, high write speed, high erase speed, and indirect or input/output-type access.

In general, a NAND flash memory array contained a higher density than a NOR flash array, according to

Toshiba. "In theory, the highest density NAND will be at least twice the density of NOR, for the same process technology and chip size," according to the company's overview of the technology. "In reality, market forces determine the highest density that will be commercially produced."

Both types of flash memory boasted their own distinct benefits, and computer system requirements usually dictated which was preferable. For example, NOR flash might be more useful for a system that needs to boot out of flash or to execute code from the flash, or when read latency was an issue. In contrast, NAND flash was highly preferable for storage applications due in large part to its high programming and erase speeds. In addition, using either type of flash carries different power implications. For write-intensive applications, NAND flash typically consumed significantly less power. In special cases, designers had to consider alternatives and trade-offs between the two types of flash. In most cases, however, the option that offered the required performance and density at the lowest cost was preferable.

According to Arie Tal in *Electronic Products,* designers weighed the following factors when considering both NOR and NAND flash memory types:

- NOR reads slightly faster than NAND.
- NAND writes significantly faster than NOR.
- NAND erases considerably faster than NOR.
- In both types, most writes first require a preceding erase operation.
- NAND contains smaller erase units, so fewer erases are necessary.

Flash memory was generally packaged as memory cards, solid-state drives, and USB flash drives. Unlike magnetic memory, flash packages were durable and capable of withstanding wide temperature extremes and even water immersion. "Furthermore," wrote Callister and Rethwisch "over time and the evolution of this flash-memory technology, storage capacity will continue to increase, physical chip size will decrease, and chip price will fall."

FUTURE OF FLASH

By 2010, flash memory sales were on the upswing. Between 2009 and 2010, the traditional enterprise storage systems market rose 18 percent. Flash-powered SSD sales increased more than 100 percent over the same year, according to research firm IDC (as noted by Steve Wexler in "Year in Review: Flash Comes of Age"). The advent of portable devices such as the iPhone and iPad tablet further boosted demand for flash technology. The shift in storage technologies was even more dramatic by the time 2012 arrived, when NAND flash revenue was expected to surpass dynamic random access memory (DRAM) revenue for the first time. Consumers were no longer compelled to utilize

DRAM chips to augment their computers and electronic devices as they once did, explained Evan Ramstad in the *Wall Street Journal,* adding, "Computer performance gains are now coming from other components, including a different type of memory, called NAND flash, which is edging into the data-storage role long played by hard disk drives."

In the meantime, Fujio Masuoka reaped awards and recognition following his flash memory development. In 1994 he became a professor at Tohoku University in Sendai, Japan. In addition, Masuoka joined Unisantis Electronics as its chief technology officer in 2007. There, he continued his chip research, particularly in three-dimensional chip technologies. Masuoka's honors are many: the IEEE Morris N. Liebmann Memorial Award (1997); *The Economist* Innovation Award (2005); and a Medal with Purple Ribbon from the Japanese emperor in 2007, among many other awards. In addition, flash memory was recognized by the IEEE in 2009 as one of "25 Microchips that Shook the World."

In the 2010s Masuoka predicted that current versions of flash might reach their technological limits in a few years. However, he was convinced that progress would continue. According to *Bloomberg Businessweek,* "There will always be another barrier, he [Masuoka] concedes, but 'someone will come up with a breakthrough technology to get around it.'"

BIBLIOGRAPHY

Aho, Alfred V., and Edward K. Blum. *Computer Science: The Hardware, Software and Heart of It.* New York: Springer, 2011.

Callister, William D. Jr., and David G. Rethwisch. *Fundamentals of Materials Science and Engineering: An Integrated Approach.* 4th ed. Hoboken, NJ: John Wiley & Sons, 2011, 513.

"Fujio Masuoka: Thanks for the Memory." *Bloomberg Businessweek,* April 3, 2006. Accessed January 8, 2012. http://www.businessweek.com/magazine/content/06_14/b3978021.htm.

Fulford, Benjamin. "Unsung Hero." *Forbes,* June 24, 2002. Accessed January 10, 2012. http://www.forbes.com/global/2002/0624/030.html.

"Intel Corporation." Austin, TX: Hoover's, 2012. Accessed January 10, 2012. http://www.hoovers.com.

Ramstad, Evan. "Fading Memory Saps Chip Makers." *Wall Street Journal,* January 7, 2012. Accessed January 10, 2012. http://online.wsj.com/article/SB10001424052970203471004577144642749390390.html.

Tal, Arie. "NAND vs. NOR Flash Technology." *Electronic Products,* February 1, 2002. Accessed January 10, 2012. http://www2.electronicproducts.com/NAND_vs_NOR_flash_technology-article-FEBMSY1-feb2002-html.aspx.

Toshiba America Electronic Components, Inc. "NAND vs. NOR Flash Memory." Irvine, CA, April 25, 2006. Accessed January 10, 2012. http://umcs.maine.edu/~cmeadow/courses/cos335/Toshiba%20NAND_vs_NOR_Flash_Memory_Technology_Overviewt.pdf.

Unisantis Electronics. "Company Profile." Tokyo, 2011. Accessed January 8, 2012. http://www.unisantis-el.jp/profile.htm.

Wexler, Steve. "2012: Flash to Supplant Disk?" *Network Computing,* December 29, 2011. Accessed January 10, 2012. http://www.networkcomputing.com/servers-storage/23230 1118.

———. "Year in Review: Flash Comes of Age." *Network Computing,* December 19, 2011. Accessed January 10, 2012. http://www.networkcomputing.com/servers-storage/2323 00786.

Flextronics's Supply Chain Management

Since opening shop in 1969 Flextronics International Ltd. made a name for itself as a turnkey manufacturer of electronics products. The Singapore-based firm produced printed circuit boards, electromechanical components, subsystems, and complete systems for a variety of technology-related industries. Flextronics additionally offered a range of services including design-engineering, assembly, and warehousing. Clients included Microsoft Corporation, Dell Inc., Hewlett-Packard Company, and Lenovo Group Limited. With manufacturing facilities on four continents, the company relied on a robust supply chain management strategy. Flextronics's supply chain management approach earned it accolades and generated copious literature on how to best manage a supply chain in the 21st century.

The company's road to supply chain excellence came as a result of continuous expansion. During the economic recession of 2008 to 2009, Flextronics grew organically by breaking into higher-end markets such as medical devices and solar panels. It also opened new facilities to handle post-recession demand, including five manufacturing plants in Asia and Europe in 2010. By 2012 the company was generating 40 percent of its revenue in China, 10 percent in Mexico, and 10 percent in the United States. To handle its supply chain needs, the company set up a separate unit, Flextronics Global Services (FGS).

Part of Flextronics's success in supply chain management came down to its ability to focus on the one thing the company did exceptionally well: contract manufacturing. "It has recognized the need of other best-of-breed supply chain companies for excellent outsourced manufacturing capabilities," wrote John Gattorna in *Gower Handbook of Supply Chain Management*. "Flextronics's focus had been on building manufacturing facilities in low-cost economies. This requires the skills of building not only the facilities but also the base of next tier suppliers around these facilities." Since fine-tuning its supply chain capabilities in the early 1990s, FGS's global network grew to include more than 20 sites and 12,000 employees in 17 countries.

DEVELOPING "TURNKEY SOLUTIONS"

When Joe McKenzie launched Flextronics in 1969, it was to provide overflow manufacturing services to companies in Silicon Valley, California. Manufacturers that found themselves with more electronic product orders than they could fulfill would send the overflow to Flextronics in those early days. McKenzie and his wife literally hand-soldered every part and returned the finished goods to the manufacturers. This overflow fulfillment service, known at the time as "board stuffing," evolved into a turnkey business over the next decade. McKenzie sold the company in 1980, at which time it was transformed from a board stuffer into a contract manufacturer.

Flextronics was one of the first companies to introduce automated manufacturing techniques in an effort to lower the various and sundry labor costs that came with board assembly, according to the *International Directory of Company Histories*. Its board-level testing procedures insured quality and in 1981 the company became the first U.S. manufacturer to go offshore by setting up manufacturing operations in Singapore. Customers would simply design a product specification and send it to Flextronics. The company would in turn handle everything from the manufacturing process to purchasing parts. The company continued to develop its package of solutions based on logistics. By accepting more of the traditional manufacturing and operational functions that had been performed by original equipment manufacturers (OEMs), Flextronics was able to help its customers remain competitive. Its expanded services included computer-aided design as well as the designing and blueprinting of circuit boards based on customer specifications. Other tasks included the logistics of building and shipping.

During the early 1990s Asian manufacturers were enjoying strong profits while U.S. firms struggled. This turn of events prompted Flextronics to spin off its Singapore operations as a separate company. Meanwhile, the U.S. facilities that had been struggling against recessionary pressures were shut down. With the assistance of outside funding, a new, privately held incarnation of Flextronics was officially christened with its headquarters in Singapore. Shortly thereafter, the company made multiple acquisitions that would cement its reputation as a leading supply chain manager. Flextronics purchased more than a dozen firms between 1993 and 1998. The acquisitions augmented Flextronic's worldwide high-volume manufacturing capabilities. In addition, the acquisitions allowed Flextronics to expand its purchasing and engineering operations while growing its employee base from 3,000 to more than 13,000 over the same period. Meanwhile, company revenue surpassed US$1 billion for the first time in 1998.

More acquisition activity followed between 1999 and 2002, including an Ericsson manufacturing plant; JIT Holdings (formerly part of Siemens's Italian holdings); and Bosch-owned Dii Group, a Danish manufacturing facility. *Harper's Magazine* writer Barry Lynn likened such growth to the breaking-up of an empire, where hundreds of vertically integrated manufacturers cast their operations to the far corners of the globe. "Most start by off-loading the manufacture of a cheap component or a light assembly operation. Many then go further: In January 2001, mobile-phone maker Ericsson sold off all its manufacturing and transport operations to a Singapore-based company named Flextronics," Lynn wrote. "Even high-end manufacturers such as Sony and IBM can't resist sloughing off a factory or four."

The first decade of the 21st century proved to be a significant period of growth for Flextronics as the company steadily added more core capabilities to its ever-expanding list of supply chain services. In late 2002, for example, it established an innovative technology center in Guadalajara, Mexico, which offered customers a full line of product analysis and test characterization services. An ocean away, the company boosted its Asian design and development operations by adding new electrical, software, mechanical, semiconductor, and test development facilities. In 2000 the company also signed the largest deal in

electronic manufacturing services history at the time by landing a US$30-billion, five-year outsourcing project for handset maker Motorola, Inc. With cell phone sales just beginning to accelerate, the Flextronics model proved to be an attractive sell to Motorola, according to Bernard Levine in *Electronics News.* That deal saw Motorola turn over as much as 40 percent of its manufacturing operations to Flextronics, including cell phones, set-top boxes, and other broadband products.

SUPPLY CHAIN SERVICES

Flextronics's acquisition activity was positioning the company to become a veritable supply chain powerhouse. Not only was the company fully engaged in the trend of purchasing the manufacturing facilities of OEMs, but it was also signing supply agreements with those same manufacturers. As more vendors sold their facilities to Flextronics to concentrate on their core capabilities, Flextronics expanded its own capabilities to meet the needs of a variety of industry segments. By the beginning of the 21st century, the company was named the third-best-managed company by *Industry Week.*

Large outsourcing contracts provided the initial fuel for Flextronics's drive to becoming a leading supply chain manager. By 2010, FGS had split its supply chain services into four distinct categories:

- Distribution and supplier managed inventory. This segment of the FGS business included traditional supply chain services such as product fulfillment, inbound freight management, and enterprise warehouse management system connectivity.
- Product transformation. In this segment, FGS configured products to meet specific market requirements or distinctive customer ship kits that could be personalized for end users. Services included build/configure to order, supply chain network design, product postponement, and flexible enterprise resource planning solutions.
- Reverse logistics and repair. Services included return logistics; like-unit repair; recovery, recycling, and e-waste; exchange fulfillment; same-unit repair; and automated IT systems.
- Service parts logistics. This segment specialized in restocking processes that were essential to reverse logistics, repair, and refurbishment services. Services included materials planning and procurement, customer order management, spare parts deployment and distribution, defective parts screening, warranty redemption and repair, integrated IT solutions, and service parts logistics control towers.

Flextronics took a decidedly collaborative approach to its supply chain management initiatives late in the first decade of the 21st century, according to James Carbone in *Purchasing*. "Flextronics's central commodity managers collaborate closely with purchasers at Flextronics manufacturing sites as well as with strategic suppliers in an effort to reduce total cost," wrote Carbone. "That's important in the electronics manufacturing services (EMS) industry because gross profit margins are in the 7–8% range, so cost reductions often can be seen on the bottom line."

Flextronics accomplished such collaboration by focusing on achieving a closer engagement with its strategic suppliers, from the CEO down through the organizational hierarchy. That included learning their expertise in certain technologies as well as involving them in the design process. By garnering their knowledge at the beginning of a relationship, cost reductions became much more likely.

Prior to working with its customers, Flextronics's central purchasing group worked with the company's six business segments as well as with purchasers at the customer's manufacturing site. By spending time with the segments and the sites, the company aimed to make the purchasing process more efficient. However, that was not always the case, noted Carbone. "As is the case with many large EMS providers and OEMs, purchasing at Flextronics has evolved over the years. It used to be done at the manufacturing level," wrote Carbone. "As a result, Flextronics did not leverage its spending from all its sites with suppliers, losing out on the chance to reduce materials cost by getting volume discounts."

Flextronics countered this challenge by moving from a completely regional site-driven procurement model to a more centralized model that took advantage of certain economies of scale. In fact, the company referred to its central procurement organization as "the main face to the supply base," and it worked on customer strategies and contracts, and negotiated requests for quotations and logistics. Flextronics furthermore broke down its purchasing by commodities, by assigning commodity managers to different production materials. These included printed circuit boards, passive components, connectors, and semiconductor materials, among many others.

Meanwhile, a purchasing council represented Flextronics's various business segments and provided input from each business unit to the central organization. Council meetings enabled the company to better understand key parts and key customers in preparation for sitting down with customers for the negotiation process. The meetings also incorporated conversations on emerging technologies and supplier selection. A central team proposed suppliers for a certain commodity. The proposal would then be discussed with council members and business units to garner more input to devise a final list of preferred suppliers. Such collaborative work, added Carbone, ultimately proved effective for Flextronics, whether it meant doing business in emerging Asian nations or managing relationships in established European and North American locations.

EXTENDING SUPPLY CHAIN

As Kevin O'Marah and Debra Hofman wrote in *Supply Chain Management Review*, the importance of supply chain services grew as manufacturing became increasingly globalized. With low-cost regional sourcing and production coming to the fore, operations management relied less on plant operations and more than ever on networks of suppliers, contract manufacturers, and outside logistics providers. Innovators like Flextronics enabled thousands of manufacturers to push their manufacturing and inventory management burdens back onto their supply bases. "These less visible elements of the extended supply chain develop extraordinary capabilities for materials sourcing and lean manufacturing by consolidating operations across branded OEMs who concentrate on channel management and marketing," O'Marah and Hofman wrote.

To remain competitive, Flextronics sharpened its focus on a few critical strengths in the first decade of the 21st century. The company's strategy of market diversification served it well in the latter half of that decade as macroeconomic disruptions led to constant demand shifts and realignments. Its sheer scale and global reach also allowed it to provide competitive pricing and flexible supply chain options to customers. In addition, Flextronics's self-contained industrial parks combined both manufacturing and supply chain operations, thereby providing even more cost competitiveness to customers. Nearly three-quarters of its manufacturing operations were located in low-cost countries, including Brazil, China, Hungary, India, Indonesia, Malaysia, Mexico, Romania, Slovakia, and Ukraine.

BIBLIOGRAPHY

Brathwaite, Nicholas. "Service Providers Keep OEMs Tech-Savvy." *Electronic Engineering Times,* March 17, 1997.

Carbone, James. "Flextronics Focuses More Spend with Fewer Suppliers." *Purchasing* 138, no 12 (December 17, 2009).

Flextronics Global Services. "About Us." Singapore, 2011. Accessed January 17, 2012. http://fgs.flextronics.com/29 /about_us.html.

"Flextronics International." Austin, TX: Hoover's, 2012. Accessed January 17, 2012. http://www.hoovers.com.

Flextronics International. "Our Company." Singapore, 2012. Accessed January 17, 2012. http://www.flextronics.com /about_us/default.aspx.

"Flextronics International Ltd.—History." Datamonitor Group, May 18, 2004.

"Flextronics International Ltd." *International Directory of Company Histories,* edited by Jay P. Pederson. Vol. 38, 186–189. Detroit: St. James Press, 2001. Gale Virtual Reference Library (GALE|CX2844200051). Accessed February 15, 2012. http://go.galegroup.com/ps/i.do?id=GALE%7CCX284

4200051&v=2.1&u=itsbtrial&it=r&p=GVRL&sw=w.

Gattorna, John. *Gower Handbook of Supply Chain Management.* 5th ed. Burlington, VT: Gower Publishing Company, 2003, 450.

Hofman, Debra, and Kevin O'Marah. "The Top 25 Supply Chains." *Supply Chain Management Review* 13, no. 7 (October 1, 2009).

Levine, Bernard. "Flextronics Deal Rocks EMS World." *Electronic News,* June 5, 2000. Accessed February 16, 2012. http://www

.edn.com/article/503218-Flextronics_Deal_Rocks_EMS _World.php.

Lynn, Barry. "Unmade in America: The True Cost of a Global Assembly Line." *Harper's Magazine,* June 2002. Accessed February 15, 2012. http://harpers.org/archive/2002/06 /0079204.

U.S. Securities and Exchange Commission. "Form 10-K: Flextronics International Ltd." Washington, DC, March 31, 2011.

Ford Motor Company's Use of the Assembly Line

The assembly line, first introduced in 1913 in the automobile industry, is a way of assembling or manufacturing goods. Assembly lines create a line of equipment and employees to gradually assemble a product by moving it from station to station consecutively, allowing each worker to add his or her own contribution to the final product. Initially, assembly lines were used to reduce manufacturing time and therefore the cost of the final product.

In the 21st century, the assembly line has been used in a variety of assembly and manufacturing situations, from food production to cars. When Henry Ford rolled out the first Model T cars in 1908, however, the assembly line was not popularly used in the production of cars. It was Ford, working to find a more efficient way to produce his Model T automobile, who is credited as one of the primary developers of assembly lines and mass production.

However, even before Henry Ford's automobiles relied on the assembly line, there were some precedents in various U.S. industries. In fact, these systems in other industries might have inspired Ford and his engineers to develop the Ford Motor Company assembly line. For example, William Klann, who would eventually join the Ford Motor Company team, had experience with conveyors and mechanized production during his work with automated flour mills in the United States in the early 20th century. At the time, U.S. flour mills used conveyor belts and other mechanized systems to move grain from one area of a mill to another for processing. According to David A. Hounshell in his book *From the American System to Mass Production, 1800–1932: The Development of Manufacturing Technology in the United States,* Klann re-

viewed this information with Ford, possibly contributing to the development of the assembly line system.

Canning companies also used conveyor belts to bring the work to the worker. Canning factories in the 19th and early 20th centuries were significant because they arranged machines in sequence. In this manner, a can of food would be gradually assembled to completion as it moved via a conveyance system through the factory.

In 1922 Ford explained that the general idea for the Ford assembly line came from "the overhead trolley that the Chicago, Illinois packers used in dressing beef," according to Ray Batchelor's book, *Henry Ford, Mass Production, Modernism, and Design.* According to Batchelor, butchers were using a type of assembly line long before Ford, hanging beef on hooks attached to an overhead rail. The beef would be disassembled piece by piece as it moved along until the entire carcass had been disassembled into sellable cuts.

In addition to the already existing processes of conveyor belts and automation in other industries, there was a popular approach to work management just around the time that Ford developed the assembly line. In 1911 Frederick W. Taylor published *Principles of Scientific Management,* marking the height of systematic management ideas. Scientific management, Taylorism, and other systems were based on the idea that efficiency in work could be measured and approached from a scientific basis in order to maximize productivity. Although the extent to which these ideas impacted Ford Motor Company has not been recorded, there was evidence that some Ford engineers created time and motion studies when developing assembly lines at Ford, suggesting that they may have been impacted by Taylor, Frank B. Gilbreth, and other writers with similar ideas.

BEFORE THE ASSEMBLY LINE

In 1908 Henry Ford's Ford Motor Company began creating the Model T, a car for the average consumer. By 1909 demand for the car was so high that Ford needed to open a new factory. According to Batchelor, by 1909 Henry Ford decided to produce only one car, the Model T. The idea was that the car would be basic and would be made with one chassis (frame) only. More than 10,000 Model T Fords were sold within the first year, making it a definite success at a time when cars were not immensely popular.

Ford's commitment to producing only the Model T and reducing the number of options available was important to the development of the assembly line system, according to Hounshell. With only one car being developed, it was possible to develop a system that took single-purpose tasks and machines to the limit. In addition, the huge demand for the car and the need to open a new factory to replace the older plant also paved the way for the assembly line. The demand for the car pushed Henry Ford and his engineers to look for more efficient ways to mass produce the car, while a new factory allowed the engineers a new space for experimenting with more effective means of production and assembly. The Highland Park, Michigan, factory was designed in a way that paved the way for assembly lines as well: the factory was one large building, which allowed for all the work to be completed under one roof.

Before the assembly line system that would eventually be used for the Model T, Ford Motor Company used the idea of interchangeable parts. At the time the Model T was created, many U.S. companies, including Singer Manufacturing Company (known for its sewing machines) and various manufacturers of typewriters, used what was known as the armory system, or the American System. The armory system involved using machine tools to create interchangeable parts that could be made by semiskilled workers and then be assembled into larger machines or finished products by unskilled workers. The parts required no fitting, just assembly, making the process of assembling much simpler, less expensive, and faster.

Before the assembly lines, teams of about 15 skilled craftsmen built each Ford car from the ground up, using the company tool room to get the materials they needed to get the job done. Each craftsman was responsible for his own tools, fixing them as necessary. Most of the parts for the cars were shipped in from manufacturers. The cars were kept up on wooden stands as they were assembled by teams. With this system, different teams could be working on different models and different cars in the same building.

In 1903 however, Ford was already considering the idea of mass production or at least the idea of producing lots of cars that were all alike. Since the Industrial Revolution in the 19th century, small household items had been made this way. Even some of the parts for Ford Motor Company cars were mass produced in this way.

THE START OF THE ASSEMBLY LINE

Before the assembly line system could be created, there were two obstacles to overcome: parts for the cars were still made by other companies and there was no system for getting the parts to the workers as they were needed. In 1906 Henry Ford hired Max W. Wollering and Walter P. Flanders as part of a plan to become less dependent on parts from other companies. Flanders became production engineer for both the Ford Motor Company and for the Ford Manufacturing Company, which Henry Ford had established to create the parts he needed for his cars. Wollering worked on creating systems that would make the assembly process simpler. For example, he worked on creating systems for getting the required parts and the necessary tools to workers in the shop so that the process of assembling the cars would be smoother.

Henry Ford then turned to making the assembly system itself more efficient. As Batchelor noted, the process by which the assembly line was introduced in Ford's business was so rapid that it is difficult to document its evolution step by step. What is known is that in 1913, a component of the car's electrical system known as the flywheel magneto was first assembled using a type of assembly line with a conveyor belt at the Highland Park, Michigan, location. The system was designed by Charles Sorensen, Peter E. Martin, C. H. Willis, and Clarence W. Avery of Ford Motor Company. Martin was the superintendent of the Ford factory and Sorensen was his assistant. Avery had been a high school teacher at Henry Ford's school.

On April 1, 1913, workers arriving at the flywheel magneto assembly found that waist-high rails had replaced the benches where the parts had been assembled before. Each worker was assigned one small task and was told to slide the partly completed flywheel magneto to the next worker in line and that worker would then complete the next task. Each of the 29 employees was given one small task to complete over and over again. Whereas before, assembling each flywheel magneto took 20 minutes, after April 1, 1913, the same 29 employees could complete the assembly of one flywheel magneto in 13 minutes and 10 seconds.

INITIAL SUCCESSES OF THE ASSEMBLY LINE

According to Batchelor, the assembly line system initially created some complaints. The benches needed to be raised between six and eight inches after workers complained of backaches. There was also a lack of uniformity in the speed at which different workers worked. To fix this problem, Ford Motor Company engineers added a chain to move the partly assembled flywheel magneto along the line at a specific speed. This caused fast workers to slow down and pushed slow workers to hurry up, essentially getting workers to adapt to a preset speed. With this new system in place, the amount of time it took to assemble one flywheel magneto dropped further, to just five minutes. Before April 1, 1913, the 29 workers who worked on the flywheel magneto could create 35 to 40 complete flywheel magnetos a day. After that date, they could produce more than 100 completed flywheel magnetos. Following the success of the assembly line with the flywheel magneto, William Klann created an assembly line for Ford engines. The Ford engine assembly line meant that the time required to assemble a Ford engine dropped from 594 minutes to 226 minutes.

Clarence Avery developed an assembly line for the Ford chassis by April 1914 and it became the assembly line that epitomized mass production. The assembly featured a large endless chain conveyor system powered by electricity. The new assembly line also fixed a previous problem: the existing assembly lines had been so efficient that they were producing more completed parts than the assembly could handle. The parts from these lines were creating a stockpile, while the total number of cars was not increasing as quickly. With the new assembly line, a line of chassis could be moved through the Ford factory, allowing employees to add parts at each individual station. Assembly lines and the feeder lines were coordinated so that the system moved smoothly.

Further adoption of assembly lines allowed Ford Motor Company to reduce the labor time required for each car by almost 90 percent, which in turn allowed the company to assemble 1,200 cars in an eight-hour shift. Before the assembly line, Ford Motor Company was assembling 475 cars over a nine-hour working day. The cost and time savings led Henry Ford to develop assembly lines for the assembly of all Ford Motor Company parts. Within one year of the first flywheel magneto assembly line, almost all assembly projects and tasks at Ford used moving line assemblies. The expansion of the Highland Park, Michigan, factory meant that supply lines needed to be automated and power driven to accommodate the increased rate of production.

The pace of production also paved the way for Ford Motor Company's River Rouge, Michigan, factory. That facility was built from the start to be fully assembly-line-based from the moment raw materials were brought in to the moment the automobiles were placed on railroad cars for shipment to customers. Uniquely, the plant also included its own glass plant and steel mill, allowing Ford to essentially convert raw materials into finished cars under one roof.

The assembly line was intended to increase production and efficiency, and it did. In 1909 the Ford Motor Company made 17,771 Model T automobiles. In 1913 the first year of assembly lines, the company manufactured 202,667. By 1924 when the entire car was made through an assembly line system, Ford Motor Company produced 1.8 million Model Ts. In addition to increasing the number of Model Ts available for sale, the mass production possible through the assembly line drove down the cost of cars so that even Ford plant workers could afford them. A fully equipped Model T was US$950 in 1909. By 1914 it had dropped to US$490, and by 1916, it was US$350.

WORKERS ON THE ASSEMBLY LINE

While engineers were eager to develop new improvements to make the assembly line even more efficient and cost-effective, the workers were initially not as impressed. According to Batchelor, workers were not eager to work at the Highland Park, Michigan plant because of the assembly line, since doing the same repetitive task over and over again at the company's pace did not necessarily provide a pleasant work environment. Employee reluctance created a new problem for Henry Ford: high labor turnover.

Worker satisfaction was the final challenge to Henry Ford's assembly line and mass production system. By 1913 high labor turnover was such a problem that Ford needed to hire 963 employees for every 100 employees needed due to the large percentage that would leave. To address the problem, on January 5, 1914, Henry Ford announced a wage increase that gave employees on the assembly line US$5 a day. This was double the going rate for the work and it helped increase employee satisfaction. In addition, Ford offered profit sharing for some employees and reduced the workday to eight hours.

THE IMPACT

According to Gregory A. Stobbs' book, *Business Method Patents,* Ford Motor Company's assembly line system revolutionized the entire "commercial landscape." The assembly line reduced the cost of making cars, and therefore reduced the cost of car ownership, making the Model T the first car to be widely available to the average consumer. According to Stobbs, this had wide-ranging consequences, including demand for better roads, and, eventually, increased freedom of travel as well as more interstate commerce.

The assembly line also produced other changes. Rather than relying on craftsmen, Ford could hire less expensive and less skilled workers. Most jobs could be taught to virtually any worker since the task of building a car was reduced to very small, unskilled units of labor that could easily be taught. During World War II, this feature of the assembly line became crucial for the U.S. economy as factories had to hire and train unskilled workers quickly to replace the workers being sent overseas to fight.

Some of the limitations of Ford Motor Company's assembly line were evident almost at once, however, and needed to be addressed. To mass produce cars, Ford had to keep large warehouses of parts ready, and if there was any breakdown in parts supply or in any part of the system, production could halt entirely. To fix this problem, Ford had to start manufacturing its own parts. In addition, the assembly system was not very flexible. Only one type of car could be made per assembly line at a time. With time, this was resolved by building larger factories that could handle multiple assembly lines, thereby creating multiple car models.

The Ford Motor Company is famous for the Model T automobile, the first popular mass-produced car. The high demand for that vehicle led the company to adopt practices already used by other industries to develop a highly efficient and mechanized system of production known as the assembly line. The assembly line used a nonstop work flow, a careful division of work, and interchangeable parts to reduce costs and improve manufacturing times.

BIBLIOGRAPHY

Batchelor, Ray. *Henry Ford, Mass Production, Modernism, and Design*. Manchester, United Kingdom: Manchester University Press, 1994, 45, 47.

Greenwood, Ronald G., and Daniel A. Wren. "Business Leaders: A Historical Sketch of Henry Ford." *Journal of Leadership Studies* 5, no. 3 (1998): 72–73.

"Henry Ford Implements the $5-a-Day Wage." *The Learning Network* (blog), *New York Times,* January 5, 2012. Accessed January 11, 2012. http://learning.blogs.nytimes.com/2012/01/05/jan-5-1914-henry-ford-implements-5-a-day-wage/.

Hooker, Clarence. *Life in the Shadows of the Crystal Palace, 1910–1927: Ford Workers in the Model T Era*. Bowling Green, OH: Bowling Green State University Popular Press, 1997.

Hounshell, David A. *From the American System to Mass Production, 1800–1932: The Development of Manufacturing Technology in the United States*. Baltimore, Maryland: The Johns Hopkins University Press, 1985, 241.

Koepfer, Chris. "Mass Producing Quantities of One." *Modern Machine Shop*, April 1998.

Samuelson, Robert J. "The Assembly Line." *Newsweek,* December 1, 1997. Accessed February 16, 2012. http://www.thedailybeast.com/newsweek/1997/12/01/the-assembly-line.html

Stobbs, Gregory A. *Business Method Patents*. New York: Aspen Law & Business, 2002, 401.

Stoddard, Scott. "Henry Ford's Moving Assembly Line Put World on Wheels." *Investor's Business Daily,* December 28, 2011. Accessed January 11, 2012. http://news.investors.com/Article/596042/201112281342/henry-ford-put-america-on-wheels.htm.

Vance, Bill. "Classic Car Showcase: Ford Model T." *Chronicle-Herald,* January 3, 2012. Accessed January 11, 2012. http://thechronicleherald.ca/wheelsnews/48371-classic-car-showcase-ford-model-t.

Genentech: Patents and Biotechnology

The year 1976 was a vintage year for high-technology businesses. It was the year that Steve Jobs and Steve Wozniak founded Apple Computer, and it was also the year that Robert A. Swanson and Herbert W. Boyer founded Genentech, Inc., a biotechnology company in San Francisco, California. Swanson, a venture capitalist who had received his degree in management from the Massachusetts Institute of Technology (MIT), was working for Kleinman, Perkins, Caufield, & Byers, a venture capital firm with a focus on high-technology companies. He heard about the launch of the world's first biotechnology company, Cetus Corporation, in Berkeley, California. Founded in 1971, Cetus was developing new biotechnology-based pharmaceuticals as well as a new technique for amplifying deoxyribonucleic acid (DNA), a process that made multiple identical copies of a DNA sequence.

Swanson was enthusiastic about the commercial potential of genetics and biotechnology, specifically DNA products. He wanted to create his own company to take advantage of the huge potential he envisioned. He began looking for a partner, ideally a molecular biologist, to provide the scientific knowledge required. Herbert Boyer, a researcher at the University of California, San Francisco, was one of the first scientists, along with Stanley Cohen of Stanford University, to create gene cells called recombinant DNA or rDNA. Swanson met with Boyer one day. Boyer agreed to give him 10 minutes of his time and the meeting ended up lasting for three hours as Swanson's enthusiasm about the commercial and medical potential of biotechnology spread to Boyer. Soon afterwards, both men left their jobs and founded Genentech.

At the time Swanson and Boyer took the leap and founded the company, genetic research, and the biotech-

nology industry itself, was very much in its infancy. The genetic code had been cracked years earlier, in 1963, when scientists led by Marshall Nirenberg, Har Khorana, and Severo Ochoa at the National Institutes of Health (NIH) and New York University were able to translate the order of the 20 kinds of amino acids in proteins. It was not until the 1970s that methods and technologies were developed that would allow biotechnology companies to explore the field to its full potential.

Swanson met with Boyer in 1976 but it was four years earlier, in 1972, that Boyer and Cohen had filed the patent with the U.S. Patent and Trademark office that became extremely important for the future of biotechnology: the patent for rDNA (recombinant DNA). Recombinant DNA allowed scientists to clone DNA sequences. Although the patent application was submitted in 1972, it was not granted to the scientists until 1980. It was rDNA technology, however, that led to many subsequent advances in the field of biotechnology, including using it to create specific proteins that could be used for pharmaceuticals and in gene therapy. By 1978 Genentech had used its technology to create the insulin gene.

PRICELESS PATENTS

Up until the time Genentech filed for patent protection, scientists and universities had not considered filing a patent which is an important part of the research process. However, through his previous experience at Kleinman, Perkins, Caufield, & Byers, Swanson recognized the value of patent protection. Although the patents that Genentech submitted in those early years did have a specific impact on the biotechnology industry, they were not considered the breakthroughs that earlier patent cases were. The patents filed by the University of California and Stanford University for rDNA were considered by legal professionals and academic researchers as the first to show that universities, as well as private companies, could benefit from patenting their intellectual property. Due to these initial Boyer-Cohen patents, all other biotechnology companies had to license the rDNA technology from the two universities, resulting in royalty payments of US$255 million each to the University of California and Stanford University. According to *Intellectual Property Management in Health and Agricultural Innovation: A Handbook of Best Practices,* as of 2007 the technology had been licensed to 468 companies and it was responsible for the development of more than 2,400 products that generated sales of US$35 billion.

The patent may never have been granted, however, if not for an earlier decision regarding the ability to patent a living organism. Considered the landmark case that started the avalanche of genetic patents, the *Diamond vs. Chakrabarty* case began in 1972 when a General Electric Company researcher named Ananda Mohan Chakrabarty developed a bacterium that could break down crude oil. His patent application was rejected because the office said it could not patent living organisms. This decision was overturned in 1980, when U.S. Chief Justice Warren E. Burger concluded that the fact that the bacterium was a living organism was irrelevant. Chakrabarty had genetically altered it into a form that did not occur in nature, which proved that it was novel and therefore patentable. Subsequently, other patents, including those pending for Genentech, were granted.

Genentech was not a passive observer of the *Diamond vs. Chakrabarty* case. Swanson and other executives recognized that the U.S. Supreme Court's decision would significantly impact their own pending patent applications, so Genentech sent one of its own legal counsels, Thomas Kiley, to speak on behalf of scientists and companies conducting biotechnology research. He argued that without patent protection, the ability of companies to research and produce innovative products would be severely limited.

GENENTECH PATENT APPLICATIONS

As a new company in an almost completely new industry, Genentech had no clear business models to emulate. Since the company had little capital when first formed, Swanson and Boyer chose to donate what funds they were able to raise to two organizations that had the facilities to create the biotechnology they needed: Boyer's previous laboratory at the University of California and the City of Hope National Medical Center of Duarte, California.

Genentech created agreements with each of these organizations such that they would receive royalties based on the revenues of product sales. These agreements were called into question later in Genentech's history. However, in these early years of the company, they were successful strategies. Within two years of founding the company, Genentech had ownership of a process that replicated human insulin. Insulin is a critical hormone for patients with diabetes. Prior to this process, insulin was taken from animal sources and purified for use in human patients. Discovering a way to biosynthesize insulin was considered an enormous breakthrough. In addition to producing the insulin, scientists eventually discovered methods for improving the synthesized hormone so that it could act faster in case of diabetic shock.

Genentech had the methodology (and the patent protection to go with it) in 1980 but not the means to manufacture and market an insulin product. The company had determined that getting the product to market would cost at least US$100 million and would take 1,000 years of labor. It was well known in the pharmaceutical industry that the drug manufacturing giant Eli Lilly and Company, headquartered in Indianapolis, Indiana, was the world leader in insulin production and marketing (claiming a 75 percent market share). Rather than viewing the company as a competitor, Genentech realized that its own methodology would be valuable to Eli Lilly and that the two companies could work together. Swanson and Boyer met with Eli Lilly executives and the two parties worked out a licensing agreement. The U.S. Food and Drug Administration (FDA) approved the human insulin product in 1982 and by 1987 Genentech was earning US$5 million per year in royalties.

Genentech was also able to isolate and clone alpha interferon, a protein involved in the immune system that signals cells to attack and break down viruses and tumors. Genentech again chose to sell the rights to this technology to another established pharmaceutical firm, F. Hoffman-La Roche Ltd., in 1987, resulting in another US$5 million in royalties. Hoffman-La Roche sold this product as Roferon-A.

With the funds from a 1980 initial public offering (which raised US$35 million) and royalties from Eli Lilly and Hoffman-La Roche coming in, Genentech focused its efforts on human growth hormone (HGH), which it had successfully cloned in 1978. It was this product that Genentech planned to manufacture and market itself. HGH is produced in large quantities in healthy children and its production slows over time. Children who have growth deficiencies are treated with HGH. It can also be used to treat specific, rare tumors in adults. Genentech received FDA approval to begin production and sales of Protropin, its HGH product, in 1985. It was the first product based on recombinant DNA technology to be manufactured and marketed by a biotechnology company. In its first year on the pharmaceutical market, Protropin, and its injectable version, Somatrem, earned US$43.6 million in sales, and by 1991 sales were more than US$155 million.

THE DOUBLE-EDGED SWORD OF PATENTS

Throughout these early years of the biotechnology industry, patent protection was considered absolutely essential for protecting each company's significant investment of clinical research and development and the very time-consuming and costly FDA approval process. Genentech was one of the first companies to realize the value of patents due to the important recombinant DNA patent filed by its founder, Herbert Boyer. However, Genentech was not the only biotechnology firm beginning to fill pharmaceutical needs based on genetic technologies. One of its biggest partners became its biggest competitor in 1989 when Eli Lilly received approval for its version of HGH. Eli Lilly had created a method for replicating the HGH found in the human body. Genentech swiftly filed a lawsuit and claimed that the FDA should decide which company could hold exclusive rights to the product. The question was settled in court, with both companies receiving exclusive rights under their respective patents for marketing HGH. However, by 1991 Genentech was the clear market leader, with more than 70 percent of the market.

Other questions were raised about Genentech and its patent and licensing agreements. Both the University of California and the City of Hope Medical Center sued Genentech claiming that they received only a portion of the royalties they were due. The issue in both cases focused on a clause that stated that the organizations would receive royalties on sales of *products,* not sales or licensing fees from the technologies developed. City of Hope also maintained that Genentech had sold and licensed products based on a technology it developed but had kept hidden from City of Hope.

These were not the only questions on patent legitimacy with which Genentech had to deal in its history. In 1987 the company received FDA approval for Activase, a drug it claimed could prevent and treat heart attacks. The product, based on recombinant DNA technology, was a clone of tissue plasmogen activator (t-PA), which is found in the blood. Its patent claimed exclusive rights to t-PA and all synthetic variations of it. This broad claim was disputed by the Wellcome Foundation Ltd. in the United Kingdom. This organization funded medical research and it challenged the idea that any company could "own" a naturally occurring biological component. It had developed its own product based on t-PA, which it planned to market in the United States. This lawsuit prevented Genentech from marketing t-PA in the United Kingdom, but Wellcome eventually lost the suit and was unable to market its product in the United States until 2005, when Genentech's patent expired.

In 1999 Genentech paid US$200 million to the University of California, San Francisco, to settle a 9-year lawsuit that claimed the company had stolen a DNA sample from the lab to develop its HGH product. The company admitted no wrongdoing in the settlement. However, the continuing legal battles, increased competition, and the rising costs of research, development, and drug approval, led to Genentech's acquisition by Roche Holding AG, the Swiss holding company, which also controlled F. Hoffmann-La Roche. At the conclusion of the merger, Roche Holding owned 60 percent of Genentech. Over the years Roche increased its ownership of the company until, in 1999, it acquired all remaining shares.

Genentech experienced a setback in 2002 when a Los Angeles County, California, Superior Court found in favor of the City of Hope Medical Center. Genentech was ordered to pay City of Hope US$500 million in royalties and damages.

LESSONS LEARNED

Genentech's founders Robert Swanson and Herbert Boyer learned in the infancy of the biotechnology industry that patent protection was essential for protecting the company's innovation. Genentech was the first company to take advantage of its founder's innovative gene-splicing technology, rDNA, and used it to patent gene sequences that could express proteins and hormones. These proteins and hormones were then used to treat medical illnesses. Genentech's foresight and recognition of the value of patent protection led to many innovative products as well as thousands of additional patents filed by other biotechnology and pharmaceutical companies that developed subsequent products using rDNA methodology.

BIBLIOGRAPHY

Feldman, Maryann P., Alessandra Colaianni, and Connie Kang Liu. "Lessons from the Commercialization of the Cohen-Boyer Patents: The Stanford University Licensing Program." In *Intellectual Property Management in Health and Agricultural Innovation: A Handbook of Best Practices,* edited by A. Krattiger, R. T. Mahoney, L. Nelsen, et al. Oxford, UK: MIHR, and Davis, CA: PIPRA, 2007. Accessed January 10, 2012. http://www.iphandbook.org/handbook/chPDFs/ch17/ipHandbook-Ch%2017%2022%20Feldman-Colaianni0Liu%20Cohen-Boyer%20Patents%20and%20Licenses.pdf.

"Genentech Inc." *Funding Universe,* 2000. Accessed January 10, 2012. http://www.fundinguniverse.com/company-histories/Genentech-Inc-Company-History.html.

Hughes, Sally Smith. "Interview with Niels Reimers." *Calisphere,* 1998. Accessed January 10, 2012. http://content.cdlib

.org/view?docId=kt4b69n6sc&brand=calisphere&doc
.view=entire_text.

Rimmer, Matthew. "Genentech and the Stolen Gene: Patent Law and Pioneer Inventions." *Bio-Science Law Review* 5, no. 6 (2002/2003): 198–211. Accessed January 12, 2012. http://papers.ssrn.com/sol3/papers.cfm?abstract_id=603221.

George Lucas and *Star Wars*

George Lucas is a U.S. filmmaker best known for the successful *Star Wars* series of motion pictures. The series shifted Hollywood's focus away from dramatic themes, to marketing summer blockbusters with high-tech special effects designed to draw huge audiences. Starting with the release of the first film in the series on May 25, 1977, *Star Wars*, the epic saga sparked massive commercial success that has affected popular culture in numerous ways.

One of the most enduring impacts of the *Star Wars* series was related to movie merchandising and the billions of dollars generated from auxiliary sales of movie-themed items, ranging from plastic action figures to beach towels to video games. Merchandising was rarely a significant consideration for film studios before the *Star Wars* phenomenon began in the late 1970s. Before the first movie was made, Lucas shrewdly negotiated a deal to keep all the merchandising rights to his movie and the rights to future sequels. That move made him a multimillionaire, and it provided funds that allowed further technological breakthroughs in moviemaking that benefited a number of other films that followed in later years.

A LONG TIME AGO. . .

George Lucas was born in 1944 in Modesto, California, to parents who owned a stationery store. He grew up on a walnut ranch in the California suburbs. He was obsessed early on with fast cars, racing at fairgrounds and planning a career as a competitive driver. However, he was seriously injured in a car accident in 1962, just a few days before his high school graduation. While recuperating from his injuries, Lucas decided he wanted to study art. When his parents would not pay for art school, he instead began studying anthropology at Modesto Junior College.

In community college, Lucas soon became interested in photography and cinematography. He began using a small camera to make his own movies, often photographing car races. He transferred to the University of Southern California (USC) so he could attend the School of Cinematic Arts, one of the few college filmmaking schools in the United States at that time. At USC he attended classes with a number of future filmmakers, most notably future collaborator Steven Spielberg. One of his eight student films, a futuristic science fiction short called *Electronic Labyrinth: THX-1138-4EB,* won the top prize at the 1967–1968 National Student Film Festival. He was also given a Warner Brothers Studio scholarship to work on a film of his choice. Lucas selected *Finnian's Rainbow,* which was being directed by the already famous Francis Ford Coppola.

After Lucas graduated he pursued a number of projects, including working as a cameraman on *Gimme Shelter,* the Rolling Stones concert film. In 1969, Lucas and his mentor, Coppola, cofounded the American Zoetrope film studio. Coppola also arranged for Warner Brothers to back a full-length version of the film that had won Lucas the national student contest. However, the 1971 *THX-1138* was not commercially successful. Later that year, Lucas formed his own studio, Lucasfilm, Ltd.

His next movie was both a critical and a box-office smash. *American Graffiti,* released in 1973, included such up-and-coming young actors as Richard Dreyfuss, Ron Howard, and Harrison Ford. (Howard and Ford would work with Lucas again in later years.) According to a Lucas profile at Biography.com, the film cost US$780,000 to make and grossed more than US$50 million. It won the Golden Globe for best picture and was nominated for five Academy Awards, including best picture, best screenplay, and best director for Lucas. The movie "is still considered one of the most successful low budget features ever made," Biography.com added. Lucas himself earned more than US$7 million from the film.

CHANNELING THE FORCE

Fresh from his first commercial success, Lucas started his next project, a science fiction epic that grew into the *Star Wars* series of movies. However, despite his previous success, Lucas struggled to sell his new film. While Universal Studios had financed *American Graffiti,* it had not expected the small film to be a moneymaker and was surprised by its success. Still, Universal passed on *Star Wars,* as did most of the other major studio executives in Hollywood, California. The sole exception was Alan Ladd, Jr., who had recently taken over as the head of financially troubled 20th Century Fox Film Corporation (Fox). Ladd had seen an early print of *American Graffiti* and was impressed by Lucas' work. According to Anne Thompson in the *Chicago Tribune,* Ladd had agreed to *Star Wars* before *American Graffiti* became a hit and put Lucas in a position to renegotiate his agreement with Fox. Ladd convinced Fox to sign a distribution and production deal with Lucas, which eventually helped return Fox to profitability. *Star Wars* was made for US$11 million and released in 1977. The movie grossed more than US$500 million globally in its first theatrical run that year and it eventually became the blockbuster movie of the decade.

However, it was the deal Lucas renegotiated with Fox that made a greater impact on the movie business for years to come. "When Lucas negotiated his deal with Fox to make *Star Wars,* the studio was shocked to learn that the red hot director was not asking for a lot of money," according to the Star Wars fan site *Supershadow.* Lucas was seeking control, and he got it. Rather than take a director's fee, he wanted 40 percent of the box office grosses, the right to make the final cut of the movie, and all merchandising rights. He had also mapped out a series of three trilogies to tell his sprawling space saga, so Lucas also negotiated the rights to future sequels. "Fox thought they were ripping Lucas off," *Supershadow* continued. "In the 1970s, science fiction films were not very profitable. Sequel and merchandising rights were virtually worthless at the time."

A UNIVERSE OF MERCHANDISING

Lucas also held rights not only for *Star Wars* toys, T-shirts, and coffee mugs; he also produced novels, video games, television series, record albums, and other products that kept the franchise in consumers' minds during the years when there were no films. For decades to follow, the merchandising rights would generate billions in revenues and provide Lucas with the funds to make other movies, as well as pursue technological innovations that continued to drive special effects in motion pictures in the 2010s.

Some reports paint Lucas as a marketing genius and perceptive negotiator who saw the potential in merchandising that studio heads had neglected. *In-Store* magazine wrote that Lucas "understood the potential gold mine that merchandising could be," and the movie's toys and action figures became "the must-have playthings of Christmas 1977." Similarly, Hugh Davies wrote in the *Telegraph* that Lucas "shrewdly persuaded 20th Century Fox in 1977 to allow him to keep the merchandising rights (the studio had expected a flop.)" The magazine *Promotions & Incentives* added, "At the time, the studio is reported to have thought nothing of it: licensing the paraphernalia that accompanies the release of a blockbuster was seen as a sideline to the serious business of making movies." The magazine *Lighting Dimensions* wrote that Fox executives "hooted at the notion of tie-ins to a movie that starred a bunch of unknowns, a couple of robots, and a walking carpet."

In fact, as the *Atlanta Journal-Constitution* noted, "George Lucas didn't discover merchandising. Charlie Chaplin and Walt Disney were on to this from the beginning," with Disney expanding the practice into television. In 1999, when Disney came out with the animated feature *Tarzan,* the *Philadelphia Inquirer* noted that Edgar Rice Burroughs had "sold MGM the movie rights to his creation, but he retained the lucrative merchandising and licensing—just as George Lucas was to do with *Star Wars.*"

However, other reports indicated that what Lucas really wanted was creative control over what would become the most successful movie franchise in history. *Supershadow* wrote that Lucas "wanted control over *Star Wars* in order to keep the movie studio from ruining *Star Wars,* not because Lucas was trying to make the best movie deal in Hollywood history." A 2012 profile in the *New York Times* made a similar case. Reporter Bryan Curtis wrote that Lucas said his first two features, *THX 1138* and *American Graffiti,* were "forcibly re-edited by the studios. Those were wrenching experiences that he has compared to someone keying your car . . . or chopping a finger off one of your children." After those films, Curtis added, "Lucas set out to gain financial independence so the final cut would be forever his."

Writing for the online news site *TG Daily,* David Konow made a similar case. He quoted Tom Pollock, an attorney for Lucas who said he did not think the director had "a giant plan to set himself up as an industry and an empire unto himself." Instead, Pollock said, Lucas wanted to make nine movies to tell the full story, "and he did not want sequel rights ending up in studio development hell where he didn't have the ability to get the movie made." Rather than foreseeing a huge hit that would generate billions, Pollock added, "I think it was more out of fear and distrust of the studios."

While Fox missed out on the merchandising gold mine, the success of the *Star Wars* franchise did help the company recoup its losses from a series of flops and put the studio back on sound financial footing. Ladd, the Fox studio head who had negotiated the deal, told *TG Daily* that Fox made so much from film rentals, it was "not unhappy about George filling his coffers . . . a little more with the merchandising." Ladd said Lucas' agent approached him seeking more merchandising rights rather than a large director salary. "We said fine, because merchandising had never been anything before."

The success of the first *Star Wars* film provided Lucas the funds to implement his strategic and creative vision for the series. While he did not direct the next two films, he wrote or cowrote the scripts and provided the money to produce *The Empire Strikes Back* in 1980 and *The Return of the Jedi* in 1983. The films grossed US$1 billion globally and generated more than US$3 billion in merchandising revenues.

CHANGING HOLLYWOOD'S BUSINESS MODEL

The multiple impacts of *Star Wars* on the movie-making industry were widespread and long-reaching. The three movies, along with Steven Spielberg's 1975 *Jaws,* ushered in the era of summer blockbusters for Hollywood studios. They made stars of newcomers like Mark Hamill (Luke Skywalker), Carrie Fisher (Princess Leia), and Harrison Ford (Han Solo), who would also portray Indiana Jones in a series of four films created by Lucas and Spielberg. The films also reenergized the science fiction genre, where high-quality special effects replaced the low budget, poor production values that had often accompanied earlier "space operas" and horror films.

The success of the *Star Wars* movies also increased Hollywood's interest in merchandising, although the results were not always as impressive as they had been with *Star Wars.* Aljean Harmetz wrote in the *New York Times* in 1989 that before *Jaws,* the "conventional wisdom was that movies didn't stay around long enough to sell merchandise," except for the popular Disney features. Harmetz wrote that before *Star Wars* was released, Fox finally sold the rights for Halloween costumes for US$500. "For *The Empire Strikes Back,* the rights for a Halloween costume sold for six figures."

While merchandising changed the ways movies are packaged and marketed, Lucas' earnings from the fran-chise also directly affected the technology used in film-making. The *Sunday Times* of London noted that an "extended family of filmmakers has benefited from the advances in digital technology forged by Industrial Light & Magic (ILM), a subsidiary of Lucasfilm, formed in 1975 to create the special effects for *Star Wars.*" Films that successfully used ILM technology included the *Jurassic Park, Transformers,* and *Harry Potter* franchises.

In fact, Lucas did not direct another feature film for 20 years. He finally resumed the *Star Wars* series with three prequels, beginning in 1999, that traced the origins of one of the main characters of the saga, Darth Vader. While the second set of films was not as critically acclaimed as the first three, they were moneymakers that introduced a new generation of fans to the saga which created new marketing opportunities. Even Jar Jar Binks, a computer-animated character from *The Phantom Menace* that was described by the *Sydney Morning Herald* as "filmdom's most irritating character," sold action figures.

Aside from directing, Lucas produced a number of films and television series, such as *The Young Indiana Jones Chronicles.* However, most of his attention went to building a multimedia empire centered around his Skywalker Ranch in Marin County, California, where he made advances in computer animation and movie special effects. In addition to ILM, he also created Skywalker Sound, an award-winning audio postproduction firm; THX Ltd., which produces high-quality theater systems for theaters and homes; LucasArts Entertainment Company, LLC, which develops interactive entertainment software; Lucasfilm Animation, which produced the *Star Wars: The Clone Wars* animated television series; and Lucas Online. He was also an early participant in Pixar Animation Studios before Apple's Steve Jobs headed the company.

Lucas Licensing is also a key part of Lucasfilm, and controls the billions of dollars in merchandising income generated by the *Star Wars* series. It has suffered occasional setbacks, such as when the magazine *Art Monthly* reported that the U.K. Supreme Court ruled in 2011 that the designer Andrew Ainsworth was able to sell replicas of the white Stormtroooper uniforms he created for the first movie. However, *Star Wars* continued to hold its position as the top film merchandising franchise. The newsletter *Licensing Letter* reported in 2006 that the films outranked those based on superheroes such as Batman and Spiderman, and Disney movies like *Toy Story* and *The Lion King.* The *Star Phoenix* of Saskatoon, Canada, noted in 2010 that *Star Wars* had been the top toy license for several years, leading the nearest competitor by 40 percent. In 2011, the *Chicago Chronicle* reported that the *Star Wars* movies had earned US$4 billion since 1977, but "the sales of toys, video games, clothing and books have earned nearly six times more, in over 100 countries."

BIBLIOGRAPHY

Academy of Achievement. "George Lucas." Washington, DC, June 7, 2011. Accessed February 10, 2012. http://www .achievement.org/autodoc/page/luc0int-1.

Ahrens, Frank. "'Final 'Star Wars' Caps Moneymaking Empire." *Washington Post,* May 14, 2005. Accessed February 10, 2012. http://www.washingtonpost.com/wp-dyn/content/article /2005/05/13/AR2005051301512.html.

Atkinson, Nathalie. "'Classic Star Wars Films Still Merchandise Force." *The Star-Phoenix* (Saskatoon, Canada), August 17, 2010. Accessed April 11, 2012. http://www2.canada.com /saskatoonstarphoenix/news/arts/story.html?id=b3edb92b -2599-4270-b8a5-61363529c28f&p=2.

Cashill, Robert. "Retail of the Jedi." *Lighting Dimensions,* September 1999. Accessed February 10, 2012. LexisNexis.

Curtis, Bryan. "George Lucas Is Ready to Roll the Credits." *New York Times,* January 17, 2012. Accessed February 10, 2012. http://www.nytimes.com/2012/01/22/magazine/george-lucas -red-tails.html?pagewanted=all.

Davis, Hugh. "Merchandising: Has Lucas Sold Out to the Dark Side?" *Telegraph,* May 7, 2005. Accessed February 10, 2012. http://www.telegraph.co.uk/news/worldnews/northamerica /usa/1489540/Merchandising-Has-Lucas-sold-out-to-the -Dark-Side.html.

Deziel, Shanda. "Toying with the Force." *Maclean's,* May 24, 1999. Accessed February 10, 2012. LexisNexis.

Emerson, Bo. "Series Looks at Birth of Film Industry." *Atlanta Journal-Constitution,* October 19, 2010. Accessed February 10, 2012. www.ajc.com.

"George Lucas." Biography.com, 2012. Accessed February 10, 2012. http://www.biography.com/people/george-lucas-9388168.

Harmetz, Aljean. "Movie Merchandise: The Rush Is On." *New York Times,* June 14, 1989. Accessed February 10, 2012. http://www.nytimes.com/1989/06/14/movies/movie -merchandise-the-rush-is-on.html?pagewanted=all&src=pm.

"'History of Star Wars." *Supershadow,* 2011. Accessed February 10, 2012. http://www.supershadow.com/starwars/history .html.

Internet Movie Database. "George Lucas." Seattle, WA, 2011. Accessed February 10, 2012. http://www.imdb.com/name /nm0000184/

Konow, David. "Lucas's Toy Story." *TG Daily,* January 13, 2012. Accessed February 10, 2012. http://www.tgdaily.com/games -and-entertainment-features/60787-george-lucass-toy-story.

Lawrence, Will. "The Emperor Strikes Back." *Sunday Times (London),* July 27, 2008. Accessed February 10, 2012. LexisNexis.

Lucasfilm Ltd. "Inside Lucasfilm/George Lucas." Nacasio, CA, January 2012. Accessed February 10, 2012. http://www .lucasfilm.com/inside/bio/georgelucas.html.

Lydiate, Henry. "What Is Sculpture?" *Art Monthly,* October 1, 2011. Accessed February 10, 2012. LexisNexis.

"May the Stores Be with You." *In-Store,* June 7, 2005. Accessed February 10, 2012. LexisNexis.

Nicholson, Tom, Deborah Prager, and Tom Kasindorf. "'The Man Who Found the Ark." *Newsweek,* June 15, 1981. Accessed February 10, 2012. LexisNexis.

Ryan, Desmond. "Blame Tarzan, or Rather, His Creator." *Philadelphia Inquirer,* June 13, 1999. Accessed February 10, 2012. http://articles.philly.com/1999-06-13/entertainment /25498582_1_tarzan-forever-edgar-rice-burroughs-tarzan -swings.

Schembri, Jim. "Top Five Reasons to Love Jar Jar Binks." *Sydney Morning Herald,* February 9, 2012. Accessed February 10, 2012. http://www.smh.com.au/entertainment/blogs/cinetopia /top-10-reasons-to-love-jar-jar-binks-20120209-1rtzr.html.

"'Star Wars' Merchandises Earn Six Times More Than Movies." *Chicago Chronicle,* October 21, 2011. Accessed February 10, 2012. http://story.chicagochronicle.com/index.php/ct/9/cid /c08dd24cec417021/id/200300842/cs/1/.

"Star Wars Ranks as Top Film Merchandising Franchise." *Licensing Letter,* September 18, 2006. Accessed February 10, 2012. LexisNexis.

"Star Wars: The Old Republic Continues Meteoric Rise in Becoming the Latest Online Phenomenon." *News Blaze,* February 1, 2012. Accessed February 10, 2012. http:// newsblaze.com/story/2012020115285600001.bw/topstory .html.

Sydell, Laura. "'Star Wars' Merchandise Still Sells After 30 Years." *National Public Radio,* March 25, 2007. Accessed February 10, 2012. http://www.npr.org/templates/story/story.php ?storyId=10431190 .

Thompson, Anne. "Reaping 'Willow': The Campaign to Capture Your Heart and Wallet: A Military Campaign." *Chicago Tribune,* May 15, 1988. Accessed February 10, 2012. LexisNexis.

"'Why Entertainment Is a Hit for Licensing." *Promotions & Incentives,* October 20, 2005. Accessed February 10, 2012. LexisNexis.

Glad Bags:
Brand Building and Integrated Marketing

The Glad brand line of plastic storage bags and garbage bags is sold commercially and is one of the more recognized brands of plastic bags for waste and food storage. Glad bags include food storage bags such as sandwich bags, zippered food storage bags, and freezer bags. The brand also includes a range of garbage bags. Low-density polyethylene is used to produce both plastic bags and plastic wraps. However, the Glad brand adds other materials to some of its bags to make them scented or to give them greater strength. As of 2012 the Glad brand was owned partly by the Procter & Gamble Company and primarily by the Clorox Company.

The first Glad bags were developed in the 1960s. However, the history of food storage and plastic bags goes back to the 1940s, when plastic garbage bags were introduced after World War II. By the time Glad was developing its range of bags, plastic food storage bags had already been invented. Robert W. Vergobbi patented a design for a plastic storage bag in May 1954. That same year they were licensed by the firm Minigrip Inc. In 1957 the winner of the National Science Fair used zippered plastic bags to demonstrate how they could keep food fresh.

THE INVENTION OF GLAD BAGS

Dr. Douglas Lyons Ford was a research chemist with Union Carbide Corporation in Australia in the early 1960s. At the Sydney Rhodes, Australia plant in 1963 he developed Glad Wrap, a sticky polyethylene wrap for covering food to prevent it from spoiling. Polyethylene (a basic plastic) had already been invented by Reginald Gibson and Eric Fawcett in 1933, and Saran Wrap was already on the U.S. market when Union Carbide introduced its own Glad Wrap in 1963. In September 1966 both Glad Bags and Glad Wrap were introduced in the United States and in Australia. Plastic disposable garbage bags were invented even earlier by Harry Wasylyk and Larry Hansen of Lindsay, Canada, in 1950. Originally intended for commercial use, they were first sold to a hospital. However, Union Carbide purchased the idea and began selling Glad garbage bags in the late 1960s.

In the middle of the 1980s Union Carbide faced some financial problems following the Bhopal gas disaster in India. This disaster occurred at the Union Carbide India Limited pesticide plant in Bhopal, India. Between December 2 and 3, 1984, a leak of methyl isocyanate gas developed, and exposure to the gas resulted in the deaths of thousands of people. Tens of thousands suffered injuries. Union Carbide faced multiple lawsuits as a result of the disaster and had to reevaluate its poorly performing assets to generate revenue for settlements.

In this situation, Union Carbide was at risk for a hostile takeover. In 1986 Harold Simmons and Samuel Heyman of GAF Corporation, a specialty chemicals and building materials company, created a plan to buy up Union Carbide. Working with other stakeholders and raising money from shareholders, banks, and a bond issuance, they were able to buy up enough of Union Carbide to take control of the business. The stakeholders, including those from GAF and others, reorganized as the First Brands Corporation. When First Brands was created in 1986, it controlled much of Union Carbide's brands, including Prestone antifreeze, Glad-Lock bags, Glad, and Simoniz wax. However, First Brands Corporation in 1987 had US$674 million of debt and only US$76.6 million in capital, putting the new entity into a precarious position.

MAKING GLAD BAGS A SUCCESS

First Brands had to take drastic measures to safeguard its new acquisition. The company slashed the staff by 9.4 percent and moved headquarters to a more affordable location in Danbury, Connecticut. First Brands also sold the manufacturing equipment used to make Glad Bags, in order to raise US$168 million for the acquisition, and then leased the same equipment back for far less.

Once the company reduced spending, First Brands started to focus on improving the brand image for its brands. For Glad Bags, the company launched recyclable garbage bags, Glad bags with handles, and Glad-Lock Zipper Bags. With an interlocking closure system that had a distinctive "Yellow and Blue Make Green" feature, the Glad-Lock Zipper Bags became the most successful product launch that First Brands had created up to that point. The unique dual-color zipper was patented in 1980 by George F. Kirkpatrick and Union Carbide Corp.

The Glad-Lock Zipper Bags were actually an initial failure in marketing tests, according to Barry Feig in *Hot Button Marketing: Push the Emotional Buttons That Get People to Buy*. Early marketing tests revealed that customers found the bags, then called Snap Lock, to be expensive, not better than the competitor brands, and not very memorable. First Brands then developed a Glad zipper bag that had a sealable strip that changed color to green when closed. Test groups did not like this new product, either, but according to Feig, test marketers found that women wanted their "husband and kids to seal the bag" to help preserve foods. This gave First Brands marketers a new idea. When they conducted the next marketing test, according to Feig, they marketed the newly named Glad-Lock Zipper Bags as "The bag that's so simple, husbands and kids get it right every time." This time, the response to the bags was positive, and Glad-Lock Zipper Bags went on the market, where they became a successful Glad product.

NEW CHALLENGES AND OPPORTUNITIES

In 1986 First Brands also launched the first "Glad Bag-A-Thon" in partnership with Keep America Beautiful Inc. The litter cleanup program started in five cities but soon expanded into a U.S. nationwide event. In 1996, according to Thomas L. Harris in *Value-Added Public Relations: The Secret Weapon of Integrated Marketing*, the Glad Bag-A-Thon collected more than 28 million pounds of recyclables and litter across the United States. More than one million volunteers took part in the event. While the Glad Bag-A-Thon program was meant to clean up litter, raise awareness about litter, and increase awareness of recycling, it was also a savvy marketing program. In 1997 alone, four million boxes of Glad bags were distributed to stores as part of the program. Each box contained coupons for Glad bags as well as information about the Glad Bag-A-Thon.

In the late 1980s First Brands also focused on distribution, in part to pay down the debts acquired during the Union Carbide deal. The rise of the big-box retail store helped with distributing Glad Bags and other First Brands products. Rather than being just sold in grocery stores, Glad Bags could now be shipped in large bulk shipments to larger retailers. By 1989 First Brands was reporting profits of US$61 million and sales of US$1.2 billion.

In 1991 First Brands faced a major challenge with its Glad Bag products. The company had been claiming that Glad Bags were degradable, in part because of media coverage about the environmental impact of plastic bags. While the bags were compostable and did break down, the U.S. Federal Trade Commission (FTC) claimed that First Brands made false claims about the degradability of Glad Bags because the bags were found not to decompose completely when they were covered up in landfills and not exposed to the elements. First Brands agreed to stop its claims about the degradable nature of Glad Bags. However, the incident had no impact on sales.

By 1992 First Brands wanted to take advantage of the popularity of the Glad-Lock Bags and also wanted to lower costs further. Therefore, it decided to move some operations to Virginia to take advantage of lower taxes and costs. With this move, the company also expanded the manufacturing capacity of its Glad Bag line. The company retained Glad Bag plants in Arkansas and Georgia.

In 1998 Industrial Equity Limited purchased the Glad brand in Australia, and by 1991 the brand was part of National Foods. By 1997 Glad in Australia was acquired by First Brands, and there was no longer as large a divide between Australian Glad and U.S. Glad brands as the brand ownership was consolidated worldwide under First Brands. In 1998 Clorox purchased First Brands for US$2 billion, including the Glad brand. By 2002 the Glad brand became a joint venture because Procter & Gamble was allowed to buy a 10 percent share in what was then known as the Glad Products Company. By 2005 Procter & Gamble owned 20 percent.

According to Jack Neff, writing in *Ad Age*, Glad Bags could face another challenge in the 2010s. While larger store chains such as Wal-Mart had been a major source of sales for Glad, Wal-Mart announced plans in 2010 to streamline its brand offerings, promoting its own Great Value brand while reducing the number of brand options available to customers. As a result of this policy, Wal-Mart would no longer offer Glad brand food bags in its stores. Instead, the retailer offered its own Great Value food storage bags. Glad trash bags would continue to be available at Wal-Mart in the near future, but the loss of Wal-Mart store shelves was a blow to the Glad food storage bags, as Wal-Mart accounted for at least a third of Glad bag sales, according to Neff in the *Ad Age* article. Other large retailers, including Walgreen Co. and CVS Caremark Corporation, also reduced the numbers of brands available in their stores, possibly indicating a larger overall trend. Many manufacturers, including Glad, increased marketing spending in response. Between 2008 and 2009 alone, Glad increased marketing spending by about 58 percent, to US$57.9 million.

GLAD PRODUCTS

Glad food bags for food storage were introduced in the 1960s. Since then, the company added many types of bags to its line of products. As of 2012 Glad offered recycling bags, compost bags, food storage bags, and garbage bags of all sizes. Glad also offered compostable bags, which were made with 40 percent vegetable-based materials so that they broke down in community compost programs.

Glad also had a wide range of garbage bags, including ones made from 65 percent recycled plastics and bags made in just about every size. Glad also made garbage bags with Glad OdorShield which, according to the company, helped contain odors. One of the more popular lines of Glad garbage bags was ForceFlex, which came in various sizes and was designed with a tear-resistant plastic that did not rip easily. The company contended that the bags were made with Stretchable Strength plastic that was originally designed for other industries. The diamond-shape pattern on the bag, claimed the company, helped change the impact of weight on the bag, making the bag more resistant to tearing. Glad also made garbage bags specifically for yard waste as well as bags for contractors. The Glad garbage bags for contractors were larger and thicker, and some featured ForceFlex or Stretchable Strength material. Some Glad bags also featured easy-tie closure methods, including the Quick-Tie drawstring tops.

Glad also made a wide range of kitchen garbage bags. In 2010 the Glad Products Company announced that some of its Glad kitchen garbage bags would be made with less plastic. The bags used 6.5 percent less plastic than previous versions of the same Glad bags. According to the company, this modest decrease was expected to reduce plastic consumption by 6.5 million pounds a year. The bags also featured reinforcing bands to make the products stronger. The company decided not to increase the costs for these products. While Glad Products Company planned to spend US$30 million to US$40 million to launch the new kitchen garbage bags, the focus was on more subtle marketing, according to a 2011 article in the *New York Times* by Stuart Elliott. The company focused on emphasizing the strength of the product with taglines such as "stronger with less plastic waste" and "strength with less plastic."

Glad also still had many Glad food storage bags, including zipper bags with the famous Yellow and Blue

Make Green Seal, as well as zipper freezer bags, twist-tie food storage bags, and fold-top bags. The Glad food storage zipper bags still featured an extra-wide seal that promised to be easy to close and open. In 2000 Glad introduced the new Glad Stand & Zip food storage bags. These bags had a wide base, so that they would remain standing up as they were filled with food. However, despite heavy advertising of the new product, the bags were discontinued a few years later.

In Australia, a different range of Glad garbage bags and kitchen tidy bags were launched. GLAD Snap Lock Bags were launched in the 1980s, and in 1993, Glad introduced GLAD® WaveTop Tie Bags. The patented design involved two ties, one to secure the bag and the other to allow the user to carry it. In Australia, the launch of GLAD WaveTop Tie Bags doubled the share of the kitchen tidy bag market that Glad enjoyed by 1994. GLAD Ice Cube Bags were introduced in Australia in 1993. Developed and patented in Denmark, the bags allow users to make ice cubes without using an ice cube tray.

GLAD BAG MARKETING

Like many companies, Glad relied heavily on advertising and marketing to position its products in the marketplace. For many years, Glad commercials and advertisements featured an older man, most famously played by actor Tom Bosley of *Happy Days,* who would give households advice about garbage and food storage. Known as the "Man from Glad," the actor would often be shown wearing a suit. One commercial from 1986, for example, showed a small child carrying a leaking (generic) garbage bag and then a Glad garbage bag, which did not leak. Bosley provided the voice-over for the advertisement and the tagline: "Why Take Chances? Get Glad." The commercial was available as of 2012 on popular video-sharing sites such as YouTube.

Another popular slogan for Glad was "Don't Get Mad, Get Glad." The slogan was used in commercials and in advertisements showing people's frustrations with other brands of plastic bags. For example, in one 1988 television commercial, a woman was shown getting frustrated when a plastic brand of resealable bags left an odor in her refrigerator. A voice-over told her that "only Glad-Lock bags change from yellow and blue to green to seal in freshness."

Glad also relied on print advertising to promote its products. In 2005, for example, the company worked with advertising company DDB San Francisco to create some print advertisements for its Glad Press'n Seal Bags. The premise of the Glad bags was that customers could roll out strips of wrap and create their own customized bags or wrap for anything they needed. The resealable product could be used to create customized wrapping around many different sizes and shapes of products. The print advertisements in the campaign showed Glad Press'n Seal Bags around a goldfish bowl, a single pea pod, a pear in a tree, and other objects that could not traditionally be contained in a plastic bag.

One thing that made Glad bags a success was the frequent launching of new products, and even more importantly, careful use of marketing and promotion to differentiate the products from those of competitors. Glad marketing played up differences in its advertising, in some cases emphasizing that it outperformed competitors or was unique because of a two-color zipper on its plastic bags. In addition, the brand made careful use of ethical advertising, stressing its commitment to the environment at a time when many people were leery about the impact of plastic bags on the environment. These savvy strategies allowed Glad to succeed, even with strong competition from Ziploc, Hefty, and other bag brands.

BIBLIOGRAPHY

"1988–Commercial–Glad-Lock Reclosable Storage Bags– Don't Get Mad, Get Glad-Lock Bags." [Video] Uploaded December 28, 2011. Accessed January 16, 2012. http://www.youtube .com/watch?v=zclBXoG3yNI.

Clorox Australia Pty Limited. "About Glad." Sydney, Australia, 2012. Accessed January 15, 2012. http://www.glad.com.au /about-glad/glad-history/.

"Clorox Company Ads & Commercials Archive." Coloribus, Creative Adverting Archive, 2012. Accessed January 16, 2012. http://www.coloribus.com/advertisers/clorox-company -6117255,brands-glad,products-glad-pressn-seal-bags/.

Elliott, Stuart. "Glad Cuts the Hyperbole for Its New Green Trash Bag." *New York Times,* October 18, 2011. Accessed January 16, 2012. http://www.nytimes.com/2011/10/19 /business/media/glad-cuts-the-hyperbole-for-its-new-green -trash-bag.html.

Feig, Barry. *Hot Button Marketing: Push the Emotional Buttons That Get People to Buy.* Avon, MA: Adams Media, 2006, 38–39.

"First Brands Corporation." *International Directory of Company Histories,* edited by Paula Kepos. Vol. 9, 180–182. Detroit: St. James Press, 1994. Gale Virtual Reference Library (GALE|CX2841200063). Accessed January 16, 2012. http:// go.galegroup.com/ps/i.do?id=GALE%7CCX2841200063&v =2.1&u=itsbtrial&it=r&p=GVRL&sw=w.

Glad. "Glad Food Storage." Oakland, CA, 2012. Available from http://www.glad.com/. Accessed January 15, 2012.

"Glad Garbage Bags Commercial (1986)." [Video] Uploaded August 13, 2006. Accessed January 16, 2012. http://www .youtube.com/watch?v=4Ide9dgoZkk.

Harris, Thomas L. *Value-Added Public Relations: The Secret Weapon of Integrated Marketing.* Chicago, IL: NTC Business Books, 1998, 201.

Kelly, Anne Marie. "Glad Trash Bags Go Greener." *Forbes,* November 28, 2011. January 16, 2012. http://www.forbes .com/sites/annemariekelly/2011/10/28/glad-trash-bags-go -greener/.

Neff, Jack. "Walmart Food-Bag Consolidation Wipes Glad, Hefty from Shelves." *Ad Age,* February 4, 2010. Accessed January 16, 2012. http://adage.com/article/news/walmart -food-bag-consolidation-leaves-glad-hefty/141918/.

"New Modern Convenience: The Plastic Bag." *Canadian Broadcasting Corporation (CBC) Digital Archives,* August 4, 2009. Accessed January 16, 2012. http://archives.cbc.ca /lifestyle/homemaking/clips/16996/.

"Plastic Bags." *Packaging Knowledge,* 2009. Accessed January 16, 2012. http://www.packagingknowledge.com/plastic_bags.asp.

Weinberg, Adam S., David N. Pellow, and Allan Schnaiberg. *Urban Recycling and the Search for Sustainable Community Development.* Princeton, NJ: Princeton University Press, 2000.

Google, Inc., and Its Ever Evolving Search Engine Business

Google, Inc., was an international juggernaut in 2011. Having risen to prominence in little more than a decade since its founding in 1998, the company's search engine claimed roughly two-thirds of the market, according to a December 2011 *Social Barrel* article. Some countries in Europe tilted even more in favor of the giant, while Beijing's Baidu retained dominance in China. In 2010, 96 percent of Google's US$29 billion in revenue came from its AdSense and AdWords campaigns, according to the company's annual report. These programs allowed businesses to promote their websites and products to targeted audiences. In the same year, the company claimed 24,400 full-time employees. Company focus was on creating and fine-tuning its search algorithm to make the web browsing interface as useful as possible. Google also reached well beyond this and offered a range of programs, such as Google Docs and Google Mail, as well as a mobile operating system, Android.

Google first achieved success through its initial innovation in web searching technology, PageRank. The idea came from the academic system used for article citations. Academicians measured an article's success, in large part, by the number of times it was cited by others. Applying the same principle to the Internet, PageRank defined the value of a web page partly by its popularity, or the number of other web pages that linked to it. Thus, increasing the number of incoming links for a given page increased that page's position on the search engine results page. In theory, the more useful web pages then received more web traffic and gravitated to the top of the rankings. Additionally, the system evaluated links depending upon source, so links coming from well-established, networked sites were worth more than their counterparts from unknown sources.

This improvement, though simple as a concept, made it significantly easier to search the Internet and more likely that search results would provide more relevant results to help Internet users. According to a case history by *The Economist* in September 2004, "Google was vastly better than anything that had come before: so much better, in fact, that it changed the way many people use the web. Almost overnight, it made the web far more useful."

GOOGLE'S PRECURSORS

In the 1990s a number of research projects, most of them academically oriented, attempted to make the Internet more searchable. The World Wide Web Wanderer and the World Wide Web Worm were two of the first attempts. These indexed page titles, addresses, and headers. In 1994 WebCrawler was created at the University of Washington and was the first metasearch engine to read the entire contents of the pages it indexed. Lycos and Infoseek came next, all with varying degrees of success.

However, they were all eclipsed by the AltaVista search program, which sprung from Digital Equipment Corporation in 1995. Conceived by Louis Monier, AltaVista used hundreds of spiders (programs to grab websites), many more than its predecessors, to sort through the Internet. These operated in parallel to search more websites than ever before. It was also successful due to its modular design, which allowed the search engine to return results quickly, even when hundreds of thousands of Internet users flocked to its homepage.

AltaVista had speed and breadth but it lacked usability because it could not distinguish between the sites that were well designed and those that were not. Without a means of distinguishing between good and bad, the algorithm forced users to do this manually, which took a considerable amount of time and effort. The website did feature a number of queries and experienced users could use these tools to narrow the results; however, most people were still frustrated by the web search experience, until Google.

PAGE AND BRIN CREATE PAGERANK

In 1995, the same year that AltaVista launched, Google founders Larry Page and Sergey Brin met as graduate students at Stanford University's Computer Science Department. Respect was mutual, but they tended to bicker more than agree. When Page started to consider ideas for his doctoral dissertation, Terry Winograd, his advisor, encouraged him to pursue his conceptualization of the Internet, which relied on connections between academia and the web. In the attempt to understand something as vast and chaotic as the Internet, Page relied on what he knew, which was the academic world. As he reported to John Battelle for *Wired*'s August 2005 issue, first, he conceptualized the Internet as a graph. From there, pursuing the topic led to a more specific idea of the World Wide Web as a system of citations. The links on a website, to him, were like the list of references on an academic paper. At the time, this conceptualization could not have been further from reality, but PageRank was to alter that.

At the time, it was easy to trace links outward, from a web page to external sites, but counting incoming links (such as from a user to a Web site) was the challenge. Page created a program called BackRub in response. Some links, Page reasoned, should carry more value than others, depending on the reputation and quality of their source. The problem lay in determining what should be measured first. Evaluating one page correctly required the values of all the sites linking to it, and the value of each of those sites could not be derived until each of *its* sources had been found. Thus, computing one value relied on what seemed to come afterward, and vice versa. That is when Sergey Brin arrived on the scene. The son of a math professor, Brin was considered a prodigy. Interested in both the nature of the project and in its author, Brin used math concepts such as recursive logic and linear algebra to find the solution.

Originally BackRub was programmed to calculate value through an iterative, or repeating, process. In the program's first run-through, each incoming link was given the same weight. Thus each site was given a score based on the sum of incoming links. Then the program went through a second calculation, which took the weight of each site into account. A new set of values was determined and the process would begin again. Eventually, the scores of each site would stabilize. The websites with the largest

systems of links gravitated toward the top scores, while the ones with fewer "connections" fell to the bottom.

Once they started playing with the results of BackRub, Page and Brin realized the algorithm was easily and usefully applied to searching the web. The makeshift search program demonstrated immediately superior results when compared to other contemporary search engines. They named the program "google" after the number googol, or 10 to the 100th power.

Brin joined the project in 1996, and by the fall of the same year, Google was known throughout Stanford and in the academic community at large. Borrowing computers and splicing servers together from friends, charity, and academic departments to continue indexing the web, Page and Brin were shocked to find Google taking on a life of its own, expanding more quickly than either could have predicted. The engine was too powerful for Stanford's Internet connection, forcing temporary shutdowns. Nevertheless, Page hesitated to start a company until 1998, when he and Brin finally formed Google, Inc.

REVOLUTIONIZING THE WEB: ADWORDS, ADSENSE, SUCCESS

Even though the Google search engine was a remarkable success in the academic community, it took some time for Page and Brin to organize a corporation. This was due in part to the death of Page's father, which motivated the entrepreneur to finish graduate school before going into business. The lag also stretched out because, according to Tony Long in his September 2011 *Wired* article, "Their technology was solid, but not solid enough to impress either the money boys or the major internet portals." Finally, on September 7, 1998, the two pitched Google to Andy Bechtolsheim, Sun Microsystems cofounder. The software tycoon interrupted the presentation, saying he had to make another appointment, but he left them with a check for US$100,000 anyway.

With funding secured, the company experienced a breakneck pace of expansion. In 1999 alone, it moved its headquarters from a garage in Menlo Park, California, to an office in Palo Alto, California. The company fielded 500,000 queries per day and had eight employees. Two years later, during which time most dot-coms suffered from the bursting financial bubble, Google gained momentum, and the company prepared for its initial public offering (IPO).

AdWords was unveiled in late 2000 as a way to secure revenue. AdWords was and continues to be a form of targeted advertising, which aims to deliver relevant advertisements to Google search-engine users. Businesses pay a fee to deliver their advertisements and links to the search results page. Advertisements are targeted depending on the specific keywords typed into the search bar.

Initially, subscribers paid an agreed fee for each click. That is, Google charged a fee only when a user clicked on an advertisement.

By contrast, the AdSense program, which was released in 2003, allowed independent businesses to post advertisements linking back to subscribers of AdWords. Members of the AdSense program could post links and advertisements on their websites and were paid each time a site visitor clicked on a link. A portion of the payment was distributed to Google as well. According to company reports, by 2003 advertising revenues increased to US$1.5 billion and investors started clamoring for stock.

In the process of designing its means of revenue (and later, while going public), the company carved out a user-oriented ethos. Google, Inc., expressed and reiterated a fundamental drive to make the Internet easier to use and to facilitate the exchange of information. Its 2004 Registration Statement to the U.S. Securities Exchange Commission (SEC) declared: "We believe strongly that in the long term, we will be better served—as shareholders and in all other ways—by a company that does good things for the world even if we forgo some short term gains."

Other definitive values emerged from the company's IPO, which was conducted as an auction. By allowing prospective investors to influence the price of its stock directly, Google ensured that investment firms could not manipulate pricing. In so doing, the company democratized the offering process. In August 2004, barely eight years after PageRank was only a notion, Google raised US$1.67 billion and was valued at US$27 billion, according to an August 20, 2004 *New York Times* article which characterized the company as follows: "Google still exudes that unabashed Silicon Valley anti-establishment attitude. . . . Nowhere was that more apparent than in the way it sought to dictate to Wall Street the terms of its own sale." Both in theory and in practice, the company sent a strong, coherent message to investors and the U.S. public. Revenue was a side effect, not a goal. Over the next seven years, as the company garnered billions of advertising dollars and swelled to gargantuan proportions, it continued to prove the irony of this declaration.

CONTINUED EXPANSION BRINGS COMPETITION, CRITICISM, AND COURT CASES

Soon after its IPO and before the company surpassed Yahoo! Inc. in advertising revenue, Google, Inc., started to expand its range of services and products. Innovation was a deep part of the corporate culture. In fact, the company's chief economist, Hal R. Varian, revealed to Steve Lohr of the *New York Times*, "The source of Google's competitive advantage is learning by doing." Corporate culture and a host of new products proved his point. For example, all

Google employees were encouraged to spend roughly 20 percent of their time looking into personal projects as opposed to completing assignments dictated by their position. As such, a host of newly developed software was released.

Some of these innovations, such as Google Desktop Search, placed the company in direct competition with other corporations. Google Desktop Search aimed to search not only the Internet but also the user's computer, pitting the newly registered company against Microsoft Corporation's operating systems. The market was competitive even before Google's entry, with Apple Inc. and Amazon.com, Inc. also developing similar technology. Other programs, such as Google Print, Google Mail, Google Chrome, and Google SMS could also be viewed as forays into already competitive markets. Later, Google's Android operating system took hold in the mobile market. In all these projects, the corporate model was to cut the unsuccessful ventures and keep the ones that worked. The method took the mindset of a Silicon Valley venture capitalist and applied it within a single company.

Meanwhile, experts continued to revise PageRank, AdSense, and AdWords. In part, these adjustments were forced by businesses who tried to gain an unfair advantage in the online marketplace through various search engine optimization techniques. For example, since the search engine placed value on incoming links, some companies created entire networks of websites to boost their value artificially. Google, Inc. computer scientists constantly adjusted the algorithm to thwart attempts to cheat the system. As of 2009, the company had allocated 70 percent of its resources on the search engine and advertising system, according to its annual report.

With revenues of US$23.7 billion that year, according to the same report, competitors were almost totally eclipsed. Yahoo!'s position was in decline, down to 18 percent of Internet searches. Microsoft's renovated and renamed engine, Bing, vied for market share but only eked out 10 percent in the same year, according to a November 2009 article in *The Economist*. When it came to light that Bing relied, in part, on data from Google's search results, Microsoft lost more of its credibility. China's Baidu was the only serious competitor and friction with the Chinese government's demands for censorship eventually caused Google to exit China in March 2010. Slightly over one year later, Baidu claimed 75.9 percent market share in its home country, according to a July 2011 study by EnfoDesk, an entity of Analysys International.

With the exception of China, Google claimed international dominance in online search requests and its prominence invited investigations, probes, and antitrust cases. Although many of these were minor, 2011 saw an escalation in the severity of litigation. In Europe, a number of business entities, some of which were owned by Microsoft, submitted claims that led to a 400-page statement of objections. The U.S. Federal Trade Commission (FTC) launched a civil probe in June, which Thomas Catan and Amir Efrati of the *Wall Street Journal* called "the most serious threat to the 12-year-old company." The company faced allegations of anticompetitive behavior, such as directing web traffic to Google, Inc. products. Among the Google, Inc. products under fire was a service, introduced in 2009, that directed users seeking information about mortgages and credit cards to the Google marketplace.

KEEPING THE SEARCH ENGINE MARKET SECURE

PageRank singlehandedly created an online market. Prior to its existence, the vastness of the Internet was an obstacle standing between would-be users and the information or services they sought. Rather than standing as a gatekeeper of this obstacle and charging a toll, Google, Inc., offered its benefits for free. Later, AdWords and AdSense brought in revenue from businesses. The entire system fell under a selfless, user-centric ethos, which made the company difficult to attack, though many companies and governments tried.

To maintain its advantage, Google reinvested most of its money into its own growth. PageRank itself was constantly being adapted to developments in business and consumer preferences to stay ahead of the competition and ensure the quality of its primary money maker. Beyond that, the company invested heavily to provide all new services for free. Google e-mail (Gmail), Google Maps, Google Books, and so on functioned as the company's advertising, bringing additional users to the Google website and furthering the site's momentum.

BIBLIOGRAPHY

"Analysys International: Baidu Occupied 76% of China Internet Search Market in 2011 Q2." Beijing, China: Analysys International, July 25, 2011. Accessed December 29, 2011. http://english.analysys.com.cn/article.php?aid=108692.

Battelle, John. "The Birth of Google." *Wired*, August 2005. Accessed December 29, 2011. http://www.wired.com/wired/archive/13.08/battelle.html?tw=wn_tophead_4.

Brin, Sergey, and Lawrence Page. "The Anatomy of a Large-Scale Hypertextual Web Search Engine." Master's Paper, Stanford University, 1997. Accessed December 29, 2011. http://infolab.stanford.edu/~backrub/google.html.

Catan, Thomas, and Amir Afrati. "Feds to Launch Probe of Google." *Wall Street Journal*, June 24, 2011. Accessed December 29, 2011. http://online.wsj.com/article/SB10001424052702303339904576403603764717680.html.

"Google Goes Public." *New York Times*, August 20, 2004. Accessed December 29, 2011. http://www.nytimes.com/2004/08/20/opinion/google-goes-public.html?src=pm.

Google, Inc. "2009 Annual Report." Mountain View, CA, December 31, 2009. Accessed December 29, 2011. http://investor.google.com/documents/2009_google_annual_report.html.

———. "2010 Annual Report." Mountain View, CA, December 31, 2010. Accessed December 29, 2011. http://investor.google.com/documents/20101231_google_10K.html.

Greenberg, Andy. "The Man Who's Beating Google." *Forbes*, September 16, 2009. Accessed December 29, 2011. http://www.forbes.com/forbes/2009/1005/technology-baidu-robin-li-man-whos-beating-google_4.html.

"How Google Works." *The Economist*, September 16, 2004. Accessed December 29, 2011. http://www.economist.com/node/3171440.

Lohr, Steve. "Google, Zen Master of the Market." *New York Times*, July 7, 2008. Accessed December 29, 2011. http://www.nytimes.com/2008/07/07/technology/07google.html?pagewanted=all.

Long, Tony. "Sept. 7, 1998: If the Check Says 'Google Inc.,' We're 'Google Inc.'." *Wired*, September 7, 2007. Accessed December 29, 2011. http://www.wired.com/science/discoveries/news/2007/09/dayintech_0907.

Markoff, John. "Google Envy Is Fomenting Search Wars." *New York Times*, October 18, 2004. Accessed December 29, 2011. http://www.nytimes.com/2004/10/18/technology/18search.html?_r=1&adxnnl=1&ref=googleinc&adxnnlx=1325193457-Cly3ZuhDP4V0FmviABr4TQ.

McDonald, Joe. "Baidu Profits Up 80 Percent, Chinese Search Engine Forecasts More Growth." *Huffington Post*, October 27, 2011. Accessed December 29, 2011. http://www.huffingtonpost.com/2011/10/28/baidu-profits-china-search-engine_n_1063485.html.

Rey, Francis. "Google Slammed with 400-Page Objection from the European Commission." *Social Barrel*, December 4, 2011. Accessed December 29, 2011. http://socialbarrel.com/google-slammed-with-400-page-objection-from-the-european-commission/28326.

Rosoff, Matt. "Yes, Bing Has Been Copying Google Search Results for Years." *Business Insider*, February 1, 2011. Accessed December 29, 2011. http://articles.businessinsider.com/2011-02-01/tech/29975847_1_bing-director-stefan-weitz-satya-nadella-msn-toolbar.

"Searching for Evidence." *The Economist*, June 23, 2011. Accessed December 29, 2011. http://www.economist.com/blogs/schumpeter/2011/06/google-and-antitrust.

TED. "Speakers Sergey Brin and Larry Page: Co-founders of Google." New York, 2004. Accessed December 29, 2011. http://www.ted.com/speakers/sergey_brin_and_larry_page.html.

U.S. Securities and Exchange Commission. "Amendment No. 4 to Form S-1 Registration Statement." Washington DC, July 26, 2004. Accessed December 29, 2011. http://sec.gov/Archives/edgar/data/1288776/000119312504124025/ds1a.htm.

Walker, David J. "Senators Khol, Lee Call for FTC Investigation of Google." *Social Barrel*, December 21, 2011. Accessed December 29, 2011. http://socialbarrel.com/senators-khol-lee-call-for-ftc-investigation-of-google/29284/.

"Web-Wide War." *The Economist*, November 25, 2009. Accessed December 29, 2011. http://www.economist.com/node/14955213.

Yared, Peter. "Google Already Knows Its Search Sucks (and Is Working to Fix It)." *VentureBeat,* January 12, 2011. Accessed December 29, 2011. http://venturebeat.com/2011/01/12 /google-search.

Google's AdWords and AdSense Equal Advertising Dollars

Larry Page and Sergey Brin founded Google, Inc., in 1998 as an improved search engine without any foreseeable revenue streams. Little more than a decade later, the corporation earned US$29 billion and employed 24,400 full-time professionals, according to its 2010 annual report. Though not part of Google's initial business pitch, the Google AdWords and AdSense campaigns brought in almost all the company's funds. According to the company's 2010 annual report, roughly 96 percent of revenues came from advertisements. Projects in freeware, such as Google Mail, Google Docs, and the Android mobile operating system, did not add profits directly, though these promoted, facilitated, and added convenience to the use of Google search. Increased traffic flowing through the website added value to business promotions conducted via AdWords and AdSense. If the search engine site's advertisements served as the main stream, then the various freeware were the tributaries.

EARLY DAYS: PAGERANK

PageRank gave the corporation its initial competitive advantage. Page and Brin developed the addition to search engine coding in 1996. As part of Page's pursuit of a doctoral degree in computer science at Stanford University in California, he conceptualized the World Wide Web, instead of the chaos of sites that it was, as a system of citation, similar to that used for academic papers. At the time, AltaVista was the most useful search engine, but one of its weaknesses was that it could not differentiate reputable sites from those that were of little value. Search results were unorganized, at best, with the most useful sites just as likely to turn up at the end of a results page as on the first page.

As a true academic, Page did not even consider the business application of his ideas when formulating his theory. Attempting to understand the web, he compared it to what he knew best, the academic world. Seeing links as a more dynamic form of citation, he reasoned that, just as the quality of an academic paper could be measured quantitatively by the number of studies that cited it, the value of a website could be determined by the number of links coming in from other web addresses. Page began to develop a program, called BackRub, to perform the necessary calculations.

The program still needed another addition to ensure accuracy. Links coming from more popular sources needed to carry more weight than others. While the first problem required a vast catalogue of all the websites and links on the web, the second necessitated a deeper level of mathematical understanding. Sergey Brin, the son of a mathematics professor and a veritable prodigy in his own right, supplied the recursive logic and linear algebra necessary to create the PageRank algorithm. In short order, Page and Brin realized that their program could be used in a powerful search engine. With the help of a US$100,000 check from Sun Microsystems, Inc., cofounder Andy Bechtolsheim, the two computer scientists incorporated Google, Inc., in 1998, roughly two years after joining forces.

PAY-PER-PLACEMENT AND ADWORDS

When Page and Brin started thinking about making their fledgling corporation profitable, banner advertisements (large advertisements often across the top of a website) were the standard revenue stream. These used images and media to attract traffic to a site but did little else. The 2010 article "Bubble Blinders: The Untold Story of the Search Business Model," indicated that, according to Ali Partovi, founder of LinkExchange, the concept of targeted, search-engine advertising was already circulating in Silicon Valley, California when Google was first incorporated. Three start-up companies, Viaweb, Submit-it, and Goto.com, played with the fundamental concept behind Adwords. Paul Graham, founder of Viaweb, even pitched an idea to Yahoo! Inc., which utilized a similar system for advertisements. The program was designed to help users find the right product to suit their needs. In return, the engine would yield a small commission from user purchases. If a consumer clicked on a product and bought it, then a percentage of the revenues would return to the search engine. Over time, the program was designed to favor the products that brought in the most revenue, a model similar to Google's search engine and AdWords campaign.

Scott Banister, founder of Submit-It, came up with the idea of pay-for-placement advertising, or what he called "Keywords." The concept was to allow companies to pay to increase the position of their websites on the search engine results page. A company could place a bid for particular keywords that were relevant to its product or website, and whenever the keyword was typed into a search, the company's website would appear at the top of the search results. Thus, small businesses that were not well known or established could have a chance to attract new clients. When Google launched AdWords in 2000, it integrated a similar bidding system with its other search factors, such as PageRank, so that the more proven sites retained their competitive advantage.

According to Partovi, Banister pitched Keywords to a number of entrepreneurs and companies, including Bill Gross, the man who takes more direct credit for pay-for-placement. Gross founded Goto.com in 1998 to execute the schema, but he did not have Google's search engine, nor Yahoo!'s prestige. Goto.com became Overture Services, Inc., and was acquired by Yahoo!. After Google Inc. became increasingly important, Yahoo! sued Google for patent infringement with Overture's patents. After two years in court, Google settled the case by paying out 2.7 million shares of its stock to Yahoo! in late 2004, according to Stefanie Olsen in her article " Google, Yahoo Bury the Legal Hatchet."

In addition to Yahoo!, Microsoft Corporation also rejected the idea, blind to its potential. Partovi reported that Banister pitched Keywords to him as well. Then, when Microsoft bought LinkExchange in 1998, Partovi shared the pay-for-placement idea freely. Microsoft even tried to implement the system as an MSN search feature as early as 2000. However, once it started to compete with banner advertisements, the Keywords option was dismantled.

Being based solely on its search engine, Google snapped up the idea. It started its AdWords program in 2000 and immediately started to reap the benefits. The next year the corporation was in the black, according to its 2004 annual report. By 2002, it claimed almost half a billion U.S. dollars in revenues, and in the same year it surpassed Yahoo!, as reported by Danny Sullivan in a 2002 article for *Search Engine Watch*. The company began preparing for its initial public offering (IPO).

In short, PageRank created the advertising market. It attracted the traffic, which attracted business, and then AdWords capitalized on businesses. The key was that it did not sacrifice user experience, at least initially.

ADSENSE

The AdSense program was built upon the strengths of PageRank and AdWords. Unveiled in 2003, the program allowed third parties to advertise products by joining the Google Network. Network members often posted information regarding the products they advertised such as product reviews and how-to articles. Users could find the information they wanted on member websites and then navigate to the appropriate supplier page to make their purchase. Third parties received money for each user that clicked on an advertisement and Google received a modest portion of the advertising fee.

For Google, revenue increased by 300 percent, according to its annual report. In his *CNET* article "Google to Sell Banner Ads," journalist Evan Hansen interpreted the move as repositioning Google "firmly into the camp of Internet advertising network providers such as ValueClick and 24/7 Real Media." The following year, 2004, saw even more revenue. With its IPO on the horizon, Google began publishing banner advertisements in May. These advertisements were not published directly on search engine results pages, but rather on the greater Google Network, where they would not impede the search process. The corporation was valued at US$27 billion, and raised US$1.67 billion in its IPO on August 19, 2004.

Google, Inc., became a household name. Yahoo!, its primary competitor, was eclipsed. Microsoft's middling attempt to compete in the search engine market with its renamed engine, Bing, resulted in unimpressive results as of 2011. Meanwhile, the search engine market continued to demonstrate its tendency toward winner-take-all. Google's revenues from AdWords and AdSense exploded, climbing to US$3 billion in 2004, US$6 billion in 2005, US$10.6 billion in 2006, and US$16.6 billion in 2007, according to U.S. Securities and Exchange Commission (SEC) filings.

One year later, Steve Lohr reported in the *New York Times* article "Google, Zen Master of the Market," that the corporation had gained over 60 percent of search traffic and over 70 percent of search advertising revenue. With such staggering market share, the reputation of the company came into question. Lohr documented a pressing question, namely: How could a company maintain such a lead, as Microsoft had in the late 1990s, without breeching antitrust laws? In the same article, Michael A. Cusumano, a professor at the Sloan School of Management at the Massachusetts Institute of Technology explained how Google's business model implemented "indirect effects" to maintain its share of the market. These effects included the company's large population of users, the ability to learn from that population, and strong brand image. Even with such explanations, experts, the media, and eventually governments came to suspect manipulation of search results, or unfair practices in general. However, it was equally clear that Google had developed a business model that stood up better to antitrust legislation than Microsoft.

CORPORATE IMAGE ERODED BY POWER

Google, Inc., continued to swell despite a global economic recession from 2008 to 2009. Not only did it retain its hold on the search engine market, its mobile operating system, Android, also demonstrated increasing success in 2010 and 2011. Like all of the company's side projects, Android was distributed without charge, which greatly aided the system's success. In 2010, only one year after it was brought to market, the operating system claimed 26 percent market share, according to "How Long Will Google's Magic Last?" in *The Economist*. Android's position only strengthened in 2011.

Increased success brought more unwanted attention. Competition and adversity welled up to quell the Google revolution. Governments launched formal investigations to ensure that the firm adhered to antitrust laws. The European Union introduced one such claim on November 30, 2010, which turned into a full-blown probe a year later. Within the same year, the U.S. Federal Trade Commission (FTC) initiated a civil probe that was designed to analyze not only Google's possible breach of antitrust law but also to analyze the efficacy of antitrust law. According to Amir Efrati and Thomas Catan of the *Wall Street Journal,* even if the latter failed to discover any illegal practices, it could change the game to restrict Google's dominance: "Many policy watchers think the Google probe ultimately could be as much of a watershed event for antitrust policy as the Justice Department's landmark lawsuit against Microsoft Corp. in the 1990s."

Additional dangers arose as well. Social media became an even larger trend than search engines, threatening to steal revenues. As reported by Experian Hitwise, an Internet analytics company, Facebook, Inc., stole the lead in U.S. Internet traffic in March 2010, with 7.07 percent

of all website visits. Although Google created its own social media outlet, Google+, it failed to gain much support in 2011.

Even with the increased pressure, the capitalization of online advertising was on a steep slope. According to a Morgan Stanley report, "Internet Trends," between 1995 and 2005, global online advertising revenue jumped from US$55 million to US$18 billion. From 2005 to 2009, it increased to US$54 billion. Mobile devices and social networking brought even more businesses to the stream. Thus, a significant increase in online advertising revenues was probable, which boded well for both Google and Facebook. Even if competition continued to steepen, the global migration of consumers to the Internet could leave enough space for the two Internet juggernauts to coexist.

CARVING OUT A STABLE POSITION

Google started with a useful, revolutionary product and quickly recognized the opportunity to capitalize on it. When the company incorporated in 1998, its search engine was its only asset, thus revenues needed to build from that strength. Pay-per-placement was the only advertising model that augmented the search engine, and Page and Brin implemented it.

BIBLIOGRAPHY

Battelle, John. "The Birth of Google." *Wired,* August 2005. Accessed January 9, 2012. http://www.wired.com/wired/archive/13.08/battelle.html?tw=wn_tophead_4.

Brady, Robert. "How Google AdWords Determines What You Pay." *Small Business Trends,* December 26, 2011. Accessed January 9, 2012. http://smallbiztrends.com/2011/12/google-adwords-auction.html.

Catan, Thomas, and Amir Efrati. "Feds to Launch Probe of Google." *Wall Street Journal,* June 24, 2011. Accessed January 9, 2012. http://online.wsj.com/article/SB1000142405270230333990457640360376471680.html.

Dougherty, Heather. "Facebook Reaches Top Ranking in US." New York: Experian Hitwise, March 15, 2010. Accessed January 9, 2012. http://weblogs.hitwise.com/heather-dougherty/2010/03/facebook_reaches_top_ranking_i.html.

"Google Goes Public." *New York Times,* August 20, 2004. Accessed January 9, 2012. http://www.nytimes.com/2004/08/20/opinion/google-goes-public.html?src=pm.

Google, Inc. "2009 Annual Report." Mountain View, CA, December 31, 2009. Accessed January 9, 2012. http://investor.google.com/documents/2009_google_annual_report.html.

———. "2010 Annual Report." Mountain View, CA, December 31, 2010. Accessed January 9, 2012. http://investor.google.com/documents/20101231_google_10K.html.

Guth, Robert A. "Microsoft Bid to Beat Google Builds on a History of Misses." *Wall Street Journal,* January 16, 2009. Accessed January 9, 2012. http://www.livemint.com

/articles/2009/01/19210503/Microsoft-bid-to-beat-Google-b .html?atype=tp.

Hansen, Evan. "Google to Sell Banner Ads." *CNET,* May 12, 2004. Accessed January 9, 2012. http://news.cnet.com/2100 -1024_3-5211662.html.

"How Google Works." *The Economist,* September 16, 2004. Accessed January 9, 2012. http://www.economist.com /node/3171440.

"How Long Will Google's Magic Last?" *The Economist,* December 2, 2010. Accessed January 9, 2012. http://www .economist.com/node/17633138.

Krazit, Tom. "Google's Primer on How It Helps the Economy." *CNET,* May 25, 2010. Accessed January 9, 2012. http://news .cnet.com/8301-30684_3-20005948-265.html.

Lohr, Steve. "Google, Zen Master of the Market." *New York Times,* July 7, 2008. Accessed December 29, 2011. http:// www.nytimes.com/2008/07/07/technology/07google .html?pagewanted=all.

Long, Tony. "Sept. 7, 1998: If the Check Says 'Google Inc.,' We're 'Google Inc.'" *Wired,* September 7, 2007. Accessed January 9, 2012. http://www.wired.com/science/discoveries /news/2007/09/dayintech_0907.

Markoff, John. "Google Envy Is Fomenting Search Wars." *New York Times,* October 18, 2004. Accessed December 29, 2011. http://www.nytimes.com/2004/10/18/technology/18search .html?_r=1&adxnnl=1&ref=googleinc&adxnnlx=13251934 57-Cly3ZuhDP4V0FmviABr4TQ.

Morgan Stanley. "Internet Trends." New York, April 12, 2010. Accessed January 9, 2012. http://www.morganstanley.com /institutional/techresearch/pdfs/Internet_Trends_041210.pdf.

Olsen, Stefanie. "Google, Yahoo Bury the Legal Hatchet." *CNET,* August 9, 2004. Accessed January 9, 2012. http://news.cnet. com/Google,-Yahoo-bury-the-legal-hatchet/2100-1024_3 -5302421.html.

Partovi, Ali. "Bubble Blinders: The Untold Story of the Search Business Model." *TechCrunch,* August 29, 2010. Accessed January 9, 2012. http://techcrunch.com/2010/08/29/bubble -blinders-the-untold-story-of-the-search-business-model.

Rey, Francis. "Google Slammed with 400-Page Objection from the European Commission." *Social Barrel,* December 4, 2011. Accessed January 9, 2012. http://socialbarrel.com/google -slammed-with-400-page-objection-from-the-european -commission/28326.

"Searching for Evidence." *The Economist,* June 23, 2011. Accessed January 9, 2012. http://www.economist.com/blogs /schumpeter/2011/06/google-and-antitrust.

Sullivan, Danny. "Google Tops in Search Hours Ratings." *Search Engine Watch,* May 5, 2002. Accessed January 9, 2012. http:// searchenginewatch.com/article/2064246/Google-Tops-In -Search-Hours-Ratings.

U.S. Securities and Exchange Commission. "Amendment No. 4 to Form S-1 Registration Statement." Washington, DC, July 26, 2004. Accessed January 9, 2012. http://sec.gov/Archives /edgar/data/1288776/000119312504124025/ds1a.htm.

"Web-Wide War." *The Economist,* November 25, 2009. Accessed January 9, 2012. http://www.economist.com/node /14955213.

Gore-Tex:
Ingredient Branding Done Correctly

GORE-TEX (popularly known as Gore-Tex) brand fabric is a type of material that is both breathable and waterproof. Gore-Tex is a registered trademark of W. L. Gore and Associates. Gore-Tex is, a modified form of polytetrafluoroethylene (PTFE), a synthetic material that in its many forms has several uses.

Gore-Tex is perhaps most familiar as a form of synthetic fabric used for clothing. In this context, it is used most commonly for outdoor clothing, as it allows athletes and outdoor enthusiasts to stay dry while also allowing the skin to breathe. Gore-Tex fabric has been popularly used in clothing since 1976. According to Philip Kotler and Waldemar Pfoertsch in their book *Ingredient Branding: Making the Invisible Visible,* more than 100 million products around the world use Gore-Tex. Although the patent for Gore-Tex expired in 1996, in the early 2010s Gore-Tex remained a multibillion-dollar product and continued to enjoy customer loyalty, despite the competing fabrics on the market.

Most Gore-Tex fabrics are in fact made from Gore-Tex laminates, whereby the Gore-Tex membrane is laminated with a fabric and sealed at the seams. This makes the fabric permanently waterproof and windproof, but breathable. The core of the process is the Gore-Tex membrane, which has nine billion microscopic pores per square inch and also has an oleophobic substance that repels oils. This helps keep sunscreens, body lotions, natural skin oils, and other oily substances from permeating the membrane and compromising it. The membrane is permanently joined with a fabric. Products and fabrics made with Gore-Tex are then seam sealed to ensure that no leaks can occur at hems and fabric edges. Seam sealing involves using GORE-SEAM TAPE to make stitch holes and seams watertight.

In the early 2010s the company manufactured Gore-Tex products in Japan, Germany, Scotland, and the United States. Although the use of Gore-Tex for athletic and outdoor clothes is well known, the material is used for a variety of purposes. PTFE is also used in medical implants for surgery, dental floss, packaging materials, industrial applications, electronics components, and more.

THE INVENTION OF POLYTETRAFLUOROETHYLENE

Gore-Tex was invented in 1958. Wilbert "Bill" Gore and his son Bob were experimenting in the family basement in Newark, Delaware. W. L. Gore and Associates was owned by Bill and his wife Genevieve. Before founding the company, Bill had worked at E.I. du Pont de Nemours and Company (DuPont), where he worked on projects concerning the conductivity of computer cables. Both Bill and Bob Gore were engineers and used a pressure cooker as well as pots and pans to modify polytetrafluoroethylene (PTFE) from a raw powder form into a type of insulation that could be used for computer cables.

By 1969 the Gores were still working with PTFE and considering computer insulation when Bob made an unexpected discovery. By accident, he discovered that the modified PTFE that was heated with a high temperature was very stretchable and could be expanded to 1,000 times its actual size. Once he discovered this, Bob called this new form of expanded PTFE "ePTFE" and started to investigate what the fluoropolymer form of the material could do. He found that the expanded material was more porous but also had a unique feature: the pores were large enough to let water vapor escape but were so small that they would not allow moisture in. In fact, the pores were 700 times larger than one molecule of water vapor but 20,000 times smaller than a water drop. Bob had found the very trait that would make the material one of the most popular fabrics for outdoor wear.

THE INVENTION OF GORE-TEX AND ITS USES

The Gores trademarked and patented their invention in 1976. They called the new ePTFE Gore-Tex. However, Bob first thought of a different idea for ePTFE. The material was initially used in hospital bed sheets. The fabric kept patients comfortable and cool while protecting the mattresses from various bodily fluids. Early commercial products including Gore-Tex were Gore-Tex Joint Sealant, which was used for industrial pipe systems, and Gore-Tex Pipe Thread Tape.

By 1972 the company had expanded into several geographic regions, including Japan, Scotland, and France, and was reporting US$10 million in annual sales. Gore-Tex was still primarily being used for industrial uses, including packaging materials for pumps, sewing threads for industrial uses, and filters. In the following year, the company began using ePTFE for filtration applications and launched its line of filter bags, also for industrial uses. By 1975 Gore-Tex was being used in medical products, starting with the Gore-Tex Vascular Graft.

A NEW USE FOR GORE-TEX

Bill Gore, however, thought up the first use of ePTFE for outdoor wear. Bill was a hiker, but at the time outerwear and waterproof gear for backpackers was made from rubberized and heavy materials. It protected the hiker from the elements, but also was uncomfortable because it was not very breathable. There were other problems with these waterproof items of clothing, too. Since the materials were waterproofed simply by rubberizing a material, the material would lose its waterproofing ability. The materials were also heavy and tended to crack after exposure to cold. In most cases, they also did not do much to keep out the cold and the wind.

Bill's wife Genevieve sewed a Gore-Tex tent, the first outdoor item to use the material. However, the tent was not an instant success. Genevieve had sewn the Gore-Tex membrane as the outside layer of the tent, with fabric as the inner layer. When Bill and Genevieve went camping at Wind Rivers in Wyoming with the tent, the tent withstood an initial rain but when the rain turned to hail, the sharp pieces of ice punctured the membrane fabric. When it began to rain again, as Genevieve told Kristin Hostetter of *Backpacker* magazine, "the floor was collecting rain like a bathtub. We almost floated away that night!"

GORE-TEX AND CUSTOMER FOCUS

It would take many more attempts to perfect Gore-Tex, but by 1976 the product was ready and was launched under the brand name Early Winters. Gore-Tex fabrics were first used in tents and in rainwear. In 1976 Gore-Tex rainwear was being marketed in the Early Winters catalog as "possibly the most versatile piece of clothing you'll ever wear."

In 1989 Gore-Tex launched what they dubbed the "Guaranteed to Keep You Dry" initiative, as Hostetter described. The program was designed to safeguard the quality of Gore-Tex products and to ensure that Gore-Tex was differentiated from other, similar products. As part of a complicated licensing agreement, all products made with Gore-Tex were tested in a climate-controlled room. Known as the "rain room," the enclosure tested product designs under a variety of conditions, including rain. Nozzles in the chamber could stimulate various rain conditions, from light misting to driving rain, to test a product.

The company eventually added other testing chambers and laboratories. These included the comfort tests to test the breathability of the fabrics under hot conditions and the windproof ability of the fabric in various types of winds. The Martindale Test focused on the durability and abrasion resistance of Gore-Tex materials. During the test, the fabric was subjected to abrasion from wool or sandpaper over a period of hours or days (depending on the fabric). The Crumple Test measured fabric durability. In the test, Gore-Tex fabrics were crumpled and stretched out in very cold temperatures repeatedly to ensure that they did not crack after being exposed to cold.

Shoes made with Gore-Tex were also subject to the Walking Test and the Wicking Test. The Wicking Test checked to ensure that the shaft of the shoe did not leak. The Walking Test involved placing the shoe, partly submerged, in a machine that simulated the movement of 300,000 steps. If a leak developed, workers could evaluate where and why moisture was entering the shoe. Gloves made with Gore-Tex were also subject to the Liner Retention Test, the Spray Test, and the Whole Glove Leak test. The Liner Retention Test and the Spray Test ensured that gloves made with Gore-Tex had a durable liner that would not come apart and that water droplets would not cling to the material in large quantities. The Whole Glove Leak test used pressurized air to ensure that the entire glove was structured well and did not leak in any area.

As a result of the initial quality testing program, all products made with Gore-Tex could be placed under a warranty that other outdoor wear manufacturers could not match. The warranty was a first in the industry and as of 2012 Gore-Tex still promised that if a Gore-Tex product leaked or failed to work as promised the company would "repair it, replace it, or refund your purchase price," according to the Gore-Tex website. Performance fabrics made with Gore-Tex in many cases also carried a multiyear warranty to function as promised.

According to Kotler and Pfoertsch, the "Guaranteed to Keep You Dry" guarantee was a watershed moment for the company because it transformed it from a manufacturer that was just creating a product to a company committed to the final product and the customer experience. The company was no longer producing a component for use in consumer products; it was involving itself with the final product. With this one program, Gore-Tex also showed its commitment to the end customer.

Rather than just being an anonymous component in a final product, Gore-Tex now became a special amenity in any product. In order for a manufacturer to use Gore-Tex in a product, the manufacturer not only had to get a license to use Gore-Tex but also had to use certified facilities to convert the material. In addition, products made with Gore-Tex featured a distinctive black and gold diamond label and the Gore-Tex brand name. Customers were made aware of the Gore-Tex warranty and the quality claims of the company through advertisements and information tags on products.

PATENT AND LEGAL TROUBLES

Although Gore-Tex was becoming a popular material, W. L. Gore and Associates did face some legal problems. Before Bill and Bob Gore had created ePTFE, John W. Cropper had independently been working on PTFE as well and had been using the material with another company. W. L. Gore and Associates accused Garlock, Inc., of infringing on its patents in the 1970s. However, the case did not turn out as the company had hoped, as the U.S. Federal District Court of Ohio invalidated Gore's patents. Gore appealed, and the U.S. Federal Circuit Court overturned the decision, claiming that while John W. Cropper had developed stretched PTFE tape and a machine to produce it, he kept it a trade secret and this, in the judge's opinion, forfeited his claim.

In 1989 a lawsuit against W. R. Grace & Company, Mobay Corporation, and E. I. du Pont de Nemours & Company involved W. L. Gore and Associates. The three companies provided a chemical known as toluene diisocyanate to W. L. Gore and Associates. The chemical was used in the production of Gore-Tex. Twenty-five workers at W. L. Gore and Associates suffered inflammatory lung disease after being exposed to the chemical. Under Maryland legislation, the workers could not sue W. L. Gore and Associates. In November 1989 a jury at the Cecil County Circuit Court found that the chemical manufacturers were not liable for the workers' injuries.

GORE-TEX AND BRANDING

Kotler and Pfoertsch noted that Gore-Tex's success was a good example of ingredient branding. Ingredient branding involved emphasizing the qualities of a specific ingredient or component of a final product to promote the final customer product. Gore-Tex's use of ingredient branding was successful for a number of reasons, according to Kotler and Pfoertsch. First, it appealed to customers because in a world of too many brand choices, ingredient branding helped with purchases. A customer who liked a Gore-Tex tent, for example, found that when shopping for a coat, finding one with a Gore-Tex label made the purchasing decision easier. Second, ingredient branding reduced marketing costs since Gore-Tex shared marketing costs with the manufacturers of products that used the material. Third, recognition of the brand allowed Gore-Tex to charge a higher price for its product. Fourth, a product with Gore-Tex in it was immediately differentiated from the competition in the mind of any customer familiar with the Gore-Tex brand.

THE W. L. GORE AND ASSOCIATES COMPANY CULTURE

In addition to advertising, the Gore-Tex success story might be due in part to the unique corporate structure at W. L. Gore and Associates. According to Jessica Lipnack and Jeffrey Stamps, in their book *The TeamNet Factor: Bringing the Power of Boundary Crossing Into the Heart of Your Business,* the company was run like a network, with sponsors instead of managers and bosses, and associates instead of employees. Bill Gore based his business on the precept that people work best in cooperation. Therefore, he avoided the strict hierarchies and large workplaces of other companies. Plants were encouraged to work together, and when the plants exceeded 150 people he divided them, believing that people could not work as effectively in teams where they were not familiar with one another.

According to Richard Daft, in his book *Organization Theory and Design,* Gore called his organization a "lattice" structure and noted that the goal of the company was to "make money and have fun." Gore's structure had six basic rules or principles. First, communication traveled in straight lines from person to person and team to team, with no middlemen. Second, there was no assigned, strongly structured authority. Third, sponsors took the form of bosses. Fourth, team and company leaders were chosen by, and needed the support of, associates to maintain their leadership. Fifth, objectives were determined by those who carried out the objectives. Sixth, commitments determined each person's tasks. Even when the company became a multibillion-dollar business, it maintained this network philosophy.

W. L. Gore and Associates also tried to provide a good environment for its associates, which included creating plants and facilities that served workers. W. L. Gore and Associates worked with architects at Bernardon & Associates and designed plants and facilities that included volleyball courts, superior indoor lighting, and other features that ensured comfort during working hours. According to an article by Maureen Milford in the *New York Times*, attention to detail included ensuring that company cafeterias were located inside the building in such a way that the sunlight did not shine into workers' eyes when they ate lunch. In most cases, Bernardon & Associates built its facilities in suburban and rural settings, so that more outdoor space could be created for associates.

In addition to being a lattice company, W. L. Gore and Associates continued to be a private, family-owned company. The stock for the company was held in a Gore trust. According to the Gores, the decision was designed to provide more control over Gore-Tex and company policy. Bill Gore founded the company as a private organization in part because he did not want undue influence from outside shareholders, according to Milford. The company's commitment to private industry was so strong that in 2011 the organization joined with two other privately held U.S. companies, Wawa, Inc., and Wegmans Food Markets, Inc., to lobby against a proposed U.S. securities rule that could require private companies to reveal financial information that typically only publicly held companies needed to disclose. The three companies created an informal coalition and hired a lobbyist, according to a December 30, 2011 article in the *Economic Times*.

In a way, Gore-Tex is an unlikely success story. The product was first developed in a basement using kitchen pans. Many successful brands, unlike Gore-Tex, were final products, but Gore-Tex succeeded through savvy ingredient branding, customer focus, and licensing agreements. Rather than focusing on relationships with manufacturers that used Gore-Tex, the makers of Gore-Tex focused on the end customer. This ensured that rather than becoming one additional component in a final product, Gore-Tex became a selling point that customers asked for by name.

BIBLIOGRAPHY

"721 F. 2d 1540 – WL Gore Associates Inc v. Garlock Inc." *Open Jurist.* Accessed January 17, 2012. http://openjurist.org/721 /f2d/1540/wl-gore-associates-inc-v-garlock-inc.

"Chemical Makers Are Cleared in Lawsuit by Textile Workers." *New York Times,* November 5, 1989. Accessed January 17, 2012. http://www.nytimes.com/1989/11/05/us/chemical -makers-are-cleared-in-lawsuit-by-textile-workers.html.

Daft, Richard L. *Organization Theory and Design.* 10th ed. Mason, OH: South-Western Cengage Learning, 2008, 554–559.

Gore-Tex. "What Is Gore-Tex Fabric?" Newark, DE, 2012. Accessed January 17, 2012. http://www.gore-tex.com/remote /Satellite/home.

Hayes, Tom, and Michael S. Malone. *No Size Fits All: From Mass Marketing to Mass Handselling.* New York: Portfolio, 2009.

Hostetter, Kristin. "Gore-Tex: The Fabric That Breathes." *Backpacker,* April 1998, 70.

Kotler, Philip, and Waldemar Pfoertsch. *Ingredient Branding: Making the Invisible Visible.* New York: Springer, 2010, 120–127.

Lipnack, Jessica, and Jeffrey Stamps. *The TeamNet Factor: Bringing the Power of Boundary Crossing into the Heart of Your Business.* New London, NH: Oliver Wight Publications, 1993, 80–84.

Milford, Maureen. "A Company Philosophy in Bricks and Mortar." *New York Times,* September 1, 1996. Accessed January 17, 2012. http://www.nytimes.com/1996/09/01 /realestate/a-company-philosophy-in-bricks-and-mortar .html?scp=4&sq=.

"Private Companies Ratchet Up Lobbying to Stay Dark." *Economic Times,* December 30, 2011. Accessed January 16, 2012. http://articles.economictimes.indiatimes.com/2011-12 -30/news/30573034_1_three-companies-wawa-wegmans -food-markets.

Got Milk?: An Enduring Advertising Campaign in the United States

DECLINING MILK CONSUMPTION

After World War II, the U.S. government, schools, and medical professionals all stressed that milk was a nutritious drink and a necessary component for a healthy lifestyle, especially for children. Schoolchildren received a cup of milk each day, and teachers included the dietary recommendations from the U.S. Department of Agriculture, which stressed the importance of dairy products, into health and nutrition education. According to Douglas Holt's article published by the Advertising Educational Foundation (AEF), by the 1950s milk was seen as the drink of choice at meal and snack times and soft drinks were viewed as "recreational leisure products."

In the 1970s aggressive marketing by soft drink companies, such as Coca-Cola Company and PepsiCo Inc., portrayed their beverages as synonymous with a youthful lifestyle. Playful, eye-catching, and convenient packaging enticed consumers away from the plain plastic or cardboard milk jug. People found that soft drink containers could be easily resealed while they did something else, like driving cars or using exercise machines, unlike bulky milk cartons. Soft drinks started to replace milk at the dinner table and soon became a staple in the U.S. home.

In the early 1990s newer beverages such as Gatorade, Snapple, Mountain Dew, and Sprite were promoted as youthful, rebellious, individualistic, and fashionable. Milk was associated with domesticity and childhood. Put simply, milk was perceived as unexciting.

The California Milk Advisory Board, an organization charged with marketing milk, noted that from 1980 to 1993 annual milk consumption dropped to just over 24 gallons per person from 30 gallons per person. Concerned with the decline in sales, California's milk processors voted to fund a single association that would be responsible for marketing milk. The processors agreed to allocate three cents from each gallon of milk to market its consumption. The California Milk Processor Board (CMPB), the body charged with using this money to increase sales, was launched in 1993 with a marketing budget of US$23 million.

WANT MILK?

The CMPB chose Goodby, Silverstein & Partners Inc. (GS&P), a San Francisco, California advertising agency, to create a marketing campaign. According to Alison Porter and Kevin Teague's essay in the *Encyclopedia of Major Marketing Campaigns*, Jeff Goodby, cochairman of GS&P, helped win CMPB's account by suggesting a strategy based on his theory that the only time people realized that they wanted milk was when they ran out of it.

Challenging GS&P's creative minds to design a campaign with stories of people who wanted milk more than other beverages, Goodby suggested using Steven Spielberg's 1971 movie *Duel* as a guideline. In the film, a malevolent truck driver hunts down a business commuter. Goodby imagined that instead of a commuter, the truck was following a second truck and rammed it from behind. The camera would pull back, Goodby proposed, and the audience would see a cookie truck chasing a milk truck. The cookie truck driver had cookies, but nothing to drink.

The campaign, named "got milk?", launched in 1993 and featured advertisements with actors in humorous situations arising from "their need to wash food down with milk," according to Porter and Teague.

THE MARKET

Previous campaigns had tried to compete with soft drink manufacturers by using the same methods that the soft drink makers used. These milk marketing attempts tried to halt the decline of milk sales by suggesting that milk was, according to Porter and Teague, "cool, fun, and cutting-edge." The problem, GS&P claimed, was that the campaigns were aimed at the wrong market. A study by CMPB revealed that approximately 70 percent of Californians reported drinking milk often. GS&P concluded that previous efforts were targeted at the 30 percent who did not drink milk or who drank it less than the average consumer.

A study conducted for GS&P by the research firm Gallup, Inc., revealed that there were three major reasons people reported drinking less milk. Consumers perceived that milk was high in fat, it was a drink for children, and, compared with sodas and other soft drinks, it was boring. Gallup's study also noted that many Californians felt they should be drinking more milk. A general guideline for the fast-moving packaged goods industry, according to Holt in "got milk?", is that it is usually easier to convince current customers to consume more of a product than it is to attract nonusers. Using this logic, GS&P, with support from CMPB executive director Jeff Manning, decided to target the 70 percent of consumers who reported drinking milk frequently.

THE STRATEGY

The "got milk?" campaign had three objectives, according to Porter and Teague. First, the idea was to change the public's perception of and behavior toward milk. This was done with some carefully placed media. The second was to create what were called "milk moments," that is, associating milk with certain foods and events in the home. The third objective was to stop the declining rate of milk consumption by persuading people already drinking milk to drink more.

The GS&P's research revealed that many of these milk-drinking consumers preferred their milk with something sweet, such as a brownie or a cookie. Using this information, Holt noted that GS&P asked market research participants to consider how they felt when they had the snack but not the milk. Focus group members reported feeling upset or deprived at being placed in this situation. "They were able to convey viscerally the feeling of having a brownie or cookie remnants stuck in their throat, calling out for a gulp of milk to cleanse the palette," Holt reported.

As a result of the focus group input, GS&P decided on a milk-deprivation campaign. Instead of selling milk as an accompaniment to snacks, the idea was to convey to consumers the feeling of deprivation that arose when milk

was not available at the very moment they needed it. The first print advertisements reflected this strategy by showing pictures of brownies and cupcakes with a bite missing and the caption "got milk?"

Using the CMPB research information that 88 percent of milk was consumed in the home, the early television advertisements depicted someone sitting at home, needing milk, then realizing there was none. The first television advertisement to create a stir in the campaign was called "Aaron Burr." In it, a history buff fails to win a prize in a radio call-in trivia show because he has just been eating a peanut butter sandwich and is barely able to speak. When he reaches for the milk carton, he finds it empty, and then the screen shows the caption, "got milk?" "Aaron Burr" won the Best in Show award at the 1994 CLIO Awards, the advertising industry's equivalent of the film industry's Academy Awards.

Other television advertisements included the portrayal of a fictional town called Drysville where town officials had implemented a milk prohibition. CMPB attracted media attention in 2002 when it announced it would make a substantial donation to the school board of the first California town willing to change its name to "Got Milk?" CMPB promised that the town would also be the centerpiece of a national publicity campaign in 2003 to celebrate 10 years of the "got milk?" advertising campaign. No town took the board up on its offer but, according to an October 2002 report by George Raine in the *San Francisco Chronicle,* the small town of Biggs, California, did consider it. "It's interesting if nothing else," the article quoted the town's mayor as saying.

Holt reported that in May 1994, in an attempt to reach a younger audience and make milk "cool," the CMPB released a television advertisement called "Heaven." In the advertisement, a young business executive discovers that hell is a place full of chocolate chip cookies but empty milk cartons. When "Heaven" turned out to be even more popular than previous advertisements, particularly with young adults facing a job market downturn in the 1990s, GS&P decided to try a strategy involving associating the drinking of milk with certain food brands. To this end, in 1995 CMPB released an advertisement that was cobranded with Oreo cookies. The advertisement, "Oreo Kane," was a parody of the famous film *Citizen Kane* It was shot in black and white and featured an executive in a management meeting demanding better ideas for the name of the company's new cookie.

MARKETING OPPORTUNITIES

While the television advertisements were successful, CMPB's research still showed that people tended to think of milk only when they ran out of it, according to Holt. From the beginning of the campaign, GS&P had placed billboard advertisements at bus stops and other strategic locations in an attempt to remind people to buy milk on their way home. In a move aimed at encouraging people who were actually in the store to buy milk, the CMPB had decals printed with the "got milk?" tag line and arranged to have them placed on the floors of convenience stores. In a similar move, agreements were made with grocery store produce sections to place the decals on fresh bananas (the logic being that bananas on cereal needed milk).

By the first decade of the 21st century, the "got milk?" tag line had become ubiquitous. To take advantage of the popularity of the campaign, CMPB launched a website and began selling merchandise such as T-shirts, mugs, and various office supplies. The board also sold licenses for the "got milk?" brand to other national dairy boards for use in their own marketing efforts and to manufacturers who used the brand on a variety of consumer products and personal clothing.

GOT ANYTHING?

CMPB tended to ignore unauthorized use of its slogan. Sites sprang up on the Internet such as "Got Wine?", "Got Junk?", "Got Breakfast?", and even "Got Jesus?", but by far the most prominent was the "Got Beer?" campaign instigated by the People for the Ethical Treatment of Animals (PETA).

In 2000 and 2002, PETA organized the "Got Beer?" promotion on campuses all across the United States in time for Saint Patrick's Day. The idea, Ellen Sorokin's March 2000 *Washington Times* article explained, was to encourage students to forego milk and drink beer, claiming that beer was more nutritious than milk and that milk promoted animal suffering. The campaign drew the ire of people, including the organization Mothers Against Drunk Driving (MADD), who were already concerned about binge drinking by students.

According to Steve Miller's December 14, 2007, article in the online magazine, *AdWeek,* CMPB threatened legal action against PETA. The board stated that it was flattered to have the "got milk?" tag line parodied and acknowledged allowing numerous other infringements. However, the article quoted Steve James, the executive director of CMPB, as saying that the board had an "obligation under federal trademark law to protect and police its use, especially when it is used in a disparaging or damaging way."

GOT RESULTS?

The longevity of the "got milk?" campaign and its international recognition suggested that the CMPB and GS&P had managed to identify a successful formula in placing milk in a context in people's lives. In 2011 the California Department of Health reported that the percentage of people who reported drinking milk or milk-based products within the previous 24 hours had increased from 52 percent in 1993 to 62 percent in 2009. Because an objective of the campaign was to increase milk consumption among people already drinking milk on a frequent basis, this would seem to indicate some success.

Another objective was to create "milk moments." This was accomplished by associating milk with events such as breakfast, snack time, and any time in the home where food could be washed down with milk. The advertisements and cobranding with companies such as Oreo provided a humorous way of linking milk with food in the public's perception.

GOING FORWARD

There have been some setbacks and a few misguided advertisements. CMPB submitted to pressure in 2011 to pull a television series of advertisements touting milk as a relief for premenstrual syndrome (PMS). As noted by Marc Babej in the July 21, 2011, issue of *Forbes,* the advertisement angered many female consumers and women's activist groups. Babej noted that the advertisement was "an example of a humorous execution of an inappropriate advertising idea."

Despite such setbacks, in the early 2010s the campaign to convert more people to drinking milk showed no sign of disappearing. The CMPB launched a website named "get fit with got milk," featuring fitness videos, nutrition information, recipes, and contests. Together with the "National Milk Moustache" campaign, featuring celebrities sporting white milk moustaches, the nation's milk processors continued to promote milk as a healthy alternative to sugary soft drinks.

BIBLIOGRAPHY

Babej, Marc E. "'Got Milk?' Pulls Its PMS-Themed Campaign Amid Controversy." *Forbes,* July 21, 2011. Accessed January 20, 2012. http://www.forbes.com/sites/marcbabej/2011/07/21/got-milk-pulls-its-pms-themed-campaign-amid-controversy.

California Department of Food and Agriculture. California Milk Processor Board. "About the Brand." 2012. Accessed January 19, 2012. http://www.gotmilk.com/#/health-benefits.

California Department of Public Health. "2009 California Dietary Practices Survey (CDPS) Data Tables." October 2011. Accessed January 20, 2012. http://www.cdph.ca.gov/programs/cpns/Pages/2009CDPSDataTables.aspx#dairy.

Holt, Douglas B. "got milk?" Advertising Educational Foundation, 2002. Accessed January 19, 2012. http://www.aef.com/on_campus/classroom/case_histories/3000.

Miller, Steve. "PETA Spars with Milk Board, Mars." *AdWeek,* December 14, 2007. Accessed January 20, 2012. http://www.adweek.com/news/advertising/peta-spars-milk-board-mars-91384.

Porter, Allison I., and Kevin Teague. "California Milk Processor Board." In *Encyclopedia of Major Marketing Campaigns.* Vol. 2, 257–260. Detroit: Gale, 2007. Gale Virtual Reference Library (GALE|CX3446600052). Accessed January 19, 2012. http://go.galegroup.com/ps/i.do?id=GALE%7CCX34466000 52&v=2.1&u=itsbtrial&it=r&p=GVRL&sw=w.

Raine, George. "Town of Biggs Weighs Request to Rename Itself Got Milk?" *San Francisco Chronicle,* October 29, 2002.

Accessed January 19, 2012. http://articles.sfgate.com/2002 -10-29/news/17565679_1_california-milk-processor-board -jeff-manning-milk-deprivation.

Sorokin, Ellen. "PETA Says 'Drink Beer, Not Milk' to Prevent Cruelty to Animals." *Washington Times,* March 13, 2000. (GALE|A60077978). Accessed January 20, 2012. http:// go.galegroup.com/ps/i.do?id=GALE%7CA60077978&v=2.1 &u=itsbtrial&it=r&p=GPS&sw=w.

Hallmark Cards: From Post Cards to Greeting Cards

Most U.S. consumers would not even give it a second thought, but sending greeting cards to mark special occasions such as birthdays, anniversaries, or events such as Mother's Day, only came about through the ideas of one man at the beginning of the 20th century. Picture postcards had been widely distributed since the first one was mailed in London in 1840. However, the format of a folded card with a message written inside, sent in a purpose-made envelope, was distinctly the invention of Joyce Clyde Hall, a U.S. entrepreneur and the founder of Hallmark Cards, Inc.

J. C. Hall helped establish a brand new industry and his company became one of the world's most recognized greeting card manufacturers. As the largest such company in the United States, Hallmark's 2011 earnings, as estimated by Forbes.com in 2012, were US$3.81 billion. Hallmark employed over 13,000 people and owned numerous well-known subsidiaries, such as Crayola LLC, a world-renowned maker of crayons and children's craft supplies. Hallmark also sold greetings under several brands, including DaySpring, Sunrise Greetings, and Blessings Unlimited. In the world of broadcast media, Hallmark also operated its own television station, the cable-based Hallmark Channel, as well as sponsored many television movies through its Hallmark Hall of Fame, a long-standing tradition with Hallmark since the 1950s. As a television sponsor, Hallmark Hall of Fame was awarded two Emmy Awards by the National Academy of Television Arts & Sciences. Hall himself received numerous accolades during his lifetime career as head of Hallmark.

A SHOEBOX FULL OF POSTCARDS

Joyce Clyde Hall was born in August 1891 to parents George Nelson Hall and Nancy Dudley Hall. His unlikely name was the result of his parents' religious nature, and he was named in honor of a Methodist bishop, Isaac W. Joyce, who happened to be visiting David City, Nebraska, where the Hall family lived. Preferring to be known by the initials J.C., the young Hall lacked formal education but made up for it with great personal ambition. At age 16, he started a small postcard company with his older brothers Rollie and William after the family moved to Norfolk, Nebraska. The Norfolk Post Card Company did not yield great profits as the demand for their product was rather low at the time.

When Hall turned 18, against the wishes of his family, he quit high school, gathered two shoeboxes full of postcards, and took a train to Kansas City, Missouri, in January 1910. Upon arrival, he moved into the local Young Men's Christian Association (YMCA) and began selling his postcards to local businesses including bookstores, drugstores, and gift shops. Slowly, he began to see some success in his efforts and gradually expanded his sales to neighboring towns. By 1911 his brother Rollie joined J.C. in Kansas City, Missouri, where they managed to open a small downtown store, selling not only postcards, but stationery, books, and gifts.

Tragedy struck the fledgling business in January 1915, almost exactly five years after J. C. Hall moved to Kansas City, Missouri. A fire broke out in the shop, destroying the brothers' entire inventory (save a small, fireproof safe). Undeterred, the brothers pressed on. Obtaining a loan for US$17,000, J.C. and Rollie bought an engraving company, allowing them to manufacture their own products. Around this time, J. C. Hall realized that the decline in the popularity of postcards may have been due to people's increasing desire for more privacy; folded greeting cards with a message inside, mailed inside envelopes, rapidly became popular.

Fueling the Halls' success further, in 1917 a busy Christmas season forced the Halls to use decorative French envelope linings to decorate gifts. These were well received and led to the company undertaking its own gift-wrap printing. In 1921, the Halls' third brother, William, also moved to Kansas City, Missouri, leaving behind the original shop in Norfolk, Nebraska. The three brothers then formed Hall Brothers Inc.

THE BIRTH OF THE HALLMARK BRAND

Always looking for new ideas, J. C. Hall was intrigued by the use of hallmarks, which were official marks, used for centuries by metal smiths and struck onto the surface of precious metals like gold and silver to indicate their provenance and purity. He liked the name Hallmark because it gave the image of high quality but also contained their last name, Hall. Until then, their greeting cards had included the words "Hall Brothers Company" on the back of each card. J.C. felt that this should be replaced by "A Hallmark Card," an idea that was criticized by just about everyone, according to Hallmark's corporate history. The change was made in 1928 and national advertising began in earnest, again to widespread criticism as J.C. was advised that advertising was a waste of money. Being the first greeting card company to advertise, it was not long before the Hallmark brand became the recognized name associated with greeting cards across the United States. This first advertising campaign appeared in the popular and widely read *Ladies' Home Journal.*

The next major milestone for J.C. Hall was establishing licensing agreements with other companies to incorporate their trademarked images into Hallmark's products. The Walt Disney Company was the first such agreement, made in 1932, and allowing some of the most recognizable cartoon characters in the United States to star in Hallmark's greeting cards. Eventually the list of licensors grew to over 75 over the decades and included such companies and well-known brands as Dr. Seuss, Garfield, Harley-Davidson, Looney Tunes, Peanuts, and Warner Brothers.

Until the 1930s, greeting cards were not bought and sold in the same way that they are in the 21st century. They were stacked in drawers or boxes, requiring potential buyers to flip through them individually in order to select the card they wanted. One of Hallmark's employees, Ed Goodman, was put in charge of inventing a new way of merchandising Hallmark greeting cards. In cooperation with architect Herb Duncan, they introduced and eventually patented Hallmark's "Eye-Vision" display system, where all the cards could be visible on a specially designed display rack, a practice that is still used today in retail stores.

The most significant development to arise in the 1940s for Hallmark were the words of one of the company's senior executives, the same Ed Goodman who came up with "Eye-Vision" store displays a decade earlier. During World War II, Hallmark was constantly looking for ways to improve its market position. Goodman was always experimenting with different catchphrases and advertising lines, so on one three-by-five-inch note card he scribbled down his thoughts. He wrote:

> Three little words that mean so much . . . A Hallmark Card. . .They tell your friends you cared enough to send the very best. —They best reflect your perfect taste . . . your thoughtfulness . . . So . . . Before you buy—look on the back—For those identifying words . . . A Hallmark Card

One day J. C. Hall was in Goodman's office. Inquisitively, he picked up the card that contained those words and asked what they were. Goodman explained that he was experimenting with different slogans. Hall was captivated by one line in particular, which was altered slightly and became the company's legacy line from then on: "When you care enough to send the very best." Hall began using the slogan immediately.

A major step in building the Hallmark brand came in 1951 when the National Broadcasting Company (NBC) aired the first made-for-TV opera, *Amahl and the Night Visitors.* Hallmark was asked to become a sponsor for the program. This presented the perfect opportunity for Hall to thank his customers for buying their products and he was happy to accept. The opera was a huge success, and after it aired, letters from television viewers poured into the company's offices, thanking Hallmark for putting the program on the air. This began a new era in Hallmark for sponsoring TV specials and movies.

In 1954, Hall Brothers Inc. officially changed the company name to Hallmark Cards. By the 1960s, Hallmark had introduced its line of Christmas ornaments, a collectible product that rapidly became popular with many consumers and continued to grow throughout the decades. In 2010, 300 different ornament designs were available for purchase. Also in the 1960s, Hallmark introduced its *Shoebox* brand of humorous greeting cards, as well as cards that were demographically aimed at the cultural and religious diversity of U.S. customers. African American, Jewish, and Hispanic product lines were introduced.

When Donald J. Hall, J. C. Hall's son, took leadership of the company in the 1960s, Hallmark International became the company's global arm, eventually expanding its reach into over 100 countries. Although Hallmark International was not an official entity until 1966, several global offices were already operating around the world. One of the first international offices, Hallmark U.K., was founded in 1958.

Hallmark Canada had a slightly different genesis. Starting out as William E. Coutts Company, this Canadian company sold greeting cards from 1916 to 1931, at which point it entered into a partnership with the Hall Brothers. After Hallmark purchased a 40 percent share of Coutts in 1948, a complete buyout followed a decade later in 1958.

With the creation of Hallmark International came Hallmark Europe, based in Schoten, Belgium, and Capelle, Netherlands. Subsidiary Hallmark Australia was created in 1979, followed by Hallmark New Zealand in 1980. In Japan, Hallmark invested in a local stationery company in 1994, which it then purchased in 1997, changing the name to Nihon Hallmark. Hallmark, through its international investments, also had wholly owned subsidiaries in Mexico, Puerto Rico, Spain, Hong Kong, Singapore, and China.

J. C. HALL'S LASTING LEGACY

In 1986, Hallmark introduced the Hallmark Gold Crown program, a chain of specialized stores that sold the wide array of Hallmark products, from cards to wrapping paper, Christmas ornaments, gifts, and other related products. By 2011, there were over 3,000 stores across the United States, only 385 of which were corporate owned, with the remainder being independently owned and operated.

J. C. Hall died in 1982 at the age of 91. According to Hallmark, he had never actually retired and had continued to work at Hallmark even after passing the torch of leadership. After he ceded executive control of the company to his son, J.C. still remained as company chairman. Following his death, the position of chairman remained in the family. The third generation of Halls, namely Donald J. Hall, Jr., and his brother David E. Hall, both grandsons of the late J. C. Hall, continued the family business. As of 2012, Donald J. Hall, Jr., was CEO and president, while David E. Hall was president of Hallmark North America.

Also in the 1980s, Hallmark pursued numerous corporate acquisitions that gave the company control over one of the most well-known children's crayon and craft supply manufacturers in the world, Crayola. In the 1990s, Sunrise Greetings, DaySpring Cards, Image Arts, and William Arthur all came under the Hallmark umbrella of companies. A significant development in this decade was the release of Hallmark Warm Wishes, a new line of greeting cards that could be purchased for only US$0.99 anywhere in the United States. In 1994, Hallmark launched Hallmark.com, its website where e-cards as well as regular paper-based cards could be purchased.

HALLMARK IN THE 21ST CENTURY

With the explosive growth of e-commerce and the Internet in the late 1990s and early 21st century, many believed that companies such as Hallmark, which continued to produce and sell traditional, paper-based products such as cards, might lose significant market share to the new digital world of e-greetings and e-mail messages. Contrary to this idea, Hallmark has continued to respond to new technology in creative ways and has also managed to find new markets in a changing market. Some of the new items of the 2010s have included recordable storybooks that capture and replay stories that have been spoken into them; cards that play music from original recording artists like the Rolling Stones, Ella Fitzgerald, and Stevie Wonder; postage prepaid cards with envelopes; and instant scrapbooks, which are kits that include a photo album with stickers and caption bubbles.

Another new direction that Hallmark took, controversial to some consumers, was the introduction in 2008 of a new line of same-sex wedding cards following the legalization of gay marriage in some U.S. states. Owners of Hallmark stores were still free to choose whether or not to stock this particular line of products. In 2011, another topical line of products was announced through news media: Hallmark-branded job loss cards, for victims of downsizing and job-cutting measures.

BIBLIOGRAPHY

"BCA Ten Hall of Fame." Washington, DC: Americans for the Arts. Accessed January 13, 2012. http://www.artsusa.org/information_services/arts_and_business_partnerships/bca/programs/bca_ten/hall_of_fame/011.asp.

Bradford, Larry. "Hallmark Launches Line of Job Loss Card." *Huffington Post,* September 27, 2011. Accessed January 13, 2012. http://www.huffingtonpost.com/2011/09/27/hallmark-layoff-cards-unemployed_n_981985.html#s374136.

"Hallmark Begins Selling Same-Sex Wedding Card." *Fox News.com,* August 21, 2008. Accessed January 13, 2012. http://www.foxnews.com/story/0,2933,407761,00.html.

"Hallmark Cards." *Forbes.com,* 2011. Accessed January 13, 2012. http://www.forbes.com/lists/2011/21/private-companies-11_Hallmark-Cards_CU50.html.

Hallmark Cards, Inc. "About Hallmark." Kansas City, MO, 2012. Accessed January 13, 2012. http://corporate.hallmark.com/Company.

————. "Founder Joyce C. Hall." Kansas City, MO, 2012. Accessed January 13, 2012. http://corporate.hallmark.com/History/Founder-JC-Hall.

————. "Hallmark History." Kansas City, MO, 2012. Accessed January 13, 2012. http://corporate.hallmark.com/history/Innovation-21st-Century.

"Hallmark Cards, U.S. Postal Service Partner for Postage-Paid Cards." *Kansas City Business Journal,* February 17, 2011. Accessed January 13, 2012. http://www.bizjournals.com/kansascity/news/2011/02/17/hallmark-cards-us-postal-service.html.

Martinez, Juan. "A Special Occasion at Hallmark Cards." *Direct Marketing News,* August 1, 2011. Accessed January 13, 2012. http://www.dmnews.com/a-special-occasion-at-hallmark

-cards/article/208063/.

"Oldest Postcard Sells for £31,750." *BBC News,* March 8, 2002. Accessed January 13, 2012. http://news.bbc.co.uk/2/hi/uk

_news/1862284.stm.

Regan, Patrick. *Hallmark: A Century of Caring.* Atlanta, GA: Lionheart Books, 2010.

Hewlett-Packard's LaserJet Printer

—■—

Hewlett-Packard Company (HP) manufactures many electronic products, and laser printers are one of the company's most well-known products. Although Hewlett-Packard did not invent the laser printer, it was the first company to introduce a relatively inexpensive laser printer that worked well with other office software. The LaserJet was instrumental in the development of the personal computer industry during the 1980s and established a product line that earned the company more than US$1 billion in revenue.

CANON PROTOTYPE

In the early 1970s, Hewlett-Packard sold thermal printers, dot-matrix printers, and daisy-wheel printers. Although these loud and sluggish printers did not perform nearly as well as laser printers, they served as the only options for small companies, as enterprise laser printers cost hundreds of thousands of U.S. dollars at the time. HP managers realized that a personal laser printer offered huge market potential, but the company lacked the technology to produce the printer itself.

Canon Inc., a well-known maker of printers, showed off a prototype laser printer at a conference in 1975, according to Jim Hall, writing for the HP Memory Project. Canon originally wanted to partner with a U.S. company that could help it sell the printers. Bill Hewlett was friends with the Canon CEO, Takeshi Mitarai, and convinced Canon's management to license the printer patents to HP instead. After HP bought the patents, the company's printer division in Boise, Idaho, started work on the project.

The Boise, Idaho team selected the name Electrophotographic Printer on Computer (EPOC) for the laser printer and also gave it a model number, HP 2680A. The 2680A designers quickly realized that the original Canon design lacked reliability, according to Hall. Canon employed many printer repair experts, so sending out an employee to fix a printer for a client was not difficult for the company. HP employed software engineers, programmers, and employees who had responsibilities other than printer repair, so HP would incur high costs if it had to send out staff to fix customers' printers on a regular basis.

The Boise division worked on EPOC for five years, completing the printer design in 1980. HP marketed the large and expensive HP 2680A to medium-sized businesses. The HP Museum listed a catalog price of US$108,500 for the machine. This did not include the price of a HP 3000 minicomputer to direct the printer, which cost another US$120,000. The 2680A boasted a maximum printing speed of 45 pages per minute, a major selling point, and offered much better reliability than the Canon prototype, as it could print hundreds of thousands of pages before it needed repair.

XEROX STAR 8010

Xerox beat HP to market with a small laser printer in 1981, which it marketed as a component of a workstation, the Xerox Star 8010. This workstation also gained fame for many other innovative features, such as Ethernet capability and a graphical user interface, which inspired the design of early personal computers (PCs). Xerox designed the workstation around the costly laser printer. At US$17,000, according to *Tech Spot*, it cost less than a fifth of the price of the HP2680A.

BONSAI

Medium-sized businesses enthusiastically bought the HP 3000 minicomputers, but the HP 2680A printer was not as popular. HP managers believed that the high cost of the printer was the reason for its low sales, and asked Canon if it had any cheaper printer technology. Canon had a cheaper desktop printer available, its LPB-10, but it suffered from major flaws. The printer drenched pages in toner that had the odor of kerosene, and HP managers worried about it burning down printer owners' offices. As Canon did not have any other suitable printing engines, HP asked its prominent competitor, Ricoh Company Limited, to provide an engine for the laser printer. This decision angered and embarrassed Canon managers and jeopardized the relationship between the firms, as the announcement that HP had switched to Ricoh technology damaged Canon's reputation.

The Bonsai project led to two new printer models for HP, the 2687A and the 2688A. With Ricoh's technology, HP managed to beat the Xerox Star on price. Canon sold the lower-end model, the 2687A, for US$12,800 in 1983, according to HP Museum. Although the 2687A was cost competitive with the other laser printers on the market, it still cost too much for many small businesses in the 1980s. The 2680A also frequently needed repairs.

PRINTER COMMAND LANGUAGE

With the Bonsai project, HP introduced an updated language for the software that controlled the printer. It was called Printer Command Language (PCL). PCL provided a single language for all types of HP printers. This was a significant innovation, because by the early 1980s, HP sold many types of printers, each of which required specific software that could send the printer commands. With the unified PCL, software developers did not have to work as hard to create new graphics software for HP printers, and this encouraged them to promote HP products.

PCL offered backwards compatibility. The first version of PCL, PCL1, included commands for the 2687A and 2688A, and HP realized that its future printer models would use additional commands. Future versions of PCL would still be able to use the old PCL1 commands, ensuring that a PC owner who had an older version of graphics software would still be able to use a newer printer. PCL included several software features that word processing software offered, which helped word processor programmers ensure that it was compatible with their software.

CANON CX

In 1983, Canon built another small printer, the LBP-CX, which addressed the flaws of the LPB-10. The LBP-CX used dry toner, eliminating the kerosene odor and fire risk issues. This time, Canon first showed the LPB-CX to several of HP's major competitors in the Bay Area of San Francisco, California. Canon managers visited Diablo

Systems Inc., which Xerox owned, offering a partnership deal. The Canon managers were surprised when Xerox rejected the partnership offer. Xerox had already agreed to a partnership with the major Japanese film manufacturer Fujifilm Holdings Corporation, and the two companies had built their own printer, the 4045, according to The Printer Works.

Canon also showed the LPB-CX to Apple Computer, Inc., and Apple agreed to license the printing technology from Canon. When Canon managers eventually showed up at HP's offices, many of HP's competitors already knew about the LPB-CX technology. LPB-CX was groundbreaking because it introduced to laser printing the all-in-one cartridge, which Canon had invented a year earlier, in 1982. Reliability continued to be a major weakness for all types of printers. However, as the all-in-one cartridge included many other printer parts along with the toner, a small business could simply buy a new cartridge instead of calling in a technician to perform expensive repairs.

PREPARING FOR THE LAUNCH

Having obtained the rights to use the LPB-CX technology, HP named its next project Sprout, with the goal of producing an inexpensive printer than the earlier Bonsai project. The Sprout project developed the printer that became known as the LaserJet. The company's goal was to complete the project by February 1984, as Canon would have the parts for the printer available at that time, according to Hall. The HP engineers worked quickly, and a LaserJet prototype was complete in January 1984.

LaserJet managers enthusiastically promoted the new printer, although HP executives remained skeptical. Ray Smelek gave a presentation to HP executives in January in which he predicted that annual sales for the LaserJet would reach 50,000, which the executives considered far too optimistic. Even a US$10,000 laser printer in 1984 was out of reach for many companies. HP depended on partners like Canon and Ricoh because it lacked many of the capabilities of a printer manufacturer, and much of its revenue came from minicomputers, calculators, tape drives, and other product lines.

The LaserJet managers realized the potential of the Microsoft Office Suite in promoting their new printer. Hall explained that two HP managers, Von Hansen and Roger Archibald, introduced themselves to Microsoft founder Bill Gates on a plane when they were leaving a conference in New Orleans, Louisiana. The managers mentioned that the Microsoft Office software would be more useful to businesses if it included support for a low-cost, high-quality laser printer.

HP also realized that the utility of its laser printer depended on the support that many software designers provided. To encourage graphics and office software makers to offer LaserJet compatibility, HP managers gave away its LaserJet printers to many software companies around the Bay Area. A competitor like Xerox would incur much higher expenses if it were to give away demonstration printers.

To create a truly mass-market laser printer, HP needed to release the LaserJet at an extremely low price. With the inexpensive parts HP received from Canon, the first LaserJet went on sale in May 1984 at US$3,495. The LaserJet cost a third of the price of other laser printers, and its price was competitive with the slow and noisy daisy-wheel and dot-matrix printers as well.

HP made its LaserJets widely available, allowing many computer shops and dealers to stock its LaserJets after their launch. However, dealers told HP that too many of their competitors sold LaserJets, which was reducing the income their stores earned. According to The Printer Works, Although HP added a few restrictions to mollify the dealers, it did not severely limit distribution, because the company knew that other firms' laser printers were not very competitive and dealers had few alternatives.

LASERWRITER

Apple continued to work on its own LPB-CX based project, the LaserWriter, throughout 1984. The LaserWriter used the Postscript language, which included many additional features and commands that the LaserJet's PCL2 did not offer. The LaserJet and the LaserWriter both offered 300 dots per inch (DPI) printing, but the LaserJet could only print 300 DPI on an eighth of a standard printer page, while the LaserWriter offered 300 DPI for an entire page. The LaserWriter was clearly the superior printer, and it gained Apple fame with graphic designers, newspapers, and other artists, greatly improving Apple's reputation in the design industry.

Developing Postscript's capabilities to produce high-quality graphics took time, and the LaserWriter did not launch until March 1985, almost a year after HP introduced the LaserJet. The high-end design features that the LaserWriter offered increased its cost, and Apple priced it at US$6,995, twice the price of the LaserJet. Ben Edwards, for *MacWorld,* reported that Apple engineers built the Appletalk network protocol into the LaserWriter, allowing an entire office of Macintosh users to print with the same laser printer.

CANON

Canon used its LPB-CX engine to develop its own printers, the LPB8-A1 and LBP8-A2, which directly competed with the LaserJet and the LaserWriter. According to The Printer Works, Canon sold the lower-end LPB8-A1 for US$2,995 in 1984, which was actually less expensive than

the LaserJet at the time. HP did reduce the price of the LaserJet to US$2,995 in 1985, eliminating Canon's cost advantage. Canon should have had an advantage over all of the companies that licensed its printing technology, as the hardware in the competing printers was mostly the same, but Canon made the wrong choice when it selected the printing software. Many printers on the market in the early 1980s used software that was compatible with the Diablo 360, a daisy-wheel-based printer from Xerox. Canon believed that software designers would continue to develop Diablo 360-compatible graphics software, so it did not develop a new printing language to compete with PCL and Postscript. This mistake cost Canon market share, although it continued to introduce new printers that competed with future LaserJet and LaserWriter models.

AFTERMATH

After the success of the LaserJet, HP continued to release new LaserJet models on a regular basis. Additional PCL versions came out that added more features, and by the early 1990s, LaserJets could also offer Postscript support. HP included hardware design upgrades such as multiple printer trays and Ethernet compatibility.

The HP LaserJet made many types of office products obsolete. Many printers relied on special and costly paper, but the LaserJet could print on standard office paper. Office supply companies designed furniture to stifle the loud noises that other types of printers produced, but the LaserJet was quiet.

FINAL (PRINTED) WORD

The HP executives had legitimate concerns about the LaserJet in 1984. The Boise division introduced a product that competed against Xerox, the company that invented the laser printer, and Apple, which had a head start on Canon's technology and employed skilled designers. The LaserJet even competed against Canon's own product line, which made dependence on Canon for parts and patent rights extremely risky. Canon could have gained control of the U.S. laser printing market with its LBP-A1 if it had not licensed its printer technology to other manufacturers.

The LaserJet succeeded because of an element that HP's own executives considered one of the firm's weak points: the company's marketing. Although HP remained a manufacturing firm, the LaserJet managers promoted their product aggressively, and the product itself created much of its own advertising buzz. By displaying the LaserJet at conferences and dropping off LaserJets at software developers' offices, HP convinced its potential customers to do much of the initial promotion for the LaserJet.

BIBLIOGRAPHY

"Canon USA LBP8-A1 and LBP8-A2 Printers." Newark, CA: The Printer Works. Accessed January 10, 2012. http://www.printerworks.com/Catalogs/CX-Catalog/CX-LBP-8A1-8A2.html.

DeCarlo, Matthew. "Xerox PARC – A Brief Nod to the Minds Behind Laser Printing, Ethernet, the GUI, and More." *Techspot,* December 20, 2011. Accessed January 10, 2012. http://www.techspot.com/guides/477-xerox-parc-tech-contributions/.

"Early Laser Printer Development." Newark, CA: The Printer Works, 1996. Accessed January 10, 2012. http://www.printerworks.com/Catalogs/CX-Catalog/CX-HP_LaserJet-History.html.

Edwards, Ben. "Four Reasons the LaserWriter Mattered." *Mac World,* April 27, 2010. Accessed January 10, 2012. http://www.macworld.com/article/150845/2010/04/laserwriter.html.

Hall, Jim. "HP LaserJet – The Early History." HP Memory Project. Accessed 10 January 2012. http://www.hpmemory.org/news/jim_hall/laserjet_page_00.htm#hp2680a.

"Laser Printers." HP Computer Museum, 2011. Accessed January 10, 2012. http://www.hpmuseum.net/exhibit.php?class=5&cat=19.

Smelek, Ray. "Making My Own Luck." HP Memory Project. Accessed January 10, 2012. http://www.hpmemory.org/timeline/ray_smelek/making_my_own_luck_00.htm.

Honda Motor Company and Their Motorcycles

A TALENTED ENGINEER PURSUES HIS DREAM

Soichiro Honda (1906–1991), born the son of a blacksmith who repaired bicycles in Hamamatsu, Japan, was a talented natural engineer and motor racing enthusiast who began his career as an apprentice in an automotive garage in Tokyo, Japan. After World War II, Japan's mass transit system had been largely destroyed, leaving remaining transit routes severely overcrowded. Seizing the opportunity, Soichiro Honda secured 500 small military-surplus motors used to power generators during the war and began to graft them onto bicycle frames, providing a transit-weary public with alternative transportation.

Following this early success Soichiro Honda opened the Honda Motor Company Ltd. in 1948. Soon thereafter he teamed up with businessman Takeo Fujisawa and the two began to craft a business that would become an international success story. The company's first creation, a motorized bicycle, was powered by a 90cc two-stroke motor of Soichiro Honda's design. However, this motor annoyed Soichiro Honda, who disliked the noise and smoke common to the two-stroke motor design. From this was born a longtime preference by Soichiro Honda for four-stroke motors. He demonstrated this preference by designing his first complete motorcycle in 1951, the four-stroke, overhead-camshaft, 146cc Dream E.

Soichiro Honda continued to show his remarkable talent for design by following up the next year with the first version of the "Cub," sporting a two-stroke 50cc motor. Consumers could buy the motor only, or the complete red and white "Auto Bai." In less than a year the Honda Motor Co. would hold 70 percent of the powered two-wheel market in Japan. In 1953 Honda Motor Company offered its most sophisticated product yet, a four-stroke 90cc motorcycle with a three-speed gear box. This vehicle carried the "Benly J" nameplate, standing for "convenience," and leaving no doubt as to the company's focus. Within a short time the company was producing one thousand Benly J's every month.

In 1954 Soichiro Honda attended the Isle of Man (a Crown Dependency of the United Kingdom) TT Grand Prix motorcycle race. Subsequently he wrote of his childhood dream of being a champion of motor racing. Soichiro Honda's dream was firmly rooted in reality however, and he laid out the requirements for fulfilling his dream, as reported in the article "Honda Motorcycle History" on Motorcycle.com: "Before becoming world champion, it is strongly required to establish a stable corporate structure, provided with precise production facilities and superior product design."

RIDING A LEGENDARY MODEL TO WORLD DOMINANCE

In 1958 Honda Motor Company was already the largest motorcycle manufacturer in Japan. The founder then used his considerable engineering talent to create the "Super Cub," also known as the "Honda 50." The Super Cub utilized Soichiro Honda's new lightweight, high-performance four-stroke motor. This model was described as a simple, low-cost, easy to operate "scooterette," so called because of its step-through design that appealed to both female and male riders. Eventually the Super Cub would be produced in both 70cc and 90cc versions and was sold around the world.

Meanwhile, Soichiro Honda fulfilled his promise by entering machines of his design in the 125cc class of the Isle of Man TT race in 1959. Around the same time, Honda Motor Company was also contemplating a momentous business decision. Taking advantage of the ceaseless drive toward technological improvement of its founder and the entrepreneurial mindset of both Soichiro Honda and Takeo Fujisawa, the company set out to enter the U.S. motorcycle market.

In 1958, with little understanding of the challenges in store, Soichiro Honda sent Kihachiro Kawashima (later to be president of American Honda) and an assistant to the United States to research the motorcycle market. Kawashima found that motorcycle sales in the United States were dominated by larger domestic machines, like the Harley-Davidson or Indian, and sports motorcycles like the Triumph, manufactured primarily in Europe. Kawashima discovered that the U.S. market was also not a market of practical transportation, as Honda Motor Company was accustomed to in Japan, but a market of lifestyle and adventure. The U.S. market was further impacted by the late 1950s perception of the motorcycle, which was widely displayed in the media as the mode of transportation preferred by anarchic outsiders bent on terrorizing an unsuspecting public.

Realizing the vast differences in the U.S. motoring public and their Japanese counterparts, Kawashima foresaw little opportunity for such Honda Motor Company stalwarts as the Super Cub. Instead he recommended to his superiors that they concentrate on pursuing the U.S. market for larger motorcycles such as 250cc and 350cc versions which were, at that time, the largest that Honda Motor Company could produce. However, early sales of these larger, little-tested Honda Motor Company models in the United States revealed some problems with the motorcycles' reliability over long distances. As the company worked to correct the flaws, its company representatives in the United States were observed by many as they buzzed around the Los Angeles, California, headquarters doing errands on the 50cc Super Cub. This led to a call from a buyer at retail giant Sears, Roebuck, & Company. That company was impressed with the Super Cub's practicality and was interested in establishing a sales arrangement with Honda Motor Company.

Initially Kawashima declined the offer, but when Honda Motor Company's sales of larger motorcycles stalled domestically, he determined that it was time to adapt company expectations. Within two years, the Super Cub became hugely popular with young U.S. consumers that wanted nothing to do with the "bad boy" image of the larger motorcycles but desired a simple, inexpensive mode of short-haul transportation. This perception was helped enormously by a clever advertising campaign that used the slogan, "You meet the nicest people on a Honda,'

showing everyday people happily whizzing back and forth on their Super Cubs carrying groceries, packages, or even other people on the Cub's rear-mounted rack. As a tribute to the design quality of the Super Cub, only minor changes were made to it over the course of the next 20 years. Eventually over 50 million of them were made and sold around the world.

WORLD LEADER

By the end of 1959 Honda Motor Company was the world's largest motorcycle manufacturer. With the success of the Super Cub, Honda now had the clout to expand its horizons. The company next set its sights on the larger sports motorcycle market then dominated in the United States and Europe by British companies. In 1959 Honda introduced the C72 Dream to the European market. This model sparked interest with its inexpensive and unusual pressed steel frame and electric starter, along with the superior, state-of-the-art aluminum engine designed by Soichiro Honda. Honda Motor Company soon followed up with the CB72, which was more in keeping with European aesthetics and handling characteristics but still sported the superior Honda engines. The 72s were enthusiastically received in the U.S. market as well, where Honda went rapidly from a new entrant to holding significant market share.

Soichiro Honda continued his passion for racing and in 1961 he returned to the Isle of Mann TT. Honda Motor Company dominated both the 125cc and 250cc classes, finishing a stunning first through fifth place in both classes. This would be the first in a long string of Honda's successes in the field of motor racing, a tradition that only a few years later would be extended to the automotive field as well. Over the next several years Honda continued to utilize its success in the field of racing to build on its development of commercially viable products. The company continued to expand its offerings into both the off-road and larger motorcycle markets.

In 1968 Honda Motor Company introduced a model called the "superbike" that would electrify the world of motorcycling and create an entirely new category of motorcycle. The CB750F, and the soon-to-be-released CB750, sported the first mass-produced four-cylinder motorcycle engine and front disc brake. It had the fastest acceleration of any production motorcycle on the market and a top speed of 120 miles per hour. In addition, Honda proved it could produce a commercially viable motorcycle with cutting-edge performance and still maintain an enviable level of reliability.

By 1973 Honda Motor Company was riding its superiority and popularity in both the small and midsize motorcycle market, boasting a commanding 63 percent of U.S. market share. During the same period British motorcycle sales had slid from 49 percent to 9 percent of the total U.S. market. In less than 10 years British motorcycle sales in the United States went from 35 million units to less than 2.5 million.

Honda Motor Company continued to build on its reputation for innovation and product quality throughout the 1990s and into the 21st century, challenging the maker of the largest U.S. motorcycles, legendary Harley-Davidson, in its own market, with an ever-expanding range of products geared to both the long-range touring and high-end sports motorcycle market. However, this market was not as robust as it once was. By 2010 U.S. motorcycle sales had been in decline for five straight years, falling by over 50 percent from the peak 2005 levels. The decline between 2008 and 2009 was historically extraordinary, with a decline in motorcycle sales of almost 41 percent in just one year.

WHAT MADE HONDA MOTOR CO. LTD. SO SUCCESSFUL?

The success of Honda Motor Co. Ltd. in rapidly expanding and dominating the world's motorcycle market has been the subject of considerable research and comment in schools of management strategy. Studies have offered differing explanations for Honda's success, particularly concerning its entry and dominance of the U.S. motorcycle market beginning in 1959.

The Analytical View. In 1975 the government of the United Kingdom employed the Boston Consulting Group (BCG) to perform a study of the decline of British motorcycle competitiveness in the international market. BCG offered a number of explanations focused primarily on the various economies of scale that Japanese competitors, and Honda in particular, enjoyed vis-à-vis its British competitors.

According to the BCG, Honda demonstrated, in its entry to the international market, a willingness to absorb losses while it learned and gained market share. Its British counterparts, on the other hand, were willing to abandon any segment of the market as soon as it became unprofitable, basically ceding the field to the Japanese competition in that segment. This process of ceding the market first occurred in the very small displacement motorcycle segment and moved slowly up to the heart of the core British product, the midsize sports motorcycle segment. Each step of the way, according to BCG, the Japanese advantages of higher production, rapid learning, and more competitive management systems allowed them to execute a strategy of "encirclement," whereby they were able, one by one, to capture every segment of the motorcycle market, except the heavyweight field dominated by Harley-Davidson in the United States.

Organizational Process View. In the mid-1980s the Pascale study (led by Richard Pascale) directly countered some of the views laid out in the BCG analysis. According to Pascale, BCG had wrongly superimposed a successful strategy over a diverse set of circumstances that occurred during the first years of Honda Motor Company's entry into the U.S. market. Pascale pointed out that Honda displayed less of a winning strategy than a willingness to learn and adapt, dubbed the "Honda effect." As a result, Honda's success, according to this view, was more the result of design (a great product) and adaptability of Honda's management. While Honda was clearly determined to enter the U.S. market, it had no clear strategy for doing so and simply reacted quickly to developments as they unfolded. Honda showed a willingness to experiment and use feedback produced from the lower rungs of the management hierarchy, who were closest to the customers.

The Idiosyncratic View. A 1991 interpretation, the Quinn study, highlighted the importance of the brilliant but eccentric Soichiro Honda, combined with the business talent of Takeo Fujisawa. In this view, the combination of Honda's perfectionist designs and the risky strategies Fujisawa undertook to support company investments deserved a lot of the credit for the company success. Out of this volatile pairing developed an organization with a focus on engineering technology and design. Fujisawa imprinted a management style on the organization that promoted outside of a traditional hierarchical approach. The organizational structure was flat, with a focus on individualism in research and development. Product development was unapologetically "trial and error," with workers often involved in creating production equipment. This production-based organization centered on a sense of equality. According to Quinn, this fostered an environment that was both creative and productive.

Other writers in the strategic study field have reflected on the value of dramatic incident and competitive breakthrough with respect to the Honda story. Both the circumstances of rapid economic growth, combined with the light weight and strong performance of Honda's novel engine designs, permitted the creation of the technologically superior and hugely successful Super Cub. Honda's success has been repeated by other Japanese companies in what is termed the "virtuous cycle" of competitiveness, whereby increased volume results in decreased unit costs, followed by increased profitability and financial power, leading to reinvestment to fuel growth.

BIBLIOGRAPHY

"Honda History." Franklin, WI: The Smoke Riders Association. Accessed February 8, 2012. http://smokeriders.com/History /Honda_History/body_honda_history.html.

"Honda Motorcycle History." *Motorcycle.com,* 2011. Accessed

February 8, 2012. http://www.motorcycle.com/manufacturer/history-honda-motorcycle.html.

Mair, Andrew. "Learning from Japan? Interpretations of Honda Motors by Strategic Management Theorists." *Nissan Occasional Paper Series,* no. 29, 1999. Accessed February 8, 2012. http://www.nissan.ox.ac.uk/__data/assets/pdf_file/0013/11812/NOPS29.pdf.

"Motorcycle Sales, Statistics, News and Information." *WebBikeWorld,* 2012. Accessed February 9, 2012. http://www.webbikeworld.com/motorcycle-news/statistics/motorcycle-sales-statistics.htm.

Richardson, Adam. "How Honda Succeeded in the United States." *Design Mind,* August 24, 2010. Accessed February 9, 2012. http://designmind.frogdesign.com/blog/how-honda-succeeded-in-the-united-states.html.

Rumelt, Richard P. "The Many Faces of Honda." Los Angeles: University of California, Anderson School of Management, 1995. Accessed February 8, 2012. http://www.anderson.ucla.edu/faculty/dick.rumelt/Docs/Papers/HONDA.

IBM's System/360 and Its Impact on the Computer Industry

International Business Machines Corporation (IBM) has a long history as a technology company, and its original reputation was built on the production of punch card tabulating machines (machines that use cards that contain digital information, conveyed through the arrangement of holes in the card, for accounting purposes). IBM gained fame for many innovations over its history, including the IBM PC. With the System/360, IBM introduced reverse compatibility (allowing older machines to use the new system) , modular design (which allows parts of a system to be made independently and then used in different systems to increase functionality), the eight-bit byte standard (a byte is a unit of digital information), and several other innovations that built the modern computer industry.

THE LEGACY OF THOMAS WATSON, SR.

IBM chairman Thomas Watson, Sr., saw the computer as a large, expensive, and specialized machine for clients like aircraft manufacturers, defense contractors, and government agencies. Although IBM sold computers, they did not produce most of the company's revenue. For businesses that could not spend millions of U.S. dollars on a computer, IBM offered much less expensive products such as tabulating machines and mechanical calculators.

Watson, Sr., was legendary for building IBM into one of the largest U.S. technology companies. He was well respected by IBM employees and other business leaders, and had a reputation as a visionary. Watson, Sr., established many cultural features of the company, like the formal business attire its employees wore. IBM adding machines contributed to the U.S. war effort in World War II by helping manufacturers and military commanders keep accurate records.

Thomas Watson, Sr., who was born in 1874, decided in the early 1950s to retire from the firm and leave his son in charge. Thomas Watson, Jr., gained control in 1952, and he faced the challenge of living up to his father's leadership record. IBM earned steady income from its punch cards, adding machines, and office calculation equipment. Any changes that Watson, Jr., made to IBM to develop his own reputation ran the risk of disrupting the company's steady growth.

ENTERING THE COMPUTER MARKET

IBM built upon its success as an accounting machine manufacturer when it introduced its own line of computers from 1952 to 1954. IBM did not place too much emphasis on marketing its computers during the first few years it sold them. The company's accounting machines brought in a lot of profits, and computers cost too much for many of its customers. As a consequence of the high cost, Remington Rand, famous for building the UNIVAC computer (the first commercial computer produced in the United States, in 1951), gained control over the market for computers. In the early 1950s, IBM held about a quarter of the market, while Remington Rand dominated much of the remaining market.

IBM's computer sales in the 1950s helped create a retail market for computers, as large organizations had built their own computers in earlier years. Although IBM now mass-produced computers, each product line was unique. IBM designed each computer to perform a certain type of calculation as fast as possible, which meant that the computer would not be as worthwhile if its owner used it for another purpose.

The IBM 701 established the feasibility of retail computer sales in 1952. The 701 was an improvement on earlier computers that operated with switches, according to IBM, because it used Williams vacuum tubes (named after its co-inventor, Frederick Williams), which were easy to replace if they broke or burned out. IBM designed the 701 to satisfy the calculation requirements of the defense industry. The vacuum-tube-based computer impressed scientific labs and finance and accounting professionals, although the calculation method the 701 used did not meet their needs. The 701 performed binary (use of only two symbols, 0 and 1) calculation, but business and scientific users needed a computer that could calculate decimals. IBM released the 702, also a Williams tube machine, that performed decimal calculation in 1953. The 701 could still handle large calculations better than the 702, so the 702 established a separate line, not an upgrade.

MARKET CHALLENGES

IBM continued to design new product lines in the 1950s. Each product line included its own hardware and instruction set. Programs that operated on the 701 did not run on the 702. This incompatibility limited IBM's sales. A customer who switched to a new IBM computer could not use any programs he wrote on the old computer, and needed to write entirely new programs to perform calculations on the new computer. This additional work discouraged existing IBM customers from upgrading, and caused customers who could afford to buy a computer to delay their purchases until a more recent computer model reached the market.

Incompatibility was not just a problem for IBM customers. IBM specifically trained its sales staff, engineers, and other product support specialists to work on specific product lines. An IBM employee who helped customers learn about the 701 would not know how to provide assistance for a customer who bought the 702. This issue became more problematic as IBM grew larger and gained more customers in the computing market. IBM incurred high costs each time it launched a new product line, because it needed to retrain every employee who would work with the new product line.

IBM addressed some of these compatibility issues with the 1954 development of its Formula Translation (Fortran) language. Fortran was a major innovation, as a computer operator could now write a program that could run on several of IBM's computers, including computers IBM would build in the future. Although Fortran provided portability for mathematical formulas, computer hardware remained incompatible.

IBM launched the IBM 1401 in 1959, which quickly gained popularity with U.S. businesses. According to Emerson W. Pugh, in a paper written for an IEEE workshop, the transistor-based 1401 was cost competitive with punch-card-based adding machines. IBM built upon the success of the 1401 and released the 1410, 1420, 1460, and 7010. These 1401-based computers were not compatible with the older, vacuum-tube-based 701 and 702.

A NEW DESIGN APPROACH

Watson, Jr., realized that hardware compatibility would be necessary in the future, and he decided to design a new architecture that would satisfy the demands of business, military, and scientific customers. However, he faced a challenge convincing his project managers to work on the new project. Separate divisions within the company produced and marketed each product line, such as the 1401. Building a new computer required the 1401 manager to assign his own employees to help design the system. The 1401 manager would have less time to improve his own product line, and potential 1401 buyers would buy the new computer instead. The 1401 project manager would have to work with IBM project managers who oversaw competing product lines to develop the new architecture.

Watson, Jr., assigned T. Vincent Learson to lead IBM's development team, and Learson recruited the team that would design the new architecture. According to Pugh, Learson assembled the Systems Programming, Research, Engineering, and Development (SPREAD) team in October 1961. To promote the unified approach of the new project, IBM chose the name System/360. Just as a circle covered a full 360 degrees, the new architecture served computer buyers in every field. Lower end System/360 components could be replaced with higher performance components, so a computer owner did not need to buy a completely new machine to improve the calculation ability of an old computer.

The System/360 project required IBM to invest a great deal of its resources. At a cost of US$5 billion, System/360 was one of the most expensive projects in technology history, and a failure risked bankrupting IBM. Watson, Jr.'s decision to introduce System/360 was not the obvious next step for IBM managers or IBM investors, as the 1401 product line was performing well.

SYSTEM/360 LAUNCH

On April 7, 1964, IBM made its five System/360 models available to its customers. IBM applied modular design to reduce the market price of the System/360. The basic System/360 calculated binary numbers. IBM sold two add-on modules, a floating point module and a packed decimal module. A customer could add these modules later as an upgrade.

The System/360 computers used the eight-bit byte to store their data. The eight-bit byte helped IBM ensure that the System/360 offered competitive performance for both binary and decimal calculations. Although using the eight-bit byte increased the price of System/360 computers, IBM believed its customers would pay for calculation speed. The specialized computers that IBM competitors offered typically used a six-bit byte, so the move to eight bits prevented the general purpose System/360 models from suffering a speed disadvantage. Since the System/360 sold so well, the eight-bit byte became the industry standard.

IBM underestimated the demand for its System/360 and announced only five models at first. The Model 40 gained the most sales, although IBM also offered a lower-end Model 30. Higher-end System/360s included the Models 50, 65, and 75. Performance differed widely between these machines, as the Model 75 performed calculations 25 times faster than the Model 30. Because IBM wanted the Model 75 to perform calculations extremely quickly, it lacked the reverse compatibility that the other four models offered. By the end of 1964, IBM had received several thousand orders for System/360 computers. IBM responded to the surge of orders by increasing production in its San Jose, California, plant. Randy Alfred, for *Wired,* reported that the company achieved sales of 1,000 System/360 computers per month by 1966.

MARKET GROWTH

The modular approach greatly increased the market for computer components. Initially, this helped IBM sell its own computer modules, but IBM competitors quickly realized that they could produce their own IBM-compatible parts. IBM even assisted this process by outsourcing semiconductor manufacturing to the large electronics company Texas Instruments Inc., and it also shared its technology with many smaller vendors. Peripherals, such as tape drives, also fit into any System/360 computer, so other manufacturers made IBM-compatible peripherals as well. IBM trained many engineers and programmers on its System/360 project, and competitors prioritized the recruitment of these IBM employees.

IBM hardware impressed organizations throughout the world, including organizations in Russia and Eastern Europe. Cold War regulations prevented IBM from selling its mainframes to Soviet bloc customers, so Russian computer manufacturers needed their own alternative. Russian manufacturers copied System/360, introducing their own IBM-compatible hardware, the ES EVM. ES EVM development extended to System/360 successors as Russian manufacturers copied System/370 and later IBM mainframes.

Remington Rand lost most of its market share to IBM, and other computer manufacturers also suffered. These hardware companies complained to the U.S. Justice Department, accusing IBM of antitrust violations. IBM struggled with antitrust regulators throughout the 1970s, which led to another historic business decision. System/360 separated the computer hardware and computer software markets, and IBM considered itself primarily a hardware manufacturer at the time. To address these antitrust complaints, IBM allowed Bill Gates to provide the operating system for IBM computers, which allowed Microsoft Corporation to develop into a major software company.

MODERN COMPUTING

The advertising campaign for System/360 established the modern computer hardware market. Future releases of System/360 retained their backwards compatibility, and IBM mainframes in the 2000s and early 2010s could still run programs from the original five System/360 models. IBM compatibility became an important selling point for computers for nearly half of a century. ES EVM programmers gained new work in the United States after the end of the Cold War, as they continued to work with System/360-compatible ES EVM mainframes after many U.S. programmers switched to personal computers, according to Matt Datilo.

The decision to carry out the System/360 initiative was a major innovation in itself. IBM produced adding machines for accountants, military contractors, and other conservative and cost-conscious clients. IBM even used its conservatism to promote the company, as its founder dressed salesmen in business suits to display their trustworthiness and credibility. When Thomas Watson, Jr., decided to develop System/360, IBM had been in business for several decades and reported revenue of US$3 billion a year. Investors relied on this blue chip company that employed many U.S. workers and reported steady earnings. Watson, Jr., correctly forecast the future growth of the computer industry and reorganized a large, conservative company to benefit from this growth.

The few weaknesses in IBM's product design actually helped cement the dominance of System/360 in the market. If IBM had successfully locked down the hardware and peripherals market so that competitors could not easily build IBM-compatible hardware, this would have reduced the number of third parties who could offer cheap upgrades. Since competitors sold upgrades, IBM was under pressure to produce its own System/360 upgrades at low prices, forcing it to rapidly improve its product line.

System/360 changed the market structure of the entire computer industry. Although Fortran gains credit for allowing programmers to transfer formulas between computers, hardware compatibility allowed multiple manufacturers to compete on price, greatly reducing the retail price of computers. About a decade later, computers became mass-market consumer products, costing several thousand U.S. dollars each instead of several million.

BIBLIOGRAPHY

Alfred, Randy. "April 7, 1964: IBM Bets Big on System/360." *Wired,* April 7, 2011. Accessed January 12, 2012. http://www.wired.com/thisdayintech/2011/04/0407ibm-launches-system-360-computers/.

Cohen, Malcolm. "Fortran: A Few Historical Details." Oxford, UK: The Numerical Algorithms Group, October 2004. Accessed January 12, 2012. http://www.nag.co.uk/nagware/np/doc/fhistory.asp.

IBM Corporation. "History of IBM: 1950s." Armonk, NY. Accessed January 12, 2012. http://www-03.ibm.com/ibm/history/history/decade_1950.html.

Pugh, Emerson. "Technology Transfer: The IBM System/360 Case." Singapore Workshop, IEEE Power Engineering Society, January 24–26, 2000. Accessed January 12, 2012. http://www.ieeeghn.org/wiki/images/f/f6/Pugh-Technology_Transfer.pdf.

Will, Steve. "System 360: From Computers to Computer Systems." Armonk, NY, 2011. Accessed January 12, 2012. http://www.ibm.com/ibm100/us/en/icons/system360/.

Zientara, Marguerite. "Think: The Story of IBM." In *Digital Deli: The Comprehensible, User-Lovable Menu of Computer Lore, Culture, Lifestyles and Fancy,* edited by Steve Ditlea. New York: Workman, 1984. Accessed January 12, 2012. http://www.atariarchives.org/deli/think.php.

IDEO: An Innovative Design and Consulting Firm

Design firm IDEO uses concepts from industrial design to improve several industries. The firm was originally established to work on technological projects such as the laptop, the mouse, and the personal digital assistant (PDA). IDEO's unique approach, known as Deep Dive, attracted other clients such as Amtrak (National Railroad Passenger Corporation), where it helped disabled passengers ride the train more comfortably. The firm also assisted hospitals by helping patients understand how a hospital functioned. IDEO later expanded into the nonprofit sector, where it used design techniques to bring clean water and improved health care to developing countries.

THREE PARTNERS

A Stanford University engineering professor, David Kelley, set up Kelley Design, a design firm, in response to the high demand for product designers in the San Francisco Bay Area during the 1970s. Computer manufacturers such as International Business Machines (IBM) Corporation and Apple Computer, Inc. were introducing personal computer products to consumers, and they needed companies that could help them create attractive laptops, monitors, computer mice, and keyboards. IDEO CEO Tim Brown and Jocelyn Watt, writing for the *World Bank Institute,* stated that Kelley Design helped Apple come up with its original mouse concept in 1982. Apple's mice were relatively unique in the personal computer industry, because they used a single button, while many IBM-compatible personal computers used a mouse that had two or even three buttons, and often included additional features such as a scroll wheel.

Since Kelley's background was in mechanical engineering, he hired industrial design firms to help him on his consulting projects. These firms employed artists and other creative professionals to help him customize the user experience for a product, while Kelley's firm made sure that the product would satisfy hardware performance expectations.

Industrial designer Bill Moggridge worked with Kelley on his design projects. Moggridge founded a London, England firm, Moggridge Associates, as well as a San Francisco, California firm, ID Two. ID Two was famous for inventing the GRiD Compass, the first laptop computer. According to Jeff Atwood at *Coding Horror,* ID Two created a laptop prototype in 1979, although the original prototype was too expensive for the mass market. The Obsolete Technology Website noted that ID Two started selling its Compass laptops to shoppers at a price of US $8,150 in 1982, which was still too expensive for most consumers, although government officials and executives did buy some of these laptops.

Mike Nuttall was a designer who had originally worked with Moggridge at ID Two. Nuttall left to start his own design firm, Matrix Product Design. Moggridge and Nuttall combined their firms with Kelley Design, creating the design firm IDEO in 1991.

IDEO PROCESS

Kelley Design and ID Two were well known during the 1980s because of the products they had invented. The management theorist Tom Peters was a fan of Kelley's company in particular and continued to praise IDEO after it was founded. Kelley modeled IDEO after Kelley Design, attempting to preserve the environment of a small design firm and eliminating bureaucracy and hierarchy whenever possible. IDEO employees were divided into smaller teams of approximately 15 individuals. Each team included both artists and engineers and they got to choose the projects on which they wanted to work. Traditional design firms were either artist-heavy or engineer-heavy, but Kelley had seen the coordination problems that this approach created.

IDEO designers were expected to go out into the field so they could experience a client's products or services as their customers experienced them. A designer might pretend to be a customer to see how a client typically treated its customers. A designer could test a product in the environment in which it was meant to be used, instead of testing it in the unrealistic environment of the studio. IDEO could also create a larger-scale model of a client's entire service environment to help its designers understand the issues that a customer experienced.

IDEO employed the concept of rapid prototyping. With rapid prototyping, a designer creates many rough prototypes, instead of working on a single prototype for a longer period of time. A prototype could be a simple model or sketch made from items that were sitting around the office, instead of a complete product that was ready to place on the shelf. Quickly developing a prototype and showing it to a focus group reduced wasted effort designing product features that a customer would not use.

IDEO named its innovation technique Deep Dive. In a Deep Dive project, the company created a "hot" team that quickly surveyed the customer's work environment, and then returned to company headquarters and proposed their ideas to solve the client's problems. The hot team then developed rapid prototypes, selected the best solution, and created a finished product. A major advantage of the Deep Dive process was its speed.

EARLY CUSTOMERS

IDEO gained prominence during the 1990s when it helped Palm, Inc. design a new Palm Pilot model. Palm released the basic Palm Pilot early in 1996, and other hardware manufacturers immediately responded by launching their own personal digital assistants (PDAs), which included other performance features. Palm wanted to add more features to the Palm Pilot so it remained competitive, but it did not want to compromise the PDA's simplicity, which was one of its primary selling points. In late 1996 Palm managers asked IDEO to help it design the Palm V.

IDEO used both customer surveys and comparisons to other mobile devices to develop the Palm V. High-end mobile devices were popular because they were very thin and very light, so IDEO investigated ways to shrink the physical size of the Palm Pilot. IDEO added new physical components to improve the Palm's design, replacing its fragile plastic shell with an aluminum case and install-

ing lithium batteries, according to the Corporate Design Foundation. IDEO also changed Palm's marketing focus. IDEO had created a stylish fashion accessory that expanded the size of the market for PDAs, instead of a product that had a marginal technological advantage over its competitors and would quickly become obsolete.

IDEO helped Polaroid Corporation come up with a new camera design in 1997. Polaroid was known for its cameras that could produce a picture after a few seconds, so the user did not have to take the film to a lab and wait for it to be developed. The photographer still had to purchase a separate Polaroid camera that could use the film, which could be expensive and inconvenient. Other camera manufacturers offered single-use cameras that were much more convenient for travelers and individuals with limited incomes, but they used standard film, which needed to be developed.

IDEO combined the advantages of both types of cameras, creating PopShots disposable Polaroid cameras. A photographer could now purchase a cheap, disposable camera that was easy to use and offered almost instantaneous pictures. IDEO added design improvements that improved the aesthetic qualities of the PopShots cameras and added features such as colored buttons that made these cameras simple to use. A disposable PopShots camera was also recyclable.

IDEO was also instrumental in designing the high-speed train service, Acela, for Amtrak. Amtrak asked IDEO to help it create a state-of-the-art train system for passengers on the East Coast of the United States. Amtrak needed to satisfy U.S. federal regulations for disability access while operating train cars that could carry enough passengers to make it financially worthwhile. Amtrak had a poor reputation in comparison to train operators in the European Union and Japan, and many potential train passengers preferred to travel by airplane.

IDEO used upscale hospitality and transportation services to develop the design concept for the Acela trains. Acela facilities were modeled after luxury hotel rooms, European passenger cars, and airline cabins, according to a report by the Center for Universal Design at North Carolina State University. IDEO developed subtle accessibility features, so it was not obvious that they were created to assist disabled passengers, and customers experienced them as high-end amenities.

SHOWCASING THE COMPANY

IDEO's clients were interested in learning how IDEO's process worked, so IDEO created IDEO University. IDEO University offered its own campus to train clients' employees to improve the products on which they were working. Ed Brown, a reporter for *CNN Money*, visited IDEO University and participated in an event called Cannonball

Run, where he worked with a team to design a cannonball launcher. IDEO had expanded beyond offering product design advice, providing services that were typically offered by a management consulting firm.

IDEO changed the relationship between design companies and their clients by offering to serve as a partner of its clients. A client was often concerned about giving the designer the size of its budget, as a client who announced that it could spend US$1 million expected to be charged US$1 million.

AFTER THE DOT-COM CRASH

IDEO continued to add employees and gain customers in the first decade of the 21st century, even as many technology companies failed. By 2005 400 employees worked for IDEO, and the company earned US$70 million a year, reported Nicole Wong of the *San Jose Mercury News*. One reason for IDEO's resilience was that its management kept it from growing too fast. IDEO could support its staff and facilities with the money it received from its clients, unlike many other technology firms that planned to become profitable later. IDEO also offered a relatively unique service. Many technology companies were simply selling groceries, household services, cars, or other products that were available offline. IDEO had a few competitors, such as frog design inc., but the market for its services was not saturated. IDEO's research approach involved additional work that many hardware designers did not perform, and helped it solve problems that competitors found intractable.

NONPROFIT WORK

IDEO had primarily worked for profit-oriented companies during the 1990s and into the new millenium. During the later years of the first decade of the 21st century it took on a few projects for nonprofit organizations to fix problems in less developed countries. Major philanthropic organizations used IDEO's design expertise to improve their services. Linda Tischler, for *Co.Design,* reported that the Bill and Melinda Gates Foundation worked with IDEO on a water purification project, and the Rockefeller Foundation worked with IDEO on an eye care project.

IDEO released its own guide for design and social responsibility in which it explained how a nonprofit could use design concepts to improve life in impoverished regions. IDEO designed its guide as a collaborative project. The nongovernmental organizations that used the guide could add their own insights to the Human Centered Design Toolkit.

Donors and U.S. government agencies were skeptical about working with a for-profit design company on philanthropic projects. To address these concerns, in 2011, IDEO created its own nonprofit design institute, IDEO .org.

THE IDEO JOURNEY

IDEO's success did not hinge on a single innovation. The company made several decisions that helped it acquire a strong reputation, even while it kept a consistent focus on its core strength, industrial design. The first innovation was combining different types of design firms. IDEO could develop a finished product much more quickly than a technology- or art-focused design firm because it did not need to contact a design firm partner to make an important project decision. IDEO later built upon this strength by adding specialists in fields that were outside of the original founders' specialties.

Deep Dive was a concept that continued to serve IDEO well. It helped IDEO designers quickly determine what was important to a client firm's customers, even if the client was in an industry such as mass transportation, health care, or grocery products that was outside of the firm's original technology industry focus. The company's management also made the decision to diversify during the late 1990s, as it could still work for hospitals and other clients during a period in which technology firms had much smaller budgets.

IDEO continued to maintain a strong reputation as it grew by expanding its reach into the global development sector. This was a significant innovation because many of the organizations that traditionally worked on these projects were large and bureaucratic, and design services were often viewed as a luxury that was not relevant to charitable projects. Working on challenges such as bringing fresh water and health care to impoverished nations helped IDEO demonstrate the functional benefits of good design.

BIBLIOGRAPHY

"Amtrak Acela Express Accommodates All." Raleigh, NC: The Center for Universal Design, North Carolina State University, May 2002. Accessed December 7, 2011. http://www.ncsu.edu /ncsu/design/cud/projserv_ps/projects/case_studies/acela.htm.

Atwood, Jeff. "Designing Interactions at IDEO." *Coding Horror,* May 15, 2007. Accessed December 7, 2011. http://www .codinghorror.com/blog/2007/05/designing-interactions-at -ideo.html.

Brown, Ed. "A Day at Innovation U." *CNN Money,* April 12, 1999. Accessed December 7, 2011. http://money.cnn.com /magazines/fortune/fortune_archive/1999/04/12/258145 /index.htm. .

Brown, Tim, and Jocelyn Watt. "Design Thinking for Social Innovation: IDEO." Washington, DC: The World Bank Institute, 2010. Accessed December 7, 2011. http://wbi .worldbank.org/wbi/devoutreach/article/366/design-thinking -social-innovation-ideo .

Clardy, Alan. "IDEO: A Study in Core Competence." Towson, MD: Towson University, Human Resources Development Program, Working Paper–05Clardy–01, November 2005. Accessed December 7, 2011. http://pages.towson.edu/aclardy /Working%20Papers/IDEO.pdf .

Corporate Design Foundation. "Beyond Techno Gadget." Boston, MA. Accessed December 7, 2011. http://www.cdf .org/issue_journal/beyond_techno_gadget.html.

"David Kelley." *TomPeters!* Accessed December 7, 2011. http:// www.tompeters.com/cool_friends/content.php?note=007994 .php.

"GRiD Compass 1101." *Obsolete Technology Website.* Accessed December 7, 2011. http://oldcomputers.net/grid1101.html.

IDEO. "PopShots for Polaroid." Palo Alto, CA. Accessed December 7, 2011. http://www.ideo.com/work/popshots/.

Pethokoukis, James M. "The Deans of Design." *US News & World Report,* September 24, 2006. Accessed December 7, 2011. http://www.usnews.com/usnews/biztech/articles/060924 /2best.htm.

Tischler, Linda. "Looking to Do More Social Good, IDEO Launches a Non-Profit Arm." *Co.Design,* March 7, 2011. Accessed December 7, 2011. http://www.fastcodesign.com /1663355/looking-to-do-more-social-good-ideo-launches-a -non-profit-arm.

Wong, Nicole C. "The Brains Behind IDEO." *San Jose Mercury News,* November 6, 2005.

IMAX: Bigger Screen Cinema

IMAX Corporation revitalized the movie theater experience by offering a much larger screen and much better sound quality than its competitors. The company started out small, displaying films at World Fair exhibitions and science museums, and later became a major player in the movie industry. IMAX created a movie theater experience that a home theater could not replicate, while allowing a movie theater to charge higher ticket prices. IMAX technology could also work in combination with other film technologies, such as three-dimensional (3-D) movies, to create an even better movie experience.

MONTREAL WORLD'S FAIR

The public was first introduced to IMAX technology during the 1967 World's Fair in Montreal. The Canadian Expo Corporation wanted to show off the talents of Canadian filmmakers, so it recruited the independent filmmaker Graeme Ferguson and asked him to create a film that could be showcased as an exhibit at the fair. Ferguson lacked the production resources to make the film himself so he turned to an old high school friend, Robert Kerr. At the time, Kerr was mayor of Galt, Ontario. According to Diane Disse, in "The Birth of IMAX," Kerr agreed to provide assistance with the business-related tasks of running the studio, while Ferguson would dedicate his time to filmmaking.

Other Canadian filmmakers were also showcasing their films at the World's Fair. Roman Kroitor, working with Colin Low, produced *Labyrinth*. The *Labyrinth* exhibit included several projectors and several screens so the film had a much wider display field than a standard movie screen could offer. Audience members walked through the exhibit instead of sitting still in the theater to view the movie. Lisa Fehsenfeld of New York University explained that the projectors were not synchronized during the *Labyrinth* showing, so, in effect, different audiences did not watch the same movie.

Ferguson and Kerr met up with Kroitor at the World's Fair, who was impressed with their film. Kroitor's *Labyrinth* was also popular with audiences. The Fuji Bank, Limited, expressed interest in funding a widescreen film that it could show at the 1970 World's Fair in Osaka, Japan. Fuji Bank asked Kroitor if he would work on the project. Kroitor recruited Ferguson and Kerr, establishing a new company, Multiscreen Corporation, in 1968, to produce widescreen films.

FILMING THE MOVIES

Two innovations helped Multiscreen create its films. A standard film camera could not capture the large images that the company wanted to display, so Multiscreen contacted a Norwegian camera engineer, Jan Jacobsen, to help them develop a new camera. Jacobsen started working on a camera that recorded images horizontally on 65 mm film, reported Courtland Shakespeare for *Good Life*. It took Jacobsen four months to produce a prototype of the horizontal capture camera, which was finished in late 1968.

The second innovation was the projector. The Australian inventor Ronald Jones had created rolling loop technology that could display the images that a horizontal capture camera produced, but it was designed to work with much smaller frames. The rolling loop projector destroyed the film when it projected it at normal speeds. Multiscreen contacted Bill Shaw, an engineer who had attended Galt Collegiate Institute.

Developing a new projector was complicated because Jones lived in Australia, while the other team members were working in Canada and Japan. The team members had to use airmail to contact one another. The other challenge was funding the projector. Multiscreen convinced Fuji Bank to give them US$100,000 to build a projector, using the projector parts as collateral to secure the loan.

In 1970 Multiscreen Corporation showed its multiscreen film *Tiger Child* to Osaka, Japan audiences attending the World's Fair. As the first movie the filmmakers had produced together at Multiscreen, *Tiger Child* is known as the first IMAX movie. *Tiger Child* was a walk-through exhibit in which the movie was displayed on multiple surfaces, and it was popular with the World Fair's visitors.

ADAPTING THE TECHNOLOGY

The filmmakers planned to build on their success at the World's Fair by showing their movies at traditional movie theaters, which would provide them with regular box office revenue. This required several other new innovations. The filmmakers moved away from multiscreen technology, developing movies that could be displayed on a single screen at a movie theater. Multiscreen would no longer be an appropriate name for the studio, so the founders changed it to IMAX. The traditional movie theater layout was designed for a much smaller screen. To ensure that every viewer could get the full IMAX experience, stadium seating was necessary.

Projecting such a large image onto the screen also required a larger light source than the one used by traditional projectors. Xenon lamps provided a brilliant light source, but they were extremely hot, reaching internal temperatures of 1200 degrees Fahrenheit. To prevent the projection booth from catching fire, IMAX used two mirrors to collect the heat, one made of quartz and the other of metal, reported Shakespeare. Technicians also had to wear special clothing to work with these lamps, as a broken xenon lamp created major safety hazards.

Sound playback was also a challenge for widescreen movies. Since it was as much as the projector could do to load the frames, IMAX film was not produced with a soundtrack, unlike standard 35mm film. The initial solution was to use a separate 35mm reel to play back analog sound while the movie was displayed synchronized with the IMAX reel. As the 35mm reel only contained sound data, IMAX films could have better analog sound quality than traditional films.

COMMERCIALIZING THE TECHNOLOGY

IMAX set up its first theater in Ontario, Canada. The company brought back the projection equipment from

Osaka, Japan, to create the first IMAX theater in 1971. Unlike the World's Fair displays, the Cinesphere was not a walk-through exhibit, and viewers remained seated throughout the show.

Scientific observers were impressed with the wide display screen that IMAX provided. The San Diego Hall of Science, which was located in Balboa Park in San Diego, California, planned to build a new planetarium. To show viewers the entire night sky effectively, the museum needed a powerful projector. The museum also wanted the capability of showing movies to the public when the astronomers were not using the planetarium, so that it could pay for its operation and maintenance costs.

IMAX modified its projection technology so that it could show a film on the dome of the planetarium instead of on a flat movie screen. The new projection technology, OMNIMAX, was introduced to the public in 1973 when the planetarium was complete. Other science museums asked IMAX to set up its projection equipment in their own planetariums, and OMNIMAX gained popularity.

THREE-DIMENSIONAL IMAX

OMNIMAX still displayed a two-dimensional image, even though it was projected on a curved screen. The first true three-dimensional IMAX movie, *We Are Born of Stars*, was released more than a decade later. Steve McKerrow, for the *Baltimore Sun*, reported that *We Are Born of Stars* opened in Japan in 1984. Viewers had to wear cardboard 3-D glasses with red and blue cellophane lenses to watch the movie.

SOUND TECHNOLOGY UPGRADE

IMAX moved to digital sound in 1988 with the acquisition of a majority stake in Sonics Associates, Inc. Sonics created the technology that newer IMAX films used, a process known as digital disc playback (DDP). An IMAX film would now use compact discs to play digital sound, instead of an analog film reel. The website In70mm.com explained that each IMAX film used three separate compact discs to store its soundtrack, in a six-channel sound system in which each disc stored two channels.

Digital disc playback had two major advantages over the sound systems that other films used. Due to the large amount of data that the compact discs stored, an IMAX film had an audio range of 10 octaves, which was greater than the six-octave range of other films. The audio information was also transmitted in an uncompressed form so the sound quality of an IMAX film did not suffer from any compression loss.

NEW OWNERSHIP

Richard Gelfond and Bradley Wechsler were two lawyers who met in the 1980s while working at the private equity firm Drexel, Burnham, and Lambert. The firm suffered large losses on its junk bond trades and several employees were convicted of felony financial crimes, including Michael Milken, which led to the firm's collapse in 1990. Gelfond and Wechsler set up their own investment firm afterward, Cheviot Capital Advisors.

Cheviot partnered with Wasserstein Perella and an IMAX competitor, the Trumbull Company, to buy out Kerr, Ferguson, and Kroitor for US$100 million in 1994. Trumbull and IMAX were merged together as part of the deal and the company kept the IMAX name. Gelfond and Wechsler took over IMAX as the new managers and under their leadership, IMAX experienced much faster growth. William Symonds, writing for *Bloomberg Businessweek,* reported that the company's profits increased by more than 400 percent in 1996, and its executives aggressively marketed IMAX technology to all of the major film studios.

IMAX continued to expand aggressively, so when a U.S. recession occurred in 2001, the company was overextended. IMAX had signed contracts with several movie theaters that were bankrupted by the recession, so it suffered from severe cash shortages. Gelfond and Wechsler responded by reducing the costs of a typical IMAX installation. IMAX rented its projection equipment to theaters instead of making permanent sales, reducing the upfront costs for the theater while establishing a permanent stream of revenue for IMAX. According to the Wharton School of Business, an installation during the 1990s could cost US$5 million, but IMAX offered a scaled down version for US$1.5 million by 2002. IMAX also developed technology that allowed it to convert standard 35mm movies to the IMAX format, so that a studio could use its existing movie library instead of filming a new IMAX movie.

DIGITAL PROJECTION

Offering studios the chance to convert their old films to the IMAX format improved the competitive position of IMAX. Competitors were starting to introduce digital projectors, which allowed them to display high-quality pictures that could compete with the IMAX experience. IMAX decided to respond by introducing its own films in digital format. Producing digital IMAX films was more challenging for IMAX because of the large screens the studio used. The larger screen made it more difficult to create a high-quality digital image on a larger screen. Gelfond and Wechsler were enthusiastic about their digital projection plan. Melanie Lindner, reporting for *Forbes,* explained that the switch to digital meant that IMAX would no longer need to use film prints, which would drastically reduce its production costs.

The challenge for IMAX was convincing movie viewers that digital IMAX provided a significant upgrade in picture quality. Digital IMAX was introduced in 2008, during a global recession. The studio had to convince a moviegoer that the improvement in picture quality was worth paying US$15 for a ticket, instead of US$10. Some film critics were not impressed, however. Peter Sciretta, for *SlashFilm,* described the digital IMAX screens as having a slightly larger size than the old analog screens, while having a significantly worse screen resolution.

Competitor Cinemark Holdings, Inc., released its own large-screen digital projection system, extreme digital cinema (XD), to compete with digital IMAX. Eugene Novikov at MovieFone reported that lawsuits followed the XD launch, as Cinemark and IMAX fought over the patent rights to large-screen digital projection technology.

REASONS FOR SUCCESS

IMAX succeeded because its founders knew when to look for help and where to look for the specialists who were needed. Roman Kroitor was willing to share the assignment he obtained from Fuji Bank with other filmmakers who had demonstrated their expertise with multichannel films. When the team of filmmakers realized that they needed new projection equipment to display their movies, they were willing to seek out skilled engineers on the other side of the world to obtain assistance. Finally, the filmmakers knew when to relinquish control of IMAX and sell it to investors who had the capital to develop it into a larger business.

BIBLIOGRAPHY

Boehm, Mike. "California Science Center Is Sued for Canceling a Film Promoting Intelligent Design." *Los Angeles Times,* December 29, 2009. Accessed December 9, 2011. http://articles.latimes.com/2009/dec/29/entertainment/la-et-science-center29-2009dec29.

Disse, Diane. "The Birth of IMAX." IEEE Canada. Accessed December 9, 2011. http://www.ieee.ca/millennium/imax/imax_birth.html.

Fehsenfeld, Lisa. "Final Report on IMAX." New York University, Fall 2006. Accessed December 9, 2011. http://www.nyu.edu/tisch/preservation/program/student_work/2006fall/06f_2910_fehsenfeld_a1.doc.

Florian, Brian. "Cinesphere, The World's First Permanent IMAX Facility." *Home Theater HiFi,* July 2001. Accessed December 9, 2011. http://www.hometheaterhifi.com/volume_8_3/feature-article-cinesphere-7-2001.html.

Hoium, Travis. "IMAX Shares Popped: What You Need to Know." *Daily Finance,* December 5, 2011. Accessed December 9, 2011. http://www.dailyfinance.com/2011/12/05/imax-shares-popped-what-you-need-to-know/?source=edddlf txt0860001.

"IMAX CEO Richard Gelfond on What's Next for the Big Screen." *Knowledge@Wharton*, July 25, 2007. (accessed December 9, 2011). http://knowledge.wharton.upenn.edu/article.cfm?articleid=1779.

IMAX Corporation. "IMAX Through the Decades: IMAX the

60s." Mississauga, Ontario, Canada. Accessed December 9, 2011. http://enews.imax.com/local/files/Communications/IMAXDecades1960.ppt.

Lindner, Melanie. "IMAX's Digital Future, Coming Soon." *Forbes*, October 17, 2007. Accessed December 9, 2011. http://www.forbes.com/2007/10/17/imax-digital-closer-markets-equity-cx_ml_1017markets41.html.

McKerrow, Steve. "'Stars': 3-D IMAX Film a Bit Too Shallow." *Baltimore Sun*, May 28, 1993. Accessed December 9, 2011. http://articles.baltimoresun.com/1993-05-28/entertainment/1993148007_1_imax-maryland-science-3-d.

Novikov, Eugene. "Revisiting Digital IMAX and Cinemark's XD Cinemas." *MovieFone*, January 30, 2010. Accessed December 9, 2011. http://blog.moviefone.com/2010/01/30/revisiting-digital-imax-and-cinemarks-xd-cinemas/.

Sciretta, Peter. "Why You Probably Shouldn't Waste $5 More for Digital IMAX." *SlashFilm*, May 11, 2009. Accessed December 9, 2011. http://www.slashfilm.com/why-you-probably-shouldnt-waste-5-more-for-digital-imax/.

Shakespeare, Courtland. "Projections: IMAX." *Good Life*, April 2011. Accessed December 9, 2011. http://goodlifemississauga.com/107-gl-2011/projections3.html.

Sorensen, Rene. "IMAX Sound System." *In70mm.com*. Last modified December 17, 2011. Accessed January 10, 2012. http://www.in70mm.com/newsletter/1997/50/imax_sound/index.htm.

Symonds, William C. "Now Showing in IMAX: Money!" *Bloomberg Businessweek*, March 31, 1997. Accessed December 9, 2011. http://www.businessweek.com/archives/1997/b3520097.arc.htm.

Incandescent Light Bulb and Thomas Edison

Although there were earlier versions of light bulbs as well as electric lamps, Thomas Edison was credited with creating the first practical incandescent light bulb. It consisted of a filament wire inside a vacuum glass globe. When the filament was heated up by an electrical current, it began to glow and produce light. This was the first economical design that lasted hundreds of hours and did not require a powerful current. Edison's other notable achievement was simultaneously inventing a complete lighting system that could power the light bulbs. With the advent of Edison's power stations, which brought electricity into homes and businesses, society soon began to benefit from many other electrical conveniences. Since the commercialization of Edison's light bulb, other scientists have made many improvements to the design over many decades.

EDISON'S EARLY INTEREST IN ELECTRICITY

Edison was born in 1847 and homeschooled by his mother, a former schoolteacher, while growing up in Ohio. Edison was an enterprising teenager and set up his first laboratory with the money he earned. He began working as a telegraph operator, which supplied background knowledge in batteries, wire circuits, and other elements of electricity. He designed an electrical vote recorder for the Massachusetts State Legislature and was awarded the patent in 1868. Unfortunately, the politicians were not interested in the device.

In 1871 Edison opened a laboratory and factory in Newark, New Jersey, with the intention of making telegraph equipment. His quadruplex telegraph system allowed four messages to be sent simultaneously (two in each direction) on a single wire. This early success allowed him to build a new laboratory in Menlo Park, New Jersey. He began a career as a full-time inventor in 1876.

This was also the year that Alexander Graham Bell patented the telephone. To get around the patent, Western Union hired Edison to improve the invention. With the help of inventor Charles Batchelor, Edison used carbon button transmitters to improve the transmission of the speaker's voice across the wires. This work led him to begin experimenting with methods for recording sound. In 1877 his design for a phonograph worked, but it would some time before it became a profitable business.

FIRST ELECTRIC LIGHTS

In 1802 English chemist Humphrey Davy created the first incandescent light by passing a current through a platinum filament. The light was not particularly bright, and although platinum had a high melting point, it did not have the longevity to be practical as a lasting light source. Around this same time, Davy also demonstrated the first arc lamp, which produced an electric arc between two charcoal rods that were spaced about four inches apart. In 1820 English scientist Warren de la Rue improved the longevity of the platinum filament in incandescent light by enclosing it in a vacuum tube. These inventions were powered by batteries and would not prove to be useful until generators were invented more than a decade later.

The first electric generator, or dynamo, was invented in 1832 by Hippolyte Pixii, a French instrument maker. His apparatus consisted of a permanent magnet and wire coil. When the magnet was rotated using a hand crank, it produced a current each time it passed the wire coil. In

1866 it was discovered that using electromagnets increased the electric output. In 1877 Charles Brush invented an arc lamp and dynamo that he intended to market as a lighting system.

Brush's arc lamps began to light department store windows, factories, city parks, and the outside of government buildings in the United States. They were also used as street lights, such as along sections of Broadway Avenue in New York City. At this same time, an arc lamp invented by Russian engineer Pavel Yablochkov was implemented as street lighting in Paris, France. Although arc lamps were suitable for commercial installations, they were too intensely bright for use in homes.

A PRACTICAL LIGHT BULB

Using the carbon filament from an arc lamp, English chemist Joseph Swan enclosed it in a vacuum glass bulb with platinum lead wires. In February 1879 he successfully completed a public demonstration of his incandescent light bulb to the Newcastle Chemical Society in England. The design had some drawbacks, however. The activated carbon released soot, which quickly covered the inside of the glass bulb and blocked the light. Additionally, the low resistance of carbon required a significant current to glow. This meant that the wires supplying the current had to be impractically short or thick.

Across the Atlantic Ocean, Edison had been experimenting with different materials for a light bulb filament without success until he began carbonizing the material. Carbonizing thread was successful in producing incandescent light, but it only lasted 40 hours. Carbonizing bristol board (uncoated paperboard) extended the filament lifespan to about 150 hours. The paper was formed into a horseshoe shape using a mold and placed in a furnace. The resulting carbonized paper filament resembled black thread. The ends were attached to platinum lead wires with platinum clamps. The lead wires ran through a glass tube and attached to copper wires that conducted the electricity. A glass globe was blown around the filament and the top of the glass tube. Exhausting the air out of the glass globe took more than an hour. The estimated cost to produce the light bulb was US$0.25.

When a *New York Times* reporter visited the Menlo Park Laboratory in October 1879, Edison had 84 light bulbs connected to an 80-horsepower generator and a machine to regulate the electrical flow to each series of lights. The reporter wrote, "It has been asserted by some persons who are supposed to be conversant with the subject of electricity that in order to furnish lights for houses in this City a copper coil as large as an ordinary barrel would be required as a conductor from the central station to the different houses in two or three blocks." Edison responded by saying, "The wire itself, which will convey the elec-

tricity, will be an ordinary No. 9 telegraph wire, the same wire that you see in use every day by the Western Union Company." These wires would be run through pipes buried along the end of the streets. Once Edison had lights in the houses and along the streets, he planned to fully test the longevity of the carbon paper by keeping the lights on for a two-week period.

LIGHT BULB EXPERIMENTATION

Edison continued to test other carbon materials, such as wood splints and plumbago (a flowering plant), looking for a longer-lasting filament. He also made some improvements to the design of the carbonized wire. The selected material was mixed with lamp-black (the soot formed by burning carbon) and tar, and rolled into a uniform wire. The wire was as thin as 0.0007 inch and measured roughly one foot long. After coiling the wire around a bobbin (spindle), the ends were secured to platinum lead wires with more lamp-black and tar before exposing it to high heat in a carbonizing chamber. Cementing the filament to the lead wires avoided having to clamp the fragile wire, and coiling the filament prevented flickering from any inconsistency in the current.

Edison's light bulb was unique in that it had a much higher resistance. Previous light bulbs had only up to four ohms, which was the unit of measure for electrical resistance, while this design had up to 2,000 ohms. The higher resistance meant that the copper wires used to supply the current could be run a longer distance. Edison filed a patent for this light bulb design in November 1879.

By Christmas of that year, Edison had extended his electrical lighting system beyond his laboratory and own house. He had successfully lit houses and streetlights up to one-fifth of a mile from the generator. The first promotional public demonstration was held on New Year's Eve. Before the patent was granted on January 27, 1880, Edison improved on the design yet again. He discovered that carbonized bamboo had an even higher electrical resistance than other materials he had used. It also lasted at least four times longer than carbonized paper.

COMMERCIALIZATION OF EDISON'S LIGHT BULB

The first commercial application of Edison's lighting system was, oddly, on a ship. It was installed on the *S.S. Columbia* docked in New York City. In February 1880 the ship embarked on a 10-week journey around the tip of South America to Oregon, during which time the incandescent lighting system functioned well. Nearly a year passed before Edison's system was installed in the first commercial building, a printing company located in New York, New York. Both of these early installations were simple in that they involved an on-site generator. Edison's factory manufactured the complete lighting system, including dynamos, sockets, and switches.

Interestingly, Edison's first power station was in London, England, not in the United States. The process of getting approval to dig up streets to lay underground wire was time consuming. The Holborn Viaduct in London, however, offered an opportunity to run wires without digging. In 1882 the power station began operating. It was a success, and Edison formed the Edison Electric Illuminating Company. By September of that year, Edison had built the Pearl Street Station in New York, New York, which lit 25 buildings in the financial district. It included a single improved generator that initially powered 800 light bulbs as well as meters to measure how much electricity each customer used. By the end of the following year, he had more than 500 customers and was powering approximately 12,700 light bulbs.

EDISON'S COMPETITION

Back in England, Swan continued experimenting with carbonized materials and found success with carbonized cellulose, the primary material in the cell wall of plants. He formed the Swan Electric Company in 1881 and began selling these light bulbs. His patents in England were strong enough to hold up in court, so Edison decided to join forces rather than wage a legal battle over patent rights. In 1883 the Edison & Swan United Electric Light Company was formed. The company began selling lights with the cellulose filament under the Ediswan brand. Edison's separate company continued to sell light bulbs with carbon bamboo filaments.

In 1889 Brush Electric Company merged with its principal arc lamp competitor, the Thomson-Houston Electric Company, which had been founded by Elihu Thomson and Edwin Houston nine years earlier. The company diversified into incandescent light in 1886 with the purchase of Sawyer & Man Electric Co. In 1890 Edison merged his various businesses together and formed the Edison General Electric Company. Two years later, it merged with Thomson-Houston and was renamed the General Electric Company. Thomson remained the chief engineer, and the company began selling light bulbs with carbon cellulose filaments.

At this time, Edison won a patent infringement case against Westinghouse Electric Company. George Westinghouse had purchased the United States Electric Lighting Company in 1888, which had been producing and installing light bulb systems since the beginning of the decade. After encountering a roadblock with selling its light bulbs, Westinghouse obtained patent rights to Sawyer & Man light bulbs, which it produced and sold until Edison's patent expired in 1897.

NOTABLE IMPROVEMENTS IN THE LIGHT BULB

In 1898 inventors began experimenting with various elements that might prove to be more efficient than carbon filaments. The element tantalum increased the efficiency from three lumens per watt (lpw) to five lpw, but only worked on alternating current. By the turn of the century the element tungsten was found to have an efficiency of eight lpw and worked with both alternating and direct current, but it was brittle. In 1909 William Coolidge, a scientist at General Electric, discovered a method of producing extremely ductile tungsten, which could be drawn into wire that was only one-sixth the diameter of a human hair, but was as strong as steel. Even before he was granted the patent on December 30, 1913, General Electric began marketing these higher-efficiency light bulbs.

In 1913 it was discovered that filling the light bulb with argon, an inert gas, rather than exhausting the air, doubled efficacy and slowed the evaporation rate of tungsten that led to bulb blackening. (Later, the element krypton was found to further boost efficacy and slow evaporation.) Chemist Marvin Pipkin joined General Electric in 1919 and began to tackle the problem of frosting the inside of a light bulb to diffuse the light. Earlier attempts using acid to etch the inside of the bulb made the glass too brittle, resulting in 50 percent breakage. One day, Pipkin poured cleaning solution into an etched light bulb and accidentally dumped it out before the etching had been removed. His discovery that this process yielded a strong light bulb occurred quite by accident when the light bulb fell off his desk. He patented the process in 1924 and invented the soft-white bulb in 1947 by coating the inside with a silica-based substance.

Although Edison was best known for his light bulb, he was granted more than 1,000 U.S. patents before his death on October 18, 1931. The journey that started with incandescent light led to the discovery of a practical light bulb and the first power station. Once the dependence on candles, oil lanterns, and gas lamps for light ended, nighttime hours became a much more social and productive time. Edison was also credited with developing the system that brought electrical power into homes. This led to many more inventions that improved life, such as General Electric's toaster in 1905, the electric range in 1910, and the refrigerator in 1917. Edison's tenacity and vision helped achieve the miracle of light and an electricity distribution system that forever changed the world.

BIBLIOGRAPHY

Bedi, Joyce. "Edison's Story." Washington, DC: The Lemelson Center for the Study of Invention and Innovation. Accessed February 8, 2012. http://invention.smithsonian.org/centerpieces/edison/000_story_02.asp.

"Competition to Edison's Lamp." Washington, DC: National

Museum of American History. Accessed February 8, 2012. http://americanhistory.si.edu/lighting/19thcent/comp19.htm.

"Edison's Electric Light." *New York Times,* October 21, 1879. Accessed February 8, 2012. http://www.nytimes.com /learning/general/onthisday/big/1021.html#headlines.

Eisenman, H. J. "Artificial Gas and Electrical Lighting Systems Are Developed That Change Living and Work Patterns." In *Science and Its Times,* edited by Neil Schlager and Josh Lauer. Vol. 5: 1800 to 1899, 553–555. Detroit: Gale Cengage Learning, 2000. Gale Virtual Reference Library (GALE|CX3408502948). Accessed February 8, 2012. http:// go.galegroup.com/ps/i.do?id=GALE%7CCX3408502948&v =2.1&u=itsbtrial&it=r&p=GVRL&sw=w.

Fletcher, Dan. "A Brief History of the Lightbulb." *TIME,* October 21, 2009. Accessed February 8, 2012. http://www .time.com/time/business/article/0,8599,1919956,00.html.

General Electric Company. "A Tradition of Innovation." Fairfield, CT, 2010. Accessed February 8, 2012. http://www.ge.com /innovation/timeline/index.html.

"History: Timeline." Interactive Nano-Visualization in Science and Engineering Education. Accessed February 8, 2012. http://invsee.asu.edu/Modules/lightbulb/1906.htm.

"Lamp Inventors 1880–1940: Carbon Filament Incandescent." Washington, DC: National Museum of American History. Accessed February 8, 2012. http://americanhistory.si.edu /lighting/bios/swan.htm.

"Lamp Inventors 1880–1940: Ductile Tungsten Filament." Washington, DC: National Museum of American History. Accessed February 8, 2012. http://www.americanhistory .si.edu/lighting/bios/coolidge.htm.

"Marvin Pipkin Lighted Our Lives." *The Ledger,* October 21, 2009. Accessed February 8, 2012. http://www.theledger.com /article/20091011/COLUMNISTS/910115010.

"Origin of Electric Power." Washington, DC: National Museum of American History. Accessed February 8, 2012. http://www .americanhistory.si.edu/powering/past/prehist.htm.

"The Practical Incandescent Light Bulb." Beaumont, TX: Edison Museum. Accessed February 8, 2012. http://www.edison museum.org/content3399.html?pageCatID=2&pageID=4.

"Promoting Edison's Lamp." Washington, DC: National Museum of American History. Accessed February 8, 2012. http://americanhistory.si.edu/lighting/19thcent/promo19 .htm.

Thomas A. Edison. "Electric Lamp." Washington, DC: United States Patent and Trademark Office, January 27, 1880. Accessed February 8, 2012. http://patimg2.uspto.gov/.piw?d ocid=00223898&SectionNum=3&IDKey=120E91948CAA &HomeUrl=http://patft.uspto.gov/netacgi/nph-Parser?Sect1 =PTO2%2526Sect2=HITOFF%2526p=1%2526u=%25252 Fnetahtml%25252FPTO%25252Fsearch-bool.html%2526 r=1%2526f=G%2526l=50%2526co1=AND%2526d=PALL %2526s1=0223898.PN.%2526OS=PN/0223898%2526RS =PN/0223898.

William D. Coolidge. "Tungsten and Method of Making the Same for Use as Filaments of Incandescent Electric Lamps and for Other Purposes." Washington, DC: United States Patent and Trademark Office, December 30, 1913. Accessed February 8, 2012. http://patimg1.uspto.gov/.piw?docid=01 082933&SectionNum=1&IDKey=78559901FA85&Home Url=http://patft.uspto.gov/netacgi/nph-Parser?Sect1=PTO2 %2526Sect2=HITOFF%2526p=1%2526u=%25252Fneta html%25252FPTO%25252Fsearch-bool.html%2526r=1% 2526f=G%2526l=50%2526co1=AND%2526d=PALL%2 526s1=1,082,933.PN.%2526OS=PN/1,082,933%2526RS =PN/1,082,933.

Intel Corporation Enters Microprocessor Industry

The engineers who founded Intel Corporation originally envisioned the company as a memory manufacturer, and during the 1970s, Intel was known for innovation in the memory chip industry. Intel did invest enough money in microprocessors to impress early computer hobbyists and, eventually, International Business Machines (IBM) Corporation. When memory sales fell rapidly in the early 1980s, Intel was able to switch over to microprocessor production because of the popularity of the IBM personal computer (PC).

REDESIGNING COMPUTER MEMORY

Gordon Moore and Bob Noyce met while working as engineers for the Shockley Semiconductor Corporation. The engineers did not like working under the direction of William Shockley, and resigned to establish a company under their own management with several other former Shockley engineers; this new firm was named the Fairchild Semiconductor Corporation. While working at the Fairchild Semiconductor Corporation, Noyce met Tadashi Sasaki, who worked for the Japanese technology firm Sharp Corporation.

Noyce and Moore left Fairchild together in 1968 to set up Intel. The start-up founders realized the great potential that semiconductors held for computer memory. Since the 1950s, computers used magnetic cores, made of ferrite, to store the results of their calculations. These metal cores were large, bulky, and expensive, and they offered very little storage capacity. Noyce and Moore planned to replace these ferrite cores with memory chips that used semiconductors to store information.

Intel gained a few customers with its first memory chip, the 3101 Schottky, in 1969. This early chip did not gain much market share, but it provided an example of Intel technology. Noyce traveled to Japan to promote the new Intel memory chips, marketing them to his friend Sasaki at Sharp.

BUSICOM

Sharp had an existing supply contract with Rockwell International, but Sasaki found a way to help Noyce anyway. Sasaki's plan also helped another friend, Yoshio Kojima, at the calculator manufacturer Business Computer Corporation, or Busicom. Busicom wanted to expand its share of the market for electronic calculators, but it needed technology upgrades and cash. Nigel Tout, for *Vintage Calculators,* explained that Sasaki offered to help Busicom if it hired Intel to design its chips. In 1969, Busicom hired Intel to design a chip for its 141-PF calculator.

Intel did not dedicate a great deal of its resources to the Busicom project. The company had introduced the Intel 1103 memory chip in 1970. The 1103 offered an effective alternative to magnetic core memory, and greatly increased Intel's revenue. Dov Frohman invented a new storage technology, erasable programmable read-only memory, which held great potential for future products. The company assigned its engineers to research memory chips while it prepared for its initial public offering (IPO). Intel eventually completed the 4004 design in early 1971.

Busicom made a significant business mistake after Intel completed the chip design as it suffered from a serious cash shortage in 1971. The original contract gave Busicom both the right to the 4004 design, and the right to buy all of the 4004 chips Intel produced, reported Sebastian Anthony for *Extreme Tech*. In exchange for a discount from Intel, Busicom gave up both of these rights, ceding its ownership of the first single chip central processor.

INTEL 8008

Although the 4004 established the feasibility of building the microprocessor, it lacked the features that Intel customers needed for advanced computing. Specifically, IBM popularized the eight-bit standard, but the less powerful 4004 used the four-bit standard, so Intel needed to produce an eight-bit processor. (A bit is a fundamental unit of digital data.) Intel also built the 8008 as a side project for a client while it concentrated its main efforts on producing the 1103 and other memory chips. Computer Terminal Corporation needed a chip for its computer terminals, which had higher processing demands than the Busicom calculators. Intel took longer than its client expected to design the 8008, and by the time the chip was complete, Computer Terminal Corporation decided it lacked the power it needed for its terminals.

Again, Intel convinced its client to give up its rights over the new chip, so it could sell the 8008 to its customers, according to Gary Marshall for *TechRadar*. Computer Terminal Corporation, like Busicom, believed it was saving money by giving up the rights to the Intel chip, as Intel would have earned US$50,000 for the 8008 rights. As with the 4004, Intel successfully marketed its 8008 chips to a Japanese calculator manufacturer, this time Seiko Holdings Corporation.

Intel continued to disregard its microprocessor business, and it did not even try to patent the 8008. Computer Terminal Corporation had also asked Texas Instruments Inc., well known for manufacturing scientific calculators, to design a chip for its terminals. Texas Instruments submitted a patent for a chip that was similar to the 8008, but Texas Instruments abandoned the manufacturing plans for its 8008 analogue after Computer Terminal Corporation decided the chip was too weak to use in its terminals, according to Stanley Mazor for the IEEE. Intel started selling the 8008 in 1972, but the 1103 memory chip provided almost all of the company's income for the year.

INTEL 8080

The 4004 and the 8008 gained enough customers for Intel to start working on a successor to the 8008, the 8080. Stanley Mazor, in *Proceedings of the IEEE,* explained that improvements in the 8080 design effectively doubled the speed of the microprocessor without making drastic changes to the chip manufacturing process. The 8080 was still similar enough to the 8008 that assembly code for the

8008 could run on the new chip. This time, Intel patented the 8080 design.

The 8080 boasted a speed of two megahertz (MHz), which was fast enough for companies to consider it a viable microprocessor for early home computers. One of these early computers, the Altair, demonstrated the potential of the new chip to the public. When Intel released the 8080 in 1974, home computer enthusiasts had to pay US$360 for the new chip. Intel chose this price to mock IBM's famous System/360 mainframe line, which consisted of much more expensive and powerful computers. Altair builder Ed Roberts wanted to offer inexpensive home computers to his customers. Intel offered Roberts 8080 chips that did not meet Intel's appearance standards, but still performed calculations normally, for US$75. This discount allowed Roberts to sell the unassembled Altair for US$395. This list price was very affordable in comparison with the IBM System/360 computers, which cost tens of thousands of U.S. dollars, and the Altair quickly gained many customers after its launch in 1975. The low price of the 8080 helped it compete with the Motorola 6800, another early microprocessor.

ZILOG Z80

Federico Faggin helped design the 4004 and the 8008 for Intel. Although these chips sold much better than Intel expected, Intel continued to focus on producing its memory chip lines. Faggin felt that Intel did not appreciate the full potential of the microprocessor market, so he decided to start a new company, Zilog, Inc., that specialized in microprocessor production. Faggin began the venture with another former Intel engineer, Ralph Ungermann. Masatoshi Shima, who worked under Faggin on the 8080 project, also left to work at Zilog.

According to the *International Directory of Company Histories,* the start-up attracted a sizable investment from Exxon of US$1.5 million. With the engineers who built the 8080 working on the project, Zilog designed a new processor relatively quickly, and the Zilog Z80 reached the market in 1976. Zilog built facilities to mass produce the Z80, and licensed the design to many other manufacturers, so Z80s were soon available at low prices.

INTEL 2117

Intel experienced delays in the development of its 16K dynamic random access memory (DRAM) chip, the 2117, which reached the market in 1977. Japanese DRAM makers had some time to market their own 16K chips to U.S. customers before Intel and other U.S. firms could make higher capacity DRAM chips. Although Intel still held a large share of the market for memory chips, the increased competition cost it some of the pricing power it needed to fund its research budget. Intel's dominance in the memory chip industry had also helped standardize memory design, which helped Japanese companies compete on price.

INTEL 8086

Intel raced to develop its next microprocessor, the 8086. Texas Instruments had already finished a 16-bit chip in 1976, the TI 9900, and Motorola and Zilog planned their own 16-bit chip launches. Zilog engineers worked on the Zilog Z8000, while Motorola engineers developed the Motorola 68000. Intel beat Motorola and Zilog to market, and released the new chip in 1978.

Intel now expected microprocessors to sell well, but the 8086 initially failed to meet the company's expectations. Computer hobbyists wanted cheap computers, and the eight-bit Z80 cost less than the 8086 and offered fair performance. Intel decided to make a lower end version of the 8086, the 8088. Although the 8088 still performed 16-bit calculations, the data bus was downgraded to eight bits. (A data bus is a pathway to and from areas where memory is stored.) Many older computer components worked with an eight-bit data bus, and various firms manufactured many components based on these older designs, so a manufacturer could build an 8088-based computer at low cost. Manufacturers also knew that the eight-bit components were reliable, and new 16-bit components might fail.

The decision to produce the 8088 gave Intel a significant competitive advantage. IBM considered both the 8088 and the Motorola 68000 for its new product line, the IBM PC. IBM and Motorola had worked together on past projects, so the IBM managers asked Motorola if it could produce a 68000 model that used an eight-bit bus. Motorola decided that modifying its 68000 would cost too much, and it considered personal computers a niche market, so it refused to make IBM an eight-bit version of the 68000. IBM decided to use the 8088 in its IBM PC instead.

125 PERCENT SOLUTION

The launch of the IBM PC occurred in the same year that Intel's main business, manufacturing memory chips, collapsed. After reporting growing sales throughout the 1970s, Intel's revenue and income shrank in 1981. Revenue fell from US$855 million to US$789 million, and income fell from US$97 million to US$27 million, Intel announced in its 1981 annual report. Many companies dealt with the early 1980s recession by conducting mass layoffs. Intel executives remembered what happened when their chip designers left to work at Zilog, and decided to keep their engineers.

Intel decided to use the market crash as an opportunity to gain an advantage over its competitors. The company continued to add staff, and by the end of 1981 it reported 16,800 employees. Intel greatly increased its research and development spending, from US$96 million to US$117 million. After the success of the IBM PC, Intel executives were confident that the company could develop a new product that would restore the firm's economic performance.

Intel also asked its engineers, and managers, to sacrifice for the company. Salaried workers had to work an additional 10 hours each week, while their paychecks remained the same. Intel referred to this initiative as the 125 percent solution. Morale remained high because of the IBM PC, so most Intel workers accepted the longer work week instead of leaving to work at other technology firms. Intel continued to report lower turnover than other companies in the tech industry.

Although Intel announced its plan to continue spending heavily on research and development, IBM executives still worried that Intel's economic problems could delay the arrival of new microprocessors. To make sure Intel could afford its research bills, IBM bought 20 percent of Intel's stock in December 1982.

ENDING MEMORY PRODUCTION

Intel continued to invest in both memory chip research and microprocessor research, but it now lacked a key technological advantage, the superior photolithography techniques known by its Japanese rivals. By 1982, Intel had fallen far behind Japanese DRAM manufacturers such as Hitachi and Fujitsu. According to Richard N. Langlois and Edward W. Steinmueller in *Economics Working Papers,* all U.S. memory chip producers, including Intel, only held eight percent of the global market for 256K chips, while Japanese companies held the other 92 percent. Intel continued to maintain its microprocessor strength in 1982 with the launch of the Intel 286.

Intel continued to invest in DRAM research over the next few years in an unsuccessful attempt to capture the 1 megabyte (1M) DRAM market. In 1985, when 1M chips came out, the Japanese firms had increased their share to 96 percent of the market. In the same year, the Intel 386 reached the market. Intel cut its losses and abandoned memory chip manufacturing.

By 1987 Intel was in significantly better economic condition. Its share price had nearly doubled during the year, and IBM was no longer worried about Intel cutting back on microprocessor development. IBM sold its remaining Intel shares, which it purchased at US$28 each, for US$54 a share in August 1987, reported Andrew Pollack for the *New York Times.*

AN UNWILLING SWITCH

The Intel founders correctly determined that their company could produce transistor-based memory that would replace the older magnetic memory, and willingly paid for research that gave the firm a technological lead. The decision to focus on memory chip sales instead of microprocessor production almost cost the company the early advantage it gained from this research. The company lost the engineers who were most enthusiastic about building its microprocessors.

Fortunately for Intel, its executives learned from their mistakes. During the early 1980s recession, they made the decision to keep spending money on microprocessor research, even though the company needed to get financial support from IBM to pay for this research. Intel left a market when it no longer held the advantage. Even though the company was founded to make products for that market, it had spent several years competing in a hopeless situation.

BIBLIOGRAPHY

Anthony, Sebastian. "Intel 4004, the First CPU, Is 40 Years Old Today." *Extreme Tech,* November 15, 2011. Accessed January 18, 2012. http://www.extremetech.com/computing/105029-intel-4004-the-first-cpu-is-40-years-old-today.

Charnock, Richard. "The '125 Percent Solution' to Beating the Recession." *Modesto Bee,* August 1, 1982. Accessed January 18, 2012. http://news.google.com/newspapers?nid=1948&dat=19820801&id=as5JAAAAIBAJ&sjid=Fx0NAAAAIBAJ&pg=2658,252192.

Daigle, Roy. "Altair." University of South Alabama. Accessed January 18, 2012. http://www.cis.usouthal.edu/faculty/daigle/project1/1975malt.htm.

Groeger, Martin. "First Products – Moore's Law." *Silicon Valley Story.* Accessed January 18, 2012. http://www.silicon-valley-story.de/sv/intel_first.html.

House, Dave, et al. "Oral History Panel on the Development and Promotion of the Motorola 68000." Computer History Museum, July 23, 2007. Accessed January 18, 2012. http://archive.computerhistory.org/resources/text/Oral_History/Motorola_68000/102658164.05.01.acc.pdf.

"In the Beginning." *Red Hill Computer Guide.* Accessed January 18, 2012. http://www.redhill.net.au/c/c-1.html.

Intel Corporation. "1981 Intel Annual Report." Santa Clara, CA, 1982. Accessed January 18, 2012. http://www.intel.com/content/www/us/en/history/history-1981-annual-report.html.

Langlois, Richard N., and Edward W. Steinmueller. "Strategy and Circumstance: The Response of American Firms to Japanese Competition in Semiconductors, 1980–1995." *Economics Working Papers.* Paper 199906. December 1, 1999. Accessed January 18, 2012. http://digitalcommons.uconn.edu/cgi/viewcontent.cgi?article=1316&context=econ_wpapers.

Marshall, Gary. "Fab at 40: Intel's Super Chip." *Tech Radar,* November 15, 2011. Accessed January 18, 2012. http://www.techradar.com/news/computing-components/processors/fab-at-40-intel-s-super-chip-1041166.

Mazor, Stanley. "The History of the Microcomputer – Invention and Evolution." *Proceedings of the IEEE,* 83, no. 12, (December 1995): 1601–1608. Accessed January 18, 2012. http://cseweb.ucsd.edu/~ngouldin/cse290/sp10/papers/Mazor.pdf.

Mote, Dave, and Christina Stansell Weaver. "ZiLOG, Inc." *International Directory of Company Histories,* edited by Tina Grant. Vol. 72, 377–380. Detroit: St. James Press, 2006. Gale Virtual Reference Library (GALE|CX3444900114). Accessed January 18, 2012. http://go.galegroup.com/ps/i.do?id=GALE%7CCX3444900114&v=2.1&u=itsbtrial&it=r&p=GVRL&sw=w.

Pollack, Andrew. "I.B.M. Ends Intel Financial Support." *New York Times,* August 29, 1987. Accessed January 18, 2012. http://www.nytimes.com/1987/08/29/business/ibm-ends-intel-financial-support.html.

Tout, Nigel. "The Calculator That Spawned the Microprocessor: The Busicom 141-PF Calculator and the Intel 4004 Microprocessor." Vintage Calculators Web Museum, 2009. Accessed January 18, 2012. http://www.vintagecalculators.com/html/busicom_141-pf_and_intel_4004.html.

Zeldes, Nathan. "Magnetic Core Memory." *Nathan's Possibly Interesting Web Site,* 2005. Accessed January 18, 2012. http://www.nzeldes.com/HOC/CoreMemory.htm.

iRobot Corporation's Specialized Robot Assistants

───────■───────

Utility robots remained costly tools for many years after their introduction. With the Roomba, iRobot Corporation introduced a robot assistant to the public at the same price as a normal vacuum cleaner, and followed it up with more consumer products, including the Scooba mop. These robot assistants became possible because of the research of Rodney Brooks, the cofounder of iRobot, who discovered that basic robots could perform tasks that more complicated robots struggled to accomplish.

SUBSUMPTION ARCHITECTURE

In the 1980s, Rodney Brooks taught students about artificial intelligence at the Massachusetts Institute of Technology (MIT). Building a robot with the intelligence of a human, or even a dog, posed a difficult challenge. Many researchers believed that the robot needed to store a model of every object it could potentially encounter in its memory, such as a car or a skyscraper, so it could navigate the environment.

Brooks built a robot, named Allen, that used sophisticated artificial intelligence to make its decisions. Brooks found Allen very difficult to manage. The computerized control system did not fit inside Allen, and electronic interference often disrupted messages between the control system and the body of the robot, according to Kevin Kelly in his book, *Out of Control: The New Biology of Machines.* Brooks simplified the control system so it fit inside his next robot, and he noticed that the more basic control system directed the robot more effectively.

Brooks realized that he had discovered a useful model for robot behavior. Small animals, such as bugs and spiders, also lacked large brains but could still make deci-

sions. A spider sitting on a car windshield did not need to understand anything about automobiles to explore its environment; it just needed to solve problems like whether a web adhered to the surface. In a 1988 MIT paper, Brooks explained that a fly robot could be designed as a simple machine, with only a few sensors to trigger hard-coded decisions and without a central processor. The simple fly robot would be much easier to design, and much less costly to make, than a robot that attempted to simulate actual intelligent decision making. Brooks even mentioned that many human behaviors that appeared to require intelligent thought could occur as a result of these instinctual decisions.

Brooks described the model for his robot as *subsumption architecture,* a behavior-based model that offered basic decision-making capabilities. A robot could walk away if a sensor detected the presence of an object within a few feet of the robot, or it could walk toward the object and use a hard-coded reflex behavior to pick it up.

GENGHIS AND ATTILA

Brooks designed a new robot, Genghis, that looked like an insect. With its insect legs, Genghis had more mobility than other robots that used wheels to move around. Sensors sent messages to a small chip inside each leg, instead of a central brain. Genghis could even continue walking if it lost one of its legs, as the sensors would automatically direct the remaining legs to compensate for the missing limb. Genghis behaved like an actual bug and successfully demonstrated its walking abilities.

Genghis impressed the other scientists at MIT. David Whelan, for *Forbes,* reported that the demonstration of

Genghis's abilities convinced MIT to offer Brooks tenure. One of Brooks's undergraduate assistants, Colin Angle, gained admittance to graduate school because of the Genghis project.

Brooks and Angle continued to work in their robot laboratory and built a more sophisticated robot, Attila. Attila included additional sensors and microprocessors, which offered better walking performance, and it also lacked a central processor. Attila retained the original design of Genghis, as it also had a six-legged insect body.

FOUNDING IROBOT

Although he received recognition from other scientists for both Genghis and Attila, Brooks was not completely happy with the two robots. The insectoid robots walked around, but they did not perform any work, effectively making them expensive toys. Brooks believed that his robots could accomplish important goals for the public, and he decided to start a new company to build robots that could carry out scientific and business tasks. Brooks recruited his assistant, Angle, and another MIT student who knew Angle, Helen Greiner, and established iRobot in 1990, according to Whelan for *Forbes*.

iRobot first needed to figure out who would buy its robots. Brooks felt that the inexpensive and plentiful insect robots could help space exploration projects. Instead of landing a probe on a planet to take pictures, a spaceship could drop off a fleet of low-cost Genghis robots. If one robot malfunctioned or fell into a crater, the other robots could keep sending back messages. The robots could also help provide funding for the mission. Brooks planned to show the video clips the robots brought back from their interplanetary missions to theater audiences, reported Helen Pitt for *COSMOS* magazine.

Subsumption architecture gained popularity when the U.S. National Aeronautics and Space Administration (NASA) conducted its 1997 Sojourner mission. The Sojourner mission landed a probe on Mars, like earlier missions, but this time the probe dropped off a robot explorer, Pathfinder. Pathfinder rolled around the surface of the planet, collecting much more information than earlier missions could provide because of its additional mobility. The Jet Propulsion Laboratory in Pasadena, California developed the Sojourner rover, and showed how it navigated Mars at science exhibits at the facility.

iRobot also gained publicity from a 1997 documentary that placed Brooks and his robot research on movie screens. Titled *Fast, Cheap, and Out of Control* after one of Brooks' 1989 research papers, the movie also included Brooks' predictions about the future of robotics. Brooks argued that subsumption architecture could be inexpensively designed into household appliances, such as refrigerators, microwaves, and personal computers, greatly improving their performance and convenience, reported Jonathan Erickson for *Dr. Dobb's*.

PACK ROBOT

The new robots impressed the U.S. Department of Defense, which in 1997 asked iRobot to develop a simple robot that could ascend a staircase, reported Lauren Drell for *Mashable*. With military funding, iRobot designed a robot that could survive on a battlefield, the Packbot. Before the military could test the Packbot on the battlefield, the terrorist attacks of September 11, 2001, occurred. The wrecked towers of the World Trade Center in New York, New York posed a risk to rescuers, as parts of the remaining structures could collapse and crush people. New York City officials needed to survey the area, so they requested support from the Packbots, which helped locate environmental hazards. The performance of the Packbot impressed both military and police observers, who ordered their own robots from the company.

During the wars in Iraq and Afghanistan in the 21st century, the Packbot gained popularity with U.S. soldiers because of its mine-clearing abilities. Improvised explosive devices lay along roads, which could detonate to destroy military vehicles. The Packbot could travel into a minefield, disarm the mines, and return to base, and if it failed to disarm a mine and the mine exploded, the mine did not take the life of a soldier.

APPLIANCE DESIGN

Brooks started working on the robot appliances he envisioned, but he quickly realized the challenges of appliance design. NASA could afford a large budget for a Mars rover, but a U.S. consumer appliance needed to be much less expensive. Brooks could repair a robot that malfunctioned in his MIT laboratory, but a consumer would not purchase an appliance that broke down frequently.

The Brooks technology impressed S.C. Johnson & Son, Inc., which hired iRobot to build industrial floor cleaners, according to Whelan. S.C. Johnson eventually walked away from the concept, but Brooks believed that his robots showed great potential in the cleaning industry. Consequently, he decided to develop an iRobot vacuum cleaner himself for the consumer appliance market in the United States.

Brooks faced additional challenges as he prepared for the U.S. consumer appliance market. He needed to order parts from manufacturers in China to reduce the cost of the iRobot, which required the scientist and his assistants to learn how to bargain aggressively. The researchers also needed to learn how vacuum cleaner buyers typically used their machines, so they watched vacuum cleaner demonstrations at Target Corporation stores to gain additional insights, reported Lev Grossman for *TIME*.

ROOMBA

iRobot released its robot vacuum cleaner in September 2002. AB Electrolux had beaten iRobot to market with its Trilobite in 2001, which had a similar disk-shaped appearance, but the Trilobite cost too much for most U.S. households, with a market price around US$1,500. At US$200, the Roomba cost much less than the Trilobite and was price competitive with the nonrobotic vacuum cleaners on the market in 2002.

The Roomba did have a few disadvantages in comparison with manually operated vacuum cleaners. A standard, US$200 nonrobotic vacuum cleaner could store a much larger quantity of dust and dirt, so the small Roomba struggled in messier environments. The Roomba decided where to vacuum using the logic that the Packbot used to clear mines on the battlefield, which produced unique vacuuming patterns that did not always completely clean a room, reported Simson Garfinkel for the *Technology Review*. Although the Roomba was meant to travel along its cleaning route without human assistance, it could not always avoid household obstacles. A homeowner needed to prepare the room for the Roomba by removing clothing, curtains, and cords that could disable the robotic vacuum. Nevertheless, it impressed many people, especially because of its low price.

SCOOBA

After designing a robot vacuum, the obvious next step for iRobot was designing a robot mop. By 2005, iRobot had completed the Scooba, a disk-shaped robot mop. In 2005, the Scooba itself cost US$399, and it required special cleaning solution that cost US$18 for three eight-ounce bottles, reported Lance Ulanoff for *PC Mag*. Although it was a relatively expensive way to clean floors, the Scooba did have one advantage over a typical mop and bucket. The Scooba always cleaned the floor with clean water, as it contained separate compartments to store clean and dirty water, which resulted in cleaner floors.

NUCLEAR MELTDOWN

iRobot continued to develop upgraded robots that could function in hostile environments. A tsunami and nuclear reactor meltdown occurred in Japan in March 2011, and the environment around the nuclear plants posed a major health risk. At the time, iRobot representatives were showing off their robots at a trade show in Singapore, and they quickly volunteered to send in their robots to provide disaster assistance in Japan, reported Wayne Rash

for *eWEEK*. iRobot performed these disaster relief services without charge.

At the time of the disaster in Japan, iRobot had a larger and more durable battlefield robot available, the Warrior 701, which could carry the sensor equipment the nuclear engineers needed to measure the radioactivity at the site. The Warrior could even pick up the smaller Packbot and drop it off in the disaster area. iRobot had also developed an improved Packbot, the 510, which also carried hazardous material monitoring equipment.

The robots carried video cameras, filming the wreckage of the nuclear facilities as they conducted their surveys. Both types of robots performed important tasks during the mission, as the smaller Packbots could crawl down small pipes that a Warrior robot could not navigate. The Warrior robots had the strength to lift concrete chunks and other impediments that blocked doors, windows, and passageways. By April 2011 the robots provided video clips from an area that was still very unsafe for human camera crews.

AVA

In 2011, iRobot demonstrated a more humanoid robot that offered a wider range of capabilities than its earlier, specialized robots. Since a tablet or a smartphone can record video and perform calculations, the iRobot designers used it as the head of the new robot. The base of the robot consisted of a motorized platform like the Roomba and Scooba. Stephen Shankland, for *CNET*, reported that the iPad and the Android could both serve as possible heads for Ava. iRobot designers were still working on Ava in early 2012, although the public did get to see the prototype at several technology conferences.

THE BENEFITS OF SIMPLICITY

Rodney Brooks took a major risk by designing simple robots, instead of complicated artificial intelligence machines, before he had gained tenure or worldwide fame. The decision to build a simple and inexpensive product offered obvious advantages for an appliance manufacturer, but it was not an obvious step in a field dedicated to building more sophisticated machines.

Although iRobot gained fame for introducing the robotic vacuum to customers, the low price of the Roomba was the main reason for its high sales. Electrolux had a much stronger brand in the vacuum cleaner industry in 2002, and the Trilobite could easily have outsold Roomba had Electrolux sold it at a competitive price. iRobot correctly performed its market analysis, realizing that the U.S. Department of Defense would pay US$100,000 for a large, armored robot, while homeowners wanted a US$200 vacuum cleaner.

BIBLIOGRAPHY

Ackerman, Kevin. "Japan Earthquake: iRobot Sending Packbots and Warriors to Fukushima Dai-1 Nuclear Plant." *IEEE Spectrum,* March 18, 2011. Accessed January 19, 2012. http://spectrum.ieee.org/automaton/robotics/industrial -robots/irobot-sending-packbots-and-warriors-to-fukushima.

Brooks, Rodney A. "How to Build Complete Creatures Rather Than Isolated Cognitive Simulators." Cambridge, MA: Massachusetts Institute of Technology, Artificial Intelligence Laboratory, 1988. Accessed January 19, 2012. http://lcs.syr .edu/faculty/Tetley/ELE%20516%20CIS%20543/brooks% 20how%20to%20build.pdf.

Drell, Lauren. "Beyond the Roomba: How iRobot's Technology Is Making War Zones Safer for Soldiers." *Mashable,* November 10, 2011. Accessed January 19, 2012. http:// mashable.com/2011/11/10/irobot-packbot-military-robot/.

Erickson, Jonathan. "Fast, Cheap, and Two Thumbs Up." *Dr. Dobb's,* September 1, 1998. Accessed January 19, 2012. http://drdobbs.com/article/print?articleId=184410674&siteS ectionName=.

Garfinkle, Simson. "iRobot Roomba." *MIT Technology Review,* October 9, 2002. Accessed January 19, 2012. http://www .technologyreview.com/computing/12978/page1/.

Grossman, Lev. "Maid to Order." *TIME,* September 23, 2002. Accessed January 19, 2012. http://www.time.com/time /magazine/article/0,9171,1003284-1,00.html.

Guizzo, Erico. "Planetary Rovers: Are We Alone?" *IEEE Spectrum,* January 2011. Accessed January 19, 2012. http:// spectrum.ieee.org/aerospace/robotic-exploration/planetary -rovers-are-we-alone/2.

Kahney, Leander. "Forget a Maid, This Robot Vacuums." *Wired,* December 24, 2002. Accessed January 19, 2012. http://www .wired.com/gadgets/miscellaneous/news/2002/12/56962?cur rentPage=all.

Kelly, Kevin. "Fast, Cheap, and Out of Control." From chap. 3 in *Out of Control: The New Biology of Machines.* Basic Books, 1995. Accessed January 19, 2012. http://www.kk.org /outofcontrol/ch3-b.html.

Pitt, Helen. "I, Rodney." *COSMOS,* June 2008. Accessed January 19, 2012. http://www.cosmosmagazine.com/node/3177/full.

Rash, Wayne. "Repurposed iRobot Military 'Packbots' Enter Damaged Japanese Nuclear Plant." *eWEEK,* April 18, 2011. Accessed January 19, 2012. http://www.eweek.com/c/a/IT -Infrastructure/Repurposed-iRobot-Military-PackBots-Enter -Damaged-Japanese-Nuclear-Plant-814538/.

Shankland, Stephen. "iRobot to Sell AVA the Android-Based Robot." *CNET,* May 10, 2011. Accessed January 19, 2012. http://news.cnet.com/8301-30685_3-20061651-264.html.

Ulanoff, Lance. "iRobot Scooba Floor Washing Robot." *PC Mag,* December 14, 2005. Accessed January 19, 2012. http://www .pcmag.com/article2/0,2817,1901372,00.asp.

Whelan, David. "Fight Wars, Lint." *Forbes,* September 8, 2006. Accessed January 19, 2012. http://www.forbes.com/forbes /2006/0904/094.html.

Kevlar: DuPont's Super-strong Lightweight Fiber

Kevlar is a super-strong, man-made fiber invented by E.I. du Pont de Nemours and Company (DuPont) in 1965. Kevlar is a lightweight fiber that is five times stronger than steel on an equal weight basis. It is best known for its use in protection vests worn by the U.S. military and is credited with saving the lives of thousands of law enforcement personnel. That is not what chemists at DuPont originally set out to do, however. Although accidental, the discovery was recognized as extraordinary, and DuPont quickly moved to patent it and explore commercialization opportunities.

Kevlar was first used as a replacement for steel in radial tires. It took another decade before it was used in life protection vests, in 1978. Next, it was expanded into military helmets and other protective clothing. In addition to continuous filament yarn used in protective clothing, Kevlar could be cut into short fibers to reinforce a wide assortment of industrial and consumer products.

FIRST SYNTHETIC FIBERS

In 1920 DuPont began licensing the process to produce rayon, which closely resembled silk. Rayon was the first man-made fiber, but it was not truly synthetic, as it was derived from plant material. Dr. Wallace Carothers joined DuPont in 1927 to research polymers that could be used to create man-made materials with specific properties. Polymers are chemical compounds. They are large molecules created by a chemical reaction that join the small molecules of one or more compounds. In 1930 Carothers' team discovered neoprene synthetic rubber and synthesized the first polyester superpolymer, the forerunner of nylon.

Carothers next set out to develop a new fiber that was stronger and less flammable than rayon. This required working with crystalline polymers that could be mechanically formed into orderly linear chains that were both long and strong. He first discovered a polyester fiber, but its low melting point made it seem unsuitable for commercialization. Carothers began researching amides, which are inorganic compounds derived from ammonia, and discovered he could produce long, linear polymer chains with a much higher melting point.

In 1935 Carothers discovered a polymer that created a highly crystalline fiber that was capable of withstanding heat and solvents. In addition to being strong, the fiber was shiny and more elastic than the common natural fibers. The company patented the new fiber but allowed the name "nylon" to become a generic term for the new type of fiber.

DuPont's expertise with rayon made it easier to quickly commercialize nylon into toothbrushes in 1938 and women's hosiery in 1940. In 1945, after Imperial Chemical Industries (ICI) had used Carothers' published research and patented polyester, DuPont purchased the patent rights to polyester and began producing its trademarked Dacron polyester fiber in 1953.

DUPONT'S FIRST HIGH-PERFORMANCE FIBER

DuPont's next goal was to develop a fiber that was more thermal resistant than nylon. (Thermal resistance is a measure of the degree to which a material resists the flow of heat.) In 1958 Paul Morgan discovered it was possible to liquefy a high-molecular-weight polymer at room temperature using amide solvents. Whereas nylon and polyester were flexible-chain polymers, meaning the molecules could not attain perfect alignment, the new polymer was characterized by a rigid chain and extremely high melting point. This resulting fiber, trademarked Nomex in 1963, had outstanding thermal and flame-resistant properties.

The next hurdle was to discover a commercially viable method of converting the polymer into a fiber. Nylon and polyester fibers were created by melting the polymer and extruding the liquid through tiny holes in a spinneret to make the individual filaments, which were solidified in cooling air. Next, the filaments were drawn, a mechanical process that stretched the filaments, in order to align the molecules along the fiber and increase the strength. Then the filaments were combined into a spun yarn. This melt-spinning process could not be used for a polymer mixed with a solvent. DuPont scientist Wilfred Sweeney discovered a dry-spinning process using hot air that did not require isolating the polymer from the solvent.

Commercialization of Nomex began, and the fiber was first used in U.S. Navy flight coveralls in 1965. Because fabric made with Nomex provided protection against intense heat and chemicals without igniting, melting, or dripping, it quickly became an essential component in firefighter apparel. Nomex also uniquely provided permanent protection. Whereas treated fabrics treated with a flame-retardant chemical could lose their flame-resistant properties, Nomex was engineered into the molecular structure of the fiber and would provide protection for the life of the garment. Eventually, Nomex was also offered in paper, felt, and fabric forms.

THE SCIENCE BEHIND KEVLAR

After Stephanie Kwolek joined DuPont as a chemist in 1946, her research contributed to the development of Nomex. In 1964 she began to develop a new high-performance fiber for reinforcing tires that could improve gas mileage. In a 2000 interview with David Brown at the Lemelson-MIT Program, Kwolek said the objective was to "find a fiber that was lightweight like the textile fibers but which could withstand very high temperatures and was very strong and very stiff." She began experimenting with aromatic polymers, which she knew were heat resistant from her previous work on Nomex, and had rigid, rod-like molecules. (Aromatic polymers are so called because many of these compounds have a sweet scent.)

In 1965 she successfully dissolved poly-p-benzamide, a polymer with rod-like molecules that would not melt below its decomposition temperature of 450 degrees Celsius. (By comparison, DuPont's nylon 6,6 [a common type of nylon] melted at 280 degrees Celsius.) The resulting liquid was watery and cloudy, not thick and clear like the flexible-chain polymers she had worked with. In fact, Kwolek had just discovered the first liquid crystal solution. The increased crystallinity made the liquid opaque as well as giving it increased rigidity and tensile strength.

When the new solution was first spun into a fiber, Kwolek was immediately intrigued by its strength and stiffness. The fiber was rigid because the molecular chains were almost perfectly extended (stretched out) and parallel in the direction of the fiber. The molecule chains in flexible-chain polymers, like nylon and polyester, were more entangled and had to be stretched during the drawing process to orient the molecules parallel to the fiber's axis. Even then, the molecules were only partially extended. This new fiber exhibited the properties of a fiber that had been drawn after only being spun.

Testing confirmed that the new fiber was very strong, but the stiffness was shocking. Kwolek went on to say in the interview with Brown, "Nylon or Aspun or some of the other ones have a stiffness number of somewhere around 25 and 50 or so. This fiber came back with a value of 450. This at the time was stiffer than glass fiber, which was considered to be very stiff." Like Nomex, Kevlar had low flammability, good chemical and corrosion resistance, and maintained fabric integrity at elevated temperatures.

SUCCESSFUL COMMERCIALIZATION OF KEVLAR

After Herbert Blades engineered the air gap spinning process in 1970 the new aramid fiber was introduced as Kevlar the following year. Mass production began and by 1973 Kevlar was used in a Firestone car tire and to provide better impact resistance in lightweight racing kayaks. Replacing steel reinforcements in tires with Kevlar of equal strength reduced the weight by two pounds per tire, and testing showed it gave better ride comfort. By 1975 nearly all of DuPont's roughly six million pounds of Kevlar was being used in radial tires. The company expected to complete construction of a second plant in Richmond, Virginia, that would increase production capacity to 50 million pounds the following year.

Whereas Nomex was softer and more textile-like, Kevlar's stiff fibers made it less suitable for use in textiles. However, DuPont had been pursuing body armor as another possible application for the new lightweight, strong fiber. In 1975 Kevlar was used in the first body armor worn by police officers. According to DuPont, "the fabric actually absorbs the energy of the bullet along the molecules of each fiber, 'catching' it in a multi-layer web of woven fabrics. These engaged fibers absorb and disperse the energy of the impact to other fibers in the weave and help reduce the amount of transferred energy that causes blunt trauma." In addition to protection from bullets, Kevlar provided cut and puncture protection from knives and other weapons.

A natural progression for Kevlar was in body protection for U.S. soldiers. In 1978 the U.S. Army began using flak jackets and the Personnel Armor System for Ground Troops (PASGT) helmet made of Kevlar, which provided protection against ballistic projectiles and explosive fragmentation. According to DuPont, "the PASGT military helmet made with Kevlar offers twice the ballistic impact energy absorbing capacity of the steel helmets they replaced."

KEVLAR OVERTAKES MILITARY PROTECTION

During the 1980s Kevlar was expanded into a host of industrial applications, such as conveyor belts, asbestos-free brake linings, jet parts, watercraft, and even the roof of the Olympic Stadium in Montréal, Canada. Developments also continued with the U.S. military, which began using the PASGT Vest in 1982, the Combat Vehicle Crew (CVC) Vest in 1987, and the CVC Helmet the following year.

The only other producer of an aramid fiber was Akzo N.V., which had begun producing Twaron in the Netherlands in 1978. DuPont responded with a patent dispute, and Akzo was barred from selling in the United States while the lawsuit was pending. In 1987 DuPont sold 9,000 tons of aramid, and Akzo was estimated to have sold 2,500 tons. Both companies were only producing about half of their capacity. The lawsuit was finally settled more than a decade later. A May 1988 article in the *New York Times* stated that DuPont agreed to let Akzo sell "a limited but steadily growing amount of aramid fibers in the United States" if the United States International Trade Commission lifted the ban.

Kevlar continued to be used extensively in the military in the 1990s. In 1991 nearly all U.S. combat soldiers in Operation Desert Storm wore a helmet made of Kevlar. Two years later, Ranger Vests containing Kevlar were used by troops stationed in Somalia. Kevlar was also used in spall liners inside certain types of military vehicles to protect occupants from shell fragments.

In 1995 Kevlar Correctional fabric was introduced specifically for corrections officers. The new fabric was more tightly woven together to provide protection against puncture and slash wounds from handmade weapons in prisons and jails. Kevlar spun yarn was primarily used in gloves that offered cut protection but remained comfortable and flexible. Gloves, aprons, jackets, and leggings were commonly used in glass industries. Kevlar was also combined with Nomex in firefighter gear and gloves for use by workers handling hot, sharp objects.

KEVLAR ADVANCEMENTS

By the dawn of the 21st century, DuPont was producing Kevlar as continuous filament yarn in two varieties. In addition to K-29 used in military and industrial applications, a more rigid fiber, called K-49, was developed for cable and rope products. Extended exposure to ultraviolet rays could cause Kevlar to lose its mechanical properties. Therefore, clothing had to be overbraided with other fibers to create a protective barrier. Ropes and cables for use outdoors had to have a protective coating applied as well.

Kevlar was also being manufactured in short fibers. The pulp could be mixed with elastomers (polymers that have the quality of elasticity), thermoplastics (polymers that turn to liquid when heated and freeze rigid when cooled), or thermoset resins (liquids usually that are hardened, or cured, after which they cannot be converted back to their original liquid form) to increase the strength and stiffness. For example, automotive brake pads or gaskets made with an elastomer reinforced with Kevlar pulp had greater strength at high temperatures and less wear and tear than natural rubber. Kevlar cut fibers could be spun into yarn that was knit into gloves or made into felt that could be used in a protective lining against punctures and cuts.

Kevlar had also expanded from its first use in the hulls of boats to a wide range of sports equipment. Kevlar was used to make cycling helmets and motorcycle components that were impact resistant, racquets for tennis, racquetball, badminton, and squash that were lightweight and ultra-rigid, racquet strings that did not stretch, skis and snowboards that were more responsive, boots and shoes that were more durable, and baseball bats with better vibration damping. Kevlar also occasionally replaced fiberglass reinforcements in race car bodies and hockey sticks, because it did not shatter on impact and produce dangerous debris.

Vests and helmets made of Kevlar were standard issue for U.S. combat soldiers in the 21st century. DuPont continued to make new innovations in Kevlar technology during this time. In 2002 the Interceptor Body Armor, also known as the Outer Tactical Vest (OTV), replaced the flak jacket as a more versatile and lighter-weight protection for troops in Afghanistan and Iraq. The vest made of Kevlar was capable of stopping a 9mm bullet from a handgun. Two armor inserts made of boron carbide could be added to the vest to stop rifle or machine-gun fire. The inserts added 8 pounds to the 8.4-pound vest, which was still significantly lighter than the 25-pound flak jacket. The Advanced Combat Helmet (ACH) improved the layering of Kevlar and resin to provide greater protection from submachine gun bullets as well as explosive shrapnel and fragmentation. The helmet was 3.5 pounds lighter than the PASGT Helmet it replaced in 2005, partially due to a larger cutout in the front to improve vision. Pads were added inside the helmet to improve fit and absorb sound.

NEW THREATS

In 2005 South Korea-based Kolon Industries Inc. began making Heracron, its own version of a Kevlar-like aramid fiber. DuPont suspected former employees had shared trade secrets with Kolon and contacted the U.S. Federal Bureau of Investigation (FBI). In February 2009 DuPont filed a lawsuit alleging Kolon had obtained confidential information. Michael Mitchell, a former DuPont engineer, pled guilty and was sentenced to 18 months in prison in March 2010. In September 2011 a jury ordered Kolon to pay DuPont US$919 million for the theft of trade secrets relating to the manufacture of Kevlar.

After being the material of choice for 30 years, Kevlar was in danger of being obsolete in U.S. military helmets in the 2010s. The U.S. Congress awarded more than US$10 million to the army to develop an Enhanced Combat Helmet made of an ultrahigh molecular weight polyethylene, which was expected to provide greater than a 35 percent improvement in ballistic protection over the ACH made of Kevlar. In July 2009 four companies were awarded a total of US$5.5 million to develop helmets for testing. The helmet by Ceradyne, Inc., performed better than expected in testing at the beginning of 2011. The helmet, which weighed four ounces less than the ACH, was expected to begin field testing at the end of 2011.

While Kevlar's future in U.S. military helmets was uncertain in the early 2010s, it continued to be an important element in body armor as well as having a wide variety of industrial and consumer applications. DuPont also continued to enhance Kevlar fibers for use in life-protection vests and helmets. As of year-end 2010, approximately half of DuPont's US$6.3 billion in revenues was attributed to its safety and security products, including Kevlar and Nomex.

BIBLIOGRAPHY

Brown, David. "Stephanie Kwolek." *Inventing Modern America: From the Microwave to the Mouse.* Cambridge, MA: The Lemelson-MIT Program, November 2000. Accessed January 24, 2012. http://web.mit.edu/invent/www/ima/kwolek_interv.html.

"Company News: Akzo-DuPont Deal Ends 11-Year Fight." *New York Times,* May 11, 1988. Accessed January 21, 2012. http://www.nytimes.com/1988/05/11/business/company-news-akzo-du-pont-deal-ends-11-year-fight.html?src=pm.

Cox, Matthew, and Dan Lamothe. "Army's New Plastic Helmet Tops Kevlar ACH." *Army Times,* August 31, 2009. Accessed January 24, 2012. http://www.armytimes.com/news/2009/08/army_helmets_083109w/.

DuPont. "DuPont Heritage." Wilmington, DE, 2007. Accessed January 23, 2012. http://www2.dupont.com/Heritage/en_US/index.html.

———. "History of Kevlar® in Life Protection." Wilmington, DE, 2006. Accessed January 21, 2012. http://www2.dupont.com/Kevlar/en_US/products/history.html.

———. "Kevlar in Sports Equipment." Wilmington, DE. Accessed January 24, 2012. http://www2.dupont.com/Kevlar/en_US/uses_apps/consumer/sports_equip.html.

———. "Law Enforcement." Wilmington, DE. Accessed January 24, 2012. http://www2.dupont.com/Personal_Protection/en_US/uses_apps/law_enforcement.html.

———. "Nomex Marks 40 Years of Safety and Protection." Wilmington, DE, March 17, 2007. Accessed January 23, 2012. http://www2.dupont.com/Personal_Protection/en_US/news_events/article20070313.html.

———. "Technical Guide Kevlar Aramid Fiber." Wilmington, DE, April 2000. Accessed January 21, 2012. http://www2.dupont.com/Kevlar/en_US/assets/downloads/KEVLAR_Technical_Guide.pdf.

Feeley, Jef, Gary Roberts ,and Jack Kaskey. "Kolon Loses US$920 Million Verdict to DuPont in Trial Over Kevlar." *Bloomberg Businessweek,* September 15, 2011. Accessed January 24, 2012. http://www.businessweek.com/news/2011-09-15/kolon-loses-920-million-verdict-to-dupont-in-trial-over-kevlar.html.

Howell, Caitlyn. "Stephanie Kwolek and Kevlar, the Wonder Fiber." Washington, DC: Smithsonian Institution, March 3, 2005. Accessed January 21, 2012. http://invention.smithsonian.org/centerpieces/ilives/lecture05.html.

Lowe, Christian. "New Helmet Blocks Rifle Shots." *Military.com,* February 4, 2011. Accessed January 24, 2012. http://www.military.com/news/article/new-helmet-blocks-rifle-shots.html.

Kimberly-Clark's Kleenex Facial Tissue

———————■———————

Kleenex tissue was one of the leading U.S. icons from the 20th century and contributed greatly to the success of the Kimberly-Clark Corporation. Kleenex was first launched as a female beauty aid in 1924. When the product was repositioned a few years later as a replacement for fabric handkerchiefs that could be used by everyone, facial tissue was established as a viable product category.

Not content with just a single product, Kimberly-Clark began a strategy of leveraging the Kleenex brand through product extensions, like the immensely successful Huggies disposable diaper. The company also maintained a 50 percent share in the facial tissue market through continuous product and packaging innovations. Since Kleenex created the facial tissue product category and maintained its market dominance for more than 80 years, many U.S. citizens use the word "Kleenex" when referring to any brand of facial tissue.

FIRST CONSUMER PRODUCT MADE FROM TISSUE

In 1872 Kimberly, Clark & Company was founded as a paper mill in Neenah, Wisconsin, to produce newsprint. When a 1911 U.S.-Canada treaty allowed Canada to ship newsprint into the United States duty-free, the mill was converted to produce creped cellulose wadding, which was being produced in Europe. Kimberly, Clark & Company trademarked its product as Cellucotton and sold the absorbent material as a substitute for cotton surgical dressings during World War I. It was five times more absorbent than cotton and cost half as much to produce. Ernst Mahler, head of Kimberly-Clark's research, technical, and engineering department, developed a thinner version of

the material that the company began developing as a filter for gas masks. The end of the war, however, brought an end to the project and the demand for disposable surgical dressing.

During World War I, field nurses had written to the company about Cellucotton's usefulness as a disposable menstrual pad. Consequently, Kimberly, Clark & Company developed the Cellucotton material into a new product that eliminated the need to wash cotton menstrual pads. The disposable menstrual pads were named Kotex, referring to its cotton-like texture. The 9-inch-long pad was made from 36 layers of absorbent Cellucotton and enclosed in a 22-inch-long gauze envelope. The company created the Cellucotton Products Company to distribute its first consumer product. A box of one dozen Kotex sold for US$0.60.

Kotex did not meet with immediate success due to comparatively prim attitudes toward menstruation. Drugstores were reluctant to stock a product that females were too embarrassed to buy from a male drugstore clerk. A breakthrough came when the company began suggesting to druggists that they stack the Kotex boxes at the counter so women could buy them more discreetly. The company was also challenged in writing magazine advertising copy that was not too offensive to be published. The term "sanitary napkin," was coined at this time.

THE FACIAL TISSUE CATEGORY

While Kotex sales remained sluggish, the company was facing an oversupply of Cellucotton. C. A. "Bert" Fourness was credited with the idea of ironing the cellulose material to make a smooth tissue. The first marketable idea was for a disposable tissue that women could use to remove cold cream, thus eliminating an unsightly face towel hanging in the bathroom. By modifying the ingredients, the company's scientists developed a softer form of the Cellucotton that was suitable for use on the face. The new product was called Kleenex Tissue, a variant spelling of the word "clean" with the same final syllable as Kotex.

Kleenex was launched in June 1924 as a disposable method of removing cold cream or cosmetics. A box of 100 tissues sold for US$0.65. The first advertisements in *Ladies Home Journal* positioned the product as "the new secret of keeping a pretty skin as used by famous movie stars," according to the Kimberly-Clark website. *Good Housekeeping, Harper's Bazaar, McCall's* and other women's magazines were soon displaying advertisements featuring female celebrities who attributed their flawless complexion to using Kleenex. In 1925, the company began marketing its consumer products in Canada.

THE FIRST DISPOSABLE HANDKERCHIEF

The idea of using Kleenex for the nose is attributed to the company's head of research, who began using the disposable tissues for his hay fever symptoms. The company's Canadian division first introduced the idea of using Kleenex for the nose in 1926. As letters began to pour in from consumers advocating the product for cold and hay fever symptoms, the company began to formulate a new marketing strategy.

In 1928 the company was reincorporated as Kimberly-Clark Corporation and began trading publicly. Around this time, Kleenex product innovations included the notable pop-up cartons. The tissues were fed through a machine that interfolded them before placing them in the "Serv-a-Tissue Box," as the company called it. When a consumer pulled a tissue out of the box, a fresh tissue popped up. In 1929 the company expanded the product line by introducing colored Kleenex, and sales exceeded US$21 million. The following year, the company began manufacturing printed Kleenex.

As consumers worldwide faced hard economic times following the Wall Street Stock Market Crash in October 1929, Kimberly-Clark began wholehearted advertising for Kleenex as a handkerchief substitute. The fact that females and males of all ages were using Kleenex helped the company maintain revenues as prices of paper products dropped during the Great Depression. With Scott Paper Company's introduction of ScotTowels, the first paper towels for the home, in 1931, the idea of disposable paper products gained considerable traction in the United States. The introduction of the Kleenex Pocket Pack in 1932 made it easier for consumers to carry Kleenex just like a handkerchief. With the end of the Great Depression,

Kimberly-Clark achieved record sales of US$22 million in 1936, and the company made nearly US$1.5 million in profits.

PAPER RESTRICTIONS

The Japanese bombed Pearl Harbor on December 7, 1941, and the United States was at war again. World War II brought paper restrictions, and the company ceased production of Kleenex in the United States. Kimberly-Clark created a separate entity, International Cellucotton Products Company, for its tissue business and focused on selling consumer products internationally. In the United States, the company returned to manufacturing Cellucotton as a sterile dressing for use by field doctors and nurses.

Before paper restrictions were lifted in 1945, the company launched an advertising campaign featuring a popular comic strip character from a well-known circulating magazine. "Little Lulu" had appeared weekly in the *Saturday Evening Post* since 1935. The Little Lulu advertisements explained why Americans could not find Kleenex on store shelves during the war. Around this time, other paper companies began to enter the facial tissue marketplace. Scott Paper Company's launch of Scottie Facial Tissues in 1943 was the first competition for Kleenex. Hoberg Paper Company's introduction of its Charmin Facial Tissues was the next new entrant.

In 1955 International Cellucotton Products was among the companies listed on the first *Fortune* 500 list of the largest U.S. corporations. Ranked number 214, the company had revenues of US$145.4 million and profits of US$7.4 million. During the year, the company had introduced Kleenex Table Napkins. International Cellucotton Products was absorbed back into Kimberly-Clark at the end of the year.

KIMBERLY-CLARK VS. PROCTER & GAMBLE

In 1957 Procter & Gamble acquired Charmin Paper Company and discontinued all Charmin products except bath tissue. Three years later, however, Procter & Gamble released Puffs, its own brand of facial tissue on a regional basis. Although Kleenex sales continued to grow, increased competition affected profits during the 1960s. Kimberly-Clark continued to expand the Kleenex product line with new packaging innovations, such as Kleenex Juniors, the Kleenex Purse Pack, and Kleenex Boutique that offered an upright box and trendier patterns. At the end of the decade, Kleenex moved its advertising to daytime television programming. One memorable television commercial demonstrated the strength of Kleenex by featuring musician Henry James trying to blow through a Kleenex tissue on his trumpet.

By the 1970s consumer product innovations were more limited, and many companies, including Kimberly-Clark, began a strategy of diversification. In 1978 the company leveraged the Kleenex brand into the premium disposable diaper market with the introduction of Kleenex Huggies. (Kimberly-Clark had introduced Kimbies disposable diapers in 1968, but the design was prone to leaking, and the product was pulled off the market in the mid-1970s.)

By making incremental product innovations, such as an hourglass shape, elastic around the leg opening, and refastenable tape, Huggies were able to steal market share from Procter & Gamble's leading Pampers brand. This new product moved Kimberly-Clark back onto a path of growth for its consumer products. Huggies were being distributed throughout the United States in 1982 and had captured about 30 percent market share by 1985. With the addition of Huggies Pull-Ups as the first disposable training pant, Huggies became the leading premium diaper brand.

While Kimberly-Clark overtook diapers, Procter & Gamble had its eye on facial tissue. A serious competitor for Kleenex was Procter & Gamble's introduction of Puffs Plus with Lotion in 1987, which promised to better soothe sore noses. Aloe was added to Puffs Plus in 1989, and all Puffs products were being distributed throughout the United States the following year. Kimberly-Clark would not introduce Kleenex with lotion until 2001.

Kleenex responded with the introduction of three-ply Kleenex Ultra in 1990, and scented Kleenex Softique the following year. Kleenex Expressions began offering unique carton designs in 1995. Kleenex ColdCare, including a product containing menthol, was introduced in 1996 for users with colds and allergies. To better compete with Kleenex, Puffs expanded its packaging options during the 1990s with Puffs To Go travel packs and the Puffs Design Cube. At the end of the decade, Puffs began selling in Canada.

In December 1995 stockholders of Kimberly-Clark and Scott Paper Company agreed to a US$9.4 billion merger. Scott Paper became a wholly owned subsidiary of Kimberly-Clark. In response to monopoly concerns by the U.S. Justice Department, Kimberly-Clark agreed to divest Scott's facial tissue and baby wipes businesses. The following year, Irving Consumer Products bought the rights to manufacture and distribute Scotties facial tissue in the United States. Considered a discount facial tissue, Scotties was the third-leading brand at the time of the merger.

CONTINUED KLEENEX INNOVATIONS

In 2004 Kleenex still dominated the US$1 billion facial tissue market with approximately a 50 percent share.

Puffs was in second place with sales of US$214.7 million. Kleenex Tissue with menthol was reintroduced, and the product category was further expanded in 2005 with the introduction of Kleenex Anti-Viral. The three-ply tissue's moisture-activated middle layer promised to kill 99.9 percent of cold and flu virus germs. Puffs followed with improvements, such as adding chamomile in 2005 and launching Puffs Plus with the Scent of Vicks in 2007.

In March 2010 Kimberly-Clark added a new product extension to the Kleenex brand with the introduction of Kleenex Hand Towels for the bathroom. The new product, packaged in a 60-count box, could sit on a bathroom vanity and offer clean, dry towels every time. In October 2011 the company improved Kleenex Menthol with a new heat-activated product called Kleenex Cool Touch. According to Kimberly-Clark, the revolutionary tissue releases cooling moisturizers and aloe to soothe a sore nose on contact.

Kimberly-Clark is highly regarded for its successful diversification into consumer products. Its Kotex and Kleenex innovations were natural extensions of its existing pulp and paper business, which did not require a major investment in research and development. Although the company had no prior experience with marketing consumer products, it recognized the importance of advertising in promoting new product categories.

After introducing Kleenex more than 80 years ago, Kimberly-Clark was able to retain 50 percent market share by incremental product innovations. As of January 2012 the Kleenex product family included everyday tissues in a variety of packaging options as well as Kleenex Expressions with designer cartons. Premium three-ply products include Kleenex Ultra Soft, Kleenex Lotion, Kleenex Anti-Viral, and Kleenex Cool Touch. Although many more brands of facial tissue became available, Kleenex achieved iconic status as the brand in the product category. Consequently, it was not uncommon to hear U.S. citizens say, "Please hand me a Kleenex," when referring to any brand of facial tissue.

BIBLIOGRAPHY

Finley, Harry. "First Kotex Sanitary Napkin Campaign." The Museum of Menstruation and Women's Health, 1999. Accessed January 9, 2012. http://www.mum.org/urkotex.htm.

"Kimberly-Clark Agrees to Sell Some of Scott's Units and Mills." *New York Times,* December 13, 1995. Accessed January 9, 2012. http://www.nytimes.com/1995/12/13/business /kimberly-clark-agrees-to-sell-some-of-scott-s-units-and-mills .html.

Kimberly-Clark Corporation. "Heritage." Neenah, WI, December 2010. Accessed January 9, 2012. http://www.cms .kimberly-clark.com/umbracoimages/UmbracoFileMedia /K-C_Timeline_umbracoFile.pdf.

———. "Kleenex® Brand through the Decades." Neenah, WI, 2009. Accessed January 9, 2012. http://www.kleenex.com /Story.aspx.

———. "Product Evolution." Neenah, WI. Accessed January 9, 2012. http://www.kimberly-clark.com/ourcompany /innovations/product_evolution.aspx.

Paper Industry International Hall of Fame Inc. "Frank J. Sensenbrenner." Appleton, WI, 1998. Accessed January 9, 2012. http://www.paperhall.org/inductees/bios/1998/frank _sensenbrenner.php.

Procter & Gamble. "Puffs History." Cincinnati, OH, 2008. Accessed January 9, 2012. http://www.puffs.com/en_US /puffs-tissue-history.shtml.

Kool-Aid: Edwin Perkins's Flavored Drink Mix

The creation of Kool-Aid in a small town in Nebraska did not keep it from becoming a staple of U.S. beverages. Invented by Edwin Perkins during the Great Depression, the powdered beverage gained a brand of its own, which persisted through one acquisition after another. It was first passed on to General Foods Corporation in 1952 and, in the following year, the iconic Kool-Aid Man was born. Initially, the enormous red pitcher was seen on print advertisements across the country, but when Philip Morris International Inc. acquired General Foods in the mid-1980s, the broad-smiling jug began to see even more time in the spotlight. As the country's biggest advertising spender at the time, Philip Morris hoisted Kool-Aid to the popularity it still enjoys in the 2010s.

Philip Morris combined General Foods and Kraft in the mid-1990s but then spun off the Kool-Aid company early in the first decade of the 21st century. Then part of Kraft Foods, Inc., Kool-Aid fruit drink was still considered one of Kraft's major power brands, comprising a significant portion of the company's international beverage sales. Of the international corporation's US\$49 billion in sales, beverage sales totaled US\$8.8 billion, according to the company's 2010 annual report. The Kool-Aid Man was a maverick in the early 2010s, standing completely on its own, regardless of ownership. This strong identity warded off competitors, but it also incurred disadvantages.

KOOL-AID AND CULTURE

As a direct result of its stalwart identity, the Kool-Aid label accrued a variety of cultural meanings and uses over the years. Perhaps the most prominent of these was the saying, "drink the Kool-Aid," which was still used in 2012 by figures such as television commentator Bill O'Reilly and columnist Marybeth Hicks. The phrase was meant to suggest that a person subscribed to a belief or an ideology in an unquestioning manner, without giving it critical thought.

In the 2010s, the phrase carried a humorous undercurrent of error and inebriation, but its origins were far more serious. In Jonestown, Guyana, in 1978, more than 900 members of a cult called the People's Temple drank a deadly punch on the orders of Jim Jones, their cult leader. The cocktail was actually a combination of punch mix, Valium, and cyanide. Meghan Daum of the *Seattle Times* described what happened in her 2011 article "Don't 'Drink the Kool-Aid'": "So in Jones' thrall were his followers that they poisoned their babies and toddlers first, using syringes to squirt the liquid into the children's mouths. In most cases, death occurred within five minutes." Daum argued that the phrase was overused, particularly considering its dark history. In fact, the deadly mixture was actually created by using Flav-R-Aid (a Kool-Aid competitor).

The saccharine powder had gained renown before Jonestown, as a result of Tom Wolfe's book, *The Electric Kool-Aid Acid Test*. Written in 1968, it associated Kool-Aid with psychedelic drugs. Whether due to Kesey's book and the Jonestown tragedy, or simply to a combination of the comical spelling, the neon-colored beverages it produced, and the ecstatic smile of the Kool-Aid Man, the brand carried mixed connotations, which added to its notoriety in the United States and the world.

EDWIN PERKINS: INEXHAUSTIBLE CREATIVITY MEETS BUSINESS

Edwin Perkins was born in 1898 in Lewis, Iowa, to a family of farmers. When he was age six, the family moved to a plot of land close to Precept, Nebraska, and then to Hendley, Nebraska, a few years later. Once in Hendley, Nebraska, the family operated a general store. Around that time, Perkins's future wife, Kitty Shoemaker, introduced him to Jell-O, a type of gelatinous dessert. Perkins was enthralled, and convinced his father to start carrying the product in the family store. Shortly thereafter, Perkins tried to create new products that his family could sell. At age 13, he could be seen in the kitchen playing the part of the mad scientist, mixing various fluids and solids. His first major attempt resulted in what he called Nix-O-Tine, a substance that purportedly helped people quit smoking.

More importantly, according to his biography in the *Gale Biography in Context* database, Perkins came up with a beverage concentrate, called Fruit Smack. Fruit Smack had a taste people enjoyed. Like Jell-O at the time, it was available in six different flavors and customers loved it. However, the bottles the product came in tended to break during shipping and the family stopped selling them.

Undaunted, the young man opened his own company, called the Perkins Product Company. It sold a number of specialty items and knickknacks, such as flavorings and household remedies. At the same time, he operated in a number of other roles in the town, editing a weekly newspaper and serving as postmaster. He married his childhood friend, Kitty, in 1918. Then, he moved his business to Hastings, Nebraska. With its three railroads, the city was better positioned to distribute Perkins's products. He was 29 when he figured out how to completely dehydrate Fruit Smack into a useable product, which he called Kool-Ade.

Although Kool-Aid was a revolutionary beverage, the Great Depression contributed to its success and popularity. The stock market crashed in 1929 in the United States, leaving many U.S. citizens destitute and out of work. Families struggled to eke out an existence, much less pay for luxury goods. At its US$0.05 per package cost (Perkins dropped the cost by 50 percent after the stock market collapse), Kool-Aid was an affordable way to celebrate with something sweet. Additionally, the fact that it was incomplete, requiring work to finish, made it appealing to many young entrepreneurs.

In the early 1930s lemonade stands made way for Kool-Aid stands. In its article about Kool-Aid, the Hastings Museum of History amusingly pointed out the new market's inefficiency. It stated: "While most of the profits were consumed by the youngsters, it was something most children enjoyed".

Kool-Aid was not the end of the entrepreneur's experimentation. Offshoots of Kool-Aid, such as ice cream mixes and pie fillings, were added to his product line. A niece reminisced to the Hastings periodical, *McCook Daily Gazette,* of receiving items from her uncle, such as packages of Bet-R-Set (a gelatin dessert), Kool-Aid flavored chewing gum, and "other products he was trying out."

ACQUISITION BY GENERAL FOODS

General Foods acquired the Perkins Product Company in 1953 in order to diversify its product line. At the time, Post cereal products and coffee brands, such as Maxwell House, were its top sellers. According to the *International Directory of Company Histories*, Maxwell instant coffee was brought to market in 1941, however, coffee markets remained inconsistent. The company looked to other sources of revenue, buying up the Gaines Dog Food Company. Acquisitions were, in part, supported by the 10-in-1 rations it supplied to the United States Army.

Kool-Aid was similar to many of General Foods's products, such as Jell-O, breakfast cereal, and Birds Eye frozen vegetables. Like these other food products, Kool-Aid was easily distributed and could be stored for long periods. It was also cheap. After the acquisition, General Foods went on to create a number of successful spin-offs. Tang, Crystal Light, and Country Time Lemonade were some of the more popular products.

In 1954 General Foods gave Marvin Potts responsibility for advertising the Kool-Aid product line. As the art director for an advertising agency, Potts was told to provide an illustration to go along with the message, "A 5-cent package makes two quarts". Perhaps the artist stumbled on the simple, straightforward message, because he ended up taking inspiration from his son's windowpane drawings. These were sketched out of the frost on the glass and depicted a large, broadly smiling face. Inserting the smiley face on a large pitcher of Kool-Aid produced the Pitcher Man. Potts attempted several other logos, but the Pitcher Man was the only success.

In the 1960s and 1970s General Foods busied itself with diversifying revenues and branching out into international markets. SOS, the scouring-pad manufacturer, was brought under the wing of the business, as was the Burger Chef fast-food chain. Also added were the Viviane Woodard Cosmetic Corporation, a toy company, and W. Atlee Burpee Company, a seed supplier.

Many of these purchases failed to turn a profit and were consequently sold. Reaching out geographically provided more reason for optimism. The company strategy began with food company acquisitions in foreign markets. A chocolate company in Venezuela was purchased, as well as Hostess Brands, Inc., in Canada. By the end of the 1960s operations were spread out to Canada, Australia, France, Mexico, Denmark, Venezuela, Italy, Sweden, Spain, and the United Kingdom. However, despite the company's best attempts to capitalize on its success through expansion, coffee was still 39 percent of revenues at the end of the 1970s, and sales started a downward trend in the early 1980s. In 1985, Philip Morris bought General Foods for US$5.6 billion reported the *International Directory of Company Histories.*

The Philip Morris acquisition signaled the start of a new effort to reorganize the company and develop its products. Philip Smith became the new chief operating officer in 1987, and he divided General Foods into three divisions: coffee, meats, and miscellaneous groceries. Philip Morris then bought Kraft Foods, Inc., and blended the two corporations under a single entity, Kraft General Foods, choosing Kraft's Michael Miles to lead the project. *New York Times* writer Richard Stevenson pointed out in 1988 the significant advertising budgets of the two companies: "Together, Philip Morris and Kraft spent nearly [US]$2 billion in advertising last year. But Philip Morris on its own was already the nation's biggest spender on advertising." The deal was seen as a veritable all-star lineup, with General Foods's drink products teaming up with Kraft's cheese brand dominance. Kool-Aid and Post cereal met Parkay and Miracle Whip. The combined advertising power carried national and even international acclaim. Potts's Pitcher Man gained legs and arms, becoming the Kool-Aid Man as known in the 2010s.

CHILDHOOD OBESITY DRIVES CONSUMER CHANGE

The first decade of the 21st century saw another transitional period for the Kool-Aid brand. On the operations side, Philip Morris completed a spin-off of Kraft, which began with a small public sell-off in 2001. In 2007, the rest of Altria (the renamed Philip Morris International Inc.) sold its shares, leaving Irene Rosenfeld as chief executive. International sales continued to rise, particularly in emerging nations. In the early 2010s, Kraft planned to split, yet again, into snack foods and high-margin domestic grocery subdivisions. Tamara Rutter, writing for *Daily Finance,* argued that the reorganization would enable Kraft to better capitalize on developing, international markets.

On the home front, Kool-Aid and many other Kraft brand items faced growing adversity. With childhood obesity rising in the United States, a number of dieticians, medical doctors, and statisticians conducted studies that did considerable damage to the reputation of fruit drinks. Health reports suggested that drinking Kool-Aid and other sugary beverages might contribute to the problem, and the media started to change the public's perception of Kool-Aid. Writing for the *New York Times,* Gary Taubes investigated the possible correlation between sugar consumption and obesity. In his article, "Is Sugar Toxic?" he

cited more than merely unhealthful caloric content and unhealthful qualities of high-dextrose corn syrup. He argued that all types of sugar were dangerous. To prove his point, he wrote, "when you bake your children a birthday cake or give them lemonade on a hot summer day, you may be doing them more harm than good, despite all the love that goes with it."

As the low-sugar and no-sugar initiative played out, public perception of the Kool-Aid Man was completely altered. The happy, broadly smiling face promoting the red drink made the *TIME* magazine 2011 list, "The 10 Creepiest Product Mascots," among other questionably healthful food company icons such as Burger King's King, Jack in the Box's Jack, MacDonald's Hamburglar, and others. What began as an innovation in convenience became tinged with negative connotations.

Kraft fought to maintain revenues, in part by switching its target demographic in the United States. Kool-Aid, in particular, shifted dramatically to Hispanic outlets, where the Kool-Aid Man's reputation was as yet untarnished. In 2009, only 3.6 percent of Kraft's marketing dollars went to Hispanic media, but in 2011 the majority of the Kool-Aid marketing budget went toward reaching Hispanic audiences, according to Andrew Adam Newman of the *New York Times.* Some of the money was used to sponsor outdoor movie screenings in major cities, such as Los Angeles, California; Chicago, Illinois; Dallas, Texas; and Houston, Texas. The movies were broadcast in Spanish and featured the Kool-Aid Man during advertising breaks. Twenty percent of Kool-Aid revenues in the United States were attributed to Hispanic consumers.

Outside the United States, the majority of growth in Kraft's beverage revenues came from emerging markets. Kraft Foods beverage revenues increased in 2010 by US$771 million over the previous year, and growth in developing markets was responsible for roughly US$430 million of the difference. The reorganization allowed by the Altria spin-off proved extremely useful in facilitating the transition.

STRONG BRAND IDENTITY

The timing of the invention of Kool-Aid was an important factor in its popular acclaim. Being a ready-to-make product, which also boasted high calorie content, Kool-Aid was in the forefront of two major trends that came out of the Great Depression. At the time they were produced, these products added a considerable value to the market in terms of flexible shipping and storage, which led to a decreased price.

The General Foods and Kraft branding strategy was powerful but it constrained product development. Once the Kool-Aid Man became an icon he could not be removed or shifted. As such, Kraft was relegated to finding the consumers who found the most benefit from its products, rather than switching or altering its products to better suit the target consumer.

In the first decade of the 21st century the standard U.S. snack foods and fruit juices, including Kool-Aid, were cast in quite a different and unhealthy light by academics, dieticians, and the media. However, even after more healthful alternatives became available, the standard U.S. snack foods brands retained a competitive advantage in developing countries, as well as in a narrowing set of U.S. consumers. By reaching out to the audiences that benefited most, Kool-Aid continued to enjoy strong prospects in the 2010s.

BIBLIOGRAPHY

"The 10 Creepiest Product Mascots." *TIME,* August 24, 2011. Accessed February 2, 2012. http://www.time.com/time/specials/packages/article/0,28804,2090074_2090076_2090112,00.html.

Daum, Meghan. "Don't 'Drink the Kool-Aid'." *Seattle Times,* November 22, 2011. Accessed February 2, 2012. http://seattletimes.nwsource.com/html/living/2016817534_daum23.html.

"Edwin Perkins." In *Gale Biography in Context.* Gale: Detroit, 2008. Gale Biography in Context (GALE|K1650006251). Accessed February 2, 2012. http://go.galegroup.com/ps/i.do?id=GALE%7CK1650006251&v=2.1&u=itsbtrial&it=r&p=GPS&sw=w.

"Food 1929–1941." In *Historic Events for Students: The Great Depression,* edited by Richard C. Hanes and Sharon M. Hanes. Vol. 2, 21–49. Gale: Detroit, 2002. Gale Virtual Reference Library (GALE|CX3424800041). Accessed February 2, 2012. http://go.galegroup.com/ps/i.do?id=GALE%7CCX3424800041&v=2.1&u=itsbtrial&it=r&p=GVRL&sw=w.

Foster, Nancy. "Pitcher This!" *Hastings Tribune,* August 11, 2005. Accessed February 2, 2012. http://www.kool-aiddays.com/index.php?option=com_content&task=view&id=26&Itemid=41.

"Hastings Gears Up for Kool-Aid Days." *McCook Daily Gazette,* August 13, 1998. Accessed February 2, 2012. http://news.google.com/newspapers?id=dZsgAAAAIBAJ&sjid=6GgFAAAAIBAJ&pg=2383,4321041&dq=kool+aid+nebraska&hl=en.

"The History of Kool-Aid." Hastings, NE: Hastings Museum, 2012. Accessed February 2, 2012. http://hastingsmuseum.org/exhibits/kool-aid/the-history-of-kool-aid.

"Kraft Foods Chief Explains Split from Altria." *NPR,* March 30, 2007. Accessed February 2, 2012. http://www.npr.org/templates/story/story.php?storyId=9237383.

Kraft Foods, Inc. "2010 Annual Report." Northfield, IL, February 28, 2011. Accessed February 2, 2012. http://www.kraftfoodscompany.com/SiteCollectionDocuments/pdf/KraftFoods_10K_20110228.pdf.

"Kraft Foods Inc." In *International Directory of Company Histories,* edited by Jay P. Pederson. Vol. 91, 291–306. Detroit: St. James Press, 2008. Gale Virtual Reference Library (GALE| CX2690700061). Accessed February 2, 2012. http://go.galegroup.com/ps/i.do?id=GALE%7CCX2690700061&v=2.1&u=itsbtrial&it=r&p=GVRL&sw=w.

Newman, Andrew Adam. "Kraft Aims Kool-Aid Ads at a Growing Hispanic Market." *New York Times,* May 26, 2011. Accessed February 2, 2012. http://www.nytimes.com/2011/05/27/business/media/27adco.html?_r=2.

Rutter, Tamara. "Will Kraft Spin Out of Control?" *Daily Finance,* January 19, 2012. Accessed February 2, 2012. http://www.dailyfinance.com/2012/01/19/will-kraft-spin-out-of-control.

Stevenson, Richard W. "A Muscular New Consumer Giant." *New York Times,* November 1, 1988. Accessed February 2, 2012. http://www.nytimes.com/1988/11/01/business/a-muscular-new-consumer-giant.html.

Taubes, Gary. "Is Sugar Toxic?" *New York Times,* April 13, 2011. Accessed February 24, 2012. http://www.nytimes.com/2011/04/17/magazine/mag-17Sugar-t.html?pagewanted=all.

Kraft Foods: From Cheese Distribution to Multi-Brand Conglomerate

In 2012 Kraft Foods, Inc., was one of the world's largest snack foods and assorted groceries corporations in the world. With almost US$50 billion in revenue and with continued growth even through the global recession of 2008–2009, the company demonstrated an ability to thrive even when general market conditions deteriorated. Many of its dairy products, such as Kraft Macaroni & Cheese and Kraft Singles, were invented by the company itself; however, many other brand-name grocery items, such as Kool-Aid, Grape Nuts, and Nabisco Wheat Thins resulted from business acquisitions. Birds Eye frozen vegetables, Maxwell House coffee, Philadelphia Cream Cheese, and dozens of other Kraft brand products were sold worldwide, as well. The acquisition of Cadbury in 2010 exemplified the corporate strategy to expand by acquiring inexpensive, processed, and packaged goods.

Historically, the company garnered the majority of its revenues in North America and Europe, though emerging nations showed strong growth in the 21st century. While North American revenues grew slightly from 2008 to 2010, developing markets exploded from US$8.2 billion to US$13.6 billion, according to the Kraft 2010 annual report. The year 2010 was the first on record in which company sales in the developing world surpassed those in Europe. Coincidentally, the company hired 30,000 employees, bringing the total workforce to 127,000 and adding almost 30 percent to global staff size.

The global recession was not a significant factor for Kraft because the company's products appealed to tight budgets. During a time when many consumers attempted to cut costs, processed snack foods offered a low-cost way to satisfy caloric intake. Additionally, innovations in packing, processing, and distribution decreased the cost of bringing snack foods to market. Extended shelf life was the significant advantage James L. Kraft discovered when he first experimented with processed cheese, and over the course of the 20th century the company learned how to bring the same type of advantage to other foodstuffs. These developments in the U.S. food industry led to products that appealed to consumers who were looking to save money, both in North America and across the globe.

In 2012 chief executive Irene Rosenfeld led the way, planning to pare down and separate the company into two main branches. On the one hand, global snack food brands, such as Oreo, Trident, and Tang, were planned to begin operating as an entity distinct from the company's North American grocery wing, which included Oscar Mayer, Planters, and Macaroni & Cheese, among other major brands. According to Emily Bryson York, in her 2012 article in the *Chicago Tribune*, the split was intended to allow the corporation to pare down its operations. Rosenfeld planned to head the global snack food entity, giving Tony Vernon control of the other division on home turf. Vernon told York about some of the significant reasons for the decision: ". . .our plan for a more nimble company, combined with the current economic and competitive pressures, led us to this point. Taking the necessary steps now will enable us to continue investing in our beloved brands to drive growth." The separation would free up the global snack foods division to step up its development in economies outside the United States and Europe, where buying power was increasing.

TOP OF THE U.S. FOOD CHAIN

Born in 1874, James L. Kraft came from a family of Canadian farmers. Once in Chicago in 1903, he realized that the grocery system was inefficient in that it required grocers to travel, individually, to cheese markets in order to purchase their cheeses. Kraft started a cheese distribution business to improve the system. Initially, the venture lost money, but it drew the attention of his four brothers. By 1909, J.L. Kraft Bros. Company was incorporated. From the beginning, the company was aggressive in its advertising campaigns and the company was one of the first to purchase color advertisements, according to *International Directory of Company Histories*.

Business development was consistent. In 1912 the company bought an office in New York, New York, and by 1914 it opened a cheese factory in Illinois and distributed 31 types of cheese. In 1916 Kraft patented "process" cheese, which did not spoil like other products. Soon after, Kraft began to acquire other businesses, beginning with a Canadian cheese company. The initial public offering came in 1924 when the company changed its name to the Kraft Cheese Company. Three years later, Kraft and Phenix Cheese Corporation merged. Their combined U.S. market presence was estimated to be 40 percent by 1930, and it owned offices in Canada, Britain, Germany, and Australia. At the same time, the National Dairy Products Corporation, which owned brands like Breyer Ice Cream and Breakstone Bros., merged with the two cheese groups to create a dairy-and-cheese conglomerate. After the merger, however, the three companies continued to act autonomously. This arrangement set a standard that the company would revisit with General Foods Corporation in the 1990s and early 21st century.

In the meantime, Kraft continued to introduce products that made the company a household name. Velveeta was brought to market just prior to the Great Depression. Miracle Whip, Kraft caramels, Macaroni & Cheese Dinner, and Parkay were all introduced prior to 1940. During World War II Kraft supplied cheese rations, roughly four million pounds per week, to Britain. Compared to the six million pounds of cheese sold to the U.S. Army over the entire course of World War I, the new figure reflected the enormous growth of the firm. In 1952 J. L. Kraft died, which brought the family leadership to an end. Directly afterward, the corporation was reorganized and the autonomous units became subsidiaries under centralized management. The company was renamed in 1976 as Kraft Inc. and John M. Richman became the chief executive in 1979.

Richman's first move was to merge the company with Dart Industries, a conglomerate of Duracell, Tupperware, and other divisions. Once again Kraft kept its distance, at first. Both companies continued to act autonomously, but management did move into a new building in Northbrook, Illinois, which, according to John Gorman of the *Chicago Tribune* may have caused resentment on both sides. Whatever the case, the future of Dart and Kraft Inc. was short-lived, and in 1986, the board voted to separate. Although the separation spelled less diversification, the food company claimed roughly 80 percent of total revenues, bringing in US$8 billion.

PHILIP MORRIS AND KRAFT

In 1985 Philip Morris Companies, Inc., acquired snack foods and coffee producer General Foods Corporation. The acquisition came with a US$5.6 billion price tag and at a good time for both parties. Looking at a shrinking tobacco market, Philip Morris sought to diversify revenue. General Foods was in the midst of a turbulent period, during which a number of the firm's divisions slipped in revenues. In 1987 the chairman of Philip Morris, Hamish Maxwell, oversaw a reorganization of the firm into three discrete units, including coffee, meat, and assorted groceries.

In 1988 Philip Morris purchased Kraft Inc. for US$13.1 billion. At the time, it was the second-largest corporate takeover in history, second to Chevron's US$13.3 billion acquisition of the Gulf Corporation. The combination brought together multiple venerable U.S. food brands, with Post cereals, Maxwell House coffee, Jell-O desserts, and Kool-Aid powdered beverages coming from General Foods. Taken together with Kraft's dairy dominance and Philip Morris' advertising prowess, the new entity was one of the biggest topics in the business world. Richman became vice-chairman of Philip Morris and was charged with managing the merger between foods divisions. Michael A. Miles, Kraft's president before the deal, was placed at the helm of Kraft.

At first, everyone seemed to win. Philip Morris diversified its portfolio. General Foods and Kraft gained leverage in a retailer's market. Moreover, Stevenson reported the potential for Philip Morris advertising practices to extend to its food divisions. With the largest advertising budget in the country before the merger, Philip Morris was expected to prop up its new acquisitions on media outlets.

Advertising expectations proved correct. The strong brand names and the icons personifying them, such as the Kool-Aid Man, gained even more prominence. In the end, however, the association with tobacco may have negatively impacted some of the strongest brands. In the United States, Philip Morris changed its name to Altria Group, Inc. It completed a spin-off of Kraft by 2007.

After the spin-off, Kraft began a process of acquisitions and spin-offs of its own. Post cereal, a General Foods brand, was sold off in 2007. Cadbury was acquired in 2010. In late 2011 the company prepared to split off its North American groceries from its international snack foods.

PUBLIC IMAGE IN THE 21ST CENTURY

Kraft Foods, Inc., continued to grow more profitable through the first decade of the 21st century, In addition to growth in emerging markets, Kraft Foods increased its advertising program in its North American division. Emily Bryson York reported that 2010 advertising expenditures rose to 6.8 percent of net revenue, up from 6.5 percent in 2009. Tony Vernon, president of Kraft Foods North America, reportedly aimed to increase that figure to 8 percent in order to charge more money for the same products.

Kraft's power brands in North America included Oreo, Ritz, Oscar Mayer, and Kool-Aid. In large part, budget increases were diverted to marketing through Hispanic media outlets. According to Adam Andrew Newman in the *New York Times,* "[In 2011] Kraft says it will triple spending on Hispanic marketing over last year. . .the percentage of overall spending would be in the double digits." In particular, the majority of Kool-Aid advertising was to focus on Hispanic markets. Seeing that the Kool-Aid Man was no longer popular in some segments of the population, Kraft sent the icon where it might be better received.

EXEMPLARY BUSINESS TACTICS

As one of the oldest corporations in the United States, Kraft Foods, Inc., has proven itself a survivor. Kraft's initial success with processed cheeses and dairy products may have given the company an initial advantage, but firm, deft management decisions were the firm's primary selling point by the 2010s.

On the far side of its numerous mergers, acquisitions, and even takeovers, Kraft seemed to always come out at least slightly better off. This was most clearly the case in its acquisitions of direct competitors. Even though the corporation invented its own successful product line, the majority of its products came from its aggressive business strategy.

When purchasing was not a beneficial option, it resorted to other means of collaboration. For example, its first big deal with the National Dairy Corporation helped to consolidate the market and lower supply costs for both parties. The merger eventually led to the subsuming of National Dairy under the Kraft brand. However, even when the other entity did not fare so well, as in the case of the merger with Dart, Kraft's progress to the top of the North American market was not hindered. Later, during the Philip Morris takeover, the firm's chief executive John M. Richman became vice-chairman, thereby retaining a position of power that helped Kraft continue to evolve under the auspices of a larger company. When it spun off from the renamed Altria, Kraft was once again in a much better position.

In all these transactions, the company's flexibility supported its success. The pattern started with the National Dairy Corporation. The two companies merged but management remained separate. When the companies finally consolidated in full, there were no doubts regarding the success of the venture. The same strategy was implemented in the deal with Dart. Shortly after the merger, when Dart began to stagnate, Kraft was able to remove itself easily. The trend continued when Philip Morris purchased the firm, helped build it up with advertising and acquisitions, and then spun it off. Shortly after the spin-off was completed, Kraft was able to reorganize itself and its advertisements around new market opportunities, both at home and abroad. Their corporate advertising strategy, which focused on individual products, made this flexibility possible. Thus, Kraft was able to buy and sell products easily.

BIBLIOGRAPHY

Gorman, John. "Dart & Kraft Separating." *Chicago Tribune,* June 20, 1986. Accessed February 2, 2012. http://articles .chicagotribune.com/1986-06-20/business/8602140126_1 _kraft-stock-john-m-richman-separation.

Jacobson, Robert R., and David E. Salamie. " Kraft Foods Inc. " In *International Directory of Company Histories,* edited by Jay P. Pederson. Vol. 91, 291–306. Detroit: St. James Press, 2008. Gale Virtual Reference Library (GALE|CX2690700061). Accessed February 2, 2012. http://go.galegroup.com/ps/i.do? id=GALE%7CCX2690700061&v=2.1&u=gale&it=r&p=G VRL&sw=w.

"Krafts Foods Chief Explains Split from Altria." *NPR,* March 30, 2007. Accessed February 29, 2012. http://www.npr.org /templates/story/story.php?storyId=9237383.

Kraft Foods, Inc. "2010 Annual Report." Northfield, IL, February 28, 2011. Accessed February 2, 2012. http://www .kraftfoodscompany.com/SiteCollectionDocuments/pdf /KraftFoods_10K_20110228.pdf.

"Kraft, from Roll-Up to Spinoff." *New York Times,* August 4, 2011. Accessed February 2, 2012. http://dealbook.nytimes .com/2011/08/04/kraft-from-roll-up-to-spin-off.

Newman, Andrew Adam. "Kraft Aims Kool-Aid Ads at a Growing Hispanic Market." *New York Times,* May 26, 2011. Accessed February 2, 2012. http://www.nytimes.com/2011 /05/27/business/media/27adco.html?_r=2.

Rutter, Tamara. "Will Kraft Spin Out of Control?" *Daily Finance,* January 19, 2012. Accessed February 2, 2012. http://www .dailyfinance.com/2012/01/19/will-kraft-spin-out-of-control.

Stevenson, Richard W. "A Muscular New Consumer Giant." *New York Times,* November 1, 1988. Accessed February 2, 2012. http://www.nytimes.com/1988/11/01/business/a-muscular -new-consumer-giant.html.

"Top 10 Creepiest Product Mascots." *TIME,* August 24, 2011. Accessed February 2, 2012. http://www.time.com/time /specials/packages/article/0,28804,2090074_2090076 _2090112,00.html.

York, Emily Bryson. "Kraft Boosting Advertising in Bid to Lift Sales." *Chicago Tribune,* February 23, 2011. Accessed February 2, 2012. http://articles.chicagotribune.com/2011 -02-23/business/ct-biz-0223-kraft-commodity-costs-2011 0223_1_consumer-analyst-group-ceo-irene-rosenfeld-kraft -plans.

———. "Kraft Slimming Down for Separation." *Chicago Tribune,* January 18, 2012. Accessed February 2, 2012. http:// www.chicagotribune.com/business/ct-biz-0118-kraft -20120118,0,2124522.story.

LED Traffic Lights Gain Acceptance in the United States and Abroad

Light-emitting diodes (LEDs) are energy-efficient bulbs that use crystal to conduct electricity and give off current. They are therefore different from the standard metal in incandescent bulbs. They generate less heat, consume less energy, and last longer than incandescent bulbs. According to a 1999 Consortium for Energy Efficiency report, LED traffic signals were between 80 percent and 90 percent more efficient than traditional incandescent lights. Whereas incandescent technology uses a single filament for each light, LED signals contain a multitude of small diodes for each bulb. Motorists can distinguish stoplights using the two technologies by inspecting the surface of the signal, which would appear fragmented in LED stop lights.

LEDs were initially invented by Nick Holynyak, Jr, in 1962, when he was working in a General Electric Company Laboratory in Syracuse, New York. At the time of his invention, Holonyak did not receive widespread acclaim, partly because the technology only emitted low-intensity red light and so was not widely applicable. LEDs went largely unseen for decades after their invention. Although they were used as electronic components, they were too expensive for private and public use.

Red and amber LEDs arrived in the 1970s, initially for use as indicator lights, and blue and green emitters were developed in the 1990s by private enterprise. White light, the frequency needed for traffic signals, could not initially be generated without blue light at the very least. However, within a few short years of white light capability, LEDs were tested in certain U.S. municipalities. Once cities such as Denver, Colorado, and Philadelphia, Pennsylvania, spearheaded retrofitting projects in the late 1990s and demonstrated the long-term fiscal benefits of converting to LED traffic signals, a trend began. City planners began to realize that the technology would pay for itself and also benefit the environment. As production increased, the price of LEDs dropped and citywide retrofitting of traffic lights became commonplace. In the first decade of the 21st century, due to environmental initiatives, U.S. federal incentives, and shifting popular opinion, the urban lighting system in the United States underwent an LED revolution.

Once private enterprise developed the capacity to produce the color white, public organizations recognized the technology as an opportunity to cut energy costs. These organizations started looking for ways to reduce greenhouse gas emissions in 1980, when the American Council for an Energy-Efficient Economy was created. The council's goal was to conduct in-depth research regarding energy expenditures and facilitate efficiency. In the early 1990s, the U.S. Environmental Protection Agency (EPA) created the Green Lights Program and the Energy Star Label. Legislation came in the form of the Energy Policy Act of 1992, which set standards for fluorescent and incandescent lamps. These measures helped to create a growing awareness of lighting inefficiencies, and people were ready to listen to proposed solutions.

In 2004, after multiple citywide traffic light retrofits took place in the United States, Holonyak was honored with a US$500,000 Lemelson-MIT prize for his invention. This award is made to outstanding inventors in mid-career who have developed a patented product or process of significant value to society. Director of the Lemelson-MIT program, Merton Flemings, dedicated the award by describing the still-untapped potential of LED technology. According to the Massachusetts Institute of Technology article, "Inventor of Long-lasting, Low-heat

Light Source Awarded US$500,000 Lemelsons-MIT Prize for Invention," "Within the next decade, LEDs could potentially make the incandescent light bulb obsolete."

RETROFITS AND NEW MARKET OPPORTUNITIES

The first municipalities to test LEDs already supported research into green technologies. The city of Denver, Colorado, began its own broad-based, energy conservation program in the late 1980s. The goal of the initiative was to address the efficient use of major utilities in the Denver, Colorado area in the hopes of saving money, conserving the environment, and setting an example for the city residents. One prong of the project aimed to research new technologies to assess their prospective use. According to Darryl Winer, the program head, in his article, "Denver Leads in LED Traffic Signals," US$1.1 million was spent on new product review in 1996. The committee decided on LED traffic signals as a potential way to save energy. At the same time, the Public Service Company of Colorado's Demand Side Energy Management programs came to the same conclusion. They offered US$50 and US$25 rebates on red light and red turn arrow traffic signals, respectively. As these were the two lights that were used most frequently, they had more potential to save energy.

Denver, Colorado, immediately put together specifications for LED traffic lights, and vendors were asked for competitive bids for the full order of 7,124 bulbs. Dialight, Inc., from New Jersey, placed the best bid, with red light bulbs priced at US$143 apiece, according to Winer. This did not include the cost of installation. Even with the seemingly exorbitant fees, Winer calculated that the investment would be paid back in 4.28 years in energy savings and maintenance. Incandescent bulbs required replacement almost every year, whereas LEDs lasted at least five years. The retrofit was such a success that Winer concluded, "LED traffic signal replacement is a public policy and environmental bonanza. . . .This project is equivalent to planting a 2,266-acre forest in the middle of Denver or removing 1,094 cars from our roads." Retrofitting Denver, Colorado, was seen as not only fiscally responsible in the long run; it was also beneficial to the environment and the health of Denver, Colorado, residents.

News of Denver, Colorado's successful test project spread across the United States, and numerous municipalities followed the example. Philadelphia, Pennsylvania combined funding with Public Technologies Incorporated (PTI) to develop specifications for a retrofit of its own. These specifications were then implemented by the State of New Hampshire and New York, New York. To facilitate the lighting revolution, the Consortium for Energy Efficiency launched the LED Traffic Signal Initiative in 1999, reporting that 25,000 LED traffic signals were installed by 1996, a figure that sextupled by the end of 1997. The initiative looked at the potential of a national effort, estimating that three billion kilowatt-hours of electricity could be saved each year by retrofitting all of the traffic signals in the United States.

Although momentum was building, there were still a number of obstacles to the widespread use of LED lights. Due to the novelty of the industry and technology, organization was a problem for both public and private sectors. On the one hand, businesses were discouraged from market entry, due to a relatively small market capitalization. Compared to incandescent bulbs, which required replacements every year, the 5 to 10-year lifespan of LEDs weakened the eventual payoff. Additionally, the price for market entry was high. Consequently, there were only a small number of LED traffic signal producers. Canada's Ecolux and Dialight, Denver's successful bidder, claimed 80 percent of the market, according to the Consortium for Energy Efficiency Inc.'s article, "LED Traffic Signal Initiative Description." These factors kept prices high and bottlenecked the supply chain.

The public sector faced problems in acquiring long-term funding, such as U.S. government subsidies. Also, new specifications were required for LED traffic lights to ensure adequate functionality and quality. No one knew how to tell the difference between a good LED bulb and a bad one, and until a set of guidelines was established, U.S. municipalities were urged to proceed with caution. Even a decade later, in June 2010, the Clinton Climate Initiative (CCI) white paper on traffic light signals described LED bulbs as a "rapidly evolving" technology, pointing attention to the potential for "unrealistic claims about product quality and performance." The paper urged city planners to create a set of project requirements and standards to ensure quality.

GREEN LIGHT COVERS THE UNITED STATES

After many cities retrofitted their traffic lights, northerly U.S. locations discovered an unexpected problem. Since LEDs were more energy efficient, they emitted much less heat than incandescent bulbs. In northern U.S. climates, the decreased heat allowed snow to occasionally pile up in front of the lights, obscuring them from view. Occurring rarely and easily fixed, the issue was not immediately given much attention.

However, on rare occasions, snow-covered traffic lights caused automobile accidents. Writing for ABC (American Broadcasting Corporation) News, Elisabeth Leamy and Vanessa Weber covered the aftermath of an intense winter storm in Wisconsin, in which a number of signals were hidden from view, although this caused more anxiety than accidents. The state was considering investing in shields to guard traffic lights against heavy snowfall. At US$40 apiece, this would have been a significant cost. Joanna Bush, Wisconsin state traffic signal systems engineer, considered a more conservative approach. She believed that drivers could be responsible, careful, and considerate of the traffic around them, telling Leamy and Weber, "You will get your green. It's just a matter of watching the cues of the vehicles around you to find it." It was also pointed out that incandescent bulbs had their own quirks. When they stopped functioning, the bulbs (and consequently the traffic lights) went completely black. By comparison, LEDs faded gradually, allowing maintenance crews to replace them before they became a problem. The issue did not deter LED retrofits, even in northern United States.

Subsidies continued to play a large role in the adoption of LED street lights. The Illinois Clean Energy Community Foundation provided US$9.9 million to upgrade traffic lights throughout the state. In fact, the Illinois Department of Transportation began mandating that communities use red-light LEDs because they were safer. Priscilla Tobias, safety engineer for the department, told *New York Times* reporter Barnaby Feder that LEDs "are much more visible to the motorist, so they have more time to see the traffic signal and react." Not only were the new traffic signals more energy efficient, they were brighter, and therefore safer, than their predecessors.

The American Recovery and Reinvestment Act of 2009 continued to spur green lighting projects across the United States. The act was designed to improve the U.S. economy during the economic recession, and a portion of the money was allocated for green projects. States still lacking LEDs were given even more incentive to install them. New Mexico, for example, upgraded traffic signals throughout the state once it became aware of the help it would receive. New Mexico received US$2.6 million in U.S. federal grants for the project, which was completed by April 2010, according to the state news release, "Governor Bill Richardson Announces New Mexico's LED Traffic Light Retrofit Completed." Many other portions of the United States followed suit.

The Clinton Climate Initiative, a subsidiary of the Clinton Foundation, also helped spur LED adoption, beginning with traffic signals. Started in 2005, the initiative researched and communicated opportunities to better control greenhouse gas emissions. The organization helped target and disseminate LED traffic-lighting technology throughout the United States. It also facilitated global development, in addition to brainstorming more LED solutions. Reviewing the global impact of energy-efficient street lighting, the organization's white paper estimated that 79 million megawatt-hours could be shaved off the annual, international electric bill with full LED implementation. This amounted to 40.5 million tons of carbon dioxide. The initiative began efforts to facilitate other types of street-lighting retrofits as well.

LED IN OTHER COUNTRIES AND APPLICATIONS

Governments in Europe, the Americas, and Asia began to take note of LED's potential. In 2011, Singapore started a festival to add notoriety and fame to LEDs. Called i Light, the month-long celebration featured sustainable light projects designed by prominent artists and professionals. The second annual celebration, slated to take place in March 2012, was expected to feature a number of award-winning light displays.

Public support increased global demand. The United Kingdom and Mexico signed contracts for LED traffic bulbs, and many countries in the European Union engaged in planning or implementation of LED retrofits in the early 2010s. All signs pointed to a large-scale, global change in city traffic lights. In "Charge of the LED Brigade," *The Economist* projected dramatic changes in the industry, stating that LED lights had a 10 percent share of the international lighting market in 2010. The same report projected that percentage to rise to 41 percent by 2016. Moreover, because emerging economies were projected to increase their demand for light, the international lighting market as a whole was expected to increase by 60 percent in the same time period. This projection indicated a drastic shift in the lighting industry and a dramatic increase in the globe's energy efficiency. If these predictions proved true, then CCI's 40.5 million tons of carbon dioxide saved was likely to become a gross underestimate.

As suppliers either jumped into the market or paid for the initial investment to begin production, prices for LEDs dropped, which opened up more possibilities for public and private use. Niche markets developed. Restaurants began to use LEDs in outdoor signs, rather than relying on neon glare to attract patrons. Automobile manufacturers implemented them in brake lights, because the new technology lit up more quickly than incandescent filaments.

IMPORTANCE OF PUBLIC INITIATIVES

Street lighting retrofits are an example of public works leading private industry, but it was only after private-sector businesses adapted the technology to emit higher frequencies of light that the public sector found widespread application in traffic signals. Government initiatives, city-wide projects, and nonprofit organizations helped build momentum for the technology, which spread to city intersections across the United States. In fact, without public initiatives, LEDs were too expensive for cities to consider.

Denver, Colorado, for instance, acted to take advantage of a U.S. federal rebate for LED bulbs, which made the hefty price tag appealing. Thereafter, continued subsidies and grants helped innumerable municipalities follow the lead and adopt the eco-friendly technology.

The speed of the adoption of LED technology in the United States testified to more than the expediency of the public sector. Simply put, LEDs were a vast improvement over incandescent bulbs in the way that mattered when they were developed. The invention demonstrated a huge leap forward in energy efficiency, but its potential was untapped until efficiency and greenhouse gas reduction became a commodity.

BIBLIOGRAPHY

American Council for an Energy-Efficient Economy. "About ACEE." Boston, MA, December, 1999. Accessed January 23, 2012. http://www.cee1.org/gov/led/led-init-desc.pdf.

"Charge of the LED Brigade." *The Economist,* August 20, 2011. Accessed January 23, 2012. http://www.economist.com/node/21526373.

Clinton Climate Initiative. "Street Lighting Retrofit Projects: Improving Performance While Reducing Costs and Greenhouse Gas Emissions." Boston, MA, June 2010. Accessed January 23, 2012. http://www.clintonfoundation.org/files/CCI_whitepaper_lighting_2010.pdf.

Consortium for Energy Efficiency, Inc. "LED Traffic Signal Initiative Description." Boston, MA, December 1999. Accessed January 23, 2012. http://www.cee1.org/gov/led/led-init-desc.pdf.

Feder, Barnaby J. "A Glimpse of a Future In a New Kind of Light." *New York Times,* February 11, 2003. Accessed January 23, 2012. http://www.nytimes.com/2003/02/11/business/a-glimpse-of-a-future-in-a-new-kind-of-light.html?src=pm.

"Inventor of Long-Lasting, Low-Heat Light Source Awarded US$500,000 Lemelsons-MIT Prize for Invention." Cambridge, MA: Massachusetts Institute of Technology, April 21, 2004. Accessed January 23, 2012. http://web.mit.edu/invent/n-pressreleases/n-press-04LMP.html.

Leamy, Elisabeth, and Vanessa Weber. "Stoplights' Unusual, Potentially Deadly Winter Problem." *ABC,* January 8, 2010. Accessed January 23, 2012. http://abcnews.go.com/GMA/ConsumerNews/stoplights-unusual-potentiall-deadly-winter-problem/story?id=9506449#.Tx7og_mroWZ.

Marusiak, Jenny. "Liveable Cities Series: Illuminating the Path to Sustainable Lighting." *Eco-Business.com,* January 19, 2012. Accessed January 23, 2012. http://www.eco-business.com/features/liveable-cities-series-illuminating-the-path-to-sustainable-lighting/.

State of New Mexico. Governor Bill Richardson. "Governor Bill Richardson Announces New Mexico's LED Traffic Light Retrofit Completed." Santa Fe, NM, April 22, 2010. Accessed April 10, 2012. www.recovery.state.nm.us/docs/press_releases/2010/042210_01.pdf.

Winer, Darryl. "Denver Leads in LED Traffic Signals." *Public Works* 128 no. 2 (1997): 47–49.

Les Paul and the Electric Guitar

A jazz man from rural Wisconsin does not seem like a likely source of one of the most influential designs in musical instruments, one that single-handedly reshaped the landscape of U.S. music in the 20th century. Yet Les Paul, more than any other musician or inventor in the music industry, is widely respected and recognized for his immeasurable contributions. He represents one of the few outstanding individuals with the rare distinction of having a permanent exhibit displayed at the Rock and Roll Hall of Fame in Cleveland, Ohio.

Although there have been designs for electric guitars before and since Les Paul, few have seen the same level of success as the one design that was born from the dreams of a lifelong inventor and talented musician. Paul was able to combine both these talents and create a legendary musical instrument and several other novel musical ideas that were instrumental to the evolution of modern music. Paul's electric guitar has had the unique power to change a wide variety of musical genres, from country, to jazz, to rock and roll. It is unsurprising that when Paul died in 2009 at the age of 94, he was eulogized by some of the world's most famous musical artists from a variety of genres, from Slash of Guns N' Roses, to blues legend B. B. King.

HOW HIGH THE MOON

Les Paul was the stage name of Lester William Polsfuss of Waukesha, Wisconsin. Born in 1915, he started his long, lucrative musical career when he was 13 years old, and he continued to entertain, invent, and experiment throughout his life. Paul's influence on the music industry transcended styles and generations, from his early days when people remembered him as a country music singer and guitar player in the 1930s, to the World War II years when he became known for his musical inventions. Undoubtedly though, it was his development of a solid-body electric guitar that earned him the most fame and a place in history as a great U.S. inventor.

According to a story related by Paul himself in a 2009 television interview with Gourmet Guitar's Holger Obenaus shortly before his death, his first foray into changing music happened when he was in his teens and working as an entertainer at a roadside drive-in barbeque stand near his home. People would drive their cars in and get served right there by the restaurant staff. Paul figured he could make some money by providing entertainment in the form of playing his guitar and harmonica, singing, and telling jokes as the people visited the roadhouse. Since it was not the ideal stage for him to be heard, Paul had taken apart the family telephone and wired the mouthpiece to be amplified through his mother's radio, which he had borrowed. In an interview with NHK's Setsuko Sato, Paul said that one day a man riding in the rumble seat of a car wrote a note that he gave to a carhop (server at the restaurant) to give to Paul. It said, "Red, your voice, and harmonica, and your jokes are okay. But your guitar is not loud enough." This is what triggered Paul to return home and start trying to resolve that problem.

Since he had already worked out how to amplify his voice and harmonica, the next thing Paul did was to take a phonograph pickup, put it through the top of the guitar, and wire it to his father's radio. This made Paul one of the first performers ever to create and use an electric acoustic guitar. It worked well enough to use and Paul would perform with both radios, on either side of the stage, amplifying his entire performance. The biggest problem that Paul found, at this point, was that the resonance created by the hollow guitar chamber caused a lot of feedback and unwanted noise in the sound being produced and amplified. This was when Paul got inspired to try using something solid rather than hollow onto which to vibrate the guitar strings.

Again, in Paul's own words from his 2007 interview with NHK, he once again disassembled the family telephone, and this time instead of using the mouthpiece, he took the receiver and placed it underneath a guitar string that he had mounted onto a solid iron railroad tie, essentially making it a one-string electric guitar. When he wired this to his father's amplifier, he finally got the sound he was looking for. He told Setsuko Sato, "Now I really have a problem because I can't see Gene Autry riding around on a horse with a railroad track." It became clear in his mind that the key to building an electric guitar would have to be a solid body made out of wood.

Over the next few years, Paul continued to work on creating just the right design for a solid-body electric guitar. His music career up to that point had taken him from his home in Wisconsin to Chicago, Illinois, and then to New York City by 1939. It was there, while living in an apartment in Queens, that he managed to convince guitar manufacturer and musical company Epiphone to allow him to use its factory for his musical experiments on Sundays. He tried everything, from stuffing hollow guitars with rags to even filling one up completely with plaster, which while solid, was unworkably heavy. The closest he had come until then was a custom guitar made for him, when he was still living in Chicago, by The Larson Brothers. It was made with a maple top that was half an inch thick and had no sound holes. Still, this was not quite right. In 1941 Paul got the idea to take a 4x4 piece of wood and attach it to a Gibson guitar neck and a set of two pickups he had made himself. He dubbed the resulting instrument "the Log."

MAGIC MELODY

Thoroughly expecting a warm response, Paul took the Log to a New York nightclub where he was playing. To his great surprise, the audience did not react at all to his invention. After all, it looked like a 4x4 piece of lumber with strings. He went home and attached two Epiphone guitar halves to either side of the 4x4, making it look just like a regular guitar. As soon as he did this, people started responding, and Paul got the applause he was anticipating. In a 1999 interview with *Jinx Magazine*'s Denver Smith, Paul said, "As soon as I put wings on it, and fastened two sides on it so that it looked like a guitar, then they applauded. So I realized that many people hear with their eyes."

Also in 1941, Paul had an unfortunate accident when he electrocuted himself with a microphone stand, which

stopped him from performing for almost two years. It was during this time that he started taking the Log to the various guitar companies, pitching them the idea for producing a solid-body electric guitar. None of them took Paul up on his idea. Most notoriously, M. H. Berlin, president of Chicago Musical Instruments, which had just bought out Gibson Guitar Corporation, dismissed Paul, calling his invention "a broomstick with pickups," according to a 2007 biography by Robert Denman. Undeterred, Paul continued to stand by his product, using it in his performances along with several other custom-modified instruments.

The year 1948 was a pivotal one for Paul and for the music industry. While driving in a car with his wife, Mary Ford, the car skidded off an icy road, nearly resulting in their deaths. At the hospital, doctors gave Paul the choice of amputating his shattered right arm or having it fixed permanently in place. Paul chose the latter option, having the surgeons put his arm at a near 90-degree angle so he would still be able to hold and play a guitar once he recovered. His recovery took about a year and half. Then, almost to add insult to injury, Fender Musical Instruments Corporation became the first company to market and release a solid-body electric guitar that year, called the Broadcaster (which was later renamed the Telecaster).

This move by Fender quickly inspired the top executives at Gibson, especially the president at the time, Ted McCarty, to rush to produce a similar instrument of their own in order to remain competitive. They managed to create a solid instrument that looked like some of the acoustic models that Gibson had released previously. It had a gold finish, two P-90 pickups, and a 22-fret fingerboard. Creating the instrument was the easy part, though. Selling it to musicians was a different matter. This was where Gibson turned to Paul. With a name like Les Paul backing their marketing efforts, Gibson believed it would be able to capture a significant market share from several important segments in country, jazz, and pop music.

While Gibson stated that the new guitar was a company creation, Paul did get a chance to provide his input, resulting in some modifications to the design and appearance of the guitar. The details surrounding the actual collaboration between Paul and Gibson, however, especially including how much input and influence Paul had in the instrument's creation, are somewhat unclear and have been subject to some debate. What is more well-known are the terms of the five-year contract with Gibson, in which Paul would only appear on stage with the new instrument that would bear his name, "the Les Paul Model."

Finally, 1948 was also the year that Capital Records released Les Paul's recording of "Lover (When You're Near Me)," which featured Paul's technique of overdubbing. This method of studio recording lays down prerecorded tracks that are then accompanied by additional instruments or vocals and then rerecorded. Paul's song involved eight different guitar parts that were overdubbed to produce the final product. This allowed Paul to play with the speed of the prerecorded parts, changing the pitch and giving the song very bright, futuristic, almost electronic effects. After its experimental infancy in the 1940s, overdubbing quickly became a commonly used technique by many artists and groups throughout the following decades.

I'M SITTIN' ON TOP OF THE WORLD

What came next for Paul was an immensely successful career recording with Capital Records. Just as significantly, however, were sales of Gibson's Les Paul Model electric guitar. The original instrument, dubbed the Goldtop, debuted in 1952 and was quickly followed by a range of four instruments, which aside from the original Goldtop (produced only between 1952 and 1958) included the Junior, the Special, the Standard, and the Custom. After the Goldtop, the next model released was the Custom in 1954. Sometimes called Black Beauty, it was all-black in color, had a mahogany top, two Humbucker pickups, and a Tune-o-matic bridge, invented by company president Ted McCarty. The Junior, also released in 1954, had a single P-90 pickup and was made from solid mahogany.

The following year, driven by the popularity of previous models, Gibson put out the Special in 1955. It was meant to be a mid-range-priced model at US$169.50, in between the Junior on the low end (retailing for US$99.50 in 1955), and the original Goldtop model, (retailing for US$235). It was made of maple and had either a natural or cherry red finish. Finally, Gibson created the Standard. This was an upgrade of the original Goldtop. Aside from a few technical improvements brought by advances in the design of the pickups, the biggest change to the original was a new sunburst finish. The original run of Gibson's Les Paul Standards from 1958 to 1960 have become iconic instruments and highly prized among collectors. In 2011 *Vintage Guitar* magazine estimated the going price of some of these instruments at US$300,000 to US$375,000.

Gibson went on to release a plethora of models but each of them harkened back to many elements of the original designs from the 1950s. These included the Deluxe, the Studio (which became a preferred instrument of Paul himself in his later years), as well as a number of different guitars made under the Epiphone label. While Epiphone had become a subsidiary of Gibson, many of its products were made in different countries and used nonpremium parts, such as less expensive woods, in production. Many of the electronic components were still the same, though, which gave these instruments much of the same quality and sound found in the more expensive Gibson Les Pauls.

At one point in 1960, Gibson produced the Les Paul SG (solid guitar). The look was significantly different from the earlier models, and when Paul saw it, he asked that his name be removed from the product. Paul subsequently divorced himself from Gibson altogether. A few years after the fallout, Paul made a new deal with Gibson and reestablished their relationship, and Gibson continued to make both the Les Paul models as before and a line of the new SG models without Paul's name on them.

IT'S BEEN A LONG, LONG TIME

Since the beginning days of the Les Paul guitars, Gibson has also collaborated with popular musicians who have used Les Paul guitars, to produce special edition versions of this classic instrument. Slash, of Guns N' Roses fame, worked with Gibson to produce the Slash "Snakepit" Les Paul, with custom styling and a very limited run. Peter Frampton, Jimmy Page, Eric Clapton, and Peter Townshend are only a few of the numerous famous musicians who have had signature model Les Paul guitars made for them.

Much of the innovation in Paul's instruments and musical techniques were experimental and revolutionary. While Paul himself cannot necessarily lay claim to having been the first to create an electric guitar, he was clearly using his self-designed and self-created instruments at a time when others were still only dreaming about it. Paul himself owned two patents to electric guitar designs, issued in 1962 (US 3,018,680) and in 1973 (US 3,725,561).

FURTHER INNOVATIONS

In addition to his famous guitars, Paul is known for his pioneering work in a number of recording techniques. The previously mentioned technique of overdubbing (recording additional music on an existing recording), also called sound-on-sound, that Paul pioneered in the 1940s had some drawbacks. The process by which he produced these multipart recordings involved repeatedly making copies, since adding a new part would entail erasing the original and using of a copy of it, and so on, until the final recording was made up of copies of copies of copies. As a result of this procedure, the quality of the sound was successively degraded.

Dissatisfied with the noise and distortion this method produced, Paul was interested in refining it by a process that came to be known as multitracking, which eliminated the problems inherent in making copies of copies. With this in mind, in 1955 Paul commissioned Ampex Corporation to custom build for his home recording studio a recorder with eight parallel tracks. This would enable separate musical elements to be recorded at different times without erasing previous takes. The Ampex eight-track recorder was delivered to Paul in 1957, and he made many hit recordings using it.

Ross H. Snyder, who worked for Ampex and takes the credit for actually creating the new method, noted in *ARSC Journal* that on the new machine the musician would be able to "hear a previously recorded track while recording a new performance part, perfectly synchronized, onto another recording head. . . .Thus all tracks would later be available as synchronized originals, to be mixed at leisure." Snyder noted that Paul nicknamed the eight-track recorder The Octopus, because of its eight channels. The machine was seven feet tall and weighed 250 pounds, and the price was US$10,000.

The invention of multitrack recording proved to be a watershed for the recording industry and led to rapid further development. By the early 1960s, 16-track and 24-track tape machines were common. Dave Tianen, in his article, "The Wizard of Waukesha," quoted Paul's remarks about the impact made by the creation of multitracking. Paul received a grateful letter from Frank Sinatra, in which the singer said, in effect (Paul did not remember the exact words), "if it wasn't for you, I'd still be recording my first song." Paul added, "It was the multitrack recording he meant." Paul also mentioned that Paul McCartney had expressed to him a similar view. "I don't care how much guitar you played, I don't care how many hits you had, you invented that multitrack recording, and that made the difference," Paul said McCartney told him.

Paul was also a pioneer in other recording techniques that have since become standard, such as tape delay (recording something and then playing it back after some time has elapsed, creating an echo effect). According to Scott Madigan in "Vidiot's Guide to the Galaxy," Paul created a tape delay by using "the space between the record and playback heads of a tape recorder. . . .Later, to increase the delay time, he tied two tape recorders together and, with the advent of variable speed playback decks, he could control the actual delay time by slowing or speeding up the second deck." Paul was also noted for his use of phasing or phase-shifting effects, since used often on electric guitars, that create an easily recognizable swirling or rippling sound. Also associated with Paul is the technique of reverb, an effect whereby the sound of an amplified musical instrument is made to reverberate slightly.

Although his achievements with the electric guitar rank as his major musical legacy, Paul's creativity in the recording studio added considerably to the range of his accomplishments. When he was inducted into the National Inventors Hall of Fame in 2005 for his contributions to music and musical recordings, he had certainly earned his place.

BIBLIOGRAPHY

Bayer, Jonah. "15 Iconic Les Paul Players." *Gibson Lifestyle,* January 8, 2009. Accessed February 9, 2012. http://www .gibson.com/en-us/Lifestyle/Features/15-Iconic-Les-Paul -Players/.

Boucher, Geoff, and Claudia Luther. "Les Paul, Guitarist Whose Innovations Paved the Way for Rock 'n' Roll, Dies at 94." *Los Angeles Times,* August 14, 2009. Accessed February 9, 2012. http://articles.latimes.com/2009/aug/14/local/me-les-paul14.

Denman, Robert. "Les Paul: The Living Legend of the Electric Guitar." *Classic Jazz Guitar.com,* September 2007. Accessed February 9, 2012. http://classicjazzguitar.com/articles/article .jsp?article=25.

"The Electric Guitar." *NPR,* August 12, 2002. Accessed February 9, 2012. http://www.npr.org/programs/morning/features /patc/electricguitar/.

Gibson Guitar Corporation. "Gibson USA." Nashville, TN, 2012. Accessed February 9, 2012. http://www.gibson.com /en-us/Support/AboutUs/.

"The Gibson Les Paul." LesPaulGuide.com. Accessed February 9, 2012. http://www.lespaulguide.com/index.php.

"Gibson USA Les Paul Guitars." *Sam Ash Buyers Guides.* Accessed February 9, 2012. http://www.samash.com/opencms /opencms/samash/buyers-guides/gibson/american-gibson-les -paul.html.

"The Inventor of the Electric Guitar Les Paul." Interview with Setsuko Sato. TV program, NHK. 2007. Accessed February 9, 2012. http://www.youtube.com/watch?v=1HKJnUWeJRM.

Les Paul—Chasing Sound! Directed by John Paulson, 2007. New York: Chasing Sound LLC, 2010. DVD, 120 min.

Les Paul Foundation. "Les Paul Bio." Accessed February 9, 2012. http://www.lespaulonline.com/bio.html.

"Les Paul – Story of the Invention of the Electric Guitar – Interview." Interview with Holger Obenaus. Gourmet Guitars, 2009. Accessed February 9, 2012. http://www .youtube.com/watch?v=rhdAWQaEsjA.

Madigan, Scott. " Vidiot's Guide to the Galaxy." Accessed April 11, 2012. http://www.interruptor.ch/scottmadigan.html.

National Inventors Hall of Fame. "Inventor Profile: Les Paul." Canton, OH, 2005. Accessed February 9, 2012. http://www .invent.org/hall_of_fame/225.html.

Schille, Paul. "Vintage Guitar Releases List of 10 Most Valuable Guitars." *The Gigging Musician.com,* December 17, 2010. Accessed February 9, 2012. http://www.thegiggingmusician .com/2010/12/17/vintage-guitar-releases-list-of-10-most -valuable-guitars/.

Smith, Denver. "Les Paul." *Jinx Magazine,* July 19, 1999. Accessed February 9, 2012. http://www.jinxmagazine.com /les_paul.html.

Snyder, Ross. H. "Self-Sync and 'The Octopus': How Came to Be the First Recorder to Minimize Successive Copying in Overdubs." *ARSC Journal* 34, no. 2 (Fall 2003): 209–213. Accessed April 12, 2012. http://www.aes.org/aeshc/docs/sel -sync/snyder_sel-sync.pdf.

Tianen, Dave. "The Wizard of Waukesha." *Milwaukee Journal Sentinel,* August 13, 2009. Accessed February 9, 2012. http:// www.pbs.org/wnet/americanmasters/episodes/les-paul/chasing -sound/100/.

"The World Has Lost a Remarkable Innovator and Musician: Les Paul Passes Away At 94." *Gibson Lifestyle,* August 13, 2009. Accessed February 9, 2012. http://www.gibson.com/en-us /Lifestyle/News/les-paul-passes-away-at-94-813/.

Levi Strauss and Blue Jeans

A LONG-STANDING TRADEMARK

By 2012, Levi Strauss & Co. resembled the weathered, rugged, enduring look of its trademark blue jeans. Since its inception almost a century and a half prior, the company experienced remarkable shifts in the fashion industry. Some of these changes, such as the post-World War II era, swung the market in its favor. Others, like the 1990s, resulted in a swing in the opposite direction. After booms and near busts, the family-owned company made roughly US$4.4 billion in annual revenue in the early 2010s.

Although blue jeans were the company trademark, a number of tweaks in style, fit, and production process gave the age-old product what it needed to survive in the face of increasing competition. Through its longstanding history dating back to 1873, its charitable donations, and its claim to the initial innovation of blue jeans, the corporate brand was tied to U.S. culture. This made its products emblematic in the United States and other parts of the world.

Both the company and its products have been the recipients of a multitude of awards, including one issued by the Smithsonian Institute in 1966. The company also garnered the German Apparel Supplier of the Year award in 1990, was a National Business Hall of Fame inductee in 1994, and was a recipient of the Ron Brown Award for Corporate Leadership in 1998. For its humanitarian contributions to research for treatment of the AIDS virus, the U.S. Centers for Disease Control gave Levi Strauss & Co. the National Business and Labor Award for Leadership on HIV/AIDS in 1997. The majority of these accolades came at a time when the company faced increasing competition from new entrants to the jeans market, such as Bugle Boy, The Gap, Inc., and others.

THE MAKING OF DENIM AND JEANS

Levi Strauss, whose original name was not Levi but Loeb, did not come up with the idea for blue jeans without precedent. Like most good ideas, blue jeans were the result of splicing together a few other major inventions that came before them. The material, denim, was developed and disseminated by English textile manufacturing plants in the 19th century. In fact, some people claim that denim was used as sailcloth, perhaps even for Christopher Columbus' ships, before being implemented for garments. In her exhaustive study on the subject, Rachel Louise Snyder debunked this story with some practical logic. Although Columbus is widely renowned for mistaking the Americas for India, Snyder humorously pointed out that "even Columbus was not so inept a sailor as to use fabric that sags and grows heavy when wet. More likely, he used a waxed canvas."

Suffice it to say, the actual origins of the material are still unknown. France claims credit via a preceding fabric called *serge de nimes*. This fabric was a silk and wool composite material, making it an unlikely predecessor for jeans, which are made of cotton twill. However, according to Snyder, there was another *serge de nimes* material made by English textile factories in the 18th century. The English variety was made of a similar cotton twill, making this derivation much more likely.

"Jean" refers to a particular type of pant, and the term was used to describe what Genoese sailors wore as early as 1500. However, it is reasonably safe to presume that those sailors did not use denim as the material for their pants, since denim did not exist until 300 years later, nor did they stitch their jeans together to make sails. Therefore, it seems likely that the material (denim) and the term for jeans existed separately until Levi Strauss brought them together in 1873.

The true invention, which gave Levi Strauss' pants their durability, came from Jacob Davis, a tailor from Nevada. Davis came up with the idea to use metal rivets to affix pant material where the most wear and tear occurred. His patent, as recorded by the U.S. Patent Office, describes "An Imporovement in Fastening Seams" (no. 139121, 1872), which took its inspiration from a riveting technique in the cobbling profession. By using metal rivets to bolster the strength of the seams, Davis was able to create pants that could last longer, even when used for hard labor. Money was the only problem. He did not have the required patenting fees.

When Davis started looking for the money, Strauss was running a dry-goods business in San Francisco, California. Loeb Strauss had emigrated from Bavaria, Germany, to New York, New York, in 1852. He then headed west for fortune and fame during the California Gold Rush and opened a small store with his brothers. Strauss's business was doing well enough to invest. Being a keen businessman, Strauss agreed to pay the initial payment for Davis' patent, in exchange for a 50 percent stake in the new company, according to an article about the company in *In an Influential Fashion: An Encyclopedia of Nineteenth and Twentieth-Century Fashion Designers and Retailers Who Transformed Dress.*

Davis and Strauss started producing a new line of waist overalls in the following year. The product was successful for two reasons. First, it was durable, and second, the cotton material shrank to fit the legs of the wearer. Other, bulkier, and loose-fitting pants caused blisters, especially after riding on horseback. Experiencing success and seeing the potential for more profit, the entrepreneur expanded his clothing product line and then incorporated Levi Strauss & Co. in 1890. Loeb Strauss was dead by 1902, bequeathing the company as a family heirloom.

FLUCTUATING FASHION TRENDS

Levi's became increasingly popular in the first decades of the 20th century as a working person's garment. They gradually became the preferred pant for ranchers and cowboys as well. Eventually, this popularity attracted the company's first competitor, Wrangler, which entered the fray in the 1930s.

Shortly afterward, the notoriety of jeans spread to the Hollywood, California, stage, where heroes and villains belted six-shooters above the blue jeans in Western movies, according to the article "Blue Jeans" in *Fashion, Costume, and Culture: Clothing, Headwear, Body Decorations, and Footwear through the Ages.* The 1939 movie *The Women* portrayed a number of women wearing blue jeans while they waited to finalize divorces. Movie stars Marlon Brando and James Dean lent their good looks to the garment as well. In turn, audiences who idolized what they saw on screen imitated their heroes' clothing, and blue jeans broke out of their earlier functional role and entered the realm of fashion. Wearing a pair of Levi's or Wranglers became a character statement.

World War II spread brand identity overseas. Used as the mainstay uniform of the U.S. Navy and worn by soldiers during shore leave, blue jeans quickly became associated with the global image of the United States. In postwar Japan, blue jeans came to signify opportunity, resourcefulness, and independence. According to Snyder, after the occupation of Japan ended, a single pair of Levi's cost nearly half a month's pay.

In the United States in the late 1960s, wearing jeans and having long hair became a social statement. In the 1970s, as former college-age protesters advanced in social status, they took their jeans with them, expanding the market to include the middle class. During this time period, consumption exploded, and Levi Strauss could hardly keep up. For the first time in the company's history, public shares were issued in order to expand quickly enough to fulfill demand.

COMPETITION TAKES THE MARKET: 1980–2000

Recognizing that the main consumer base for jean products could afford pricier clothing, designer jeans hit the market in the 1980s. Product lines from companies such as Calvin Klein Inc., The Gap, Eddie Bauer Holdings Inc., and Gloria Vanderbilt Apparel Corp. were sold in department stores, in direct competition with Levi's and Wranglers. For wealthier consumers, the Levi brand seemed too simple, pared down, and cheap. According to a *New York Times* article "Gap to Drop Levi's," The Gap originally sold Levi's when it opened in 1970. At the time, more Levi's sold than any other brand. In 1991, however, The Gap retail stores recorded that only 2 percent of their jean purchases were Levi's, and all 1,100 locations stopped selling them.

Whereas designers took the high-end market, mass-marketing companies took the low end. Wal-Mart Stores, Inc., Sears Roebuck & Co., Old Navy, and other lower-cost retailers began offering new, trendy designs to younger or less affluent U.S. consumers. There was little room left for the company, which was quickly viewed as an article of the past. Writing for the *Los Angeles Times* in 1999, Bettijane Levine wondered whether Levi Strauss would survive as a company: "Is this the end of Levi's as an icon right up there with the flag and apple pie? To those who love style, does this signal the end of denim as America's bedrock fashion statement?"

In part, Levine blamed corporate hubris for Levi Strauss's troubles. However, whereas Wal-Mart and other low-end competitors were setting up their operations in countries outside the United States, Levi Strauss continued to bolster the U.S. economy with its factories. Of course, this incurred a higher cost of production, which drove consumers away. Initially, the company held to its old practices.

Levi Strauss, as a family-owned business, was an example of the American Dream, having pulled itself up by its bootstraps and begun one of the largest fashion trends in the world. Yet by the end of the 20th century, the corporation was almost destitute. It closed stores and factories in the United States, laying off thousands of workers. Leslie Kaufman reported that sales declined by 13 percent in 1998, to US$6 billion, worldwide. In Kaufman's article, Robert Haas, Levi chairman and chief executive officer at the time, summarized the reasons for the collapse: "We took our eye off the consumer, and we weren't as nimble as we should have been." While Levi remained headstrong in the assumption that 501s, its blockbuster product, would always be a staple of U.S. fashion, competitors stole market share with cheaper production on one side, and with flashy new trends on the other.

CHANGES

Finally, in spite of its heavy traditions, the corporation was forced to adapt in order to compete. Stymied by defeat in the department store, the brand first took the fight to the courtroom, claiming patent infringement. Jordache Enterprises was sued for its Jordache Basics 101 product line's use of the number 101, as noted in the article "Patterns" in the *New York Times*. Abercrombie & Fitch Co. and Ralph Lauren Corporation were also sued. However, these claims were unsuccessful, as judges pointed out that use of the number 101 did not lead consumers to mistake 101s for a Levi's product. As it turned out, the company did not own all triple-digit numbers ending in 01.

Knowing that it could no longer rely on continued success from old patents, the company turned to other, more creative fronts. Robert Haas, who was chairman and chief executive for a decade and a half, retired from his post in 2007. His successor, John Anderson, immediately began to make some significant attempts to bring the business back to the forefront of fashion. In 2009, the company joined the international nonprofit organization Better Cotton Initiative, which promoted water conservation, reduced use of pesticides, and improved child labor practices. As noted in the *New York Times* article, "Changes in the Air; Stone-Washed Blue Jeans (Minus the Washed)" although the organization was four years old at the time, with other retailers already signed up, such as Adidas, Cotton, Inc., and The Gap, the move demonstrated Levi

Strauss &s Co.'s willingness to show that it was environmentally responsible.

Forging ahead, the company formed a bold new initiative in the attempt to rebrand itself as a contemporary label. It conducted consumer research in the development of the Curve ID fit system, which demonstrated a completely new way of measuring fit for women's jeans. According to the corporation's 2010 annual report, it conducted over 60,000 body scans, internationally, and surveyed consumers to garner an accurate conception of popular opinion. This approach was a business trend at the time, after Facebook's interactive approach to consumer relations proved a remarkable success in the 2010s. For Levi Strauss, what resulted was a new way of measuring women's clothing, which was based on body shape as opposed to body size.

The initiative, which involved thousands of potential consumers, also improved customer loyalty. Although the corporation's profits remained flat, at around $4.4 billion annually, recapturing a portion of the market was possible. The name Levi's was still known by households all over the world, and by adjusting to accelerating consumer demands, the brand was in a position to regain some former glory.

FLOW, EBB, AND REPOSITIONING

Levi Strauss & Company created an entire market that changed modern wear, although its market-maker status could not protect it from the inevitable upstart competition. The company's long history and the close ties between the brand and U.S. culture helped keep the company operating for well over a century. In addition to a strong brand, Levi Strauss eventually adapted to changing market conditions. It did take some time for the family-owned business to do so, but it started imitating the competition by producing goods outside the United States. Levi Strauss also began to invent new ideas, such as the Curve ID Fit System, showing that the company founded in the 19th century was working to remain relevant in the 21st century.

BIBLIOGRAPHY

"Blue Jeans." In *Fashion, Costume, and Culture: Clothing, Headwear, Body Decorations, and Footwear through the Ages,* edited by Sara Pendergast and Tom Pendergast. Vol. 3, 612–615. Detroit: UXL, 2004. Gale Virtual Reference Library (GALE|CX3425500391). Accessed January 30, 2012. http://go.galegroup.com/ps/i.do?id=GALE%7CCX34255003 91&v=2.1&u=itsbtrial&it=r&p=GVRL&sw=w .

"Changes in the Air; Stone-Washed Blue Jeans (Minus the Washed)." *New York Times,* November 2, 2011. Accessed January 30, 2012. http://www.nytimes.com/2011/11/02 /science/earth/levi-strauss-tries-to-minimize-water-use\

.html?pagewanted=all.

Davis, Jacob W. et al. Improvement in Fastening Pocket-Openings. U.S. Patent 139,121, filed August 9, 1872, issued May 20, 1873. Accessed February 24, 2012. http://www.google.com/patents/US139121.

"Gap to Drop Levi's." *New York Times,* July 31, 1991. Accessed January 30, 2012. http://www.nytimes.com/1991/07/31/business/company-news-gap-to-drop-levi-s.html?src=pm.

Kaufman, Leslie. "Levi Is Closing 11 Factories; 5,900 Jobs Cut." *New York Times,* February 23, 1999. Accessed January 30, 2012. http://www.nytimes.com/1999/02/23/business/levi-is-closing-11-factories-5900-jobs-cut.html?src=pm.

Lamothe, Keisha. "Levi's Sues the Pants Off of Polo." *CNNMoney,* July 24, 2007. Accessed January 30, 2012. http://money.cnn.com/2007/07/24/news/companies/levi_polo/index.htm.

Levine, Bettijane. "End of the Line?" *Los Angeles Times,* March 1, 1999. Accessed January 30, 2012. http://articles.latimes.com/1999/mar/01/news/cl-12777.

Levi Strauss & Company. "2010 Annual Report.' San Francisco, CA, April 13, 2011. Accessed January 30, 2012. http://

levistrauss.com/sites/default/files/librarydocument/2011/4/levistrauss-annualreport-2010.pdf.

"Patterns." *New York Times,* October 1, 1991. Accessed January 30, 2012. http://www.nytimes.com/1991/10/01/news/patterns-155791.html?pagewanted=2&src=pm.

Snyder, Rachel Louise. *Fugitive Denim: A Moving Story of People and Pants in the Borderless World of Global Trade.* New York: W. W. Norton, 2008, 138–144.

"Strauss, Levi and Company." In *In an Influential Fashion: An Encyclopedia of Nineteenth and Twentieth-Century Fashion Designers and Retailers Who Transformed Dress,* edited by Ann T. Kellogg, et al, 279–281. Westport, CT: Greenwood Press, 2002. Gale Virtual Reference Library (GALE|CX2884900147). Accessed January 30, 2012. .http://go.galegroup.com/ps/i.do?id=GALE%7CCX2884900147&v=2.1&u=itsbtrial&it=r&p=GVRL&sw=w .

United States Court of Appeal for the Tenth Circuit. "Levi Strauss & Company v. Abercrombie & Fitch Trading Company. No. 09-16322. Opinion." February 8, 2011. Accessed February 22, 2012. articles.law360.s3.amazonaws.com/0224000/224534/09-16322.pdf

Magnetic Resonance Imaging: Its Discovery and Usage

Magnetic resonance imaging (MRI) technology is an important medical tool as well as a big business. MRI technology has allowed for imaging of the soft tissue of the human body by using computers, radio waves, and magnets. MRIs allow doctors to get clear images of patients' soft tissue without exposing the patient to X-rays, toxic dyes, surgical procedures, and many other medical risks. MRI technology has become an important medical tool for the diagnosis of tumors as well as soft tissue injuries and other health problems.

Tissues and organs of the body emit radio signals and when they are exposed to a magnetic field, these signals have different relaxation times. Relaxation times refer to the decay speed of the signals. MRI scanners work by exploiting the differences in the relaxation times between normal and abnormal tissue. These differences create a clear image for doctors. In fact, MRI images provided between 10 and 30 times more contrast than standard X-rays, according to the FONAR Corporation. The term FONAR refers to a type of MRI known as field focused nuclear magnetic resonance.

Early experiments with the MRI technology suggested that cancerous tissue has a longer relaxation time, meaning that it takes longer for the signal to decay. With an MRI, the decay rate or relaxation rate is shown visually as a varying brightness. MRI scanners create computer images of the tissue being scanned, and healthy tissue as well as abnormal tissue show up at different rates of brightness on the images, showing that they have different relaxation rates. Analyzing these images allows physicians to make determinations about the pathologies (diseases) that may be present in a scanned area.

Prior to MRIs, X-rays were the medical imaging technology available. However, the MRI has several important advantages over past medical imaging options. For example, MRI scans can detect tumors and other abnormal tissues that other medical imaging devices cannot. MRIs also allow physicians to administer chemotherapy directly into tumors and further allows for monitoring of a tumor's reaction to chemotherapy treatments. In addition, MRIs can be used to diagnose ligament damage and other problems in soft tissue, as well as joint problems.

THE INVENTION OF MRI

Medical doctor Raymond Vahan Damadian is credited with the initial concept and the technology that would lead to MRI technology. Damadian was experimenting with potassium and sodium in living cells in the late 1960s at the State University of New York Health Science Center in Brooklyn, New York, when he began researching and experimenting with nuclear magnetic resonance (NMR). He and other researchers used NMR devices to track potassium deposits and Damadian got the idea that the technology could have a medical application. At the time, NMR had already been extensively used during World War II to check inanimate objects, but the technology had never been used for scans related to humans. Damadian is credited with being the first to try to apply NMR to living tissue in order to use it as a scanning device. By 1969 Damadian had a theory that normal tissue and abnormal tissue had different relaxation times, something that could be shown *in vivo* with the use of NMR.

In 1970 Damadian found that there was a difference between the relaxation times of abnormal soft tissues and normal tissues in the body. He also found that there were different relaxation times between different types of healthy tissues in the human anatomy. This discovery paved the way for the development of what would become known as MRI technology. In 1971 Damadian published his discovery and by 1972 had filed a patent (U.S. Patent 3,789,832) for the practical uses of his findings. Over time, he would file 40 patents related to NMR and MRI technology.

Working with postgraduate assistants Michael Goldsmith and Lawrence Minkoff, Damadian created NMR scanners for practical medical use. By 1976 the researchers created an image of a tumor by scanning a live animal. This was the first time that NMR had been used for medical purposes.

The year 1977 was a notable one for Damadian and his research team. They created a superconducting scanner magnet and what became known as the first NMR scanner. Known as the Indomitable, which required seven years to create, the scanner showed the first images of a human subject on July 3, 1977. These first images were of Minkoff's chest area. According to a December 4, 2003, report in *The Economist,* Damadian had originally attempted to scan himself, but the machine was too small, and Minkoff's smaller frame was a better fit. The first MRI scan took four hours and 45 minutes as the machine carefully scanned 106 points to create one image. According to *The Economist,* Damadian sent out a press release after the scan announcing "a new technique for the non-surgical detection of cancer anywhere in the human body."

FONAR AND MRI TECHNOLOGY

By 1978 Damadian and other scientists were using the scanner to create images of cancer patients' tissue. That same year, FONAR was created and incorporated. Based in Melville, New York, the small company relied heavily on Damadian's early patents to protect itself from larger companies, some of which were able to invest millions of U.S. dollars into developing MRI technology. FONAR was the first company to create MRI scanners, launching the first commercial full-body MRI scanner in 1980. By 1980 NMR was renamed to the now-familiar MRI, in part because it was generally felt that the term "nuclear" might have a negative connotation for patients and the general public.

By 1981 FONAR had become a public company. The first MRIs, however, were not a big success. They were unfamiliar and much slower and more expensive than X-rays, which were the standard for medical imaging in the late 1970s and early 1980s. Getting approval from the U.S. Food and Drug Administration (FDA) was also a slow process. MRI scanners were not FDA-approved until 1984. However, Damadian persisted, certain that his invention was valuable due to its accuracy and the fact that it

did not expose patients to the risk of radiation, a concern with X-rays.

In 1982 FONAR publicized its iron-core technology, a patented technology that allowed for the creation of Open MRI scanners. Previously, all MRI scanners had been enclosed, leaving some patients to feel claustrophobic. Open MRI scanners were seen as less confining and could more easily accommodate patients of many sizes.

In 1984 the company created and patented Oblique Imagining. This technology allowed medical professionals to take multiple images of human tissue from various angles. In fact, the technology allowed physicians to request and receive images from any angle required and by allowing multiple images to be taken with one scan, this technology allowed FONAR to reduce the time required for MRI scans. This was very important, as one of the early complaints about MRI medical imaging was that it was slower than the traditional X-ray. In 1985 FONAR extended the Oblique Imaging technology by creating the Multi-Angle Oblique (MAO) scanning protocol. That same year, FONAR created a mobile MRI device, the first in the world.

For decades, patients had to lie down to get MRI scans. However, this position could allow some abnormalities in human tissue to remain undetected. A scanner was needed that could scan patients in weight-bearing positions, including standing and sitting. This was especially important for scanning and diagnosing conditions related to joints and weight-bearing areas of the body. In 1996 FONAR launched just such a scanner, the Stand-Up MRI. The open scanner used Position Imaging (pMRI), so that patients could be scanned in a variety of postures. In 2004 FONAR renamed the device the Upright MRI.

In 1997 FONAR established the Health Management Corporation of America (HMCA). This subsidiary was a physician practice management firm, tasked with managing imaging centers and other health care facilities and practices. Also in 1997 FONAR announced plans for a surgical MRI room, the OR-360°, which would allow physicians to operate inside of an MRI room-size scanner, allowing doctors to get real-time images of the tissue being operated on in order to guide the medical procedures. The imaging room allowed doctors to see how surgical procedures affected the soft tissue of the body, allowing for very precise surgeries, especially in cases where physicians were trying to remove cancerous tissue and needed to accurately distinguish between healthy and abnormal tissue.

In 1997 Damadian and FONAR researchers were also working on ways to make MRIs less expensive. Indeed, one of the biggest obstacles to more widespread MRI use has been the high cost of the machines. In 1997 MRI scanners cost over US$1 million, meaning that individual tests could cost insurance companies and patients US$1,000 or more. This meant that many patients were still being tested with older technologies due to cost considerations and were only being sent for MRIs in situations where other tests failed to disclose a problem, according to a *New York Times* article by Claudia H. Deutsch.

DAMADIAN, MRI, AND AWARDS

Damadian was the cowinner of the National Medal of Technology in 1988 for his work with MRI. The award was also won by Dr. Paul C. Lauterbur that year. Lauterbur was a chemistry researcher who was able to create a way of generating images from radio signals, a vital process for modern MRIs and medical imaging. Damadian also became a part of the National Inventors Hall of Fame of the United States Patent Office. In 2001 Damadian was awarded the Lemelson-MIT Lifetime Achievement Award by the Massachusetts Institute of Technology (MIT) and in 2008 was awarded the Caring Award by the Leslie Munzer Neurological Institute of Long Island (LMNI). Damadian also acted as president and chairman of FONAR since its inception, and he remained in that position as of 2012.

In 2003 Damadian suffered a serious setback. That year, Lauterbur and Sir Peter Mansfield were awarded the Nobel Prize for their work in magnetic resonance imaging, but Damadian was not awarded the prestigious honor, although up to three people can be awarded a single Nobel Prize. Damadian, in full-page advertisements in national newspapers, including the *Washington Post, Los Angeles Times,* and *New York Times,* decried the decision of the Nobel Prize committee and called the omission "the shameful wrong that must be righted," according to a 2004 *New York Times* article by Kenneth Chang. The advertisements showed a Nobel Prize medal upside down. Much commentary about the advertisement was made in the press, especially since full-page advertisements cost a large amount of money.

PATENT BATTLES

MRI technology was not just a potential life-saving technology. It was potentially a lucrative market, and in the world of medical technology, FONAR was a relatively small company. As a result, a number of other companies, including larger corporations such as Toshiba Corporation and General Electric Company, among others, started to roll out their own versions of MRI-based devices. FONAR defended its patents in U.S. courts.

The first court case was against Johnson & Johnson, which in the late 1970s developed its own medical imaging machine. FONAR sued and initially won. However, that decision was later overturned. Then, in 1988, Hitachi created an open MRI machine. Prior to that, most of the machines made by competing companies were closed cyl-

inders, so FONAR felt that it could still remain competitive in the market.

By 1989 FONAR faced more bad news. The U.S. Congress made it illegal for doctors to refer patients to their own MRI facilities. At the time, according to Deutsch in the *New York Times,* an estimated 65 percent of MRI machine sales went to doctors who set up such centers. Sales dropped further when some health groups condemned the practice of sending patients for MRI tests. Some groups alleged that doctors were prescribing unnecessary tests because the MRI machines were so expensive that they needed to get more use out of the technology to make it economically feasible. Then there was yet another patent problem: Damadian's original patent expired in 1989.

According to Hedieh Nasheri in her book *Economic Espionage and Industrial Spying,* the FONAR story is also one of espionage. Once it became evident that MRI would be a huge success, FONAR had to deal with underhand tactics from competitors. According to Damadian's testimony before the 1996 U.S. House Committee on the Judiciary Subcommittee on Crime, a competitor hired FONAR service engineers to get access to FONAR software and schematics. Even when FONAR was able to gather evidence of the corporate espionage, a judge was not able to do much to punish the perpetrators. Damadian also recounted how Toshiba hired a FONAR engineer and paid his legal bills while FONAR pursued him. Other competitors, the inventor claimed, used similar underhand tactics, in one case allegedly intoxicating a FONAR employee to get access to an MRI scanner.

Damadian and FONAR decided to continue pursuing patent infringement claims, despite the obstacles. To do so, they hired Robins, Kaplan, Miller & Ciresi. The law firm told Deutsch for the *New York Times* that the unique position of Damadian and FONAR did in fact give them an advantage: "Usually, inventors don't make things, so you can only sue for royalties. Here, we could sue for lost profits, too." This was an important distinction, and one which would ultimately allow FONAR to triumph and to get compensation.

Armed with new attorneys, FONAR sued Hitachi Corporation and General Electric in 1992. The court battles that FONAR waged against General Electric were particularly notable. For years, FONAR argued in court that General Electric violated FONAR's Cancer Detection and Multi-Angle Oblique patents. General Electric alleged that it had been developing its own magnetic resonance scanning technology from the beginning, but according to Deutsch, Damadian alleged that this was not the case and that, "No sooner did we invent [it] than the big guys took it away." He also claimed in the interview that, "With their marketing and financing strength, big companies don't need to risk doing things first. For entrepreneurs to keep taking risks, they need temporary exclusive rights to their inventions."

Finally, in May 1995, a jury decided that FONAR was in the right. General Electric appealed but the U.S. Federal Circuit Court of Appeals upheld the jury's findings. General Electric appealed again. In 1997 the U.S. Supreme Court enforced the original patents held by Damadian and ordered General Electric to pay US$128,705,766 to FONAR for copyright infringement. FONAR had originally asked for US$450 million.

The other patent infringement lawsuits FONAR filed did not result in such high payments, but many of the lawsuits were successful. Hitachi settled before the case went to trial. In 1992 FONAR had not sued other companies producing MRI scanners but had sent letters to Toshiba, Philips, Siemens, and other companies, informing them that FONAR might sue. Siemens and Philips went to court, hoping to get Damadian's patents invalidated, but they ended up settling with FONAR, as did the other companies that had created MRI scanners.

With the money from the patent infringement lawsuits, FONAR was able to bolster its finances after shares dropped from a high of US$15 in 1982 to US$3.15 in 1997. The money also went into creating the HMCA. Despite its small size and the considerable obstacles it faced, FONAR managed not only to survive but to thrive. According to FONAR, net income for the company in the first quarter of fiscal year 2012 was US$1.8 million, a 360 percent increase over the previous quarter. Revenues were US$9.6 million for the period ending September 30, 2011.

Although the technology that helped develop MRI scanners came from many sources, Raymond Vahan Damadian's early inventions and the establishment of his company FONAR led to the use of MRIs for medical imaging. Millions of patients rely on MRI technology for medical diagnoses. Despite setbacks, including espionage and patent battles involving much larger competitors, FONAR managed to remain a multimillion-dollar MRI company.

BIBLIOGRAPHY

"2001 Lemelson-MIT Lifetime Achievement Award Winner." Cambridge, MA: Massachusetts Institute of Technology, April 2008. Accessed January 11, 2012. http://web.mit.edu/invent /a-winners/a-damadian.html.

Chang, Kenneth. "Denied Nobel for M.R.I., He Wins Another Prize." *New York Times,* March 23, 2004. Accessed January 10, 2012. http://www.nytimes.com/2004/03/23/science /denied-nobel-for-mri-he-wins-another-prize.html.

Deutsch, Claudia H. "Patent Fights Aplenty for M.R.I. Pioneer." *New York Times,* July 12, 1997. Accessed January 11, 2012. http://www.nytimes.com/1997/07/12/business/patent-fights -aplenty-for-mri-pioneer.html?pagewanted=all.

FONAR Corporation. "About FONAR." Melville, NY, 2005. Accessed January 11, 2012. http://www.fonar.com /fonargroup.htm.

Judson, Horace Freeland. "No Nobel Prize for Whining." *New York Times,* October 20, 2003. Accessed January 10, 2012. http://www.nytimes.com/2003/10/20/opinion/no-nobel -prize-for-whining.html.

Lipton, Michael L. *Totally Accessible MRI: A User's Guide to Principles, Technology, and Applications.* New York: Springer, 2008.

"Magnetic Resonance (MR) Scanning Machine." Cambridge, MA: Massachusetts Institute of Technology, April 2008. Accessed January 11, 2012. http://web.mit.edu/invent/iow /damadian.html.

"MRIs Inside Story." *The Economist,* December 4, 2003. Accessed January 11, 2012. http://www.economist.com/node/2246166 ?story_id=E1_NNQGTGG.

Nasheri, Hedieh. *Economic Espionage and Industrial Spying.* New York: Cambridge University Press, 2005.

Wade, Nicholas. "Doctor Disputes Winners of Nobel in Medicine." *New York Times,* October 11, 2003. Accessed January 11, 2012. http://www.nytimes.com/2003/10/11/us /doctor-disputes-winners-of-nobel-in-medicine.html.

Mattel, Inc.'s Barbie Doll

Very few women can say they look as beautiful at age 50 and beyond as they did at 20. However, Barbie can. Barbie, a doll created in 1959 by Mattel, Inc., was as glamorous and popular in the 2010s as she was when she was first introduced. She was also considered a blockbuster toy, with sales of nearly US$1 billion and with both domestic and worldwide sales increasing in 2010. In its 2010 annual report, Mattel posted a 14 percent increase in domestic sales and a 2 percent increase in worldwide sales. But in 1959, the company was unsure whether Barbie would be successful.

MATTEL FINDS ITS NICHE

The three partners who laid their life savings on the line to found Mattel in 1945 were Ruth and Elliot Handler, and Harold "Matt" Matson. Ruth had worked at Paramount Pictures as a stenographer, and Elliott spent years working as a light fixture builder. Mattel began its operations in a Southern California garage workshop, manufacturing Plexiglas furniture, jewelry, candleholders, and other decorative items.

Elliott Handler used the scraps from their picture frame products to build plastic dollhouse furniture. The furniture sold so well that the company decided to make toys its sole focus. By this time, Matson had sold his share of the business to the Handlers. The company's first musical toy, the Uke-A-Doodle, was launched in 1947. The company had found its niche and was profitable, but it had not yet found a true market-leading product.

Barbie was modeled after a German doll named Lilli that Ruth found on a trip to Switzerland. Ruth actually had the idea, prior to that trip, to develop a three-dimensional doll that would look like a teenager. Ruth had come

up with the idea while watching her daughter, Barbara (for whom Barbie was subsequently named), playing with cut-out paper dolls. She realized that as her daughter got older, she could use a teen-like doll to act out her thoughts and dreams of the future.

The design and production team at Mattel did not want to pursue the idea. They said such a toy would be much too expensive to produce, and they would have to set the price so high that it would be inaccessible to the mass market. It was after this conversation took place that Ruth found the Lilli doll at a bar in Switzerland. Lilli was a doll for the adult male market, and she was considered much too sexy for the American toy market. By this time, however, the toy market was booming in a manner it never had before. The timing and market conditions were perfect to launch an innovative toy.

The United States was at peace during most of the 1950s, with the Korean War ending in 1953, and the baby boomer generation being conceived and born, creating a much bigger market for toys than in years past. It was during these years that toys with enduring market appeal such as Mr. Potato Head (1952) and Legos (1955) were first introduced. Television was also changing the way toy companies could message and sell to their target market. Kids were gathering around the television every afternoon to watch favorite programs such as *The Mickey Mouse Club Show,* a program which was the first in television history to be sponsored by a toy company, Mattel. Mattel advertised its Tommy Burp Machine Gun on the *The Mickey Mouse Club Show* and by Christmas the company had sold out of the toy.

In addition, Mattel hired designer Jack Ryan to assist the design team. Ryan was a former designer with Raytheon Corporation, where he helped design missiles for the U.S. government and the war effort. Ryan had an open and creative mind when it came to design. All of these factors led to the decision to move ahead with the production of the Barbie doll, to be launched in 1959.

BARBIE MAKES HER DEBUT

Barbie's introduction occurred at the 1959 American International Toy Fair in New York City. Mattel's fashion designer, Charlotte Johnson, designed Barbie's first outfits, including the zebra-striped swimsuit she wore at her introduction. Mattel had set the price for Barbie at a low US$3.00, and the accompanying outfits were priced between US$1.00 and US$3.00 each. Still, buyers at the toy fair were not enthusiastic. This was not the typical doll. In fact, Barbie was the first doll to be introduced to the market that was not a baby. Also, Barbie looked too adult and sexy, and the buyers feared girls' parents would not allow them to buy her or play with her. They were wrong. A few buyers took the chance on Barbie, and by the summer of 1959, stores were selling out of their supplies faster than they could receive new shipments.

Once Barbie had established her market appeal, Mattel executives capitalized on it by introducing new versions of Barbie, as well as new clothes and accessories, all sold separately. Since Mattel started out in the dollhouse business, it was a natural next step to build Barbie her dream house. Mattel also had the foresight to introduce Ken in 1961, who was also named after one of Ruth Handler's children. Ken was marketed as Barbie's new boyfriend. Kids could take Barbie and Ken on a date in Ken's convertible, for example.

Throughout the 1960s, sales of Barbie dolls continued to increase. Mattel sustained the interest of its market by continuing to introduce new versions of Barbie and many new outfits, all designed to mirror the fashions of the day. However, society was quickly changing in the United States, and Barbie would need to change with it.

BARBIE LAUNCHES HER CAREER

During the 1960s, more women in the United States were working than ever before. It was not just women's fashions that were changing, but how women looked at themselves and how they saw their future. New women's movements demanded that women receive equal rights and pay. One women's organization in particular, the National Organization for Women, felt that Barbie reflected a sexist view of women.

As a consequence, sales of Barbie began to dip. The baby boomer generation was growing up. Mattel felt it was time to diversify. They began manufacturing and selling pet supplies. However, this move did nothing to change the downturn in overall sales and revenues the company had begun to experience.

By 1973 Ruth Handler was forced to resign as Mattel's president, and it was not until 1981 that another dynamic and innovative leader replaced her. Jill Barad, a former executive with Coty Cosmetics, was hired as president. Barad understood that if Barbie were going to keep her appeal, she needed to reflect the new goals and dreams of the girls who were playing with her. This generation was not as focused on getting married as it was on choosing a career and being independent.

New versions of Barbie began to reflect this change. There are estimates that Barbie has had more than 125 careers since 1959, from stewardess to computer engineer complete with her own laptop. Some of Barbie's other occupations include Olympic athlete, doctor, scuba diver, rock star, and astronaut. Yet the key to her success was Mattel's understanding of her market, and what the market liked.

OTHER KEYS TO BARBIE'S SUCCESS

Another factor that led to the huge market success of Barbie was Mattel's drive to continuously improve her and the manufacturing process. One of the first things the company did after Barbie was on the market was to look for ways to redesign her so that she would be less costly to manufacture and any existing glitches in the process would be resolved. The company was also one of the first in the United States to use a much more scientific and analytical process in developing their products. They spent a great deal of time observing girls playing with their prototypes to ensure that they were truly engaged. These sessions were often videotaped and analyzed by psychologists. The company used the information to improve Barbie and to develop new products and accessories for her. They wanted to understand the entire experience kids had with Barbie, rather than whether Barbie simply functioned the way she should.

Mattel's design-to-product process was considered innovative for the time. Designers were encouraged to consider all aspects of the product and include this in their design and production plan. Mattel's process was from idea to design, design to creating a testable prototype, prototype to manufacturing evaluation, and evaluation to production with as few redesigns as possible. This process enabled Mattel to get creative designs to the marketplace faster than its competitors.

There were no serious competitors for Barbie's market until the Bratz dolls, manufactured by MGA Entertainment, Inc., were introduced in 2001. The dolls were similar to Barbie and specifically targeted the same market. However, Bratz dolls looked more like teens than

Barbie did, and these dolls had an attitude and an edge. The name alone was able to send that message. While Bratz dolls held their own against Barbie, they did not actually claim too much of Barbie's market share. However, when the latest version of Barbie was released in 2005, MGA executives noticed that her eyes closely resembled the Bratz dolls' eyes. MGA Entertainment sued Mattel for stealing its eye design. In response, Mattel countersued MGA for US$500 million, saying that one of the company's designers, Carter Bryant, had been working at Mattel when he got the idea for Bratz. Bryant joined MGA in 2000, one year prior to the launch of Bratz. As of 2011, each company had won a court decision in their respective legal battles, and attorneys for both sides planned to appeal the decisions. In the meantime, Barbie held tight to her leading market position.

OTHER BARBIE ISSUES

In addition to the Bratz lawsuit, Barbie encountered other problems throughout her existence. However, Barbie's makers have succeeded in overcoming these problems, or at least assuaging them enough to continue in a profitable vein. First, beginning in the 1970s, women were tired of the unrealistic body image Barbie epitomized. Eating disorders were becoming more prevalent, and Barbie's appearance was not helping. In fact, one doll, Slumber Party Barbie, introduced in 1965, had come complete with a book on how to lose weight. Its advice: Don't eat.

When Barbie's dimensions are extrapolated to life-size, she would be just over five feet nine inches tall. Her bust size would be 36 inches, her waistline 18 inches, and her hips would measure 33 inches. A study by the University Central Hospital in Helsinki, Finland, as noted by Yona Zeldis McDonough in the *New York Times*, estimated that Barbie's body mass index (BMI) was so low that she would lack the 17 to 22 percent body fat required for a woman to menstruate. Mattel explained that it had initially designed Barbie's waist as tiny as it was because the clothing that was designed for her included a lot of belts and other accessories that added bulk to her figure. However, by 1998, Mattel had created a Barbie with a more realistic, wider, waistline.

Barbie and Mattel were also labeled as racist because only Caucasian versions of the doll were produced and sold. Even though Mattel reacted by introducing *Colored Francie* in 1967, she was not much of a success. Francie had originally been introduced as Barbie's cousin, a Caucasian doll, in a previous year. Mattel simply created the same doll only with darker skin. The following year Christie was introduced. She was considered the first real African American Barbie. However, she did not do well on the market, and it was not until 1980 that realistic African American and Hispanic Barbies were introduced and sold well.

PACKAGING IS EVERYTHING

Mattel had also been innovative when it came to developing and selling a complete package of products to promote and sell Barbie. Over the years, additional products that have been created and sold included books that told Barbie's personal story; several sisters, cousins, and friends; various vehicles and homes; and hundreds of accessories.

By the 1990s and continuing into the 2000s, Mattel took marketing and packaging to an even higher level when it introduced Barbie movies. Mattel took a traditional tale and created an animated version of it, starring Barbie. The movie would be shown on television near the Christmas holiday season, and the corresponding Barbie and all of her accompanying accessories were sold. Movies included *Barbie in the Nutcracker, Barbie as Rapunzel, Barbie of Swan Lake,* and Barbie as *The Prince and the Pauper.* Each movie came out on VHS and later on DVD so children could watch it whenever they wanted. There was also the large, head-only version of Barbie, which was sold with hair accessories and makeup so kids could create new hairstyles and makeup looks on a much bigger doll surface.

Another innovative marketing campaign by Mattel took place in 2010, when the company announced that Barbie and Ken had broken up but would always be friends. This was in anticipation of Ken's reintroduction to the market on his 50th birthday in 2011. Although many wedding dresses were designed for Barbie and she wore them, she remained single. She also became a collector's item, with vintage Barbies still in their boxes fetching prices as high as US$4,000 and limited edition Barbies worth as much as US$10,000. While many things about Barbie changed since her inception, her enduring appeal remained.

BIBLIOGRAPHY

do Rego Barros, Isabel. "The Business of Barbie." Chicago: Illinois Institute of Technology, February 1999. Accessed January 12, 2012. http://trex.id.iit.edu/~ibarros/cases /Barbie99.pdf.

Mattel, Inc. "2010 Annual Report." El Segundo, CA. Accessed January 12, 2012. http://investor.shareholder.com/mattel /annuals.cfm.

———. "Mattel History." El Segundo, CA, 2012. Accessed January 12, 2012. http://corporate.mattel.com/about-us /history/default.aspx.

McDonough, Yona Zeldis. "Barbie." *New York Times,* October 21, 2010. Accessed January 12, 2012. http://topics.nytimes .com/topics/reference/timestopics/subjects/b/barbie_doll /index.html.

Townsend, Allie. "Barbie vs. Bratz: It's a Doll-Eat-Doll World." *TIME,* April 22, 2011. Accessed January 12, 2012. http:// www.time.com/time/business/article/0,8599,2067001,00 .html.

Medtronic, Inc.: Medical Device Pioneer

INAUSPICIOUS ORIGINS

In 1949, Earl Bakken and his brother-in-law, Palmer Hermundslie, opened a medical equipment repair shop in Bakken's Minneapolis, Minnesota, garage. At the time, Bakken was an electrical engineering graduate student at the University of Minnesota, employed part time repairing medical equipment at a local hospital, while Hermundslie was employed full time with a local Minneapolis lumber firm. During the first year of operation, Medtronic, Inc., as the business came to be known, was sufficiently prosperous for both partners to leave their other professional endeavors to concentrate full time on building the fledgling company.

During its second year of operation, Medtronic expanded its business by offering to do service work for several medical equipment manufacturing companies located in the upper Midwestern United States. Bakken and his partner expanded slowly at first, adding another garage to their company operations and then an apartment. As the company grew and added employees it eventually began to modify devices, and design and build new devices as needed for medical research.

In 1957, an electrical blackout across Minnesota and Wisconsin on Halloween (October 31) created an event that led to a turning point in Medtronic's history, according to a 2007 story by Lorna Benson for Minnesota Public Radio. The University of Minnesota hospital had started using pacemakers to help children recover from heart surgery. The hospital thought it had redundancy in its electric supply by being connected to two different power sources, but the widespread power outage, which brought down both of their suppliers, left them without power. Drama ensued as the local police department was enlisted to park its cars outside the hospital with their lights on while surgeons performed operations within. In the children's cardiac unit that night, doctors scrambled to give their patients drugs to keep their hearts going, after the bulky plug-in AC pacemakers they were attached to quit operating. In spite of their efforts, one child died during the three-hour hospital blackout.

OUT OF TRAGEDY

Pioneering Minnesota heart surgeon C. Walter Lillehei was shaken by the event and, seeing the familiar figure of Bakken in the hospital the next day, discussed with him what they might do to prevent the recurrence of such a disastrous event. Lillehei suggested to Bakken the possibility of creating a portable, battery-operated pacemaker, one that would not be vulnerable to electrical system failure. Bakken was willing to give it a try, and they quickly produced a device that ran on a conventional six-volt automotive car battery. Unfortunately, the car battery provided too much power, and Bakken was forced to look for a more suitable alternative. Remembering an article he had read about a new circuit used in a metronome, which had a pulse very similar to a heart rhythm, he decided to conduct the experiment along that avenue of research. Within a short time, Bakken's new device, powered by nine-volt mercury batteries and small enough to be worn by pediatric cardiac patients, was ready for trials.

Initially the device was installed on a laboratory dog that had been given an artificial heart. Following the successful test, Bakken thought he had the prototype for a device that could be used on humans, and he prepared to make a suitable version. However, when he returned to the hospital the next day to retrieve his device, he found it already in operation, keeping a child alive in the cardiac recovery unit of the hospital. Seeing the device in action Bakken later said, according to the Benson article, "What a great feeling. . .something we made with our own hands keeping this child alive." This attitude would help to shape Medtronic's future mission statement.

Bakken later characteristically diminished his own importance in the development of the device, saying he felt the Halloween blackout simply highlighted the need for a battery-operated pacemaker. Surgeons were making rapid advances in treatment during the 1950s and such a development would have occurred eventually without his fortuitous intervention. Nonetheless, Medtronic's device kicked off a new era in the use of electrical stimulation in cardiac medical treatment.

During the rest of the 1950s, Bakken and Medtronic went on to build about 100 medical devices, only 10 of which eventually became part of the company's product line. Early products concentrated in the cardiac area and included pacemakers, external defibrillators, a cardiac rate monitor, an animal respirator, and a physiological stimulator. By 1960, Medtronic was an established maker of heart pacemakers, with devices in use at hospitals across the United States and in other countries around the globe. That year two doctors, William Chardack and Andrew Gage, experimented with the development of a totally implantable pacemaker device at a veterans' hospital in New York. Medtronic's founders quickly found out about the device, and realizing its importance, secured the exclusive rights to produce it. Within two months they had orders for 50 of the US$375 devices.

In 1960, the company implemented its mission statement, which more than 50 years later continues to be the ethical framework and guiding directive behind the company's operations. Medtronic's commitment to its mission runs deep, and senior executives give each new employee at the company a medallion, inscribed with the ideals, as a reminder of the seriousness of the company's mission. In the statement, the following principals were laid out for Medtronic's operations:

Medtronic Mission Statement

- To contribute to human welfare by application of biomedical engineering in the research, design, manufacture, and sale of instruments or appliances that alleviate pain, restore health, and extend life
- To direct growth in the areas of biomedical engineering where we display maximum strength and ability
- To strive without reserve for the greatest possible reliability and quality in our products
- To make a fair profit on current operations to meet our obligations, sustain our growth, and reach our goals

- To recognize the personal worth of employees by providing an employment framework that allows personal satisfaction in work accomplished, security, advancement opportunity, and means to share in the company's success
- To maintain good citizenship as a company

MEDTRONIC BEGINS ITS METEORIC RISE

The 1960s saw dramatic company growth, as revenues went from US$500,000 in 1962 to US$12 million in 1968. Employees grew from 36 to 348 during the same period. Twice during the decade, company expansion necessitated moving the headquarters and manufacturing facilities to new locations. During this period the company refocused its efforts away from less profitable products and concentrated more on prosthetics and surgically implanted devices, including heart valves, pacemakers, stent grafts, and balloon angioplasty. Company scientists and researchers also ventured into projects to relieve spinal cord pain, and explored the development of both infant and gastrointestinal pacemaker devices. By the end of the decade about a third of Medtronic sales were international, with most of that coming from Europe. By 1970, the company was divided into four international regions geographically, with direct sales offices in 19 countries.

As the company moved into the 1970s, it continued to expand its operations internationally. During the decade the company established a regional European headquarters in Paris, as well as a Latin American headquarters in São Paulo, Brazil. By the end of the decade the company also had manufacturing facilities in Canada, France, and Puerto Rico. This period also saw the company make its first acquisitions and introduce computerized technology into its product line. The company reached a milestone in 1974, when founder Bakken stepped down from day-to-day operations. In 1976, under the new leadership of CEO Dale R. Olseth, the company went public.

Product emphasis continued to evolve, with a shifting of focus toward more chronic conditions. A neurological division was established in 1976, followed by the introduction of deep brain and spinal cord stimulators to relieve chronic pain, as well as a product to treat scoliosis (crooked spine). An independent heart valve division was also created, and a valve was introduced that had been developed by Dr. Karl Hall. It became the first implantable valve containing no welds, joints, or bends that might weaken the device.

MEDTRONIC IN THE 1980S AND 1990S

With a number of new products and business acquisitions beginning in the mid-1980s, Medtronic continued its evolution as an important international medical research and product development company. Research spending doubled between 1985 and 1988 and led to the introduction of implantable defibrillators and drug delivery devices. Acquisitions allowed the company to enter new markets in a number of surgical equipment specialties. Medtronic sales reached the milestone of US$1 billion in 1989.

During the 1990s, Medtronic continued its meteoric growth; by the end of the decade the company employed 22,000 people worldwide and products made by the company were involved in treating over 1.5 million patients annually. By 1992, the company's international sales contributed 40 percent of total company revenues. Strategic acquisitions again played a significant role in the company's growth, with the company doubling in size following the acquisition of nine key companies that were involved in a number of therapeutic areas. European headquarters were moved first to Belgium and finally to Switzerland. By 2000, company sales had grown to over US$5 billion annually. Nevertheless, the company continued to live up to its mission statement developed 30 years earlier and was named by *Fortune* magazine in 1998 as one of "The One Hundred Best Companies to Work For," according to Medtronic's company website.

During the first decade of the 21st century, Medtronic did not rest on its past success in terms of growth. Having reached the economic milestone of US$5 billion in sales by 2000, company sales doubled in the next five years to reach over US$10 billion in 2005, only to grow an additional US$5 billion by the end of the decade, reaching almost US$16 billion in 2010. During this period company employee growth was also strong, with 21,600 employees in 2000 growing to over 40,000 by 2010.

In 2001, as Arthur D. Collins took over leadership of the company, he again refocused the business on developing treatments for chronic conditions, by now an exploding international market. During the following years the company introduced a number of devices attending to this market, including a protein product to treat degenerative spinal disc disease, the first deep brain stimulator used to treat obsessive-compulsive disorders, and the first artificial cervical disc.

WHY HAS MEDTRONIC BEEN SO SUCCESSFUL?

Certainly, a good deal of Medtronic's success can be attributed to favorable positioning in a field, and sector of that field, which has experienced enormous growth in revenues since the 1950s. According to an April 2011 report by the Kaiser Family Foundation, with rapidly aging populations, per capita expenditures on health care in the United States, Europe, and Japan have increased sharply. The highest rate of growth in industrialized countries has occurred in the United States, where per capita expenditures have gone from US$356 per year in 1970 to over US$7,500 in 2008. While growth rates in other industrial countries have been slower than in the United States, their expenditures still averaged US$3944 annually in 2008, up from an average of US$225 in 1970.

Additionally, Medtronic's placement in the sectors of cardiology and chronic diseases has been favorable, given that these are areas of growth and concern for aging populations in particular. High technology and its melding with modern medicine has also been a major trend in medical treatments during the past 50 years. Medtronic has been well positioned to take advantage of this trend.

An outside analysis of Medtronic's success, performed in July 2006 by Rene Cveykus and Eric Carter for *Strategic Finance,* mentioned the company's use of Lean Sigma (a form of business management strategy) process improvement initiatives in its financial operations, a process first used in manufacturing by Toyota Motor Company. Medtronic began using these methods in its global operations in 2003, in areas as diverse as information technology, sales, and quality control. Using trained operators (called Master Black Belts and Black Belts) in four-week training sessions, the company refocused employees on the "DMAIC" principals: Define (the opportunity), Measure (performance), Analyze (causes), Improve (performance), and Control (causes). In over 800 projects where the techniques were applied between 2003 to 2006, actual improvements usually exceeded expectations, with approximately US$150,000 saved per project.

With its placement in over 120 countries worldwide, and its recognition as the global leader in medical technology devices, a Medtronic device is used every five seconds around the world, as of 2012. Utilizing its core values expressed in its mission statement, and continuing its policy of aggressive innovation and strategic acquisition, the company seems well placed to continue strong annual revenue growth for many years into the future.

BIBLIOGRAPHY

Benson, Lorna. "Halloween Blackout of '57 Spurs Creation of Portable Pacemaker." *Minnesota Public Radio News,* October 31, 2007. Accessed January 30, 2012. http://minnesota.publicradio.org/display/web/2007/10/29/batterypacemaker/.

"Company Profile – Medtronic." Denmark: EcoMerc, 2008. Accessed January 30, 2012. http://www.ecomerc.com/help/case/company_profile.html.

Cveyku, Renee, and Erin Carter. "Fix The Process Not the People." *Strategic Finance,* July 2006. Accessed January 30, 2012. http://www.imanet.org/PDFs/Public/SF/2006_07/07_06_cveykus.pdf.

The Henry J. Kaiser Family Foundation. "Health Care Spending in the United States and Selected OECD Countries." Menlo Park, CA, April 2011. Accessed January 30, 2012. http://www.kff.org/insurance/snapshot/OECD042111.cfm.

Medtronic, Inc. "About Us." Fridley, MN, 2012. Accessed January 30, 2012. http://www.medtronic.com/about -medtronic/our-story/shifting-to-disease-management/index .htm.

———. "A Legacy of Innovation." Fridley, MN, 2012. Accessed January 30, 2012. http://wwwp.medtronic.com/newsroom /content/1281109242470.pdf .

Merrill Lynch: Innovative Financial Services

BRINGING WALL STREET TO MAIN STREET

In the 2010s, Merrill Lynch and Company, Inc., offers wealth management, securities trading and sales, corporate finance, and investment banking services in more than 40 countries worldwide. The company grew from its roots as a small investment firm headed by Charles Merrill and Edmund Lynch to its billion-dollar acquisition by Bank of America Corporation in 2008.

According to an article in *Bloomberg Businessweek* by Marcia Vickers, Charles Merrill believed "passionately" that the buying and selling of stocks should not just be for the ultrarich, but that the middle class should also benefit from buying good, well-researched stocks. He brought a strong sense of ethics to the firm and insisted on separating stock research from banking activities. At a time when most people thought the stock market dealt in livestock rather than paper, wrote Vickers, Merrill Lynch's corporate motto was "investigate, then invest." The firm published numerous how-to articles and advertisements and held investment seminars in Airstream trailers advocating lifetime investing. It was Merrill's foresight in mailing a cautionary letter to his firm's investors in 1929, however, that showed his business acumen and his ethics.

1929 STOCK MARKET CRASH

In the *Journal of Economic History* article, "The Bubble of 1929: Evidence from Closed-End Funds," J. Bradford DeLong and Andrei Schleifer noted that the incredibly sharp rise and then drastic fall of stock prices in 1929 was "perhaps the most striking episode in the history of American financial markets." The nominal Standard and Poor's (S&P) composite index rose 64 percent between January 1928 and September 1929 as stock prices soared to levels never seen before. Many investors were convinced that stocks were a sound investment and borrowed heavily to invest more money in the market.

In a 1956 obituary of Merrill, the *New York Times* noted that if Merrill "had been addicted to the I-told-you-so attitude," he could have pointed to 1929 as a moment in the history of the United States when he was "painfully right." He was convinced that the boom in the stock market and the ever-increasing stock values could not last. In the *Journal of Business and Economic History,* Edwin J. Perkins described how Charles Merrill, "sensing that the stock market was ripe for a sharp correction," mailed a form letter to all of his firm's retail customers strongly suggesting that they carefully look at all their current investments and reduce any debts they may have in connection with purchasing securities. In Merrill's obituary, it was noted that the letter said in part, "We do not urge you to sell securities indiscriminately, but we advise you in no uncertain terms that you take advantage of present high prices and put your own financial house in order. We recommend that you sell enough securities to lighten your obligations, or better yet, pay them entirely."

Although Merrill's partner, Edmund Lynch, and other junior associates in the firm were skeptical of his dire predictions for the market, his judgment was proven correct by the Stock Market Crash of October 1929. It is mentioned in Merrill's obituary that his action in mailing the letter probably saved approximately US$6 million for his firm's clients.

NOVEL COMPENSATION SCHEME

In the early 1940s, according to Perkins, Charles Merrill retained Ted Braun, a California public relations consultant, to perform a thorough analysis of a branch of E.A. Pierce & Company, with which Merrill, Lynch & Co. had merged in the winter of 1940. Braun was also instructed to survey a random sample of the branch's 3,000 clients regarding their opinions about the company. The results of the survey, according to Perkins, "had a tremendous impact on the policies and strategies adopted by Merrill Lynch in the early 1940s—and in due course on the procedures and practices of every firm in the brokerage field."

Based on the results of the survey, Braun suggested a strategy to Merrill that was completely unheard of in the industry at the time: brokers should not be compensated by receiving a share of the percentage of the commission linked to specific transactions, but instead should receive an annual salary based on their overall contribution to the profitability of the firm. Each branch manager would be given the authority to grant raises as deemed appropriate. While no other company on Wall Street had ever considered such a radical idea, Braun warned that it was necessary to differentiate Merrill Lynch from other investment companies and to gain the trust of a clientele still suspicious of brokerage firms after the market crash of 1929.

Braun's research revealed that almost every client who maintained an active account with an investment firm had, at times, wondered whose interest was actually being served when a broker suggested buying or selling stocks. Merely saying that Merrill Lynch brokers were honest was not enough, advised Braun. Although some of Merrill Lynch's senior management were astounded that the partners were even considering such a move, and despite the fact that it was risky for the firm (with a large amount of variable costs suddenly becoming fixed costs), the company set a minimum salary for its sales force.

In an effort to assuage the perceived loss of status, Merrill Lynch renamed its brokers "account executives," a term borrowed from the advertising industry. Merrill, noted Perkins, was keen for the company's employees to maintain higher ethical standards than were usual in the financial services industry. He "envisioned the sales staff as trusted advisors to a group of valued clients."

NOVEL BANKING

In 1970, Merrill Lynch created another stir in the financial services industry by introducing a previously unheard of account called the cash management account (CMA). Former chairman and chief executive officer Donald T. Regan moved Merrill Lynch from a brokerage house to a full-service financial provider. A major step in this process was the creation of the CMA in 1977. Merrill Lynch saw a marketing opportunity for integrating all of a client's accounts (checking, savings, and brokerage accounts) under one umbrella. The company created a solution that

was able to meet its clients' banking and investment needs while complying with U.S. regulatory standards.

According to the December 1985 article "Information Systems for a Competitive Advantage: Implementation of a Planning Process," by Nick Rackoff, Charles Wiseman, and Walter A. Ulrich in the *MIS Quarterly*, the CMA not only depended on creative thinking by Merrill Lynch about the banking and investment services industry, but its introduction was dependent on database and laser printing technology, neither of which were commonplace at the time. The introduction of the CMA was made possible by a strategic information systems (SIS) alliance between Merrill Lynch and Banc One of Columbus, Ohio. Banc One developed systems to process the debit card and check transactions on a CMA account. Rackoff, Wiseman, and Ulrich noted that the introduction of this unique account enabled Merrill Lynch to sign up over one million clients, approximately 10 times the amount of its closest rival, and reap over US$60 million annually in fees.

At a July 16, 2003, conference sponsored by the U.S. Federal Deposit Insurance Corporation (FDIC) titled "The Future of Banking: The Structure and Role of Commercial Affiliations," John Qua, a senior vice president and head of global banking at Merrill Lynch, discussed the company's role in pioneering the concept of an interest-only mortgage. Merrill Lynch first introduced a mortgage with a 25-year adjustable interest rate and the feature of interest-only payments for the first 10 years. According to Qua, "It provides clients with the benefits of liquidity and diversification, as lower initial down payments make more cash available for investments or other purposes. At the same time, it offers the tax advantages of interest deduction and the ability to pre-pay principle without penalty." At the time of speaking, Qua noted that US$35 billion had been extended to clients through this product.

In 2011, the financial services magazine, *The Banker* named Merrill Lynch as the "Most Innovative Bank in North America." The firm was also named the "Most Innovative Bank for Initial Public Offerings," and the "Most Innovative Bank for Prime Brokerage." It was the second consecutive year that Merrill Lynch made the magazine's award list.

Many other companies have followed Merrill Lynch's lead. In the 2010s, cash management accounts and interest-only mortgages are widely available through numerous financial institutions. Many banks and credit unions employ financial advisors paid on salary rather than commission, and industry and governmental regulations have forced brokerage houses into the transparency and honesty that Merrill advocated.

CHANGE IN FOCUS

Harking back to Charles Merrill's philosophy that investing should not just be for the ultrarich and that success for the firm meant listening to the customer, Qua titled his remarks at the FDIC conference, "Banking at Merrill Lynch: A Function of Client-Driven Innovation." He pointed out that there had been major changes in the financial services industry since Charles Merrill's day, and that competitive advantage based on new ideas, whether client driven or not, was harder to maintain. Indeed, Jonathan Stempel, in his Reuters article, noted that 1999 was the last time that Merrill Lynch was the world's largest underwriter of stocks and bonds. The following year, the company was overtaken by Citigroup Inc.

In a January 8, 2012, article in *Investment News,* Andrew Osterland detailed how Merrill Lynch Wealth Management, a division of Bank of America Merrill Lynch, had changed its compensation package for brokers to encourage them to pursue wealthier clients. While encouraging brokers to attract such clients was widespread in the industry, Osterland noted that Merrill Lynch was taking the lead. The article quoted Alois Pirker, a senior industry analyst with Aite Group Inc., as stating that, "Small clients don't bring in enough revenue to compensate for providing them a full-service advisory offering." The division hoped to encourage smaller investors to move to less costly accounts at its Merrill Edge division, a platform for self-directed investments.

Merrill Lynch was not the only financial services group searching for ways to increase revenue, shed unprofitable accounts, and cut expenses. In a June 16, 2011, *New York Times* article, Susanne Craig reported that even Goldman Sachs, Wall Street's most profitable firm, ordered the re-examination of every aspect of the business to cut US$1 billion from noncompensation expenses. Morgan Stanley planned to reduce its low-income-producing brokers by 300, while Barclays Capital reduced its worldwide staff by 2 percent.

TOWARD POSSIBILITIES

As Vickers noted in her *Bloomberg Businessweek* article, in 1940, just 16 percent of U.S. citizens invested in stocks. In the 21st century, more than half of the population invested. This was primarily due to the explosion of 401(k) plans, the wide variety and easy access of mutual funds, lower trading costs, and more accessible research.

In addition, credit must be given to Charles Merrill and his firm. Merrill, as noted by an associate and recorded in Stempel's Reuters article, "could imagine the possibilities," and although in the early 2010s Merrill Lynch was facing tough times and increased competition, the possibilities for new ideas were still available.

BIBLIOGRAPHY

"The Banker's Investment Banking Awards 2011." *The Banker,* October 7, 2011. Accessed January 10, 2012. http://www.thebanker.com/Awards/Investment-Banking-Awards/The-Banker-s-Investment-Banking-Awards-2011.

"Charles Merrill, Broker, Dies; Founder of Merrill Lynch Firm." *New York Times,* October 7, 1956. Accessed January 11, 2012. http://www.nytimes.com/learning/general/onthisday/bday/1019.html.

Craig, Susanne. "Wall Street Braces for New Layoffs as Profits Wane." *New York Times,* June 16, 2011. Accessed January 12, 2012. http://dealbook.nytimes.com/2011/06/16/as-profits-wane-wall-street-braces-for-new-layoffs.

DeLong, J. Bradford, and Andrei Schleifer. "The Bubble of 1929: Evidence from Closed-End Funds." *Journal of Economic History* 51, no. 3 (September 1991): 675–700.

"Donald T. Regan, Former Chairman and Chief Executive Officer of Merrill Lynch & Co., Inc., Dies at 84." *Business Wire,* June 10, 2003. Accessed January 12, 2012. http://findarticles.com/p/articles/mi_m0EIN/is_2003_June_10/ai_102957082.

Merrill Lynch. "About Us." New York, NY, 2011. Accessed January 11, 2012. http://www.ml.com/index.asp?id=7695_8134_8296.

Osterland, Andrew. "Merrill Lynch Raises the Bar for Small Brokers." *Investment News,* January 8, 2012. Accessed January 12, 2012. http://www.investmentnews.com/article/20120108/REG/301089982.

Perkins, Edwin J. "New Strategies for Stockbrokers: Merrill Lynch in the 1940s." *Journal of Business and Economic History* 28, no. 2 (Winter 1999): 173–184.

Qua, John. "Banking at Merrill Lynch: A Function of Client-Driven Innovation." "The Future of Banking: The Structure and Role of Commercial Affiliations." A Conference Sponsored by the Federal Deposit Insurance Corporation Washington, DC, July 16, 2003. Accessed January 12, 2012. http://www.fdic.gov/news/conferences/future_qua_speech.html.

Rackoff, Nick, Charles Wiseman, and Walter A. Ulrich. "Information Systems for a Competitive Advantage: Implementation of a Planning Process." *MIS Quarterly* 9, no. 4 (Dec 1985): 285–294.

Stempel, Jonathan. "TIMELINE: History of Merrill Lynch." *Reuters,* September 15, 2008. Accessed January 10, 2012. http://www.reuters.com/article/2008/09/15/us-merrill-idUSN1546989520080915.

Vickers, Marcia. "Charles Merrill: Selling Stocks to the Masses." *Bloomberg Businessweek,* April 19, 2004. Accessed January 10, 2012. http://www.businessweek.com/magazine/content/04_16/b3879045_mz072.htm.

Microsoft's Savvy Licensing
of Operating Systems

An operating system (OS) is the program that manages memory and other system resources and allows a computer user to interact with the computer programs and applications on the system. The main purpose of the OS is to manage the kernel, the connection between applications and the system hardware and components. Modern OS systems are so seamless that they allow computer users to manage applications, such as web browsers and word processing programs, without having to worry about any of the programming languages or inner workings of a computer.

Earlier computers had more distinct operating systems. For example, on early personal computers (PCs), users might have had Microsoft Disk OS (MS-DOS) and would need to add Windows 3.1 as a user interface that made it easier to interact with the OS. After the release of Windows 95, Microsoft had erased the distinction between an OS and a user interface by packaging both into one system.

As of 2012 the Microsoft Windows OS was the most commonly used OS on PCs and mobile devices worldwide. Microsoft Corporation was founded in 1975 and initially it developed programming languages rather than an OS. The company was founded by Bill Gates and Paul Allen, two longtime friends who had an interest in computer programming. The founding date of Microsoft is significant because it ensured that the company was not a late arrival to the OS market. In fact, Microsoft was established before the first PCs were launched and therefore the company was able to grow as technology developed. Microsoft's first OS was introduced in the early 1980s.

As of 2012 the company not only developed operating systems and software, but also licensed the software to companies and sold software directly to consumers. Part of the success of Microsoft has had more to do with licensing than with the development of new software. Microsoft's early successes were with software that the company did not even create, but instead licensed or purchased from third parties. Microsoft licensed its operating systems to companies that were creating devices that could utilize the software, thus ensuring that the software was available on a wide range of computers and devices. In the 2010s, while many brands of devices compete with each other, the popularity of Microsoft products and licensing agreements ensure that customers across many brands can buy products with a Microsoft OS pre-installed.

Although Microsoft is one of the most recognized names in OS and software develoment, it has not generated widespread goodwill. Many computer experts acknowledge that Microsoft Windows and other programs are susceptible to more security threats than competitors such as Apple Inc., which have their own OS. Microsoft's licensing agreements have also garnered criticism for being somewhat harsh. For example, in their essay, "Who Is Microsoft Today?" Don E. Waldman and Rochelle Rupper noted that Bill Gates used his "knowledge of licensing agreements and his strategic abilities to write licensing agreements with the explicit objective of gaining advantages over his competitors."

EARLY PROGRAMS AND AGREEMENTS

Even before Microsoft was developing operating systems, it was creating programs and licensing agreements that gave it a distinct advantage. Well before the company launched its first OS, Microsoft created a software program for the new 8080 computer chip, one of the earlier computer processors. After developing the program, Gates and Allen signed a licensing agreement with Micro Instrumentation and Telemetry Systems, Inc. (MITS), which gave MITS exclusive rights for licensing the program. The licensing agreement that was signed between Gates, Allen, and MITS contained a clause, according to Waldman and Rupper, in which MITS "agree[d] to use its best efforts to license, promote, and commercialize the Program." The contract further explicitly stated that the licensing agreement would be null and void if MITS failed to meet this requirement.

Eventually, MITS was purchased by Pertec Computer Corporation, and Gates and Allen were able to invalidate the MITS contract, alleging that the company did not do its best to promote BASIC. Once out of the contract, Gates and Allen were free to enter into licensing agreements with other companies, including competitors of MITS. A similar pattern of advantageous licensing agreements and work with multiple parties would be the hallmark of Microsoft's success when the company started licensing operating systems.

MS-DOS

It was with MS-DOS that Gates and Allen were really able to use licensing to a great advantage. According to Waldman and Rupper, "Gates's knowledge of contracts and his willingness to push the envelope beyond industry norms helped Microsoft establish MS-DOS as the PC industry standard."

The story of MS-DOS began in 1980 when IBM contacted Microsoft because it needed a BASIC interpreter system for the IBM PC, a new personal desktop computer that IBM was about to launch. During discussions about that product, IBM also told Microsoft that it needed a new OS for its new PC too. IBM had initially approached Digital Research Inc. (DRI) for an OS, but the two companies were not able to reach a deal. Microsoft told IBM that it would find an OS for the new computer.

Microsoft signed a licensing agreement with Seattle Computer products for their 86-DOS (QDOS) software. Microsoft was the exclusive licensing agent for QDOS and by 1981 it owned the software outright. The licensing agreement between Microsoft and IBM essentially saw IBM and Microsoft developing parts of the DOS program at the same time, with IBM funding the bulk of the development. Microsoft adapted the program for IBM's needs and the program became, in its two permutations, MS-DOS and PC DOS. PC DOS was used on IBM computers but Microsoft retained the right to license MS-DOS, a key factor that would lead to Microsoft's dominance.

THE SIGNIFICANCE OF THE MS-DOS LICENSING AGREEMENT

According to Matt Haig's book, *Brand Success: How the World's Top 100 Brands Thrive and Survive,* in the early 1980s, when Microsoft was a growing company, the focus was on the hardware component of computers. Haig wrote that IBM outsourced the OS because it seemed like the less important component of the desktop computer. An intangible part of the computer, the OS at the time seemed as though it would never become very important. This would become a costly mistake, as Microsoft eventually outstripped IBM in revenues and in brand marketing.

At the time that MS-DOS was created, original equipment manufacturers (OEMs) like IBM usually held legal rights over the source code on their equipment. In the agreement between IBM and Microsoft, however, Microsoft received US$500,000 for the rights to a few computer languages as well as another payment for adapting MS-DOS for IBM computers. Unusually for the time, the licensing agreement between IBM and Microsoft placed few restraints on Microsoft and did not give IBM the right to license MS-DOS. The agreement gave Microsoft money to adapt the OS for IBM, but Microsoft remained the sole entity allowed to license the OS to other parties. This important part of the agreement set the stage for Microsoft's dominance in the OS marketplace. While IBM faced increased competition from more and more computer companies in the 1990s, Microsoft thrived, since essentially every new computer brand meant a new market for its OS.

The MS-DOS licensing agreement with IBM was significant for a number of other reasons as well. Since IBM at the time was the larger company, the licensing agreement allowed Microsoft to use IBM's huge reach in the desktop computer market, which meant that it could use IBM's brand name and marketing to get its own products into consumers' homes.

In addition, the licensing agreement gave Microsoft a competitive advantage because it allowed the company to market its own version of MS-DOS to other companies, including Texas Instruments Inc. and Compaq Computer Corporation. These computer competitors were able to run their own versions of DOS on their machines, allowing Microsoft to develop a much larger market share than what could be encompassed by IBM PCs alone. This also allowed manufacturers to create computers that were not compatible with PC DOS but could still run some form of the DOS software. By the 1990s computer manufacturers saw that it was no longer profitable to create machines that were not compatible with IBM and a wave of so-called IBM clones running MS-DOS was the result. Microsoft marketed MS-DOS to IBM clones, ensuring that a majority of PCs sold in the 1980s used MS-DOS.

IBM launched its PCs in 1981 and they ran using MS-DOS. Just five years later, by 1986 Microsoft was generating revenues of US$60.9 million a year, with about half of that amount coming from licensing agreements involving MS-DOS. The OS had become the industry standard for PCs. By 1999, according to Haig, Microsoft had captured 90 percent of the OS market for desktop computers.

Microsoft's immense success with MS-DOS was in part due to its licensing agreement, something which Haig claimed could be shown by contrasting Microsoft's success with the experience of Apple and IBM. According to Haig, Microsoft succeeded because it was willing to license its product to many other companies, and IBM and Apple failed to achieve the same level of market dominance simply because they failed to branch out in this same way. For example, while many considered the Apple OS better than MS-DOS, Apple only sold its system on Apple computers, thereby reducing its market reach. Similarly, IBM ultimately did not retain its level of dominance in the PC market because it focused on its personal brand of computers and faced increasing pressure from multiple competitors.

WINDOWS

Once MS-DOS had been established as the industry standard, the next big revolution in the OS was the graphical user interface (GUI) OS. While MS-DOS relied on command lines, so that users had to type specific information into a computer in order to open programs and files, GUI systems allowed users to click on icons on a desktop in order to open files or programs. After Microsoft launched its first GUI OS, Windows 2.03, Apple sued the company in March 1988, alleging that the new system looked very similar to Apple's own GUI OS. Apple attempted to stop the sale of the new Windows program and tried to get copies of the program destroyed and to recover the profits Microsoft had earned for Windows.

Microsoft responded by noting that it had a licensing agreement that the company had previously signed with Apple. That 1985 agreement permitted Microsoft to use graphical aspects for several programs, including for Windows 1.0. The defense for Microsoft claimed that the 1985 licensing agreement implicitly allowed Microsoft to use visual displays in other programs. Apple pursued its claim, even when Microsoft launched Windows 3.0. Microsoft spent US$9 million on legal costs and eventually won when Apple's case was dismissed in 1992. It was Microsoft's savvy use of legal systems and especially licensing agreements that allowed the company to prevail.

In the 1990s Microsoft used licensing agreements to ensure that the vast majority of systems sold came with Windows pre-installed. This ensured a huge market share. Since computer buyers were given the OS with their computer, if they wanted a different one they would need to pay extra and then go to the trouble of removing the Microsoft system to install a new system. Not surprisingly, few customers did so. According to Haig, Windows 95 was used in 250 million businesses and homes, while Windows 7 sales rose to 175 million in the first nine months the OS was on the market.

CHALLENGES TO THE MICROSOFT WAY

Microsoft's route to OS success was not without challenges. In the 1990s many entities voiced concerns about Microsoft's practices and even claimed that the company's licensing practices were predatory. In May 1998 Microsoft executives testified at a trial in the *United States v. Microsoft* civil action. Twenty U.S. states as well as the U.S. Department of Justice sued the software company, alleging that Microsoft used unfair trade practices that were in violation of the Sherman Antitrust Act of 1890. The main issue at hand was the fact that Microsoft packaged its Internet Explorer (IE) web browser with its OS, ensuring that all users of Windows had the web browser. Prosecutors accused the software company of using a number of tactics to ensure that Netscape, Opera, and other web browsers would be harder to install and that the OS might not work properly if IE were removed. In 2001 the case was settled, and under the terms of the agreement Microsoft was compelled to disclose its application programming interfaces to others and to create a committee that would ensure compliance with the settlement.

MOBILE DEVICES

Microsoft's licensing has also enabled the company to make a switch to mobile devices. However, the move has not been without controversy. In early 2012 U.S. International Trade Commission judge Theodore Essex rejected a claim made by Barnes & Noble Inc. that Microsoft was unfairly undercutting competition from Google Inc.'s Android system through misuse of patents. According to a 2012 article by Susan Decker in *Bloomberg,* Microsoft signed licensing contracts with over 70 percent of companies that developed the Android smartphones used in the United States.

According to a 2012 article by Paul McDougall in *Information Week,* the future of Microsoft's OS will likely rest in a common OS, Windows 8, for multiple types of devices, including tablets, PCs, mobile phones, and other electronic devices. According to McDougall, most companies have separate mobile and desktop OSs, so that if Microsoft is able to create a common OS, this could give the company an advantage in the marketplace as it would permit more seamless sharing between different devices.

UNDERSTANDING MICROSOFT'S SUCCESS

Microsoft is generally viewed as primarily a software company, but the company's success is due more to its licensing agreements than its software. In fact, Microsoft's success is staggering when one considers the negative press and security concerns that are routinely voiced over Microsoft products. Despite this, Microsoft operating systems continue to dominate the market.

Microsoft's early success with MS-DOS is even more remarkable, considering that Bill Gates and Paul Allen did not even create the software for which they would eventually become famous. Instead, they used licensing agreements to get the software and ensure that IBM took care of much of the investment to get the OS on computers. From BASIC to MS-DOS and the many versions of Windows, Microsoft has always retained advantageous rights to its software, ensuring that products under multiple brands can be sold with Microsoft OS pre-installed.

BIBLIOGRAPHY

Cusumano, Michael, and Richard W. Selby. "How Microsoft Competes." *Research Technology Management* 39, no. 1 (1996): 26–27.

Decker, Susan. "Barnes & Noble's Patent-Misuse Claim against Microsoft Thrown Out by Judge." *Bloomberg,* January 31, 2012. Accessed February 2, 2012. http://www.bloomberg .com/news/2012-01-31/barnes-noble-s-patent-misuse-claim -against-microsoft-rejected.html.

Haig, Matt. *Brand Success: How the World's Top 100 Brands Thrive and Survive.* Philadelphia, PA: Kogan Page, 2011, 89–93.

Kraemer, Sylvia K. *Science and Technology Policy in the United States: Open Systems in Action.* Piscataway, NJ: Rutgers University Press, 2006, 144–255.

Lowe, Janet. *Bill Gates Speaks: Insight from the World's Greatest Entrepreneur.* New York: John Wiley & Sons, 1998, 110–171.

McDougall, Paul. "Microsoft Windows 8 Unification Plan: Grand, but Risky." *InformationWeek,* February 4, 2012. Accessed February 2, 2012. http://informationweek.com /news/windows/microsoft_news/232600242.

McMichael, Andrew. *History on the Web: Using and Evaluating the Internet.* Wheeling, IL: Harlan Davidson, 2005, 155–361.

Metz, Cade. "Meet Bill Gates, the Man Who Changed Open Source Software." *Wired,* January 30, 2012. Accessed February 2, 2012. http://www.wired.com/wiredenterprise /2012/01/meet-bill-gates/.

Microsoft Corporation. "About Microsoft." Redmond, WA, 2012. Accessed February 2, 2012. http://www.microsoft.com /about/en/us/default.aspx.

Waldman, Don. E., and Rochelle Rupper. "Who Is Microsoft Today?" In *Industry and Firm Studies,* edited by Victor J. Tremblay and Carol Horton Tremblay. 4th ed., 293–316. Armonk, NY: ME Sharpe, 2007.

Watson, Jon. *A History of Computer OSs.* Ann Arbor, MI: Nimble Books, 2007.

Monopoly: The Evolution of an Iconic U.S. Board Game

THE LANDLORD'S GAME

The history of the board game Monopoly stands as an example of tenacious entrepreneurism. Without the efforts of Charles Darrow, Monopoly would never have been a best-selling game. Sometimes, the work of one person willing to invest in an idea can help change an industry and win over an entire market. Darrow may not have invented the concept of Monopoly or the successful marketing campaign that helped it grow in popularity, but he refused to give up on the game.

The history of the Monopoly board game actually began in the early 20th century, although the classic, popular version of the game was released much later, during the Great Depression. Its origins lay with Elizabeth "Lizzie" Magie, who took out a patent for a game in 1904 known as the Landlord's Game. Landlord's Game and Monopoly shared many concepts. Magie focused on the nature of rentals and how renting out properties created cash flows moving from the tenants to the property owners. The game was intended to be educational. Magie believed people had difficulty understanding how renting could lead to financial problems, and hoped the board game would reveal the dangers of renting in the prevailing economic times. The nature of gameplay in the Landlord's Game also laid the foundation for Monopoly, as players rented properties, paid utilities, and attempted to avoid being sent to jail while dealing with realistic, changing tax systems.

Several years later, the Landlord's Game found a publisher in the Economic Game Company of New York, New York, which released the game in 1910. Demand, however, was slow to build. At first the game garnered interest primarily among supporters of renting alternatives and students studying economic theory. Yet people continued to play throughout the next decade, and important changes started to develop. With such a select market (sales often spreading via word of mouth), players had more freedom to alter the game and its rules. The result was a more streamlined version of the original game, eventually dubbed Auction Monopoly. Players in the United States customized the board game to fit their own neighborhoods, renaming properties after streets and buildings in their towns, which made it even more popular.

By 1933 the Great Depression was sweeping through the United States, leaving millions of workers jobless and desperate for income. One of these workers was Charles Darrow of Pennsylvania, who had been a sales representative for a local engineering firm. Accounts said that Darrow either played the game while visiting friends or in his own house while entertaining. Captured by the unique concept of the game, Darrow began to envision ways that it could be improved for a much wider audience.

CHARLES DARROW AND HUMBLE BEGINNINGS

Darrow's first work on Monopoly showed he had pinpointed the key areas of interest in the original Landlord's Game. Magie had designed the game to combine entertainment and education, but Darrow understood the reasons people were still playing decades later. In the middle of the Great Depression, the lure of financial conquest and bets without consequences proved strong. While people lost jobs and homes in the real world, the board game allowed them to pretend to be tycoons, landlords, and real estate moguls.

The alterations Darrow started to make highlighted the competitive aspects of the game. He moved the game from a rental basis to a purchasing structure where players could buy and exchange deeds to the properties. Fake money and dice helped move the game along, and Darrow constructed the board in a wide circle pattern, made from oilcloth. He also used the customization features of the previous version to create permanent lots, all based on the resort town of Atlantic City, New Jersey, including local details to make the game feel more authentic. Finally, Darrow created a color-code system for all the properties and altered the rules of taxation and jail time. He called this new game by the title that had won popularity through the lean years of the early 1930s: Monopoly.

INITIAL REJECTION

The first sets of Monopoly were the result of an engineering service worker with a lot of time on his hands. He took the customization features of the Landord's Game as far as they would go, actually carving out houses and hotels to use, hand-painting both the pieces and the board. He created the original cards and money by typing up information on small cut cards.

As a result of Darrow's detailed work and the new property baron fantasy, interest in Monopoly quickly outgrew his own household and spread amongst family, then friends. Soon people throughout Pennsylvania were hearing about this unique version of Monopoly. Darrow continued to handcraft board sets and sell them to interested parties for US$4 each. However, within a short time he had far more demand than he could supply, and stores in Philadelphia wanted their own copies to sell. Darrow knew he needed to turn the hobby into a firm source of profit, so he wrote to one of the largest game makers of the era, Parker Brothers.

In 1934 Parker Brothers reviewed Monopoly and rejected the game. The company claimed that it had found a total of 52 design errors in the game that prevented it from being marketable. The problem centered on the concept of the family board game, still a relatively new idea during the Great Depression. Parker Brothers and other game manufacturers had clear expectations of the parameters for a board game. The few games that had already been produced and sold successfully were suitable for children and kept the premise light. The company did not realize the adult appeal of a financial conquest game at the height of financial disaster.

In summary of the 52 flaws, Monopoly was dismissed as being far too long for a good family game. It had too many rules, which closely mirrored real property laws instead of rules that could be easily understood by young children. The concept of winning in Monopoly was nebulous at best, since a stasis was eventually reached as one player simply became more successful than all others. Darrow had also created more than 200 pieces in all for the game, which could be lost or destroyed if they were not treated with care. These departures from the accepted board game criteria made Parker Brothers too wary to invest in the reinvention.

PERSEVERANCE AND SUCCESS OF MONOPOLY

The initial rejection did not faze Darrow, who remained eager to supply local demand for his game. What Darrow encountered in Philadelphia stood in direct contrast to the beliefs of Parker Brothers. Families and friends had found a relatively inexpensive source of entertainment for the long and often hungry evenings of the mid-1930s. Darrow moved on to the next alternative. He partnered with a local printing shop and, using the money he had collected from his personal sales of the game, invested in the more professional production of 500 units. Some of the work for each set still required personal attention, but Darrow was able to create enough models to temporarily satisfy the requests of nearby stores.

The first order was followed by a second, and then a much larger third order as stores across Philadelphia, Pennsylvania, began buying the game. By 1935 the previous holiday season and continued demand were starting to make Darrow's Monopoly a sensation. The skyrocketing order numbers reached the attention of Parker Brothers, which began to rapidly reconsider its original stance. Any game that could generate so much interest and (more importantly) profit was worth a second look.

After negotiations with Charles Darrow, Parker Brothers purchased the rights to Monopoly in exchange for providing Darrow with royalties from the resulting sales. Backed by the production and marketing power that Parker Brothers held, Monopoly started selling on a national scale. The original success in Philadelphia was mirrored in cities across the United States. By the end of 1935 Parker Brothers was selling thousands of units per week, and Monopoly had become the most popular board game in the United States.

Darrow was eventually able to retire from the proceeds of the Monopoly project, marking his transition from unemployed engineering worker to millionaire in only a few short years. Parker Brothers, meanwhile, set to work dealing with one of the more curious problems that the success of Monopoly had created. Darrow was not the only person who had created a personal version of the Landlord's Game. A number of variations on the original game existed in cities across the East Coast of the United States.

Parker Brothers began by purchasing the original patent first created by Lizzie Magie 30 years prior for US$500 and no royalties. However, one of the first attractions of the Landlord's Game was the ease with which it could be customized according to individual preferences. Parker Brothers wanted to ensure its legal hold on the cash cow Monopoly had become. A version called Finance had surfaced in Indianapolis, Indiana, which required US$10,000 in settlements and legal actions to safely differentiate itself from Monopoly. Another version in Texas was known as Inflation, which involved suits and countersuits with Rudy Copeland, who eventually settled for a similar amount. This left the way clear for Monopoly to be accepted as a unique, unrivaled game by the U.S. public.

THE NEXT HUNDRED YEARS

Board games changed. Names were updated, color schemes were changed, rules and wording evolved with the times. Game companies attempted to reimagine games for new generations and often replaced games altogether as new technology or interests slowly took over. However, Monopoly remained unchanged throughout the years of its success. The square board eventually overtook the circular shape designed by Darrow, but that was one of the necessary changes Parker Brothers made when repackaging the game for a national U.S. market. In most aspects, Monopoly stayed the same, both visually and thematically.

The Great Depression passed, World War II came and went, the boom of the 1950s and the style changes of the 1960s swept through the United States, but Monopoly remained Monopoly. The problems created by ruthless landlords and economic collapse in the Great Depression passed in later decades, but new generations remained attracted to the board game and its surprisingly complex rules. The original versions of Monopoly and those produced in the early 1990s remained remarkably similar. The

illustrations and names, from Water Works to Go to Jail, stayed in place. The layout itself was altered only slightly.

The appeal of Monopoly has been debated, but its takeover tactics, without the issue of real-world consequences, appeared to have won the board game universal appeal. The friendly atmosphere of fake money and chance rolls of the dice, mixed with unbridled competition, continued to attract people. Parker Brothers never had a reason to change from Darrow's original design. By the late 1990s over 500 million people had played Monopoly, and 200 million units had been sold around the world. By the mid-1990s Hasbro (which by then owned Parker Brothers) had begun to release customized versions of the board game based on specific regions, movies, and cultural movements, but even this was a throwback to the original adaptability that had given Darrow his idea.

BIBLIOGRAPHY

Ament, Phil. "Monopoly." Troy, MI: The Great Idea Finder. Last modified November 30, 2006. Accessed December 21, 2011. http://www.ideafinder.com/history/inventions/monopoly.htm.

"Charles Darrow." Cambridge, MA: Lemelson-MIT Program, October 1997. Accessed December 21, 2011. http://web.mit.edu/invent/iow/monopoly.html.

"Darrow Editions." *World of Monopoly,* 2011. Accessed December 21, 2011. http://www.worldofmonopoly.com/history/darrow.php.

Hasbro. "History & Fun Facts." Pawtucket, RI, 2011. Accessed December 21, 2011. http://www.hasbro.com/monopoly/en_US/discover/history.cfm.

"Inventions from the Great Depression: Monopoly." *Bloomberg Businessweek,* 2011. Accessed December 21, 2011. http://images.businessweek.com/ss/08/12/1205_sb_necessity/8.

Taylor, Patrick. "The Game Monopoly." PatrickTaylor.com, May 13, 2006. Accessed December 21, 2011. http://www.patricktaylor.com/game-monopoly.

Muhammad Yunus and Microfinancing

Dr. Muhammad Yunus and his Grameen Bank research project (now the Grameen Bank) stand testament to the global impact that Yunus's innovative credit financing ideas had on the lives of the poor. Concepts he created, such as solidarity lending, benefit millions of people around the world, from a hairdresser in New York City needing a loan to buy supplies to a goat farmer in a small village in Bangladesh buying animal feed. Yunus's resourcefulness has helped spawn countless other microfinance projects such as Kiva.com, Prosper.com, and Kickerstarter.com. Using microfinancing, entrepreneurs who would be turned away by traditional banking institutions are able to secure small but critically important loans with little or no collateral that can help start their businesses and allow them the opportunity to be successful.

The concept of microfinance is not new. Examples of small loans to the poor or disadvantaged have been around since at least the 19th century. The most noted pioneer of the microfinance concept was a German mayor named Friedrich Wilhelm Raiffeisen. In 1846 he founded the first rural credit union. Unlike large central banks, a small and local credit union could assist local farmers, a very underrepresented demographic. Traditional banks shunned this group because of the small amounts of money involved and because of the high perceived risk of loan defaults.

THE NEED FOR MICROFINANCING

Historically, many regions of the world have practiced various forms of bonded labor or debt bondage. This is a system where poor individuals or families will exchange anything from physical labor to prostitution for loans of money, food, accommodation, or other basic necessities for living or working. On the Indian subcontinent, countries like India, Pakistan, and Bangladesh have been particularly susceptible, making it nearly impossible for the poor to improve their situations due to the continuous need to rely on money lenders for subsistence. Children are often exploited and forced into labor, such as making carpets or leatherworking. Most debts incurred by the poor are small amounts, such as loans ranging from US$14 to US$214, but interest rates demanded by lenders can be as high as 60 percent, making repayment difficult, if not impossible. Even though women and children are the most frequent victims, men also are exploited. This problem is so prevalent that international human rights organizations have estimated that on the Indian subcontinent alone, 15 to 20 million people were living as indentured workers at the beginning of the 21st century. In 2011, according to the CNN Freedom Project, there were anywhere between 10 and 30 million slaves worldwide, depending on the source and terminology used.

MUHAMMAD YUNUS

Born on June 28, 1940, in Bathua, Bangladesh, Muhammad Yunus was the third of 14 children. Yunus learned about altruism from his mother, who had the kindness to help any poor person who asked her for assistance. Growing up primarily in the city of Chittagong, Bangladesh, he attended Dhaka University in 1957, earning his bachelor's degree in economics. He completed his master's degree in 1961. After becoming a lecturer at Dhaka University, he was offered a Fulbright scholarship in 1965 to study in the United States. In 1969 he received a doctorate in economics from Vanderbilt University, and he served as assistant professor of economics at Middle Tennessee State University until 1972.

Returning to his native Bangladesh Muhammad Yunus became a professor of economics at Chittagong University. Yunus's first encounter with microlending, and how incredibly small amounts of money could make a disproportionately major difference in people's lives, was in 1976 when he was visiting the village of Jobra, near his hometown of Chittagong, Bangladesh. In Jobra he met with some poor women who were making bamboo furniture but could not achieve profitability because in order to purchase materials and supplies to manufacture the furniture, they had to borrow money. Since no bank or government institution would lend to them, they had to accept the services of local usurers (sometimes called loan sharks) who demanded exorbitant interest rates. As a result, any profit these women earned in their furniture business was paid back to the loan sharks. Seeing the problem, Yunus loaned US$27 of his own money to the 42 villagers, allowing them to break free from the vicious cycle of borrowing and repaying money to the loan sharks without being able to make a profit.

YUNUS'S VISION

For Yunus the solution was simple. Provide loans to the poor and give them a chance to turn their lives and their businesses around. However, he soon discovered that existing banks were unwilling to offer such services. Poor borrowers were seen as an unacceptably high credit risk, especially due to their inability to provide any collateral or security to guarantee repayment of the loan. While not an unreasonable thing to ask, the lack of collateral immediately disqualified the vast majority of would-be borrowers, even if they could make good on their promises of repayment.

Yunus firmly believed that poor borrowers were no less likely to repay than richer ones, if only they were given a chance. In order to prove it he put his own creditworthiness on the line and managed to secure a line of credit from Janata Bank, with himself as the guarantor. What started out as a small, simple project to help the villagers of Jobra evolved into the foundation of Grameen Bank, meaning "Village Bank" in Bengali, on October 2, 1983.

Yunus and Grameen Bank faced many of the same questions that traditional banks asked their clients. The question of what could be done to ensure repayment of a loan was one of the most significant hurdles to overcome. Another was the set of criteria on which lending decisions should be based. Under normal circumstances banks demanded some form of collateral or security. If a borrower defaulted on a loan the bank could repossess and monetize the collateral in an effort to recover the money they

loaned. Yet the vast majority of Yunus's clients had no such creditworthiness, so he devised a system that satisfied the bank's need for security and that could ensure loan repayment while still remaining accessible even to the poorest of the poor. One of the founding principles of Grameen Bank was that credit should be considered a basic human right rather than a privilege. As such, decisions on loans would be made on a person's future potential and not on his or her material possessions.

Grameen Bank operates on a concept of *solidarity lending*. Rather than demanding collateral or a traditional guarantor in order to get a loan, no legal instrument exists between the bank and the borrower. Instead, borrowers are required to be a part of a "borrowing group," typically of around five people. Only one member of the group needs to receive the loan, but the other members serve as encouragers and if needed, a source of peer pressure for the loan to be repaid. These "guarantors" are not legally obliged to cover the loan in case of default. They are simply a means to provide a method of accountability and oversight, so that the lender makes responsible decisions with the money he or she was loaned. The responsibility for repayment then is a moral one and rests on the honor and reputation of the group.

According to some reports, in situations of nonrepayment it is common for the group members to take responsibility in repaying the owed amount even though they are not obliged to do so, with the anticipation of recovering outstanding debts from the defaulting member on their own terms in the future. The success of this system speaks for itself. Grameen Bank boasts a repayment rate of over 98 percent. This figure is also consistent with many other microfinancing projects that have come into existence all around the world since Grameen Bank's inception in the early 1980s.

Microfinancing generally charges far lower interest rates than many traditional banks and money lenders. Since microfinancing institutions are put in place to serve the poor, they are not held to the same high money-earning standards demanded by boards of directors and investors in traditional financial institutions. Grameen Bank, for instance, offered several interest rates depending on the purpose of the loan. Income-generating loans were charged a 20 percent rate, while loans for housing were only 8 percent. Student loans were 5 percent and struggling members (i.e., beggars) could obtain interest-free loans. Loans are typically repaid on a weekly schedule, but there is no binding, legal agreement between lender and borrower, meaning that payments may be delayed even if they are eventually made. This latter aspect is a commonly cited criticism of the microfinancing system.

Another unusual feature of Grameen Bank's system of microfinancing is that it provides additional benefits to its members that could vastly improve standards of living, such as products and services that are generally reserved for those with some degree of wealth. Life insurance, pension funds, education loans, and scholarships are all available for the bank's members.

THE SUCCESS AND FUTURE OF MICROFINANCE

From its humble beginnings, Grameen Bank has grown tremendously. It is completely self-sufficient and does not require infusions of money or donations in order to operate. Profits from interest-generating loans are fed back into the bank and are used to expand the bank's ability to service the community and its poorest members. In 2011 there were 2,565 branches working in 81,379 villages and employing 22,124 people. Since it began, Grameen Bank has disbursed over US$11.35 billion. In the 2010–2011 year, over a 12-month period, an average of US$123.38 million was disbursed each month. A total of 8.35 million borrowers have benefited from Yunus's achievements, 96 percent of whom were women. Since 1983 Grameen Bank has grown far beyond being just a microfinancing bank in Bangladesh. It now operates its own telecommunications arm, capital management company, fabric and fashion company, employment agency, health care company, and fisheries company, to name only a few. The Grameen Foundation does not just function in Bangladesh. It also supports microfinancing endeavors all across the Asia-Pacific region, including the Indian subcontinent; North, Central, and South America, including the United States; and several countries in Africa.

Drawing inspiration from Yunus's work, dozens of other, similar microfinancing efforts have started up around the world. Statistics provided by the World Bank estimate that over 160 million people worldwide benefit from microfinancing. In fact, microfinance has become so popular that in 2007, *Forbes.com* published the first ever "50 Top Microfinance Institutions" list. Others, such as investment bloggers and companies, have put up microfinance institution review sites for those considering supporting these institutions. Some microfinance sites such as Kiva.com, established in 2005, have become incredibly popular, drawing support from celebrities such as former U.S. President Bill Clinton, Hollywood actor Kevin Connolly, and popular music group Maroon 5.

The concept behind Kiva is taken directly from the methods of Yunus and Grameen Bank, even including solidarity lending as a means of loan security. But what differentiates Kiva is the introduction of crowdsourced funding. This is when many individuals collaborate, with each person contributing a small amount of money, to help fund a larger project. In the case of Kiva, this is as little as US$25, allowing just about any individual in the world with an Internet connection and US$25 to contribute

and take part in something of which they can feel proud. Kiva borrowers receive loans of several hundred or even several thousand U.S. dollars, which they repay on a fixed schedule. When lenders are repaid, they have the choice of feeding the money back into another Kiva loan, donating it to Kiva to be used for operating costs, or withdrawing the funds entirely. In 2011, Kiva had given over US$261 million in loans in 61 different countries, and boasted a repayment rate of 98.93 percent.

BIBLIOGRAPHY

"Biography of Professor Muhammad Yunus." Johannesburg, South Africa: Nelson Mandela Centre of Memory. Accessed January 10, 2012. http://www.nelsonmandela.org/images /uploads/Yunus_Bio_LT.pdf.

Ethirajan, Anbarasan. "Bangladesh City to Pay Beggars During Cricket World Cup." *BBC News,* January 31, 2011. Accessed January 10, 2012. http://www.bbc.co.uk/news/world-south -asia-12320172.

"Friedrich Wilhelm Raiffeisen, Brief Biography." Russia: Raiffeisen Bank. Accessed January 10, 2012. http://www .raiffeisen.ru/en/about/bankgroup/wraiffeisen/.

"Grameen at a Glance." Dhaka, Bangladesh: Grameen Bank, October 2011. Accessed January 10, 2012. http://www .grameen-info.org/index.php?option=com_content&task =view&id=26&Itemid=175.

Hammond, Claudia. "'I'm Here for Survival'." *Guardian,* January 9, 2008. Accessed January 10, 2012. http://www.guardian.co .uk/world/2008/jan/09/gender.humantrafficking.

"How GA Works." New York: Grameen America, 2012. Accessed January 10, 2012. http://www.grameenamerica.com/how-we -work/how-we-work/the-model.html.

Human Development Foundation. "Dr. Akhtar Hameed Khan: Hero of the Poor." Schaumberg, IL, June 2, 2004. Accessed January 10, 2012. http://www.yespakistan.com/ahkhan.asp.

Kiva. "Kiva: About Us." San Francisco, CA, 2012. Accessed January 10, 2012. http://www.kiva.org. Accessed January 10, 2012.

"Kiva Celebrity Supporters & Events." *Look to the Stars,* 2012. Accessed January 10, 2012. http://www.looktothestars.org /charity/613-kiva.

Mehta, Swathi. "A Report on Debt Bondage, Carpet-Making, and Child Slavery." Boston, MA: American Anti-Slavery Group, 2010. Accessed January 10, 2012. http://www .iabolish.org/index.php?option=com_content&view =article&id=184:a-report-on-debt-bondage-carpet-making -and-child-slavery-&catid=5:essays-on-slavery&Itemid=8.

"Nobel Winner Yunus: Microcredit Missionary." *Bloomberg Businessweek,* December 26, 2005. Accessed January 10, 2012. http://www.businessweek.com/magazine/content/05 _52/b3965024.htm.

Perkins, Anne. "A Short History of Microfinance." *Guardian,* June 3, 2008. Accessed January 10, 2012. http://www .guardian.co.uk/katine/2008/jun/03/livelihoods.projectgoals1.

"Profile: Muhammad Yunus, 'World's Banker to the Poor'." *BBC News,* March 2, 2011. Accessed January 10, 2012. http:// www.bbc.co.uk/news/world-south-asia-11901625.

Swibel, Matthew. "The 50 Top Microfinance Institutions."

Forbes.com, December 20, 2007. Accessed January 10, 2012. http://www.forbes.com/2007/12/20/microfinance -philanthropy-credit-biz-cz_ms_1220microfinance_table .html.

Tanneeru, Manav. "The Challenges of Counting a 'Hidden Population'." *The CNN Freedom Project,* March 9, 2011. Accessed January 10, 2012. http://thecnnfreedomproject .blogs.cnn.com/2011/03/09/slavery-numbers/.

Nano-Tex Creates Stain-resistant, Breathable Fabrics

Nano-Tex is the name of the fabric treatment technologies owned and licensed by Nano-Tex, Inc., to textile producers. Nano-Tex uses molecular engineering, polymers, and the principles of nanotechnology to control fabric design at a molecular level. The aim is to create improved clothing that looks and feels like traditional materials. Nano-Tex fabrics look like traditional fabrics but they have features such as stain resistance, fibers that wick moisture away from the body, breathability, waterproofing, wrinkle resistance, odor control, and more. Nano-Tex fabrics have a number of uses, but are perhaps most recognizable in apparel. Nordstrom, Inc., Eddie Bauer Holdings Inc., Dockers, L.L. Bean, Inc., The Gap. Inc., Old Navy, Bass Pro Shops, and many other retailers sell clothing made with Nano-Tex fabrics. Nano-Tex is also used in home textiles, mattresses, furniture upholstery, and other fabrics. The Nano-Tex company has 17 patents for its technologies, as of February 2012.

In many cases, before 1998, waterproof fabrics were created simply by laminating a waterproof fabric over an existing fabric or by coating a fabric with a rubberized surface. While these methods made a fabric temporarily waterproof, the weatherproofing could wear off and fade, especially with excessive use, use in extreme temperatures, and with washing. The fabrics treated in these ways would also usually be stiff and uncomfortable, and, in many cases, not very breathable or comfortable for the wearer. Since Nano-Tex fabrics are waterproof and stainproof at the molecular level, they remain stain-resistant and waterproof for the life of the fabric. The protection cannot be washed away. They also do not coat the fabric and still allow for a porous, breathable fabric.

HOW NANO-TEX WORKS

All Nano-Tex fabric treatments work by attaching tiny polymer hairs, sometimes called "whiskers," to every fiber of a specific fabric. The whiskers are attached with a dipping process and, once attached, stand up perpendicular to the fabric they are attached to and prevent molecules of oil and water from attaching to the fiber. The whiskers essentially create a barrier of air around the fabric, making it harder for stains and water to approach and penetrate the fabric. This makes the fabric stain-resistant, since any spills are pooled on the surface and can be brushed away. The nanotechnology component of the technology is that the whiskers are a billionth of a meter, or the size of a nanometer.

The process used for attaching the Nano-Tex whiskers to the fabric uses high heat. While Nano-Tex treatments can be used successfully with most traditional fabrics, including cotton, wool, and other fabrics, the treatments as of 2012 could not be used with olefin. Olefin is the one fabric that could not be used with Nano-Tex as the olefin fibers would melt during the treatment process.

The Nano-Tex treatment begins with the engineering of molecules. The molecules can be designed to have specific traits, such as the ability to repel oils, or the ability to repel water and moisture. Next, the molecules must be engineered in such a way that they can adhere to the surface of a fabric in a specific and precise way. In most cases, for example, the molecules need to be spaced evenly and need to be standing perpendicularly in order to have the desired effect. Nano-Tex uses a patented binding system to attach the Nano-Tex to the fabric. This binding technology ensures that the stain resistance and other attributes of the fabric will not wash away or simply wear away with time.

According to David Offord, Nano-Tex's chief scientific officer, interviewed in a 2006 article in *Contract* magazine, this ensures that Nano-Tex becomes an inherent part of the fabric at a molecular level.

Since the nanoparticles are so tiny, they do not coat the surface of the fabric. Instead, they are attached to the very fibers of the fabric. This allows the fabric to maintain its strength, natural texture, and breathability, while still offering the benefits that the tiny Nano-Tex molecules confer. Since the fabric is not heavily coated, it does not provide the heavy-duty protection of heavily rubberized fabrics. However, it can repel regular spills and water.

THE INVENTION OF NANO-TEX

David Soane, a chemical engineer, founded Nano-Tex, Inc., in 1998. In his book, *Nanotechnology 101*, John F. Mongillo wrote that Soane came up with his idea for nanoparticles for clothes when washing a peach and noticing that "on the fruit's surface, there are all these little pointed whiskers" which "prop up the liquid drops, allowing the liquid drops to roll off." In a 2004 interview in the *Daily News Record*, Soane stated, "I had a brainstorm and figured out how to change the properties of the fabrics." He also told the interviewer that he focused on nanotechnology and fabrics specifically because the area was less explored and less government regulated than other areas where nanotechnology could be applied. In addition, Soane was intrigued by some of the flaws in fabric treatments, including Scotchgard, which coated the fabric but did not become part of the material.

By 1999, he had patented the fabric treatment used for Nano-Tex. He then met with Burlington Industries executives and showed them samples of Nano-Tex fabric. George Henderson, then the CEO of Burlington, was impressed, and the company decided to mass produce Nano-Tex fabrics as well as to invest in the technology. However, Burlington Industries did not make Nano-Tex fabrics themselves. Instead, they focused on forming lucrative licensing agreements with textile mills, including mills in Asia, to make the products. Burlington also got involved in marketing the Nano-Tex products. By 2003, the company had a 51 percent investment in Nano-Tex.

At the dawn of the 21st century, Nano-Tex was facing a number of challenges, according to Jane Tanner, writing for the *New York Times*. The entire U.S. textile industry, in fact, was in trouble. By 2001, 116 U.S. textile plants had closed, eliminating approximately 13 percent of the workforce in the industry, and five major textile companies filed for bankruptcy. The U.S. textile industry was facing increased competition from Asia, especially from China and India, two countries able to produce fabrics and apparel at greatly lower prices when compared with U.S. competitors. In addition to the shaky textile industry

overall, by 2003 Burlington Industries was facing bankruptcy. In part due to the strength of the Nano-Tex brand, a number of investors offered to buy the flailing company. In 2003, Warren Buffett made a US$579 million offer for Burlington Industries. That offer was rejected by a judge, but by late that year WL Ross & Co. acquired Burlington Industries. Through this purchase WL Ross gained a large interest in Nano-Tex.

In 2002, Renee Hultin, Nano-Tex's executive vice president of marketing and business development, had a specific plan for marketing the Nano-Tex products more effectively. In the late 1990s and into the new millenium, Nano-Tex had been marketed primarily to the textile mills that could be persuaded to sign licensing agreements with Nano-Tex. In 2001 however, the company started targeting brands directly, showing them that use of Nano-Tex in their products would be beneficial. In 2002, the company started marketing directly to retailers, to convince them that they could successfully use the technology in their private in-store brands. Within a few years, Nano-Tex was appealing directly to consumers with media coverage, tags describing the benefits of Nano-Tex, a website, and other marketing efforts.

MAKING NANO-TEX A SUCCESS

In 2003, Donn Tice became the executive officer of Nano-Tex, and while the products using Nano-Tex were getting good reviews, at that time there were only 40 companies licensing the Nano-Tex product. Tice had to convince customers to pay a little more for Nano-Tex, and he had to convince more companies to license the product. He decided to do this in part by focusing on new products and developments. As Tice told the *Daily News Record* in 2004, "The remaining textile industry is spending precious little on real R&D."

Nano-Tex focused on creating new products and on ensuring that Nano-Tex made products could perform better without affecting the smell, texture, care, or durability of the product. The company also tested the products for comfort and safety. This ensured that no customers would get skin irritation from Nano-Tex-treated fabrics, for example.

Tice's strategy seemed to pay off. In 2005, Nano-Tex was expanding rapidly. Between 2004 and 2005, the company added seven positions to its management staff, including some marketing positions. In March 2005, the company received US$35 million in investments from WL Ross & Co. (already a large shareholder), Masters Capital, LLC, Norwest Venture Partners, Howard Hughes Medical Institute, and Firelake Capital Management, LLC. The money was earmarked for marketing, product development, and expansion efforts. According to a 2005 article in *WWD* magazine, Nano-Tex doubled the number of facilities and the number of products using the Nano-Tex technology between 2004 and 2005.

In 2005, the company named Wendy Riley as vice president of business development for the home furnishings department. This move marked a new focus on Nano-Tex home interiors. Starting that year, Nano-Tex came to be used for bedding, cushions, mattresses, upholstery, window treatments, table linens, and other fabrics in the home. Nano-Tex was able to make these fabrics more stain-resistant and water-resistant, appealing to customers. By 2007, both Target Corporation. and J.C. Penney Company, Inc., were selling sheet sets made with Nano-Tex fabrics. The cotton bedding felt just like cotton but provided temperature control, moisture wicking, and breathability.

CONCERNS ABOUT NANOTECHNOLOGY AND CLOTHING

Some customers have voiced concerns about Nano-Tex fabrics and products. In 2005, a group called Topless Humans Organized for Natural Genetics (THONG) spoke out against the Nano-Tex line of Eddie Bauer khakis and shirts by protesting outside of an Eddie Bauer store in Chicago, Illinois. The group argued that nanotechnology and the process of altering clothing at the molecular level could have unprecedented consequences for those who wear such clothing, and that the fabrics may be unsafe.

Some scientists have also expressed concerns about the safety of nanotechnology in clothing. According to Professor Lynn Frewer of the Marketing and Consumer Behaviour Group, based at the University of Wageningen in the Netherlands, if the whiskers or fibers get loose they may potentially be inhaled or pose other risks. According to Frewer, interviewed by juststyle.com in 2008, if the whiskers can get beyond the subcutaneous layer of the skin they can penetrate the body. The Natural Resources Defense Council has also criticized the growing use of nanoparticles in various everyday products. In the past, nanoparticles were often enclosed in appliances or devices, but there is some concern in the scientific community that the new nanoparticles are not enclosed and are becoming more a part of everyday life.

A number of calls for studies have been made, and the European Chemical Industry Council (CEFIC) and other organizations have begun to study the use of nanoparticles in clothes as well as other consumer materials. Among the questions scientists are exploring is whether the nanoparticles can enter the human body, and especially the human cell. Researchers have also explored whether nanoparticles detach during washing and regular wear and whether detached nanoparticles have an impact on the environment or on sewage and water systems. In the United States, The National Nanotechnology Initiative was launched in 2000 to study nanotoxicology and the toxicity of nanoparticles. However, despite research, no conclusive link between nanoparticles and serious health effects had been found by 2012. With no verified health concerns and all the benefits the technology promises, nanoparticles have become a hot market in the 2010s. According to the National Science Foundation, nanotechnology is expected to be a US$1 trillion business by 2015.

NANO-TEX TECHNOLOGIES

Nano-Tex, Inc., produces a number of fabric treatments. Among them is Nano-Dry, which makes fabrics wrinkle-resistant and stain-resistant. The treatment will not wash out with repeated use, wear, or dry cleaning. Nano-Dry is a wicking technology that draws moisture away from the fabric. Other Nano-Tex fabric treatments include Nano-Care for cotton and Nano-Pel, which is specifically for synthetics and wool fabrics.

Nano-Tex Resists uses nanowhiskers to prevent static cling and also to keep pet hair as well as lint off clothing. Nano-Tex Neutralizer is designed to trap odor molecules and hold them rather than releasing them into the air. According to Nano-Tex, the molecules are trapped until the garment is washed, creating an odor-controlling fabric. Nano-Tex + BioAM, used mostly in health care settings, contains antimicrobial treatment to control any microorganisms, including bacteria, that can cause odors.

In 2010 and 2011, Nano-Tex announced a number of new products. For example, in 2010, the company launched All Conditions, Repels Water, and Speed Dry. All Conditions was specifically designed for outdoor wear, providing wearers with rain resistance and weatherproofing as well as breathability. Speed Dry was designed for rapid drying, promising to dry 50 percent faster than traditional fabrics. The technology was used in active wear and swimwear for use in chlorine water, fresh water, and salt water. Repels Water was designed for awnings, outdoor furniture, and other fabrics designed to be placed outdoors. The technology made fabrics more rugged and repelled water. That same year, Nano-Tex opened a research and development center in China to develop new products and to attract new scientists to its research and development teams.

In 2011, the company launched Aquapel, a fabric technology that used a hydrocarbon (a compound consisting entirely of hydrogen and carbon) polymer, rather than the fluorocarbon (a compound containing only carbon and fluorine) polymer usually used in many Nano-Tex products. The change allowed fabrics and the process to be more ecologically conscious, according to the company, but still provided breathable, wickable, and moisture-resistant clothing comparable to the rest of the Nano-Tex line.

According to a 2011 article in *Apparel Online,* the new process did not leave clothes resistant to oil and alcohol, however.

Nano-Tex also produced Nano-Touch, a fabric treatment that promised to make synthetic fabrics as soft and touchable as cotton while allowing them to retain the strength and durability of a synthetic material. In 2011, Nano-Tex announced the release of its Fortify DP technology, which penetrated the fabric in order to make fabrics wrinkle-resistant. According to a 2011 article in juststyle.com, the Nano-Tex wrinkle treatment was different from traditional treatments, which were so harsh that they reduced the strength of the fabric. Traditional treatments also usually required fabric manufacturers to strengthen the material being treated and made it impossible for some lighter materials to be treated. Since Nano-Tex relied on nanowhiskers to provide wrinkle resistance, thin fabrics could be used, and the treatment did not affect the strength or the comfort of the fabric. According to the juststyle.com article, the Fortify DP technology made use of "a longer and more flexible crosslinking chain" to ensure that fabrics were just as strong after treatment.

WHAT MAKES NANO-TEX A SUCCESS?

The success story of Nano-Tex, both the fabric and the company, shows that in many cases the simplest ideas can be the most successful. Built on the idea that peach fuzz causes water to bead up and roll off the fruit, Nano-Tex has become a highly successful private company. As a private company, Nano-Tex has consistently refused to disclose financial details, but close relationships with companies such as The Gap and the Donna Karan Company certainly suggest a profitable company. Nano-Tex releases new products and announces new partnerships and licensing agreements annually.

When Nano-Tex was first developed it marketed exclusively to textile mills, but since has expanded to market to others in the production chain, all the way to the end consumer. Nano-Tex was able to position its products, through this marketing strategy, in stores such as Eddie Bauer and J.C. Penney. These were stores that customers already trusted and visited, ensuring good product placement for visibility.

Investment in research and development made Nano-Tex stand out from other companies in the textile industry and allowed the company to develop new products that appealed to the customer. The company was able to offer the promise of affordable, stain-resistant, breathable fabrics that meant less care and work for consumers worldwide. That combination proved to be extremely attractive to buyers.

BIBLIOGRAPHY

Barrie, Leonie. "US: Nano-Tex Develops New Wrinkle Free Treatment." just-style.com, September 29, 2011. Accessed January 21, 2012. http://www.just-style.com/news/nano-tex -develops-new-wrinkle-free-treatment_id112301.aspx.

Bellah, John. "What's New in Uniforms." *Law & Order,* October 2002, 34.

Cornell, Susan. "Uniform Fabric: Terminology and Technology." *Law & Order,* May 2003, 64.

Eisenberg, Anne. "The Chemist's Find: A Way to Shrug Off Spills." *New York Times,* August 27, 2006. Accessed January 20, 2012. http://www.nytimes.com/2006/08/27/business /yourmoney/27novel.html?_r=1&scp=1&sq=chemist&st=nyt.

"Fluorocarbon-Free Finish by Nano-Tex, Perfect for Work-Wear." *Apparel Online,* September 1, 2011. Gale Virtual Reference Library (GALE|A265914504). Accessed January 21, 2012. http://go.galegroup.com/ps/i.do?id=GALE%7CA265914504 &v=2.1&u=itsbtrial&it=r&p=GPS&sw=w.

Galadza, Sofia. "Nano First: Innovative Technology That Made a Splash in the Apparel Market Finds Its Way into the Commercial Interiors Arena." *Contract,* May 2006. Gale Virtual Reference Library (GALE|A146344193). Accessed January 21, 2012. http://go.galegroup.com/ps/i.do?id=GALE %7CA146344193&v=2.1&u=itsbtrial&it=r&p=GPS&sw=w.

Greene, Joshua. "Textile Firms Try to Reel in Consumers." *WWD,* September 17, 2002. Gale Virtual Reference Library (GALE|A93460857). Accessed January 21, 2012. http:// go.galegroup.com/ps/i.do?id=GALE%7CA93460857&v=2.1 &u=itsbtrial&it=r&p=GPS&sw=w.

Malone, Scott. "Burlington Gets Small: Makes Breakthrough In Nanotechnology." *WWD,* June 29, 2000. Gale Virtual Reference Library (GALE|A63511917). Accessed January 21, 2012. http://go.galegroup.com/ps/i.do?id=GALE%7CA6351 1917&v=2.1&u=itsbtrial&it=r&p=GPS&sw=w.

Mongillo, John F. *Nanotechnology 101.* Westport, CT: Greenwood Press, 2007, 128

Moyer, Michael. "Protesting High-Tech Trousers." *Popular Science,* August 2005, 98.

Nagappan, Padma. "Nanotechnology: Burlington's New Avenue for Revenue." *Bobbin,* November 2002. Gale Virtual Reference Library (GALE|A94264654). Accessed January 21, 2012. http://go.galegroup.com/ps/i.do?id=GALE%7CA9426 4654&v=2.1&u=itsbtrial&it=r&p=GPS&sw=w.

"Nanoparticles in Clothing: How Safe Are They?" just-style.com, November 13, 2008. Gale Virtual Reference Library. Accessed January 21, 2012. http://go.galegroup.com/ps/i.do?id=GALE %7CA188909343&v=2.1&u=itsbtrial&it=r&p=GPS&sw=w.

Nano-Tex. "About Us." Oakland, CA, 2012. Accessed January 20, 2012. http://www.nanotex.com/company/aboutus.html.

"Nano-Tex Introduces Performance Bed Sheets." *Apparel,* February 2007. Gale Virtual Reference Library (GALE|A159644637). Accessed January 21, 2012. http:// go.galegroup.com/ps/i.do?id=GALE%7CA159644637&v=2 .1&u=itsbtrial&it=r&p=GPS&sw=w.

"Nano-Tex Introduces Three New Repellency Innovations." *Apparel,* June 2010. Gale Virtual Reference Library (GALE|A230256460). Accessed January 21, 2012. http:// go.galegroup.com/ps/i.do?id=GALE%7CA230256460&v=2 .1&u=itsbtrial&it=r&p=GPS&sw=w.

"Nano-Tex to Open R&D Center in China." *Nonwovens Industry,* January 2010. Gale Virtual Reference Library (GALE|A217063617). Accessed January 21, 2012. http://go.galegroup.com/ps/i.do?id=GALE%7CA217063617&v=2.1&u=itsbtrial&it=r&p=GPS&sw=w.

"The Next Small Thing; Taking Fabric Innovation Down to the Molecular Level, Nano-Tex Builds Market Share . . . and Repels Stains." *Daily News Record,* March 22, 2004. Gale Virtual Reference Library (GALE|A114605008). Accessed January 21, 2012. http://go.galegroup.com/ps/i.do?id=GALE%7CA114605008&v=2.1&u=itsbtrial&it=r&p=GPS&sw=w.

Robertson, Campbell. "Responsible Party/Dr. David Soane; Armor against Stains." *New York Times,* October 13, 2002. Accessed January 20, 2012. http://www.nytimes.com/2002/10/13/business/responsible-party-dr-david-soane-armor-against-stains.html?scp=1&sq=%22Nano-Tex%22&st=cse.

Sloan, Carole. "Riley Joins Nano-Tex." *Home Textiles Today,* September 5, 2005. Gale Virtual Reference Library (GALE|A136121237). Accessed January 21, 2012. http://go.galegroup.com/ps/i.do?id=GALE%7CA136121237&v=2.1&u=itsbtrial&it=r&p=GPS&sw=w.

Tanner, Jane. "Business; A Bet on Textiles, Despite the Doomsayers." *New York Times,* May 11, 2003. Accessed January 20, 2012. http://www.nytimes.com/2003/05/11/business/business-a-bet-on-textiles-despite-the-doomsayers.html?scp=2&sq=.

Tucker, Ross. "Nano-Tex Adds Executives for North American Push." *WWD,* August 9, 2005. Gale Virtual Reference Library (GALE|A135006148). Accessed January 21, 2012. http://go.galegroup.com/ps/i.do?id=GALE%7CA135006148&v=2.1&u=itsbtrial&it=r&p=GPS&sw=w.

Williams, Court. "Good Chemistry." *WWD,* December 4, 2007. Gale Virtual Reference Library (GALE|A172527211). Accessed January 21, 2012. http://go.galegroup.com/ps/i.do?id=GALE%7CA172527211&v=2.1&u=itsbtrial&it=r&p=GPS&sw=w.

NASCAR: Growing Fan Base Builds Marketing Opportunities

The National Association for Stock Car Auto Racing (NASCAR) is an organization that oversees and authorizes car racing events. NASCAR drivers have become celebrities, earning millions of U.S. dollars as well as lucrative advertising contracts. NASCAR events and even practices are televised and the events draw millions of spectators. According to *Contemporary Sport Management*, NASCAR has a fan base of 75 million individuals.

NASCAR races take part on four basic types of tracks: superspeedways, speedways, short tracks, and road courses. Superspeedways are banked high and are longer in length than speedways, allowing for maximum speeds. Speedways are ovals of one to 2.5 miles in length, while short tracks are less than one mile. Road courses have twists and turns, much like country roads.

NASCAR has national, regional, and local series. The organization also has two international series: The NASCAR Canadian Tire and the NASCAR Mexico Series. The three national NASCAR series are the NASCAR Sprint Cup Series, the NASCAR Nationwide Series, and the NASCAR Camping World Truck Series. The NASCAR Sprint Cup Series includes 36 points races while the NASCAR Nationwide Series is a 34-race series that includes an international race in Canada. The NASCAR Camping World Truck Series is designed for full-sized trucks.

NASCAR regional and local series include the NASCAR K&N Pro Series, the NASCAR Whelen Modified Tour, the NASCAR Whelen Southern Modified Tour, and the NASCAR Whelen All-American Series. The NASCAR K&N Pro Series is considered the most prestigious series at the regional and local level, with racing in the eastern and western United States. The NASCAR Whelen Modified Tour is the only open-wheel NASCAR division and is also the oldest NASCAR division. The NASCAR Whelen Southern Modified Tour is based in the southwestern United States, while the NASCAR Whelen All-American Series is held in the United States and Canada.

In addition to being sporting events, major NASCAR events have become a form of entertainment for spectators. NASCAR Sprint Cup Series events, for example, which are arguably the most prestigious of NASCAR events and are among the best advertised, usually take place over several days, even though the NASCAR Sprint Cup Series race itself may only last a few hours. Fans often arrive well in advance of the racing events to take part in tailgate parties and other entertainment staged by fans and event organizers. Practices are held a few days before the race itself and are intended to help drivers get used to the course and determine any car repairs they may need before the race. Qualifying rounds are held on days before the race to determine which cars will be used in a race and the order in which cars will be raced.

NASCAR'S HUMBLE BEGINNINGS

NASCAR did not start out as a huge organization. Initially, it was a very loosely organized group of car enthusiasts who raced each other on weekends. The early history of NASCAR is closely linked to the history of the U.S. South, according to some historians. In the 1920s and 1930s, illegal sales of alcohol in the South made speeding cars not just a pastime, but a business necessity. O. C. Ferrell and Michael Hartline, in their book, *Marketing Strategy*, note that the moonshine connection is likely "overemphasized." Nevertheless, the idea of the moonshine bootlegger modifying a car and racing to escape the long arm of the law was a popular motif in early racing history.

Early races in the South, before NASCAR, often involved drivers racing their own modified cars around an unofficial, rough track. Track owners determined most of the racing rules, including the prizes race winners could earn and when the races would take place. There were few safety measures for racers. In the 1940s, in Daytona Beach, Florida, there were also races along soft and packed sand. Eventually, the racing groups in Daytona Beach, Florida and the racing groups in the South organized and joined together to form NASCAR.

William Henry France, more popularly known as "Big" Bill France, is credited with bringing the various racing parties together under one organization. France worked at a car dealership but in his spare time during the 1930s and into the 1940s, he raced cars in Daytona Beach, Florida. Like many drivers, he was unhappy with the conditions that racers faced. France was also unhappy with the low amount of money that race car drivers were getting and felt that the races were poorly organized. Since races were held across many U.S. states in the South and were organized in different ways by different track owners, there was no consensus about who the best drivers were. France's objections were echoed by many fellow racers.

In 1947 France met with a group of drivers, car owners, and mechanics at the Streamline Hotel in Daytona Beach, Florida to create a new racing organization. Over a few days, the group created new rules and outlined the basis for a professional stock car association that France hoped would make the sport lucrative and respected. They called the new group the National Association for Stock Car Auto Racing and elected France as the CEO and president. Through 2012, NASCAR has remained a family run business, managed largely by the France family. After Bill France left NASCAR in 1972, his son took over as CEO and president, and in 2003, Bill France' grandson Brian France became NASCAR CEO.

NASCAR was incorporated on February 21, 1948. By 1948, the first NASCAR races took place. The first NASCAR race, won by Red Byron, was held on February 15, 1948. In most of these races, drivers raced cars that they had modified for speed.

By 1949, the group organized larger car races all under one set of NASCAR rules and regulations. Rather than the different rules determined by different track owners, all drivers racing at NASCAR events earned points for each of the races they completed. The points received depended on how well a driver finished a race. At the end of the season, the driver who accumulated the highest number of points would be named the winner, or the "Grand National" winner. The first Grand National champion was Red Byron.

NASCAR'S EARLY YEARS

By the late 1940s, race car driving (and NASCAR) was popular in the South, attracting large audiences. Once NASCAR was established and races were organized by the group, the next step was to build better and larger race tracks. The tracks served several purposes. They attracted more fans, who could now sit in larger seating areas. In addition, the turns of the new racetracks featured higher banking, which allowed drivers to maintain higher speeds at the turns. The first racetrack built in this manner was the Darlington Raceway in South Carolina. Opened in 1950, it had paved asphalt and two kilometers (1.25 miles) of track for racing, making it the largest speedway in the United States at the time.

By 1959 the Daytona International Speedway opened. This venue had more accommodations for fans as well as a 2.5-mile paved track and an enclosure. By 1969, France had opened Alabama's Talladega Speedway, a 2.7-mile oval track.

In the early 1950s, NASCAR took an important step by creating sponsorship deals with car makers such as Chrysler Corporation, Ford Motor Company, and General Motors Company (GM). The step gave NASCAR more money and car dealers were convinced that sponsorship of the races would lead to better car sales. According to Ferrell and Hartline, car manufacturers believed that when their cars won it would improve sales. Many car companies adopted the motto "Win on Sunday, Sell on Monday."

BIG MEDIA SUCCESS

In the 1970s, NASCAR's success increased, and the reasons were simple: sponsors and television. The first NASCAR race fully broadcast on television was the 1979 Daytona 500. There were 120,000 fans in the stands that day at the track and millions of U.S. viewers tuned into the race on television. It was an auspicious race to broadcast because it was full of drama. Donnie Allison, Dale Earnhardt, A. J. Foyt, Cale Yarborough, and Richard Petty all led the pack at various times during the race. In the final lap, Allison and Yarborough were in front when Yarborough attempted to pass. The pass resulted in a collision and Petty won the race. Yarborough and Allison's brother got into a fight after the race.

By the 1980s, all NASCAR Premier Series races were broadcast on television. This was important for two main reasons. First, it allowed more people to watch the event. Second, wider television broadcasting meant that fans could develop loyalty to drivers that they could watch regularly. Early racing celebrities such as Dale Earnhardt became celebrities as fans across the United States watched the drivers race and tuned in to see their favorite driver.

Sponsorship also became increasingly important for NASCAR beginning in the 1970s when the organization looked beyond auto makers as a source of sponsorship dollars. NASCAR created branding sponsorships and partnerships with R.J. Reynolds Tobacco Company, The Goodyear Tire and Rubber Company, and gasoline station chain Union 76. Sponsorship was a familiar phenomenon to racing fans by the 1990s, but it was quite new in the 1970s. Sponsorship was closely tied in with television. Since more fans were watching the sport, companies could advertise to larger audiences using sponsorship.

THE 1990S: MORE FANS

While the number of fans watching NASCAR events had been growing since the 1940s, the number of spectators jumped in the 1990s. According to Ferrell and Hartline, between 1993 and 2002 the number of U.S. citizens watching NASCAR races on television grew 48 percent and "by 2006 about 6 percent of U.S. households watched NASCAR races on television." Part of the trend was due to more widespread television coverage of NASCAR races. According to *Contemporary Sport Management,* by the late 1970s the American Broadcasting Company (ABC) aired race highlights and the Daytona 500 was the only race to be shown fully on television. By the 1990s, however, 28 Winston Cup series events were shown by major networks, including Turner Broadcasting System (TBS), Entertainment and Sports Programming Network (ESPN), and The Nashville Network (TNN).

A number of factors contributed to the spectator boom. By 1995, NASCAR had a number of branding partnerships, which generated revenue for marketing and advertising. As part of marketing efforts that year, NASCAR launched an interactive website, allowing fans to interact more with the sport and with other fans. According to the website NASCAR.com, the site received seven million unique visitors monthly as of 2012.

Another major change in NASCAR in the 1990s was the introduction of female competitors. Racers such as Kelly Sutton, Tina Gordon, and other women helped NASCAR entice a new fan demographic. According to Ferrell and Hartline, this change ensured that 40 percent of the NASCAR fan base was female. According to *Contemporary Sport Management,* the fastest-growing demographic of the 2004 Nextel Cup Series in terms of a television audience was young women.

NASCAR used a number of techniques to attract a female audience. For example, television shows such as *NASCAR Drivers: 360* focused not only on the sport but also on human interest pieces. In addition, NASCAR also ensured that there were fan items available for female spectators at fan events, including tank tops, shorts, and hats designed specifically for female fans.

THE 21ST CENTURY AND BEYOND: NEW CHALLENGES AND OPPORTUNITIES

By 2000, according to Contemporary Sport Management, corporate sponsorship became a major avenue for NASCAR to make money and a major way for sponsors to obtain valuable advertising. By 2005, primary sponsors were paying US$15 million to US$20 million to sponsor a racing team with NASCAR. In return, primary sponsors could place a prominent logo on team cars and could use drivers to endorse their product. Secondary sponsorship cost US$500,000 to US$1 million that same year and would ensure a bumper sticker on the car as well as suit patches on the drivers. By 2005, NASCAR had 42 official sponsors, generating sponsorship revenues of US$3.7 billion.

In addition to sponsorship dollars, NASCAR also increased revenues by charging track owners for the opportunity to host a NASCAR event. According to Robert G. Hagstrom's book, *The NASCAR Way: The Business That Drives the Sport,* NASCAR has built a lucrative licensing business, licensing the NASCAR name to companies willing to establish NASCAR entertainment parks, restaurants, publications, merchandise, stores, and other business ventures. In addition, companies can rent spaces at corporate hospitality tents at NASCAR events, can sponsor special awards, and can advertise at NASCAR events.

While the first decade of the 21st century was a lucrative time for NASCAR, concerns were raised about the safety of races. In 2001, NASCAR driver Dale Earnhardt, Sr., was killed during the Daytona 500 when his car plowed into a wall on the final turn. Earnhardt's death was the subject of a NASCAR inquiry and an official police investigation. As a result of the accident, NASCAR made a number of changes to its tracks to make walls safer and also made it mandatory for drivers to wear head and neck support (HANS) devices which can help prevent brain injuries in an accident. The debates about safety also led many teams to implement voluntary changes to keep drivers safer.

In 2012, NASCAR faced a number of new challenges and opportunities. For example, the organization announced that in the future, when drivers were penalized with fines, it would no longer keep that fact secret from the public. The move may have been a reaction to undisclosed fines issued to driver Denny Hamlin in 2010. When it was revealed in the media that Hamlin had allegedly been fined over some comments he had made via Twitter, NASCAR received criticism in the press over its handling of the matter. In late January 2012, NASCAR announced that it would publicly announce all fines against NASCAR event participants and organizations.

In 2010, a report by Sean Gregory in *TIME* magazine highlighted some of the economic woes NASCAR was facing as a result of the sluggish economy. According to Gregory, attendance at NASCAR events dropped 10 percent in 2009. Even television viewing of Sprint Cup races dropped 25 percent on major television networks. The drop in fan attendance and viewership also led to a decrease in sponsorship dollars. While Gregory noted that NASCAR fared better in 2010 than most sports, he also noted that many fans were finding the sport boring, especially as the organization struggled to balance concerns about safety with fan expectations of a high-adrenaline sport.

Despite the challenges, however, NASCAR was well ahead of competitors in 2012. In a 2012 article in Toronto's *Globe and Mail,* Jeff Pappone noted that NASCAR had "40-million hard core fans" in 2012, despite the allegations made by some experts that the technology of the races did not match Formula One (F1) open-wheel racing. Pappone noted, however, "NASCAR is the second-most watched sport in the U.S. behind the National Football League, while F1 battles with championship darts for TV ratings."

From early dirt-road races in the U.S. South, NASCAR grew from a small organization designed to organize the sport under one set of rules into the second most popular sport in the United States. Still a family organization, NASCAR has judiciously used sponsorship dollars and television exposure to create a racing empire. From building race venues that could seat hundreds of thousands of fans to televising NASCAR events, NASCAR has made it easy for fans to enjoy the sport. By attracting large audiences, NASCAR has been able to attract sponsors and advertising revenues.

BIBLIOGRAPHY

"Auto Racing: NASCAR Will No Longer Keep Fines Under Wraps." *Arizona Daily Star,* January 26, 2012. Accessed January 27, 2012. http://azstarnet.com/sports/motor-sports/auto-racing-nascar-will-no-longer-keep-fines-under-wraps/article_4ef23ab2-e79c-56b3-adf3-9bfcc730cd49.html#ixzz1kbURSd8l.

Ferrell, O. C., and Michael Hartline. *Marketing Strategy.* 5th ed. Mason, OH: South-West Cengage Learning, 2011, 415–416.

Goff, Brian. *From the Ballfield to the Boardroom: Management Lessons from Sports.* Westport, CT: Praeger, 2005, 45–75.

Gregory, Sean. "NASCAR: A Once Hot Sport Tries to Restart Its Engine." *TIME,* April 26, 2010. Accessed January 26, 2012. http://www.time.com/time/magazine/article/0,9171,1982299,00.html#ixzz1kh8ZWPXT.

Hagstrom, Robert G. *The NASCAR Way. The Business That Drives the Sport.* Hoboken, NJ: John Wiley & Sons, 1998, 13.

Howell, Mark D. *From Moonshine to Madison Avenue: A Cultural History of the NASCAR Winston Cup Series.* Bowling Green, OH: Bowling Green State University Popular Press, 1997.

NASCAR. "NASCAR 101." Daytona Beach, FL, 2012. Accessed January 26, 2012. http://www.nascar.com/kyn/.

Pappone, Jeff. NASCAR's Fan-Pleasing Formula Beats F1's Technology." *Globe and Mail,* January 23, 2012. Accessed January 26, 2012. http://www.theglobeandmail.com/globe-drive/nascars-fan-pleasing-formula-beats-f1s-technology/article2311888/?utm_medium=Feeds%3A%20RSS%2FAtom&utm_source=Home&utm_content=2311888.

Parks, Janet B., Jerome Quarterman, and Lucie Thibault, eds. *Contemporary Sport Management,* 3rd ed. Champaign, IL: Human Kinetics, 2007, 237–295.

Netflix, Inc., Disrupts the Traditional U.S. Movie Rental Market

BREAKING INTO THE MOVIE RENTAL BUSINESS

Netflix, Inc., is a DVD rental and online video company. Founded in 1997 by Marc Randolph and Reed Hastings, the company initially distributed DVDs via mail. Rather than choosing movies by going to a brick-and-mortar store, customers only needed to peruse Netflix.com's offerings online, which entailed a completely different user experience. Under Hastings' deft leadership, the company quickly became a leader in the entertainment retail industry, outflanking competitors such as Blockbuster LLC and Wal-Mart Stores, Inc. When Netflix began to offer streaming services in 2008, it met with even more formidable competition. By 2011, only 14 years after its inception, the company vied for market share with media companies such as HBO and Time Warner, which revised their infrastructure and business models to respond to the upstart.

In 1997 when Netflix was founded, established DVD rental and sales outlets, such as Blockbuster and Movie Gallery, were leading a seemingly mature market in the United States. The territory of the rental market was divvied up among geographical boundaries, and store locations marked that territory. Blockbuster was the clear winner. According to an article in the *Journal of Industrial Economics* by James Dana, Jr., and Kathryn Spier, the movie rental industry grew to an estimated US$8.1 billion in revenue in 1999. There were roughly 3.1 billion rental transactions each year, and between 25,000 and 30,000 outlets in the United States. Blockbuster had 4,790 stores and claimed 30 percent of industry revenues. True to its name, Blockbuster emphasized extensive inventories of the latest, most sought-after releases. Whereas other national chains charged US$3.32 per rental and had a 60 percent chance of having the video their customers wanted, Blockbuster charged US$3.81 per rental and boasted an 86 percent chance of having the desired video in stock. A rental company's ability to match the ebbs and flows of U.S. consumer demand was directly correlated to the value of its products.

DVD technology changed the rules of the game. Although the new format became available in the spring of 1997, rental companies were slow to adopt it. DVD players were too expensive for most people in the United States, and there were only an estimated 1,000 titles available for distribution. With a firm belief that DVDs would dominate videos in the future, Marc Randolph and Reed Hastings aggressively seized the opportunity. In August 1997, they founded Netflix, a company that took advantage of the lightweight portability of the DVD by offering movie rentals by mail.

The company experimented with over 200 potential mailing packages before arriving on a reuseable envelope that contained both the DVD and the return mailing label. The package, DVD included, was light enough to warrant only one U.S. first-class stamp. Customers could sort through movie selections by using Netflix.com, choose the item they wanted to see, and the DVD of that item would arrive within days. By setting up its storefront online and disbursing videos through the mail, the company was able to keep initial costs to a minimum. Netflix opened for business in April 1998, with 30 employees and a 925-title catalogue. Rentals cost US$4 with US$2 for shipping, which was more expensive than Blockbuster, but the service was new, exciting, and high tech. Within 48 hours of opening, Netflix.com was shut down by an unexpectedly large influx of traffic; it was an auspicious beginning.

SUBSCRIPTION-BASED PAYMENT AND CINEMATCH

Netflix quickly differentiated itself from the competition. In late 1999 Netflix adopted its subscription payment system. Rather than ask for US$6 per DVD, it started charging a monthly fee for access to the entire Netflix catalogue. Customers simply chose what titles they wanted, and the movies were sent to their address. Around the same time, former MGM Studios, Inc. executive and CEO of the Screen Actor's Guild, Bob Pisano, became a member of the Netflix board of trustees, giving the company access to the U.S. moviemaking industry.

Over the following year, Netflix secured a number of agreements with studios, which added volumes of titles to its increasing collection. The vast majority of these deals were revenue-sharing agreements. Netflix purchased the DVDs at cost and then distributed funds whenever the title was rented. (Blockbuster had successfully pioneered this model with VHS videotapes.) Sharing revenues for rentals allowed the company to purchase more copies of a film and offer them as rentals during periods of increased demand. In their 2001 case study of the video rental industry published in the *Journal of Industrial Economics,* Dana and Spier concluded: "Unlike two-part tariffs, revenue sharing achieves the first best outcome by softening retail price competition without distorting retailers' inventory decisions." Rental companies could afford to keep more movies in stock, allowing more U.S. customers to rent what they wanted when they wanted it.

Netflix's subscription-based model made the adoption of revenue sharing extraordinary, because the company was not being paid directly for each DVD it rented, although it paid suppliers for each rental. With a few tweaks, the company was able to adopt a useful practice from its competition while still differentiating its product on the user end. Another such tweak came in 2000, when the company unrolled the Cinematch system. At no extra cost to the consumer, Cinematch automatically kept track of the movies customers rented. Customers could choose to rate what they had seen, and then the system made suggestions based on previous selections and user ratings. Not only did this make the experience more personalized, it also encouraged customers to explore Netflix's collection more deeply. As Jeffrey O'Brien noted in *Wired,* "CineMatch doesn't focus on the mass market; it caters to the individual. . . . Such customization is foreign to Blockbuster, which has a massive database of rental data and no idea which films customers enjoy." Since Netflix's customers paid a monthly fee, Cinematch came off as a service designed solely for the user's enjoyment.

MANEUVERING PAST BLOCKBUSTER AND WAL-MART

By the time Hastings took the company public in early 2002, Netflix was positioned for success. With 500,000 subscriptions, the company had numerous distribution centers near Los Angeles, California and Boston, Massachusetts. It was not yet profitable, but with US$74.3 million in revenue, roughly US$95 million in expenses in 2001, and an accelerating subscription rate, it had attracted significant attention from investors. In May 2002, Netflix held its initial public offering (IPO) which earned US$82.5 million. It quickly used the income to expand. Distribution centers opened in Atlanta, Georgia; New York, New York; Seattle, Washington; Washington, D.C.; Denver, Colorado; Detroit, Michigan; and Houston, Texas. By December Hastings was quite confident about the company's prospects, telling *Wired's* O'Brien, "The dream 20 years from now is to have a global entertainment distribution company that provides a unique channel for film producers and studios. . . .Starbucks is a great example. . . .As Starbucks is for coffee, Netflix is for movies."

After the IPO brought Netflix from regional to national U.S. markets, the company began to face national and even multinational competition. Under two percent of the US$8 billion in video rental revenues in 2002 belonged to Hastings' company, but there was plenty of evidence of its growing clout. Its inventive business model and growth rate were impressive, and achieving national distribution in less than four years was another sign that its competitors needed to be concerned.

Alarmed by the potential impact Netflix could have on its rental sales, Blockbuster began to strategize an effective counter. It tried an in-store subscription service with unlimited rentals in order to take away a competitive advantage, and it bought another DVD movie rental company as well. In the same year, Wal-Mart also tried to beat Hastings at his own game. It began its own DVD rental program in early 2003, offering a 12,000-DVD catalogue at a rate that undercut the small company's price by US$1. The competition was staunch enough to scare off some Netflix shareholders, and stock value halved. Nonetheless, the company continued to open more distribution centers in major metropolitan areas across the United States, increasing subscribers to one million by February 2003. In contrast, Wal-Mart's DVD program did not gain significant traction in the marketplace. By 2005 Wal-Mart decided to cut its losses and closed the program. It even referred its clientele to the Netflix website, in exchange for video-purchase referrals from Netflix. Having successfully navigated some of the fiercest competition in the movie rental industry, Netflix fared well during the first decade of the 21st century. One competitor capitulated and turned ally. The other, Blockbuster, filed for bankruptcy in 2010.

THE UNSTEADY TRANSITION TO ONLINE STREAMING

Before Netflix had a chance to enjoy its well-earned success, technological progress forced the company to turn its attention from DVDs to online streaming. The company achieved early success by positioning itself for the upsurge of DVD technology. In 2007 online streaming of movies began to emerge as the growing trend, due to superiority in convenience and portability. Broadband access was the largest obstacle to streaming, but such access was becoming standard in homes in the United States. The rise of mobile devices allowed many users to view media from the car, the train, home, or work, and as these technologies were popularized, online streaming became the consumer choice. By 2010 an estimated 12 percent of purchased television sets came with Internet connections, and this figure was projected to continue to rise steeply.

In anticipation of the trend, Netflix and other major television networks were forced to reposition themselves as online streaming sites. Not one to delay, Hastings was at the forefront, enabling a "Watch Now" option that was available for both Macs and PCs by 2008. Over the course of the next three years, the company forged deals with Microsoft Corporation, Apple Inc., and Google Inc., making its interface standard on the Xbox 360 gaming console, the Apple TV digital media receiver, and the Google Television software platform.

Acquiring content licenses for online streaming proved to be a more significant problem. There were not the same standards for sharing revenues on an as-watched basis, and Netflix was forced to spend massive amounts of capital in order to stay competitive. As the market entrant, Netflix was at a disadvantage, and content was expensive. Nonetheless, the company aggressively reached for prized content. A deal with Starz in 2008 provided rights to the Walt Disney Company and Sony Corporation. In 2010 the company signed a contract for Paramount, MGM, and Lion's Gate Films, at a cost of US$900 million over five years. In 2011 Hastings acquired rights of a new series, called *House of Cards,* in which Kevin Spacey was slated to play a leading role. In May, a Sandvine study, as noted by Richard Lawler in *engadget,* reported that Netflix comprised an estimated 22 percent of total Internet bandwidth usage in North America. In the summer of 2011 stock reached an all-time high of nearly US$300 per share.

However, in September 2011, the Starz deal fell through. The media company hiked up its asking price by an estimated 1,000 percent, and Hastings refused to pay. Around the same time, Hulu LLC entered the arena with its new subscription plan for Hulu Plus. Owned by NBCUniversal Media, the Walt Disney Company, and News Corporation, Hulu was a newcomer to the market with industry connections. In addition, earlier that year Netflix announced that it was planning to separate its subscription plan, which included both DVD rental and online streaming, into two separate services, each with its own price. The decision cost the company a portion of its 25 million subscriptions, and declining subscribers became another cause for investor concern. As Hulu Plus took off over the summer of 2011, Netflix, Inc.'s stock prices declined. By December 2011, stock was valued near US$70, less than 25 percent of its worth just five months prior.

POTENTIAL AND VOLATILITY

Netflix, Inc., exemplifies the reason for investing in leaders, not ideas. Although there were plenty of companies that attempted to take advantage of DVD technology in the late 1990s, Hastings successfully carved out a new niche. Subscription-based fees and Cinematch allowed Netflix to sail past regional and even national competitors in the United States. In addition, day-to-day management decisions played a large part. Putting Bob Pisano on the board of trustees, for example, and convincing Wal-Mart to give Netflix referrals, helped to propel Netflix to the remarkable success it achieved.

BIBLIOGRAPHY

Dana, James D. Jr., and Kathryn E. Spier. "Revenue Sharing and Vertical Control of the Rental Industry." *Journal of Industrial Economics* 49, no. 3 (2001): 223–245. Accessed December 12, 2011. http://www.law.harvard.edu/faculty/spier/pdf/revenuesharingjie.pdf.

Fritz, Ben, and Claudia Eller. "Netflix and Epix Working on Major Digital Partnership to Shake Up Pay TV Landscape." *Los Angeles Times,* August 9, 2010. Accessed December 12, 2011. http://latimesblogs.latimes.com/entertainment newsbuzz/2010/08/netflix-and-epix-working-on-major -digital-partnership-to-shake-up-pay-tv-landscape.html.

Gullo, Karen. "Netflix Wins Dismissal of Antitrust Case Over Online Rentals." *Bloomberg Businessweek,* November 28, 2011. Accessed December 12, 2011. http://www.business week.com/news/2011-11-28/netflix-wins-dismissal-of -antitrust-case-over-online-rentals.html.

Helft, Miguel. "Netflix to Deliver Movies to the PC." *New York Times,* January 16, 2007. Accessed December 12, 2011. http://www.nytimes.com/2007/01/16/technology/16netflix .html?pagewanted=all.

"Hogging the Remote." *The Economist,* September 2, 2010. Accessed December 12, 2011. http://www.economist.com /node/16944911.

Kang, Cecilia. "CES: Netflix CEO Hastings Sets Eyes on Global Expansion." *Washington Post,* January 8, 2011. Accessed December 12, 2011. http://online.wsj.com/article/SB100014 24053111904583204576545051871923760.html.

Lawler, Richard. "Study Finds Netflix Is the Largest Source of Internet traffic in North America." *engadget,* May 17, 2011. Accessed December 12, 2011. http://www.engadget.com /2011/05/17/study-finds-netflix-is-the-largest-source-of -internet-traffic-in.

Mullaney, Timothy J. "Netflix: The Mail-Order Movie House That Clobbered Blockbuster." *Bloomberg Businessweek,* May 25, 2006. Accessed December 12, 2011. http://www.business week.com/smallbiz/content/may2006/sb20060525_268860 .htm.

"Netflix, Inc." *International Directory of Company Histories.* Farmington Hills, MI: The Gale Group, 2010. Accessed December 12, 2011. http://www.answers.com/topic/netflix -inc.

Netflix, Inc. "Netflix 2007 Annual Report." Los Gatos, CA, 2007. Accessed December 12, 2011. http://files.shareholder .com/downloads/NFLX/1560905767x0x188779/a5de0034 -8320-4d49-b13b-80c9845e49d4/AR_10K_final.pdf.

"Netflix Locks Up Rights to Its First TV Series, 'House of Cards.'" *Huffington Post,* March 18, 2011. Accessed December 12, 2011. http://www.huffingtonpost.com/2011/03/18 /netflix-house-of-cards-tv-series_n_837673.html.

O'Brien, Jeffrey M. "The Netflix Effect." *Wired,* December 2002. Accessed January 14, 2012. http://www.wired.com/wired /archive/10.12/netflix.html .

Shaughnessy, Haydn. "How the $1million Netflix Prize Spurred a Radical Innovation, Accidentally." *Forbes,* June 28, 2011. Accessed December 12, 2011. http://www.forbes.com/sites /haydnshaughnessy/2011/06/28/how-the-1million-netflix -prize-spurred-a-radical-innovation-accidentally.

Wauters, Robin. "BookRenter Adds Netflix Co-Founder Marc Randolph to Its Board of Directors." *TechCrunch,* May 7, 2010. Accessed December 12, 2011. http://techcrunch.com /2010/05/07/marc-randolph-bookrenter.

Netscape Communications: Internet Software Development in the 1990s

The founders of Netscape Communications Corporation designed the first web browser while they were still college students, and then released a superior version of the browser that made the World Wide Web accessible to the public. With its rapid growth and surprisingly successful initial public offering (IPO), Netscape popularized investment in Internet companies.

VIOLAWWW

When Tim Berners-Lee built the web browser ViolaWWW, he introduced the concept of hypertext markup language (HTML) to Internet users. By clicking on these hypertext links, an Internet user could quickly find other documents that were relevant to the one he or she was reading, a major innovation in 1992, when ViolaWWW came out. ViolaWWW was a text-based browser so a user needed a separate graphics viewing program to display an image.

ViolaWWW was very simple and its graphics display weaknesses were obvious. However, the new browser still impressed viewers, including Dave Thompson, who demonstrated it to computer science students at the University of Illinois at Urbana-Champaign. Two people knowledgeable about computer programming and who were at the university in late 1992, Marc Andreessen and Eric Bina, decided to improve the picture display features of ViolaWWW. The graphical browser would function on a terminal running UNIX, which was a common operating system for universities and large businesses that owned a mainframe computer. Andreessen and Bina named their web browser Mosaic.

MOSAIC

Andreessen worked for the National Center for Super-computing Applications (NCSA) at the university while he studied computer science. According to Douglas Wagner, writing for the History of Computing Project, Andreessen and Bina wrote Mosaic in six weeks as a side project and their employee contract with NCSA assigned the institution the rights to Mosaic.

NCSA, a nonprofit science research facility, made Mosaic freely available from its servers instead of charging for downloads. Due to the convenience Mosaic offered, it rapidly gained popularity, and Andreessen realized the commercial potential of a web browser. After he received his diploma, Andreessen left Urbana-Champaign, Illinois, to work as a computer programmer at Enterprise Integration Technologies in the San Francisco Bay Area in California.

At the same time, Jim Clark, the CEO of Silicon Graphics, Inc., was also unsatisfied with his job, as Clark later told Michael Goldberg for *Wired*. Clark saw the rising potential of the personal computer (PC) market and wanted to develop less expensive chips for consumers, but the other Silicon Graphics executives were happy selling graphics chips to high-end customers. According to Adam Lashinsky for *CNNMoney*, Mosaic impressed Clark and he sent an e-mail to Andreessen asking the recent graduate if he was interested in forming a partnership. Clark continued to work at Silicon Graphics throughout 1993, leaving in early 1994 to work on his new venture with Andreessen.

DEVELOPMENT

Clark originally wanted to use Mosaic as browser software for television sets. He believed that the television would eventually merge with the computer, creating a simple and easy-to-use machine that offered access to all types of media and provided communication capabilities. Goldberg, for *Wired,* reported Clark's prediction that handheld devices would have all the features of televisions and PCs by 2009. Andreessen believed that the growing PC market offered more than the TV industry and he convinced Clark to start work on this project first. The partners named their company Mosaic Communications Corporation.

In 1994, very few potential employees had experience designing web browsers. Andreessen recruited Eric Bina and other fellow NCSA workers for their new company and Clark recruited some of his former employees from Silicon Graphics, who were much more experienced. The company also hired business and sales staff, who quickly got to work figuring out how to market a web browser.

Clark realized that he needed help financing Mosaic Communications as the company was quickly spending his US$3 million investment. Clark knew that the venture capitalists who funded Silicon Graphics received many of its shares and he decided to set a high price for Mosaic Communications so that he could keep control of the company. The venture capitalists Kleiner Perkins Caulfield & Byers accepted a valuation of US$21 million, much higher than other dot-coms (Internet companies), which were typically priced at US$4 million or less in 1994, and invested US$5 million in the company, reported Lashinsky for *CNNMoney.*

SPYGLASS

The NCSA did not sell commercial products itself, so it worked with a partner company, Spyglass, Inc., which helped market products invented by University of Illinois students. Before the development of Mosaic, Spyglass developed statistical analysis software, according to former Spyglass developer Eric Sink in "Memoirs from the Browser Wars." Spyglass assigned most of its staff to browser development in 1994 as a web browser offered much higher potential revenue than niche scientific products. Although Spyglass had obtained the rights to use the original Mosaic code, its employees decided to write their web browser with their own code, although they could still promote it as the legitimate version of Mosaic.

The NCSA threatened to file a lawsuit against Mosaic Communications. NCSA claimed that Spyglass was the only company that had the right to sell Mosaic, and that Clark and Andreessen were violating its trademarks. To mollify the NCSA, Mosaic Communications agreed to change its name to Netscape Communications Corporation and renamed its browser Netscape Navigator.

According to Eric Sink, Spyglass Mosaic and Netscape Navigator initially offered many of the same features. However, Jim Clark had more experience in the software industry, and a large cash stockpile, so his browser quickly

surpassed what Spyglass could offer. By the end of the year, Netscape had developed a superior browser in terms of speed and reliability and gained the attention of the news media. Nevertheless, Netscape rushed to finish version 1.0 of its browser because of the competition from Spyglass.

LAUNCH

Netscape Navigator 1.0 reached the market in December 1994. At first, Navigator cost an individual consumer nothing as Netscape wanted to popularize web browsers. Netscape planned to sell corporate licenses for its browser and also offered web design software and web server software. The decision to offer Netscape 1.0 as a free download was risky for the company. Netscape had spent a large portion of the money that Kleiner Perkins Caulfield & Byers and Jim Clark had invested by the end of the year.

The company's financial health quickly improved. Clark gauged corporate demand correctly, and corporations were eager to buy thousands of Netscape licenses for their employees. Publishers and news organizations offered to invest in the software company. Lashinsky reported that Netscape revenue reached US$5 million in the first quarter of 1995 and US$12 million in the second quarter.

MICROSOFT OFFERS A DEAL

After the successful launch of Netscape, Microsoft executives realized that they needed a better web strategy. In early 1995, the company planned to release Windows 95, which would greatly improve the features the Windows operating system offered. Microsoft believed that software companies would design their upcoming products primarily to run on Windows 95. After Microsoft saw Netscape Navigator, Microsoft realized that the browser threatened the market for Windows 95. If games, spreadsheets, and other programs could run in a browser, companies might design their software for the browser instead of the operating system. Windows would lose a major competitive advantage, software compatibility, as customers could use Netscape in a Mac, Linux, or Unix environment and their programs would still function.

Microsoft offered to help Netscape. Netscape could use the features that were built into Windows 95 to launch programs and Microsoft would share information about these features with Netscape and a few other companies. The Netscape browser could still serve as a software platform for non-Windows operating systems and obsolete versions of Windows.

Netscape refused the deal. Netscape believed that future programmers would write their software for the web, so that it could take on Microsoft as a software platform and win.

THE DAWN OF JAVASCRIPT

In order build and expand web activity, a programming language was needed for the Netscape browser. Web programming languages had already been around before Netscape tried to create its personalized version, but the company hoped to break from past languages and create a language for the new Information age. Netscape hired Brendan Eich to help create this new web programming language, which became known as JavaScript.

JavaScript did not evolve directly from the Java programming language, developed in 1991 and marketed in the 1990s by Sun Microsystems, Inc. Instead, it started as Mocha, became Livescript, and then eventually changed into JavaScript as Eich incorporated several ideas from Java in the language and, after negotiations between Netscape and Sun Microsystems, the name was approved. This was a shrewd marketing move on the part of Netscape, as it drew the many users of the Java programming language to the JavaScript web development language, despite the differences between the two.

For web developers, the benefits of JavaScript were immediately noticeable. JavaScript became a glue that programmers could use to experiment with and build the Internet, using images, plugins, and applets (chunks of Internet-based code that could be used to put objects into cyberspace). Instead of the boring lines of flickering text the Internet had begun with, developers could now create bold, interesting interfaces or dynamic websites that moved and responded to users. Eventually, JavaScript also became popular for building documents offline that could be easily transitioned online if necessary, such as PDF documents and desktop objects. JavaScript allowed code on the client, or viewer, side to handle these site changes so the browser did not need to keep loading new pages with every change.

Easy for the growing segment of amateur web developers to pick up and use, JavaScript grew to dominate the Web just as Netscape began to dominate the browser market. An industry standard version, called ECMAScript, was released, and Microsoft created an imitation called JScript. Eventually, JavaScript became so popular that, in its future versions, it would long outlast Netscape itself as a primary feature of Web sites.

SECURE SOCKETS LAYER (SSL)

The success of Netscape was as unprecedented as the success of the Internet as a commercial medium. While 1995 is considered the starting line for online stores, advanced network structures, and other Internet features that users were taking for granted only a few years later, it was also the year Netscape dominated the online scene. During the mid–1990s, use of the Netscape browser became so common that more than 85 percent of Internet users chose Netscape.

Part of this instant popularity was due to supply. Netscape was one of the only browser systems available for online developers and viewers to use, so it became the most popular. Few of the first serious Internet users considered using anything else, because Netscape was all they knew. However, the company also excelled at determining what its brand new market would need and how to provide those features in its browsers. A classic example is the creation of Secure Sockets Layer (SSL). When networks became more complex in the middle and later 1990s, people began to worry about security. The early stages of the Internet had very little protection against hackers and viruses. If businesses were going to send private information online, they needed a solution to ease their security worries.

Netscape had been working on just such a solution since 1994. The concept of SSL was very simple. Every online message was provided with two different keys, one key that the sender had and one key that the receiver had. The first key encrypted the message, encoding it so it could not be read by external devices and even if intercepted would not give away any information. The second key decrypted the message when it arrived at its destination, allowing the receiver to read (and eventually view, watch, or listen) to it.

This simple concept revolutionized the Internet and paved the way for secure web browsing and e-commerce. Other applications, such as file transfers, could also use SSL to send data safely. As time went on, Netscape realized users also needed a way to verify websites and server connections that had the necessary decryption but might still not be trustworthy. Therefore it added a new concept to traditional SSL known as SSL certificates. These certificates were a second layer of security provided by web browser creators that certified websites as trustworthy, or warned users of the dangers of advancing forward.

THE INITIAL PUBLIC OFFERING

Spyglass, which had been in business several years longer than Netscape, announced its initial public offering (IPO) during the summer of 1995. Clark saw the Spyglass announcement and decided that he wanted Netscape to go public as well. This decision surprised the other executives as Netscape had only been in existence for about a year. The executives also believed that launching an IPO in late summer was bad timing.

Stock analysts and the public heard the Netscape IPO announcement with more enthusiasm. Many investors had avoided buying Microsoft stock during its early years, lacking knowledge about the PC industry, and had missed out on large profits. Like Microsoft, Netscape offered a new type of product and Netscape controlled the market for browser software.

Investors were so eager to buy Netscape stock that the stock opened late its first day in 1995. Many inexperienced investors did not tell their brokers the maximum price they would pay for a share of Netscape, and nobody wanted to sell a share, which made it difficult to establish an initial price for the stock. The founders priced Netscape stock conservatively, at US$28 per share, and investors bid it up to US$71 per share. Netscape was now worth more than US$2 billion. The Netscape IPO launched the dot-com era as employees and investors of start-up Internet companies believed that other software companies could declare an IPO with similar results.

INTERNET EXPLORER

Microsoft released Internet Explorer 1.0 shortly after the Netscape IPO in August 1995, licensing Spyglass Mosaic to obtain the technology for the new browser. It did not impress many observers, as it lacked many features that Netscape offered, and Netscape kept its high share of the market. Explorer could be acquired only with the optional Plus Pack add-on, so obtaining it was not convenient. Nevertheless, Microsoft planned to establish it as the new web browser standard, and continued development. At the time, many PC owners used older versions of Windows, like Windows 3.1, and upgrading to a new operating system to use the new browser was an unattractive proposition. Daniel Penrice, writing in Harvard Business School's *Working Knowledge,* also noted that Netscape Navigator ran on the more costly, business-focused Windows NT, unlike the first version of Internet Explorer. When Microsoft introduced Internet Explorer 2.0, it was also met with low demand.

However, with the 1996 release of Internet Explorer 3.0, Microsoft introduced a browser comparable to Netscape Navigator. Microsoft made Internet Explorer 3.0 much more convenient to obtain than earlier editions. Internet Explorer came with new editions of the Windows 95 software package and it was available as a free download from Microsoft itself. This decision had a negative impact on Netscape's pricing power, since the company did not offer its browser free, although Netscape still earned US$8 billion in 1996.

Many web developers were confused because the two browsers displayed pages differently and Microsoft and Netscape had developed incompatible methods for implementing advanced features. Although both Microsoft and Netscape were working together to develop the HTML standard as members of the World Wide Web Consortium (W3C)(an international community whose goal is the long-term growth of the World Wide Web), web designers frequently optimized their sites for either Internet Explorer 3.0 or Netscape Navigator 3.0. Internet Explorer used Microsoft ActiveX to implement many features, while Netscape Navigator relied on JavaScript.

LEGAL WARS

Netscape believed that Microsoft had abused its position in the operating systems market by releasing Internet Explorer for free, and in 1997 the company asked the U.S. Department of Justice (DOJ) to investigate Microsoft. Microsoft had already been investigated in earlier years, leading to an agreement between Microsoft and the DOJ in 1995 that required the software maker to sell its software products separately.

Microsoft sold many PC programs, such as Word, Excel, and Powerpoint, and designing Internet Explorer cost Microsoft a lot of money. Netscape accused Microsoft of illegal bundling, claiming that Microsoft included Internet Explorer in the price of Windows 95 to force a PC user to buy two separate products as a single purchase. Microsoft also used Windows 95 as leverage to force hardware manufacturers to remove Netscape Navigator from the software that came with home computers, and required them to display Internet Explorer prominently on the desktops of PC buyers.

Microsoft went even further in 1997 as it fully integrated Internet Explorer 4.0 into new editions of Windows 95. A PC would now load Internet Explorer when it loaded Windows, so that Internet Explorer would appear to start up faster than Navigator. A user who ran Navigator would have both browsers loaded, thus degrading overall system performance.

The DOJ agreed with Netscape, and with a preliminary injunction, Judge Thomas Penfield Jackson ordered Microsoft to separate Internet Explorer 4.0 from Windows 95. Even though Netscape had won the battle, it had weakened Netscape significantly. Netscape reported a US$88 million loss for 1997. In 1998 the DOJ launched a full–scale antitrust investigation of Microsoft.

Netscape released the code that made up Navigator to open-source programmers in 1998. Microsoft could afford to hire thousands of programmers and Netscape realized that it needed help from volunteers to match the feature set of Internet Explorer. As a result, open-source programmers started work on the Mozilla Project.

AOL ACQUISITION

Even though the courts sympathized with Netscape's argument, Netscape lost control of the browser market, and Internet Explorer gained the upper hand. Although the major Internet service provider America Online had changed its default browser to Internet Explorer, it still decided to buy Netscape. Netscape announced the US$4.2 billion acquisition in November 1998, when Netscape stock traded for US$39 per share, reported Jon Swartz for *SFGate*.

In 1999, the deal looked like it would make AOL the dominant Internet company, and consumer activist Ralph

Nader even tried to stop the deal on antitrust grounds. In later years, the Netscape acquisition became known as one of the worst corporate decisions ever, as James Quinn explained in the *Telegraph*. AOL spent US$4.2 billion that it could have used to buy Google, eBay, or another future tech success, and it bought a company that produced technology that even AOL no longer recommended to its users.

AOL continued to support and update Netscape Navigator. After the Mozilla Project coders established the Mozilla Foundation in 2003, AOL donated money to the foundation. Netscape releases continued during the first decade of the 21st century, although they relied heavily on code from the Mozilla browser, which was much more popular. AOL released Netscape Navigator 9.0 in October 2007 but announced the end of the Navigator project shortly afterward, in December.

FIRST GLIMPSE OF THE WEB

Netscape's time in the spotlight as a groundbreaking company was relatively short-lived. The company failed to capitalize on its early dominance of the market because it attempted to beat Microsoft, a much larger software company, by developing a software platform. However, although Internet Explorer won the "browser wars," in the 1990s many people had their first experience surfing the web courtesy of Netscape Communications Corporation.

BIBLIOGRAPHY

Drapeau, Tom. "End of Support for Netscape Web Browsers." *Netscape Blog,* December 28, 2007. Accessed January 24, 2012. http://blog.netscape.com/2007/12/28/end-of-support-for-netscape-web-browsers.

Economides, Nicholas. "The Microsoft Antitrust Case: A Case Study for MBA Students." Stern School of Business, New York University, April 2003. Accessed January 24, 2012. http://www.stern.nyu.edu/networks/homeworks/Microsoft_Case.pdf.

Goldberg, Michael. "Why Jim Clark Loves Mosaic." *Wired,* October 1994. Accessed January 24, 2012. http://www.wired.com/wired/archive/2.10/jim.clark.html?topic=&topic_set=.

"The History of the Internet." *Tech-FAQ,* Accessed April 12, 2012. http://www.tech-faq.com/history-of-the-internet.html.

"The History of JavaScript." *Techtopia,* 2009. Accessed April 12, 2012. http://www.techotopia.com/index.php/The_History_of_JavaScript.

"History of SSL." *ISM,* Accessed April 12, 2012. http://publib.boulder.ibm.com/infocenter/iseries/v5r3/index.jsp?topic=%2Frzain%2Frzainhistory.htm.

Hurd, Andrew. "The Web and the Internet Explosion." Troy, NY: Hudson Valley Community College, December 2004. Accessed January 24, 2012. http://acaddb.hvcc.edu/~a.hurd/ciss220/web03/notes/w1TheWebandtheInternetExplosion.htm.

Jackson, Judge Thomas Penfield. "Microsoft's Attempt to Dissuade Netscape from Developing Navigator as a Platform." Albion.com, November 5, 1999. Accessed January 24, 2012. http://www.albion.com/microsoft/findings-21.html.

"JavaScript: How It All Began." *2ality,* March 23, 2011. Accessed April 12, 2012. http://www.2ality.com/2011/03/javascript-how-it-all-began.html.

Lashinsky, Adam. "Remembering Netscape: The Birth of the Web." *CNNMoney,* July 25, 2005. Accessed January 24, 2012. http://money.cnn.com/magazines/fortune/fortune_archive/2005/07/25/8266639/index.htm.

Mozilla Foundation. "History of the Mozilla Project." Mountain View, CA, August 24, 2011. Accessed January 24, 2012. http://www.mozilla.org/about/history.html.

"Netscape: A History." *BBC,* February 10, 2000. Accessed January 24, 2012. http://news.bbc.co.uk/2/hi/in_depth/business/2000/microsoft/635689.stm.

Penrice, Daniel. "Throwing Your Opponent: Strategies for the Internet Age." *Working Knowledge,* Harvard Business School, October 12, 1999. Accessed January 24, 2012. http://hbswk.hbs.edu/item/2826.html.

Quinn, James. "Final Farewell to Worst Deal in History—AOL-Time Warner." *Telegraph,* November 21, 2009. Accessed April 11, 2012. http://www.telegraph.co.uk/finance/newsbysector/mediatechnologyandtelecoms/.

Sink, Eric. "Memoirs from the Browser Wars." EricSink.com, April 15, 2003. Accessed January 24, 2012. http://www.ericsink.com/Browser_Wars.html.

"SSL Certificates History and Background." *SSL Certificate Reviews,* Accessed April 12, 2012. http://www.sslcertificatereviews.net/blog/ssl-certificates-history-background.html.

Steinert-Threlkeld, Tom. "Can You Work in Netscape Time?" *Fast Company,* October 31, 1995. Accessed January 24, 2012. http://www.fastcompany.com/magazine/01/netscape.html?page=0%2C0.

Swartz, John, and David Einstein. "AOL Near Deal for Netscape." *SFGate,* November 23, 1998. Accessed January 24, 2012. http://articles.sfgate.com/1998-11-23/news/17737609_1_aol-and-netscape-netscape-s-web-aol-netscape-sun.

Wagner, Douglas. "Marc Andreessen." *The History of Computing Project,* October 18, 2002. Accessed January 24, 2012. http://www.thocp.net/biographies/andreesen_marc.htm.

Nike, Inc.: Building a Global Brand

Nike, Inc., rose to prominence as a track shoe (running shoe) company, later expanding into other sports and introducing lines of athletic apparel and sports equipment. After signing Chicago Bulls basketball star Michael Jordan to an endorsement deal, the company established its brand in markets throughout the world. Nike brands itself and its products with the spirit of athletic competition, represented by the Greek goddess of victory (Nike) and its "Swoosh" logo.

THE SEARCH FOR BETTER TRACK SHOES

University of Oregon coach Bill Bowerman faced challenging competition at track meets because coaches at rival universities could recruit more talented and athletic players, and his athletes were simply average, according to the article "Just Do It: More Than an Athletic Prescription," in *Knowledge@Wharton*. Bowerman, who coached at Oregon from 1948 to 1972, addressed this problem by inspiring and motivating his track team and by searching for better shoes that could stand up to the hardships of athletic competition but were also light weight. He looked at Adidas shoes, but they cost too much, so he made the shoes for his runners himself.

One of the track team members coached by Bowerman in the late 1950s was Philip Knight, who graduated from the University of Oregon in journalism and went on to business school at California's Stanford University. Frank Shallenberger, a Stanford Business School professor, gave Knight and his fellow students an assignment in which they had to create a business plan. By the early 1960s, the radios, cars, and electronic goods that U.S. retailers im-

ported from Japan had improved significantly, and these products competed successfully in price with U.S. high-tech goods. Knight decided that a U.S. shoe retailer could import shoes from Japan and sell less expensive, durable shoes in the U.S. market. Although Shallenberger was not very impressed, Knight continued to pursue his business plan while he worked as an accountant.

SETTING UP A SHOE IMPORT COMPANY

Knight traveled to Japan in 1962 in search of a manufacturer that could build track shoes similar to Adidas shoes. He visited the Tiger division of Onitsuka Company Ltd., which produced Adidas-style running shoes. The Tiger managers were looking for a way to export their shoes to the United States. After Knight told the Tiger managers he had a shoe company, Blue Ribbon Sports, Tiger agreed to let Knight become their U.S. distributor.

Knight returned to the United States and told Bill Bowerman that he had obtained the distribution rights from Tiger, and asked him to help set up a shoe import company. The two partners each invested US$500 in Blue Ribbon Sports, officially founding the company in 1964. Bill Bowerman also helped Tiger design better shoes for U.S. runners. Knight ran the company as a part-time job, selling the Tiger shoes out of the trunk of his car.

Blue Ribbon earned US$3,240 from its shoe sales in 1964, and Knight and Bowerman decided to recruit another employee to help sell shoes. Jeff Johnson, a track athlete from Stanford, joined the company and helped develop a new marketing strategy. Johnson expanded the Blue Ribbon brand outside of shoes, placing the company logo on shirts and other apparel goods, and gave Blue Ribbon-branded products away to star athletes, improving the exposure of the company. Blue Ribbon also set up a store in Santa Monica, California. Jackie Krentzman, for *Stanford Magazine,* reported that the company reached US$1 million in annual income by 1969.

INTRODUCING NIKE SHOES

Knight and Bowerman decided to establish their own line of shoes to sell along with the Onitsuka Tiger. According to Krentzman, Knight considered calling the shoes Dimension Six, but Johnson suggested Nike, a name that came to him in a dream, and which Blue Ribbon employees preferred. As the goddess of victory, Nike represented the ultimate hope of athletes throughout the world.

Blue Ribbon needed a logo for its Nike shoes. Caroline Davis, a Portland State University graphic design student, performed freelance work for Knight, and he offered her US$35 to create a Nike logo. Davis created the Nike Swoosh, which appeared on Nike shoes in 1972. That same year, Blue Ribbon Sports ended its distribution agreement with Onitsuka.

Nike contracted out manufacturing to Nippon Rubber Industry Company, Ltd., and other Japanese firms soon afterward, but manufacturing costs rose quickly because of the strong Japanese yen, explained Richard Locke in a Massachusetts Institute of Technology (MIT) paper. Nike set up a few of its own factories in the United States and sourced components from less wealthy Asian nations to deal with the rising costs.

WAFFLE SHOES

Knight wanted to build shoes with better traction that remained lightweight, so he poured rubber into his wife's waffle maker, creating a waffled sole. Drawing on the moonwalks of U.S. astronauts in the early 1970s for inspiration, Knight called these shoes Moon Shoes, and they rapidly gained popularity with athletes. Nike demonstrated its Moon Shoes to the public during the Olympic tryouts in Oregon in 1972.

Nike decided to sponsor the athletes who wore the new Moon Shoes. Ilie Nastase, a Romanian tennis star with an aggressive attitude, signed on first in 1973, followed by the track star Steve Prefontaine. Nike developed a new shoe design for Prefontaine to show off, the Nike Premontreal, with design assistance from Prefontaine. Prefontaine set several track records, bringing much publicity to Nike. Tragically, an automobile accident in 1975 ended Steve Prefontaine's life.

PROMOTING THE NIKE BRAND

In its early years, Nike primarily relied on recommendations from track stars to spread awareness of its shoes. By 1977, Nike was ready for a larger-scale advertising campaign, and the John Brown advertising agency created the slogan "There Is No Finish Line." Nike showed off its new slogan with a series of posters that showed an athlete running alone along a road in several harsh environments to perfect his abilities. These posters became collectors' items and motivational tools for aspiring track stars.

The year 1978 was critical for the company. Blue Ribbon Sports capitalized on the popularity of its Nike shoes by changing its company name to Nike. In January that same year, rising tennis star John McEnroe signed an endorsement contract with Nike. McEnroe would win five tennis titles that year. Nike also introduced shoes that had air-filled soles in 1978, which were invented by designer Frank Rudy, and demonstrated the air-cushioned Nike Tailwind at a marathon in Hawaii.

By 1980, Nike finally surpassed Adidas, selling the majority of the athletic shoes that U.S. consumers purchased during the year. Ben Jacklet, for *Oregon Business,* reported that Nike revenue reached US$150 million in 1980 and the company went public that year. The Chinese government had invested in its factories and opened up its export market, and Phil Knight traveled to China to find contractors who could manufacture Nike shoes at lower cost, although it would take some time before the Chinese manufacturers were ready. Locke, in his MIT paper, stated that Nike continued to produce most of its shoes in South Korea and Taiwan in 1982.

MICHAEL JORDAN

Nike continued to expand beyond its track beginnings into other sports, sponsoring hockey players and basketball players. In 1984, a crucial moment occurred for the company when basketball star Michael Jordan was signed to an endorsement deal, and Nike introduced a new line of shoes called Air Jordan. Jordan quickly became the public face of the company and by 1986 annual revenue exceeded US$1 billion.

Nike created a new slogan, "Be Like Mike," encouraging a customer who bought Air Jordan shoes to identify with the basketball star. The Chicago Bulls team that Jordan led won several championships and the popularity of Air Jordans continued to rise. Jordan became a well-known athlete throughout the world, introducing the Nike brand to foreign markets. In 1988, Nike introduced one of its best-known slogans, "Just Do It."

MANUFACTURING CONTROVERSY

Nike continued to outsource shoe manufacturing to low-wage Asian nations, resulting in condemnation from human rights organizations. Although many U.S. retailers also purchased products from overseas suppliers, Nike had a strong brand, which made it a prominent target for criticism. Knight defended his sourcing policy, stating that he offered better wages than the Asian workers could earn performing other work, but Nike continued to receive criticism. In the midst of the early 1990s recession, many out-of-work U.S. citizens blamed Nike and other retailers for moving their factories out of the United States.

Nike established a new code of conduct for its Asian contractors in 1992 and hired U.S. audit firm Ernst & Young to ensure that Nike adhered to its code of conduct. Nike issued specific reports for China and Vietnam, which mentioned issues such as making sure workers earned national minimum wages and received mandatory employment benefits, preventing contractors from hiring underage workers, and establishing health and safety standards. Nike also worked with other U.S. apparel retailers to establish a code of conduct for the apparel industry.

TROUBLESOME CELEBRITIES

Starting with its first professional endorser, Ilie Nastase, Nike recruited temperamental and unpredictable athletes to promote its products. The brand promoted an image of victory at all costs and signed athletes who did not always demonstrate good sportsmanship. In 1994 Nike signed Tonya Harding. While the Olympic ice skater Nancy Kerrigan was well known for her athletic talents, Tonya Harding was more familiar to audiences as a jealous rival who was involved in covering up an attack on Kerrigan. (Harding's ex-husband and her bodyguard hired a man to injure Kerrigan so she would be unable to skate in an important competition.) Krentzman reported that Adidas had signed Kerrigan, so Nike also used the endorsement to get back at its main rival.

In 1996, Nike signed a contract with a promising young golfer, Tiger Woods. The contract promised Woods so much money that investors initially sold their Nike stock after hearing about the deal. Woods quickly became an effective spokesman for Nike, and the Nike brand became a popular one for golfers. Nike signed two more contracts with Woods, promising him an additional US$100 million in 2000 and 2005, according to Kevin YC Chung and colleagues at the Tepper School of Business at Carnegie Mellon University. Nike started selling golf clubs and golf balls along with its golf shoes, and because of Woods's popularity, the revenue of Nike's golf division grew rapidly.

Nike also went after the football market, signing Atlanta Falcons quarterback Michael Vick. However, in 2007 government agents raided Michael Vick's house, finding dogs that had been trained to fight in illegal dog fighting matches and reported that the dogs had been severely abused. Vick agreed to a plea bargain and went to prison. Nike canceled its agreement with the disgraced quarterback, taking Vick merchandise off the market.

In 2009, Tiger Woods crashed his car into a fire hydrant and the public learned that he had left his house in a hurry after angering his wife. It soon transpired that Woods had cheated on his wife with multiple mistresses and the ensuing scandal eroded his reputation. By 2009, Woods had become as prominent as Jordan as a representative of the Nike brand, so his loss of reputation cost Nike some golf product sales. Although some sponsors abandoned Woods, Nike continued to use the golfer to promote its brand. The decision surprised some observers who expected Nike to let Woods go because it had fired Michael Vick.

After Vick completed his prison sentence, the National Football League allowed him to come back to football. Nike also forgave Vick, signing a new contract with the troubled quarterback. The sponsorship agreement drew controversy for Nike because football watchers still remembered the crimes Vick committed, and some football fans boycotted Nike over the decision to bring him back.

NIKE CREATIONS

Phil Knight came up with the most valuable Nike idea, the company business plan, at Stanford Business School. Manufacturing shoes in Japan was not an obvious decision at the time because many managers believed that Japan could not meet the quality requirements of the U.S. market during the 1960s. Although the decision to make shoes overseas got Nike into trouble in the 1990s, Knight responded to the criticism by introducing reforms.

Nike introduced several successful strategies in the advertising arena. When Nike used the strength of its shoe brand in the 1960s to market shirts and other apparel products, cross-marketing was not a widely used strategy for shoe manufacturers. Nike created general slogans that promoted athletics instead of more specific jingles that applied solely to its shoes. This built a loyalty to the brand greater than any single product.

BIBLIOGRAPHY

Chung, Kevin YC, Timothy Derdenger, and Kannan Srinivasan. "Economic Value of Celebrity Endorsements: Tiger Woods' Impact on Sales of Nike Golf Balls." Pittsburgh, PA: Tepper School of Business, Carnegie Mellon University, September 26, 2011. Accessed January 26, 2012. http://www.contrib.andrew.cmu.edu/~derdenge/CelebrityEndorsements.pdf.

Jacklet, Ben. "Nike's Great Leap." *Oregon Business,* August 2008. Accessed January 26, 2012. http://www.oregonbusiness.com/articles/22/325.

Jordan. "The Evolution of Nike Advertising." *Union Room Blog,* December 2, 2009. Accessed January 26, 2012. http://www.unionroom.com/blog/the-evolution-of-nike-advertising.

"Just Do It: More Than an Athletic Prescription." *Knowledge@Wharton,* March 30, 2005. Accessed January 26, 2012. http://

knowledge.wharton.upenn.edu/article.cfm?articleid=1152.

Krentzman, Jackie. "The Force Behind the Nike Empire." *Stanford Magazine,* January 1997. Accessed January 26, 2012. http://www.stanfordalumni.org/news/magazine/1997/janfeb/articles/knight.html.

Locke, Richard M. "The Promise and Perils of Globalization: The Case of Nike." Cambridge, MA: MIT Sloan School of Management, 2002. Accessed January 26, 2012. http://mitsloan.mit.edu/50th/pdf/nikepaper.pdf.

McCorkle, Henry, and Matt Vespa. "Michael Vick Faces Bad Newz." *The Dickinsonian,* August 23, 2007. Accessed January 26, 2012. http://www2.dickinson.edu/dickinsonian/detail.cfm?2585.

"Nike Founder Defends Paterno Response to Scandal." *CBS News,* January 26, 2012. Accessed January 26, 2012. http://www.cbsnews.com/8301-400_162-57367005/nike-founder-defends-paterno-response-to-scandal.

Nike, Inc. "Nike Timeline." Beaverton, OR, 2011. Accessed January 26, 2012. http://nikejobs.com/company_overview/timeline/.

Nintendo's Wii: The Interactive Game Console That Crossed Generations

───────■───────

Nintendo Co., Ltd., has a very long history as a Japanese gaming company, although the company only became well known in the United States after it released its famous Nintendo Entertainment System in 1985. By 2001, Nintendo was struggling, but it still dedicated its employees to work on the development of a new video game console. When the Wii came out in 2006, its low cost and motion capture technology attracted new players to video games and helped the company gain a lead over rivals Sony Corporation and Microsoft Corporation.

EARLY STRENGTH

The eight-bit Nintendo Entertainment System quickly became popular with game players in the mid-1980s. (A bit is a unit of data in a computer, and the term eight-bit refers to a generation of computers that used eight-bit processors.) This console offered much better performance than the Atari 2600 that introduced many players to video games, and it provided a wider selection of games than the eight-bit Sega Master System that followed the eight-bit Nintendo in 1986. Nintendo adeptly negotiated deals with movie studios, toy makers, and other entertainment companies, and introduced its own popular characters Mario and Luigi, Donkey Kong, and Link.

During the 1980s, Nintendo primarily competed with another video game console manufacturer, Sega Corporation. When Sega released the 16-bit Genesis, Nintendo followed with its 16-bit Super Nintendo. The two video game companies faced limited competition from personal computer (PC) manufacturers such as IBM, Inc., and Apple Computer, Inc., because a gaming PC often cost thousands of U.S. dollars, making it much more expensive than a console that cost a few hundred. The Panasonic 3DO and the SNK Neo Geo cost too much for many video game buyers, at more than US$600 each, even though they offered arcade-quality hardware and games.

Nintendo and Sega offered their consoles at low prices so that their younger buyers could afford them, relying on game cartridge sales for most of their income. Nintendo, Sega, and other manufacturers installed proprietary software on their consoles. A cartridge maker needed to gain the console maker's permission to create a game that would run on a specific console, which required paying the console maker a percentage of the cartridge sales. This approval process also helped Nintendo and Sega ensure that all of their games remained family friendly, whereas PCs could run adult-oriented games. Although consoles could be accessed illegally by hackers to run unlicensed games, the process was difficult as well as illegal.

NEW COMPETITORS

The growing video game console market in the 1990s attracted the attention of several other technology companies. Microsoft had built a reputation for its business and home software via its Windows software, but the company believed that a family would not go to the expense of purchasing a computer simply to play games. Microsoft therefore decided to create a scaled down computer for video games, the XBox. Sony, which introduced the Walkman (a small portable cassette player with light headphones) and sold televisions, camcorders, and other electronics, successfully launched its first video game console, PlayStation, in 1995. The PlayStation offered high-quality games, and the console itself had a competitive price of US$299.

The Sega Saturn, released in 1995 in North America, never gained widespread acceptance, while the Nintendo 64, Nintendo's third video game console, became very popular following its North American release in 1996. After Sega's sixth-generation video game console, the Dreamcast, also failed to gain popularity following its 1998 release in Japan and 1999 release elsewhere, Sega responded by ending its console manufacturing operations in 2001 and concentrated on developing games that ran on other manufacturers' platforms. Microsoft benefited greatly from Sega's decision, as it lacked the large library of characters and concepts that Sega had built up during the 1980s and 1990s, such as Sonic the Hedgehog, and it needed games for the Xbox launch.

FINANCIAL POSITION

When Nintendo released its financial statements in March 2001, it was clear that they were not in a good position. According to the British Broadcasting Corporation (BBC), the company reported 13 percent lower sales and 42 percent lower profits compared to the previous fiscal year. Nintendo's main competitor for nearly two decades had just abandoned the market, and two firms that did not depend on the revenue from their video game consoles planned to introduce their products for the holiday season. Both Sony's PlayStation 2 and Microsoft's Xbox were priced at US$299. Nevertheless, Nintendo decided to stay in the video game console market, promoting its new GameCube.

Nintendo announced that the GameCube would cost US$100 less than the PlayStation 2 and the Xbox when it reached markets in late 2001. The GameCube did not include additional features that its competitors offered, such as the ability to play music CDs and movie DVDs, and it lacked a hard drive. Leaving these features out helped Nintendo prevent piracy. Nintendo believed that younger buyers remained extremely price sensitive, and that the dot-com crash of 2000–2001 reduced the disposable income of young video game players' parents. However, the pricing decision meant that Nintendo would lose money on the GameCube hardware.

Nintendo managers predicted that GameCube game sales would bring in more cash in the next few years, so the company could still afford to start working on its next console. The GameCube successor, which was also known as the Nintendo fifth-generation console, received the code name Revolution. According to *N-Sider,* Nintendo employees were already at work on the Revolution project before holiday shoppers could purchase the GameCube in late 2001.

A SATURATED MARKET

Sony's PlayStation 2 drastically outperformed its rivals, as its games were of much higher quality than the games that Microsoft and Nintendo offered. By 2003, PlayStation 2 sales were far ahead of GameCube and Xbox sales. Zev Borow, for *Wired,* reported that gamers had purchased 40 million PlayStation 2 consoles, while Xbox and GameCube console sales combined amounted to only around 12 million.

Nintendo designers realized that competing with Sony for the traditional younger male gaming demographic would remain very difficult. All video game makers realized that they could improve their sales by making games for older people, but designing and marketing a game that older people could enjoy posed a major challenge. Many older adults continued to see gaming consoles as toys for their children.

Nintendo continued to invest in console and handheld technology. Sony and Nintendo planned to release their own next generation systems and Nintendo had enough cash to continue funding its research. According to *N-Sider,* in early 2003 Nintendo announced that it had US$6 billion in cash, and it planned to spend a large portion of its cash to produce future consoles. Nintendo continued to keep its Revolution project unknown to the public.

The handheld market had always been one of Nintendo's main strengths. The company's GameBoy beat early competitors such as the Sega Game Gear and the Atari Lynx, and by 2004 Nintendo controlled almost all of the handheld gaming market. Nintendo planned a new handheld system, the GameBoy Advance, but competitor Sony had also announced a handheld system, the PlayStation Pocket (PSP). Daniel Terdiman, for *Wired,* noted that Sony planned to promote the PSP to young adult gamers who had more cash to spend than the children who owned GameBoy systems. The PlayStation itself gained much of its popularity because it offered more adult-oriented games than the child-centered Nintendo consoles.

NINTENDO REVOLUTION

Nintendo described its Revolution project to gamers in early 2004, according to *N-Sider.* Since the eight-bit era, console manufacturers had promoted the hardware capabilities of their systems. Games included features such as three-dimensional graphics to provide a more lifelike experience. Nintendo designers argued that consoles already had hardware capabilities that were good enough to provide a fun gaming experience. The Revolution would feature energy-saving and noise-damping technology, and it would not compete primarily on its processor and graphics capabilities. The Revolution designers left out some cutting-edge technologies, such as the capability to display high-definition video, in order to reduce costs.

Nintendo designers believed that the technical challenges of new gaming systems scared off many potential players, as recent games had become very complex and detailed. Complexity was a problem for older players, who did not have the time to learn the mechanics of a new game, and young children, who could not comprehend complex game elements. Nintendo continued to keep many of the system specifications for the Revolution secret in late 2005, although it did tell gamers that graphics chip maker ATI Technologies Inc. and PC-maker IBM were helping to build the hardware for the console.

Sony continued to dominate the video game console market with its PlayStation 2 and announced its next console, the PlayStation 3. Microsoft promoted its own next-generation console, the Xbox 360. The three companies had demonstrated their prototype consoles to gamers by late 2005, and planned to sell their consoles in 2006. Alfred Hermida, for the BBC, reported that gamers looked forward to the PlayStation 3 the most, and were least enthusiastic about the Revolution. GameCube sales continued to lag behind the Xbox, and remained far behind the PlayStation 2.

INTRODUCING THE WII

In April 2006, Nintendo announced the official name of its next-generation console, the Wii (pronounced like "we"). Nintendo claimed that gamers in every country could easily pronounce the name Wii, and English audiences would feel a sense of community by hearing the new name, reported Chris Morris for *CNNMoney.*

Gamers wondered why Nintendo had adopted such an unusual name, and the new console quickly became the focus of widespread mockery. However, Nintendo managers decided to keep the name, even after hearing the gamers' complaints, as many technology firms had achieved commercial success by selling products that had silly names.

GameCube games could be played on the Wii, although offering reverse compatibility with a manufacturer's previous system was not that unusual. The option of playing older Sega games was a major change. While Nintendo and Sega were bitter rivals, gamers had to choose the console that had the games with their preferred characters. The Wii no longer had that conflict. With the Wii, Sega gamers could now play Sonic games on their Nintendo.

Nintendo promoted the immersion capabilities of the Wii remote. The Wii included two controllers, one of which looked similar to a television remote control (the Wii remote), and another that looked like a traditional console controller (the Nunchuk controller). The Wii remote included motion sensors, so that the game could record the physical actions the gamer performed. If the gamer played a golf game, he/she could swing the remote through the air instead of pushing a button to take a swing. The Wii

remote allowed the player great flexibility while performing arm gestures. This design feature had some unexpected consequences for Nintendo, as gamers were not used to performing the physical motions that their characters performed in video games. Some gamers accidentally threw the Wii remote across the room or dropped it on the floor, in spite of the fact that a wrist strap is provided to prevent such accidents.

MOTION TECHNOLOGY

Central to the success of the Wii was its motion-sensor technology. Nintendo (and other console companies) had experimented with motion sensing technology in the past, using infrared and other signal-based science concepts, but an entire console devoted to sensing moves made by the player had never been tried before. The few games that had included the technology came with expensive extra parts, which made it difficult for many customers to afford. This old sensor equipment was designed for only one game, giving it very limited appeal. Nintendo wanted to change the whole idea by making motion-sensing the most interesting and attractive aspect of the Wii. The plans began with investment in the research company Gyration, which specialized in interactive controllers.

The idea was simple from a technological point of view. Motion sensing parts had been used in cars and factories for years. They often used internal parts such as accelerometers and gyroscopic sensors. Accelerometers measured how fast an object, such as a Wii remote control, moved through the air, while gyroscopic sensors detected how high or low an object was by measuring its angular velocity. More advanced gyroscopes were made from a sphere that kept its own position relative to controller movement, allowing it to sense any angle in which the controller moved, according to player actions. Gyration had been working on a dual-axis gyroscope patent that Nintendo was interested in using. With this technology in hand, Nintendo developed two different parts for its controller, a remote piece and a joystick piece, one to be held in each hand, although motion sensor controls were primarily located in the remote half.

As a result, Nintendo was able to produce controllers that could track every arm position and orientation that players made. Instead of pushing a button, players could swing their arms, make specific motions, and point their controllers at places on the screen. Buttons were still used to start or stop actions within games, but movement was almost entirely determined by the player's own position. Many games needed to be played standing up, with broad motions that had the benefit of exercise as well as hands-on control. The only side effect, from the consumer standpoint, was the potential for lags in reaction time and the need for an extra part, which was a sensor bar arranged on the television to help track the movements the controllers made.

The effects of this motion sensor technology were widespread. The change in the market was especially promising. Before the Wii, only customers seriously invested in gaming would buy Nintendo consoles: they were largely relegated to presents for children or hobbies for a particular submarket. Anyone who wanted to play a game had to learn a complex button layout that often changed with each new game. Motion sensing technology removed barriers that customers faced. All newcomers had to do was move the Wii controllers in the right patterns, which were simple hand gestures anyone could pick up. At first this revolution seemed to be only a curiosity, but the market quickly realized what it meant. Young kids, interested parents, daring grandparents, and people of all ages could swiftly learn to play the Wii and enter into family competitions. The Wii quickly entered a potential market much larger than anything Sony or Microsoft held.

REGAINING MARKET DOMINANCE

During 2007, the Wii outsold the Xbox 360 and the PlayStation 3 by a large margin. The success of the Wii surprised gamers and market analysts. Nintendo pulled off a feat that Atari, Sega, and other companies could not accomplish, by recapturing its lead in the video game console industry.

One of the main advantages of the Wii, like older Nintendo systems, was its low cost. Sony and Microsoft loaded their systems up with expensive, latest-generation processors and graphics chips, while Nintendo used its older GameCube technology. Even though these systems cost hundreds of dollars more than the Wii, Microsoft and Sony still lost money on each sale of their consoles. Nintendo priced its Wii at US$250, earning US$50 with each sale, reported John Gaudiosi for *Business 2.0*. The pricing advantage allowed Nintendo to use an old console marketing strategy, offering a game (Wii Sports) with each system purchase, that demonstrated the capabilities of the machine.

A TEMPORARY ADVANTAGE

Wii sales remained strong throughout 2008. By 2009, sales started to decline as many customers already owned Wii systems. Sony and Microsoft planned next-generation systems that could match the popular motion control features that the Wii offered. The economic recession also dragged down Wii sales. Martyn Williams, for *IDG News*, reported that Nintendo earned ¥69 billion during the first two quarters of its 2009 fiscal year, less than half of its earnings in the first half of fiscal 2008.

Ryan Kim, for *SFGate*, reported that third-party developers were also dissatisfied with the Wii. It was difficult for a gaming company to port a Wii game to other consoles easily because of the unique control system that the Wii used. Developers also felt that Nintendo placed too much emphasis on selling its own Wii games instead of helping other companies that made games for its platform.

Wii sales continued to shrink during 2010 and 2011 and Nintendo suffered large losses in 2011. Brad Moon, for *Investor Place,* reported that Nintendo probably lost around US$844 million during the 2011 fiscal year. Nintendo had crafted a strategy to beat competing console and handheld game manufacturers, but it had failed to predict the popularity of smartphones. A smartphone provided Internet access, business applications, phone service, and video games on a device that weighed about the same as a dedicated portable video game player like the Nintendo DS and often cost about the same. Nintendo had failed to create Mario and Zelda games for the iPhone and Android or introduce its own Nintendo-branded smartphone. Kyle Orland, for *Gamasutra*, reported that Sega did develop a smartphone version of its 1993 Sonic CD game. Console game companies were wary of competing in the smartphone gaming market because smartphone games often sold for a few dollars, instead of the US$50 or more that a console game could fetch.

AN OLD STRENGTH, A NEW INNOVATION

Nintendo learned, via its own past history, about one of the factors that made the Wii popular. Instead of attempting to upgrade its hardware to match competitors, Nintendo continued to market products that its customers could afford, and this strategy remained effective against the PlayStation and the Xbox. The other factor was the introduction of motion capture technology. Nintendo managed to create an innovative, new gaming experience while keeping hardware costs low and its control system simple.

BIBLIOGRAPHY

Borow, Zev. "Why Nintendo Won't Grow Up." *Wired,* January 2003. Accessed February 1, 2012. http://www.wired.com/wired/archive/11.01/nintendo.html?pg=1&topic=&topic_set=.

Chen, Vincent, et al. "Motion Sensor Technology Moves Towards Maturity with Related Markets to Hit US$63.8 Billion." *Digitimes,* October 14 2010. Accessed April 12 2012. http://www.digitimes.com/supply_chain_window/story.asp?datepublish=2010/10/14&pages=PR&seq=201.

Gaudiosi, John. "How the Wii Is Creaming the Competition." *Business 2.0,* April 25, 2007. Accessed February 1, 2012. http://money.cnn.com/magazines/business2/business2_archive/2007/05/01/8405654/index.htm.

Hermida, Alfred. "Nintendo Reveals Its Revolution." *BBC,* May 17, 2005. Accessed February 1, 2012. http://news.bbc.co.uk /2/hi/technology/4557443.stm.

Kim, Ryan. "New Challenges for Nintendo." *SF Gate,* November 30, 2009. Accessed February 1, 2012. http://www.sfgate .com/cgi-bin/article.cgi?f=/c/a/2009/11/29/BUPI1AQGOD .DTL&type=tech.

Mainelli, Tom, and Grace Aquino. "Let the Game Console Wars Begin." *PC World,* May 17, 2001. Accessed February 1, 2012. http://www.pcworld.com/article/50330/let_the_game _console_wars_begin.html.

Moon, Brad. "Nintendo Is Getting Its Lunch Eaten." *Investor Place,* February 1, 2012. Accessed February 1, 2012. http:// www.investorplace.com/2012/02/nintendo-is-getting-its -lunch-eaten-ntdoy-msft-sne/.

Morris, Chris. "Nintendo Goes 'Wii'." *CNN Money,* April 27, 2006. Accessed February 1, 2012. http://money.cnn.com /2006/04/27/commentary/game_over/nintendo/.

"Nintendo GameCube to Undercut Rivals." *BBC,* May 22, 2001. Accessed February 1, 2012. http://news.bbc.co.uk/2/hi /business/1344849.stm.

"Nintendo Profits Fall 42%." *BBC,* May 24, 2001. Accessed February 1, 2012. http://news.bbc.co.uk/2/hi/business /1348698.stm.

"Nintendo Revolution." *N-Sider,* October 5, 2005. Accessed February 1, 2012. http://www.n-sider.com/contentview.php ?contentid=248.

"Nintendo's Gyration." *Gamecubicle,* 2001. Accessed April 12, 2012. http://www.gamecubicle.com/news-nintendo_gyration .htm.

Orland, Kyle. "Sega Confirms Sonic CD Release for Consoles, PC, Smartphone." *GamaSutra,* August 25, 2011. Accessed February 1, 2012. http://www.gamasutra.com/view/news /36793/Sega_Confirms_Sonic_CD_Release_For_Consoles _PC_Smartphone.php.

Terdiman, Daniel. "Game Makers' Hand-to-Hand Combat." *Wired,* May 6, 2004. Accessed February 1, 2012. http://www .wired.com/gaming/gamingreviews/news/2004/05/63201?cu rrentPage=all.

"Thinking Out of the Box." *The Economist,* December 10 2011. Accessed April 12, 2012. http://www.economist.com/node /21541161.

Williams, Martyn. "Nintendo Profits Halved as Console Sales Slow." *IDG News,* October 29, 2009. Accessed February 1, 2012. http://www.pcworld.com/article/174633/nintendo _profit_halved_as_wii_console_sales_slow.html.

Oral Contraceptives:
From Discovery to Approval

Oral contraceptives took several decades to develop. When researchers identified the hormones that prevented pregnancy, mass production of these hormones was challenging, as they needed to be extracted from living animals. Advances in hormone synthesis made oral contraceptive work much easier, but scientists faced a new challenge: getting government officials to approve their new drugs. Oral contraceptives triggered a series of events that caused widespread changes in society, including the famous *Griswold v. Connecticut* legal decision in the United States.

CONTRACEPTIVE THEORY

Scientists knew that a pregnant animal could not become pregnant again while carrying a fetus (unborn yet developing organism) or fetuses, although they did not know exactly how the animal's body prevented a second pregnancy. Ludwig Haberlandt, a German professor, predicted that the ovaries of a pregnant animal released hormones that prevented conception. Haberlandt carried out a rabbit study in 1919 that supported this hypothesis. Haberlandt removed the ovaries of a pregnant rabbit and placed them inside a second rabbit. Haberlandt then allowed a male rabbit to have intercourse with the second rabbit, but the second rabbit did not become pregnant, according to Bob Weintraub in his article "Pincus, Djerassi, and Oral Contraceptives." The experiment proved the feasibility of human oral contraception, as a similar hormone could be given to a woman to prevent pregnancy. Ottfried Otto Fellner reported similar results from his own experiments in 1919 and suggested that the hormones could be used to sterilize human patients.

The scientists Edgar Allen and Edward Doisy identified the hormone inside the rabbit ovaries as estrogen and searched for other animals to use as a source of estrogen. Horses appeared promising because of their large size and virility. Pharmaceutical companies studied estrogen for its potential therapeutic effects as well as its potential birth control uses, as scientists believed that it could reduce the symptoms of menopause and help rejuvenate older women, potentially creating an extremely profitable drug.

In 1938, scientists at the Schering AG pharmaceutical company figured out how to produce estrogen, which eliminated the need to extract estrogen from rabbits and horses. When scientists gave the estrogen orally to female patients, it was not very effective, as it could not easily reach the ovaries through the digestive system. Hans Innhofen and Walter Hohlweg, who also worked for Schering, researched estrogen compounds that could be taken orally. Also in 1938, Innhofen and Hohlweg announced the discovery of the estrogen compound ethinyl estradiol, which did not break down in the digestive system.

STRATEGIC IMPLICATIONS

The discovery of synthetic estrogen impressed British and U.S. researchers, but the United Kingdom and the United States knew that Germany was likely to declare war in the near future, and the new hormone could give the Third Reich a military advantage. The British researcher Charles Dodds knew that Schering could earn high profits if it could obtain the patent for estrogen, so Dodds rushed to create his own artificial estrogen, diethylstilbesterol.

Although Schering could still patent ethinyl estradiol, every pharmaceutical company could now produce diethylstilbesterol without paying royalties. This greatly reduced the value of Schering's research as well as the tax revenue the German company received. Dodds gave up his own opportunity to become wealthy from the sale of artificial estrogen, but he believed strongly in sharing scientific knowledge for the benefit of all nations rather than restricting it for his own personal gain.

U.S. pharmaceutical manufacturers wanted to sell diethylstilbesterol in the United States. Since Dodds had given up his right to collect royalties, the artificial estrogen offered a much better profit margin than other drugs. Although several pharmaceutical companies asked the U.S. Food and Drug Administration (FDA) to grant them the right to sell diethylstilbesterol, reports suggesting that artificial estrogen could cause cancer complicated the approval process. The companies decided to work together to convince the FDA to approve the drug. With this in mind, the U.S. manufacturers canceled their individual drug applications in late 1940 and decided to set up a new organization that would lobby the FDA to approve estrogen sales from all manufacturers, organizing testimonies from physicians and research from several drug companies. Drug companies continued to fund their lobbying organization after the FDA approved estrogen sales in 1941, and the organization eventually became the Pharmaceutical Research and Manufacturers of America (PhRMA).

CORTISONE RESEARCH

Carl Djerassi left his home in Austria to escape Nazi Germany and became a student at the University of Wisconsin. Djerassi worked with estrogen at the university, selecting it as his thesis topic, but pharmaceutical companies were more interested in synthesizing cortisone. The U.S. Department of Defense used cortisone to treat combat stress, so many hormone researchers focused on cortisone synthesis during the war. In the late 1940s cortisone appeared more commercially promising than estrogen and progesterone, as scientists discovered that cortisone could also alleviate the symptoms of arthritis, according to Weintraub. Djerassi traveled to a Laboratorios Syntex S.A. facility in Mexico to research lower cost pathways of cortisone synthesis.

Meanwhile in the United States, Margaret Sanger was searching for a way to replace physical contraception methods such as condoms with a more effective oral contraceptive. In 1950 Sanger met the hormone researcher Gregory Pincus in New York, New York at a party and told him about her search for oral contraceptives. Pincus agreed to help, but he needed money to conduct his hormone research. Pincus was already famous because he had invented *in vitro* fertilization for rabbits while working at Harvard University, but conservative groups complained

about this research and it had cost him a tenured research position. Sanger convinced Katherine McCormick, whose husband had inherited a large amount of money from the International Harvester Corporation, to pay for the research. Katherine McCormick held a degree from the Massachusetts Institute of Technology and was familiar with a large amount of the science involved in hormone therapy.

Although Djerassi did discover a better way to synthesize cortisone, The Upjohn Company researchers found an even better method of their own, so Djerassi started working on progesterone compounds. A physician could administer estrogen orally, but commonly available forms of progesterone broke down in the digestive system. With the research of Djerassi, Syntex developed an orally available progesterone derivative, norethisterone, removing the necessity for painful progesterone injections.

HORMONE PILLS

Pincus realized that norethisterone held potential as an oral contraceptive in pill form. Researcher and chemist Frank Colton had announced the discovery of another hormone, norethynodrel, which also showed promise, in Pincus' opinion. Pincus needed to make sure that his birth control research would not get him into legal trouble. Massachusetts considered birth control illegal and some people did not trust Pincus because of his work with *in vitro* fertilization. He decided to recruit scientist John Rock, who held a reputation as a devout Catholic, to help him research oral contraceptives.

Rock had advocated birth control techniques in the past, such as the rhythm method, that did not offend the Catholic Church authorities. Rock knew that the church could excommunicate him if its leaders believed he was promoting immoral activities. Although the Catholic Church was aware of Rock's birth control advocacy, he still remained in good standing and had the respect of church authorities. Rock was old enough to retire, but he remained a strong advocate of birth control, so he decided to help Pincus despite the personal risks.

The pill effectively prevented conception, but Pincus and Rock noticed that they also contained another estrogen compound, mestranol. Considering mestranol an impurity, the scientists removed it, but they discovered that by doing so, the pill had become less effective. The scientists continued their work on a pill that contained both active ingredients, which became known as a combined oral contraceptive pill. Enovid, the first pill, contained norethynodrel and a smaller amount of mestranol.

Pincus and Rock released a preliminary study of their pill in 1955. The researchers knew that Massachusetts would not let them test Enovid for birth control in the

United States, so they tested the pill in Puerto Rico in 1956. Pincus and Rock suspected that the FDA would be cautious about approving a birth control pill, so they decided to demonstrate that the pill was safe before they revealed its true purpose. The researchers asked the FDA to approve Enovid for menstrual disorders, showing that it treated female ailments without severe side effects, and the FDA approved Enovid in 1957.

GAINING APPROVAL

Rock remained faithful to the Catholic Church and he decided to use the same strategy that he had used with the FDA and the Commonwealth of Massachusetts to convince Pope Pius XII to approve the pills. After Rock told Pope Pius that the pills treated female illnesses related to menstruation, Pope Pius agreed in 1958 to allow Catholic women to take Enovid pills. Pope Pius died of a heart attack later in 1958 and Pope John XXIII became the new leader of the Catholic Church.

Rock realized that the FDA would be more skeptical, so he explained that the pill simply used the same hormones the body used to prevent pregnancy, so it would not harm female patients. The decision to approve Enovid involved unusual safety issues because women could potentially take it for several decades, unlike most medications at the time, which treated temporary illnesses. The FDA accepted the scientists' argument and authorized Enovid prescriptions for birth control in 1960. Enovid quickly became very popular in the United States.

Enovid did not gain popularity as quickly in Europe. European women could already get prescriptions for intra-uterine device implants which effectively prevented pregnancy. European officials were concerned that legalizing the pill would lead to immoral behavior. Schering introduced the pill to Europeans as Anovlar, a medicine for menstrual disorders, following the strategy of Pincus and Rock, while claiming that infertility was simply a side effect of the medication. European officials remained wary, limiting the pill to married women who already had children. The European pill contained a smaller concentration of active ingredients than the U.S. pill.

Rock continued to promote Enovid throughout the United States, writing a book in 1963 that explained why the pill did not violate Catholic theology and discussing the book in magazines and television shows. Scientists and religious leaders met with Vatican leaders and discussed the pill, as the Catholic Church considered whether to allow its congregants to use oral contraception. Many priests continued to believe that the church would authorize birth control and Pope Paul VI (who succeeded Pope John XXIII in 1963) set up the Birth Control Commission to study the issue.

GRISWOLD V. CONNECTICUT

Estelle Griswold, a member of Planned Parenthood (an organization that provides reproductive health services), decided to make Enovid available to more U.S. women by opening up Planned Parenthood clinics in Connecticut that sold the drug. Like Massachusetts, Connecticut also prohibited hormonal birth control, and the state sued Griswold to shut down her clinics. Griswold expected to face conflict with government authorities, so she appealed the initial rulings, and the *Griswold v. Connecticut* case eventually reached the Supreme Court.

The U.S. Constitution did not include any guidance for the court that specifically referred to oral contraceptives. Although the Constitution did not directly grant citizens a right to privacy, several amendments in the Bill of Rights covered privacy-related issues. For example, a court needed to approve a law enforcement request to search a citizen's house because of the Fourth Amendment of the U.S. Constitution, which guarded against unreasonable searches and seizures. The justices decided that the Founding Fathers had written these amendments to protect privacy rights, so these amendments established a penumbra (literally, a kind of shadow) that prevented future attempts to limit the rights of citizens. The U.S. Supreme Court ruled in favor of Estelle Griswold in 1965, preventing Connecticut from closing down her Planned Parenthood clinics.

The *Griswold v. Connecticut* ruling was extremely controversial, not only because it made oral contraceptives legal but also because the judges established the concept of the penumbra. Conservatives argued that the court had exceeded its authority by creating new rights that were not present in the Constitution. Liberals realized that the concept of the penumbra could also apply to other religion- and morality-based court rulings.

CHANGING SOCIETY

The Catholic Church finally made its decision in 1968, stating that it would not allow Catholic women to use oral contraception. Priests could no longer advocate birth control. However, by 1968, oral contraception had become widespread within the United States and many Catholic couples simply ignored the ruling. As for John Rock, he had always believed that the pope would accept his argument, and after the final decision, he stopped going to church.

The precedent that *Griswold v. Connecticut* set became very important, as litigants successfully used the penumbra concept to challenge laws that criminalized homosexuality, made abortion illegal, and prevented single women from buying birth control pills. The U.S. Supreme Court struck down many of the state laws that restricted the sale of contraception products in the United States.

BIBLIOGRAPHY

Li, Raymond Hang Wun, and Sue Seen Tsing Lo. "Evolutionary Voyage of Modern Birth Control Methods." *HKJGOM,* 5, no. 1 (2005): 40–45. Accessed February 3, 2012. http://www.ogshk.org/documents/2005V5N1/V5N1-p40-GYN4.pdf.

Pedersen, Thoru. "A Tale of Pincus and the Pill." *Worcester Telegram,* July 2, 2009. Accessed February 3, 2012. http://www.telegram.com/article/20090702/NEWS/907020630.

"The Pill." *PBS,* 2002. Accessed February 3, 2012. http://www.pbs.org/wgbh/amex/pill/index.html.

"The Story of the Pill: A Forgotten Revolution." MUVS.org. Accessed February 3, 2012. http://www.en.muvs.org/topic/the-story-of-the-pill-en.pdf.

Vile, John R. "Review of *Griswold v. Connecticut: Birth Control and the Constitutional Right of Privacy.*" *Law & Politics Book Review* 15, no. 3 (March 2005): 246–249. Accessed February 3, 2012. http://www.bsos.umd.edu/gvpt/lpbr/subpages/reviews/johnson305.htm.

Weintraub, Bob. "Pincus, Djerassi, and Oral Contraceptives." *Bulletin of the Israel Chemical Society,* August 2005. Accessed February 3, 2012. www.chemistry.org.il/booklet/19/pdf/Bob_weintraub.pdf .

Otis Elevator Company

EARLY YEARS IN A RISING BUSINESS

Elisha Graves Otis (1811–1861), born on a farm outside of Halifax, Vermont, was the youngest of six children. Otis's several attempts at starting a business in his early years were all cut short by his persistent poor health. In 1845, while working as a master mechanic for a bed frame manufacturer in Albany, New York, Otis began to demonstrate a talent for invention. While there, he devised a railroad safety brake that the locomotive's engineer could control, a device to build rails for four-poster beds, and a mechanism to improve the operation of turbine wheels.

Following a move to Yonkers, New York, where Otis was employed by another bedstead firm, his talents for mechanical invention again came to the fore. Asked by management to create a method to move equipment and supplies between floors in their manufacturing facility, Otis took an entirely fresh look at a conventional hoist design used in that era. Mid-19th century hoists involved significant risk to those in close proximity, given the lack of protection against mechanical failure of the device and a resulting sudden reversal of the hoist cart's direction. Otis devised a means to prevent such catastrophic reversals by use of a strong steel wagon spring meshing with a ratchet. Using his device, the car or platform would be locked in place should the lifting cables be broken or damaged.

Sudden direction reversals, and the possibility of severe injury as a result, had plagued the hoisting and elevating industry for years, causing many to avoid such hoisting devices and consequently limiting their acceptance. Realizing his safety brake's potential, Otis quit his job and with two US$300 orders in hand, opened his own factory.

A year later Otis demonstrated his hoist break, used on an elevator device initially known as an "ascending room," at the 1854 Crystal Palace Exposition in New York, New York. Showing a flair for the dramatic, Otis placed himself in a demonstration elevator, and while it was being hoisted, had the cable severed with an axe. The large audience on hand witnessed the success of his safety brake.

Shortly thereafter, Otis began manufacturing passenger elevators and received a patent for a steam-powered version in 1861. An early version of his steam-powered elevator was installed in a five-story department store in Manhattan, New York and became the first public elevator in operation in the world.

THE SONS TAKE OVER

Otis was a talented inventor, but his abilities did not extend to the world of business. At his death in 1861 from nervous depression and diphtheria, he left an estate to his two sons, Charles and Norton, worth only US$5,200, a sum counterbalanced by over US$8,000 of debt. His sons did receive the elevator company, which they quickly named Otis Brothers and Company. The sons showed a talent for business and during their careers received a total of 53 patents for elevator and elevator safety devices.

By the mid-1870s the two brothers had installed over 2,000 steam-powered elevators and gained what was then an impressive total of more than US$1 million in total receipts. In 1878 Otis Brothers and Company introduced a faster, less expensive, hydraulic-actuated elevator. In the next four years, the company would install elevators in the U.S. Capitol Building, the White House, and the Washington Monument.

In 1889 the company introduced the first electric-powered direct connection elevator and demonstrated the first "escalator," a term that was an exclusive company trademark until 1950. Nine years later, in a merger with 14 other elevator companies, the Otis Elevator Company was created. In 1904 the company introduced an electric gearless-traction model elevator, a design so effective that it was still the basis for most elevators constructed in the 21st century.

By 1912 Otis Elevator Co. had seven factories , as well as subsidiaries in Canada and three European countries. In 1922 Otis Elevator began to sell service contracts on the equipment it manufactured and installed, and this became a key profit center for the company for many years. Innovations continued during the 1920s and early 1930s, such as the introduction of an elevator that would self-stop precisely and reliably at any floor. Speeds improved as well, and a double-deck model was introduced. In 1929, just prior to the onset of the Great Depression, Otis Elevator Company saw its net income reach US$8.4 million. In 1931 Otis Elevator became the contractor for the elevator system in the Empire State Building in New York City, which would remain for decades the tallest building in the world.

THE AUTOTRONIC DEBUTS

Following World War II Otis Elevator introduced an elevator that no longer needed an attendant. The "Autotronic" put an end to the occupation of elevator operator, whose job had been to control the elevator up and down via a lever. In those same postwar years Otis introduced the first elevators with automatic doors.

During the 1950s the elevator industry began to mature and Otis started looking for ways to diversify while still maintaining a hold on its key line of business. In 1953 the company made its first acquisitions in over 50 years with the purchase of Transmitter Equipment Manufacturing Company (TIMCO) and a U.S.-based forklift manufacturer. However, neither of these acquisitions was particularly profitable and even with revenues increasing fourfold between 1955 and 1968, company profits would grow by less than half that rate.

By 1968 Otis Elevator held nearly half of the U.S. elevator market but the company was still searching outside of the United States to increase sales and profitability. Trying to stay in fields related to its core competency, Otis bought five companies over the next few years, all of which were involved in materials handling, including lift truck and hoist and crane manufacturers. The company also branched out to horizontal people-moving systems (also known as moving walkways or sidewalks)in 1969, taking advantage of the rapidly expanding need for such equipment in airports and other areas of high pedestrian congestion.

By the early 1970s Otis Elevator Company sales had begun to close in on the US$1 billion in annual sales milestone. The company had plants in 17 countries and derived 37 percent of its profit from overseas operations. In 1974 company revenues surpassed US$1 billion for the first time, with half its revenues coming from foreign sales. Taking advantage of strong economic activity, both in the United States and overseas, company profits rose every year between 1968 and 1975.

OTIS ELEVATOR BECOMES PART OF A CONGLOMERATE

In 1975 United Technologies Corporation (UT), seeking to end its overreliance on military contracts, made an unsolicited tender offer and purchased Otis stock. Otis management, which at first resisted the takeover, went along when UT sweetened the purchase price by US$2 per share and agreed to purchase or exchange all outstanding Otis stock. The total purchase price was estimated at US$276 million.

As a subsidiary of UT, Otis Elevator continued to thrive and grew its sales and profitability as never before. Sales rose to US$2 billion in 1986, US$3 billion in 1989, and US$4 billion in 1990. Otis then had 24 percent of the world market for elevators, twice the amount of its next largest competitor.

By 1990 Otis had introduced an array of computerized microprocessors into the control function of its elevator systems, allowing for an increasingly sophisticated and high passenger-carrying capability. When linked to a base operating system, building managers could control up to 64 elevators in one building. By the year 2000 Otis had become the most international division of the UT family of companies and its many multilingual employees were often used as translators for other company divisions. Otis continued its successful policy of acquisition to further growth, a policy that now occurred primarily in foreign markets, where rapid industrialization and urbanization provided the highest growth markets for the elevator industry.

OTIS BECOMES A RECOGNIZED NAME WORLDWIDE

In the first decade of the 21st century, Otis began to take advantage of the largest new elevator market in the world, China. The company established seven joint ventures with Chinese elevator companies, including one in Suzhou, China, with the largest elevator manufacturer in China. During these years Otis did not neglect the country of its origin in its efforts to continue growth, purchasing Amtec Elevator Services, the largest independent elevator and escalator service company in the United States. This purchase enabled Otis to continue expansion of its profitable service operations.

In the 2010s Otis has continued to expand upon its two core strengths, product improvement and continued acquisition. New markets have opened up in management of green technology for elevators that exist within low-operating-cost buildings. In 2011 Otis purchased Marshall Elevator Company, the largest privately held elevator service business in Pennsylvania. This acquisition capped a decade of growth in the firm's service business, made through acquiring 60 companies.

By 2011 Otis had over 60,000 employees in 200 countries, with 53,000 of those employees working outside of the United States. Revenues in 2010 were US$11.6 billion, with more than 80 percent of that coming from foreign operations. Over 2.4 million Otis elevators were in operation worldwide and the company's service division maintained over 1.7 million elevators across the globe.

THE SOCIAL AND ECONOMIC IMPACT OF ELEVATORS

The elevator played a significant role in the rapid urbanization that took place in North America and Europe starting in the mid-19th century. Without a safe and reliable means of vertical transportation, the heights of buildings were limited. Elisha Otis's application of his braking system to elevators significantly reduced public anxiety regarding the safety of this technology. As the speed and reliability of these devices improved, the practical height of any building increased correspondingly. Companies often viewed the height of their headquarters buildings as a mark of prestige, and they took advantage of improvements in elevators to construct taller and taller buildings. As the intensity of land use increased, land prices in urban areas rose significantly, partly due to improvements in elevator technology.

Otis played a significant role in the urbanization of the United States and Europe and continued in the 21st century to play a significant part in that trend throughout the developing world.

WHAT HAS MADE OTIS SO SUCCESSFUL?

Otis Elevator's rise to the position of the leading elevator company in the world is due to successful company strategies, many of which have been maintained since early in the firm's existence. One such quality is leadership. Since the company's beginnings in the 1860s, Otis has consistently placed itself at the forefront of elevator technological development. In the 2010s the company's philosophy continued in that tradition, with a strong commitment to development of green technologies, both in its products and manufacturing processes.

Since the company's founding on the basis of development of the first safe people-moving elevator system, it has maintained a policy of "safety first." Otis employs a stringent Product Development Process (PDP) for all of its products, and major components to systems are tested to ensure a 20-year life expectancy between overhauls. Otis has utilized this strategy to become dominant in the development of systems for large buildings, where reliability is generally more important to the customer than cost. Otis has developed and continued to expand its highly regarded service organization, which operates throughout the world.

BIBLIOGRAPHY

Kluger, Jeffrey. "An Elevator to Space? Better Take the Stairs." *TIME,* November 21, 2011. Accessed January 31, 2012. http://www.time.com/time/health/article/0,8599,2099830,00.html.

Otis Elevator Company. "About Otis." Farmington, CT. Accessed January 31, 2012. http://www.otisworldwide.com/d1-about.html.

———. "Proven Flat Belt Elevator Technology." Farmington, CT. Accessed January 31, 2012. http://www.otisgen2.com/index.shtml.

"Otis Elevator Company, Inc." *International Directory of Company Histories,* edited by Tina Grant. Vol. 39, 311–315. Detroit: St. James Press, 2001. Gale Virtual Reference Library (GALE|CX2844300090). Accessed January 31, 2012. http://go.galegroup.com/ps/i.do?id=GALE%7CCX2844300090&v=2.1&u=itsbtrial&it=r&p=GVRL&sw=w.

"Who Made America?" *PBS,* Accessed January 31, 2012. http://www.pbs.org/wgbh/theymadeamerica/whomade/otis_hi.html.

Pacemaker: An Evolving Global Medical Innovation

A cardiac pacemaker is a small medical device used to correct faulty electrical signaling in the heart. Modern pacemakers are implanted in the user's chest and use low-level electrical pulses to correct the heart's faulty signaling, thereby inducing the heart to beat at a normal rate. A pacemaker system consists of a miniaturized battery, a computerized generator, and sensors that connect the pacemaker to the heart. Placing of a pacemaker typically requires a surgical procedure, usually done in a laboratory or hospital setting, with most patients being released the following day or within a few days, depending on the patient and type of device implanted.

Pacemakers can be used to correct a number of abnormal conditions, including dangerous arrhythmias (heart disorders in which the heart may beat too fast, too slow, or irregularly), or poor synchronization between heart chambers. Newer pacemakers have taken advantage of advances in microprocessor technology to include monitoring of such factors as breathing rate and blood temperature to adjust the heart rate to the user's activity level. Depending on the conditions being corrected, pacemakers can be installed either on a temporary or permanent basis. Pacemakers may also be used to alleviate symptoms such as shortness of breath, fatigue, or fainting. A related device is an implantable cardioverter defibrillator (ICD). An ICD can use either low- or high-energy pulses administered to the heart to prevent dangerous arrhythmias leading to sudden death.

While pacemakers are usually installed in adults, and most frequently in elderly adults, they can also be used in children and adolescents who are suffering from some forms of congenital heart disease.

PACEMAKER DEVELOPMENT

While electro-stimulation of the heart was attempted as far back as the late 18th century, proof that electrical stimulation of the heart muscle could cause ventricular fibrillation (an arrhythmia in which there is a rapid series of contractions in the lower chambers of the heart) did not occur until the late 1890s. After this discovery, the first portable electric resuscitation devices (which stimulate the heart electronically until it starts beating again) were developed for ambulances.

In 1930, Albert Hyman and his brother, an engineer, developed and patented the first device to which the term "artificial pacemaker" was applied. This device, which used a hand crank magneto (a machine used to generate electrical current) to provide the electrical pulses, did not receive widespread attention. Despite Hyman's claims, later investigation of his device found it ineffective and no commercial development of the device was ever attempted. In the early 1950s external pacemakers, using straps placed over the chest of a patient, were successfully used by Dr. Paul Zoll at the Beth Israel Hospital in Boston, Massachusetts. These devices, large tabletop electrical instruments, were effective under limited circumstances for patients with transient heart arrhythmia (an arrythmia that comes and goes).

By the mid-1950s and the early years of open-heart surgery, a condition characterized by a persistent slow heart rate, called atrioventricular block or AV block, was being studied, and the link to this impairment and the electrical workings of the heart was known. However, AV block required stimulation of the heart for too long a time for the type of device Zoll had developed. University of Minnesota heart surgeon C. Walter Lillehei, struggling with this problem, began to work with a local student named Earl Bakken, who was employed part-time at the hospital. Their efforts produced the first device that used electrodes attached directly to the heart. (An electrode is a conductor through which electricity enters or leaves.) This method of direct stimulation permitted the use of much lower levels of voltage and was better tolerated by patients requiring long-term treatment.

INNOVATION FOLLOWING A TRAGEDY

In 1957, according to a 2007 story by Lorna Benson for Minnesota Public Radio, a Halloween (October 31) electrical blackout across Minnesota and Wisconsin created an event that led to a turning point in the development of the pacemaker. The University of Minnesota hospital had started using pacemakers to treat children with heart defects, but the blackout that night brought down both of its electricity suppliers. Doctors in the cardiac unit had to give their child patients drugs to keep them alive in the absence of the pacemakers. One child died.

Later, Lillehei discussed with Bakken what might be done to prevent a similar event from happening in the future. By this time Bakken had dropped out of school and founded Medtronic, Inc., a medical device repair company. Lillehei and Bakken collaborated in the development of a portable, battery-operated pacemaker. The new device was powered by nine-volt mercury batteries and was small enough to be worn by a child. Bakken was elated by the invention, knowing that it would be capable of saving children's lives. This battery-powered device would become a watershed in the development of the pacemaker, and a defining moment in the future of Bakken's new company. While Medtronic made fewer than 100 of these devices in the following three years, the company would go on to become a leading producer of pacemaker devices for decades to come.

By 1960, Medtronic was already an established maker of external heart pacemakers, with devices in use at hospitals in the United States and other countries around the globe. Also in 1960, two doctors, William Chardack and Andrew Gage, were developing an implantable pacemaker at a veterans' hospital in New York, New York. At the same time, Wilson Greatbatch, often described as the inventor of the implantable pacemaker, was working on similar technology. Greatbatch, Chardack, and Gage eventually installed an implantable pacemaker in a laboratory dog. Medtronic's founders secured the rights to produce and sell the first implantable pacemakers, and between 1961 and 1963 Medtronic produced a total of 2,178 implantable devices, more than all other producers combined.

By 1972 pacemaker implantations in the United States had grown to 110 per million population, similar to rates in France, Germany, and Sweden but five times that of the United Kingdom. Barriers to entrance in the industry remained low until the mid-1970s, and about two dozen companies had by that time introduced new versions of the devices. Research in this period was concentrated in two areas: increasing the battery life of pacemakers to limit frequent replacement and reduction in the overall size of the devices.

A nuclear-fueled device with a battery life of 10 to 20 years was also tried during this period, but the drawback of radiation exposure soon stopped those efforts. Finally, the lithium battery was accepted as the best power source then available. Simultaneously, new integrated circuits were developed, which improved the functionality and further reduced pacemaker size.

INDUSTRY LEADERS

Both of these advances were successfully brought to the market, based on U.S. National Aeronautics and Space Administration (NASA) miniaturization technology, by Pacesetter Systems Inc. of Sylmar, California. Pacesetter would eventually be bought by St. Jude Medical, Inc., which would become one of the big three manufacturers of heart-pacing devices for years to come.

In 1972 Cardiac Pacemakers Inc. (CPI) was formed in St. Paul, Minnesota. This firm quickly became a leader in the industry with the improvement of a sealed titanium case for implantable devices. Eventually a subsidiary of Boston Scientific Corporation, this entity would go on to become one the three largest pacemaker manufacturers in the world, along with Medtronic and St. Jude Medical.

Acceptance of implantable pacing devices had grown significantly by 1989, despite national headlines in the United States reporting fears that physicians were implanting more devices than were necessary. Pacemakers in 1989 all had lithium batteries and integrated circuitry with reliable life spans of up to eight years. In that year, estimates of implantation rates in the United States had grown over 300 percent in just 17 years, to a total of 359 implants per million residents, according to Kirk Jeffrey in his book, *Machines in Our Hearts: The Cardiac Pacemaker*. Northern European countries showed similar rates of increased acceptance and use.

By 1997 U.S. estimates of implantation reached an estimated 571 implants per million residents. Estimates of the number of devices installed worldwide in 1997 were as high as 317,000. Growth during these years was attributable to aging populations, greater acceptance of the pacemaker devices, and a greater variety of conditions that such devices were able to treat. In the 21st century, this spectrum of usage continued to expand, with pacemaker-type devices able to provide prolonged relief for an increasing range of heart conditions. The creation and improvement of multichamber devices, begun in the 1990s, led to reduced risk, increased life spans, and a higher quality of life for recipients. By 2004 it was estimated that 150,000 pacemakers were installed annually in the United States alone.

PACEMAKERS: A GROWING GLOBAL MARKET

In the 21st century the cardiac pacemaker device has continued to experience rapid change and technological improvement on both a short-term and long-term basis. Demand for this product is not subject to fluctuation due to ups and downs in the economy, and this, combined with a growing population of older potential users worldwide, has contributed to forecasts of positive growth for the industry through 2015. According to the report, "Global Cardiac Pacemakers–Market Growth Analysis, 2009–2115," global sales are expected to reach US$5.1 billion by 2015, with a compounded annual growth rate (CAGR) of 11 percent between 2009 and 2015. Thus far the high cost of the devices has served to concentrate the market in wealthier, developed countries. In 2009 the North American market accounted for approximately 40 percent of global sales, with Europe accounting for a little less than 30 percent. However, the Asia-Pacific region is the fastest-growing segment of the market, where growth (on a CAGR basis) for 2009 to 2015 is expected to exceed 13 percent.

However, countertrends exist in the market for these devices. Relatively mature conditions and intense competition in the United States and Europe, as well as competition from ICD and cardio-resynchronization therapy (CRT) devices, have resulted in softening prices for traditional cardio-rhythm management (CRM) pacemakers. Reimbursement trends in health insurance companies and Medicare have also placed downward pressure on pricing, which is expected to continue in the 2010s. Additionally, trust concerns developed in the pacemaker market, following a series of recalls in the middle of the first decade of the 21st century, and device manufacturers struggled to regain the confidence of potential users.

After several years of strong growth from 1993 to 2001, implantation of the more advanced dual-chamber devices leveled off in the United States for some years afterward. Meanwhile, implantation of the single-chamber devices has been in a downward trend since before the turn of the century.

THE FUTURE OF PACEMAKING

While the market for pacemakers in the developing world is growing at a double-digit rate, that growth is hampered by one major obstacle: the high price of implantable pacemakers. While incomes in third world countries in the 21st century grew more rapidly than in much of the developed world, the price of cardiac pacemakers is still an insurmountable hurdle for most people in Asia, Latin America, and Africa.

In January 2012, at the World Economic Forum in Davos, Switzerland, Medtronic CEO Omar Ishrak outlined Medtronic's ongoing commitment to bringing the same revolution in pricing to the pacemaker industry that has made the computer a globally available product. Medtronic had already segmented the pacemaker market specifically for Asian users in its development of the Champion product line, a lower-priced, less-feature-laden model of the offerings available in the developed world. In keeping with the company's long-held mission statement and commitment to "contribute to human welfare," Ishrak outlined Medtronic's efforts to extend its product differentiation strategy to bring low-cost medical devices to the world's poor. Although research was still in the beginning stages, Ishrak saw pacemakers as the device with the greatest potential for fulfilling that promise in the near future. In an article by Ben Hirschler for the *Huffington Post*, Ishrak was quoted as saying, "I'd like to challenge all our businesses to start thinking this way, but the area where we are furthest ahead is perhaps pacemakers, where we're thinking of real disruption in terms of cost and simplicity." Ishrak said he expected to see these results in three to five years.

Another outlook for the industry is the dramatic reduction in size of pacemaking devices anticipated in the near future. As reported in March 2011 by Aaron Saenz in *Singularity Hub*, Medtronic vice president of medicine and technology, Stephen Oesterie, announced Medtronic's plans for development of a new generation of pacemakers that are about half the size of the average person's smallest fingernail. These devices would be placed directly on the user's heart, would require no leads, and could be installed via a catheter without invasive major surgery. Medtronic had already developed most of the technology necessary to build such a device. The largest hurdles that remained were the development of a reliable and appropriately miniaturized power source and the time involved in meeting U.S. Food and Drug Administration trial requirements.

BIBLIOGRAPHY

Benson, Lorna. "Halloween Blackout of '57 Spurs Creation of Portable Pacemaker." *Minnesota Public Radio,* October 31, 2007. Accessed February 6, 2012. http://minnesota.public radio.org/display/web/2007/10/29/batterypacemaker/.

"Global Cardiac Pacemakers–Market Growth Analysis, 2009–2115." *ReportLinker,* February 2011. Accessed February 6, 2012. http://www.reportlinker.com/p0407311-summary /Global-Cardiac-Pacemakers-Market-Growth-Analysis.html.

Hirschler, Ben. "After $35 Tablet Computer, Are Inexpensive Pacemakers Next?" *Huffington Post,* January 25, 2012. Accessed February 6, 2012. http://www.huffingtonpost .com/2012/01/25/inexpensive-pacemaker-medtronic-cheap _n_1230853.html.

Jeffrey, Kirk. *Machines in Our Hearts: The Cardiac Pacemaker.* Baltimore, MD: The Johns Hopkins University Press, 2001, 263–290.

"Medtronic's Market Segmentation Strategy." YouSigma, 2008. Accessed February 6, 2012. http://www.yousigma.com.

Mohee, Kevin. "Cardiac Pacing: A Brief History in the Development of Pacemakers." Society for Cardiothoracic Surgery in Great Britain and Ireland. Accessed February 6, 2012. http://sscts.org/HistoryPacemakers.aspx.

"Pacemaker." MedicineNet.com. Accessed February 6, 2012. http://www.medicinenet.com/pacemaker/article .htm.

Saenz, Aaron. "Medtronic's Tiny Pacemaker–No Leads, No Surgery, Wireless." *Singularity Hub,* March 3, 2011. Accessed February 6, 2012. http://singularityhub.com/2011/03/03 /medtronics-tiny-pacemaker-no-surgery-no-leads-wireless -communications/.

Pandora Radio/Music Genome Project

Pandora Media, Inc., began life as Savage Beast Technologies, Inc., in January 2000. Founded by Tim Westergren and friends, Jon Kraft and Will Glaser, Savage Beast was a music recommendation service that grew into the Music Genome Project. In July 2005 the company launched an Internet radio service and changed its name to Pandora Media, Inc.

The Music Genome Project is a sophisticated database using technology that attempts to understand an individual's taste in music and make appropriate, personalized listening recommendations. With a computer program and employees trained in music, songs are evaluated and classified using over 400 attributes covering the qualities of melody, harmony, rhythm, form, composition, and lyrics. According to the company's musicologist and recognized architect of the Music Genome Project, Nolan Gasser, the basic idea was to approach music from an almost scientific perspective. Once the database was organized, an Internet radio service seemed a logical extension and Pandora Radio was launched in August 2005.

FROM MUSICIAN TO ENTREPRENEUR

According to a 2008 Harvard Business School article by Noam Wasserman and L. P. Maurice, Tim Westergren conceived of the idea of using musical attributes to connect songs while working as a musical composer in the film industry. His work entailed establishing the type of music a movie director wanted by listening to songs that the director thought might work with the film. Westergren would then break this music down into a set of attributes and translate the set into a composition with similar attributes.

Aware that existing music websites at the time were simply "content repositories," Westergren wanted to take the process used in his composing work and develop it into software that could produce intelligent recommendations for a music listener based on previous selections. As a musician himself, he was also aware of the difficulty that new or lesser-known musicians had in connecting the listening public to their music. He thought that a software product recommending music choices based on the types of songs enjoyed by the listener could alert them to new music and new artists.

Although originally reluctant to take on the role of entrepreneur, Westergren became convinced that his idea had a chance of success. He explained the concept to a college acquaintance, Jon Kraft, who had already successfully founded and subsequently sold his own enterprise database start-up. Kraft was a big music fan and saw merit in Westergren's proposal. In December 1999 they began drafting a business plan.

The original business model called for the development of a music recommendation technology (the Music Genome Project) and then licensing it to other Internet radio service providers and possibly radio kiosks in record stores. Asked why he changed the business plan from simply selling licenses for the music recommendation software to operating an online personalized radio station, Westergren responded that Pandora knew that there was an enormous potential in the intellectual property. By 2005 broadband had become the accepted norm for Internet access and this made a huge difference for the streaming of music on computers.

PERSONALIZED RADIO

According to the Pandora website, the name "Pandora" was taken from Greek mythology and means "all gifted."

In the Greek myth Pandora received many gifts from the gods including the gift of music. She was also renowned for being very curious. Putting these two attributes together, Pandora Media, Inc., devised a mission statement that aimed "to reward the musically curious among us with a never-ending experience of music discovery."

The Music Genome Project, the essence of Pandora, was initiated in 2000. Pandora Media, then named Savage Beast Technologies, began by recruiting Gasser, the musicologist, and a number of trained musicians to analyze and log over 100 attributes of songs and work with engineers to develop algorithms. These first results were recorded on an Excel spreadsheet and formed the basis of the project.

In an October 2011 interview with *Third Coast Digest,* an online arts and culture magazine, Westergren explained how the musicians tested the first algorithms by playing a Beatles tune to see what the computer came up with as a recommendation for similar listening. It took several minutes before the computer presented a song by a contemporary group, the Bee Gees. Initially, the team believed the test was a failure, but then Westergren realized that the two songs contained a number of similar components. The computer had, in fact, made a logical connection.

After the original US$1.5 million start-up financing from initial investors for the Project ran out, the early years proved to be challenging as sources of traditional financing and venture capital evaporated during a recession of 2001. By the end of 2001 Savage Beast had 50 employees and no way to pay them. Every two weeks Westergren called a staff meeting to beg people to continue working without pay. This routine continued for two years.

In a *New York Times* article by Claire Cain Miller, Westergren recalled pitching his business plan to over 300 venture capitalists, charging 11 credit cards to their maximum limits, and even contemplating a corporate trip to Reno, Nevada, to gamble for more money to keep the company alive. Savage Beast was able to sell its music recommendation services to companies such as Best Buy Company, Inc., but this was not enough. In March 2004, after his 348th sales pitch for financing, Westergren was able to convince Larry Marcus, a venture capitalist at Walden Venture Capital and a musician, to lead a US$9 million investment in Savage Beast. Marcus later said he did not find the sales pitch that tempting, but was impressed with Westergren himself. At the next staff meeting, Westergren was able to hand out paychecks to employees, some of whom were owed US$150,000, instead of pleading for more unpaid work.

INTERNET RADIO TRUMPS THE SAVAGE BEAST

In July 2005 Savage Beast Technologies, Inc., officially changed its name to Pandora Media, Inc., and launched its Internet radio service. The Pandora radio site was the consumer's interface with the Music Genome Project serving as the technology backbone. Listeners created a personal radio station with the name of an artist and then received recommendations of similar music to add to their station.

The Pandora service had no concept of genre, user connections, or ratings. When a radio station was created, Pandora used a radical approach to delivering personalized selections. Having analyzed the musical structures present in the songs the listener chose, it played other songs that possessed similar musical traits.

Initially, Pandora offered a subscription-only service without commercials. The idea of paying did not sit well with most U.S. consumers and the company had to consider alternative business models to offer a free service. In December 2005 Pandora sold its first advertisement.

ROYALTY PAINS

In 2007 Pandora, along with other Internet radio broadcasters, was dealt another challenge when the U. S. Copyright Royalty Board (CRB) raised the amount per song that online radio stations had to pay to the record labels. "Overnight our business was broken," the *New York Times* quoted Westergren as saying in March 2010. "We contemplated pulling the plug."

However, instead of "pulling the plug," Westergren hired a lobbyist in Washington, D.C., and enlisted the help of Pandora's listeners to appeal to their U.S. state representatives. The strategy worked and, in the face of mounting public pressure, the CRB agreed to negotiations. Although it took two years, the CRB finally settled on a lower rate. Pandora had proven the loyalty of its listeners.

OUT OF THE BOX AND INTO THE SMARTPHONE

In July 2008 Pandora released what Chief Technology Officer Tom Conrad called, in a blog entry on the Pandora website, "maybe the best form of Pandora yet: Pandora for the iPhone." Almost immediately after the release of the Pandora Radio iPhone application, 35,000 new users per day listened to Pandora on their mobile phones, thereby doubling the daily audience. Suddenly, online music was not just for the computer. People could take their personalized selections with them in the car, on the treadmill at the gym, or even plug the phone into speakers at home. On Christmas Day 2009 Pandora added 250,000 new mobile phone subscribers, which Westergren theorized was due to the large number of people receiving iPhones for Christmas.

By late 2009 Pandora had doubled its subscription base to 40 million users and recorded US$50 million worth of revenue, although roughly 60 percent of that revenue had to be paid in royalty fees to the record labels. The company also announced a partnership with U.S. automaker Ford Motor Company that would allow users to listen hands-free through a Bluetooth device in their cars. Other automotive brands, such as Hyundai, Buick, Toyota, and Mercedes, as well as radio manufacturers Alpine Electronics of America, Inc., and Pioneer Corporation, have since signed partnership agreements with Pandora to offer an online radio experience in new vehicles. In October 2010 Westergren told the *Los Angeles Times,* "Our goal is to be in every new car that rolls off the manufacturing line."

Pandora issued an initial public offering (IPO) in June 2011 on the New York Stock Exchange, raising over US$235 million. As of January 2011 Pandora reported over 80 million registered users. However, its competitors were catching on and catching up.

FACING THE COMPETITION

Pandora revolutionized online music listening in the first decade of the 21st century. Early Internet offerings in the radio domain were either terrestrial broadcasters streaming programs online, or music repositories, such as iTunes, where music could be downloaded to a computer, iPod, or other portable MP3 player. Pandora was the first radio offering that allowed the listener to develop a personalized radio station based on previous listening preferences and to listen to that station online on their mobile device. However, in the early 2010s relatively new entrants into the market, such as Grooveshark, iHeartRadio, Mog.com, Rhapsody, and Europe's Spotify, are threatening to use the concept of true on-demand access to online music as a challenge to Pandora's personalized radio.

In January 2008 the online magazine *Tech Crunch* reported that Pandora Media sent an email in mid-2007 to its subscribers in the United Kingdom. The communication advised that Pandora was withdrawing all radio offerings to any location outside the United States due to "the lack of a viable license structure for Internet radio streaming in other countries." While Westergren noted in a September 2011 *Forbes* article that he thought this was the right decision due to non-U.S. licensing being "complicated," it did limit Pandora's market potential.

Seeing no such complicating challenge with the U.S. licensing arrangements, Spotify, one of Europe's most popular online streaming music services, announced its official arrival in the country in mid-2011. Spotify boasted a catalogue of over 15 million songs compared to Pandora's library of around 800,000. In addition, Spotify allows users to upload their own songs to the online library. While Pandora allows listeners to connect to the social media site Facebook to see what their friends are listening to, Spotify users can quickly and easily share playlists with their friends through Facebook, Twitter, email, and SMS text messages.

A service that is targeting Pandora's personalized radio appeal is iHeartRadio. Owned by Clear Channel Communications, Inc., the largest radio operator in the United States with 237 million listeners and 800 stations in 150 markets, iHeartRadio, like Pandora, offers listeners the opportunity to like or dislike a song in order to receive recommendations on other tunes. It also offers custom tools that allow the listener to discover new artists or more songs based on existing choices. The service has joined Pandora as a feature in Toyota vehicles and it plans to introduce an application for TV and mobile devices.

MUSIC GENOME PROJECT STILL SHINES

The mainstay of Pandora's business is still the Music Genome Project. While other online radio stations may be able to offer a semi-personalized experience, it is generally based on the user "training" the computer by rating each requested song. The listener may also be able to use add-on tools to discover new music and artists. At the core of Pandora's Music Genome Project, however, are trained musicians who have classified and logged the music so that a computer can refer to the database and, without regard to genre or artist, recommend a song with similar attributes to the user's initial choice.

As for the efforts of iHeartRadio to offer a personalized online music service to compete with Pandora, Westergren was thrilled. "The largest traditional broadcaster is recognizing that personalized radio is the future," he said in a September 2011 interview with Jefferson Graham in *USA Today.*

BIBLIOGRAPHY

Conrad, Tim. "Pandora on the iPhone." Oakland, CA: Pandora Media, Inc., July 11, 2008. Accessed January 11, 2012. http://blog.pandora.com/pandora/archives/2008/07/pandora-on-the.html.

Goldman, David. "Pandora Rises Out of Streaming Music Rubble." *CNNMoney,* February 18, 2010. Accessed January 11, 2012. http://money.cnn.com/2010/02/18/technology/pandora/.

Graham, Jefferson. "Clear Channel's iHeartRadio Takes on Pandora." *USA Today,* September 13, 2011. Accessed January 11, 2012. http://www.usatoday.com/tech/products/story/2011-09-13/iheart-radio-clear-channel/50393228/1.

Lasar, Matthew. "Digging into Pandora's Music Genome with Musicologist Nolan Gasser." *Ars Technica,* January 12, 2011. Accessed January 11, 2012. http://arstechnica.com/tech-policy/news/2011/01/digging-into-pandoras-music-genome-with-musicologist-nolan-gasser.ars.

McBride, Sarah. "Pandora's Radio Head." *Wall Street Journal,* March 11, 2010. Accessed January 11, 2012. http://magazine.wsj.com/hunter/rebel-yell/radio-head.

McNicholas, Kym. "Pandora's Tim Westergren on Defending His Turf." *Forbes,* September 21, 2011. Accessed January 11, 2012. http://www.forbes.com/sites/kymmcnicholas/2011/09/21/pandoras-tim-westergren-were-right-where-we-want-to-be.

Miller, Claire Cain. "How Pandora Slipped Past the Junkyard." *New York Times,* March 7, 2010. Accessed January 11, 2012. http://www.nytimes.com/2010/03/08/technology/08pandora.html.

Pandora Media, Inc. "About Pandora." Oakland, CA, 2011. Accessed January 11, 2012. http://www.pandora.com/corporate/.

Pham, Alex. "What's Next for Pandora Radio?" *Los Angeles Times,* October 21, 2010. Accessed January 11, 2012. http://articles.latimes.com/2010/oct/21/business/la-fi-1021-ct-facetime-pandora-20101019.

Riley, Duncan. "Memo to UK: No Pandora for You." *Tech Crunch,* January 7, 2008. Accessed January 11, 2012. http://techcrunch.com/2008/01/07/memo-to-uk-no-pandora-for-you/.

Shafer, Dan. "Opening Pandora's Thoughts." *Third Coast Digest,* October 14, 2011. Accessed January 11, 2012. http://thirdcoastdigest.com/2011/10/opening-pandoras-thoughts.

Trefis Team. "Pandora Suffers Blow to Outlook from Clear Channel Competition." *Forbes,* September 14, 2011. Accessed January 11, 2012. http://www.forbes.com/sites/greatspeculations/2011/09/14/pandora-suffers-blow-to-outlook-from-clear-channel-competition.

Walker, Rob. "The Song Decoders." *New York Times,* October 14, 2009. Accessed January 11, 2012. http://www.nytimes.com/2009/10/18/magazine/18Pandora-t.html?pagewanted=all.

Wasserman, Noam, and L. P. Maurice. "Savage Beast (A)." Boston, MA: Harvard Business Publishing, November 19, 2008. Accessed January 11, 2012. http://cb.hbsp.harvard.edu/cb/product/809069-PDF-ENG.

PayPal: Global E-commerce
Payment Processing

■

PayPal, Inc., is a U.S.-based e-commerce business that offers a paperless, fast, global online payment and money transfer system to consumers and businesses. PayPal allows users to pay for purchases via the Internet without sharing financial information. Consumers may use several methods of payment through PayPal, including credit cards, bank accounts, and PayPal's three different payment services: PayPal global payment service, the Payflow Gateway, and Bill-Me-Later. PayPal derives its revenues from fees collected for payment processing services for sellers, via currency exchange, and other service-based fees. PayPal's main industry competitor is Google Checkout.

The company, headquartered in San Jose, California, was founded in 1998. Since 2002 the company has been a subsidiary of global auction site eBay, Inc. PayPal has an international headquarters in Singapore and a European headquarters in Luxembourg. The company operated localized websites in 21 markets throughout North America, Europe, and Asia. In 2011 it had 160 million active accounts in 190 world markets using 25 different currencies. Revenues in 2011 totaled US$4.4 billion, up 28 percent from the previous year. According to *CrunchBase,* an online directory of technology companies, PayPal had 300,000 employees worldwide.

THE START-UP

Like many early e-commerce start-ups, PayPal had its roots at Stanford University. Peter Thiel, a graduate of Stanford and former securities lawyer and options trader, got together with a few of his Stanford alumni associates and founded a company called Confinity Inc. Confinity

sought out and financed University of Illinois software engineer Max Levchin's development of a secure software payment system for e-commerce transactions. The payment software system Levchin developed, initially designed to reconcile payments from mobile devices, attracted the attention of venture capitalists interested in broadening the application's capabilities. PayPal became the vehicle for these venture investments and system development efforts.

The use of the name Confinity was eventually dropped when the company merged with and adopted the name X.com. X.com, an online bank founded by Elon Musk, helped recruit other talent needed to expand the company's reach, and a worldwide payment and money transfer company began to take shape. Many of the employees Musk and Thiel brought on board would later become known as the "PayPal Mafia," largely on the basis of their success in founding other high-technology companies following their tenure at PayPal.

Bolstered by the merger and increased number of employees, Musk and Thiel soon had a platform from which anyone with an e-mail account could make payments for goods and services worldwide, using the latest in secure payment and fraud prevention technology. Included in this technology, the PayPal service pioneered the use of the CAPTCHA system, where users entered a series of blurry numbers and letters shown on the log-in screen to gain access to the system. In the 2010s, this system was still widely used.

In spite of its promise, PayPal faced numerous challenges during its first years, including three changes in CEOs in the first full year of operation. Other banking firms and online businesses also saw the promise of a secure online payment system, and PayPal quickly had a number of budding competitors.

ACQUIRED BY EBAY

Taking advantage of the rapid rise and success of e-commerce, by early 2001 PayPal had 1.5 million account holders with account throughput of US$2 million per day. Many of these accounts were held by customers of online auction giant eBay Inc. eBay soon named PayPal as its primary online payment service. By early 2002 PayPal went public with a total stock value of US$900 million, and the stock rose 54 percent on the first day of trading.

In July 2002 PayPal active accounts mushroomed to a total of 16 million, with almost 300,000 individual payments made daily. In October 2002, having recognized the increasing importance of PayPal to its own business and its potential as a stand-alone operation, eBay purchased PayPal for approximately US$1.5 billion. eBay's own online payment system, Billpoint, which had been started to compete with PayPal, was quickly phased out following the acquisition.

By 2004 PayPal launched its first application programming interface (API), offering merchants and application developers a means to develop their own individually tailored payment systems. By the end of the year, PayPal had over 50 million account holders and offered their services in 45 different countries. Revenues for the year grew nearly 300 percent year-over-year, totaling US$1.4 billion. In 2005 PayPal acquired Verisign, Inc.'s Payment Gateway and combined it with its own merchant payment platform.

In spite of its success, not everything went smoothly for PayPal. Its early success also made it highly visible to U.S. regulators, who often questioned its business practices. Following the September 11, 2001, terrorist attacks against the United States, congressional enactment of the Patriot Act produced inquiries about PayPal's involvement in transactions by terrorists. The office of New York Attorney General Elliot Spitzer became involved, and the company had to pay a US$150,000 fine because its user agreement was not clear enough. In addition, the U.S. Federal Trade Commission (FTC) opened an investigation into the company's frequent practice of freezing its users' accounts.

Fraud became another persistent problem. "Phishing," fraudulent e-mail communications to PayPal users, duped hundreds into turning over their passwords to thieves and produced considerable negative publicity for the company in the process. Criminal organizations in Eastern Europe and Asia developed malicious software containing code to log keystrokes, designed to gather credit card information and PayPal log-in information. Overseas purchasers scammed merchants by having merchandise sent to untraceable foreign addresses, then claiming they did not receive the package and demanding a refund through PayPal. Despite these obstacles and the persistent efforts of capital-rich potential competitors to start similar services, PayPal prevailed and developed a brand that continued to attract new users.

M-COMMERCE

In 2006 PayPal reentered the mobile device market, where it had begun with Confinity in 1998, by providing mobile e-commerce payment capability. Also in 2006, PayPal expanded significantly overseas, adding 103 markets and 10 currencies during the year. A big step occurred for PayPal in 2007 when the European Union issued the company a banking license, facilitating continued growth of its service in this key e-commerce market. Northwest Airlines became the first U.S.-based airline to accept PayPal for ticket purchases in August 2007. By 2011 this acceptance would spread to all of the 10 largest U.S. airlines and to many overseas airlines as well.

PayPal continued its expansion efforts in 2008, acquiring Bill-Me-Later Inc., a company offering e-commerce credit on a revolving basis. Rapid expansion overseas also continued as the company offered services in nine new languages and added three new localized websites. To continue its efforts to remain a secure site for Internet payments, PayPal also acquired Israeli-based Fraud Sciences Ltd. for US$169 million. This purchase allowed the company to bolster its fraud management system technology and stay ahead of constant efforts to attack its platform. Responding to increased competition from Google, Inc., and Amazon.com, Inc., which created their own online payment systems, PayPal launched a new platform, PayPal X, in 2009. PayPal X further opened PayPal's payment system to third-party development, including the development of a Twitter-based payment platform and offered a number of new or expanded features, including expanded peer-to-peer payment systems across multiple platforms.

SOCIAL MEDIA IN THE SPOTLIGHT

Keeping pace with the expansion of social media, PayPal began the year 2010 by offering account holders payment support for advertising and virtual goods on Facebook. In March, PayPal announced an expanded relationship with Magento Inc., a global open-source e-commerce platform. The arrangement allowed for a seamless integration between PayPal and Magento's open-source shopping solutions. Also in March, PayPal announced its first payment application designed for the increasingly popular iPhone. With it, account holders could receive, split, and transfer payments worldwide from their iPhone.

In April 2010 PayPal announced it had further expanded its reach into the business-to-business arena by formulating an agreement with small-business website Alibaba.com Limited, which allowed small businesses to tailor their orders, make smaller quantity orders, and establish an escrow service for buyers and sellers. PayPal ended the year by establishing a relationship with Vivo Participações S.A., the largest mobile phone service provider in Brazil, to allow payments for all forms of goods and services. With this agreement Vivo's customers could purchase and make payment for goods purchased from millions of PayPal merchants around the world.

PAYPAL'S ILLUSTRIOUS ALUMNI

Many of PayPal's founders and key executives went on to experience extraordinary success. The PayPal Mafia, so called due to a *Fortune* story that featured some of the executives dressed in gangster attire, went on to start up a number of successful Silicon Valley, California, e-businesses. The most well-known of these alumni include:

- Peter Thiel, who founded the US$2 billion Clarion Fund and produced the movie *Thank You for Smoking*. Thiel started the "Founders Club" with other PayPal founders, and they went on to make early investments in a number of Silicon Valley, California, successes, including Facebook, LinkedIn, and Yelp.com.
- Max Levchin, who invested in Slide.com and made the founding investment of US$1 million in Yelp.com.
- David Sacks, who founded start-ups Geni.com and Yammer and created the movie production company that produced *Thank You for Smoking* with Thiel.
- Engineers Steve Chen and Jawed Karim, who were two of the three founders of YouTube.
- Elon Musk, who co-founded electric car company Tesla Motors, Inc. and founded the space exploration business SpaceX (with US$100 million of his own money).
- Reid Hoffman, former executive vice president at PayPal, who founded LinkedIn and was an early investor in Friendster.

WHY DID PAYPAL PREVAIL?

In his book *The PayPal Wars,* Eric M. Jackson wrote about some of the elements he felt made PayPal a success; his points were summarized by Sachin Rekhi, founder and CEO of Connected, in a blog post. Other founders and early employees expressed their views as to the success of the company, and how it influenced its employees, on Quora, a question-and-answer website. These views were summarized by Vincent Chan on *Power of Scale* in June 2010. Together these two sources covered several key points:

- Managerial ability: The ability of Thiel and Musk to recognize people with extraordinary capabilities was a definite boon. At PayPal, managing was foremost about assembling a top-notch group that was both smart and hungry for success.
- Focus: Former vice president of the company Keith Rabois mentioned Thiel and Musk's requirement that every employee be tasked with one priority, and they would virtually refuse to discuss anything with that person other than that priority. Each employee was required to indicate his or her key contribution to the company in an annual review.
- Individual accomplishment: Teams were not considered desirable at PayPal, and any meeting of more than three to four people was considered undesirable. Rabois believed that most of the top 25 innovations at PayPal were individually created, then championed to others by those creators. The annual review form asked employees to rate their peers on "not imposing on other's time" by scheduling unnecessary meetings.
- Self-sufficiency: Individuals and small teams were expected to find their own resources to accomplish their tasks. If they needed something from outside they were expected to pick up the phone and order it instead of engaging in a long approval process. Decision making was extended as far down in the organization as was practically possible.
- A willingness to try: While many organizations produced a culture of fear, based on an unwillingness to receive blame, PayPal management placed so much emphasis on action that individuals and their managers were often likely to give something a try and let performance data determine its value.
- Transparency: Business metrics and performance data were widely circulated rather than restricted to key decision makers. Management felt all employees should be well versed on the business metrics. Otherwise, management reasoned, employees would not be able to make rational decisions.
- High-pressure environment: PayPal was a rapidly evolving business that needed employees who did not rest on their laurels but constantly looked to stay ahead in an extremely competitive environment.

THE FUTURE OF PAYPAL

In October 2011 PayPal held a "sneak peek" in Los Angeles, California at what the company saw for the future of shopping. At its Customer Summit, an invitation-only event, the company unveiled the PayPal Shopping Showcase, a behind-the-scenes look at PayPal's newest products. Highlights of the showcase were outlined on the *PayPal Blog,* by PayPal's Senior Director of Emerging Opportunities, Carey Kolaja. PayPal asked participants to imagine a "digital wallet" where all of a customer's credit cards, gift cards, loyalty points, and special offers were kept. All of these offers would then automatically be applied at the point of sale. If a customer purchased an oversized item, it would automatically be shipped to his or her home. Overall, PayPal's focus was to become a source of added convenience for both customer and merchant to make it an indispensible link in the shopping experience.

BIBLIOGRAPHY

Chan, Vincent. "Why Did So Many Successful Entrepreneurs and Startups Come Out of PayPal? Answered by Insiders." *Power of Scale,* June 28, 2010. Accessed February 6, 2012. http://primitus.com/blog/why-did-so-many-successful -entrepreneurs-and-startups-come-out-of-PayPal-answered -by-insiders/.

Jackson, Eric M. *The PayPal Wars: Battles with eBay, the Media, the Mafia, and the Rest of Planet Earth.* Los Angeles, CA: World Ahead Publishing, 2006.

Kolaja, Carey. "PayPal Brings the Future of Shopping to Manhattan." *PayPal Blog,* October 10, 2011. Accessed January 31, 2012. https://www.thePayPalblog.com/2011/10 /PayPal-brings-the-future-of-shopping-to-manhattan/.

O'Brien, Jeffrey M. "Meet the PayPal Mafia." *CNNMoney,* November 26, 2007. Accessed February 6, 2012. http:// money.cnn.com/2007/11/13/magazines/fortune/paypal_mafia .fortune/index.htm.

"PayPal." *CrunchBase,* 2012. Accessed February 6, 2012. http:// www.crunchbase.com/company/PayPal.

PayPal, Inc. "About PayPal." San Jose, CA, 2012. Accessed February 6, 2012. https://www.PayPal-media.com/about.

"The PayPal Story." *WebProNews,* November 10, 2004. Accessed February 6, 2012. http://www.webpronews.com/the-PayPal -story-2004-11.

Rekhi, Sachin. "The PayPal Wars and Its Lessons for Today's Entrepreneurs." SachinRekhi.com, October 10, 2011. Accessed February 6, 2012. http://www.sachinrekhi.com /blog/2010/01/11/the-PayPal-wars-and-its-lessons-for-todays -entrepreneurs.

"Why Did So Many Successful Entrepreneurs and Startups Come Out of PayPal?" *Quora,* 2010. Accessed February 25, 2012. http://www.quora.com/Why-did-so-many-successful -entrepreneurs-and-startups-come-out-of-PayPal.

Pixar Animation Studios:
It Started as a Toy Story

In just two short decades, Pixar Animation Studios turned film animation on its head and rewrote the rules of family entertainment. Since its groundbreaking 1995 release of *Toy Story*, Pixar has produced a series of award-winning animated feature films that by 2011 had generated US$7.2 billion in worldwide box-office revenue. Notable films include *Monsters, Inc., Finding Nemo,* and *Toy Story 3*. As of 2011 *Toy Story 3* was the highest-grossing animated film of all time with more than US$1 billion in revenue. The studio's ascent to the upper echelons of animation, not to mention Hollywood filmmaking, became a blueprint for a slew of companies that helped to push computer animation into exciting new realms.

ORIGINS OF THE COMPANY

Pixar sprang from rather obscure beginnings. In 1984 John Lasseter left an animation job at the Walt Disney Company to join the computer graphics division of Lucasfilm, Ltd. There, Lasseter experimented with computer animation and developed a short film, *The Adventures of Wally and Andre B.,* which represented a significant advance in the field. "The programmers had created a program that randomly generated the movement of every leaf, blade of grass, and branch in the film, eliminating the need for animators to define every element in the film," wrote Tom Hormby in *LowEndMac*. While it premiered prior to Pixar's incorporation, the film was ostensibly the company's first animated product.

In 1986 Apple Computer cofounder Steve Jobs purchased the computer graphics division from Lucas for US$10 million and spontaneously renamed it "Pixar." The newly independent company developed the Pixar Image Computer, a device that enabled the storage and display of images on a computer screen. Priced at US$135,000 per unit, the device failed to sell, and Pixar's future became uncertain. However, another Lasseter-helmed short film, *Luxo Jr.,* impressed computer scientists and filmmakers alike, and was nominated for Best Short Animated Film at the 1986 Academy Awards. The honor gave Pixar a new level of pedigree in the film industry.

RETHINKING ANIMATION

Pixar's revolutionary animation technology actually began to take shape more than a decade before the company's founding. Dick Shoup, who held a doctorate from Carnegie Mellon University, recorded the first-ever digital video on a computer at Xerox Coprporation's Palo Alto Research Center (PARC) in 1973. Shoup developed the technology so it could grab footage from any video source and modify it. SuperPaint, as Shoup called it, continued development but received little support at Xerox until Alvy Ray Smith toured the PARC with Shoup. Smith, a mathematician and economist who had recently taken a teaching job at the University of California, Berkeley, and was likewise a devotee of moving images, was so impressed with SuperPaint that Shoup invited him to help develop the technology. "Shoup was able to construct incredible video sequences that were impossible to create in any other medium," wrote Hormby. "He took an image of his girlfriend's face and transformed it into a kaleidoscope of colors that was still very organic in nature. He created a gecko's hide that cycled through colors and modified *Star Trek* episodes with new psychedelic effects." Before long, however, Xerox dismissed Smith and dismantled SuperPaint.

Not long after his PARC work, Smith took a position with the computer research group of the New York Institute of Technology, where he was introduced to Ed Catmull. Catmull, who held a doctorate in physics, had created a computer-generated film in his teens, according to Hormby. With funding from New York millionaire Alex Schure, Smith and Catmull's charge was to develop the first computer-generated feature film. One system the researchers developed helped accelerate the creation of conventional, hand-drawn animated films by digitally tracking their lines and using virtual paint to fill them (a technology that later became the Disney computer animation production system).

While Smith, Catmull, and their researchers persisted under Schure's patronage, they began to seek another sponsor who might better help bring their ideas to the fore. Upon seeing *Star Wars* in 1977, they reached out to George Lucas as someone who might be interested in adopting computer-generated effects. The team moved to California to start a new computer division at Lucasfilm, named Industrial Light and Magic, and began work on the computer effects used in *Return of the Jedi*. Soon after, Paramount Pictures approached the team to create a scene for *Star Trek II: The Wrath of Khan* showing the destruction and reintegration of a planet, dubbed "Genesis." Catmull and his colleagues developed a scene that ended up becoming one of the most popular in the film, and convinced Lucas to utilize the team and its technology for even more special effects.

Disney CEO Michael Eisner was also impressed with Genesis, noted Hormby, and invited Catmull to develop a program that would trace and color every animation cell, thereby replacing the formerly hand-drawn process. The team's creation was the computer animation production system (CAPS), which presented a SuperPaint-like interface to allow animators to fill in hand-drawn cells. CAPS also enabled the storage of hundreds of thousands of high-resolution images, a feat that most computers of that time could not perform. A key component of CAPS was RenderMan, which enabled animators to turn simple models into high-resolution images. Added Hormby, "RenderMan would form the basis for every project that the researchers would undertake for the next two decades and allowed traditional animators to begin working with computer animation with relatively little training." It would also be the essential technology that powered the Pixar films.

RENDERING RENDERMAN

The animation advances developed by Shoup, Smith, and Catmull opened a new era of computer animation graphics. In 1982 Catmull, Loren Carpenter, and Rob Cook developed an algorithm at Lucasfilm known as REYES (Renders Everything You Ever Saw). REYES effectively became the engine that powered RenderMan. REYES basically processed geometric shapes for the RenderMan renderer. The rendering process begins with geometric "primitives" taken from an animation package such as Autodesk's Maya or Side Effects's Houdini. This three-dimensional data was sent to RenderMan in RIB (RenderMan Interface Bytestream) files. Pixar likened this process to a large, mechanical robot that consumed and digested a scene.

Step One of the rendering process involved sending the geometry to the rendering robot. The geometry arrived as a "banquet platter" of RIB files, which was then fed into the "mouth" of the robot. In this case, the mouth was actually a viewing area that the animator's camera had of a particular scene. Items that were visible got processed, while other items that were not visible consequently were culled and discarded from the process.

Step Two involved bounding, splitting, and dicing the geometry. The REYES machine examined the size of each geometric primitive in a process called bounding to determine what fit in the viewing area. The renderer checked the bounding box of each primitive; everything completely outside the box was discarded. However, some items that sat halfway inside the mouth of the renderer were split into smaller pieces. This repetitive process of breaking down the geometry into smaller, bite-sized subprimitives was known as splitting. Thus the REYES robot essentially chewed the geometry until it could be easily digested. Next, split primitives were swallowed by the robot and further subdivided into clusters of "subpixel-sized micropolygons" in a process called dicing. Groups of these micropolygons were referred to as grids.

In the third step of the rendering process, the grids moved further into the stomach of the rendering robot, where they were shaded together. When the shading process was complete, RenderMan busted the grid into individual micropolygons, tested each micropolygon for visibility, and then sent them to the screen to create pixels. Finally, RenderMan divided the entire image into pixel groups otherwise known as buckets. When the pixels inside one bucket were fully rendered, RenderMan moved on to the next bucket. The image was complete when all buckets were rendered.

RenderMan was particularly adept at creating specialized image elements: namely, motion blur, depth of field, fur and hair, and displacement. Motion blur resulted from objects moving during the exposure of film. When exposure was fast, images would blur less often. Conversely, when exposure was slow, more motion blur resulted. A moving image would look unnatural without some level of motion blur; therefore, RenderMan rendered motion blur with a variety of options that an animator could choose from to fine-tune the final image.

RenderMan's depth-of-field features enabled the animator to control the effect of an image's background. For example, the animator could choose between a finite or infinite background, as well as an instantaneous shutter speed or long shutter speed that created a blur. These options controlled RenderMan's virtual camera in ways that created lifelike three-dimensional imagery.

RenderMan also drastically changed the way animators rendered fur and hair. Films including *Monsters, Inc., Ratatouille,* and *Up* all utilized RenderMan's fur and hair features to enhance the three-dimensional look of their characters. In particular, the product featured a "Sigma Hiding" option that could be used to render a small sub-pixel geometry such as fur using techniques that Pixar perfected over the course of its own film productions. Its riCurve feature also allowed for smooth curves, and the deep shadows tool enabled the animator to capture translucency, create motion blur, and smooth out shadows.

RenderMan's displacement tool allowed animators to add varying amounts of depth and detail to an image by displacing different geometric points along a surface or plane of the image. The tool was used to a great extent in Pixar's *WALL-E,* in which animators were challenged by creating hundreds of shots of a world covered in garbage. They relied on a displacement shader in RenderMan to generate small garbage, thereby generating many types of different looks quickly and efficiently. Physically placing the garbage on the plane would make the scene geometrically heavy and difficult to alter. Using a displacement shader to create the scene, however, made adding garbage to any scene much easier. Different parameters could be fine-tuned to change the look. For instance, animators could control the density of garbage on the ground. Another parameter allowed animators to paint where the garbage should appear in a scene. Displacements could additionally be layered and augmented with elements such as grime and hills, as was the case in the garbage mounds in *WALL-E.*

TO INFINITY AND BEYOND

"As Ed Catmull described it, 'Just like a car's user interface—the steering wheel, gear shift, accelerator, and brake—lets you use a car without having to know how the much more complicated engine inside works, the RenderMan interface lets you use the renderer without having to know the details of how it operates,'" wrote Karen Paik in *To Infinity and Beyond!: The Story of Pixar Animation Studios.* In a scene that required a door opening and light shining from inside onto the sidewalk and a car in front of a building, RenderMan translated a digital artist's effects into levels of instructions that a computer could follow. Such instructions could even specify how light reflected off a concrete slab as opposed to how it reflected off metal-flake paint.

Powerful features such as motion blur, fur and hair, and displacements gave animators a large amount of leeway in determining the final look of their moving images.

Often mistaken as a software program in and of itself, RenderMan was perhaps more accurately described as an application programming interface. It was developed to help define how animation and modeling software should communicate with rendering software. "This separation of modeling from rendering benefits developers of modeling software, developers of renderers, and end users," wrote Ian Stephenson in *Essential RenderMan.* RenderMan, explained Stephenson, was developed at the same time that Pixar was building its custom-rendering hardware in the late 1980s. Developers wanted to make sure that anyone could develop modeling software that could communicate with Pixar's hardware.

"[Steve] Jobs hoped that products like RenderMan would spark a consumer revolution, empowering untrained people to create computer animation on their home computer, the same way the Macintosh allowed untrained people to create professional-appearing documents like newsletters and flyers," wrote Hormby. "Unfortunately for Jobs, that revolution didn't occur. Other companies created animation packages based on RenderMan, like PixelPutty for the Macintosh, but none were designed for consumers to use."

When Pixar realized its hardware devices were too prohibitively expensive to generate substantial income, it refocused its efforts on RenderMan. The product was first commercially released in 1989, according to Paik, just as Pixar's hardware division was stalling. RenderMan underwent additional refinement throughout the 1990s as it gained popularity among animators for offering quality, artistic control, and technical reach required for feature-length films. The renewed focus on RenderMan paid off for Pixar. By 2011 RenderMan had been used in every visual effects Academy Award winner for 15 years, and 47 of 50 prior nominees for the honor had incorporated the product in their films. Pixar's first 10 feature films alone earned 35 Academy Award nominations, nine Oscars, six Golden Globes, and a slew of other accolades. Such achievements subsequently garnered the interest of Disney, which purchased Pixar in 2006 for US$7.4 billion and maintained its animation production studios under the creative control of Lasseter.

BIBLIOGRAPHY

"Box Office History for Disney-Pixar Movies." *The Numbers,* 2011. Accessed December 20, 2011. http://www.the-numbers.com/movies/series/Pixar.php.

Hormby, Tom. "The Pixar Story: Dick Shoup, Alex Schure, George Lucas, Steve Jobs, and Disney." *LowEndMac,* January 22, 2007. Accessed December 20, 2011. http://lowendmac.com/orchard/06/pixar-story-lucas-disney.html.

Paik, Karen. *To Infinity and Beyond!: The Story of Pixar Animation Studios.* San Francisco, CA: Chronicle Books, 2007.

Pixar. "The Industry Standard." Emeryville, CA. Accessed December 20, 2011. https://renderman.pixar.com/products /whats_renderman/standard.html.

Stephenson, Ian. *Essential RenderMan.* 2nd ed. London: Springer-Verlag, 2007.

Plastic: Its Discovery, Use, and Reinvention

Since the 1950s plastics have grown into a major industry that affects almost every aspect of modern daily life. Plastic is involved in packaging to keep food fresher, new electronic gadgets such as mobile phones and laptop computers, industrial construction, water bottles, and thousands of other products. In every decade since its discovery, plastic has evolved and been developed to fill an ever-increasing number of uses. In 1925 the trade journal *Plastics* was launched and the word "plastic" was used for the first time.

According to a 2008 article by Brian Black and Donna L. Lybecker in *Great Debates in American Environmental History*, plastic has been the most used material in the world since the mid-1970s. Its evolution has been called one of the top 100 news events of the 20th century. In 2002 North America produced approximately 107 billion pounds of plastic with an estimated one-third of that production used to package other products.

BEGINNING WITH BILLIARD BALLS

An organic material called cellulose had been known in the United States since the mid-19th century, according to the Society of the Plastics Industry (SPI). In the 1860s, according to the entry for "Plastic" in *Inventions and Inventors,* the New York, New York, billiard table manufacturer, Phelan and Collender, offered a prize of US$10,000 to anyone able to produce a substance that could provide a lower cost substitute for the ivory used to make billiard balls.

John Wesley Hyatt experimented with adding camphor to nitrocellulose and found that, under certain con-

ditions, it formed a white material that could be molded and machined. He named this substance "celluloid" and it has been acknowledged as the first synthetic plastic, according to "Plastic." Celluloid was used in the manufacturing of baby rattles, shirt collars, dentures, and other consumer goods.

Celluloid failed miserably for billiard ball use, however. As a thermoplastic material that softened if heated, the material was too soft to be effective as a billiard ball cover. It is also highly flammable and a "widely circulated, perhaps apocryphal, story claimed that celluloid billiard balls detonated when they collided," according to "Plastic."

GENUINELY ARTIFICIAL

The first completely synthetic plastic appeared in 1907 with the discovery by a New York, New York, chemist, Leo Baekeland, of a liquid material that hardened into any form desired when cooled. Baekeland called this resin material bakelite and it became the first thermoset plastic, meaning that it would not lose the shape that it had taken and could not be reheated or melted back to a liquid form. Bakelite was introduced to the scientific community on February 15, 1909, at the annual meeting of the American Chemical Society. The rapidly growing automotive industry used bakelite in the manufacture of vehicle ignition parts.

Bakelite became the first in a class of polymers called "synthetic polymers." A polymer, meaning "having many parts," is a giant molecule consisting of smaller molecular parts whose combined physical properties are stronger and more flexible than the individual components. There are many natural polymers, such as cotton, but the discovery of a completely man-made compound led to a surge of research and attempts to produce other artificial materials that could be useful to manufacturing both industrial and consumer goods.

In the decades following Baekeland's discovery, firms such as E.I. DuPont de Nemours and Company (DuPont), Tupper Plastics Company, Dow Chemical Company, and others took this completely man-made synthetic and created a variety of products that are considered indispensable in the 21st century.

E. I. DUPONT DE NEMOURS AND COMPANY

Dupont was one of the first companies to recognize the importance of the synthetic polymers, now called plastics. Although novel products from this company are numerous, two products that became quickly enmeshed in consumers' daily lives were cellophane and Teflon.

Cellophane. Cellophane was invented in 1908 by Swiss textile engineer, Jacques E. Brandenberger, and was patented in 1912. According to the book *Inventors and Inventions*, Brandenberger was sitting in a restaurant in 1900 when a patron at another table spilled wine on the tablecloth. As the tablecloth was made of untreated fabric, the waiter needed to change it. It occurred to Brandenberger that, as tablecloths were constantly being soiled by food and drink, it would be advantageous for them to be made from a fabric that repelled the spillage rather than absorbed it.

His first idea was to spray the material with a dissolved cellulose solution. However, this turned out to be ineffective. Tablecloths treated with cellulose became too stiff to fold or drape when the solution dried, were not durable, and peeled off in large transparent sheets when dry. This last consequence inspired Brandenberger to think bigger than tablecloths. He experimented further and realized that these sheets were thin and transparent like glass but that, unlike glass, the material was flexible. Also, by adding various salts to the material, he could make it fire resistant.

In 1912 Brandenberger found a commercial market for his invention in eyepieces for gas masks. The material was lighter than glass, absorbed water vapor so it did not fog up, and did not shatter like glass. He formed a company, La Cellophane S.A., a combination of the French words cellulose and diaphane (transparent), and named his product the same.

In 1923 Brandenberger sold the rights to produce and distribute cellophane in the United States to DuPont. After further research and development, a DuPont scientist, William Hale Charch, discovered a process to make the material waterproof by coating both sides of the cellophane with thin layers of resin, plastic, and wax. DuPont's

sales of the new and improved cellophane tripled between 1928 and 1930, and in 1938 cellophane accounted for 10 percent of DuPont's sales and 25 percent of its profits.

The invention and perfection of the cellophane process, combined with modern transportation methods, radically changed the way the food industry operated. Food could now be produced in a central facility (instead of numerous scattered local providers), wrapped in cellophane, and shipped to restaurants and retailers.

Teflon. In 1938 DuPont scientist, Ray Plunkett, discovered a material that was impervious to acids, cold, and heat by pumping Freon gas into a cylinder and leaving it in cold storage overnight. The gas dissipated into an unexpected white solid powder that could withstand high temperatures without melting and it had surface properties that made it very slick. At the time there were no suggested applications for the product.

A conversation between Leslie R. Groves, the head of the Manhattan Project (which was the code name for the research and development program that resulted in the construction of the first atomic bombs), and another DuPont scientist regarding Plunkett's discovery led to DuPont using the material to manufacture gaskets for uranium enrichment facilities during World War II and immediately thereafter. The secrecy surrounding the Manhattan Project delayed the commercial introduction of the material, called Teflon, until the late 1950s. The best-known use for Teflon is as a nonstick coating for cookware. However, it has also proven to be a useful material in producing devices that are implanted into the human body. It is easily formed into various shapes and is one of the few materials that the human body does not reject. Teflon has also been used in space applications to make the outer skin of suits worn by astronauts and as insulating material on wires and cables in spacecraft.

TUPPERWARE

In the 1940s Earl S. Tupper held a belief that plastic was about to become the product of the future. He also had an interest in improving refrigeration techniques. Tupper was a self-taught chemical engineer and got his start with DuPont in the 1930s. Due to the limited availability of raw materials at the time, major chemical companies such as DuPont received priority for the use of these materials in the production of plastic. Although DuPont was not willing to accede to Tupper's request to provide some raw materials for his experiments, the company did allow him to take the polyethylene slag. This malodorous waste product of oil refining was practically unusable. Not to be deterred, Tupper devised methods for purifying the slag and then designed an injection-molding machine to form bowls and other containers out of the resultant material.

In 1938 he founded the Tupper Plastics Company and in the first few years formulated the design for his well known Tupperware seal. With the advent of electric refrigerators, consumers found that the dry interiors and low temperatures caused food to wilt and dry out. Tupper realized that his containers could help solve this problem. The key to his solution was the Tupperware seal. Tupper took the idea from paint can lids, inverted it, and created a tight seal with a partial vacuum that protected food from the dry refrigeration processes. It also stopped the transfer of odors from one food to another.

While Tupperware is credited with changing way U.S. citizens viewed plastic products, another offshoot was the opportunities it offered to women. Tupper opted to sell his products via "home parties," where the hosts were predominately women. At a time when society disapproved of women working outside of the home, selling Tupperware offered a type of employment that women could schedule around their homes and families. Annual training conventions centered on marketing skills also gave these women the opportunity to network and establish contacts. According to the "Tupperware" entry in *Inventions and Inventors,* these new opportunities proved invaluable to women as they entered the workforce in ever-increasing numbers in later decades.

DOW CHEMICAL AND POLYSTYRENE

In the 1930s Dow Chemical Company began producing and marketing the polystyrene products first invented by Marcellin Pierre Berthelot in 1866 and subsequently marketed by the Naugatuck Chemical Company in 1925. Dow's Styron 666 was the first product on the market to demonstrate the ease of production and market potential for polystyrene.

When the United States' supply of rubber was interrupted at the beginning of World War II, there was an increased need for plastics. As chemists worked to experiment with synthetic substitutes for rubber, they found that the addition of substances called "elastomers" gave a rubber-like quality to the usually brittle polystyrene. In the post-World War II era, polystyrene found its way into a multitude of consumer and commercial products such as disposable kitchen utensils, plates, cups, videocassettes, insulating foams, egg cartons, food packaging, paints, and appliances, to name just a few. The production of polystyrene, according to the "Polystyrene" entry in *Inventions and Inventors,* has risen to exceed five billion pounds per year.

RECYCLE AND REPLACE

According to Jon Evans in his article "Filling Up: Converting Plastics into Fuel," published in the trade magazine

Plastics Engineering, only approximately 8 percent of all the plastic waste generated in 2010 was recycled. This was mainly due to the cost of separating and recycling of a material that covered such a wide range of synthetic and chemical fibers with diverse characteristics. The vast majority of plastic waste, stated Evans, was either incinerated or placed in a landfill. There are disadvantages to both methods. Incineration generated some energy but also introduced carbon dioxide and a number of other pollutants into the atmosphere. Dumping plastic into landfills can result in chemicals leaching into the soil.

Plastic found its way into every aspect of society because of its durability and versatility, but has proven difficult, even poisonous, in its waste form. However, showing the same creative spirit that led to the creation of plastic in the first place, scientists are attempting to find less environmentally damaging alternatives together with new ways of disposing of or transforming the end product. According to Evans, research is being done regarding the possibility of heating the plastic waste at high temperatures and (in the absence of oxygen) breaking the chemicals down into their component molecules. The intention is to eventually generate vehicle fuel.

Necessity being the mother of invention, German scientists have turned to researching a liquid wood material to replace plastic in many products due to the increasing cost of crude oil. Bryn Nelson reported in his article, "A Greener Alternative to Plastics: Liquid Wood," that petroleum is the basis of the chemicals used in plastics and the increasing cost of oil has encouraged scientists to develop a bioplastic that is derived from wood and can be mixed with hemp, flax, or other additives such as wax to generate a strong, nontoxic alternative.

In the early 20th century, scientists worked to develop less organic materials with higher man-made synthetic content to fill consumer demand for more convenience and manufacturer demand for more cost-effective and durable alternatives to natural products. In the early 21st century, a new generation of scientists work to uncover a more organic, back-to-nature solution that offers the same strength, durability, and ease of use as plastic.

BIBLIOGRAPHY

Black , Brian, and Donna L. Lybecker. "Plastics Form the Core of America's Disposable Society." In *Great Debates in American Environmental History.* Vol. 2, 78–80. Westport, CT: Greenwood Press, 2008. Gale Virtual Reference Library (GALE|CX3252800119). Accessed February 9, 2012. http://go.galegroup.com/ps/i.do?id=GALE%7CCX3252800119&v=2.1&u=itsbtrial&it=r&p=GVRL&sw=w.

Dow Chemical Company. "History." Midland, MI, 2012. Accessed February 9, 2012. http://www.dow.com/about/aboutdow/history/timeline.htm.

DuPont. "Plastics." Wilmington, DE, 2012. Accessed February 9, 2012. http://www2.dupont.com/Heritage/en_US/related

_topics/plastics.html.

Evans, Jon. "Filling Up: Converting Plastics into Fuel." *Plastics Engineering,* January 2012. Accessed February 9, 2012. http://www.plastics-ebooks.com/ebooks/pe/2012/january/.

"The History of Plastic: From Billiards to Bibs." *NPR,* 2012. Accessed February 9, 2012. http://www.npr.org/templates/story/story.php?storyId=114331762.

Inventors and Inventions. Vol. 1. Tarrytown, NY: Marshall Cavendish, 2007, 166–169. Gale Virtual Reference Library. (GALE|CX4097100025). Accessed February 9, 2012. http://go.galegroup.com/ps/i.do?id=GALE%7CCX4097100025&v=2.1&u=gale&it=r&p=GVRL&sw=w.

Nelson, Bryn. "A Greener Alternative to Plastics: Liquid Wood." *MSN,* December 22, 2008. Accessed February 9, 2012. http://www.msnbc.msn.com/id/28283260/ns/technology_and_science-innovation/t/greener-alternative-plastics-liquid-wood/#.TzW2fSPDPJw.

"Plastic." In *Inventions and Inventors,* edited by Roger Smith, 571–575. Pasadena, CA: Salem Press, 2001. EBSCOhost. Accessed February 9, 2012. http://web.ebscohost.com/ehost/ebookviewer/ebook/nlebk_72893_AN?sid=5cb5faea-69f0-4f9e-b782-4a78e56c88fb@sessionmgr14&vid=22012.

"Polystyrene." In *Inventions and Inventors,* edited by Roger Smith, 597–600. Pasadena, CA: Salem Press, 2001.

Society of the Plastics Industry (SPI). "History of Plastics." Washington, DC, 2012. Accessed February 9, 2012. http://www.plasticsindustry.org/AboutPlastics/content.cfm?ItemNumber=670&navItemNumber=1117.

"Tupperware." In *Inventions and Inventors,* edited by Roger Smith, 799–806. Pasadena, CA: Salem Press, 2001.

Polaroid Camera: An Iconic Brand with Staying Power

TEENAGE SCIENTIST

In 1926 17-year-old Edwin Land decided to pursue his interest in the research of polarization rather than return to Harvard University after his freshman year. According to the *International Directory of Company Histories,* Land developed a prototype synthetic polarizer before returning to his studies at Harvard in 1929. With the assistance of Harvard physics professor George Wheelwright III, Land was able to gain access to a laboratory where he began producing small sheets of polarizing material. In June 1932, Land and Wheelwright founded Land-Wheelwright Laboratories to explore the possible practical applications of the polarizing process.

Polarizing material selectively screens light waves and is capable of allowing some waves through while blocking any waves that create glare. Land-Wheelwright Laboratories focused its efforts on creating no-glare material for car headlights and windshields. Although this application of the polarizing process was perfected, the company had no success in convincing the large automobile makers of Detroit, Michigan, to incorporate it into the car manufacturing process.

Land-Wheelwright Laboratories' first commercial success came when Eastman Kodak Company, the photography firm, contracted with Land-Wheelwright to provide US$10,000 worth of photographic polarizing filters. The filters consisted of polarizing material sealed between two glass discs, and they worked to increase contrast while decreasing glare in photographs that had been shot in bright light. Around the same time, Professor Clarence Kennedy of Smith College called the material "polaroid," which became the common term used to describe the filter.

In 1937 Land established the Polaroid Corporation and acquired the business operations of Land-Wheelwright Laboratories. Wheelwright left the company in 1940, and an arrangement with investors and shareholders allowed Land control of the company for a decade. Polaroid Corporation conceived other uses for polarized film such as in desk lamps, variable-density windows, lenses, and three-dimensional (3D) photographs called Vecto-graphs, but had little commercial success.

In 1939, Polaroid Corporation tried to convince automakers to demonstrate its headlight system at the New York World's Fair. Although all the car manufacturers declined, Chrysler Corporation agreed to show a promotional 3D movie at its display booth. The public loved the 3D film, dodging water that seemed to spray out of the screen, and were thrilled with the 3D glasses made of oppositely polarized lenses that made a Chrysler vehicle appear to dance in the air. However, the movie industry, still in awe over the introduction of color films with sound, was not interested in the polarized 3D technology.

During World War II the company had some financial success providing the United States military with products such as a device that determined an aircraft's elevation above the horizon, an infrared night-viewing device, goggles, lenses, color filters for periscopes, and range finders. However, Land knew that his company was in financial trouble after the war as military contracts declined. He believed that Polaroid Corporation's research into instant photography was the only way to save the company.

THE ILLUMINATING QUESTION

F. W. Campbell of the Royal Society quoted Land as reminiscing about a sunny afternoon in 1944 when he was walking with his three-year-old daughter in Santa Fe, New

Mexico, and she asked him why she could not immediately see the picture he had just taken of her. As they continued to walk around town, Land said that he puzzled over the answer to her question. "Within an hour," he is quoted as saying, "the camera, the film and the physical chemistry became so clear to me."

Land went on to say that it appeared to him that everything he had discovered and the various other discoveries of the time, such as the laminating of plastic sheets, had been preparing him for the moment when he suddenly knew how to develop a one-step dry photographic process. However, a sudden revelation is one thing. Bringing the product to market is quite another, as he discovered.

ALMOST INSTANT PHOTOGRAPHY

In 1946, according to the *International Directory of Company Histories,* Land announced that he would demonstrate an instant camera system at the winter meeting of the Optical Society of America the following year. Research on the process was far from complete, and Polaroid scientists and researchers worked long hours to develop a working model for Land to use in his demonstration. The image of Land peeling back the negative paper from a photograph of himself taken just a minute earlier made headline news in the *New York Times,* a full page spread in *Life* magazine, and was reported by the international press.

F. W. Campbell noted in his description of the occasion that "instant" was a "slight exaggeration." The time it took for a fully formed picture to be produced depended on the temperature. At room temperature, a picture emerged after a few seconds and was sufficiently well formed for the photographer to see that the camera had been aimed correctly and that it was in focus. It took several more minutes, however, for a high contrast to appear. Campbell noted that on one occasion when Land demonstrated the camera, he held the resulting photograph under his arm to speed the process.

The camera was made available for general sale within two years of the Optical Society of America demonstration. Land chose to sell the camera through Jordon Marsh department store in Boston, Massachusetts, where it retailed for US$89.75, and the film cost US$1.75 for eight sepia-toned exposures. The unit weighed four pounds when loaded with film and flash.

BRISK SALES

On the initial sales day, all 56 available units were sold. Cameras continued to sell as quickly as the company could make them. Sales in the first year exceeded US$5 million, and by 1950 more than 4,000 retail outlets sold Polaroid cameras. Just one year earlier, Kodak had practically mo-

nopolized the camera market in the United States, noted the *International Directory of Company Histories.* Polaroid Corporation embarked on an aggressive television advertising campaign, which increased sales dramatically. After all, the instant camera could be easily and effectively demonstrated on television.

In 1950 Polaroid introduced black-and-white film, to initial public excitement. The enthusiasm for the new film quickly turned to disappointment, however, when it was discovered that the black-and-white images first faded and then disappeared entirely. Polaroid was unable to develop a black-and-white film that did not fade and so provided consumers with a sponge-tipped tube of a liquid polymer that needed to be hand applied to each image to set the picture. This clumsy procedure was in effect until 1963 when the company introduced color film and a pack-loading black-and-white film that did not require the liquid setting polymer.

During the 1960s Polaroid continued to develop and improve the original instant camera. In 1965 the company introduced the "Swinger" camera aimed at the teenage market. For less than US$20, U.S. consumers could purchase a camera that took only black-and-white photographs. Proving popular with the younger market, the camera also sustained Polaroid's black-and-white film sales in the United States.

An offshoot of the Polaroid instant camera was launched in 1966. The ID-2 Land Identification system produced full-color laminated cards in two minutes. This innovation allowed for the instant production of drivers' licenses and other identification cards. In 1972 the first fully integrated camera and film system, the SX-70, was introduced. While the camera was immensely popular, and sales were growing at an annual rate of 20 percent, the high cost of research, manufacturing, and marketing of the SX-70 meant that company earnings began to fall.

DIGITAL CAMERAS

In "What Was Polaroid Thinking?" an article written for *Qn,* a publication of the Yale School of Management, Andrea Nagy Smith noted that Polaroid Corporation was researching digital cameras as early as the 1960s. In the mid-1960s the company applied for and received some of the earliest patents for electronic shutters for cameras. In 1981 Polaroid established an electronic imaging group to develop an instant camera that would produce a film-based print from a digital image, and by 1989, 42 percent of Polaroid's research and development funding was dedicated to digital imaging.

By the late 1990s, noted Smith, Polaroid was a top seller of digital cameras. Nonetheless, as other digital cameras flooded the market, Polaroid was unable to retain its major customers in the real estate, insurance, and photo-identification business, customers that had embraced and relied on the instant camera technology that originally brought the corporation success. The reason, suggested Smith, was that the company, starting with Edwin Land, always believed that chemistry and media came first, and that there was little interest in developing hardware. That logic, claimed former Polaroid Corporation Chief Executive Gary DiCamillo, in Smith's article, was based on the belief that instant film, not the instant camera, was at the core of the company's success and financial sustainability.

Another mistaken belief of the Polaroid Corporation was that consumers would always want a hard-copy print of their photographs. In a 1985 letter to Polaroid shareholders, the chief executive officer at the time, I. MacAllister Booth noted that there would always be "a basic human need for a permanent visual record." When customers began to abandon prints, Polaroid was taken by surprise.

LAND AND HIS LEGACY

Edwin Land felt that his legacy was the instant camera. He imagined that instant photography would change people's lives and, according to Smith, felt that the camera should "go beyond amusement and record-making to become a continuous partner of most human beings. . .a new eye, and a second memory."

Polaroid, recovering from its surprise and dismay at the popularity of digital photography, refocused research on its original success, the instant camera. In late 2011 the company collaborated with singer Lady Gaga to introduce an instant digital camera and printer. According to an advertisement, Polaroid described the camera as taking on the function of instant digital photography and combining it with instant photo printing while allowing the consumer to select various borders based on personal preference. The product used a technology that required zinc rather than ink to print the pictures, thus appealing to environmentally conscious consumers.

This new approach became known as the Impossible Project, a business financed by Austrian backers and aimed at keeping Polaroid instant film available. Polaroid itself had stopped manufacturing its instant film in 2009, turning instead to its digital product lines. The Impossible Project stepped in to take over Polaroid instant film and preserve it. As it happened, a number of amateur photographers and artists preferred the sepia tones of traditional Polaroid film to the starkness of digital images. The value of Polaroid film had shifted to a niche market, where its classic approach found new meaning thanks to a new group of fans.

While the Impossible Project was turning Polaroid film into a highbrow art form, Polaroid stayed busy working on its digital line. In January 2012, it announced the pending release of the SC1630 Smart Camera, a device that resembled a smartphone in size and touch screen, but came equipped with 16 megapixel camera and a 3x optical zoom. The touch screen allowed users to sort and send photos through a variety of applications, using included wireless and Bluetooth connectivity.

Meanwhile, the instant printer division of the company allowed Polaroid to market instant digital cameras and printer packages. Users took pictures with the digital camera, then immediately printed the image, with a classic option that created a print the same size as traditional Polaroid film. Photographers could also choose to include the white border from the classic film or create borderless images. In addition, connectivity options allowed users to post their pictures to social networks if they had no reason to immediately print them out. While the instant digital camera line could not replace the lesser cameras included on ubiquitous smartphones, the products offered more serious photographers dedicated camera options with greater clarity.

By the early 2010s the Polaroid brand saw a clean split between its new digital incarnation and the Impossible Project. The instant digital camera lines brought Polaroid into the digital age and helped the company create new value with its connections between digital imaging and photograph printers. Meanwhile, the Impossible Project showed that the original Polaroid inventions still had undeniable attraction, even after the camera industry had moved on. Few businesses can claim such success that their products develop a life of their own even after production stops. However, the decades of popularity that turned Polaroid into an iconic name also maintained its brand worth even when the market had moved on.

BIBLIOGRAPHY

Belsito, Elaine and and David E. Salamie. " Polaroid Corporation. " In *International Directory of Company Histories,* edited by Jay P. Pederson. Vol. 91, 345–353. Detroit: St. James Press, 2008. Gale Virtual Reference Library (GALE|CX3079200076). Accessed February 2, 2012. http://go.galegroup.com/ps/i.do?id=GALE%7CCX3079200076&v=2.1&u=gale&it=r&p=GVRL&sw=w.

Campbell, F. W. "Dr. Edwin H. Land (1909–1991)." Cambridge, MA: The Rowland Institute at Harvard University. Accessed February 20, 2012. http://www.rowland.harvard.edu/organization/land/index.php.

Festa, Anthony. "Instant Gratification." New York: Adorama, August 4, 2011. Accessed February 20, 2012. http://www.adorama.com/alc/article/Instant-Gratification.

Meyer, Sarah. "Polaroid at CES 2012." *Printer Comparison,* January 12, 2012. Accessed February 20, 2012. http://www.printercomparison.com/default.asp?newsID=1301.

Pepitone, Julianne. "Polaroid Goes Digital with Android

Camera." *CNNMoney,* January 16, 2012. Accessed February 20, 2012. http://money.cnn.com/2012/01/16/technology /polaroid_android/index.htm.

"Polaroid Announces Landmark 2012 CES Program." *Business Journals,* January 10, 2012. Accessed February 20, 2012. http://www.bizjournals.com/prnewswire/press_releases/2012 /01/10/NY33067.

"Polaroid and Impossible Present INSTANT REVOLUTION." *PR Newswire,* Accessed February 20, 2012. http://www .prnewswire.com/news-releases/polaroid-and-impossible -present-instant-revolution-138569204.html.

Smith, Andrea Nagy. "What Was Polaroid Thinking?" *Qn,* Fall 2009. Accessed February 20, 2012. Accessed February 20, 2012. http://qn.som.yale.edu/content/what-was-polaroid -thinking.

Trewe, Marti. "Instant Polaroid Film Development, 2012 Style." *AG Beat,* January 4, 2012. Accessed February 20, 2012. http://agbeat.com/real-estate-sales-marketing/photography -real-estate-sales-marketing/instant-polaroid-film -development-2012-style/.

Polyester:
Enduring Versatile Synthetic Fiber

Polyester, like other products of the modern era, has been hailed as a clever, useful creation and a versatile fabric woven to mimic silk, wool, or cotton, a fabric of comfort. "Polyester could be called the tofu of manufactured fibers since its appearance takes on many forms," the *Encyclopedia of Clothing and Fashion* noted in its entry on the subject.

The history of plastics forms part of the ever-changing attitudes toward man-made materials, as Martijntje Smits noted in the essay "Plastics" in the *Encyclopedia of Science, Technology, and Ethics*. Polyester is no exception. Hailed as a strong, easy-care fiber when first produced, it later became a symbol of a plastic age, a product that exemplified a retreat from the times when organic fabrics were the norm. Time was on polyester's side, however, and in the 21st century the man-made fabric returned in a variety of new forms matched to an age of outdoor pursuits and sophisticated living.

Its revived reputation, combined with the emergence of vast worldwide markets for consumer goods, has ensured polyester's survival and continued growth. In 2010 global production of polyester topped 34 million metric tons, according to a study by IHS, Inc., and despite a slow global economy, polyester production was expected to rise by 4.1 percent per year through 2015 and by 3.2 percent per year through 2020. While the United States and Europe once dominated the global polyester marketplace, Asia, led by China, took the lead in polyester manufacturing in the first decade of the 21st century.

Asia dominated the production of polyester fiber and was the market leader for polyester products. In addition to yarn utilized in weaving fabric, polyester manufacturers also produced filament yarn for use in the manufacture of tires, seat belts, and ropes. The versatility of polyester fiber inspired its use in a wide variety of consumer goods from yacht sails to wall coverings. By the 2010s polyester fleece clothing had crossed over from the hiking trails and ski slopes to the sidewalks. High-fashion designers were singing polyester's praises for the fabric's versatility and suitability to modern living.

A MODERN FABRIC FOR MODERN TIMES

Polyester was the invention of two British chemists, J. T. Dickson and J. R. Winfield, working for the Calico Printers Association in Manchester, England, according to *Bowling, Beatniks, and Bell-Bottoms: Pop Culture of 20th Century America*. The search for manufactured fabrics that would hold up to extended wear dated back to the 19th century. An artificial silk was created in the 1880s, according to *How Products Are Made: An Illustrated Guide to Product Manufacturing*, and in the 1920s U.S. scientists at E. I. du Pont de Nemours and Company (DuPont) had developed nylon. British chemists continued the synthetic fabric research at Imperial Chemical Industries, where they produced polyethylene terephthalate (PET) by combining terephthalic acid and ethylene glycol, both petroleum derivatives. In 1945 DuPont bought the rights to PET and launched commercial production of Dacron polyester, the name by which polyethylene terephthalate would be marketed.

The new synthetic fiber had many excellent properties. It was easy to maintain; washable and quick-drying; strong; wrinkle-, shrink-, moth-, and stain-resistant; not easily stretched out of shape; and long-lasting. However, early forms of the fabric were also hot to wear and did not breathe like natural fabrics. The surface also formed "pills" that gave it an unpleasant appearance, and the fabric soaked up oil easily, making stains difficult to wash out. Despite these detractions, the fact that it was easy to care for in an increasingly busy world made polyester garments attractive to consumers in the 1950s. According to the *Encyclopedia of Clothing and Fashion,* "When polyester first reached the market in the 1950s, it was hailed as a wonder fabric. Travelers could wash a garment, hang it up, and have it ready to wear in a couple of hours. It needed no ironing." Polyester suits could be worn for 68 days without dry cleaning, early advertisements boasted.

This was a fabric well suited to the latter half of the 20th century. More women were working outside of the home, with little time for a tedious day of ironing. Entertainment was more relaxed and less formal. The leisure suit, casual bell-bottom trousers, and easy-to-wear, relaxed-form dresses became the attire of the day. As reported by Miles Socha in *W Magazine,* by the 1960s polyester was welcomed as a godsend by consumers and was being utilized in a wide range of consumer goods from clothes to bedding. "It crystallized the modern life because it was wrinkle-free and easy to care for. You could just pop it in the washing machine," Pamela Golbin, chief fashion curator at the Arts Decoratifs museum in Paris, stated in the Socha article.

Although polyester was well received in the 1950s and early 1960s, as the decade progressed, a new generation, the "hippie culture," grew and derided their parents' polyester as a symbol of the unnatural and artificial. Polyester was set to enter its Dark Ages.

SPINNING OUT OF CONTROL

By the late 1960s, polyester, the plastic polymer that had led to the abandonment of the ironing board, was being held in disdain. "Polyester leisure suits for men and polyester pantsuits for women were embraced by the middle-aged and elderly," according to the *Encyclopedia of Clothing and Fashion.* "College students, on the other hand, hated polyester." This disdain for synthetic fabrics in popular culture was illustrated in the classic 1967 Hollywood movie, *The Graduate,* a dark comedy that sought to capture some of the cynicism of the time. The star, a recent college graduate named Benjamin Braddock, played by Dustin Hoffman, is advised to consider one thing as he looks to his future: plastics. In his essay on "Plastics," Smits noted, "most viewers of the film. . .immediately recognized its praise of plastics as a cynical joke, as a metaphor for the phony, banal and materialist world the protagonist has entered."

Another filmmaker chose to reinforce the metaphor by naming his satirical, over-the-top depiction of suburban U.S. life after the ubiquitous synthetic fabric. *Polyester,* a movie directed by filmmaker John Waters in 1981, was

named after "the dirtiest word you could say in fashion," Waters told Socha in 2008. Yet even while the hippie look focused on organic cotton blouses reminiscent of a bygone romantic age, both haute couture designers and clothing manufacturers were taking aim at the practical consumer concerned with easy care and long-term durability. Therefore, designers (notably the Japanese) continued to work with polyester.

IN FROM THE COLD

By the 1990s polyester once again emerged both on the runway of high-fashion houses and in outdoor clothing catalogs. A key player in the resurgence of polyester as a favored U.S. fabric was Aaron Feuerstein, whose family owned Malden Mills in Lawrence, Massachusetts. In 1981 the company founded by Feuerstein's grandfather was in Chapter 11 bankruptcy and reduced to making faux fur fabric to stay in business. Desperate to work his way out of an economic abyss, Feuerstein turned to his company's researchers for a solution. They devised a new polyester fleece fabric that would offer more warmth and did not absorb body odors as the older polyester fabrics had. The company took the new fabric to one of its customers, Patagonia, Inc., an outdoor clothing manufacturer, which quickly embraced the new lighter, windproof fabric. Patagonia dubbed it Polarfleece, and the result was new life for Malden Mills and the creation of a US$3 billion polyester fleece market, according to *Fortune* magazine.

Polyester fleece is a two-sided fabric with a soft pile on both sides that, unlike earlier polyester fabrics, resists pilling. It is lightweight and warmer than wool, according to *How Products Are Made,* leading to a variety of uses, from ear warmers for winter-born calves to underwear for astronauts. The popularity of polyester fleece led Patagonia to develop a product line, in 1993, made from recycled plastic soda bottles, which in turn had been made from the same PET used to make polyester fabric. The company also pledged to take in recycled Patagonia fleece or Polartec fleece from any manufacturer and recycle it into new fabric. With this emphasis on recycling and reuse, as well as the reengineering of polyester fabric to make it more comfortable and lightweight, polyester was back in the good graces of the consumer.

SPINNING A NEW TALE

A parade of fashion headlines began in the 1990s, marking the return of polyester (admittedly often under fashionable pseudonyms). In 1991 the *New York Times* hailed polyester's new look and new name, microfiber. The new polyester mimicked silk and suede, prompting top designers like Donna Karan to use it in their designs. Washable, breathable, and still stain-resistant, the new microfiber polyesters quickly gained a fashion foothold. In 2000, the *New York Times* also hailed what it called the new "techno fabrics;" man-made fabrics, among them new durable polyesters, that resisted stains, making them ideal for upholstery. Four years later, again the *New York Times* lauded the polyester uniforms being donned by top athletes on the playing fields. The paper-thin, lightweight polyester uniforms were the creation of a Maryland-based company, Under Armour, Inc.

Under Armour's push for market share was aimed at dislodging cotton sports clothing from the top spot. The company's success was helped when the cotton industry's 70 percent market share was threatened in mid-decade as droughts occurred in Asia and Australia. As Robert Johnson noted in the *New York Times,* in 2004 polyester was one-fourth the price of cotton. In addition to a price advantage, sports clothing manufacturers continued to market their new polyester fabrics under names like microfiber. The ultimate irony, Johnson pointed out, was the attempt by cotton sports clothing manufacturers to make their uniforms look like polyester. Using a process dubbed mercerizing, high-end golf shirts were soaked in chemicals and then treated with caustic soda. The process swelled the fabric's fibers and gave the shirts a shiny, polyester appearance.

WHAT'S OLD IS NEW

In the 1960s, as Johnson noted, famed U.S. talk show host Johnny Carson, a man known for his sartorial relaxed elegance, had once observed that polyester was made from the same material used to make soda bottles. By 2011, wearing recycled soda bottles had become emblematic of social responsibility for a generation, and Patagonia claimed on its website that over 13 years since the project's launch, some 86 million soda bottles had been utilized to create recycled polyester. Even the polyester-taunting filmmaker Waters found himself an advocate of the revived plastic fabric. Waters told *W Magazine* in 2008 that he was a fan of Japanese designer Rei Kawakubo, one of the proponents of the polyester revival.

BIBLIOGRAPHY

American Fiber Manufacturers Association. "Polyester Fiber." Arlington, VA. Accessed February 19, 2012. http://www.afma.org/f-tutor/polyester.htm.

"Global Polyester Market to Reach 39.3 Million Tons by 2015, According to a New Report by Global Industry Analysts, Inc." *SFGate,* February 9, 2011. Accessed February 19, 2012. http://www.sfgate.com/cgi-bin/article.cgi?f=/g/a/2011/02/09/prweb8121171.DTL&type=printable.

Hofmann, Deborah. "Polyester: A New Look, a New Name." *New York Times,* July 21, 1991. Accessed February 19, 2012. http://www.nytimes.com/1991/07/21/news/polyester-a-new-look-a-new-name.html?src=pm.

IHS Inc. "Polyester Fibers." Englewood, CO, January 2011. Accessed February 19, 2012. http://chemical.ihs.com/WP/Public/Reports/polyester_fibers/.

Johnson, Robert. "Incognito, Polyester Boogies onto the Playing Field." *New York Times,* March 21, 2004. Accessed February 19, 2012. http://www.nytimes.com/2004/03/21/business/business-incognito-polyester-boogies-onto-the-playing-field.html?pagewanted=all&src=pm.

Kavilariz, Parija. "Two New Products a Week, $2 Million in Sales." *CNNMoney,* November 17, 2011. Accessed February 19, 2012. http://money.cnn.com/2011/11/17/smallbusiness/betabrand_products/index.htm?iid=SF_SB_Lead.

Lowe, Elizabeth D. "Polyester." In *Encyclopedia of Clothing and Fashion,* edited by Valerie Steele. Vol. 3, 52–54. Detroit: Charles Scribner's Sons, 2005. Gale Virtual Reference Library (GALE|CX3427500462). Accessed February 19, 2012. http://go.galegroup.com/ps/i.do?id=GALE%7CCX3427500462&v=2.1&u=itsbtrial&it=r&p=GVRL&sw=w.

Patagonia, Inc. "Fabric: Recycled Polyester." Ventura, CA. Accessed February 19, 2012. http://www.patagonia.com/us/patagonia.go?assetid=2791.

"Repreve Warp Knits in Ford Focus Electric." *Knitting Industry,* January 9, 2012. Accessed February 19, 2012. http://www.knittingindustry.com/articles/1633.php.

Rohrlich, Marianne. "Personal Shopper; Techno Fabrics Suffer Red Wine Stylishly." *New York Times,* September 28, 2000. Accessed February 19, 2012. http://www.nytimes.com/2000/09/28/garden/personal-shopper-techno-fabrics-suffer-red-wine-stylishly.html?src=pm.

Rose, Julie. "How We Began: From Burgers to Beer to Berhas, Nine Innovators Tell Their Tales of Grit, Luck, and Inspiration." *Fortune,* May 1, 2000. Accessed February 19, 2012. http://money.cnn.com/magazines/fsb/fsb_archive/2000/05/01/279461/index.htm.

Routledge, Chris. "Polyester." In *Bowling, Beatniks, and Bell-Bottoms: Pop Culture of 20th-Century America,* edited by Sara Pendergast and Tom Pendergast. Vol. 4: 1960s–1970s, 959–960. Detroit: UXL, 2002. Gale Virtual Reference Library (GALE|CX3425100584). Accessed February 19, 2012. http://go.galegroup.com/ps/i.do?id=GALE%7CCX3425100584&v=2.1&u=itsbtrial&it=r&p=GVRL&sw=w.

Smits, Martijntje W. "Plastics." In *Encyclopedia of Science, Technology, and Ethics,* edited by Carl Mitcham. Vol. 3, 1418–1421. Detroit: Macmillan Reference USA, 2005. Gale Virtual Reference Library (GALE|CX3434900499). Accessed February 19, 2012. http://go.galegroup.com/ps/i.do?id=GALE%7CCX3434900499&v=2.1&u=itsbtrial&it=r&p=GVRL&sw=w.

Socha, Miles. "Synthetically Speaking." *W Magazine,* March 2008. Accessed February 19, 2012. http://www.wmagazine.com/fashion/2008/03/polyester.

Woodward, Angela. "Polyester Fleece." In *How Products Are Made: An Illustrated Guide to Product Manufacturing,* edited by Jacqueline L. Longe. Vol. 4, 384–388. Detroit: Gale, 1999. Gale Virtual Reference Library (GALE|CX2896800090). Accessed February 19, 2012. http://go.galegroup.com/ps/i.do?id=GALE%7CCX2896800090&v=2.1&u=itsbtrial&it=r&p=GVRL&sw=w.

Procter and Gamble:
Purpose-driven Products and Brands

In the 2010s the Procter and Gamble Company (P&G) was a global leader in the manufacture of household products, with products ranging from soaps (Tide, Ivory) to cat food (Iams) to cosmetics (Olay, Clairol). Revenue was more than US$82 billion in 2011. In part, P&G achieved this leadership position as a result of its novel approach to brand management as well as advertising, marketing, and market research. However, before the vaunted position as market leader was reached, Procter and Gamble consisted of just two brothers-in-law.

CANDLES AND SOAP

William Procter, originally from England, and James Gamble, fleeing poverty in Ireland, met in Cincinnati, Ohio, when they married two sisters. In 1837, at the suggestion of their father-in-law, they formed the partnership of Procter and Gamble. Operating initially out of a storeroom in Cincinnati, Ohio, Procter, a candle maker, took care of the store while Gamble, a soap maker, ran the manufacturing operation. While the new company manufactured both candles and soap, candles were the most important product at a time that predated widespread electrical lighting.

According to "P&G: A Company History," 1837 was not the ideal time to start a business in the United States. Cincinnati, Ohio itself was a bustling center of commerce, but there was widespread concern that the United States was on the verge of bankruptcy as financial institutions closed around the country. However, Procter and Gamble concerned themselves more with the challenge of competing with 14 other soap and candle makers in the city than with the possibility of a financial meltdown in the United States.

The partners soon expanded their operations to other locations in the region and took advantage of Cincinnati's location on the Ohio River to move their products to other areas. In 1848 Cincinnati, Ohio was linked to the major cities of the eastern United States by railroad, and Procter and Gamble expanded their sales area further. In the 1850s and in the wake of rumors about an impending Civil War, the partnership built a new plant to cope with increasing demand.

In 1851 the company's famous stars and moon logo was introduced. According to the *Gale Encyclopedia of U.S. Economic History*, the design of a simple cross on Procter and Gamble's Star brand candles was made by a shipper to help the mostly illiterate dock workers identify the goods. Subsequently, another shipper replaced the cross with an encircled star, and later, according to company legend, William Procter added 13 stars to represent the original 13 colonies of the United States.

The logo became synonymous with quality to Procter and Gamble's growing loyal customer base, and the company also became closely linked to such novel concepts as brand marketing.

BRANDING

In 1879 James Norris Gamble, son of one of the founders and a trained chemist, became the company's first full-time chemist. He researched possible new products, particularly a soap with the same quality as the expensive olive oil-based soaps of the time but with a less expensive production cost. Soon after, P&G introduced its White Soap. The most distinctive characteristic of the soap, noted the *Gale Encyclopedia of U.S. Economic History*, was the fact that it floated. Eager consumers contacted Procter and Gamble to purchase this "floating" soap, perplexing the company until it was discovered that a worker had accidentally left a soap mixer on while he was at lunch. This introduced more air than usual into the soap, resulting in a tendency to float. The product was redesigned to include this inadvertent process and was renamed Ivory Soap, a name that was inspired by a Bible passage favored by Harley Procter, William Procter's son.

Harley Procter urged the company's board of directors to market the purity and floating characteristics of the soap to consumers by way of advertising. At the time, it was only the mainly disreputable firms that advertised, using outrageous claims in an attempt to promote their products. Nonetheless, the board awarded Harley Procter an annual budget of US$11,000 in 1882, and the company began advertising Ivory with the more reasonable claim, "99 and 44/100 percent pure." The slogan was perceived by consumers to be a welcome alternative to the outlandish claims of the firm's competitors. In 1896 Procter and Gamble's first color advertisement, for Ivory, was featured in *Cosmopolitan* magazine. Ivory soap represented the company's first effort at mass marketing by continuous advertising to consumers.

However, according to the *Gale Encyclopedia of U.S. Economic History,* Harley Procter was of the opinion that "advertising alone couldn't make a product successful—it was merely evidence of a manufacturer's faith in the merit of the article." To this end, he insisted on testing the products for quality and improving them before they were even placed for sale. This tactic was the beginning of Procter and Gamble's reputation as the manufacturer of superior-quality products and also its brand marketing initiative.

Almost 30 years later, in 1924, Procter and Gamble created one of the first market research departments in the industry to study consumer preferences and buying habits. In the same year, it became the first company to conduct deliberate database market research with consumers. The company hired female college graduates to go door-to-door to interview homemakers about their use of household products and to document those usage patterns. The first brand to incorporate the research into the design process was Camay.

CAMAY

Camay was introduced in 1926 in response to consumer demand for perfumed soap. According to a November 2010 article by Ricki Morell in the *New York Times,* the soap was marketed as "the soap of beautiful women," and its original wrapper featured a cameo of an elegant woman in profile. The advertisement campaigns for Camay were focused on young brides who marveled at their soft complexions. This bar of soap, stated Morell, evoked a femininity and sensuality wheras other soaps, such as Ivory, seemed utilitarian.

The company's website noted that in 1931, Procter and Gamble's brand management system began to evolve in earnest. Neil McElroy, the promotion department manager at the time, turned Procter and Gamble into a marketing organization with competing brands, each with its own marketing strategy and managed by separate teams. In 1933 one of those brands, Oxydol, sponsored a nationally aired radio serial program, *Ma Perkins.* The popularity of the program led other Procter and Gamble brands to sponsor many "soap operas," and faithful listeners of the programs became regular and loyal Procter and Gamble customers.

CREATING NEW PRODUCTS

Harley Procter's statement that advertising alone does not sell a product seems to be behind Procter and Gamble's philosophy of first determining the consumer's unarticulated needs and then developing a quality product that fills those needs. After filling a consumer demand for perfumed soap with its Camay soap bar in 1926, the company went on to become an industry leader on numerous other product fronts.

Laundry Detergent. In the 1920s, after learning that homemakers were peeling strips of bars of Ivory soap to use for washing clothes and dishes, the company developed Ivory Soap Flakes. However, soap flakes performed poorly in hard water, often leaving a ring around sinks, dulling colors, and turning whites gray. Researchers at Procter and Gamble discovered two synthetic molecules that worked together to pull grease and dirt from clothes and suspend it until it could be rinsed away. In 1933 this discovery led to the introduction of a product called Dreft. Further refining and improving the product resulted in Tide, a detergent that could handle heavily soiled clothes.

Toothpaste. In the 1940s it was estimated that tooth decay was one of the most prevalent diseases in the United States, with citizens developing an estimated 700 million cavities per year. According to the Crest website, Procter and Gamble began a joint collaboration with Indiana University in 1950 to research, develop, and test a new toothpaste containing fluoride. Results from the research showed that children ages 6 to 16 showed a 49 percent reduction in cavities, and adults showed a similar reduction in overall tooth decay. Crest with Flouristan toothpaste was launched nationally in 1956, and by 1962 it had become one of the best-selling toothpastes in the United States.

Disposable Diapers. Victor Mills was a chemical engineer who worked for Procter and Gamble in the 1950s.

Dissatisfied with the diapers used on his grandchild, Mills assigned researchers at Procter and Gamble to find a better-quality, lower-cost, disposable diaper. At the time, it was estimated that disposable diapers were used in less than 1 percent of the billions of diaper changes in the United States. After manufacturing, largely by hand, and testing 37,000 disposable diapers, Pampers became the first brand of practical, disposable diapers.

According to its corporate website, Procter and Gamble interacted with more than five million consumers in almost 100 countries, conducted 20,000 research studies, and invested over US$400 million in "consumer understanding" per year. Recognizing that many of its products were produced by many of its competitors, albeit in different forms, the company strived for innovation through collaboration. It developed a program, "Connect and Develop," that invited other companies or individual inventors to contact it with new ideas. The corporation estimated that 50 percent of its new product initiatives involved a significant collaboration with an outside party.

P&G AS AN EMPLOYER

In 1886 Procter and Gamble started production at the Ivorydale, Ohio factory, north of Cincinnati, which had been designed by the industrial architect Solon Beman. The plant incorporated the latest technological advances and a pleasant work environment for the employees. This was seen as a progressive approach to employee management at a time of significant local and national labor unrest in the United States. In 1887 the company instituted a pioneering profit-sharing program for factory workers. The program was conceived by William Cooper Procter, grandson of the founder, to help workers understand their vital role in the company's success, a sentiment voiced in a revision to the company's articles of incorporation in 1919 to include the statement that the "interests of the Company and its employees are inseparable."

According to "P&G: A Company History," available on the corporate website, seasonal purchases of the firm's products by wholesalers led to uneven production levels and the necessity of layoffs at the Ivorydale factory. In 1919 the company announced that it planned to sell directly to retailers and hired an additional 450 salespeople. The change stabilized production, reduced layoffs, and changed the way the grocery industry operated.

In 1994 Procter and Gamble received an award from the U.S. Department of Labor for its commitment to "instituting equal opportunities and creating a diverse workforce." In 2011 the company reported over 129,000 employees and estimated that its workforce represented over 145 nationalities.

NEW MILLENNIUM, NEW APPROACH

In the 21st century, Procter and Gamble's continued view of brand marketing as the way to promote its products was emphasized on the company's website in the form of "Core Strengths." The first strength, consumer understanding, involved uncovering the unarticulated needs of the consumer. Innovation translated the customer's articulated desires into new products, and brand building sought to develop "purpose-inspired, benefit-driven brands."

As Procter and Gamble's competitors, most notably Johnson & Johnson, incorporated brand packaging and marketing into their own marketing techniques, the company created a shift away from individual brand marketing to generic corporate brand awareness and brand bundling. One such approach to creating corporate brand awareness occurred in 2010 when, as a sponsor of the Team USA Olympic athletes, Procter and Gamble released several television and video advertisements titled, "Proud Sponsor of Moms." In the commercials, no specific brands were advertised other than a flash of the most high-profile product labels at the end. The emphasis was on promoting the Procter and Gamble brand itself by targeting the people who were the most frequent buyers of its household and beauty products, such as women and particularly mothers.

While co-branding with another company's product was not unusual in the advertising world, one brand commandeering another brand's advertisement had never been done before Procter and Gamble tried it in 2012, according to Andrew Adam Newman's article in the *New York Times*. Using the muscular actor and former NFL football player, Terry Crews, to utter the words, "Old Spice is too powerful to stay in its own commercial," Procter and Gamble's advertising agency, Wieden and Kennedy, developed a series of advertisements in which Crews promoted the body wash and men's aftershave, Old Spice, while dramatically entering an in-progress advertisement for other corporate products, such as Bounce dryer balls or Charmin toilet paper. Newman quoted Barbara Lippert of the ad agency Goodby, Silverstein & Partners as saying, "One commercial crashing into another commercial is really dead-on brilliant because it mimics the chaotic clutter of advertising."

CORE VALUE

The company's purpose, as stated on the corporate website, was "to provide branded products and services of superior quality and value that improve the lives of the world's consumers. . . .As a result, consumers will reward us with leadership sales, profit, and value creation." Or, as the company's global marketing and brand officer Marc

Pritchard said in a February 2011 video available on the website, "At Procter and Gamble, a brand is not a brand until it makes a difference in your life. A P&G brand must have a purpose that transcends its benefits."

BIBLIOGRAPHY

Crest. "Crest Heritage." Cincinnati, OH, 2011. Accessed February 1, 2012. http://www.crest.com/about-crest/crest-heritage.aspx.

Morell, Ricki. "When a Trusted Brand Disappears." *New York Times,* November 30, 2010. Accessed February 1, 2012. http://www.nytimes.com/2010/12/02/fashion/02SKINDEEP.html.

Newman, Andrew Adam. "A Brand Too Strong to Stay in Its Own Ad." *New York Times,* January 31, 2012. Accessed February 1, 2012. http://www.nytimes.com/2012/02/01/business/media/old-spice-too-strong-to-stay-in-its-own-ad.html.

Procter & Gamble. "A Company History." Cincinnati, OH, 2011. Accessed February 27, 2012. www.pg.com/translations/history_pdf/english_history.pdf.

———. "Heritage." Cincinnati, OH, 2011. Accessed February 1, 2012. http://www.pg.com/en_US/company/heritage.shtml.

"Procter and Gamble Company." In *Gale Encyclopedia of U.S. Economic History,* edited by Thomas Carson and Mary Bonk. Vol. 2, 821–823. Detroit: Gale, 2000. Gale Virtual Reference Library (GALE|CX3406400753). Accessed February 1, 2012. http://go.galegroup.com/ps/i.do?id=GALE%7CCX3406400753&v=2.1&u=itsbtrial&it=r&p=GVRL&sw=w.

Rayasam, Renuka. "Procter Gamble Takes Marketing into a New Era." *U.S. News,* March 23, 2007. Accessed February 1, 2012. http://www.usnews.com/usnews/biztech/articles/070323/23pg.htm.

Refrigeration: Its Development, Application, and Use Over Time

In many parts of the developed world, refrigeration is so common in the 21st century that most people seldom give it thought. The techniques of mechanical refrigeration and cooling enable people to keep foods fresh for days, control the temperature of homes and cars, maintain sterile hospital operating rooms and blood banks, and preserve and ship meats and vegetables for consumption thousands of miles away and hundreds of days later.

While refrigeration is commonplace throughout the industrialized world, the industry is actually less than 200 years old. The modern conveniences enjoyed today are the direct result of several inventors who had to overcome not only technological challenges but, in many cases, resistance from entrenched industries fighting to maintain the status quo. Such people as John Gorrie, Frederick McKinley Jones, and Gustavus Swift battled railroad barons, racism, and Frederick Tudor, the "Ice King," to develop the refrigeration technologies and underlying industries that are all too often taken for granted today.

EARLY REFRIGERATION METHODS

For centuries, humanity has used natural means for refrigeration, which is defined as the process of cooling a material or an area below the temperature of its surrounding environment. Barbara Krasner-Khait reported in *History Magazine* that in ancient times, the Greeks, Romans, and Hebrews filled pits with snow and covered them with materials to insulate the snow from the warmer climate. "Ice was harvested and stored in China before the first millennium," Krasner-Khait continued, while 17th-century Europeans placed their bottles in a mixture of water and saltpeter to cool beverages. Most food was consumed soon after it was grown, and most people lived close to the farms where meat and vegetables were produced. Before the 1830s, food that was not consumed during the harvest season was preserved through traditional methods such as pickling and smoking.

However, those practices became inadequate as the Industrial Revolution progressed. In the United States from 1830 to 1860, health concerns, a diet reform movement, and consumers with more disposable income created higher demand for fresh produce and other foods. Krasner-Khait commented, "As the cities grew, so grew the distance between the consumer and the source of food."

The initial response to these trends was to harvest the world's natural supply of wintertime ice. Krasner-Khait wrote that the commercial ice trade began in 1799, when ice cut in New York City was shipped to Charleston, South Carolina. She added, "Unfortunately, there wasn't much ice left when the shipment arrived." A number of entrepreneurs began experimenting with methods and materials to cut, store, and insulate ice for transportation from the northern United States to other markets. Early pioneer Nathaniel Wyeth developed standardized techniques to score, cut, and harvest ice blocks. Another early pioneer was Frederick Tudor, dubbed the "Ice King" after his efficient insulation materials allowed him to export ice to tropical markets. Minna Scherlinder Morse wrote in *Smithsonian* magazine that by 1846, Tudor was "shipping tens of thousands of tons of ice from Boston to destinations around the globe. His monopoly would remain unchallenged for decades." Households began buying ice boxes, insulated containers that held foods for longer periods of time. However, they needed to add new ice every few days, spawning companies that delivered ice to homes on a regular basis.

Natural ice was not an ideal solution for commercial use, however. By the late 19th century, industries in the United States were polluting lakes and streams, contaminating many sources of water and ice. Meat and produce that came in contact with ice during transport became discolored, making them less desirable to consumers. While competition and improving technology reduced the costs involved, it was still relatively inefficient to insulate and transport heavy blocks of ice over long distances.

ICE THROUGH MECHANICAL MEANS

In response, inventors and investors pursued methods to manufacture ice through mechanical means, a path that would eventually create the refrigeration industry. As early as 1748, William Cullen demonstrated artificial refrigeration in Scotland, but he never pursued the concept. In the United States, Oliver Evans is credited with designing the first refrigerator in 1805, with Jacob Perkins building a practical machine in 1834. In London, England Michael Faraday used liquefied ammonia to create a cooling effect in 1820.

Another key player was Carl von Linde, a German engineer whose work with gas compression and extracting oxygen from the atmosphere led to the creation of the Linde Air Products Company (now known as Praxair). Linde's research also "led to his invention of the first reliable and efficient compressed-ammonia refrigerator" in 1877, according to the Chemical Heritage Foundation. "The company he established to promote this invention was an international success: refrigeration rapidly displaced ice in food handling and was introduced into many industrial processes."

Even with these improvements, the road to refrigeration success was not always straight. In the 1840s Dr. John Gorrie built a machine that manufactured ice and cooled air for his yellow fever patients in Apalachicola, Florida. By the early 1850s "Dr. Gorrie's artificial ice machine would be patented in London, England and the United States, and the doctor would largely forgo his practice, devoting himself to promoting his device," Morse wrote in *Smithsonian*. The idea of creating ice artificially "bordered on blasphemy," Morse continued, and Gorrie was widely ridiculed in the press. Still, he created a demonstration model, received a patent, and lined up investors. "Gorrie became the first person to create a commercially available refrigeration machine," but he "quickly fell on hard times," Morse wrote. His lead investor died, and others backed out. "Gorrie suspected that Frederic Tudor had spearheaded a smear campaign against him and his invention," Morse continued, as the "Ice King" fought to protect his ice-harvesting monopoly from mechanical competition. Without funds, Gorrie eventually returned to Apalachicola, Florida, convinced that his invention had appeared before the United States was ready for it. He died soon afterward, in 1855.

In the years following, the ice industry evolved from harvesting to manufacturing. James McSwain wrote in the *Journal of Southern History* that in the southeastern United States, "The block ice business flourished from 1900 through World War II. Movie theaters bought vast amounts of block ice to provide customers with air-conditioned viewing." By the 1950s, however, more U.S. households had their own refrigerators, eliminating the need for ice boxes, McSwain continued. Automatic ice makers and air conditioning soon followed. By the 1960s, the block ice industry had "almost disappeared except for a few plants that catered to niche markets," he added.

Over time, continued improvements and efficiencies in refrigeration technology brought the practice into wider use, first among industries, then in commercial establishments and eventually in homes. Brewing was the first industry to embrace refrigeration. In the 1860s, Anton Dreher "introduced refrigeration to the fermentation and conditioning stages of beermaking," according to *Modern Brewing Age*. Krasher-Khait wrote in *History Magazine* that commercial refrigeration was "primarily directed at brewers in the 1870s," with all breweries equipped by 1891. The Chicago, Illinois, meat-packing industry followed a decade later, she added, with many other industries soon adopting the practice.

MOBILIZING REFRIGERATION

While stationary refrigeration was an important breakthrough for manufacturing, it solved only part of the problem. Companies still faced logistical hurdles in keeping their products cold while moving them from processing centers to widespread markets.

A major transportation innovation was the refrigerated railroad car, which was primarily driven by the meat industry. During the 1870s, cattle raised in Texas were driven to the Great Plains of the United States for feeding, then taken to railheads in the Midwest and shipped to the Chicago, Illinois, stockyards. Buyers in Chicago, Illinois, then shipped live cattle to the major markets on the Eastern Seaboard of the United States. It would have been more efficient to slaughter the cattle in Chicago, Illinois, and ship the dressed beef east, but that method could only be pursued in the cold winter months.

When cattle buyer Gustavus Swift moved to Chicago, Illinois, he quickly determined that the current practices were inefficient. Cattle often lost weight during the long train trips to market and their meat became less tender. "The cattle had to be fed along the way, some died in transit, and—since the railroads charged per pound—huge freight charges added tremendously to the cost of doing business," according to the entry in the *Gale Encyclopedia of World Biography*. Also, many parts of the slaughtered animal were discarded, adding no value at the ultimate destination. Swift "believed that butchering cattle and shipping dressed beef was a far more profitable idea," the article continued, both because of the lesser shipping cost and because Swift could find other uses for the inedible parts of the cattle. After one successful attempt to ship a railway carload of dressed beef during the winter of 1877, Swift put all his attention on building up the dressed beef business.

However, he soon encountered a number of challenges. Eastern U.S. consumers had concerns that if the cattle were not killed locally, the meat would not be safe. Their butchers also warned of possible health risks, and Swift was unable to convince the railroads to develop refrigerated container cars. The rail companies had already invested in massive pens and cattle yards. They wanted to protect the higher rates they charged for shipping animals. "Forming a cartel against Swift, they began charging exorbitantly high prices for dressed meat," the *Gale Encyclopedia of World Biography* noted.

Swift responded by hiring his own engineer, Andrew Chase, who designed a workable refrigerated railcar in 1877. Swift then partnered with a manufacturer to build his cars. He ran advertisements promoting dressed beef and partnered with local butchers on the East Coast of the United States to sell his products. Locked out by the major railroads, he negotiated a favorable shipping rate with the Grand Trunk Railway, which drew little business from shipping live cattle. The Grand Trunk carried his beef from Chicago, Illinois, through Michigan and into Canada en route to the eastern U.S. markets. Soon the other major Chicago, Illinois, packers followed Swift's lead, building their own cars to transport dressed beef. "Once meat could be reliably shipped east, the Chicago slaughterhouse industry boomed, and such meat-packing companies as Swift and Armour made fortunes," the *Gale Encyclopedia of Science* noted. Refrigerated cars (also called "reefers") were then developed to bring fruits, vegetables, and other perishables to markets around the United States.

REFRIGERATION UNITS IN TRUCKS

While reefers solved the long-distance issues of rail transport, shippers still faced challenges away from large cities or railheads. "An obvious problem with iced refrigeration of transported perishable foods is that the food may spoil if the ice melts before the shipment reaches the market," the *Gale Encyclopedia of Science* observed. Ice and salt were used on trucks, but with limited success. Electric refrigeration

units were heavy and used too much energy to be supported by the truck's battery, so they had their own batteries that required frequent stops for recharging. The trucks also had minimal suspension systems, so the jarring and bouncing during transit damaged produce in the truck bed.

The solution came in the 1930s from Frederick McKinley Jones, who would become the first African American to receive the U.S. federal government's National Medal of Technology. Jones faced considerable racism in segregated society as he pursued a career as an engineer. According to the *International Directory of Company Histories,* Jones was first involved with automobile racing. He built and designed cars until he left his job because, as an African American, he was unable to attend the races where his cars were competing. After serving as a mechanic and engineer in France during World War I, he went to work at a movie theater in Hallock, Minnesota. During the transition from silent movies to "talkies," Jones developed a sound-on-film system that landed him a job as an engineer with Ultraphone Sound Systems.

While at Ultraphone, Jones also developed an early air conditioner for his automobile but was unable to persuade his bosses that there was a market for the device. Not long afterward, entrepreneur Joseph Numero, who headed Ultraphone, made a golfing bet that his company could develop an ice-free, automatic air cooling system for the transportation industry. "Jones applied his knowledge of race car shock proofing and automobile air conditioning to the transport refrigeration project," the *International Directory of Company Histories* stated. The early product, the Thermo-King, met with skepticism until Numero convinced Armour & Company to try the system on its meat trucks. Shortly afterward, the United States entered World War II, and Thermo-King landed a military refrigeration contract. "Jones's lightweight, portable refrigeration units performed so well in the field that they became designated equipment for all the armed forces," the article continued, cooling water, blood plasma, airplane cockpits, and soldiers around the world.

The company's military success enabled Thermo-King to develop refrigerated containers that could be transported from trucks to trains to ships. "Jones designed the first practical and automatic refrigeration unit for trucks and railcars, allowing the transport of food and other perishables across long distances," *Fleet Owner* stated. "This device helped lead to the creation of the fast food and frozen food industries," and enabled the growth of large supermarket chains.

FROM INDUSTRIAL TO CONSUMER GOODS

Industrial uses drove much of the early improvements in refrigeration technology, which took more time to move into the consumer sector. The *Encyclopedia of American Industries* noted that home refrigerators presented more challenges than commercial ones. "The home unit had to be small enough to fit easily into the house. It had to be automatic and not require an operator as the commercial units did. It also had to use safer chemicals than the highly toxic or flammable ones used in commercial units. And the unit had to be affordable, which meant mass production."

In the meantime, U.S. homemakers relied on ice boxes to store perishables. By 1884, according to Krasner-Khait, ice boxes were "as common as stoves or sewing machines in all but the poorest tenements." Ice wagons were a common site as they made regular deliveries to households.

The first working home refrigerator was the Domelre, introduced in 1912. The Kelvinator in 1918 was the first mass-produced unit. After General Motors (GM) bought the small Frigidaire company in 1919, GM "proceeded to pour money and talent into the company," Bernard Nagengast wrote in *Mechanical Engineering.* "All of GM's research and engineering divisions were ordered to assist in solving problems," ultimately driving down the units' costs and boosting sales of the technically advanced products. General Electric's "Monitor Top," introduced in 1927, "leapfrogged everyone else" with a model that was "quieter, more energy-efficient and less expensive than competing models," Nagengast continued. Frigidaire soon responded with the "Meter Miser." Refrigerator shelving, automatic ice makers, and self-defrosting models soon followed.

As competition intensified among refrigerator manufacturers, *Air Conditioning, Heating and Refrigeration News* reported that ice box sales fell from 1.3 million in 1924 to less than half a million in 1931. After World War II, "Mass production of modern refrigerators began in earnest," Krasner-Khait wrote in *History Magazine,* with refrigerators present in more than 90 percent of urban U.S. households and 80 percent of farms by 1950 in the United States.

Manufacturers also introduced home freezers, which allowed the frozen food industry to expand from institutional to retail customers. Stand-alone freezers had been introduced in the 1920s but did not gain popularity until the 1940s. GE introduced the first combination refrigerator-freezer in 1939 and other companies followed suit. Clarence Birdseye, the "father of frozen food," designed freezing equipment and organized "companies pioneering in the processing and marketing of quick-frozen foods," according to *Frozen Food Digest.*

With refrigerated appliances becoming common, related techniques were introduced to address the challenges of "refrigerated rooms." According to Nagengast in *Mechanical Engineering,* the first "complete comfort air conditioning system was engineered in 1901 for the New York Stock Exchange" by Alfred Wolff. Willis Haviland Carrier built on Wolff's work and "really perfected the art of precision cooling," Nagengast wrote. Like the other refrigeration technologies, air conditioning grew from commercial applications to retail businesses and movie theaters, and eventually to homes across the United States. Just as refrigeration had eliminated the distances between foods and markets, air conditioning brought comfortable living conditions to people living in hot deserts and muggy southern swamps.

Air conditioning, refrigerators, freezers, and reefers evolved over the years from common roots and similar technical backgrounds to become an integral part of modern society. The comfort and convenience often taken for granted today exists because of the creativity, drive, and ambition of a handful of entrepreneurs and engineers who applied technology to the basic need to keep people, food, and materials cool.

BIBLIOGRAPHY

"After Long Wait, Improved Refrigerated Rail Car Right on Track." *Quick Frozen Foods International,* October 1, 2010. Accessed February 13, 2012. LexisNexis.

Burnson, Patrick. "A Convergence of International Issues." *Logistics Management,* September 1, 2008. Accessed February 13, 2012. LexisNexis.

Chemical Heritage Foundation. "Carl von Linde." Philadelphia, PA, 2012. Accessed February 13, 2012. http://chemical heritage.net/discover/online-resources/topics/people-and -organizations/linde-carl-von.aspx.

"Early Frozen Food History Facts." *Frozen Food Digest,* October 1, 2009. Accessed February 13, 2012. LexisNexis.

Encyclopedia of American Industries. Farmington Hills, Michigan: Gale/Cengage Learning, 2005.

"Fredrick McKinley Jones, The Father of Portable Refrigeration, to Be Honored." *Fleet Owner,* November 2, 2010. Accessed February 13, 2012. http://blog.fleetowner.com/trucking -straight-talk/2010/11/02/fredrick-mckinley-jones-the-father -of-portable-refrigeration-to-be-honored/.

Gale Encyclopedia of Science. Farmington Hills, Michigan: Gale/Cengage Learning, 2008.

Glaser, Gregg. "Speaking of Beer." *Modern Brewery Age,* January 29, 1996. Accessed February 13, 2012. LexisNexis.

"Gustavus Franklin Swift." In *Encyclopedia of World Biography.* 2nd ed. Detroit: Gale, 2004, 407–409. Gale Virtual Reference Library (GALE|CX3404708121). Accessed March 1, 2012. http://go.galegroup.com/ps/i.do?id=GALE%7CCX3 404708121&v=2.1&u=itsbtrial&it=r&p=GVRL&sw=w.

Hall, Gary. "Keeping It Cold with Style." *Contracting Business,* August 2001. Accessed February 13, 2012. LexisNexis.

International Directory of Company Histories (digital edition). Farmington Hills, Michigan: Gale/Cengage Learning, 2007.

Keep It Cool, Inc. "The History of the Refrigerator." Lake Park, FL, 2012. Accessed February 13, 2012. http://www.keep itcool.com/history_of_the_refrigerator2.htm.

Krasner-Khait, Barbara. "The Impact of Refrigeration." *History Magazine,* July 1, 2003. Accessed February 13, 2012. http:// www.history-magazine.com/refrig.html.

"A Look Back on the HVACR Industry of the Early 1930s." *Air Conditioning, Heating & Refrigeration News,* January 5, 2009. Accessed February 13, 2012. LexisNexis.

McSwain, James B. "Cooling the South: The Block Ice Era. 1875–1975." *Journal of Southern History* 75, no. 2 (May 2009): 518.

Morse, Minna Scherlinder. "Chilly Reception." *Smithsonian,* July 1, 2002. Accessed February 13, 2012. http://www.smithsonianmag.com/history-archaeology/Chilly_Reception.html.

Nagengast, Bernard. "It's a Cool Story!" *Mechanical Engineering,* May 2000. Accessed February 13, 2012. http://www.memagazine.org/backissues/membersonly/may00/features/coolstory/coolstory.html.

Soule, Alexander. "For Praxair, Another Century Begins." *Fairfield County Business Journal,* February 2007. Accessed February 13, 2012. LexisNexis.

Texas State Historical Association. "Swift and Company." Denton, TX, 2012. Accessed February 13, 2012. http://www.tshaonline.org/handbook/online/articles/dis02.

Saran Wrap: Serendipitous Plastic Wrap

Saran Wrap held high standing in popular culture as evidenced by the diverse number of uses, both practical and wacky, featured in YouTube videos and in the pages of do-it-yourself magazines. This resilient, transparent, plastic film was created by accident in an industrial laboratory, utilized in an historic war effort, and eventually found its way into kitchen drawers and pantries across the world. Along the way, it contributed to a cultural revolution in the marketplace and the home, and liberated shoppers and chefs by allowing foods to be showcased, stored, transported, preserved, and protected.

Like Xerox and Google, Saran Wrap also became a genericized tradename, the modern slang for any plastic film. While the chemical composition of the trademarked product changed over the years, reflecting environmental sensibilities and pressures, its ubiquity and usefulness made it one of the world's best and most well-known inventions. From a stubborn, foul-smelling substance coating a laboratory beaker to a household staple, Saran Wrap was a serendipitous discovery that became a clingy, clear part of modern daily life.

WRAPPED AND READY

The search for a food wrapping that would preserve flavor and prevent food from spoiling, either by losing moisture or succumbing to it, began in the mid-19th century. In 1862, according to the book *How Products Are Made: An Illustrated Guide to Product Manufacturing*, Alexander Parkes, an English chemist, developed a material he dubbed Parkesine. It was made from cotton, nitric acid, sulfuric acid, castor oil, and camphor. Two years later, U.S. chemist John Wesley Hyatt improved the product and called it celluloid. Building on this work, Swiss chemist Jacques Brandenberger developed cellophane in 1911, a transparent packaging that gained wider use in the 1920s.

A decade later, English scientists developed polyethylene and later polyvinyl chloride (PVC), both man-made materials derived from hydrocarbons, including methane and ethylene. These materials were utilized in a wide variety of products in industrial and military sectors, from insulating wiring to protecting materials from corrosion. Following World War II, the chemical industry repurposed these new plastics, extruding them into thin films designed to meet packaging needs in a burgeoning consumer marketplace where convenience and self-service were hallmarks. In 1945 the Visking Corporation introduced a plastic film made from polyethylene. In the next decade, manufacturers began to produce plastic film made from PVC.

The E. I. du Pont de Nemours Company (DuPont) started producing cellophane in the 1920s. Following World War II, DuPont recognized a new opportunity for the wrap in the growing number of suburban self-service supermarkets, and the company embarked on a major advertising push for the product. Unlike the hydrocarbon-sourced plastic films that were gaining market share, cellophane was derived from cellulose extracted from wood pulp or cotton fibers. According to Cory Bernat, who detailed the history of grocery store packaging in a 2012 story for *The Atlantic,* DuPont's market research section developed consumer surveys to help market cellophane. The company persuaded grocery store owners that modern shoppers were susceptible to impulse buying, thereby making attractive packaging an advantage in the ever-widening aisles of the new supermarkets. Butchers were told that pre-wrapped meats in self-service counters, according to Bernat, prompted shoppers to buy more.

Both cellophane and wax paper were widely used until the late 1950s when plastic wraps began their push into the food packaging marketplace. The new films were suited to foods that required segregation from air or outside moisture. They also helped to contain odors and held moisture in when necessary. Foods frozen in plastic film had a longer shelf life and were less susceptible to freezer burn than foods wrapped in aluminum foil. The new plastic films were much better at creating a barrier between the food and the outer environment, but they did not completely block out air from interacting with food or block all aromas.

Plastics and plastic film became indispensable to everyday life, Martijntje W. Smits noted in his essay, "Plastics," in the *Encyclopedia of Science, Technology and Ethics*. "It would, for example, be impossible to have twenty-first century supermarkets without plastic packaging, because the supermarket system is dependent on lightweight, airproof, and pre-packaged goods," Smits wrote. "In fact the transition from the traditional grocery store to the supermarket system was strongly encouraged by the emerging availability of plastic packaging materials in the 1950s and 1960s." Given their vital role in the marketplace, the search for a better plastic wrap, one with greater barrier qualities, had begun.

FROM GREEN SLIME TO CLEAR SHINE

In 1933 a young college student was working at Dow Chemical Company with an eye to a future in industrial chemistry. Ralph Wiley was washing glass laboratory vessels and working on the development of an improved dry cleaning chemical when he came upon a beaker lined with a green, smelly film that resisted his cleaning efforts. He dubbed the substance "eonite," inspired by a chapter in the popular U.S. Depression-era cartoon, "Little Orphan Annie," in which the mop-haired heroine befriends a down-on-his-luck inventor named Eli Eon, creator of an indestructible substance he hopes will change the world.

Wiley embarked on a 10-year exploration of the green film. Dow changed the name to Saran, got rid of the green color and odor, and used the new substance, polyvinylidene chloride (PVdC), to coat and protect sensitive optical and aircraft components from corrosive materials in World War II. Following the war, the company produced a film from the PVdC that would eventually launch Dow into the consumer goods sector and make Saran Wrap a household name.

In 1994 the 83-year-old Wiley said in an interview published in the *Ludington Daily News* that initially he "wasn't enthusiastic about Saran film. I thought Saran fibers would be the bigger market." After the initial discovery, Wiley worked with PVdC fibers, incorporating them into automobile seat covers. While increasing the strength, the fibers also helped produce static electricity that proved discomforting to passengers and drivers as they slipped in and out of their cars. Dow therefore took the PVdC in a new direction, plastic film, and the new product proved such a hit with consumers it pushed Dow into the consumer goods marketplace. The new plastic film had better barrier properties than other plastic wraps and it was tenacious in attaching itself to the tops of bowls or around food products.

Briefly, Dow allowed two former employees to market the new plastic film in the U.S. Midwest, according to Wiley, but after watching their success, two years later Dow took back control and launched the Dow brands division, introducing Saran Wrap to the U.S. marketplace in 1953. "Dow at the time was sort of resistant to the retail market. They liked to sell by the ton and let other people worry about the retail market," Wiley said in the *Ludington Daily News* 41 years after the product launch, when the market for Saran Wrap topped US$30 million annually. As he prepared to retire from his life's work at Dow, Wiley, whose patents had been held by the company, acknowledged he had not made a fortune for his discovery, but said he did get a "lash of pride" whenever he passed Saran Wrap on grocery store shelves.

Dow's plastic film became a household favorite because its chemical composition allowed it to withstand extreme temperatures and also gave it excellent barrier properties. Those same properties that made it a household name in the 1960s continue to make PVdC one of the top plastic packaging materials among food producers worldwide in the 2010s. "PVdC's outstanding barrier properties make it ideal for use in food packaging, and it is particularly effective for products with a high fat content and strong flavours and aromas," according to PlasticsEurope, the association of plastic manufacturers. "It is often used in the packaging of confectionary, dehydrated foods, dairy products, sausages, patés, meat, smoked fish, and dried products such as herbs, spices, tea and coffee."

For Dow, Saran Wrap became the foundation of a flourishing consumer goods division that included household names, such as Ziploc bags and Fantastik cleaners. When the division was sold to S.C. Johnson and Son, Inc., in 1998, it was valued at US$1.13 billion. Saran Wrap then became a brand-name product under the S.C. Johnson label, a company based in Racine, Wisconsin, that had grown from a family furniture wax business into a global giant. Dow would continue to produce food and pharmaceutical packaging utilizing its trademarked Saran resins, touting PVdC as the standard for barrier protection.

BACK TO GREEN

In 2000 H. Fisk Johnson became head of S.C. Johnson. It signaled a change in leadership as the fifth generation of the Johnson family stepped into the top spot at the company, soon to be renamed S.C. Johnson and Son. Ranked at 171 on the *Forbes* 400 list of the richest U.S citizens in 2011, Johnson was estimated to be worth US$2.3 billion, and the magazine noted his passion for the environment as a board member of Conservation International. Under his leadership, the company, *Forbes* noted, had embarked on a wide variety of efforts to make it more environmentally conscious and to reduce greenhouse gases. H. Fisk Johnson led an effort to utilize methane at a S.C. Johnson factory from a dump in Racine, Wisconsin, and wind turbines were installed at plants in the Netherlands. A year after his accession to the company top spot, H. Fisk Johnson launched what would become Greenlist, a database of S.C. Johnson product ingredients ranked by their environmental impact, according to Hoover's writer Gene Bisbee. The ranking led to changes in product formulas, including several famous brands. The formula for Windex, the window cleaner, was changed, and the company also switched from using PVdC in Saran Wrap to low-density polyethlene (LDPE) to make the plastic film. The Greenlist was hailed by the U.S. Environmental Protection Agency (EPA) with a 2006 award that noted S.C. Johnson had eliminated "the use of nearly 4 million pounds of polyvinylidene chloride (PVdC) annually."

PLASTICS AND THE MODERN WORLD

One of the most fascinating aspects of the history of plastics in the United States and Europe was the on-again, off-again, love-hate relationship consumers had with the man-made creations that had such a profound impact on their daily lives. Plastics made possible medical devices like heart valves and hearing aids, rust-free sewer systems, lightweight automobiles, and a host of other modern amenities, but they also prompted controversy and provoked intense debate over their impact and safety. "In all European and North American countries, the public appreciation of plastics exhibits a whimsical pattern, filled with opposite emotions and paradoxes, soaked with utopian and dystopian fantasies," Smits noted in his "Plastics" essay. "From the beginning, plastics were unlike natural raw materials, because they were artificially synthesized and therefore products of culture. This led to the interpretation of plastics as a miracle. Then in the climate of increasing environmental concern the nondegradability of plastics turned the miracle into monster." Saran Wrap, the miracle plastic wrap, became caught up in the spirited debate about plastics that periodically roiled the public arena in the last decades of the 20th century.

Concerns about overflowing landfills were matched with worries about product safety. Plastic products, particularly those used in packaging, were the object of increasing public scrutiny and often subject to Internet rumor and fraudulent e-mail campaigns. Some consumer and environmental groups highlighted studies warning of health dangers. In 1999 the *New York Times* reported on a call from the Consumers Union to ban a commonly used plasticizer known as DEHA in many PVC films because it could be an "endocrine disrupter, which can mimic or interfere with hormones in the body." The Society of the Plastics Industry responded that both the Food and Drug Administration (FDA) and the EPA had given DEHA a clean bill of health.

Concerns were also raised about the manufacture of chloride in the PVdC process. S.C. Johnson chose to switch from PVdC to LDPE in response to concerns, noting on its website: "This formulation change represents the company's commitment to use more environmentally responsible ingredients in our products." Dow Chemical continued to produce Saran resins and also laid out its position on PVdC on its website, noting that Saran Wrap was no longer made from Saran resins in the United States and Canada, but "continues to be commercialized" using Saran resins in Europe. The Saran resins and films, Dow stated, "are considered safe for humans, wildlife and the environment. They are approved for food packaging by every regulatory agency in the world that sets food packaging regulations for polymers."

In the 2010s the "greener" version of Saran Wrap can be found in supermarkets, refrigerators, and lunch boxes around the world.

BIBLIOGRAPHY

Beranbaum, Rose Levy. "My Favorite Plastic Wrap!!!" *Real Baking with Rose Levy Beranbaum,* January 8, 2006. Accessed February 18, 2012. http://www.realbakingwithrose.com/2006/01/my_favorite_plastic_wrap.html.

Bernat, Cory. "Supermarket Packaging: The Shift from Glass to Aluminum to Plastic." *The Atlantic,* January 25, 2012. Accessed February 18, 2012. http://www.theatlantic.com/health/archive/2012/01/supermarket-packaging-the-shift-from-glass-to-aluminum-to-plastic/251875/?single_page=true.

Bisbee, Gene. "Exceeding Expectations—S.C. Johnson & Son." Austin, TX: Hoover's, November 6, 2007. Accessed February 18, 2012. http://www.hoovers.com/business-information/--pageid__16297--/global-hoov-index.xhtml.

Burros, Marian. "Eating Well; Plastic Wrap and Health: Studies Raise Questions." *New York Times,* January 13, 1999. Accessed February 18, 2012. http://www.nytimes.com/1999/01/13/dining/eating-well-plastic-wrap-and-health-studies-raise-questions.html?pagewanted=all&src=pm.

Dow Chemical Company. "Product Safety." Midland, MI. Accessed February 18, 2012. http://www.dow.com/productsafety/finder/saran.htm#uses.

———. "Saran PVDC Resins and Films." Midland, MI. Accessed February 18, 2012. http://www.dow.com/product safety/finder/saran.htm#environ.

"H. Fisk Johnson." *Forbes,* September 2011. Accessed February 18, 2012. http://www.forbes.com/profile/h-fisk-johnson/.

Henze, Doug. "Dow's Plastic Wrap Celebrates 40th Birthday." *Ludington Daily News,* March 5, 1994. Accessed March 2, 2012. http://news.google.com/newspapers?nid=110&dat= 19940305&id=pDRQAAAAIBAJ&sjid=yFUDAAAAIBAJ &pg=4910,5139514.

"Saran Wrap, Marking 40 Years in Use: Began as Lab Byproduct." *Toledo Blade,* January 25, 1994. Accessed February 18, 2012. http://news.google.com/newspapers?nid= 1350&dat=19940125&id=-zExAAAAIBAJ&sjid=WQME AAAAIBAJ&pg=6662,6618518.

S.C. Johnson & Inc. "Saran Wrap." Racine, WI. Accessed February 18, 2012. http://www.saranbrands.com/.

"S.C. Johnson & Son, Inc." In *International Directory of Company Histories,* edited by Jay P. Pederson. Vol. 89, 382–389. Detroit: St. James Press, 2008. Gale Virtual Reference Library (GALE|CX2690500086). Accessed February 18, 2012. http://go.galegroup.com/ps/i.do?id=GALE%7CCX26905000 86&v=2.1&u=itsbtrial&it=r&p=GVRL&sw=w.

Secrest, Rose. "Plastic Wrap." In *How Products Are Made: An Illustrated Guide to Product Manufacturing,* edited by Kyung-Sun Lim. Vol. 2, 351–355. Detroit: Gale Research, 1996.

Gale Virtual Reference Library (GALE|CX2896600082). Accessed February 18, 2012. http://go.galegroup.com/ps/i.do ?id=GALE%7CCX2896600082&v=2.1&u=itsbtrial&it=r&p =GVRL&sw=w.

Sevenster, Arien. "PVdC." Brussels, Belgium: PlasticsEurope. Accessed February 18, 2012. http://www.plasticseurope.org /what-is-plastic/types-of-plastics/pvdc.aspx.

"Simple Solution for Cork Taint." *Los Angeles Times,* March 28, 2007. Accessed February 18, 2012. http://articles.latimes .com/2007/mar/28/food/fo-wineside28.

Smits, Martijntje W. "Plastics." In *Encyclopedia of Science, Technology, and Ethics,* edited by Carl Mitcham. Vol. 3, 1418–1421. Detroit: Macmillan Reference USA, 2005. Gale Virtual Reference Library (GALE|CX3434900499). Accessed February 19, 2012. http://go.galegroup.com/ps/i.do?id=GAL E%7CCX3434900499&v=2.1&u=itsbtrial&it=r&p=GVRL &sw=w.

Stimpson, Jennifer. "10 Uses for Plastic Wrap." *This Old House.* Accessed February 18, 2012. http://www.thisoldhouse.com /toh/article/0,,20206915,00.html.

U.S. Environmental Protection Agency. "Designing Greener Chemicals Award, 2006: S.C. Johnson & Son, Inc." Washington, DC. Last modified August 10, 2011. Accessed February 18, 2012. http://www.epa.gov/greenchemistry/pubs /pgcc/winners/dgca06.html.

Sears Shifts from Mail Orders to Retail Stores

The Sears, Roebuck and Company (Sears) catalog brought the urban, mass-manufactured way of life to U.S. farms and small towns. At the dawn of the 20th century, Sears was the world's largest merchandising corporation and its catalog set the standard for mail-order retail that is still used in the 2010s, even by online shops such as Amazon.com. However, in the early decades of the 20th century in the United States the urban population was growing and increasing numbers of rural residents were going into towns for their shopping. Sears' decision to venture into retail was risky, but largely through the vision and determination of one man, it was successful in turning the most trusted mail-order company in the United States into one of its largest retail stores.

In 1890, 65 percent of the U.S. population was rural. Traveling salesmen and general stores offered the only shopping options in much of the United States, and these options were limited. Mail-order catalogs, with the help of newly built railroads, brought a wider variety of goods to rural communities. Sears, which had begun its mail-order catalog in 1893, had surpassed the industry's undisputed leader, Montgomery Ward & Company, Incorporated by 1900.

Residents of farms and prairie towns bought faithfully from the Sears catalog for many years, but the United States was becoming increasingly urban. Labor-saving mechanical technology on farms meant that fewer workers were required, and this drove jobseekers to the cities to look for factory work. At the same time, farmers were becoming more prosperous. They could now afford automobiles to drive into town and purchase mass-produced consumer goods such as electrical appliances, power tools, and radios. More options for shopping were becoming available to them.

ENTER THE GENERAL

General Robert E. Wood was a U.S. Army logistics officer in World War I. Before this conflict, Wood helped coordinate the construction of the Panama Canal. After the war, Wood entered the business sector, bringing with him an obsession with statistics and a love of methodical testing and experimentation. His first position in the business sector was with Sears' competitor Montgomery Ward. Noting that automobile sales were increasing and farm income was dropping, he proposed to the company that it begin expanding by opening retail stores. However, Montgomery Ward executives were not receptive to the idea and in 1924 Wood quit the company in frustration over its lack of interest. He then moved to Sears, where President Charles Kittle and former President Julius Rosenwald, impressed with Wood's business acumen and military background, handpicked him to become vice president.

Wood brought his ideas about the changing U.S. landscape with him to Sears. He believed that with the growth of the cities, the company needed to begin aggressively opening retail stores in urban areas. He also realized that the automobile was the future of U.S. transportation and that better mobility would mean a decrease in mail-order shopping.

Sears management saw things differently. The company's success was entirely due to its mail-order catalogs and it had no experience whatsoever with retail stores. Catalog sales were still growing and management believed that opening retail stores would take away from its mail-order business. Furthermore, its customer base had always been the nation's rural population. According to archives on the Sears website, founder Richard Sears wrote in 1906,

"We do comparatively very little business in cities, and we assume the cities are not at all our field—maybe they are not—but I think it is our duty to prove they are not."

THE RETAIL EXPERIMENT BEGINS

Rosenwald and Kittle did not agree with the idea of retail expansion for Sears, but they had great faith in their new vice president. With their support, Wood prevailed and the first experimental store opened in 1925 inside the main Sears mail-order plant in Chicago, Illinois. This store was Wood's first project for the company, initiated after he had been employed for only two months.

Opening inside one of the company's mail-order plants meant that the experimental store was able to overcome many of the challenges and risks of retail operation. There were already personnel there, as well as space. Stock was on hand, inventory was ready, and there were no additional shipping costs. The store was a tremendous success and led to the opening of seven more stores by the end of the year.

Wood was not one to take risks lightly. He devised a plan to test three different types of stores: stores within mail-order plants, stores in the same towns as mail-order plants, and stores in towns that had no Sears presence. All stores' sales figures and expenses were closely monitored, and store openings continued. Wood also studied census figures in order to plan the expansion of Sears. These figures showed that population growth was slowing down in the following U.S. geographic regions: New England, the Mid-Atlantic, and the Upper Midwest. Wood focused the store's expansion instead on the South, Southwest, and West regions of the United States, where the U.S. population was growing more rapidly.

Wood's strategy for siting store locations was unorthodox. While most retailers focused on central downtown districts, Sears' stores were built on the outskirts at highway junctions and other main traffic arteries. A Sears store might be surrounded by its massive parking lot and little else. Wood chose these isolated locations because he believed that the automobile was the future of U.S. transportation. He reasoned that downtown districts would gradually lose their traffic to these areas. This proved to be the case, as new shopping districts often grew up around Sears stores.

Sears stores were also unique for their wide variety of merchandise. Retailers had traditionally focused on selling goods to women, but Sears offered goods for the whole family. According to the Sears website archives, Wood was quoted as saying, "The [existing] department stores were essentially for women. Eighty percent of their business was in women's wear, hosiery, and all other apparel. A man in a department store was lost. We made it a store for the family; in other words, for the men, too. We added hardware, tires, service parts and other items of particular interest to men." This decision was in keeping with the merchandising methods of the Sears catalog, which had sold everything a farm family needed, including clothing, household goods, appliances, bicycles, musical instruments, and firearms.

BRANDING

In the late 1920s Sears began launching its own brands such as DieHard, Craftsman, and Kenmore. Until this time, department stores had focused largely on selling food, clothing, necessities, and occasionally luxury goods. However, with the increase in U.S. home ownership, Sears began to change its merchandise and offer hardware, paint, electrical goods, building materials, and other items homeowners could use.

Sears also took a unique approach to its store design. It organized every aspect of its stores around merchandise requirements and traffic flow. Stores at this time were designed from the outside in, but Sears took the opposite approach, starting with its merchandise and designing the entire store around it. A special store planning department was created by Wood in 1932 for the purpose of analyzing data and designing stores accordingly.

Wood's facts and figures told him that a majority of the city dwellers who were the store's target market lacked insurance for their automobiles. To meet the growing demand for insurance, he created the Allstate Corporation in 1931. Allstate sold its policies to customers inside Sears stores at its Allstate counters. No store had ever done this before.

"A 100% RECORD OF MISTAKES"

In the years following the opening of the experimental stores, Sears grew at an extraordinary pace. By 1928 its 27 stores had grown to 192, and by the next year there were a total of 319. During one 12-month period, a new store opened every other business day. In 1930 store sales eclipsed catalog sales for the first time. Although store sales were increasing, this rapid expansion was not without its challenges and difficulties. Sears' retail stores quickly gained a reputation for the chaos and confusion one would find inside.

According to *Fortune* magazine's Jerry Useem, Wood said in later years, "We had a 100% record of mistakes." However, Wood believed that if value was provided, people would keep coming back even if small errors were made. "Business is like war in one respect," he said, "If its grand strategy is correct, any number of tactical errors can be made." Indeed, it was trust in the Sears name that kept customers loyal even with its many blunders.

Wood's design concept was to keep stores simple and austere. He believed that frills and fancy furnishings were not necessary because it was the high-quality goods that customers wanted. The early stores were essentially warehouses where customers were allowed to come in and rummage. Goods were piled on tables haphazardly and there were few store displays. When management learned that customers were turned off by the lack of order and cleanliness, Sears began to rethink its store design.

The organization of the stores was highly centralized, following the model of the mail-order business. In the world of mail-order, a highly centralized organization was effective for handling large numbers and predicting sales figures, but in the retail environment this style of organization was inappropriate. No matter how precise its estimations were, Sears found the behavior of retail shoppers much less predictable than those of its mail-order customers. As a result, Sears' stores often faced overstocks, shortages, and shipping mix-ups.

Wood's response to the company's organizational problems was to decentralize. He created a democratic management system, establishing five regional territories, each with its own management team that was given a large degree of autonomy. Responsibility and authority were designated as far down the line as possible. The logic behind this organizational system was that at each store regional circumstances were different.

It also took time for Sears to adapt its internal communication style to the retail environment. In a mail-order business, work was highly routine and the use of manuals and written guidelines was high. In the retail environment, where employees had constant face-to-face contact with customers and often had to adapt quickly to their needs, there was no time for written procedure. The company flooded its retail stores with memos and other written instructions, many of which contradicted each other. While these written instructions worked well in the standardized mail-order environment, they often caused confusion among its retail staff.

The company's lack of retail skill and experience presented great challenges in staffing the stores. Realizing that it lacked this experience, it began recruiting management staff from other established retail chains. Despite their experience, these managers found it hard to fit into the Sears mold, with its wider array of merchandise and unique store policies. In response, Wood created a large and ambitious executive personnel department to manage the hiring and promoting of employees from within the company. It took many years before the retail stores were staffed with well-trained, competent management. Through the difficult years of adjustment, Wood personally visited stores and talked to staff about their problems and concerns. He then used this information to create new company policies.

A SYMBOL OF U.S. PROSPERITY

The Great Depression of the 1930s hurt Sears' sales, but the company cut costs wherever it could and continued to build new stores. Despite the hard times, Sears grew to 600 stores by the end of the decade. As the United States prepared to enter World War II, military spending and consumer panic boosted Sears' sales to US$975 million in 1941. It turned some of its plants into munitions plants and sold goods to the U.S. military.

While other companies were saving their pennies during the war, Sears was spending its capital liberally. From 1945 to 1953, Sears spent over US$300 million on store improvements. During this same time sales nearly tripled. Sears opened its first international stores in Cuba and Mexico.

Wood also spent a great deal of money researching postwar demographic and economic trends. Wood's research told him that there would be an economic boom after the war. The company began a new campaign of aggressive expansion, building stores near urban areas in the Sun Belt states of the South and Southwest of the United States, where the population was expected to grow. It also began changing its merchandise to suit its new suburban customers' needs. Furniture and appliance sales had slackened after suburbanites bought what their newly purchased homes needed, so the store shifted its focus to clothes, luxury appliances, and new luxury items such as televisions, record players, and tape players.

In the years following World War II Sears became a symbol of U.S. prosperity. According to the *International Directory of Company Histories* the Moscow bureau chief of the Associated Press stated that the Sears catalog was the most effective piece of propaganda to reach the Soviet Union. The company continued to grow through the 1950s and 1960s, focusing more on apparel and further decentralizing its management. Wood retired in 1954 but stayed on the board of directors of both Sears and Allstate to continue oversight of the company's expansion until his death in 1969. This growth culminated in the building of the Sears Tower in Chicago, Illinois which, at its completion in 1973, was the tallest building in the world, with 110 stories.

DESCENDING THE TOWER

Sears hit an all-time sales peak in 1972, but skyrocketing oil prices, competition from discount specialty shops, and management problems led to difficulties for the company. Wood's vision was no longer viable in the changing times of the 1970s. Sales steadily declined throughout the 1970s and 1980s, eventually resulting in a restructuring in 1993. Under the leadership of new chief executive Arthur C. Martinez, a massive marketing drive was launched to better understand how customers viewed the store, which led to Sears targeting female shoppers in their 20s and 30s with its new slogan, "Come See the Softer Side of Sears." This change revitalized the store's sales.

There is no doubt that Wood was ahead of his time. Although it was through his ideas that Sears made the change from mail-order to retail, he also had some ideas for which the world was not yet ready. Only in the 1990s did "no frills" warehouse stores such as Costco Wholesale Corporation and Home Depot, Inc., begin attracting a customer base with their stripped-down and austere design. In his 2005 *Fortune,* article, Useem remarked that a windowless Sears built in 1934 was the world's first big-box store.

The strategies that Sears developed under Wood's leadership to overcome the challenges of becoming a retailer had a major impact on U.S. retail stores. Other companies copied Sears' methods, opening stores in outlying areas to attract automobile traffic, decentralizing and localizing management, and honing their marketing skills through careful observation of economic and demographic trends. His vision alone successfully turned Sears from the favorite mail-order merchandiser into one of its major retail chains in the United States.

BIBLIOGRAPHY

Risland, Susan, Ed Dinger, and Candice Mancini. "Sears, Roebuck & Co." In *Encyclopedia of Major Marketing Campaigns.* Vol. 2, 1487–1495. Detroit: Gale, 2007. Gale Virtual Reference Library (GALE|CX3446600255). Accessed February 3, 2012. http://go.galegroup.com/ps/i.do?id=GALE%7CCX3446600255&v=2.1&u=itsbtrial&it=r&p=GVRL&sw=w.

Roell, Craig H. "Sears, Roebuck & Co. Catalogue." In *Encyclopedia of Leadership,* edited by George R. Goethals, Georgia J. Sorenson, and James MacGregor Burns. Vol. 4, 1395–1400. Thousand Oaks, CA: Sage Reference, 2004. Gale Virtual Reference Library (GALE|CX3452500342). Accessed February 3, 2012. http://go.galegroup.com/ps/i.do?id=GALE%7CCX3452500342&v=2.1&u=itsbtrial&it=r&p=GVRL.

"Sears Holding Corporation," In *International Directory of Company Histories,* edited by Karen Hill. Vol. 119, 406–414. Detroit: St. James Press, 2011. Gale Virtual Reference Library (GALE|CX1722100085). Accessed February 3, 2012. http://go.galegroup.com/ps/i.do?id=GALE%7C CX1722100085&v=2.1&u=itsbtrial&it=r&p=GVRL&sw=w.

"Sears, Roebuck and Co." In *Company Profiles for Students,* edited by Donna Craft and Amanda Quick. Vol. 2, 1179–1184. Detroit: Gale, 1999. Gale Virtual Reference Library (GALE|CX3427200244). Accessed February 3, 2012. http://go.galegroup.com/ps/i.do?id=GALE%7CCX3427200244&v=2.1&u=itsbtrial&it=r&p=GVRL&sw=w

"Sears, Roebuck and Co." In *Gale Encyclopedia of U.S. Economic History,* edited by Thomas Carson and Mary Bonk. Vol. 2, 903–905. Detroit: Gale, 2000. Gale Virtual Reference Library (GALE|CX3406400839). Accessed February 3, 2012. http://go.galegroup.com/ps/i.do?id=GALE%7CCX3406400839&v=2.1&u=itsbtrial&it=r&p=GVRL&sw=w.

"Sears, Roebuck and Company." In *In an Influential Fashion: An Encyclopedia of Nineteenth- and Twentieth-Century Fashion Designers and Retailers Who Transformed Dress,* edited by Ann T. Kellogg, et al. 272–274. Westport, CT: Greenwood Press, 2002. Gale Virtual Reference Library (GALE|CX2884900143). Accessed February 3, 2012. http://go.galegroup.com/ps/i.do?id=GALE%7CCX2884900143&v=2.1&u=itsbtrial&it=r&p=GVRL&sw=w.

Sears, Roebuck and Co. "Sears First Free Standing Retail Store Opened October 5, 1925 in Evansville, Indiana." Hoffman Estates, IL, 2012. Accessed February 3, 2012. http://www.searsarchives.com/stores/history_indiana.htm.

———. "Sears History 1925." Hoffman Estates, IL, 2012. Accessed February 3, 2012. http://www.searsarchives.com/history/history1925.htm.

Useem, Jerry. "1925: Sears Gets Physical." *Fortune,* June 27, 2005. Accessed February 4, 2012. http://money.cnn.com/magazines/fortune/fortune_archive/2005/06/27/8263412/index.htm

Woloson, Wendy. "Sears Roebuck Catalogue." In *St. James Encyclopedia of Popular Culture,* edited by Sara Pendergast and Tom Pendergast. Vol. 4, 346–347. Detroit: St. James Press, 2000. Gale Virtual Reference Library (GALE|CX3409002201). Accessed February 3, 2012. http://go.galegroup.com/ps/i.do?id=GALE%7CCX3409002201&v=2.1&u=itsbtrial&it=r&p=GVRL&sw=w.

Worthy, James C. "Sears Roebuck: General Robert E. Wood's Retail Strategy." *Business and Economic History* 9: 61–73. Business History Conference, 1980. Accessed February 3, 2012. http://www.thebhc.org/publications/BEHprint/v009/p0061-p0073.pdf.

Sony Walkman:
Portable Music Player in the 1980s

The Sony Walkman was one of the most successful electronic products in history. Developed by Sony Corporation and released in the early 1980s, it completely changed the way people enjoyed music and spawned an entire industry of handheld devices for personal listening. Doubted by Sony management and ridiculed by the press, it was largely due to the vision of Sony founders Akio Morita and Masaru Ibuka that the revolutionary electronic device was put on the market.

HISTORY OF THE CASSETTE

Since the development of the first compact cassette in 1963 by Dutch company Royal Philips Electronics N.V., cassette players had become increasingly smaller in size. By the 1970s the smallest was approximately the size of a trade paperback. These devices offered some portability but were still inferior in sound quality to long-playing (LP) vinyl records. The cassette tape player had become a fixture in most homes, but the LP was the preferred medium for listening to music.

Sony Corporation of Japan, which had established itself as a world leader in consumer electronics and especially miniaturized electronic products, had a number of its own portable cassette players on the market. However, by the late 1970s, Sony's tape recorder division was not doing well financially. Sony's portable tape recorders were made for the high-end market and there was little demand for them. Its portable "boom boxes" (luggage-sized stereo systems) and other mid-sized products were outsold by its competition. The company had just gone through reorganization, and many within Sony believed that its tape recorder division might be eliminated.

The Walkman began with a simple idea by Sony founder Masaru Ibuka. He wanted a stereo small enough to fit in his coat pocket to take on airplanes with him. He often traveled by airplane, and when he did so, he took Sony's bulky TC-D5 tape recorder. The TC-D5, which was developed specifically for Ibuka's use, was small but too heavy to be truly portable. Retailing at around ¥100,000 per unit (roughly US$1,000), this high-end device was popular only among audiophiles. When he took it with him, Ibuka would attach a set of headphones so that he could enjoy it in stereo.

Ibuka asked Sony executive deputy president Norio Ohga to design for him a stereo version of the Pressman, a Sony tape recorder released in 1978. The Pressman was made for journalists and was designed for recording. Ibuka wanted a version of the Pressman that would be designed for private listening with playback only and no record function. He asked Ohga to develop this prototype and Ohga immediately contacted the tape recorder division. The development of the Walkman was underway.

EARLY VERSIONS

Sony engineers quickly made a prototype for Ibuka by modifying the Pressman and attaching a pair of stereo headphones to it. The sound was excellent, but it was still far too large and heavy. The tape recorder division created a second prototype that used miniature headphones that were placed inside the listener's ears. These headphones would be central to the Walkman's success because they allowed people to listen without disturbing those around them.

This prototype was given to Ibuka to try on a business trip to the United States. Sony staff hurried around

Akihabara, Japan, the electronics district of Tokyo, Japan, to find special batteries that could be used in the unit. They also put together a small collection of classical music tapes for Ibuka to try.

Despite the batteries dying halfway over the Pacific Ocean and the cassettes turning out to be blank, Ibuka was greatly impressed with the prototype and considered it a success. Upon returning to Tokyo, Japan, he showed it to Akio Morita, who was also impressed. Ibuka and Morita decided that the world was ready for its first handheld tape player. The two believed that there was high demand for a handheld stereo cassette tape player among consumers who wanted to take their music with them wherever they went.

THE TAPE RECORDER WITH NO RECORD

In February 1979 Morita held a meeting with Sony engineers and marketing staff to announce that the modified Pressman would go into production. He also announced that the new product would be released just days before the beginning of the Japanese summer vacation. This meant that they had only four months to create and market the product.

Morita had noticed that young people always wanted to carry their music with them, and he believed that a miniature version of the tape recorder with small headphones was marketable. He ordered engineers to make two major changes to the portable products already on the market. First, the speakers would be removed entirely. This device would be listened to only with headphones. Second, he proposed removing the record function. Morita insisted that teenagers wanted music to travel with and did not care whether or not they could record.

While there was a certain level of excitement among engineers, few believed the device could actually be produced in four months. Sony's marketing department was outright hostile to the idea. It argued that cassette players had already become small enough. Furthermore, its marketing research had found absolutely no demand for the product among consumers.

Morita and Ibuka ignored the advice of the marketing department. They believed that consumers would buy it. In his book *Brand Royalty,* Matt Haig quoted Morita as saying years later, "I do not believe that any amount of market research could have told us that it would have been successful. The public does not know what is possible. We do."

Sony had a reputation for innovation, and especially for miniaturizing consumer electronic goods. The company gave Japan its first transistor radio and invented the world's first all-transistor television. Sony's scaled-down radios, televisions, and reel-to-reel tape recorders had found an unexpectedly large market among U.S. families, even when those families already owned larger versions of the products.

Morita faced further resistance to the idea when he suggested that it be sold at a lower cost so that teenagers could afford it. When Sony's marketing team told him that it would need to sell 30,000 units in order to make the new product profitable, he offered to resign if all 30,000 were not sold. Based on production costs, it was decided that the portable stereo tape player would be sold for ¥35,000, but Morita lowered the price to ¥33,000 since Sony had been in operation for 33 years.

In Japan, the new pocket-sized stereo would be called the "Walkman," modeled after the Pressman that spawned its early prototype. Sony's marketing department believed that "Walkman" sounded awkward in English and felt that it would not go over well in English-speaking markets, so it chose a variety of names to suit each country in which it would be sold. In the United States, it would be the Soundabout. The British version was the Stowaway. Sweden's version was to be named the Freestyle. Before the release, however, it was decided that a single name should be used in all of the world's markets because it would be too difficult to secure names that were not already copyrighted in each country. While Morita was visiting stores in Paris, France, a group of French children asked him when they could expect to be able to buy a Walkman, referring to the device using its Japanese name, and the name stuck. It would be named the Walkman in every market worldwide.

The first Walkman was the TPS-L2. It was a blue and silver model that weighed 14 ounces. The only controls were play, stop, rewind, and a volume control. The TPS-L2 came with a leather case and a second headphone jack so that two people could listen together. Although primitive compared to later models, the TPS-L2 retailed for about US$200. Sony's slogan for its advertising campaign was, "Remember the name: Walkman."

The audio industry praised it for its unusual qualities but treated it as nothing more than a novelty. The press outright lampooned it, ridiculing it as a tape player with no speakers and no record button. Sony's own marketing department saw the Walkman as a clever gimmick and did not expect it to sell.

DEBUT OF THE WALKMAN

The TPS-L2 went on sale in Japan on July 1, 1979, the first day of summer vacation for Japanese students. In the first month it sold only 3,000 units, which was far below Sony's expectation of selling at least 5,000. For the second month, Sony workers hit the streets to promote the new product. They strapped on Walkmans and walked the streets of Tokyo, Japan, listening to music, approaching people in busy shopping districts such as Ginza (a district of Tokyo) to let them try out the Walkman for themselves. Sony gave the small tape players to celebrities and arranged a bus tour where they would travel through the city and give a series of mini press conferences with Walkmans in hand.

The marketing efforts were successful. In August 1979, sales figures skyrocketed, and the Walkman sold out of all available stock. In the first two months nearly 50,000 units were sold. The Walkman was not only popular among the students and young adults Sony targeted, but among people of all ages as well.

Japanese consumers were accustomed to listening to music on headphones, but this was not the case in the United States. There, the Walkman was slower to catch on. Sony surmised that a major reason for the lack of sales was the TPS-L2's high price tag. In 1981 it released the Walkman II, the first in a series of newer models that would become progressively smaller, more inexpensive, and better sounding. The Walkman II was designed with U.S. consumers in mind and was priced considerably lower than the TPS-L2.

The Walkman II was a tremendous success in the United States. There was a giant market for the Walkman that no one even knew existed among a young generation of U.S. citizens who were more active and mobile. Just as Morita predicted, they wanted to take their music with them, and they did not mind the sacrifice in sound quality. The idea that the Walkman gave a person freedom and mobility was central to Sony's marketing strategy in the United States.

By the time the Walkman II was released, it had begun to spawn imitators such as Toshiba's Stereo Walky and Panasonic's Stereo-To-Go. However, Sony continued to hold 30 percent of the Walkman market worldwide and ensured that it continued to rule the market by constantly introducing new products. It made over a hundred different Walkman models for every possible niche of the buying public. There were waterproof models, shock-resistant models, and models that were solar powered. Newer models grew increasingly smaller until they were only slightly larger than the cassette tape itself.

Sony worked to improve the sound quality by introducing better stereo reproduction and higher fidelity, largely by making improvements to the headphones. It added Dolby noise reduction circuits in 1982. New features such as bass boost and auto-reverse were added in later years. Newer models came with AM/FM receivers in addition to tape decks. In 1985 Sony released the WM-W800, the only Walkman ever produced with twin tape decks.

THE WALKMAN DECADE

Sony sold 50 million Walkmans in the 1980s. Half of these sales were in the United States, where the market for

the handheld stereos was around 20 to 30 million units per year. In 1983 cassette tape sales surpassed record sales. Largely due to the Sony Walkman, cassette tapes would continue to outsell LPs until compact disc sales eventually replaced them both. During the 1990s Sony continued to sell 30 million Walkmans per year. By 1998 the company had sold around 250 million total.

By 1986 the word "Walkman" had appeared in the *Oxford Dictionary* to mean any handheld device for listening to music. The effect of the Walkman on popular culture was immense. In the book *Bowling, Beatniks, and Bell Bottoms: Pop Culture of 20th Century America*, Chris Routledge wrote, "The Walkman was not only a major technological advancement but a cultural one as well. It broke all the unwritten rules about the size of consumer products and changed the way people listened to music." He also noted that it was largely responsible for the rise of the compilation tape, where music fans would make their own cassettes of their favorite songs. The Walkman, he said, matched the fast pace of modern life and allowed people in crowded urban environments to feel that they were alone. "By adding a soundtrack to everyday life, the Walkman changed the way people experienced the world."

In a 2009 *TIME* article, Meaghan Haire wrote, "The 1980s could well have been the Walkman decade." She also wrote that the Walkman was likely to have had a positive impact on the health of U.S. citizens. During the peak years of its popularity from 1987 to 1997, U.S. citizens reported walking for exercise 30 percent more than in other years.

The idea of a portable music player for personal listening with no external speakers and no record function had not been taken seriously in the late 1970s. However, Sony founders Morita and Ibuka accurately predicted that handheld devices would one day be the norm. Although the cassette tape era came and went, the Sony Walkman's influence could be seen in every portable electronic device that developed since.

BIBLIOGRAPHY

"The First Sony Walkman Goes on Sale." History.com, 2012. Accessed February 10, 2012. http://www.history.com/this-day-in-history/the-first-sony-walkman-goes-on-sale.

Haige, Matt. "Sony: The Pioneer Brand." In *Brand Royalty*. 11–12. London: Kogan Page, 2004. Gale Virtual Reference Library (GALE|CX3472900008). Accessed February 10, 2012. http://go.galegroup.com/ps/i.do?id=GALE%7CCX3472900008&v=2.1&u=itsbtrial&it=r&p=GVRL&sw=w.

Haire, Meaghan. "A Brief History of the Walkman." *TIME*, July 1, 2009. Accessed February 10, 2012. http://www.time.com/time/nation/article/0,8599,1907884,00.html.

Hormby, Tom. "The Story Behind the Sony Walkman." *Low End Mac*, September 15, 2006. Accessed February 10, 2012. http://lowendmac.com/orchard/06/sony-walkman-origin.html.

Millard, Andre. "Walkman." In *St. James Encyclopedia of Popular Culture,* edited by Sara Pendergast and Tom Pendergast. Vol. 5, 66. Detroit: St. James Press, 2000. Gale Virtual Reference Library (GALE|CX3409002608). Accessed February 10, 2012. http://go.galegroup.com/ps/i.do?id=GALE%7CCX3409002608&v=2.1&u=itsbtrial&it=r&p=GVRL&sw=w.

Routledge, Chris. "Walkman." In *Bowling, Beatniks, and Bell Bottoms: Pop Culture of 20th Century America,* edited by Sara Pendergast and Tom Pendergast. Vol. 4: 1960–1970, 994–995. Detroit: UXL, 2002. Gale Virtual Reference Library (GALE|CX3425100605). Accessed February 10, 2012. http://go.galegroup.com/ps/i.do?id=GALE%7CCX3425100605&v=2.1&u=itsbtrial&it=r&p=GVRL&sw=w.

Sisson, Mary. "Akio Morita." In *Inventors and Inventions,* Vol. 4. Tarrytown, NY: Marshall Cavendish, 2008. Gale Virtual Reference Library (GALE|CX4097100142). Accessed February 10, 2012. http://go.galegroup.com/ps/i.do?id=GALE%7CCX4097100142&v=2.1&u=itsbtrial&it=r&p=GVRL&sw=w.

Sony Corporation. "Promoting Compact Cassettes Worldwide." Minato, Tokyo, Japan. Accessed February 10, 2012. http://www.sony.net/SonyInfo/CorporateInfo/History/SonyHistory/2-05.html.

"Sony Walkman Advertisement." In *American Decades Primary Sources,* edited by Cynthia Rose. Vol. 8: 1970–1978, 202–203. Detroit: Gale, 2004. Gale Virtual Reference Library (GALE|CX3490201501). Accessed February 10, 2012. http://go.galegroup.com/ps/i.do?id=GALE%7CCX3490201501&v=2.1&u=itsbtrial&it=r&p=GVRL&sw=w.

"WM-W800." Walkman Central.com. Accessed February 10, 2012. http://www.walkmancentral.com/products/wm-w800.

Springfield Armory: Military Standardization and Interchangeable Parts

THE ARMORY ON A BLUFF

The Springfield Armory (1777–1968) was located overlooking the Connecticut River in Springfield, Massachusetts. General George Washington, the first President of the United States, established the armory initially as a site to manufacture and store cartridges and other war material. The location of the armory was chosen for a number of reasons: Springfield, Massachusetts was well situated for access to water power and good roads; the site was located above a waterfall, which rendered it inaccessible to ocean-going enemy military ships; the area was already well supplied with the artisans and metal workers needed for arms production; and the site was easily defended owing to its location on a high bluff above the river. For much of its useful life, the armory would serve as the chief location for production of shoulder firearms and cutlery, for use by U.S. military fighting forces.

Many notable firearms were developed and produced at the Springfield Armory during its long and illustrious history as a manufacturing facility, starting with the venerable musket, first produced at the site in 1795. Prior to World War II, the first mass-produced semiautomatic rifle, the M1 Garand rifle, was developed at the armory. The M1 took advantage of many novel manufacturing processes first developed in Springfield and became one of the most venerated personal firearms in military history. More M1s were produced at the armory than any other firearm.

While the greatest fame of the Springfield Armory will rest with its place in military history, out of its role in this vital capacity arose a number of important techniques and processes that also gave it great significance in the history of the Industrial Revolution in the United States.

THE ARMORY AS CREATIVE WELLSPRING

In many ways the armory, and the Connecticut River Valley in which it was situated, could be compared to the modern Silicon Valley, California, the locus of technological innovation in the United States in the late 20th century. Almost from its beginning, the armory was a focal point of change in early U.S. industry. From the late 18th century until well into the 20th century, the armory was renowned for its collection of skilled craftsman and engineers. The Springfield Armory would become a highly analyzed prototype of the large factory, which would come to dominate industrial manufacturing throughout the modern era.

Its first superintendent, David Ames (who was appointed by George Washington), retired in 1802 and entered the paper manufacturing industry with a process he had developed to infuse paper with gypsum, making it heavier and more durable. His son would remain in the Connecticut River Valley and develop and patent a cylindrical printing system for newsprint and books. They would become the prototype for generations of Springfield Armory and Connecticut River Valley entrepreneurs.

Superintendent Benjamin Prescott (in charge from 1805 to 1813) inherited a complicated situation at the armory. The physical layout of the site had led to the separation of workshops between two areas, known as the Hill Shops and the Water Shops. This separation necessitated considerable inefficiencies and a great deal of hauling of product between different manufacturing locations. In order to compensate for these problems and to track production at the dispersed shop sites, Prescott instituted the first crude comprehensive manufacturing record-keeping system known to exist in the United States. In addition to regulating cost and productivity, Prescott's various improvements increased production at the armory by nearly 300 percent between 1805 and 1812.

THE ARMORY UNDER LEE

In 1815 Colonel Roswell Lee was hired as superintendent. Lee was able to institute a number of changes in manufacturing and business practices that brought increased discipline and control to the operation of the armory. Among those changes were increased centralized authority and the employment of cost accounting for both labor usage and materials. In product fabrication during this era, it was common for there to be considerable variation in the final specifications of products such as bayonets and muskets. Lee instituted the use of gauges during the production of musket components, developed by Springfield master armorer, Adonijah Foot. Prior to this, gauge use at any point other than final inspection of the finished product was unknown. This increased usage of gauges, the first step toward interchangeability, was so successful it was also instituted at the army's other armory at Harper's Ferry, West Virginia (then part of Virginia), and in private contractor work as well. By 1824 it was possible to fit a bayonet made at the Harper's Ferry Armory to a musket made at the Springfield Armory, a significant achievement by the standards of early 19th century manufacturing.

In 1819 Thomas Blanchard, an engineer working at the armory who was already a respected inventor, developed an improved metal lathe for boring gun barrels. Blanchard then turned his skill to a more complicated problem and created a revolutionary lathe for turning irregular shapes, needed in manufacturing rifle stocks. This "copying lathe," which could reproduce a shape from a pattern, became a major improvement in the production of long-barreled guns and was later applied successfully to the manufacturing of a number of previously handmade wooden implements, such as axe handles. Later, this same copying principle was successfully applied to metal lathe manufacturing. By the time of the U.S. Civil War in the 1860s, Blanchard's lathe allowed for the manufacture of 450 gun stocks in a 10-hour production shift, where previously a single gun stock had taken 10 man-hours to produce.

According to Thomas Moore and William Goss, authors of "The Springfield Armory," a history written for the dedication of the armory site as a National Mechanical Engineering Landmark, Blanchard's lathe is one of history's 10 most important mechanical engineering innovations. Following his tenure at the Springfield Armory, Blanchard would go on to develop his ideas in a number of fields, including an 1826 steam-powered vehicle many considered the first automobile.

INCREASED INTERCHANGEABILITY

By the 1820s the U.S. military had developed a strong interest in standardizing weapon production by using interchangeable parts. Military planners reasoned interchangeability would be simpler and more efficient than manufacturing custom repair parts for small arms in the field, and perhaps provide a significant tactical military advantage in the process. This new form of manufacturing, which took several decades to fully evolve, came to be called "mass production." Mass production required greater use of machines, improved quality, and greater tolerance control to make interchangeability possible.

By the early 1840s the first practical example of a weapon with interchangeable parts was developed in the form of the U.S. Model 1841 percussion rifle. Soon, these same improvements in production techniques spread to other industries and to European manufacturers as well. With these changes, a new way of organizing labor production, known as the assembly line, came into use. Another armory engineer, Thomas Warner, stepped forward with the engineering knowledge to help bring this idea to fruition. Warner also developed a technique for manufacturing bayonets that eliminated the health-threatening stone-grinding process.

By 1865 the breech-loaded weapon had been developed and proved a significant technological improvement over muzzle-loaded rifles. In response, Springfield Armory developed a method of converting previously manufactured muzzle loaders to this new technology. Such a development would not have been possible without the earlier advent and exploitation of interchangeable parts, and improved tolerance control, developed at the Springfield Armory.

In their 1997 essay in the journal *Business and Economic History*, Richard Fleischman and Thomas Tyson wrote that workers in the early 19th century would be considered lax and unruly by modern standards. Workplace drinking, conversing, and socializing were common in the era and little effort was made to control the pace of work. Eventually, Fleischman and Tyson maintained, shifts in the workplace environment toward greater efficiency led to work being increasingly subdivided into smaller, more precise tasks. The authors credit the armory, along with the nearby Lowell Textile Mills, with the development of these changes in work processes based partly on the use of manufacturing accountancy.

The development of these techniques was closely tied to the ascendency of superintendents at the armory trained at the U.S. Military Academy West Point in New York. West Point was the first institution of higher learning that routinely taught its students cost-accounting practices used by army regimental quartermasters to account for men and materials. The armory was also expected to justify its value to the U.S. Congress, in terms of comparing expenses to the private workplace. According to Fleischman and Tyson, accounting practices at the Springfield Armory were developed primarily to establish benchmark cost data against which private contractors were required to compete in securing government contracts. This cost data was developed by using piecework pay methods, which in turn led to rates of pay commensurate with skill levels and market expectations. Piece-rate pay was established by Superintendent Lee in 1816, and was still utilized as late as 1855. These accounting methods and controls were widely regarded as the most sophisticated techniques used prior to the 1840s.

Meanwhile, the new methods taking place at the armory, called the "American System," were producing widespread effects. Manufacturing processes developed at the armory spread throughout the Connecticut River Valley and New England manufacturing. Prior to the 1840s much of the high-quality machinery needed to manufacture firearms was made in Britain; by the 1850s Britain was importing machines made in New England. Solyman Merrick of Springfield, Massachusetts, patented the first adjustable wrench in 1835, and a handheld hole punch in 1838. Horace Smith and Daniel Wesson, also of Springfield, Massachusetts, entered into a partnership in 1856 and produced a lever action repeating pistol. Their company, the Smith and Wesson Company, would secure a key government contract to supply handguns to the U.S. Cavalry, and go on to become a world leader in production of handheld firearms. From the 1820s on, equipment such as milling machines, rifling machines, and drop forges increasingly were manufactured in the Connecticut River Valley and sold in both the United States and Europe.

THE ARMORY OF THE UNION

With the coming of the U.S. Civil War, and with the only other armory in the United States being in Confederate hands, efforts to create a more productive weapons manufacturing capacity at the Springfield Armory produced another round of growth. With only 200 workmen at the beginning of the war, employee count would increase to 2,600. In 1861 steam power was introduced along with new machinery to increase production processes. In a process begun in the 1820s skilled artisan workers increasingly lost control of the pace of production, as machinery run by semiskilled labor (producing individual components) determined production levels. Between 1860 and 1865 the number of worker classifications at the armory, brought on by increased task specialization, increased from 113 to 390. By 1864 the new machinery and production processes had proven their worth, with the annual production of weapons at the armory rising to 276,200, a

10-fold increase over early war efforts. By the end of the war the armory was producing more shoulder arms than all U.S. private contractors combined.

Following the Civil War, exhaustion set in, both among the congressional overseers of the armory and the U.S. public in general. As funding declined, the efforts that had made the armory so famous shifted to the private sector where production processes and machinery continued to improve. Nowhere was this more evident than in the outcome of the Battle of the Little Big Horn (also known as Custer's Last Stand) in what was then known as the Eastern Montana Territory of the United States. There, in 1876 a combination of Colonel George Custer's incompetence, and the fact that the Native Americans were equipped with better weaponry developed in the private sector led to the massacre of a significant portion of the U.S. Seventh Cavalry.

Later analysis of the battle by army experts led to the conclusion that the Springfield rifle used at the time was antiquated and inadequate. Improvements in gunpowder further necessitated the development of a new weapon for the U.S. Army. However, the decreased status of the armory in this era led to the nation turning instead to Europe for the development of the next main weapon used by U.S. military forces.

SHIFT IN FOCUS

By the 1890s the country was again ready to see the armory play a significant role. However, the development of manufacturing processes begun at the armory had led to a shift in priorities. With the transformation of production to simple steps increasingly handled by semiskilled labor, and the rapid improvement of tolerances fueled by ever more sophisticated machinery, the focus at the armory shifted from improving production process to improving the product itself.

In 1891 an experimental department of the Springfield Armory was formed, designed to determine the best way to take advantage of the opportunities created by improved technology. Out of this department came the design for the M1903 Springfield, a clip-loaded military bolt-action rifle, eventually produced for use in World War I. The M1903 Springfield featured a new loading and firing method developed in Springfield's experimental department. However, manufacturing was not ignored in this period either, and the armory made extensive purchases of new machinery in the 1910s to expand production.

In 1919 a new employee named John Garand came to the armory to work on the development of a new semi-automatic shoulder-fired weapon. In 1924 Garand developed the design for such a weapon, which would eventually be adopted by the military in 1936. This weapon, the famous M1, became the most well-known and highly praised personal firearm of World War II. A total of 4.5 million of the weapons were made at the Springfield Armory.

The armory would continue to play a role in weapons development and manufacturing into the 1960s. The M-14, a rapid-fire personal shoulder weapon, began production there in 1957. However, the M-14 was quickly superseded by the M-15, a weapon developed and produced by private industry. Following the adoption of the M-15, the Springfield Armory was found to have outlived its usefulness, and in 1968 was shut down as a manufacturing facility.

A LEGACY PRESERVED

Since being acquired by the U.S. National Park Service, the Springfield Armory has become a museum. It contains the largest collection of small arms in the world, with approximately 20,000 rifles. In the collection are the first of each weapon manufactured at the facility. The museum also contains the original Blanchard lathe, the oldest of its type in existence. Springfield Technical Community College, providing instruction in engineering technology is also located on the grounds.

BIBLIOGRAPHY

Fleischman, Richard K., and Thomas N. Tyson. "Developing Expertise: Two Episodes in Early Nineteenth Century U.S. Managerial Accounting History." *Business and Economic History* 26, no. 2 (Winter 1997): 365–380. Accessed February 6, 2012. http://www.thebhc.org/publications/BEHprint /v026n2/p0365-p0380.pdf.

Moore, Thomas A., and William P. Goss. "The Springfield Armory." Dedication of the National Historical Mechanical Engineering Landmark. February 19, 1980. Accessed February 6, 2012. http://files.asme.org/asmeorg/communities /history/landmarks/5646.pdf.

Norman, Richard. "Industry and Innovation in the Connecticut River Valley." *Our Plural History.* Springfield, MA: Technical Community College. Accessed February 6, 2012. http:// ourpluralhistory.stcc.edu/index.html.

"The Springfield Armory: Forge of Innovation." University of Massachusetts. National Park Service. Accessed February 7, 2012. http://www.forgeofinnovation.org/index.html.

U.S. Department of the Interior. National Park Service. "Springfield Armory: Technology in Transition." Springfield, MA. Accessed February 7, 2012. http://www.nps.gov/spar /forteachers/upload/Springfield%20Technology%20Lesson .pdf.

Swanson Successfully Markets and Sells TV Dinners

■

THE BIRTH OF THE TV DINNER

The average U.S. citizen ate 72 frozen meals every year, according to information published by the American Frozen Food Institute in 2005, but it was not always like this. A few inventions had to be developed and successfully marketed before the first "television dinner" (TV dinner) would appear. In addition to the dinner itself, freezers had to be a part of every household, as did TVs. While C.A. Swanson & Sons was the company to cleverly market the frozen TV dinner in 1953, it was a concept whose development had started several years prior, beginning with Maxson Food Systems, Inc., which manufactured a complete frozen meal in 1945.

The first refrigerators were developed for commercial applications, such as transporting fresh foods like fruits and vegetables in railroad cars or James Harrison's 1856 invention of a machine that cooled beer for a brewery. The first real consumer refrigerator was introduced by General Electric Company (GE) as early as 1911. By 1920 there were more than 200 different models or brands of refrigerators on the market. Kelvinator led the market by 1923, claiming a 20 percent share. However, it was not until 1939 that the first refrigerator with a freezer section was introduced to the market by GE. By 1947 GE was first to market again with a refrigerator-freezer side-by-side combination.

In the meantime, the television was being developed. In fact, its development somewhat mirrors that of the freezer. Philo Taylor Farnsworth, a 21-year-old inventor, demonstrated the first television system in 1927. However, it was RCA Corporation, with the financial resources to invest in extensive research and development, which actually launched the television business. 11 years

and US$50 million later, RCA produced its first broadcast, President Franklin Roosevelt speaking at the World's Fair in New York, New York. Television networks were formed to broadcast shows. The Columbia Broadcasting System (CBS), National Broadcasting Company (NBC), and American Broadcasting Company (ABC) were the first networks. Commercial broadcasting across the country officially began in 1947, the same year GE's side-by-side freezer entered the market.

The two inventions needed for frozen TV dinners to be developed occurred almost simultaneously; however, there were other factors that led to the huge success of Swanson's TV dinners. During World War II many women entered the workforce because so many U.S. men were overseas serving in the military, and factories needed workers to produce their goods and services, including those needed for the war effort. After World War II ended and men returned home, not all women stopped working. In fact, many continued working and more entered the workforce to supplement incomes or to support themselves until they married. By the end of the 1940s, women, who traditionally cooked the meals, were looking for convenient ways to prepare meals that would save them time. Frozen foods were a solution.

Processed, packaged, and frozen foods were all becoming more popular at this time. Not only were they convenient, but with both parents working, many families had more disposable income.

BIRDSEYE

Clarence Birdseye developed the first techniques for freezing food in 1923. Birdseye's inspiration to develop frozen foods occurred while he was working for the U.S. government as a naturalist in the Arctic. He caught fresh fish to eat, which, in the harsh environment, immediately froze. Later, when he thawed the fish and prepared it to eat, he discovered it had retained its fresh taste and appearance. This realization inspired him to create methods for freezing foods. He invested US$7 in his initial experiment, which he used to purchase an electric fan, buckets of brine, and some ice. This led to his method for packing and flash-freezing boxes of fresh foods.

The first frozen foods were ready to be sold by stores in the 1930s. However, grocery store owners were not enthusiastic about adding them to their product lines. It would be expensive to purchase and run the freezers, and it would take up a lot of valuable floor space.

By 1945 Maxson Food Systems, had developed frozen meals that could be reheated and served on military and commercial passenger air flights. These meals were prepared and served in plastic trays with individual compartments for each of three food groups, including meat, vegetables, and potatoes. The meals were successful on these flights, but they were never introduced to the retail market, primarily due to the cost of production as well as the death of the company founder. However, they eventually inspired the development of TV dinners.

Back on the ground in Pittsburgh, Pennsylvania, Albert and Meyer Bernstein organized Frozen Dinners, Inc., in 1949. Their One-Eye Eskimo meals were sold in aluminum, three-compartment trays exclusively at grocery stores in Pittsburgh, Pennsylvania. They became so popular that within a year they had sold 400,000 of them. Demand for the meals continued to grow over the next few years. In 1952, the Bernsteins renamed the company Quaker State Food Corporation. and expanded their market until they were selling the meals throughout the U.S. Midwest. Shoppers continued to buy these meals, and by 1954, Quaker State had sold more than 2.5 million of them. Unfortunately for Quaker State, however, a competitor with a clever marketing idea hit the market in 1953.

THANKSGIVING LEFTOVERS BECOME PROFITABLE FOODS

C.A. Swanson & Sons, based in Omaha, Nebraska, started out as a company that sold butter and poultry. These two products made it highly successful, especially through World War II when it supplied these foods to U.S. troops. However, by Thanksgiving of 1953, a major U.S. holiday in late November, the market was changing. That season proved to be a less successful one for the food company. The article, "TV Dinners," in *CooksInfo.com: The Encyclopedia for Cooks,* noted that according to a story circulated for years by Gerry Thomas, a salesperson for Swanson at the time, the company had invested in hundreds of thousands of pounds of turkey, which did not sell out. The two brothers who owned the company, Gilbert and Clark Swanson, were facing the dilemma of what to do with 520,000 pounds of frozen poultry. They did not have adequate storage space at their facility, so the poultry was loaded onto refrigerated train cars that had to keep moving to keep the turkey from thawing. The brothers asked employees to help them come up with a solution to this problem.

It later turned out that not all of the details in this story were correct, including the traveling turkeys. In fact, a bacteriologist who also worked for Swanson during this time, Betty Cronin, said in 2002, according to the same article, that Thomas may have contributed to the development of the dinners, but that it was actually the two Swanson brothers who had all the ideas. The actual date the dinners were introduced was also a point of contention, although John Fuller, in his article, "Sept. 10, 1953: Swanson Sells First TV Dinner," suggested it was September 10, 1953. However, the popular story remained that the company needed to find a market for surplus turkey and it was looking for a new product.

According to Thomas, he was traveling by plane for his job with Swanson when he received his previously frozen meal, one of the Maxson Food System dinners, on its plastic tray. This inspired him to suggest a three-compartment aluminium tray that could be manufactured at a reasonable cost and could hold three foods, with turkey being the primary food in the meal. Thomas recognized that if the company could somehow tie these meals to television, which was becoming enormously popular, the meals would stand a very good chance of succeeding. He passed the idea on to the Swansons, and the company began to research the matter.

Although the debate continued over who actually coined the phrase "TV dinners," it did stem from the Swanson company, according to Fuller. Regardless of who first came up with the idea and the name, it was considered a good vehicle for marketing the company's turkey.

PACKAGING IS EVERYTHING

Despite the fact that there were already frozen dinners on the market, Swanson was able to succeed on a much greater scale than Quaker State for a number of reasons. At first glance, it would seem that Quaker State had all the advantages. For example, it had already developed five dinners that were selling well: turkey and dressing, beef pot roast, Swiss steak, chicken, and Salisbury steak. Swanson hit the market with just one dinner, which contained turkey, corn bread stuffing, buttered peas, and sweet potatoes. Quaker State also held the price advantage with its dinners priced at US$0.49 each, while Swanson's dinners initially cost double the price, at US$0.98 each.

However, Swanson did have some advantages over Quaker State that tilted the market in its favor. One of these advantages was that the company already had a national market and distribution system for its existing products. This was simply a new product launch, which was easier to accomplish for an established brand name. In addition, this was not the first frozen food item Swanson had produced and marketed. Its first product was a frozen chicken pot pie put on the market in 1950. Another advantage was Swanson's large marketing budget, which allowed it to advertise and promote its dinners in a much broader way than Quaker State could. The link to television, and naming the product TV dinners, also proved to be brilliant marketing strategies for the company.

However, what may have been the most successful element was the packaging. Prior to Swanson's TV dinners, not much thought was put into frozen meal packaging. In fact, some consumers found them unappealing. In contrast, Swanson developed packaging that would make its meals more attractive to consumers and would further reinforce the TV dinner idea. The box was designed to look like a television set. At the time, television consoles were cased in wood, so the box was complete with a wood grain look and control knobs in the corners. On the box's "television screen" was a photo of the turkey dinner. The aluminium tray, which could go directly into the oven for easy preparation and little cleanup, was also a hit with female consumers. In addition, people liked the fact that the compartments kept the food items from touching each other. Overall, the concept was an immediate success, much to the surprise of the Swanson brothers.

While the Swanson brothers had been willing to give the TV dinner idea a try, they were not convinced it would be a success. They decided to be cautious and produced just 5,000 of the meals in the first production run. This very small number did not come close to meeting consumer demand. Less than a year after its introduction, the company had sold 10 million TV dinners. The following year, its first full year on the market, 25 million TV dinners had been consumed. With so much demand, Swanson decided to add other meals to the product line. Soon, consumers were also able to eat fried chicken, Salisbury steak, and meatloaf while watching their favorite TV shows, such as *I Love Lucy.*

Not everyone was a fan of Swanson TV dinners, however. The company received what it called "hate mail," mainly from husbands who preferred their wives' cooking over the precooked Swanson dinners. However, the product was selling so well that Swanson sold off its butter business in 1954 so the company could focus solely on frozen dinners and foods. The following year, the company, which was attracting attention in the retail food business, was acquired by Campbell's Soup Company,

based in New Jersey. The meals continued to be produced and sold under the Swanson label, although their production was moved to the New Jersey location by 1958.

THE EVOLUTION OF FROZEN FOODS AND SWANSON

Swanson took full advantage of its success with the TV dinner. After the meals were an established market success for a few years, marketing executives at the company decided it was time to make them even more appealing to consumers. The primary food missing from the existing dinners was dessert. In response, in 1960 the company redesigned the aluminum tray, adding a fourth compartment that could house a dessert, usually a peach or apple cobbler that would taste good when heated.

In addition to the new meals and desserts, it did not take long for the company to realize that it could be limiting its success by emphasizing the fact that the meals were for dinner. What Swanson customer would not love a Swanson frozen meal for lunch as well? Thereafter the meals were produced under the Swanson Frozen Meals name so that consumers would eat them for other meals as well. Seven years later, Swanson introduced its first frozen breakfasts. All mealtimes were covered; a consumer could conceivably eat a Swanson frozen meal for breakfast, lunch, and dinner.

However, times change, and throughout the 1980s and 1990s U.S. citizens became more educated about the foods they ate. Processed and frozen foods became less popular as more people returned to fresh foods. To keep consumers buying, many frozen food companies changed the food in their dinners to more healthful versions, such as grilled chicken rather than fried. Swanson was no exception to this trend, as it dropped desserts from its meals in 2001. It struggled to maintain market share, however, due to intense competition.

There were also significant developments in Swanson's corporate history at the end of the 20th century and into the new millenium. In 1998, Campbell Soup spun off Swanson's TV dinner business to a new company, Vlasic Foods International (renamed Pinnacle Foods Group, LLC, in 2001), which was given a 10-year license to use the Swanson name on its frozen meals. When the license expired in 2009, Pinnacle Foods discontinued the use of the Swanson name, thus bringing an era of the TV dinner to a close.

BIBLIOGRAPHY

Fuller, John. "Sept. 10, 1953: Swanson Sells First TV Dinner." HowStuffWorks.com. Accessed February 3, 2012. http://people.howstuffworks.com/swanson-dinner.htm/.

Gust, Lauren. "Defrosting Dinner: The Evolution of Frozen Meals in America." *Intersect* 4, no. 1, 2011.

LeBeau, Mary Dixon. "At 50, TV Dinner Is Still Cookin'." *Christian Science Monitor,* November 10, 2004. Accessed February 3, 2012. http://www.csmonitor.com/2004/1110/p11s01-lifo.html.

"TV Dinners." *CooksInfo.com: The Encyclopedia for Cooks,* November 22, 2004. Accessed February 2, 2012. http://www.practicallyedible.com/edible.nsf/pages/tvdinners.

"Who Invented the TV Dinner?" Washington, DC: Library of Congress Science Reference Services, August 23, 2010. Accessed February 3, 2012. http://www.loc.gov/rr/scitech/mysteries/tvdinner.html.

Swatch Group: Reinvigorating the Swiss Watch Industry

A NEW KIND OF SWISS WATCH

For many years, Swiss watches were considered the best of the best. They were known for their precision, quality, and luxurious-looking styles. It became a status symbol for certain people to own a Swiss watch such as a Rolex or an Omega. They were expensive but long-lasting, and wearing one was a declaration of financial success. Other Swiss watch brands were also successful, although they were not as strong as the Rolex.

Two companies in the Swiss watch industry, Allgemeine Schweizerische Uhrenindustrie AG (ASUAG) and Société Suisse pour l'Industrie Horlogère (SSIH), had experienced a roller-coaster ride of success and failure throughout their respective histories. ASUAG manufactured and marketed well-known and previously successful watches, like Omega, while SSIH primarily marketed and sold watch parts to other watch manufacturers. Each company had struggled in the 1930s due to the Great Depression, but each company endured this crisis. However, by the 1970s, another economic recession and increasing competition led to difficult times for both companies.

By that time, several new watch technologies and products had been introduced to the market and proven successful. Two examples included the Hamilton electric watch, which was introduced in 1957, and the Bulova Accutron tuning fork watch that hit the market in 1961. Yet it was the competing low-cost but high-technology watches produced in Japan, such as those sold under the Seiko brand, that proved to be the ultimate undoing of the two companies. Across multiple markets, the Japanese developed methods for mass producing lower cost electronics that competed successfully with long-standing brands, including the Swiss watches. The Swiss watch export market had dropped by half, with Japanese and Chinese products taking over most of this business. One of these competing watches was an ultra-thin version that was just two millimeters thick. ASAUG responded by developing its own ultra-thin version that was less than one millimeter in thickness. It was successful but not sufficient to turn the tide of consumers back to Swiss watches. The Swiss watch industry was in a slump; it needed a way to compete and still remain true to its reputation of quality and accuracy.

This was when entrepreneur Nicholas G. Hayek entered the picture. In the early 1980s Hayek was chief executive officer of Hayek Engineering AG, a consulting firm. ASUAG's and SSIH's bankers hired Hayek to dissolve the failing companies. Instead, he conducted some research and then devised a plan for merging the two companies and revitalizing them by launching new brands that could compete with the less expensive brands that were taking over the market. His goal for the newly combined company, which would be called Swatch Group SA, was to develop, manufacture, and market a watch that was completely made from plastic parts, and that would need just about half the parts of contemporary models. He assigned this task to Ernst Thomke and his group of young engineers and designers.

Although Swatch is credited with being the first watch of its kind, there actually was a forerunner on the market that did not succeed. In 1971 the Swiss watch company Tissot SA demonstrated its watch made entirely from plastic at that year's International Watch Fair. This watch could be manufactured using fewer parts than the watches then on the market. It was a mechanical watch, whose parts numbered just 52, compared with the average

90 parts needed to make most other watches being sold at the time. Called the Astrolon, it was self-lubricating and required only 15 steps in its manufacturing process. It was also lightweight and highly reliable.

Reliability aside, the time for an all-plastic watch just had not arrived. The Astrolon was sold by U.S. companies such as Sears, Roebuck and Co. Its price ranged from US$8.00 per watch to US$22.00 per watch. This was inexpensive, yet widespread sales and market success like that experienced by Swatch years later never materialized. However, it did prove to Hayek that his model was doable. His goal then was to make it successful.

WHAT SWATCH DID DIFFERENTLY

In developing a marketing strategy for his Swatch, Hayek did several things differently from earlier marketing efforts. One of the major differences between Swatch's approach and Tissot's was that Hayek had a better appreciation for and understanding of the value of the right marketing approach. Throughout the Swiss watch industry history, manufacturers were known to be conservative in their approach to marketing, and with good reason. The quality of their products spoke for themselves, and there was no need to spend a lot of time and effort on a marketing campaign. Watches were not a commodity. However, the different market environment of the 1970s and 1980s had created a commodity market for watches and Hayek recognized that he had to create and implement a much more aggressive marketing campaign if the brand was going to be successful. He had to get consumers to change their thinking about watches. He also realized that he needed to devote a great deal of financial and human resources to create a successful marketing campaign.

One of the first things Hayek did was hire a master marketer, Jacques Irniger, who had previously been a top marketing director with Colgate-Palmolive Company. Irniger and Hayek then hired one of the top advertising agencies of the time, McCann Erickson Advertising Limited, to develop and implement a global campaign. No other watch company had thought of doing this before. It was unheard of because Swiss watches had seemed to sell themselves, but the Swatch watch was meant to be a retail fashion accessory, not a traditional timepiece. Up to this point, while people wanted attractive watches, they were expensive purchases, and people usually had and wore only one watch. The point of Swatch watches was to entice consumers to buy several, with each timepiece correlating to different outfits or activities.

In the 1980s companies were also just beginning to realize that they needed to understand who was buying their products. Hayek was one of the first CEOs of this generation who seemed to know instinctively who would buy the new Swatch watches and how to appeal to this market. His goal was to create inexpensive watches that were accurate and reliable but were also designed fashionably with several different designs from which to choose. He knew that young, fashion-conscious buyers would be the market to which these watches would appeal most. Yet despite Hayek's focus on the customer, he was not one to conduct extensive market research. Similar to Steve Jobs at Apple Computer, he believed that using the right marketing approach would create a product's success.

Another major difference between the Swatch watch and others of its day was that a great deal of attention was paid to its appearance. Even though other watch manufacturers made sure their watches were attractive, they all tended to look alike. As the Swatch was plastic, rather than gold or silver metal, there was practically no limit to the colors and designs that could be created for the brand. To ensure that it would appeal to his target market, Hayek hired artists and fashion designers who were well versed in creating retail products.

Hayek and his marketing team also made sure that all Swatch marketing and advertising efforts, as well as the products themselves, clearly conveyed a strong brand message. The watches were characterized by vivid colors and bold combinations, striking geometric designs and smooth, distinctive curves. When the watches were first introduced in Germany, Japan, and Spain, Swatch hung giant 165-meter watches from the cities' skyscrapers. Hayek challenged his marketing team to convey an overall marketing message for the swatches: he wanted the watches to be portrayed as high technology and exciting in a fresh and upbeat way.

Marketing glamour aside, the watches were not going to be successful if they were not inexpensive to produce. To that end, the Swatch's fewer parts and manufacturing steps led to an 80 percent reduction in the cost of producing them. However, that did not mean that the watches did not perform with the same quality as more expensive watches. They did, which made them even more popular with consumers who felt they were getting the ultimate deal: the precision and quality of Swiss watches, in lots of colors and designs, at a price that almost anyone could afford.

Hayek also had the foresight to protect the company by filing for patent protection, something that most retail product manufacturers did not often do. By the 2010s Swatch had more than 2,000 registered designs. The company also filed for patent protection for all of the technology it used in manufacturing the watches.

MAINTAINING A LEADING POSITION

Swatch and Hayek's marketing ideas quickly proved to be successful. Millions of Swatch watches were produced and sold. Just three years after its launch Swatch had produced 50 million watches, and four years later in 1992 it had doubled that number, having produced 100 million watches. It hit the 200 million mark in 1996. As of 2011 the company reported that it was unable to keep up with demand and would add both factory capacity and nearly 2,000 employees to its payroll to increase manufacturing capability. The demand for Swatch watches in Asia accounted for much of the increased demand. This success presented an interesting contrast to the company's position in its earliest years. The company reported a 42 percent increase in profits in 2010 and it appeared that demand for the watches would remain strong throughout the 2010s. In fact, brand loyalty had become so high that the original Swatch watches became collector's items and sold at auction for thousands of dollars.

One reason for the ongoing popularity of the Swatch watches is the company's creative marketing approach, which has helped the company succeed since the launch of the initial models. For example, in 2000 Swatch launched a new Scuba watch with a media campaign that included unveiling the new watch in the Death Valley desert in California. The company also sponsored extreme sports stars and popular music bands, cultural icons of the generation and the market to which Swatch intended to appeal. Swatch also opened its own stores. As of 2012 there were 600 stores worldwide, each designed to attract the consumer with interactive games and exhibits, the kind of activities that would appeal most to the young, active generation that represents the Swatch market.

In order to compete with all types of watches, the company also introduced more expensive gold and silver Swatch watches that offered the same quality in a thin or wide profile band. When these watches were first launched in 1986, there were few watches that had a similar design. The company has also continued to market its watches as innovative and creative, and has enlisted well-known artists to design them. For example, artist Keith Haring designed some limited edition Swatch watches, and in 1992 a Swatch by Kiki Picasso, a pseudonym of the French artist Christian Chapiron, sold at an auction at Christie's in London for US$28,000.

As of 2012 Swatch Group was one of the largest watch companies in the world. The company's creator, Hayek, has been credited with restoring the Swiss watch industry to its glory days and he received many honors, rewards, and recognition for his role in the Swiss business. The University of Neuchâtel and the University of Bologna conferred honorary doctorates on him, and he has received honors or awards from the governments of Austria and France. In January 2007 Hayek received the Swiss Lifetime Award. In 2002 Hayek stepped down from handling the day-to-day operations of the company. His son, Nick Hayek, Jr., succeeded him as CEO, and his daughter, Nayla, became chair of the board of directors. Hayek remained active as a board member and as a management consultant. He died in 2010, at the age of 82, while working at his office.

BIBLIOGRAPHY

Bradley, Simon. "The Man Who Revolutionized Watch Marketing." *SwisInfo.ch,* June 30, 2010. Accessed February 10, 2012. http://www.swissinfo.ch/eng/business/The_man _who_revolutionised_watch_marketing.html?cid=15331650.

Freedman, Jack. "The Amazing 'Swatch' Story." *TimeZone.com,* March 3, 1998. Accessed February 10, 2012. http://www .timezone.com/library/archives/archives0085.

Minder, Raphael. "At Swatch, an Enviable Problem: An Excess of Eager Customers for Its Products." *New York Times,* Accessed February 10, 2012. http://www.nytimes.com/2011/04/23 /business/global/23swatch.html?_r=1&pagewanted=all.

Pope, Stephen. "Swatch Billionaire Nicholas Hayek, Who Saved the Swiss Watch Industry, Dies." *Forbes,* June 29, 2010. Accessed February 10, 2012. http://www.forbes.com/sites /billions/2010/06/29/swatch-billionaire-nicolas-hayek-who -saved-the-swiss-watch-industry-dies/.

The Swatch Group. "Swatch Watch History." Biel, Switzerland, 2012. Accessed February 10, 2012. http://www.swatchgroup .com/en/group_profile/history.

Taiwan Semiconductor
Manufacturing Company

THE FABLESS AND THE FOUNDRY

The Taiwan Semiconductor Manufacturing Company (TSMC) grew to be the first dedicated semiconductor foundry in the world and remained the largest of its kind for years. Semiconductors are the ubiquitous, silicon-based chips found in nearly every kind of electronic device. They are the physical key to producing digital information, transforming binary language into real-world expression by flipping millions upon millions of transistors on or off.

Semiconductor technology took giant leaps forward in the 1960s and 1970s, primarily in the United States. As Silicon Valley, California began to grow as a locus of technological innovation, commercial companies started embracing the potential of the semiconductor market. Semiconductors began with calculators and large-scale computation systems, and these early devices look outdated in comparison to the processors created in the 2010s.

TAIWAN AND SILICON VALLEY

Since all semiconductor planning occurred in Silicon Valley and similar environs, production stayed in close proximity as well. The United States used Taiwan's ample labor force primarily for low-wage, basic manufacturing contracts to supply other product components needed to house the semiconductors, but not for advanced products like the semiconductors themselves. If Taiwanese workers wanted more advanced training, they left for the United States to study electrical engineering. By the 1980s Taiwan was sending more doctoral candidates for science and engineering to the United States than any other country.

With the lack of suitable jobs in their home country, most immigrants chose to remain in the United States.

This cycle proved destructive for Taiwan, draining some of its most talented workers without any appreciable returns. The trend would probably have continued had it not been for a single immigrant called Morris Chang. Chang, born in China, left for the United States to attend Harvard University and then the Massachusetts Institute of Technology (MIT). After getting his master's degree in mechanical engineering he quickly moved into the semiconductor field. In 1958 he joined Texas Instruments Inc., where he proved integral to that company's meteoric rise in the following decades.

Chang left Texas Instruments in 1983, after reaching the position of vice president over its international semiconductor business. For a brief time he served as president and COO for General Instrument Corporation, but then in 1985, the Taiwanese government made him a fascinating offer. Taiwan, eager to reverse the trend of losing its best people to the overseas technology industry, asked Chang to form a partnership with the government to help make key changes. In return, Chang would get the opportunity to influence the technology policy of an entire nation and a potentially lucrative job if enterprises developed based on the work he did.

Chang agreed to the Taiwanese request and moved to the island nation. His work with the government soon led to a revolutionary way of thinking about the semiconductor industry, and it provided a chance to propel Taiwan forward as an international leader in manufacturing. The idea was simple at its core: Taiwan would attempt to separate semiconductor manufacturing from semiconductor design. U.S. companies could keep their plans, research, and designs, but they could also choose to contract Taiwan to build the semiconductors according to specifications, avoiding the need for complex manufacturing facilities in the United States.

The move led to the coining of the term "fabless," meaning without fabrication. In an era where tech companies had begun to embrace vertical integration (where a company works to control all parts of the supply chain for a product), the plan Chang made astounded others with its vertical *fragmentation* approach, and its immediate success. By splitting the semiconductor manufacturing process, Chang enabled greater focus on efficiency and quality control for both the supply side and design side. The challenge was to win the trust of tech companies in the United States so they would send their business to Taiwan.

In 1987 Chang, the Taiwanese government, and Panasonic Corporation worked together to found TSMC. It became the first semiconductor business devoted entirely to the production of semiconductor parts, known as a dedicated foundry (foundry being the traditional term for a factory involved in producing resources). External clients sent in designs, orders, and requirements, while TSMC focused entirely on producing semiconductor wafers on demand. Chang became known as the "father of the Taiwan semiconductor industry" or the "father of the foundry business."

SEMICONDUCTOR JUGGLING ACT

Initial suspicion of the fabless or foundry process quickly gave way to acceptance as U.S. firms realized they could avoid costs associated with the complex semiconductor production process, focusing instead on the other features of their products. The low-grade manufacturing orders sent to Taiwan began turning into specific, complex requirements for new semiconductors.

TSMC stood ready to deliver, backed by the Taiwan Industrial Technology Research Institute, both led by Chang. Chang accurately predicted that the fabless manufacturing process would eventually invigorate semiconductor business on an international level. A host of companies had been eyeing the technology market eagerly but did not have enough experience or capital to start production themselves. The fabless option allowed them to outsource the most complex parts of fabrication so they could enter the market. Suddenly, a number of smaller businesses could operate at a profit by designing and ordering computer chips.

As the Taiwanese economy improved, indigenous engineers started to think twice about moving away from Taiwan, and TSMC achieved swift growth with healthy revenues, primarily from the United States. However, the success TSMC achieved went far beyond lowering market

barriers. Computer chips were the wave of the future, and as the 1990s started TSMC found itself at the center of most cutting-edge technologies being developed for commercial networking and home computers.

Succeeding at fabless manufacturing required skilled juggling at every level. First came the suppliers. TSMC needed the silicon and broad variety of doping materials to doctor wafers according to client needs. The company needed to order these materials in time to complete expected client orders, and quality needed to be as high as possible. Due to advancing refining techniques, this often meant a greater purity than the previous contract, which could cause some trouble with supplier relationships. However, Taiwan managed to arrange sufficient raw materials contracts in nearby locations in Asia in order to compensate for changing demand needs into the 1990s.

Next, TSMC needed to consider client requirements for the manufacturing process. Detailed contract negotiation helped, but it took both time and talent to find a middle ground both sides could accept. Clients wanted their semiconductor chips as soon as possible and flawless, while TSMC wanted deadlines that would make good service possible while keeping cross-Pacific Ocean transportation expenses under control. Communication barriers also made it difficult to exchange information across the ocean, especially before the Internet era. If not for the quickly proven high efficiency of the foundry model, it might have taken clients much longer to begin trusting the young manufacturer with their delicate specifications.

Such delicate specifications created quality-control concerns. Semiconductors depended on the smallest amount of additional elements placed into pure silicon using precise methods, temperatures, and timing. Small mistakes would erode trust and cause clients to revert to other methods. Proving the fabless process worthwhile required an excellent track record. TMSC hired talented engineers who had been educated in the United States and understood what technology companies needed.

Even with supplier and client relations properly managed and quality control under strict parameters, TSMC still had to deal with rapidly progressing market conditions. Contracts in the 1990s technology world were frequently updated as companies created newer, better designs for their chips. Semiconductors grew constantly smaller, while companies kept discovering new element-doping mixtures. TSMC could not find a winning formula and stay with it for several profitable years. Instead, it needed to constantly revise its own factory plans and workflow to keep up with better techniques. Equipment, storage, and software all needed frequent attention. Despite the challenge, TSMC not only survived the 1990s but also managed to thrive, going public in 1994. By the start of the 21st century, the era had changed, but TSMC was still the largest dedicated semiconductor foundry in the world.

BETTER THAN THE REST: TSMC ENTERS THE 21ST CENTURY

In the 1990s multiple new markets were created for TSMC. Early computers were already a distant memory. Most printers, cameras, phones, appliances, cars, and music players, to name just a few items, all needed a semiconductor to operate. Fabless manufacturing had become so popular that thousands of competitors had emerged in the 1990s, offering the same types of services as TSMC. In order to stay ahead, TSMC needed additional competencies to keep its old clients and attract new operators. It found the extra edge in acquisitions, an early start, and skilled use of information technology.

TSMC invested heavily in acquisitions beginning in the mid-to-late 1990s, and continued using acquisition as a strategy. In 2000 the company completed the acquisition of Acer Semiconductor Manufacturing Inc. and acquired Worldwide Semiconductor Corporation as well. These moves, which continued throughout the first decade of the 21st century, helped stave off fabless competition while also giving TSMC access to other design options and revenue streams.

As the first foundry for fabless manufacturing, TSMC had an additional first-mover advantage, especially when it came to cost. During the 1980s and 1990s the cost of starting a manufacturing plant for semiconductors was high but attainable, around US$750 million for a new plant. Around 2005, costs had soared to between US$4 billion and US$5 billion for a typical 8-inch semiconductor wafer laboratory, in addition to high operating costs. This made it increasingly difficult for other companies to enter the market, creating a natural barrier that protected TSMC. By 2006 at least 750 fabless companies existed, but only 15 were fully independent foundries.

Even with the limited number of competitors, the service model TSMC used kept it in first place. Technology had reached a point where information could be exchanged between the fabless companies and the foundry very easily. Chang envisioned virtual design services that allowed companies to create and modify their designs as needed, with immediate results in the factory. TSMC fulfilled these dreams with online research and development compatibility. This solved problems companies had with intellectual property and capital investment in research, drawing in many new clients. It also helped TSMC survive the sharp downturn in business due to the dot-com bust, which made the first couple of years of the 21st century difficult for the semiconductor industry.

As an extra service, TSMC also began offering advanced testing of its products. This move was another revolutionary step for the fabless industry. Companies rarely had the ability to conduct product testing in their own facilities, and even when they did, it was at considerable cost. Mistakes or defects in the design were even more expensive. By offering design testing and additional elements of product control or consultation for its clients, TSMC added even more value to the fabless process. Original tests of memory, logic, and mixed-mode circuits led to other types of technology testing.

BIGGER, BRIGHTER, AND MORE CUSTOMIZABLE

As the 2010s approached, TSMC invested in further changes to meet new markets halfway. Although Rick Tsai had been leading the company for the previous several years, in 2009 a switch put Morris Chang back in charge as CEO. The company followed this announcement with a new focus on energy efficiency and emerging technology. Another evolution occurred in the testing division of TSMC with the introduction of the open innovation platform. The manufacturer began to sell not only manufacturing services, but the references, process technologies, methods, and intellectual property it used. The company had been sitting on the intellectual property it used to support chip design and production for years. Now it was able to capitalize on this knowledge, bringing in revenue not only from sales but from ongoing licenses for its tools and procedures.

In 2011 TSMC began working on a major contract from Apple Inc. as the technology giant switched from Samsung Group to the TSMC process in an attempt to diversify. As the company entered 2012, it held a production capacity of 13.2 million eight-inch wafers, with three additional 12-inch factories, four eight-inch factories, and one six-inch factory, in additional to several subsidiaries.

THE SWEET SPOT

In 2011 alone, TSMC budgeted US$7.8 billion for updates and new processes. This type of dedication to the best service and quality possible made TSMC successful. Its short history, spanning only a few decades, was filled with examples of new features and options that met needs the market was only beginning to understand. By reaching out to clients in these ways, TSMC was able to single-handedly start the fabless segment of the industry and stay at the top, despite the rise of competitors. TSMC also owed much of its success to the insights and plans of Morris Chang, who stayed with the company from its founding. It was a famous formula: the actions of a single brilliant person often directed or inspired great business.

BIBLIOGRAPHY

Doraiswamy, Deepa. "Fabless Semiconductor Model." Mountain View, CA: Frost & Sullivan, March 17, 2006. Accessed February 6, 2012. http://www.frost.com/prod/servlet/market -insight-top.pag?docid=63842246.

Hadavi, Kameron. "Fabless Semiconductor Planning: Between a Rock and a Hard Place!" *Adexa Supply Chain Planning Blog,* 2012. Accessed February 6, 2012. http://web.adexa.com /adexa-blog/bid/44358/Fabless-Semiconductor-Planning -Between-A-Rock-And-A-Hard-Place.

IEEE. "Morris Chang, Pioneering Leader of the Semiconductor Industry, to Receive 2011 IEEE Medal of Honor." New York, August 10, 2011. Accessed February 6, 2012. http://www .ieee.org/about/news/2011/honors_ceremony/releases_moh .html.

Jim, Clare, and Argin Chang. "TSMC to Manufacture New Chips for Apple as Samsung Battle Heats Up: Report." *Huffington Post,* September 14, 2011. Accessed February 6, 2012. http://www.huffingtonpost.com/2011/07/15/tsmc -apple-chips-samsung_n_899634.html.

Norton, Rob. "The Thought Leader Interview: Henry Chesbrough." *Strategy + Business,* May 24, 2011. Accessed February 6, 2012. http://m.strategy-business.com/article /11210?gko=af24f.

Shilov, Anton. "Fabless Semiconductor Developers Boost Orders at TSMC and UMC. " *Xbit Labs,* March 24, 2009. Accessed February 6, 2012. http://www.xbitlabs.com/news/other /display/20090324145944_Fabless_Semiconductor

_Developers_Boost_Orders_at_TSMC_and_UMC.html.

"Taiwan Semiconductor Manufacturing Company Ltd." In *International Directory of Company Histories,* edited by Jay P. Pederson. Vol. 47, 383–387. Detroit: St. James Press, 2002. Gale Virtual Reference Library (GALE|CX2845100105). Accessed February 6, 2012. http://go.galegroup.com/ps/i.do ?id=GALE%7CCX2845100105&v=2.1&u=itsbtrial&it=r&p =GVRL&sw=w.

Tano Capital LLC. "China." Shanghai, China, 2011. Accessed February 6, 2012. http://www.tanocapital.com/china-2.

TSMC. "Company Profile. " Hsinchu, Taiwan, 2011. Accessed February 6, 2012. http://www.tsmc.com/english/aboutTSMC /company_profile.htm.

"TSMC Announces Power Trim Service for Leakage Power Reduction." Los Gatos, CA: Tela Innovations, April 15, 2008. Accessed February 6, 2012. http://www.tela-inc.com/nr _041508_tsmc.php.

Vance, Ashlee. "Taiwan Semiconductor Manufacturing Company Ltd. " *New York Times,* June 16, 2009. Accessed February 6, 2012. http://topics.nytimes.com/top/news/business /companies/taiwan-semiconductor-manufacturing-company -ltd/index.html.

Telephone Improves with Edison's Innovative Device

THE RACE TO INVENT THE TELEPHONE

Thomas Alva Edison was a prolific inventor. By the end of his life, he held more than 1,000 patents. While he was best known as the inventor of the incandescent light bulb, he was also credited with inventing the phonograph and the motion picture camera. In addition to these inventions, he invented parts that improved other inventions, including the telegraph and the telephone.

Edison was born in 1847 and grew up in Michigan, where he was a poor student. His mother decided to educate him at home. Edison later said that his mother's faith in him inspired him to learn and become a better student. Even at a young age, he demonstrated a strong understanding of all things chemical and mechanical. At the age of 12, Edison became almost completely deaf, and no one knew exactly what caused the condition. Some historians theorized that it was due to a bout of scarlet fever, while others attributed it to the fact that he was grabbed by the ears or boxed on the ears. The result of his deafness, though, was that he became shy and focused more on his studies and research.

EDISON AND THE TELEGRAPH

Edison's introduction to the telegraph industry had heroic beginnings. Edison happened to be standing near a train where a three-year old boy was playing. The little boy was on the train track and a boxcar was about to roll on top of him. Edison rescued the little boy. It so happened that the boy's father was proficient in railroad telegraphy, and out of gratitude to Edison for saving his son, he taught Edison telegraphy. Shortly afterward, Edison landed a job as a telegraph operator in Port Huron, Michigan. This was the beginning of a long-time interest in the telegraph and its equipment. In fact, it was such a large part of Edison's life that he later nicknamed his first two children "Dot" and "Dash" for the Morse code used by telegraph operators to send messages.

By 1869 Edison left Michigan and moved to Boston, Massachusetts, where he worked for the Western Union Company. However, he was determined to work on his inventions, and this led him to resign his position so he could work on them full time. In 1869 he invented an electric vote recorder. It was the first of his inventions to receive a patent. However, the local politicians were not interested, and the electric vote recorder never became successful.

Over the course of the next five years, Edison combined his telegraph experience with his inventiveness and formed several partnerships that involved developing telegraph instruments or improvements. These included the telegraph printer, a multiplex telegraphic system for Western Union, and a quadruplex system that could send two messages in both directions at the same time along the same wire.

In 1876 Edison moved into his first full-fledged laboratory in Menlo Park, New Jersey. It became known as the "Invention Factory," due to the many inventions Edison and his employees would be working on at one time. One of the first inventions that came out of Edison' Invention Factory was an improved transmitter for the telephone.

BELL'S INVENTION

While Alexander Graham Bell was considered the inventor of the telephone, he was not the only inventor to be working on a similar instrument at the time. In fact, another leading inventor, Elisha Gray, filed his "Caveat," an official notice that he would be patenting his invention within three months, just hours after Bell's patent application was filed. Gray's invention specifically addressed transmitting sounds, while Bell's focused more on his method for improving telegraphy. However, Bell had written down the key element needed to transmit sounds on the side of the patent application; he called it variable resistance. When Gray filed a patent lawsuit against Bell and his telephone, the court subsequently decided in Bell's favor. In addition to Gray, other inventors, such as Emile Berliner, the inventor of the music record, and Edison, also created similar inventions or parts for them.

Bell and his business partner and future father-in-law, Gardiner Greene Hubbard, had actually decided to abandon the telephone in 1876, less than a year after the patent for it was granted. They were concerned about the invention for a number of reasons. First, there was the fact that a number of patent lawsuits against Bell had been filed, including suits filed by Edison, Berliner, and Gray. These suits were proving costly and more suits were being threatened. In addition to this, the telephone itself was a long way from perfection as there were issues with it that needed to be resolved.

For instance, the design of the telephone was not suitable for long conversations, and physically using it was awkward and uncomfortable. This was due to the fact that both the transmitter and receiver were housed in the same boxlike apparatus. Users would speak into one spot on the box, and then have to tilt their heads to the side of the box to hear the answer from the other end. While this was not an insurmountable obstacle, another technical difficulty with the telephone would be quite difficult to correct: the fact that his telephone was unable to transmit sounds over long distances. Even though Bell continued to work on his telephone to see if he could overcome these issues, there was already a patented invention that would improve it.

One month before Bell's patent application was filed, Edison had filed his own patent for a transmitter. The transmitter was not part of a telephone. In fact, Edison created it to conduct sound analysis research. Despite this, Edison's transmitter proved to be quite valuable to the telephone industry.

OPERATION OF BELL'S TELEPHONE

Bell's telephone worked by converting the sound waves made by a human voice into electric impulses. He used a wire to conduct these impulses to the receiver, where they were converted back into a human voice at the other end of the wire. Bell's original transmitter consisted of a parchment membrane that vibrated in response to sound. He used a metal button attached to the membrane to send the varied movements to an electromagnet. Electric current that corresponded to these vibrations was induced. Then, the induced current traveled to the receiving device, where the process was reversed: the electricity caused the magnet to move, which then caused a membrane to vibrate, and the corresponding sounds came out.

The problem with Bell's approach was that the parchment membrane in the receiver was not very sensitive to the electricity produced by the instrument. That was why the sender and receiver needed to be somewhat close to each other for the parchment device to pick up the sound. Edison's transmitter, on the other hand, used a disc of compressed carbon between two metal plates.

However, not just any carbon would work. Edison had to experiment with several different forms of carbon before finding one that would respond with sensitivity to sound. He used oil and burned it at a very low temperature, which created hydrocarbons in the form of powder. He then compressed the powder and shaped it into a button that contacted the electromagnet. It was this device that he patented and that was later used in Bell's equipment. The patent covered metal diaphragms, other diaphragms using two contacts to produce the varying resistance, as well as all the materials that could be used to make the contacts. Although this was far-ranging, the patent did not cover multiple contacts or nonmetallic diaphragms. This oversight led to many lawsuits filed against Edison. Unlike Bell, Edison did not always win these lawsuits.

Several other events occurred, however, before Edison's transmitter became widely used. Despite the fact that the telegraph ruled the telecom industry during this time, several people recognized that the telephone could have remarkable market potential. Gray and Berliner, for example, were quick to file patent infringement suits against Edison and Bell to stake their own claims in the market.

Meanwhile, the giant of the industry, Western Union, was weighing its options and playing its own role in the development of the telephone. Initially, in 1876, Bell and his financial backer, Hubbard, approached Western Union president William Orton to purchase the patent for Bell's version of the telephone for US$100,000. It seemed a natural fit for the company, which already had extensive telegraph infrastructure in place that could be easily converted to the telephone. Orton assembled a team of executives and engineers to examine Bell's invention and make a recommendation on his proposal. The decision this group came to was that the telephone did not have much of a future. After all, telecommunication needs were already being well met by their telegraph system. Plus, Bell's invention was not really a finished product that could be introduced to the market with little or no refinement. When this offer was rejected, Bell and Hubbard also tried to sell the patent to the telephone to the British Post

Office Department, which operated the telegraph system in Great Britain. They received the same answer.

In response, Bell and Hubbard decided to pursue the opportunity themselves, and founded Bell Telephone Company in 1877. Within a year, their business was successful enough that Western Union realized that they needed to enter the telephone industry, and quickly. The other leading contenders, including Edison, also continued to expand the market for the telephone.

EDISON'S TRANSMITTER BECOMES PART OF BELL'S PHONE

In 1878 Western Union entered into an agreement with both Gray and Edison for their inventions. Edison's transmitter was then used in Western Union's phones. However, Edison was also interested in producing and selling his own telephones. So Edison decided to take his invention overseas, where he launched his own telephone company, the Edison Telephone Company, in London, England. While Edison was operating his telephone company in England, Bell was operating his in the United States, and Western Union was operating its own new telephone company.

There were no fewer than 600 patent disputes filed in the fight to control this hot new invention; in the meantime, Bell continued expanding his phone company and working to come up with a transmitter that worked as well as Edison's. Another inventor, Frances Blake, invented a transmitter similar to Edison's, and it was this transmitter that allowed Bell and Bell Telephone to continue operations. Western Union also continued to operate its phone system. Still, the patent lawsuits and cross suits continued to be filed, including one that became notorious.

On January 13, 1887, the U.S. government sought to revoke Bell's patent, saying he had received it under fraudulent terms and misrepresentation of the invention. It became known as the Government Case. However, the suit was quickly dropped when it was publicized that the U.S. attorney general at the time, Augustus Hill Garland, had been bribed to file the suit by being given millions of dollars of stock from a competing company.

By 1892 the patent lawsuit filed against Edison and his transmitter was finally settled, and its settlement established an agreement in which Edison's transmitters would be used in Bell telephones throughout the term of the patent. As other suits settled, the future of the telephone began to take shape. Western Union was forced to close its telephone operations and surrender all of its patents. Bell had also filed a suit against Edison and his operation in London, England, which he won. All of Edison's phone subscribers became part of Bell's company.

Because Western Union had the rights to Edison's transmitter at that time, Bell was required to pay 20 percent of its telephone rental revenue to Western Union until Edison's patent expired 17 years later. The transmitters were so successful, however, that even after the 17 years they continued to be used, in revised and improved forms, in analog telephones. In fact, it was not until the 1970s that Edison's transmitter was discontinued. Without these transmitters, the telephone might not have been as successful and as widely used.

BIBLIOGRAPHY

"The Case Files: Thomas Alva Edison." Philadephia, PA: The Franklin Institute, 2004. Accessed February 13, 2012. http://www.fi.edu/learn/case-files/edison/telephone.html.

"The Life of Thomas A. Edison." Washington, DC: Library of Congress. Accessed February 13, 2012. http://memory.loc.gov/ammem/edhtml/edbio.html.

"Telephone History." Telephonymuseum.com, 1998. Accessed February 13, 2012. http://www.telephonymuseum.com/telephone%20history.htm.

"The Telephone Patent Follies." Telecommunications Virtual Museum. Accessed February 13, 2012. http://www.telcomhistory.org/vm/sciencePatentFollies.shtml.

Texas Instruments and Digital Light Processing Technology

In 1987 the idea of putting hundreds of microscopic mirrors on a chip seemed a far-fetched notion to many, but that was precisely what Dr. Larry Hornbeck succeeded in doing while working at Texas Instruments Inc. In 1989 Seiko Epson Corporation began producing the first full-color, liquid crystal display (LCD) projectors and that was the direction that Texas Instruments headed with its new digital light processing (DLP) technology, which was used in the first business projectors in 1996. Since that time, DLP has been incorporated into high-definition televisions (HDTVs); projection systems, ranging from pocket-size to projectors for large venues; and a host of other applications requiring an optical semiconductor that can digitally manipulate light. Texas Instruments also developed DLP as a three-chip projection system for cinemas that could achieve more than 35 trillion colors. Since 2008 DLP projectors have been available with three-dimensional (3D) capabilities.

TEXAS INSTRUMENTS

Texas Instruments is one of the world's largest semiconductor manufacturers and is credited with many firsts in the industry. In 1958 Jack Kirby invented the integrated circuit while working at Texas Instruments. Although Intel Corporation invented the first microprocessor and in March 1971 began shipping the first chips for use in a printing calculator, two engineers at Texas Instruments, Gary Boone and Michael Cochran, invented the first microcontroller, which integrated the computer processing unit (CPU) on a single semiconductor chip. Texas Instruments became a household name after it began shipping the first handheld calculators with a light-emitting diode (LED) display in 1972.

In 1977 the U.S. Defense Department contracted Texas Instruments to make a spatial-light modulator with mirrors for use in optical computing, and Hornbeck began working on the project. The company had developed analog micromirrors (extremely small mirrors operated electromechanically), but as of 1986 had been unsuccessful in getting enough uniformity and optical efficiency to do simple copying. In 1987 Hornbeck solved the problem by inventing the first digital micromirror, called the digital micromirror device (DMD). Each hinged mirror tilted either toward or away from the light source. The new design with two states made it easier to control the angle and maintain uniformity. Since the mirrors were bi-stable, meaning they held their position until changed, they operated at a lower voltage than analog micromirrors.

DMD technology was first used in an airline ticket printer in 1990, which was composed of 840 linear micromirrors. Around that time, Texas Instruments received funding from the Defense Advanced Research Projects Agency (DARPA, a military research agency) and started development of a high-definition DMD chip that could be used in HDTVs. Rank Brimar Ltd., a subsidiary of the Rank Group Plc in the United Kingdom, also invested money in Texas Instruments to develop a three-chip DMD projector that could be used in theaters and auditoriums. In 1992 Texas Instruments formed the Digital Imaging Venture Project to develop projectors that could possibly lead to technology that would work in HDTVs.

FIRST PROJECTORS WITH DLP

The first digital projectors used 3LCD technology, which was developed by Epson Corp. The technology was commercialized in the 16-pound Epson VPJ-700 projector in January 1989, which had a resolution of 320-by-220 pixels and cost US$6,000. (A pixel is s single point in an image.) Epson took a wrong turn with the release of the VPJ-2000 in July 1991. The projector achieved 480-by-440 resolution but weighed 24 pounds and cost US$11,000. However, the ELP-3000 released at the end of 1994 had notable improvements and cost half as much. It achieved 640-by-480 resolution, so projected images were identical to how they appeared on a personal computer (PC) display, and images were twice as bright. Portability also improved with the more compact projector that weighed 17 pounds. With the release of Microsoft Windows 95, the popularity of PowerPoint soared, and so did demand for projectors.

Texas Instruments believed it could reduce the size and cost of projects with its DLP technology so the company began developing it for the business and educational projector market. The first array of micromirrors was equivalent to 512 pixels. When the mirrors were tilted toward the light, they were in the "on" position and reflected the light through the projection lens to create an image on a screen. Light hitting mirrors in the "off" position was reflected away from the projection lens and into a light absorber. The mirrors were capable of switching on and off thousands of times per second. This technology was called DLP.

In 1993 the Digital Imaging Division was formed to focus on commercializing the DLP technology. A key design improvement moved the hinges under the mirrors, which allowed a smaller gap between mirrors. Each rectangular array could have up to two million mirrors, each one measuring less than one-fifth the width of human hair. To create color, the light source first shone through a spinning wheel with filters of red, green, and blue to create 16.7 million colors.

The division began demonstrating its prototype projector in 1994 and signed its first customer contracts for the production of projectors by InFocus, nView, and Proxima the following year. Texas Instruments initially provided the DLP technology as a complete digital light engine to the projector manufacturers, which began shipping units in 1996. The Infocus LP610 weighed 24 pounds, but the InFocus LP420 released a year later weighed just 6 pounds. This more compact projector was brighter and achieved a resolution of 800-by-600 pixels.

DLP IN CINEMA PROJECTORS

The digital imaging division was also working on a three-chip projection system for use in a large venue. Rather than using a spinning wheel to create color, a separate DMD chip was dedicated to red, blue, or green. A prism split the light into the three colors and directed it toward the appropriate DMD chip. The reflected light combined in different proportions to produce the desired color in the projected image. In addition to increasing the range to 35 trillion colors, more light was reflected off the three DMD chips to create a brighter image on the screen.

In February 1997 DLP was established as the technology used to project onto the screens at the Academy Awards, an entertainment awards show. Texas Instruments began working with the Digital Cinema Initiative (DCI), a consortium of six major Hollywood studios, to develop projectors that would meet the standards established for digital cinema. Storing movies digitally on a server would greatly improve the quality of the projected image. There would no longer be issues with the film jumping or degradation of color and quality over time. DLP Cinema projectors were used for the first time at the premiere of *StarWars: Episode I—The Phantom Menace* in 1999.

DLP EXPANDS INTO HDTVS

In January 2002 the first DLP HDTV, manufactured by Samsung, hit the marketplace at a price of US$4,000. RCA Corporation joined the DLP HDTV business in August of that year. Texas Instruments continued to obtain contracts with other leading HDTV makers, including LG Electronics Inc. and Toshiba Corp. These HDTVs used rear-projection technology; therefore, they were too thick to hang on a wall. However, DLP had a competitive advantage over LCD or plasma in large-screen TVs in that they cost about half as much.

Entrance into the HDTV market dramatically stimulated sales, and the company sold three million DLP systems in only a year (making it five million since 1996). DLP had captured an estimated 28 percent of the large-screen HDTV market, with DLP sales peaking at US$920 million in 2004. Approximately 16 percent of HDTVs had DLP chips in them. In August 2005, Mitsubishi Corp. became the first manufacturer to begin shipping 1080p DLP HDTVs (with a resolution of 1,920-by-1,080). By the end of the year, Texas Instruments had additional contracts with Hewlett-Packard Company (HP), Samsung, and Toshiba. DLP was the number one technology for 1080p HDTVs.

Texas Instruments also announced its new BrilliantColor technology. It added yellow, cyan (aqua), and magenta (pink) to the spinning color wheel to project more colors than were available with LCD technology. The result achieved colors that were up to 50 percent brighter, had better color saturation, and had a more realistic image. The company introduced BrilliantColor in chip sets for 720p and 1080p HDTVs. BrilliantColor was also used in some high-end models of home theater projectors.

IMPROVEMENTS IN DLP PROJECTORS

Developments continued for DLP projector technology throughout 2005. Hewlett-Packard Company and Tandy

Corporation (Radio Shack), among other companies, introduced home entertainment projectors that included sound and a DVD player in single consumer-friendly units. A new category of pico projectors, or handheld projectors, weighing less than one pound were launched by Mitsubishi Group, Samsung Group, and Toshiba Corporation. By the beginning of 2006, DLP technology had succeeded in obtaining at least a 50 percent market share of the front-projection market once dominated by 3LCD technology.

Texas Instruments continued to make strides with its three-chip DLP technology, which was incorporated into the first 1080p projectors for home entertainment in 2006. DLP Cinema projectors continued to experience growth, with the number of DLP projectors in cinemas worldwide exceeding 3,000 by the end of the year. Texas Instruments reached a milestone of 10 million DLP systems shipped by the technology's 10-year anniversary. At this time, DLP was used in 350 front-projector models and more than 100 HDTV models.

REAR-PROJECTION HDTV MARKET

While the DLP projector business was doing well, the rear-projection HDTV market, which had greatly contributed to the technology's growth in 2004, was drying up. Advances were being made in flat-panel LCD TVs that led to plummeting prices, and DLP technology was quickly losing its price advantage in the large-size TV market. When rear-projection TV sales in the United States fell from 3.1 million in 2006 to 1.6 million units in 2007, it was clear that consumers' preferences had shifted away from rear-projection TVs.

Consequently, Sony Corporation and Royal Philips Electronics were among the first TV makers to announce they were dropping rear-projection TVs from their product lines. This shift in demand caused Texas Instruments' DLP revenue to drop from a high of US$920 million in 2004 to US$635 million in 2009. Mitsubishi was one of the few companies that continued to make DLP HDTVs.

DLP'S RENEWED GROWTH

In 2008 Texas Instruments enhanced the capability of its large-venue projectors with the introduction of the world's first WUXGA DLP chip, which had a resolution of 1,920-by-1,200 pixels. The rise in popularity of 3D movies had fueled the implementation of DLP Cinema projectors, which had doubled over the previous two years to 6,000 installations worldwide.

In June 2009 Texas Instruments began demonstrating prototypes for a new lamp-free LED projector and the first 3D front projector. The 3D projector worked by project-

ing a separate image for the left and right eye, which were then combined using 3D glasses. Several manufacturers began offering these 3D-ready projectors, which were targeted at the education market as a way to help engage students and improve test scores. The ability to project either a 2D or 3D image from a single projector was a new competitive advantage over LCD.

After Texas Instruments released its DLP Pico Projector Development Kit at the beginning of 2009, pico projectors began to experience explosive growth. Pico projectors were small enough to fit in a pocket or could be embedded into a cell phone, but were capable of projecting up to a 50-inch-diagonal image on a wall. A pico projector made it easy for anyone to share photos, movies, video games, or any other images. Nearly one million pico projectors with DLP technology shipped in 2010.

The concept of using microscopic mirrors to reflect light was a remarkable innovation, but the real success story was in the development and commercialization of DLP. After persevering through the decline of rear-projection TVs, DLP reinvented itself with advancements that were better poised to steal market share from LCD projectors. In 2010 DLP sales rose to US$790 million, the most significant growth in six years.

BIBLIOGRAPHY

Bouchaud, Jeremie. "DLP Revival Returns Texas Instruments to MEMS Market Leadership in 2010." El Segundo, CA: IHS iSuppli, April 5, 2011. Accessed January 31, 2012. http://www.isuppli.com/MEMS-and-Sensors/News/Pages/DLP-Revival-Returns-Texas-Instruments-to-MEMS-Market-Leadership-in-2010.aspx.

DLP Technology. "DLP History." Cincinnati, OH, 2009. Accessed January 31, 2012. http://www.dlp.com/technology/dlp-history/default.aspx.

———. "How DLP Technology Works." Cincinnati, OH. Accessed January 31, 2012. http://www.dlp.com/technology/how-dlp-works/default.aspx.

Johnson, R. Colin. "TI Fellow on DLP: We Did It with Mirrors." *EE Times,* January 29, 2007. Accessed January 31, 2012. http://eetimes.com/electronics-news/4069251/TI-fellow-on-DLP-We-did-it-with-mirrors.

Kanellos, Michael. "Texas Instruments Revs Up TV, Theater." *CNET,* January 10, 2005. Accessed January 31, 2012. http://news.cnet.com/Texas-Instruments-revs-up-TV%2C-theater/2100-1047_3-5519902.html.

Park, Andrew. "Texas Instruments Inside?" *Bloomberg Businessweek,* December 6, 2004. Accessed January 31, 2012. http://www.businessweek.com/magazine/content/04_49/b3911045_mz011.htm.

Perenson, Melissa J. "Texas Instruments Boosts DLP Color Processing." *PC World,* June 20, 2007. Accessed January 31, 2012. http://www.pcworld.com/article/133207/texas_instruments_boosts_dlp_color_processing.html.

Seiko Epson Corporation. "Epson Projector Marks Twentieth Anniversary." Suwa, Nagano, Japan, 2009. Accessed January

31, 2012. http://global.epson.com/company/corporate
_history/epson_story/pdf/EpsonStory03E.pdf.

Shim, Richard. "TI Ships 5 Millionth DLP System." *CNET,*

December 5, 2004. Accessed January 31, 2012. http://news
.cnet.com/TI-ships-5-millionth-DLP-system/2100-1041_3
-5492775.html?tag=mncol.

Thermos: From Scientific Invention to Insulated Container Brand

Thermos has become known as the brand name of a vacuum-insulated bottle equally useful for keeping liquids (such as soups or beverages) either hot or cold. However, it was not originally invented with this intent in mind. It was originally invented by a British scientist for storing and keeping liquefied gases at a constant temperature. A glassblower in Germany saw an opportunity to use the concept in insulated flasks and named the product Thermos. Several companies began producing Thermos beverage bottles, and the product line was soon expanded to other types of insulated containers. The original glass-lined containers were adapted and replaced with more durable stainless steel. These products include bottles, mugs, and tumblers for beverages, food jars, and carafes and pump pots for serving hot beverages. The company has also enjoyed success producing and marketing lunchboxes and coolers.

THE INVENTION OF A VACUUM-INSULATED FLASK

The invention of a vacuum-insulated container depended on the long road toward liquefying gases. The French scientist Gaspard Monge liquefied sulfur dioxide in 1784, but little headway was made toward liquefying other gases until Michael Faraday stumbled on a way to liquefy chlorine in 1823. Faraday used a similar method to liquefy other gases. However, oxygen, hydrogen, and helium were among the gasses he was unable to liquefy under pressure, due to a lower "critical temperature" (the point at which the gas turned into a liquid).

Two scientists were independently working on the problem of liquefying oxygen by using other liquefied gases to cool it below its critical temperature. The French physicist Louis Cailletet and the Swiss chemist Raoul Pictet were successful in liquefying oxygen around the same time, in 1877. Cailletet used similar methods to liquefy nitrogen and carbon monoxide, but hydrogen and helium were still considered to be "permanent" gases.

Also in the 1870s, James Dewar was a gifted chemist who had been appointed as a professor of chemistry at the Royal Institution in London, England at the age of 35. Dewar began studying the properties of liquefied gases. Since liquefying gases was a time-consuming process, he wanted a container that would keep the gases at a constant cold temperature for a longer period. Dewar had used a double-walled vacuum calorimeter (used to measure the heat from chemical reactions or change in the state of matter) made of brass in the early 1870s and modified that concept.

The first design consisted of a double-walled vessel made of glass. Dewar used a pump to evacuate most of the air out of the narrow gap between the walls to create a vacuum. The cold liquid gas was placed in the container and the opening covered. Without many air molecules, there was very little heat transfer, and the liquid gas remained at a constant temperature. Later, the glass flasks were coated with mercury to block heat transfer through thermal radiation. This design, which became known as the Dewar Flask, was first shown in public in 1893. The vacuum was also improved by the addition of a bit of charcoal to absorb any remaining gas in the gap. The Dewar Flask helped James Dewar to liquefy hydrogen successfully in 1898.

THE COMMERCIALIZATION OF THE THERMOS BRAND

Glassware used in scientific laboratories was made by glassblowers. After a German glassblower discovered the

Dewar Flask kept his baby's milk warm for hours, he and his partner decided to patent and commercialize the product in 1904. The glass-insulated liner was encased in aluminum, and the bottle had an aluminum screw-on cap. Dewar filed a lawsuit against Thermos GmbH and lost.

William B. Walker licensed the production and marketing of the Thermos brand in the United States in 1907 and formed the American Thermos Bottle Company. At the same time, the German company sold trademark rights to Thermos Limited in England and Canadian Thermos Bottle Company Ltd. in Montreal, Canada. Walker imported vacuum-insulated bottles from Germany until his plant in Brooklyn, New York began operating. In 1908 the company began a U.S. advertising campaign in the *Saturday Evening Post*. One advertisement featured a family using the Thermos Bottle on a picnic and guaranteed to keep beverages cold for three days or hot for 24 hours.

Walker's clever marketing strategies, such as a car in the shape of a Thermos bottle in a New York City parade and at the Vanderbilt Cup races on Long Island, New York, helped Thermos gain visibility with locals. By 1909 Walker had established a network of 30,000 dealers. Thermos gained international exposure through its appearance at eight world expositions. Apparently no notable polar exhibition was complete without a Thermos, as Ernest Shackleton had one on his journey to the South Pole, and Robert E. Peary had one on his successful journey to the Arctic in 1909.

The Thermos Bottle was particularly popular with construction workers and other outdoor laborers. The Thermos Jug was a pitcher with a lid, and the Water Can had a handle like a pail for keeping boiling water hot for hours. They were available with either nickel or silver plating on the outside. The Thermetot was a nickel-plated jar for keeping food hot. All products were available in pint and quart sizes.

THERMOS BECOMES A HOUSEHOLD NAME

By 1910 sales exceeded US$381,000, and the company moved to larger production facilities in Chelsea, in New York City. The following year, Thermos began to produce machine-made glass fillers. The company built a new plant in Norwich, Connecticut, in 1912 and relocated its corporate headquarters there.

By the time other companies entered the vacuum bottle market, the word "thermos" had become a generic term for any insulated bottle. After Walker's death in 1922, the family's interest was sold to a group of investors. Annual revenues were approaching US$1.5 million at this time. The influx of capital allowed Thermos to add a 24-pint "Blue Bottle" and a gallon-sized insulated food jar known as the Thermos Jumbo Jug to its product line.

After acquiring Thermos Limited of London in 1920, the American Thermos Bottle Company purchased Icy Hot Bottle Company in 1925 and Keapsit Company in 1929. However, with the start of World War II in 1939, Thermos Limited produced insulated flasks for the British troops. The American Thermos Bottle Company's efforts were also refocused on the U.S. military. When the war ended in 1945, the popularity of Thermos products resumed, and sales exceeded US$5 million. In 1946 a second plant was built in Norwich, Connecticut.

THE LUNCHBOX BUSINESS

In 1950 Aladdin Industries Inc. introduced the first character-theme lunchbox. Baked-on enamel in red or blue covered the steel lunchbox, which had a picture of the fictional cowboy character Hopalong Cassidy on the front. The company sold half a million units in the first year. The accompanying half-pint vacuum bottle featured Hopalong Cassidy and his horse. In 1953 Thermos followed suit with its first character lunchbox and Thermos bottle. In the first year, the company sold over two million fully lithographed lunchboxes and accompanying Thermos bottle, featuring Western movie star Roy Rogers. Roy Rogers' horse Trigger even got his own lunchbox.

The company also diversified by acquiring companies that produced complementary insulated products as well as outdoor grills. To better reflect the company's diversification, American Thermos Products Company and Canadian Thermos Products Limited were adopted as new company names in 1956. Operations at a new plant in Anaheim, California, began in 1958. By the end of the 1950s, sales reached US$13 million. In 1960 both companies were acquired by King-Seeley, a supplier of cooking appliance controls and timers. The two companies were renamed as the Thermos Division of King-Seeley Thermos Company.

The legality of using "thermos" as a generic term for vacuum bottles was made official by a judge in 1962. Thermos had filed a patent-infringement against Aladdin four years prior. The judge ruled that Aladdin could proceed with using the term "thermos bottles" in lowercase for its vacuum bottles. In 1966 Thermos began producing the world's first stainless-steel vacuum bottle.

The company continued to license characters like Looney Tunes in 1959 and Barbie in 1962. Many licensed themes were of children's television shows, such as *Lost in Space* in 1967 and *The Brady Bunch* in 1970. The Harlem Globetrotters were featured on a Thermos lunchbox in 1971. Sometimes the metal was embossed to add a three-dimensional effect to the characters on lunchboxes. In the early 1970s glass-insulated lunchbox Thermos were replaced with more durable plastic Thermoses with foam insulation.

Lunchbox sales increased dramatically in 1982, "after the U.S. Congress cut subsidies for school lunch programs and tightened eligibility requirements for reduced-price and free meals," according to N. R. Kleinfield in the August 6, 1989 *New York Times*. Molded plastic lunchboxes began to replace the metal ones, which cost more to produce. When metal lunchboxes were completely phased out in 1987, Thermos and Aladdin were each offering about 20 themes a year. A few soft-sided lunch boxes with foam insulation and a zipper closure began to appear at this time and would eventually overtake plastic lunchboxes.

REFOCUS ON STAINLESS-STEEL BOTTLES

The King-Seeley Thermos Company was acquired by Household Finance Corporation in 1968. Within three years, Thermos products were being exported to more than 100 countries. In 1982 Household consolidated its Thermos and Structo (a manufacturer of outdoor grills) operations as Household Manufacturing. In 1984 the original Thermos plant in Norwich, Connecticut, and the plant in Anaheim, California were shut down. Although more expensive, the indestructible nature of stainless steel completely overtook the glass-insulated market. After the remaining glass manufacturing plant in Norwich, Connecticut was closed in 1986, the Thermos division was relocated and the company name became the Thermos Company.

In 1989 the Thermos Company (then operating in Australia, Canada, the United States, and the United Kingdom) was sold to Nippon Sanso Corporation of Japan, a manufacturer of industrial gases, for US$134 million. At this time, Nippon Sanso's subsidiary Nissan Thermo K.K. was manufacturing its own stainless-steel thermoses under the Nissan brand. To take advantage of the Thermos brand, Nissan products were rebranded as Thermos Nissan. In October 2001 Nippon Sanso merged the Thermos Division with Nissan Thermo K.K. and spun it off as Thermos K.K.

STAINLESS-STEEL SALES SWELL

The concern over the chemical compound bisphenol A (BPA), used to make clear plastic baby bottles and beverage bottles, helped to fuel sales of stainless-steel bottles. The U.S. Centers for Disease Control and Prevention had conducted a study from 2003 to 2004 and found detectable amounts of BPA in the urine of all 2,517 participants. In 2008 the National Toxicology Program Center for the Evaluation of Risks to Human Reproduction released the results of a study to determine the health effects of BPA (as reported by the U.S. Food and Drug Administration). The study found "some concern for effects on the brain, behavior, and prostate gland in fetuses, infants, and children at current human exposures to bisphenol A."

Thermos had already responded to parents' concern over BPA by introducing its Foogo line of BPA-free products for infants in 2007. The sippy cup, hydration bottle, and food jar were made with a stainless-steel, vacuum-insulated container and were BPA-free. Foogo sales dramatically increased over the first year, and parents were also turning to Thermos stainless-steel water bottles in droves for older children.

The Intak hydration bottle was another BPA-free product targeted at school-age children. The stainless-steel bottle had a single-wall construction for a more attractive price. The outside of the bottle was imprinted with temperature-sensitive ink, so the design changed after chilled water was added. In September 2008 Thermos added a BPA-free, all-plastic water bottle to its Intak product line. The new 24-ounce bottle targeted at adults had a stylish, ergonomic design.

THE NEW FACE OF THERMOS

As of 2011 the product lineup consisted of Thermos brand and the premium Thermos Nissan brand made with 18/8 stainless steel. Many of the beverage bottles for adults and children featured a push-button lid with a pop-up silicon straw. Stainless-steel travel mugs and tumblers were expanded into 30 different products, ranging from 14- to 18-ounce sizes, and an array of color choices. Food jars were also big business. The company offered about 30 different sizes and options plus numerous character themes in the 10-ounce FUNtainer Food Jar for kids. The company continued to make a few glass-insulated beverage bottles and food jars in a variety of colors. The company also offered about a dozen vacuum-insulated carafes and pump pots for serving hot beverages.

BIBLIOGRAPHY

Calafat, Antonia M., Xiaoyun Ye, Lee-Yang Wong, John A. Reidy, and Larry L. Needham. "Exposure of the U.S. Population to Bisphenol A and 4-tertiary-Octylphenol: 2003–2004." *Environmental Health Perspectives* 116, no. 1 (January 2008). Accessed February 4, 2012. http://ehp03 .niehs.nih.gov/article/fetchArticle.action?articleURI=info:doi /10.1289/ehp.10753.

"Classic Kit: Dewar's Flask." *Chemistry World*, August 2008. Accessed February 4, 2012. http://www.rsc.org/chemistry world/Issues/2008/August/DewarsFlask.asp.

"Dewar, James." In *Chemistry: Foundations and Applications*, edited by J. J. Lagowski. Vol. 2, 11–12. New York: Macmillan Reference USA, 2004. Gale Virtual Reference Library (GALE|CX3400900157). Accessed February 4, 2012. http:// go.galegroup.com/ps/i.do?id=GALE%7CCX3400900157&v =2.1&u=itsbtrial&it=r&p=GVRL&sw=w.

Gay, Hannah. "Technical Assistance in the World of London Science: 1850–1900." *Notes & Records of the Royal Society* 62, no. 1 (March 2008): 51–75. Accessed February 4, 2012. http://rsnr.royalsocietypublishing.org/content/62/1/51.full.

Kleinfield, N. R. "Another August Under the 'Whine Sign'." *New York Times,* August 6, 1989. Accessed February 4, 2012. http://www.nytimes.com/1989/08/06/business/another-august-under-the-whine-sign.html?pagewanted=1.

Oswald, Alison L. "Aladdin Industries Inc. Records, 1889–2003." Washington, DC: Archives Center, National Museum of American History, December 2003. Accessed February 4, 2012. http://www.americanhistory.si.edu/archives/d8844.htm.

Prince, Mark. "Thermos Nissan Review–Nissan Product Review." *CoffeeGeek.com,* June 1, 2004. Accessed February 4, 2012. http://www.coffeegeek.com/proreviews/detailed/thermos nissan/overview.

Smith, Tima. "Thermos Company Collection." Storrs, CT: Archives & Special Collections at the Thomas J. Dodd Research Center, June 2002. Accessed February 4, 2012. http://doddcenter.uconn.edu/asc/findaids/Thermos/MSS19890098.html.

"The Thermos Building, Keeping It Hot (and Cool) in Chelsea." *The Bowery Boys New York City History,* December 2, 2011. Accessed February 4, 2012. http://theboweryboys.blogspot.com/2011/12/thermos-building-keeping-it-hot-and.html.

"Thermos Company." In *International Directory of Company Histories,* edited by Tina Grant. Vol. 16, 486–488. Detroit: St. James Press, 1997. Gale Virtual Reference Library (GALE|CX2842000150). Accessed February 4, 2012. http://go.galegroup.com/ps/i.do?id=GALE%7CCX2842000150&v=2.1&u=itsbtrial&it=r&p=GVRL&sw=w.

Thermos LLC. "Lunch Kits." Schaumburg, IL, 2007. Accessed February 4, 2012. http://www.thermos.com/lunchbox/.

———. "Our History." Schaumburg, IL, 2004. Accessed February 4, 2012. http://www.thermos.com/history.aspx.

U.S. Food and Drug Administration. "Update on Bisphenol A for Use in Food Contact Applications." Washington, DC, January 2010. Accessed February 4, 2012. http://www.fda.gov/NewsEvents/PublicHealthFocus/ucm197739.htm.

Timberland Company:
Made the Duck Boot Better

DEVELOPING THE DUCK BOOT: THE ORIGINS OF TIMBERLAND

The duck boot is highly distinctive, with its leather or fabric top, usually equipped with a full set of laces, and its rubber base guarding the bottom of the shoe from the ankle to the sole. The history of the duck boot did not start with the Timberland Company, although Timberland played a key role in making the duck boot practical and popular. The origins of the waterproof footwear actually can be dated to the 19th century, when footwear companies began experimenting with more useful water-repellent shoes.

Wellingtons (rubber boots based on leather Hessian boots), the forerunners of all rubber shoes, had been in existence since the 18th century, thanks to an early understanding of the waterproofing properties of rubber. Production techniques improved in the 19th century and increased the popularity of Wellington boots, but the boots were made primarily of rubber and were often ill-fitting and subject to decay. In addition, the rubberized textiles were often too uncomfortable to wear in any but the wettest conditions.

Duck boots bridged the gap between rubber clothes and common fabrics by combining the two. With a fabric top, including laces, the boots could fit feet more easily and be tightened or loosened at will. With the rubber base, the boots resisted soaking upwater from puddles, mud, or snow. Timberland did not have much to do with the original design of duck boots, which were named for duck cloth canvas. The boots were created by long-time competitor Leon Leonwood (L.L.) Bean himself. L.L. Bean fashioned the boots out of leather and rubber in 1912 to sell to hunters in Maine.

L.L. Bean Incorporated's first line of duck boots were not successful. Almost every customer returned the boots because of problems due to faulty design. Although Bean eventually developed a more commercially successful version, duck boots still had issues that outdoor lovers had to accept. The rubber was joined to the top of the boot through stitching. Stitching required holes which were located at the very place where water protection was needed most. As a result, duck boots made in this fashion could leak through the stitches or could quickly crack if the stitching was damaged.

While L.L. Bean and other shoe companies struggled with this problem, a shoe store in Massachusetts, Abington Shoe Company, incorporated in 1933. The shoe store stayed small and local for nearly 20 years, until Nathan Swartz bought half of the interest in the store in 1952. Swartz worked as a stitcher by trade and understood the problems inherent in duck boots. After three years he purchased Abington Shoe Company and hired his sons to work with him. Having started his shoemaking career in Boston, Massachusetts before achieving recognition throughout New England, Swartz was well placed to find a solution for the hybrid boot problem.

WHAT WATERPROOF REALLY MEANS

Innovation came to the Swartz family thanks to the strides made in manufacturing technology. After World War II, dozens of inventions made and processes learned in the war began making their way into commercial markets. One of the greatest impacts proved to be plastics and the processes used to manufacture plastic products. Research eventually spread the use of injection molding to produce a high number of units quickly.

Injection molding solved several problems with which plastic factories had been struggling. A series of identical molds rotated past an injection machine. The machine would pump a precise amount of molten plastic into each mold, where the plastic would set. By altering the process slightly, factories could create plastic products of many sizes, including difficult bottle and cup shapes.

As the injection-molding technique became widely accepted, it caught the eye of the Swartz family. Shoes had been made using molds for hundreds of years, so the concept of working with tailored molds was a familiar one. The process used for plastic worked just as easily with rubber, so switching materials posed no problems.

After 10 years of full ownership in Abington Shoe Company, the Swartz family began producing boots and shoes using this injection-molding process. It was a revolutionary step not practiced by any other shoe company. By extruding the bottom part of the duck boot, Swartz could effectively fuse the rubber sole to the leather top without needing stitches. No stitches meant no chance of leaks or gradual deterioration. The duck boot Swartz began to sell was an entirely different product, the first truly waterproof hybrid shoe on the market. Swartz immediately capitalized on this fact, producing other shoe lines the same way and with advertising that emphasized the waterproof features.

After a few years, the new production techniques paid off. Boot sales rose, and Swartz worked on a branding strategy, giving his boots the name Timberland in 1973. Through further marketing work, the Timberland name became associated with truly waterproof duck boots. Swartz began the tradition of harsh testing to prove water could not enter the boot, famously leaving it in a toilet overnight to ensure the fusion process was working properly. In 1976 the company produced the six-inch premium Waterproof Boot in wheat color. This particular model became so popular that the other lines revolved around it. Consumers naturally linked the style and color of the boot with Timberland, and sales quickly rose. The company would manufacture the same boot, product number unchanged, for more than 30 years.

Swartz had crafted a winning formula with his injection-molding process. Abington became well known for both its waterproof lines and the quality of its hand-sewn shoes. The family decided to transform the successful brand into a successful company. They changed the name of the shoe store to The Timberland Company in 1978, the same year it started manufacturing hand-sewn casual shoes in addition to its more outdoor-oriented products.

THE BOOT CRAZE

If the 1970s were good years for Timberland, the 1980s were transformational. Before that time, Timberland and rivals like L.L. Bean, Inc., had made a profit primarily by selling utility boots designed for protection and durability instead of style. This was one major reason the injection-molding process was such an important breakthrough. To customers, waterproofing was the chief, sometimes only, reason to purchase duck boots. However, as the 1970s waned, a change took place.

Distinctions between utilitarian shoes and shoes purchased for style and casual use started to blur. In previous generations, expanding more fully into the casual shoe market would have been a dangerous move, but Timberland chose expansion at the right time. Consumers started flocking to the company for casual shoes as well as boots, and Swartz made sure core product lines received attention, too, introducing a boating shoe in 1979. The next year, Timberland took its first jump into international sales, shipping shoes to Italy. This was the first in a line of exports to countries throughout Europe and Asia, providing some of the strongest long-term sales for Timberland.

The 1980s were also an important time for Timberland internally. By 1985 the manufacturer had sold more than one million classic duck boots. In 1986 Nathan Swartz stepped down from his leadership position and his son Sydney took charge of the company, becoming sole proprietor of the business. Sole ownership only lasted for a year, however, before Timberland went public on the American Stock Exchange to raise capital. The timing coincided with the first Timberland advertisements for shoes on U.S. television, which featured the classic duck boot.

The Swartz family began planning again, this time with an eye on expansion into dedicated retail stores. The first retail store opened in Newport, Rhode Island, in 1986, close to the time Timberland began manufacturing a version of the classic duck boot for women, which the company aggressively advertised. With styles available for both men and women, the classic boot swiftly became the number one seller in the retail store.

NOT JUST FOOTWEAR

The opening of the Newport store was the beginning of Timberland's worldwide expansion that eventually saw more than 700 retail stores open across the world. At the start, however, the company understood that selling only shoes and boots in retail stores would be a missed opportunity, despite growing lines that including hiking boots and professional sled dog racing books. Therefore, the company expanded not only into storefronts, but also into apparel. In the late 1980s Timberland introduced a line of clothing for men to complement its boots. It followed this in the early 1990s by releasing apparel options for women as well as waterproof leather outerwear and accessories for a variety of activities.

Timberland repeated the strategy it had used with boots to promote its clothing products, focusing on the qualities that had made the company famous, including waterproof abilities and practicality. This appealed to consumers looking for trustworthy outdoor gear, making the enterprise profitable enough to continue growing.

The company continued to be successful in the 1990s as the craze in Italy over Timberland boots during the previous decade was repeated in the urban United States. The rugged Timberland had become a full-fledged style, including backpacks, purses, watches, and shoes for kids. The change in trends toward Timberland was not entirely unusual. After all, in the 1930s U.S. consumers fell in love with the canvas-style boots baseball players wore. In the 1950s motorcyclist boots caught the attention of customers across the nation. Timberland and its duck boots caught the interest of the United States consumer in the same way. The store had help too, when notable rappers (a type of singer) of the day started wearing Timberland boots and included references to them in their songs, a sure sign of cultural success in the 1990s. The shoes even made it onto popular television sitcoms in the United States.

In 1998 the Timberland Company celebrated its 25th anniversary. Buoyed by continued success, the next generation of the Swartz family took the helm, with Jeffrey Swartz (son of Sydney) moving from his COO position to CEO and president of the company.

TIMBERLAND AND RESPONSIBILITY: SOCIAL LEGACY

By the late 1990s Timberland was doing more than making waterproof shoes. It also started winning awards, placing in several lists of the 100 best companies to work for and winning a place in the 100 Best Corporate Citizens list as well as the Corporate Citizenship Award from the Business Ethics Corporate Social Responsibility Report. Social responsibility had been a distinguishing feature of the company since the 1980s when it first started working with the "urban Peace Corps" movement in Boston, Massachusetts donating shoes and helping the movement expand into 13 different cities.

Soon Timberland was fostering a reputation for social ethics alongside its famed waterproof brand. The Swartz family decided their brand could represent more than a waterproofing improvement and the duck boot style. Within a decade, the name Timberland became synonymous with a number of charities and social projects, from the Give Racism the Boot awareness campaign to the annual Serv-A-Palooza, first held in 1998 (the same year Timberland reached 40,000 total hours given to community aid). Timberland projects fell under the collective Path of Service program, which encouraged employees to become involved in community service by offering them paid leave for service projects.

Timberland thrived under the dual identity of stylish outdoor gear and community involvement. From donations for New York rescue workers who helped the victims of the September 11, 2001, terrorist attacks against the United States, to a Save Darfur product launch to promote awareness of the crisis in Darfur, Sudan, the company continued to garner respect for its efforts on an international level. As 2010 approached the company began an extensive campaign to reduce its carbon emissions, using LED lighting and energy reclamation technology. Timberland also began releasing shoes made with recycled rubber, reused lining materials, and organic cotton, accessing a growing environmentally conscious market it had already been winning over for years.

Work with the classic duck boot also continued. Timberland experimented with climate-control linings, removable orthotic insoles, and a choice of outer moldings so customers could pick a focus on gripping ability, density, or overall traction.

FUTURE BOOTS, CLASSIC IMPROVEMENTS

By 2007 Timberland had appeared on the 100 Best Companies to Work For list in *Fortune* magazine for 10 consecutive years. It had also placed in the 100 Best Corporate Citizens list for eight years. Other awards, commendations, and nominations followed for work in community service, sustainability, and workplace environment. By 2008 the company was generating US$1.36 billion in revenues.

Despite the decades of success, Timberland did not forget the tenets that made it an award-winning company in the first place. In 2009 the company reinvented the shoe mold-making process once again by investing in digital shape sampling and processing (DSSP). In the past, shoe companies used more than 100 molds per year to create major product lines, throwing away old molds as shoe lines became outdated or molds wore out. DSSP allowed Timberland to create digital models of shoes using a three-dimensional scanner. This digital mold could then be moved between software programs until it was used to construct a new shoe. This process not only saved considerable time and expense usually spent on molds, but also allowed for easier customization, better shoe design, and instant overseas transfer of new product information.

It was this long-lasting understanding of its brand and well-timed strategic shifts that made Timberland such a successful business. The Swartz family closely observed the market, making quick moves forward within core competencies when the time was right. This effective strategy preserved the strength of the Timberland brand for decades, reinvigorating it with new technologies and policies when necessary. The brand was helped by the jump to high-quality duck boots, which Timberland made before any of its competitors tried similar technology.

In 2011 Timberland arranged its own sale to V.F. Corporation, an apparel giant that already owned such notable brands as Wrangler and The North Face. The deal was made for US$2 billion, at a 40 percent premium for the Timberland shares, which had never been selling higher. While in the early 2010s the future of the Timberland brand was uncertain, the legacy the company has established cannot be doubted.

BIBLIOGRAPHY

Cramblitt, Bob. "Using DSSP to Reinvent Footwear Manufacturing." *Mold Making Technology,* January 1, 2009. Accessed February 3, 2012. http://www.moldmakingtechnology.com/articles/using-dssp-to-reinvent-footwear-manufacturing.

"Duck Boots: Go Anywhere in Them. " *The Snow Boots.* Accessed February 3, 2012. http://thesnowboots.org/duck-boots/.

Nelson, Debra L., and James Campbell Quick. *Organizational Behavior: Science, The Real World, and You.* 6th ed. Mason, OH: South-Western Cengage Learning, 2010, 72–73.

Primack, Dan. "Can Timberland Get a Better Deal?" *CNNMoney,* June 13, 2011. Accessed February 3, 2012. http://finance.fortune.cnn.com/2011/06/13/can-timberland-get-a-better-deal/.

Swartz, Jeff. "Endings and Beginnings." *The Bootmakers Blog,* September 13, 2011. Accessed February 3, 2012. http://blog.timberland.com/category/jeff-swartz/.

"Timberland Boots." *Hiking Beginner,* 2012. Accessed February 3, 2012. http://www.hikingbeginner.com/Timberland_Boots.html.

Timberland Company. "Our History. " Stratham, NH, 2011. Accessed February 3, 2012. http://www.timberlandonline.co.uk/on/demandware.store/Sites-TBLGB-Site/default/Page-Show?cid=about_timberland_corporate_timeline .

———. "The Timberland Premium Waterproof Boot: History of a Classic." Stratham, NH, 2011. Accessed February 3, 2012. http://www.timberland.com/category/index.jsp?categoryId=4089424.

———. "Timberland Responsibility." Stratham, NH, 2012. Accessed February 3, 2012. http://responsibility.timberland.com/climate/reducing-impact-benefits-bottom-line/.

Toyota Prius: The World's First Mass-Produced Hybrid Vehicle

It is hard to believe that electric vehicles have been around since the 1880s, but using electric motors to propel cars really is a very old concept. Yet to the Toyota Motor Corporation's credit, many new ideas went into creating the world's first commercially produced hybrid model car, the Prius. Wildly successful, this model celebrated its 15th anniversary in 2012 and has been shipped to 80 countries. By March 2011, sales had topped three million units.

Although other hybrid cars have existed before and since, none have achieved the same iconic status as the Prius, which has nearly become synonymous with the term "hybrid." While some of this fame is undoubtedly due in part to a very active, hard-working marketing department at Toyota, the fact remains that the company produced a long-awaited product that does what the company says it can do at a reasonable cost, and is durable and reliable too. By some accounts, including a 2011 Clean Fleet Report, 97 percent of all Prius cars were still on the road since their North American debut in 2000. With gasoline prices continually causing concerns for consumers, the impressive, ever-improving fuel economy of the Prius model has also been a major factor contributing to the acclaim that the vehicle has received. The estimated fuel economy of its 2012 model plug-in hybrid was 50 miles per gallon (MPG), far higher than that of any other hybrid model or manufacturer, according to a 2012 survey by the U.S. Department of Energy.

Toyota first released the Prius domestically in Japan in late 1997. This first generation of hybrid was a compact four-door sedan, the format changing to a hatchback style in the second- and third-generation models. The world had to wait two years for the official global launch of an export model Prius, but when it finally occurred in the year 2000, the United States rapidly became the largest market for the cars. Fuelled by its success with the Prius, Toyota expanded its hybrid car lineup to include other models like the Camry, Highlander, and even its luxury class Lexus vehicles, including the CT 200h, HS 250h, and RX 450h. For fuel economy and popularity, however, none could top the Prius.

21ST CENTURY CARS

Several key people at Toyota are generally credited with having dramatically shaped and influenced the development of the Prius. From the top down, the Toyoda family, which has led the Japanese auto manufacturer since its inception in 1937, saw company chairman Eiji Toyoda share his vision of cars in the 21st century, which focused on the concern over gasoline prices and protection of the environment.

Concurrently, Toyota had also released its Environmental Action Plan in 1993, which contained the seeds of inspiration for the production of future vehicles that would be more efficient and greener than their predecessors. With this document, along with Toyota's senior executives' concerns about the future of their industry, the board members came together to compile a list of qualities that would characterize the car of the future. This was named the G21 Project. The project included features such as safety, ease of use, demographic appeal factors, low emissions, and much-improved mileage. Vice president of research and development Yoshiro Kimbara's goal was to produce a car that would get 48 miles per gallon or better, a challenge he put to his team. At the time, president Hiroshi Okuda was a driving force behind the Prius's development who insisted that the production timeline of the vehicle be accelerated by a year from its original planned release date.

Takeshi Uchiyamada, the senior engineer among Toyota's ranks who is often given the title "Father of the Hybrid," was charged with the task of making G21 a reality in 1994. During the same year he also became project general manager of Vehicle Development Center 2, the incubator for what would become the Prius project. One of Uchiyamada's first tasks was to recruit 10 of the company's top engineers to work on the G21 Project. These men were in their early 30s and viewed by Toyota as experienced but still young enough to have high flexibility in thought and problem solving.

THE BIRTH OF TOYOTA'S HYBRID

Uchiyamada's team worked for several months to create a proposal for the senior executives, one that would see the production of a small family car that would improve the fuel economy of their already successful and economical Corolla model by 50 percent. Vice president Akihiro Wada, the man who had handpicked Uchiyamada for leading the G21 Project, was unimpressed. He told Uchiyamada that he wanted a 100 percent improvement. This sent the team back to the design tables, where they abandoned the idea of improving on existing drivetrain technologies in favor of something completely new and untested. This was the birth of the hybrid engine concept. Although Toyota had been experimenting with hybrids for some time, it was a very bold move to recommend its inclusion in its next production model car.

During the early years of development, Uchiyamada and his team started looking at different hybrid systems; they considered a host of factors, including issues of noise, heat, reliability, and cost. One significant stumbling block that had prevented not only Toyota but all other manufacturers from releasing a viable hybrid were the high costs involved, not just in development but also in specialized components: a hybrid car would require both a gasoline engine and an electric motor, as well as a way to integrate the two. In the beginning, according to Bonnie Juettner in her book *Hybrid Cars,* the team started with over 80 different engine prototypes. They would run each through computer simulations until they eventually brought the number of prototypes to just four, based mainly on fuel efficiency. From the final four they added technical and cost considerations, which brought them to a single prototype that made its way from the drawing board to being built into an actual, "working" model in the later months of 1995.

The term "working" was actually a misnomer at first. The design team found that even though their computer

kept telling them that the car should work, reality dictated otherwise, and they spent over a month overcoming electrical and software issues trying to get their model to start. They finally succeeded, and not a moment too soon, as they were able to reach their goal of completing the prototype in time for the Tokyo Motor Show. By then, the G21 Project car had been given the name *Prius,* which meant "to go before" in Latin.

PROTOTYPE DIFFICULTIES

The newly created Prius prototype was far from becoming a reality, however. In those early days of development, even though Uchiyamada's team had managed to make the car start and run, they could not get it to go more than a few hundred yards down a test track before the engine died, leaving them stranded. One major problem for the fledgling design was that the large batteries needed to drive the electric motor were prone to shutting down when they were too hot or too cold. According to one Toyota employee, Hideshi Itazaki, quoted in a 2006 *Fortune* article, they had to have someone ride in the vehicle with a laptop, monitoring battery temperatures so that the batteries would not spontaneously burst into flames. Early road tests were limited to about two laps around the track due to the poor performance of the batteries.

By December 1996 company president Okuda was getting restless and he wanted to announce Toyota's new hybrid technology to the world. Uchiyamada and hundreds of engineers were working feverishly, but an operational prototype still eluded them. The team refused to give up, however, and problems were solved one at a time. These solutions were sometimes creative or required outside support, in spite of Toyota's general go-it-alone attitude. In the end, the company decided to enlist the support of Matsushita Electric Industrial Company, Ltd. to help develop the specialized hybrid batteries, in a joint venture that would later allow Toyota the option to sell the technology to other manufacturers.

Another major obstacle to overcome was the production of certain electronic components that were highly specialized and critical in managing the power distribution between the electric motor and the gasoline engine. Even third-party suppliers were unable to satisfy Toyota's requirements adequately. The company was therefore forced to build its own specialized factory for the manufacture of these parts, along with a team of semiconductor engineers to operate the facility.

The body of the Prius was designed in-house, but interestingly, not in Japan. As part of an internal design competition, Japanese designers were pitted against Toyota's U.S.-based design studio in Newport Beach, California. Accustomed to having several months to submit model designs, the designers were shocked to learn that they had only two or three weeks. Erwin Lui and his team settled on a small, four-door sedan design, which top executives back in Japan ultimately adopted as the winning proposal.

Finally, everything came together in October 1997, two months earlier than the expected December completion date. At a total development cost of US$1 billion, Toyota was poised to release the Prius to the Japanese domestic market. Two months later, in December, and in conjunction with an alternative-fuel vehicle show, Toyota held a press release announcing the new Prius, and sales began in earnest the very same month. Originally, the company had envisioned a production rate of 1,000 units per month.

MARKET CONCERNS

Of course, Toyota's executives in the United States were eagerly waiting and watching from the sidelines to see how the vehicle would be received in Japan. Anticipating an eventual arrival into the North American market, everyone within Toyota Motor Sales was nervously considering whether the vehicle would even sell, and how the company would deal with educating both dealers and consumers. Everything from how to sell the vehicle and how to drive it, to servicing and repairs, would have to be reinvented at least to some degree. Feasibility studies and survey results done two years prior had warranted skepticism as it showed U.S. citizens were leery of such radical new changes to drivetrain designs and whether the price of the vehicle, being noticeably higher than other similar designs, would be justified by the promise of long-term savings through superior fuel economy.

Prior to its introduction to North America, a rift between the U.S. and Japanese divisions over the vehicle's price point became a major point of contention. While Japanese executives insisted that the Prius have a manufacturer's suggested retail price (MSRP) of over US$20,000, U.S. executives countered that based on their consumer research, it would not sell for that amount. Eventually a compromise was reached in which dealer margin was reduced, allowing Japan to make more on the cars, while still keeping the selling price reasonable. The car went on sale for US$19,995, but Japan still took a loss on the first batch of cars.

A SUCCESS THAT SHOULD NOT HAVE BEEN

When the Prius finally arrived in the United States in July 2000, it was an immediate success, even though there were problems. Slow acceleration times, a jerky ride, and inexplicable engine noises all plagued the new hybrid, and yet, in spite of it all, people lined up to buy one. According to *Fortune,* consumers were willing to overlook all these things and focus instead on emissions, which were reduced almost 80 percent, and great fuel economy. They seemed not to mind paying a price that was almost US$3,000 more than what it would otherwise have been in order to own a car that was high technology and environmentally friendly. Resale value on the Prius was relatively high; it retained 57 percent of its value after three years. Only 2 percent of all Prius owners chose to lease their cars; almost universally, customers opted for ownership.

What really cinched the outstanding success of the Prius was when U.S. celebrities and other world notables got behind the wheel and started buying the new hybrids. Leonardo DiCaprio bought one in 2001, as did Cameron Diaz, making them among the first of a long list of celebrity Prius owners. In 2003, five of the cars were provided and chauffeured to transport the top of Hollywood's A-list to the Academy Awards ceremony that year, something that did not go unnoticed with U.S. car buyers. The Prius achieved royalty status when Prince Albert II of Monaco bought one, as well as another one of Toyota's hybrids, the Lexus 600h hybrid.

In terms of sales, the year 2000 saw 5,562 units sold in the United States. In 2001, there was an increase of 180 percent over 2000, or 15,556 units. The following year, sales increased to 20,119, and in 2003 sales reached 24,600. At this point, Toyota was ready to release its second generation of Prius in a brand-new body design. The redesigned Prius was a hatchback, more fuel efficient, faster and more powerful, and reduced emissions even further. In 2004, sales skyrocketed. Doubling previous years' numbers, 53,991 were put on the road in the United States.

Continuing the doubling trend in 2005, 107,897 units were sold in the United States. Between 2004 and 2005 gas prices in many parts of the country shot up from US$1.50 a gallon to US$2.50 a gallon, making people very amenable to the concept of owning a hybrid vehicle. In 2006, 106,971 cars were sold, while that figure shot up to 181,221 in 2007. In 2008, sales did drop somewhat, but not unreasonably. In spite of the global recession and financial crisis, 158,574 Prius cars were sold. When the U.S. automotive industry almost collapsed between 2008 and 2010, the "Big Three" automakers, Ford Motor Company, Chrysler Corporation, and General Motors Company, all had extremely tough years, with two of the three requiring financial bailouts in order to keep operating. However, Toyota still managed to sell 139,682 units of the Prius in 2009 and 140,928 units in 2010. Numerous recalls made by Toyota, starting in 2009 and continuing into 2010, may have been a factor in the relatively flat sales from 2009 to 2010. One of these recalls was a worldwide brake recall for 2010 Priuses in February 2010.

DRIVING INTO THE SUNSET

As other automakers began releasing hybrid vehicles of their own, Toyota still enjoyed a dominant position in the market, with the most number of hybrids sold. In 2012, Toyota was poised to release as many as ten new hybrid models into the market, of which only four were redesigns and six were brand new models. That year was also the inaugural year of the plug-in Prius in the United States, a US$32,000 model that promised to match the performance of previous Prius models and also travel as much as 14.3 miles on electricity alone. While the success of this new model is unknown, consumers continue to demand highly fuel-efficient, low-emissions cars, making it very likely that U.S. citizens will see even more Prius vehicles on the road in the coming years.

BIBLIOGRAPHY

Addison, John. "Ford Challenges Toyota in Hybrid and Plug-in Hybrid Cars." *Clean Fleet Report,* November 22, 2011. Accessed January 19, 2012. http://www.cleanfleetreport.com /hybrid-cars/ford-toyota-plugin-hybrid/.

"Cumulative Worldwide Sales of Toyota Hybrids Top 3M Units." *Green Car Congress,* March 8, 2011. Accessed January 19, 2012. http://www.greencarcongress.com/2011/03/cumulative -worldwide-sales-of-toyota-hybrids-top-3m-units.html.

Juettner, Bonnie. *Hybrid Cars.* Chicago, IL: Norwood House Press, 2009, p. 17.

Slywotzky, Adrian. "The Upside of Strategic Risk: How Toyota Turned Its Greatest Threat into a Growth Breakthrough." New York: Marsh & McLennan Companies, 2007. Accessed January 19, 2012. http://www.mmc.com/knowledgecenter /viewpoint/Slywotzky2007.php.

Taylor, Alex III. "Toyota: The Birth of the Prius." *Fortune,* February 21, 2006. Accessed January 19, 2012. http://money .cnn.com/2006/02/17/news/companies/mostadmired_fortune _toyota/index.htm.

Toyota Motor Sales USA, Inc. "Takeshi Uchiyamada." Torrance, CA. Accessed January 19, 2012. http://pressroom.toyota.com /article_display.cfm?article_id=2279.

"Toyota Prius Chronological History." Toyoland.com, 2003. Accessed January 19, 2012. http://www.toyoland.com/prius /chronology.html.

U.S. Department of Energy. "Alternative Fuels & Advanced Vehicles Data Center." Washington, DC, November 7, 2011. Accessed January 19, 2012. http://www.afdc.energy.gov/afdc /data/vehicles.html#afv_hev.

———. "Compare Hybrids Side-by-Side." Washington, DC, 2012. Accessed January 19, 2012. http://www.fueleconomy .gov/feg/hybrids.jsp.

Twitter: Social Networking and Microblogging Service

INTERNET COMMUNICATION: BLOGS AND INSTANT MESSAGING

While Twitter did not explode in popularity until the middle of the first decade of the 21st century, the foundations of the addictive microblog service stretched back to the 1990s. In fact, the first instant messaging service was technically UNIX Talk in the 1980s, which let users send text updates to one another through the network. Instant messaging grew along with the Internet, becoming an integral part of the Information Age.

On the phone front, companies worked on allowing people to type quick text messages through their mobile phones, known traditionally as short message service (SMS). The idea caught on in the early 1990s and spread throughout major phone carriers around the world. It quickly became apparent that customerswould pay for the ability to send simple messages rather than make a call. Many people liked the non-vocal aspect, others enjoyed the ability to multitask conversations, and some just found texting (as it became to be known) fun.

After a few years of texting, the Internet adopted the same type of service. America Online, Inc. (AOL) came out with one of the first versions in 1995, calling it AOL Instant Messenger (AIM). PowWow and ICQ offered messaging services, too, followed by MSN Messenger by Microsoft Corporation. Instant messaging went hand in hand with e-mail, although it was often limited to friend lists wherein both parties agreed beforehand to receive messages from the other. Some Internet providers experimented with voice chatting services as well, but text chat services proved to have the most staying power.

Internet usage increased and by the late 1990s users began developing weblogs, soon shortened to blogs. Companies sprang up to facilitate blog creation and social networks. One of these projects was Blogger.com, launched by Evan Williams in 1999. Xanga.com was another, cofounded by another entrepreneur and developer, Christopher "Biz" Stone. After several years Google, Inc., recruited these developers for its own blogging projects.

By the early 21st century, both instant messaging and blogging had become well-developed aspects of the Internet. Users had shown their interest in sending easy messages to one another and broadcasting their views to an online audience. However, no hybrid service existed to combine these two pastimes. Evan Williams, Biz Stone, software writer Jack Dorsey, and a handful of others were about to change that.

SAVING ODEO

In 2004 Biz Stone and Evan Williams left Google to become part of a new project called Odeo. Odeo was the brainchild of Noah Glass, who began the software project in his apartment. Odeo took the podcasting concept of publishing audio clips online and mixed it with traditional phone services, allowing people to call a number, speak a message, and automatically turn it into an online file. Williams came onto the project as the primary financial backer, eventually becoming CEO of the company. Stone and Jack Dorsey also joined the project.

Just as Odeo was becoming an official company with offices and additional employees, Apple, Inc., released the bomb that would shatter the nascent business. In 2005 Apple developers finished working on a podcasting platform for iTunes and announced the software would be included in all future versions of the iPod. The services Odeo offered, based on a different, self-made platform, became obsolete almost overnight. The founders also realized the impracticality of basing a company solely on podcasting personal messages, a service that held little attraction to the common Internet user. Odeo, with only 14 full-time employees and a small circle of anxious investors, appeared doomed.

Williams split the employees into groups for frequent brainstorming, known in the office as "hackathons." The developers and founders exchanged ideas for new projects or channels that would render Odeo viable again. At one group, Glass and Dorsey began discussing the possibility of switching to an SMS-like service. Dorsey, inspired by social networks, believed people would be interested in the ability to send short texts to an entire group of people, sharing their current status. At first the idea centered around location and event updates, but after discussion Dorsey realized the applications could be far broader. Before long, the old Odeo work paled compared to this new concept.

In early 2006 the team presented the status idea to the company as a whole, calling it Twttr after both the noise of birds (particularly apt for describing online group messaging) and popular services like Flickr. More resources were dedicated to the project, and Glass took a leading role. Before long he experimented with a working prototype of the concept on his laptop. The name eventually changed to the more user-friendly Twitter when the product was finally ready for its first public trials.

What began as a last-ditch effort to save Odeo blossomed into a project with a momentum all its own. Odeo employees experimented with the service and soon found out they could not stop. By the middle of 2006, some in-house workers were using the service so often they had text messaging bills of hundreds of dollars. (Odeo offered to pay these expenses.) Only a couple of months after its first beta launch, Twitter had 5,000 registered users.

Williams followed the release of Twitter with a buy-back, purchasing all shares from the old Odeo company and moving the concentration of the business toward the Twitter project. The first public signs of the Twitter phenomenon occurred in March 2007, when Twitter won the blog award at the South by Southwest (SXSW) Interactive event in Austin, Texas. Several months later, a correspondent used the microblog to tweet live updates from the MTV Video Music Awards, garnering increased interest.

LIMITLESS POTENTIAL IN 140 CHARACTERS

The Twitter concept remained so simple and so easy to understand that the public had no problems grasping its use and function. The few core rules, such as the 140-char-

acter limit, needed little explanation. Originally the SMS service had no character limits at all, and if texts were too long the program automatically broke them down and sent them in separate bundles but, as Twitter went public, this became impractical. The company chose 140 maximum characters because of the 160-character limit adopted by SMS carriers of the day. This left 20 characters for an automatic username.

The first years of Twitter, Inc., had their trials. The value of the service became difficult to express to newcomers and especially investors. Only eight employees worked at the project until 2008. The service was subject to delays and slowdowns, which became more widely publicized as subscribers grew. Odeo also suffered, in part, because the employees clearly preferred to work on Twitter. The original staff was cut back to save on costs, and eventually Twitter operations moved over to Obvious Corporation in a separation move, after which Odeo was shuttered.

The public also showed some initial misunderstandings regarding the use of Twitter. When Twitter first went public, most phone carriers still charged for their text services. Calling Twitter an SMS service made people suspect they would have to pay a fee for any message they sent, no matter the source. This was one reason the word "microblog" became so useful for pinpointing exactly what Twitter was and how people could use it. After some initial confusion, the time for Twitter had already arrived. After 18 months of use, Twitter accounts had grown from 5,000 largely local users to 500,000 subscribers spread out across the United States, and the momentum had only just begun.

By this time, Internet users had become accustomed to the status update, a key function in social networks. It had taken on a life of its own, distinct from the phone-based text message in its group-oriented applications. Friends found it easier to share information with their followers in one tweet than to select multiple friends for a traditional SMS message. Phones soon evolved data plans, allowing users to access their Twitter accounts on the move and send tweets from nearly any location, an enormous advantage in the world of media.

On a deeper level, the era of Internet personalization had also arrived. The grasp of news and reports had begun to slip from the hands of more traditional media sources like newspapers and television. People went online and consulted blogs or friends to find out news, especially entertainment stories. Even so, blogs were difficult to maintain and share compared to the usefulness of Twitter.

With only a few words, users could send commentary and updates to all of their followers on a play-by-play basis. The potential won over thousands of fans eager for the fastest news, especially from individuals responsible for it. Even actors, politicians, and newscasters could find the time to send a short "tweet" to communicate information directly without any intervening interpretation. Before long, those thousands of fans were turning into millions, and Twitter had found its place in society.

THE ATTRACTION OF TWEETS

As subscribers grew in number, additional Twitter features arose, making the service even more attractive. One of the most important was the ability to link to images, blogs, or other websites within tweets. Soon many tweets pointed toward other, more complete sources of information (or advertised products with links to online stores, a use that businesses were quick to exploit).

Some Twitter ideas originated with Twitter users themselves. The famous hashtags, which allowed users to title, connect, categorize, and sort tweets by including a pound sign at the beginning of a line, began with a single user, Chris Messina, in 2007. Messina simply asked his followers if they wanted to create a group surrounding one particular topic by setting that topic apart with a hashtag (his example was "#barcamp"). Before long people started using hashtags to search for specific tweets, bind shared viewpoints together, and exchange popular jokes or memes.

The hashtag also led to a better understanding about how companies could use Twitter for their benefit. As a sounding board, Twitter excelled at tracking discussions on new products or brands. Not only could businesses tweet direct marketing, but they could also use Twitter tracking programs to analyze current communication trends, judging the success of their advertising campaigns while keeping an eye on movements made by their competitors. As services increased, so did the acceptance of Twitter. Before long the microblog had birthed a new lexicon, moving far beyond tweeting into twitpic, twictionary, tweetup, tweetometer, twitterverse, and twitterati, among almost innumerable other examples. Of particular note was the twitpocalypse in 2009, when the number of tweets exceeded the limits of coded integers, causing a Twitter application blackout.

By March 2008 Twitter had 1.3 million registered users. One year later, that number increased to six million and was firmly on an exponential pattern of growth. Three years after opening to the public, tweets totaled one billion. The company began hiring more staff to deal with the growth. The 6 million users grew to 105 million within a year, then more than 200 million registered users with at least 50 million who used Twitter once a day or more. New features included promoted tweets, promoted trends, and promoted accounts. By the middle of 2011, 350 billion tweets were created every day, and Twitter employees had grown from 8 to 400.

By that time, the death of Al Qaeda leader Osama Bin Laden had generated the fastest flow of tweets, topping the charts at 3,000 tweets per second, or TPS, for more than three hours. In 2011, U.S. President Barack Obama had a significant amount of Twitter followers, but politics was still no match for entertainment as he was outnumbered by the several million followers of pop singer Justin Bieber and the approximately 14 million followers of singer Lady Gaga, who was at the top of the list. Actors and singers dominated the rest of the top 10 list.

The value of Twitter continued to be secondary to its popularity. The company once denied a US$500 million buyout offer, but analysts put the total value of the business around US$250 million in 2011. How it made its revenues remained nebulous. Certainly a large portion came from selling firehose access. The firehose was the full and constant stream of all public tweets, which Twitter began to sell to major companies in 2009 for analysis purposes. Google and Bing, along with many smaller companies, purchased access for millions of dollars.

REINVENTION: THE POWER OF A GOOD IDEA

Twitter owed much of its remarkable rise to its usability. Many online applications were attractive in concept but got bogged down in execution. Users were easily distracted or turned away by complex instructions, difficult interfaces, or an overwhelming number of features. Twitter avoided these pitfalls by keeping an extremely basic design directed entirely toward a universal purpose. This provided a focal point on which the buzz surrounding Twitter could build.

BIBLIOGRAPHY

Buck, Stephanie. "A Visual History of Twitter." *Mashable,* September 30, 2011. Accessed February 9, 2012. http://mashable.com/2011/09/30/twitter-history-infographic/.

Carlson, Nicholas. "The Real History of Twitter." *Business Insider,* April 13, 2011. Accessed February 9, 2012. http://articles.businessinsider.com/2011-04-13/tech/29957143_1_jack-dorsey-twitter-podcasting.

Gannes, Liz. "The Short and Illustrious History of Twitter #Hashtags." *GigaOM,* April 30, 2010. Accessed February 9, 2012. http://gigaom.com/2010/04/30/the-short-and-illustrious-history-of-twitter-hashtags/.

"The History of Twitter." *Smart Solutions,* July 21, 2011. Accessed February 9, 2012. http://www.smartz.com/blog/2011/07/21/the-history-of-twitter/.

Malik, Om. "A Brief History of Twitter." *GigaOM,* February 1, 2009. Accessed February 9, 2012. http://gigaom.com/2009/02/01/a-brief-history-of-twitter/.

Maxwell, Kerry. "Twhatever Next? The Lexicon of Twitter." *MED Magazine,* October 2010. Accessed February 9, 2012. http://www.macmillandictionaries.com/MED-Magazine/October2010/59-WTM.htm.

Percival, Sean. "The Story (So Far) of Twitter." *Manolith,* June 21, 2009. Accessed February 9, 2012. http://www.manolith.com/2009/06/21/the-story-so-far-of-twitter/.

Picard, Andre. "The History of Twitter, 140 Characters at a Time." *Globe and Mail,* March 22, 2011. Accessed February 9, 2012. http://www.theglobeandmail.com/news/technology /tech-news/the-history-of-twitter-140-characters-at-a-time /article1949299/.

Sagolla, Dom. "How Twitter Was Born." *140 Characters,* January 30, 2009. Accessed February 9, 2012. http:// www.140characters.com/2009/01/30/how-twitter-was-born/.

UPS: Package Delivery Plus Logistics and Supply Chain Management

In 1907 Jim Casey established a bicycle messenger service in Seattle, Washington. At a time when most people did not own telephones, telegraph messages were carried by hand to their recipients, in many cases detracting from the urgent nature of the telegrams. The unwieldy system prompted 19-year-old Casey to propose a bicycle service to deliver the messages, along with lunches and other items his customers might need, more quickly. Within a few years, the business evolved into delivering packages for large retail stores around Seattle, Washington, and the "American Messenger Service" started using automobiles and motorcycles to speed the process.

Seattle, Washington, had at least eight rival messenger companies when Casey started American Messenger Service, wrote Mike Brewster and Frederick Dalzell in *Driving Change: The UPS Approach to Business*. To set themselves apart and win over customers, Casey and his crew vowed to stick to competitive pricing, work harder for longer hours, and provide better service than their competitors. This corporate culture, based on superior service and work ethic, continued to drive United Parcel Service, Inc. (UPS).

In 2010 UPS had US$49.55 billion in annual sales and approximately 400,000 employees, making it the world's largest package shipper. It owned its own airline and delivered packages worldwide. UPS in the 2010s was more than familiar brown uniforms, brown trucks, and brown-wrapped boxes, however. Just as founder Casey saw potential in the bicycle to fill a need for faster local message delivery, UPS leadership continued to invest heavily in the latest technologies over the years to meet the logistics and supply chain needs of businesses that operated on a global scale.

UPS invested US$1 billion per year on information technology, according to the *Gale Encyclopedia of E-Commerce*. The company used the latest technological innovations to grow its business beyond its shipping roots and become one of the foremost providers of logistics services for multinational corporations.

AN IDEA FOR GROWTH

In 1997 a reported 185,000 UPS drivers walked off their jobs in the largest strike in the United States in over a decade. Package deliveries to millions of customers were disrupted for more than two weeks, Charles Krause reported on the *PBS NewsHour*. The strike allowed competitors the U.S. Postal Service and FedEx Corporation to gain a share of UPS's shipping business and revenues, grabbing a combined US$350 million during the 15 days of the strike, according to the January 2000 article, "Logistics in Brown," by Kelly Barron in *Forbes*.

UPS eventually settled the strike and repaired its customer relationships. However, the labor dispute and the resulting business disruption led UPS to make a change in its core business. The company's leadership realized that to remain competitive, UPS had to venture beyond simple package delivery to meet the changing needs of its customers. "The strike opened up all the gates that we wanted to open in terms of developing more aggressive strategies," Joseph Guerrisi, a former UPS executive, told *Forbes*.

UPS's customers were in transition, moving beyond simply selling and shipping goods to dealing in information, knowledge, and complex logistics to manage operations scattered around the globe. Guaranteeing to ship packages and paperwork from one place to another on time was no longer enough to satisfy basic business needs. Therefore, UPS decided to diversify its business into the logistics and supply chain management areas. By doing so, it would help its customers find the most efficient, cost-effective ways to fulfill orders, maintain inventory, process returns and repairs, finance operations, and maintain business processes. UPS's ultimate goal was to become a one-stop solution for keeping customers' supply chains running smoothly, even when their corporate offices were located in one country, manufacturing plants in another, and customers somewhere else in the world.

MAKING A LOGICAL MOVE

By recognizing its package-shipping operations had reached maturity and it was time to diversify into a new business model, UPS carved a new niche for itself in the global business world that would keep it profitable and ensure its growth, even as the needs of its customers changed over time. UPS grew its shipping business serving brick-and-mortar retailers. These sellers increasingly moved into the virtual realm, and UPS had to boost its technology assets to support higher volumes of online sales, shipments, and returns.

Brewster and Dalzell described the early days of the transition to e-retail in one UPS market, Europe, in *Driving Change*: "By 2000, the Internet and globalization sparked a huge increase in premium packages within Europe. The volume was growing at twenty percent each year, and the big strategic accounts were growing especially fast. According to Paul White, UPS Europe's vice president of marketing at the time, the revenues really exploded when the most lucrative UPS customers—those small-to-medium five-package-per-day customers that get only small discounts—started to order via the Internet as well."

RAISING FUNDS TO BUY TECHNOLOGY

In preparation for its shift to logistics, UPS conducted a large initial public offering (IPO) on November 10, 1999, selling 109 million shares for US$5.5 billion, according to the article "United Parcel Service, Inc.," in the *Gale Encyclopedia of E-Commerce*. The IPO represented a major change for the company, which had been privately owned and insular for nearly a century. With the revenue gained through the stock offering, UPS invested billions in technology, "purchasing mainframes, personal computers, handheld devices, wireless modems, and cellular networks," as well as hiring 4,000 programmers and technicians, wrote Barron in *Forbes*.

UPS also acquired six logistics companies, a brokerage, freight specialists, and a bank. In 2002 UPS com-

bined 19 companies and services related to global supply chain management to form UPS Supply Chain Solutions (SCS). Over the next few years, the company diversified beyond its packing and shipping origins to become a world leader in supply chain management, international commerce, and global transportation. By 2004 the supply chain services division had more than 750 locations worldwide. This infrastructure, technology, and personnel boost gave UPS the tools and power it needed to enter the world of global commerce and offer a new menu of logistics services to its customers. "UPS used to be a trucking company with technology. Now it's a technology company with trucks," Barron wrote.

UPS also launched a full-scale worldwide marketing effort in 2010 to promote its technologically enhanced logistics offerings. The 103-year-old company changed its slogan "What can Brown do for you?" to "We ♡ Logistics," retooled its logo, and launched an onslaught of print, television, and digital-media advertisements in the United States, China, Mexico, and the United Kingdom, according to Jennifer Levitz's 2010 article in the *Wall Street Journal*. The campaign signaled UPS customers it was now open for a different kind of business.

MOVING INFORMATION, NOT JUST PACKAGES

In the late 1980s UPS was still largely dependent on manually writing down and tracking pickups and deliveries. A decade and a half later, according to *Driving Change*, the company owned the largest IBM relational database in existence and became the heaviest user of cell phone minutes in the world, as it transitioned to wireless-enabled, handheld tracking devices and Internet-enabled systems to drive its business. In the 2010s UPS drivers around the world carried handheld Delivery Information Acquisition Devices (DIADs) made by Honeywell International Inc. The mobile computers featured cellular technology that allowed them to seamlessly switch between wireless network providers on the fly, so they never lost carrier signal. The DIAD had a color display and powerful microprocessor that could support Global Positioning System-enabled maps and satellite tracking, a camera to enhance proof of delivery and process customer claims quickly, Wi-Fi support enabling drivers to download information quickly, and sophisticated imaging software enabling the device to recognize a wide variety of signatures, bar codes, and symbols.

"Moving information is just as important to us as moving goods," former chief executive officer of UPS, Michael Eskew, told *MIT News* in 2002. "UPS moves 14 million packages through the system every day and scans each of those packages three to five times so the packages can tell us where they are." The handheld DIAD computers dovetailed with the sophisticated technology UPS used on the logistics and international shipping sides of its business. The company's WorldShip, Quantum View Manage, and UPS Billing services, for example, allowed customers to search, sort, filter, e-mail, and download shipment data; view scanned images of customs documentation required for international shipping, including bills of lading and delivery receipts; and import inventory and shipment details from spreadsheet programs into the UPS system, according to the 2007 article, "New UPS Technologies Aim to Speed Worldwide Package Delivery," in *Information Week*. Advanced technologies gave UPS's customers an inside view of their operations right from their own computers. UPS's technology platforms also captured data and transferred it seamlessly from one part of the supply chain system to another, saving customers from keying data multiple times or maintaining multiple systems, which could raise both cost and likelihood of errors.

THE THE END OF THE RUNWAY

In his article "Surprise Package," in *Fast Company*, Chuck Salter described the logistics operation that UPS employees called "the end of the runway" as "six unmarked, off-white monolithic buildings" on campus at the company's sprawling Louisville, Kentucky, hub. Inside those buildings, Salter wrote, employees of SCS wore blue antistatic laboratory coats rather than the familiar, brown uniforms. It was here that companies around the world outsourced every part of their supply chain, hiring UPS as a third-party provider to handle the entire lifecycle of their products and services. The term "supply chain" could describe nearly every function a company performed as it strived to get its products and services to customers worldwide. Rather than building and staffing high-cost operations near their corporate home bases, multinational corporations increasingly opted to outsource, putting their raw materials, inventory, and repair specialists near the people who bought their products. "Or, because the customers are spread out, then close to the next best thing: the end of the runway," Salter wrote.

UPS Supply Chain Services had the transportation available via its "package cars" and proprietary airline to move raw materials and products easily and inexpensively. Its logistics operation also encompassed financial institutions that could lend money to pay for supplies and materials, call centers and order processing centers, fully staffed warehouses, repair technicians, and parts suppliers. By consolidating these varied services under one massive umbrella, UPS parlayed the experience it gained creating one of the world's largest and most efficient transportation networks into a solution for the global business landscape of the 2010s.

Even more important to its multinational customers, UPS had one computer system to create an unbroken chain of information across a customer's operations, and even between different countries. If a corporation hired different companies to provide services along each step in the chain, it would also have to contend with potentially incompatible hardware and software solutions. By contracting with one supply chain service from end to end, companies ensured materials, goods, services, revenues, and other aspects of their business could be easily tracked throughout the chain. UPS ensured that desired continuity and tracking, much like it guaranteed a package traveling from one destination to another.

The supply chain management arm of UPS's business was largely hidden from actual consumers. Customers might go online to exchange a pair of Nike sneakers that did not fit or call Toshiba about getting their laptop computer repaired. They would never realize that SCS handled the entire process, including the service call, the shipping, and the actual repair or replacement.

According to Salter in *Fast Company*, SCS made US$2.5 billion in 2002, which accounted for just 8 percent of UPS's total business. While the bulk of the company's revenue was still made shipping packages from one destination to another, the shipping part of the business was largely static. On the other hand, the behind-the-scenes supply chain and logistics areas represented the fastest-growing area of UPS's business.

SCS had locations all over the world. It operated automated warehouses in Singapore to handle the many types and huge volumes of goods manufactured in Asia. "In Germany, it installed six-ton X-ray machines in hospitals. In Paris, it repairs cash registers for McDonald's. It even used to tune guitars in Europe for Fender," Salter wrote in "Surprise Package." However, the Louisville hub was the largest, and its proximity to UPS's proprietary airline and airport runways made it able to accommodate last-minute shipping requests and cut down on international shipping costs because the planes were located right next to where the inventory was stored and, in many cases, pieced together and repaired as well.

STILL IN TOUCH WITH ITS SHIPPING ROOTS

Michael Eskew, who started out as a UPS driver and package sorter in the early 1970s and worked his way up to serve as CEO and chairman until 2007, was largely responsible for the technological advancements and overall push into logistics that allowed UPS to transform itself into a global partner for so many successful companies. Eskew reportedly accomplished this with a lack of ego that set him apart from many company leaders of the time. David J. Lynch described Eskew in a 2006 *USA Today* article as someone who would "rather highlight the people and processes that have transformed this once-staid delivery service into a technology-rich mainstay of global commerce" than talk about his own accomplishments. "Our ambition is not just to get things from here to there," Eskew told Lynch, "but to enable commerce, and enabling commerce can encompass an awful lot."

In many ways, the logistics branch of UPS's business is a natural outgrowth of its shipping history, mirroring its ability to transport packages smoothly from one place to another in the smooth transfer of information and services, as well as physical goods, from one part of a company's supply chain to the next. UPS's supply chain management and logistics operation, although it generates smaller profit margins than its shipping operations, benefits its business as a whole. It allows UPS to capitalize on its existing network of planes, trucks, computers, and warehouses, creating economies of scale and, ultimately, ensuring a steady stream of customers for the shipping side of its business. UPS's logistics and shipping branches support each other. Logistics draws in customers looking for a virtual partner to support their business from end to end, while shipping ensures their goods arrive where they are supposed to be on time and in accordance with global regulations.

BIBLIOGRAPHY

Barron, Kelly. "Logistics in Brown." *Forbes,* January 10, 2000. Accessed February 11, 2012. http://www.forbes.com /forbes/2000/0110/6501078a.html.

Brewster, Mike, and Frederick Dalzell. *Driving Change: The UPS Approach to Business.* New York: Hyperion, 2007, 13, 149–161, 170.

Brown, Paul B. "Mail Call." *Fast Company,* November 1, 2005. Accessed February 11, 2012. http://www.fastcompany.com /magazine/100/wikn.html.

Gardner, David W. "New UPS Technologies Aim to Speed Worldwide Package Delivery." *Information Week,* March 20, 2007. Accessed February 11, 2012. http://www.information week.com/news/198100187.

Krause, Charles. "UPS Strike: Package Deal." *PBS NewsHour,* August 19, 1997. Accessed February 11, 2012. http://www .pbs.org/newshour/bb/business/july-dec97/ups_8-19a.html.

Levitz, Jennifer. "UPS Leaves 'Brown' for New Love." *Wall Street Journal,* September 13, 2010. Accessed February 11, 2012. http://online.wsj.com/article/SB10001424052748704621204 575487840032479922.html.

Lynch, David J. "Thanks to Its CEO, UPS Doesn't Just Deliver." *USA Today,* July 24, 2006. Accessed February 11, 2012. http://www.usatoday.com/educate/college/careers/CEOs/7 -24-06.htm.

Salter, Chuck. "Surprise Package." *Fast Company,* February 4, 2004. Accessed February 11, 2012. http://www.fastcompany .com/magazine/79/ups.html?page=0%2C1.

Smith, Nancy DuVergne. "Technology Is Driving UPS." *MIT News,* March 6, 2002. Accessed February 11, 2012. http:// web.mit.edu/newsoffice/2002/ups-0306.html.

"United Parcel Service, Inc. (UPS)." In *Gale Encyclopedia of E-Commerce,* edited by Jane A. Malonis. Vol 2, 722–724. Detroit: Gale, 2002. Gale Virtual Reference Library (GALE|CX3405300444). Accessed March 1, 2012. http:// go.galegroup.com/ps/i.do?id=GALE%7CCX3405300444&v =2.1&u=itsbtrial&it=r&p=GVRL&sw=w.

"UPS and Honeywell Set State for Next High-Tech Handheld for UPS Drivers." *BusinessWire,* January 13, 2010. Accessed February 11, 2012. http://www.businesswire.com/news /home/20100113005851/en/UPS-Honeywell-Set-Stage -High-Tech-Handheld-UPS.

Weiss, Todd. "UPS Deploys Its Fourth-Generation Handheld Delivery Terminals." *Computerworld,* May 9, 2005. Accessed February 11, 2012. http://www.computerworld.com/s/article /101629/UPS_deploys_its_fourth_generation_handheld _delivery_terminals.

U.S. Military Becomes More Eco-Savvy

The United States Army, Navy, and Marine Corps were established in 1775 at the time of the American Revolution. Headquartered at the Pentagon in Washington, D.C., it is estimated that the U.S. Department of Defense (DoD) utilizes over 30 million acres of land around the world. With approximately 1.4 million active duty personnel and 718,000 civilians at more than 800 bases worldwide, the DoD is one of the country's highest energy consumers as well as the largest employer in the United States.

In an article by Cheryl Pellerin published on the DoD website in January 2012, Oliver Fritz, deputy director for policy for the Office of the Under Secretary of Defense for Acquisition, Technology, and Logistics, noted that the department's own largest consumer of energy is the U.S. Air Force, which uses approximately 84 percent of the 2.5 billion gallons of fuel purchased by the DoD annually. Energy, he added, can be a decisive factor in war when it needs to be moved in increasing quantities across a war zone that has no front line, such as in Iraq and Afghanistan. "Many American lives have been lost on such convoys," Fritz elaborated, "moving fuel or protecting it."

In an April 2010 *USA Today* article, Brian Winter noted that the DoD, which introduced the gas-guzzling Hummer to the world, has not always been concerned about the environment or energy conservation. However, in a strategy review published in early 2010, the DoD recognized that cutting its reliance on foreign oil and reducing the carbon footprint of the armed forces was both fiscally responsible and critical to the long-term safety of U.S. troops.

SAFETY VERSUS ENVIRONMENTAL CONCERNS

In his review in the Journal of Public Administration, Research & Theory of Robert Durant's 2007 book, The Greening of the U.S. Military, Steven Cohen noted that the book provides extensive detail about the environmental crisis facing the military. By the end of 1989, the DoD had identified some 15,257 contaminated military sites with an estimated cleanup price tag of US$42.2 billion. An additional challenge was the base closures after the end of the Cold War, a time of hostility (but no overt fighting) between Western democratic nations and Communist countries. As bases were closed and land returned to the governing authorities, the question arose as to who was responsible for cleanup.

However, as Cohen observed, the "greening of the military" is also an interesting reflection of the greening of the United States. For decades, support for environmental protection together with environmental goals and regulation has grown amongst the U.S. public. The military, viewing its mission as one of defense rather than environmental protection, saw that every U.S. dollar spent on cleanup represented a dollar taken away from defense spending. However, there was also the realization that costs could be reduced and troop safety improved by taking steps to limit the environmental footprint of the military. This created the impetus within the military to examine operations both at home and abroad. This mirrored the public's growing awareness that economic development is not divorced from environmental protection, but rather the sustainability of economic development is dependent on environmental protection.

SUSTAINABLE ENERGY

One of the goals of the military's move toward sustainable energy is to be free of a product that originates in volatile places with unsavory regimes, according to Ray Mabus, secretary of the U.S. Navy. In an interview with Quil Lawrence of National Public Radio (NPR) in December 2011, Mabus noted that during the 2011 NATO action in Libya, the spike in oil prices had the effect of increasing the cost to the U.S. military by US$1 billion. "It really is a question of national security. [We may be] better stewards of the environment, but that's not the reason we're doing it," Mabus explained.

For the military, the incentive is clear. "One out of eight U.S. Army casualties in Iraq was the result of protecting fuel convoys," reported Steve Hargreaves in his August 17, 2011, article for *CNNMoney*. This statistic came from an army study that looked at the fuel convoys in Iraq between 2003 and 2007. A fighting army that is restricted by the availability of a tanker truck of conventional fuel or obliged to carry heavy batteries is also less able to respond as readily to insurgent conflict.

In Afghanistan, stated Hargreaves, oil arrived in convoys that had to travel through Pakistan. Other truck convoys then needed to distribute the fuel to smaller regional centers. The trucks were slow-moving targets and susceptible to attacks. In some instances, the fuel had to arrive by helicopter. In addition to the risk to lives, this was an expensive proposition. Hargreaves quoted the army as saying that it could cost up to US$40 per barrel of oil to transport the fuel to the most remote and dangerous places.

The project to "green" the United States military began in the United States. Beginning in 1998, the Pentagon underwent a major renovation. The Pentagon Renovation Team worked with guidance and support from the U.S. Environmental Protection Agency's Environmentally Preferable Purchase (EPP) program to develop environmentally friendly building initiatives. These included removing hazardous waste already present in the buildings, using wood from "sustained managed forests," installing low water use plumbing fixtures, and developing a design consisting of energy- efficient material. While part of the first phase was severely damaged in the September 11, 2001, terrorist attacks against the United States, the EPP website noted that studies indicated that the newly reinforced material had saved sections of the Pentagon from more widespread destruction.

In an article on the U.S. Army official website, Paul MacPherson reported on "The 'Greening' of Army Housing." Using the slogan, "Go Green, Be Green, Live ARMY Green," the army has implemented building designs for residential units that incorporate solar energy power and water systems, use recycled old concrete slabs for new roads, and emphasize the retention of shade trees. In his *USA Today* article, Winter reported that between 2004 and 2010, the army reduced water usage in its facilities around the world by up to 31 percent. In addition, the amount of energy used per square foot of army buildings declined by 10.4 percent during the same period.

Although Iraq and Afghanistan were not included in the calculations (due to an increase in energy use because of an increase in troop presence at the time), the article went on to detail a number of energy-efficient measures in both of these countries, including US$100 million spent on spray-foam insulation for tents that reduced the leakage of air cooled by air conditioning by at least 50 percent. Joe Sikes, director of facilities energy for the DoD, estimated that the environmental initiatives by the army in Iraq and Afghanistan would result in savings of at least US$1.6 billion over the lifetime of the projects. Other facility improvements included using more energy-efficient lighting, low-flow toilets, heating and air-conditioning upgrades, and solar panels.

To reduce its dependence on foreign fuel, the army is moving toward substituting solar energy and biodiesel fuel together with other technologies that are cleaner and have a lower carbon footprint. In June 2011, the DoD released an operational strategy that called for "more fight with less fuel, more options with less risk, and more capability with less cost," according to Pellerin's article. In Afghanistan, this took the form of a suite of new generators and centralized power.

ECO-AMMO

One of the options the military is exploring is the "greening" of its firepower. In the November 2011 issue of *Nature,* a scientific journal, Erika Hayden reported on the ongoing debate amongst scientists about receiving money from the military to develop "green" explosives. The article, "Bioengineers Debate Use of Military Money," discussed the resistance of many scientists to receiving funds from the military for research into adapting biological systems to replace chemical methods for manufacturing explosives. The article quoted Drew Endy, a bioengineer at Stanford University in California:"We need to figure out what the right relationship is between the worlds of defense and synthetic biology,"

In 2011, the U.S. Navy and Marine Corps experimented with forward operating bases (FOB), according to Pellerin. These bases used small-scale water purification, energy-efficient lighting, and photovoltaic (solar-based) energy harvesting to help reduce the need to transport fuel and water over long distances. After testing in the United States, the bases were expected to be deployed in Afghanistan.

The U.S. Air Force, the largest user of energy of the DoD, has been modifying how it flies aircraft by changing routes and optimizing aircraft loading. This alone, according to Pellerin's article, was estimated to save US$500 million in fuel costs. In March 2010, as noted in an April 26, 2010, article by Bruce Rolfsen in the *Air Force Times,* the U.S. Air Force conducted a test flight from the Elgin Air Force Base in Florida using a 50/50 mix of synthetic fuel refined from camelina oil and traditional jet fuel. Rolfsen pointed out that, according to a report by the Pew Charitable Trusts, the air force cut energy consumption by 20 percent in the previous six years.

Air force bases were doing their part for the "greening of the military," according to the Pew Report. As of 2010, 37 air force bases were drawing at least part of their power from renewable energy sources. In 2007, the Nellis Air Force Base in Nevada built what was then the largest solar photovoltaic system in the United States. It rated 14.2 megawatts and generated more than 30 million kilowatt-hours of electricity per year. There are plans in the 2010s to build another solar farm at Luke Air Force Base in Arizona. In addition, the Soaring Heights Community at Davis-Monthon Air Force Base, Arizona, relies on solar power for 75 percent of its residential needs.

In a February 2011 video interview with Rebecca Ward at *Voice of America,* Ray Mabus noted that the U.S. Navy made a tactical decision to find cleaner fuel alternatives. The navy had successfully tested biofuels in various air and sea craft and, instead of buying new vehicles that used biofuel, found biofuels that worked with the existing fleet. Mabus's point, again, was that the armed forces purchased fuel from volatile nations. The United States would not sell air or sea craft to many of these nations yet, indirectly, they had a "vote" on whether the nation's vessels fly or sail, Mabus said.

MILITARY INNOVATIONS HELP PRIVATE BUSINESS

Just as the world benefited from the military's use of global positioning systems (GPS), radar, and the Internet, so private businesses reported benefits from military research into more environmentally friendly and efficient fuel. In his article for *CNNMoney,* Hargreaves wrote that one of the biggest obstacles for companies offering renewable energy products, often start-up enterprises, was credibility. "Having the military buy these systems proves they are reliable," said Ron Helfan, an executive with Israeli-based Essence Solar Solutions. Essence Solar is negotiating to sell an advanced solar power system to the U.S. Marine Corps known as the Sun Spider.

Hargreaves also noted that the U.S. military was in a position to purchase products that were too expensive for private businesses or the general public. By purchasing solar panel installations or biofuels, the military helped support the industries pioneering the sale of the

technology until the products gained wider commercial appeal.

MISSION FAR FROM ACCOMPLISHED

While the U.S. military has been working hard to change its image as one of the highest power users and land contaminators, it recognizes that it still has some way to go before deserving the tag of "environmentally friendly." Environmental groups, while noting the military's efforts in the area, cautioned that there was much more to be done. In Winter's *USA Today* article, Scott Slesinger of the Natural Resources Defense Council noted that the Pentagon still needed to address the matter of toxic waste sites.

However, Kevin Geiss, the army's program director for energy security, commented in the same article, "The Army's mission is not to be green. Our mission is to defend the nation. In that context, we've found it's in our interest to develop sustainable projects."

BIBLIOGRAPHY

Cohen, Steven. "The Greening of the U.S. Military." *Journal of Public Administration, Research & Theory* 19, no. 3 (2009): 684–687. Accessed January 24, 2012. http://jpart.oxford journals.org/content/19/3/684.full.pdf+html.

Hargreaves, Steve. "For the Military Clean Energy Saves Lives." *CNN Money,* August 17, 2011. Accessed January 24, 2012. http://money.cnn.com/2011/08/17/technology/military _energy/index.htm.

Hayden, Erika. "Bioengineers Debate Use of Military Money." *Nature,* November 22, 2011. Accessed January 26, 2012. http://www.nature.com/news/bioengineers-debate-use-of -military-money-1.9409.

Lawrence, Quil. "U.S. Military Tests Out Green Tech in Afghanistan." *NPR,* December 29, 2011. Accessed January 24, 2012. http://www.npr.org/2011/12/29/144395953/u-s -military-tests-out-green-tech-in-afghanistan.

MacPherson, Paul C. "The 'Greening' of Army Housing." Washington, DC: United States Army, January 10, 2012. Accessed January 24, 2012. http://www.army.mil/article /71722/The__Greening__of_Army_housing.

Pellerin, Cheryl. "Smaller Carbon Footprint Means Fewer Risks, Official Says." Washington, DC: U.S. Department of Defense, January 19, 2012. Accessed January 24, 2012. http://www.defense.gov//News/NewsArticle.aspx?ID=66860.

Rolfsen, Bruce. "Pew Report Says Air Force Is Going Green." *Air Force Times,* April 26, 2010. Accessed January 24, 2012. http://www.airforcetimes.com/news/2010/04/airforce_green _042610w.

U.S. Department of Defense. "About the Department of Defense (DoD)." Washington, DC. Accessed January 24, 2012. http://www.defense.gov/about.

U.S. Environmental Protection Agency. "Greening of the Pentagon." Washington, DC, May 12, 2010. Accessed January 24, 2012. http://www.epa.gov/epp/pubs/case/penren .htm.

Ward, Rebecca. "Biofuels Powering Navy Jets, Helicopters and Boats." *Voice of America,* February 1, 2011. Accessed January 25, 2012. http://www.voanews.com/english/news/environment/The-Navy-Going-Green-115011269.html.

Winter, Brian. "U.S. Military's Green Projects to Save $1.6 Billion Over Time." *USA Today,* April 12, 2010. Accessed January 24, 2012. http://www.usatoday.com/news/military/2010-04-11-military-going-green_N.htm.

Velcro: How Biomimicry Inspired Innovative Design

Velcro drew on a concept from nature to greatly improve adhesive technology. Consumers no longer had to worry about tying their shoelaces when they could simply press together two Velcro strips. Velcro became a cultural icon, as its characteristic ripping sound and strong binding properties were unlike other fastener products on the market. The uniqueness of Velcro almost cost the company its trademark, as few used the generic term, "hook and loop strips," to describe the product.

HIKING TRIP

Georges de Mestral enjoyed nature and wildlife, and the Swiss electrical engineer frequently hiked through forests with his dog. During a hike in the Swiss Alps in 1941, de Mestral and his dog passed through a thicket of burdock. Burdock greatly annoyed travelers because its burrs stuck to their clothing very easily. The plant evolved this ability to help spread its seeds, as the burrs on its seeds would attach to the fur of a dog or other animal.

While he removed the burrs, de Mestral wondered how they attached to his coat and his dog so easily. The burrs lacked sticky sap and other obvious mechanisms. Using a microscope, de Mestral discovered that burdock burrs contained many miniature hooks that could get tangled in loops of cotton cloth, dog fur, or other soft materials.

De Mestral realized that a piece of fabric that held hooks shaped like burdock burrs could easily attach to another article of clothing that contained lots of small loops, and one could then simply pull on the two pieces of fabric to separate them. People would not need to struggle with laces, knots, and zippers to put on an outfit. Instead, they could simply press a few pieces of fabric together to get dressed in the morning.

DESIGNING THE FABRIC

De Mestral stitched a few prototype fabric strips, but they did not stick together as strongly as the burdock burrs stuck to his clothing. Creating all of the tiny hooks and sewing the small loops proved challenging, and de Mestral needed to test several hook sizes. The engineer decided to seek out a weaver to help with his project.

De Mestral told Swiss and French clothing makers about his discovery, but they did not take him seriously. Although de Mestral had attended a well-regarded technical school, the École Polytechnique Fédérale de Lausanne in Switzerland, he had studied electrical engineering, so the clothing makers believed he did not know much about fabric. After a French weaver and Swiss loom maker finally agreed to help him, de Mestral started work on cotton cloth that contained hooks and loops.

Cotton fabric stuck together at first, but its soft loops and hooks broke apart when de Mestral pulled the fabric apart, so it had a short lifespan. De Mestral realized that he needed to use a more durable material. By exposing nylon to infrared light to harden it, de Mestral produced much more resilient nylon loops and hooks. The hard nylon loops attached to the hooks very well, which made the detachment process difficult. De Mestral realized that cutting off part of each loop made the fabrics easier to separate.

MARKETING THE PRODUCT

When de Mestral finished his adhesive strip in 1955, he used the words "velour" and "crochet" to develop a brand name for the strips, Velcro. Few customers initially purchased the Velcro strips because of their tacky appearance: a customer preferred a stylish zipper to a plain black velcro strip that looked like a piece of masking tape.

De Mestral added strips in other colors, which improved his sales, but he still had trouble selling large amounts of Velcro from his location in Switzerland. He decided to license Velcro to a firm in Canada, granting it the right to sell Velcro in many nations outside of Europe. Velok Limited, the Canadian firm, successfully launched its product in the Canadian and U.S. markets. The Canadian firm soon renamed itself Velcro Industries. Enthusiastic reporters described the hook and loop strips as the "zipless zipper."

THE SPACE AGE

Velcro made changing into a bulky suit of clothing much more convenient, and the strips of tape could securely fasten an item to many surfaces temporarily. The new fabric impressed astronauts. An astronaut could conveniently fasten parts of his spacesuit with Velcro strips, and the strips proved useful in the weightless environment of space. Any unattached item drifted away, but permanently gluing everything inside the spaceship to a surface would inconvenience astronauts.

Space flight boosted the profile of the adhesive strips. Athletes realized that if Velcro could make changing into a spacesuit more convenient, it would also help a diver put on a bulky wetsuit or help a skier change into a ski outfit. Athletic shoe manufacturers realized that Velcro strips offered more convenience than traditional shoe laces.

Velcro found uses in other industries. It helped hospitals dress their patients, and automakers used it to attach devices inside their vehicles. Homeowners could use it to secure decorations inside their homes. Trampoline owners used Velcro to create a new game, as a person could put on a Velcro suit, bounce off the trampoline, and stick to a wall.

A CHANGE IN OWNERSHIP

Velcro Industries struggled in the early 1970s, and its stock price dropped substantially, falling from US$81 to US$5, according to *International Directory of Company Histories.* The British investor and philanthropist C. Humphrey Cripps used this opportunity to buy most of the company from de Mestral. The secretive Cripps used his offshore holding company to conduct the transaction so that he owned few shares himself while holding a great deal of control. Cripps gave other Velcro Industries stockholders few details about how he conducted business for the company, but he did successfully turn the firm around.

THE VELCRO BRAND

Velcro was both a product and a company name. Low-cost manufacturers started making hook and loop prod-

ucts after the patent on Velcro expired in 1978. These companies suffered from a marketing disadvantage because they did not have the right to sell their products as Velcro, and Velcro Industries aggressively defended its trademark. Several well-known products, such as Kleenex and Aspirin, originally received trademark protection but lost their protection when courts decided that the product name had become a generic term for an item. Velcro Industries knew this was a real risk with its own product, because other hook and loop makers competed on price and had not established strong brands of their own, so the company tried hard to encourage the use of the generic term "hook and loop strips."

In the early 1980s Velcro sneakers became extremely popular. Velcro Industries could not produce enough strips for the shoe companies, and it charged high prices for the strips it did make, so shoe companies purchased hook and loop strips from its competitors. According to *International Directory of Company Histories,* some of these competitors had paid licensing fees to manufacture official Velcro strips in the 1970s, so they already knew how to manufacture the strips. Velcro Industries decided to market its products to different industries. Shoe manufacturers wanted low-cost adhesive strips, but hospitals, car companies, and aerospace companies would pay more for a high-quality product.

NEW MATERIALS

Velcro Industries sales grew during the 1980s, as the company invested in research and developed hook and loop strips made from new materials. Auto manufacturers wanted alternatives to nylon Velcro, so Velcro Industries used other plastics to attach floor mats, carpets, seat cushions, and even fenders. Velcro substantially reduced the weight of new cars, improving their gas mileage and maneuverability. Velcro Industries used Nomex, a plastic that protected race car drivers from fires, to create fireproof Velcro.

Velcro Industries also introduced metal hook and loop products. Metal could withstand much higher temperatures than nylon, and it created much stronger bonds. Velcro Industries did continue to make its nylon products, as metal Velcro became useless after it was pulled apart a few times, so it was not suitable for clothing makers. The new materials attracted many new customers, and annual revenue reached US$64 million in 1986, reported the *Chicago Tribune.*

STOCKHOLDER TROUBLES

C. Humphrey Cripps continued to successfully lead the company during the late 1980s, and its revenue reached US$93 million in 1988, according to *International Di-*

rectory of Company Histories. Cripps owned most of the stock in Velcro Industries, and he continued to hide information from investors who owned fewer shares. These smaller shareholders could not easily get tickets to attend Velcro board meetings on Dutch Caribbean islands, where the holding company was based. Despite this, Queen Elizabeth II knighted Cripps in 1989.

In 1990 the minority shareholders decided to force Cripps to allow them more input into the management of the company. Cripps planned to buy out the minority investors in Velcro Industries, but the minority shareholders believed that the Cripps plan offered them much less cash than the company was worth. They were also angry because Velcro Industries had not paid dividends for the previous two years, even though Velcro Industries reported rapidly rising income.

Velcro Industries held its own stock portfolio, which was worth nearly as much as the market capitalization of the company. This valuation suggested that market analysts were not assigning much value to the operations of Velcro Industries itself, possibly because Cripps was not giving them enough data to perform the calculations. Velcro Industries conducted research and introduced new products without informing its shareholders.

The angry shareholders chose the stockbroker Alan Kahn to represent them. The Kahn group owned about a quarter of company shares in 1990, while the Cripps holding company Cohere held about two-thirds of the shares. Cripps had also stacked the Velcro Industries board with his relatives. After Kahn threatened to sue Cripps, Cripps cancelled his plan to buy out the other shareholders.

NEW MARKETS

Although Velcro Industries continued to use its adhesive strips in new products, such as diapers, analysts believed that manufacturers in its traditional markets were already purchasing most of the Velcro products that they could use. Low-cost competitors continued to capture market share. Changes in international tax law raised the company's tax bills. By 1996 Cripps realized that Velcro Industries needed new markets to improve its sales.

Expansion into overseas markets offered a long-term boost at the short-term cost of the stock performance of the company. This plan held down the value of Velcro Industries shares, which continued to make the minority stockholders angry, but Cripps believed it was a better strategy for the long term. Although some investors saw the sudden drop in earnings and sold off their Velcro Industries shares in 1995 and 1996, other investors concluded that these one-time expenses had made Velcro Industries shares temporarily available at a bargain price.

COMBAT VELCRO

Velcro Industries promoted its adhesive strips to the U.S. Defense Department. A soldier could put on bulky military clothing much quicker if it included Velcro straps, and the speed advantage that Velcro provided held a potential combat use, as a soldier would not want to worry about buttons or shoelaces while enemy forces were firing. Nylon strips weighed less than metal zippers and buttons, and soldiers already had to carry heavy weapons and supplies, so the weight advantage could improve mobility and reduce fatigue. The U.S. Department of Defense issued soldiers clothing that included Velcro strips in 2004, reported Claire Suddath for *TIME*.

However, many soldiers did not like the Velcro strips. The U.S. army stationed troops in Middle Eastern nations, such as Iraq, where soldiers frequently traveled through the desert. The desert sands easily gummed up the Velcro strips, reducing their effectiveness. Velcro was also ineffective in combat, as a soldier preferred to leave tools inside his pockets rather than rip apart the Velcro strips on his uniform and give away his position.

MOBILE DEVICES AND VELCRO

Compact and powerful tablets and smartphones made high-performance computers much easier to transport, and these handheld devices included video-recording capabilities. Although a camcorder tripod could hold a mobile device in place, the tripod was awkward and bulky to transport. Travelers quickly realized that a Velcro strip on the back of a mobile device could establish a strong enough bond to secure the device in a vehicle or attach it to a wall, so the traveler could conveniently record video while driving.

BIOMIMICRY

Buttons and zippers lacked close analogues in nature. When de Mestral introduced fabric strips that used burdock characteristics to bond products much more strongly to one another, he popularized the concept of biomimicry. Designers realized that other plants and animals might have evolved strategies that offered much better performance than products on the market, and engineers searched for biologists to improve product design.

The unique concept behind Velcro made the product much harder for de Mestral to develop. Fabric makers had no experience producing similar adhesive strips, and de Mestral needed almost a decade to convert burdock burrs into a market-ready product. The product initially suffered from a lack of a market, as de Mestral did not know who would purchase his adhesive strips. These disadvantages became strengths once athletic companies learned about Velcro. De Mestral created a new industry that lacked competitors for nearly two decades, allowing his company to dominate the market by the time his patent rights ran out. By the time other firms could introduce their own hook and loop products, Velcro had high name recognition, and the company held large capital reserves that it could use to fund Velcro research.

BIBLIOGRAPHY

Brush, Michael. "Investing IT; It Keeps Your Pants On, but Can It Fasten Your Wallet?" *New York Times,* April 14, 1996. Accessed February 8, 2012. http://www.nytimes.com/1996 /04/14/business/investing-it-it-keeps-your-pants-on-but-can -it-fatten-your-wallet.html?pagewanted=all&src=pm.

"How a Swiss Invention Hooked the World." *Swissinfo.ch,* January 4, 2007. Accessed February 8, 2012. http://www .swissinfo.ch/eng/index/How_a_Swiss_invention_hooked _the_world.html?cid=5653568.

Ingram, Frederick C. "Velcro Industries N.V." *International Directory of Company Histories,* edited by Tina Grant. Vol. 72, 361–364. St. James Press, 2006. Gale Virtual Reference Library (GALE|CX3444900110). Accessed February 8, 2012. http://go.galegroup.com/ps/i.do?id=GALE%7CCX34449001 10&v=2.1&u=itsbtrial&it=r&p=GVRL&sw=w.

"Inventor of the Week: George de Mestral." Cambridge, MA: Lemelson-MIT, April 2004. Accessed February 8, 2012. http://web.mit.edu/invent/iow/demestral.html.

Suddath, Claire. "A Brief History of: Velcro." *TIME,* June 15, 2010. Accessed February 8, 2012. http://www.time.com /time/nation/article/0,8599,1996883,00.html.

"USA: Velcro Comes Unstuck." *Management Today,* March 1, 1991. Accessed February 8, 2012. http://www.management today.co.uk/news/408887/USA-Velcro-comes-unstuck /?DCMP=ILC-SEARCH.

"Velcro Latching On with Industrial Uses." *Chicago Tribune,* November 30, 1986. Accessed February 8, 2012. http:// articles.chicagotribune.com/1986-11-30/business/86033 00683_1_mestral-buttons-and-zippers-nylon.

VisiCalc, Lotus 1-2-3, and the Advent of Spreadsheet Software

Before VisiCalc, business managers needed to share time on expensive mainframes to perform financial calculations and estimates, or use a pencil and paper. When Personal Software introduced VisiCalc in 1979, even small-business owners who owned an Apple II personal computer (PC) could easily make forecasts, predict inventory levels, and determine whether a decision would be profitable. Although increased competition and a dispute between the VisiCalc vendor and the programming team cost VisiCalc its market share a few years later, the concepts behind VisiCalc led to Lotus 1-2-3 and eventually Microsoft Excel.

MAINFRAME SPREADSHEETS

In a 1961 research paper, "Budgeting Models and Systems Simulation," University of California, Berkeley, professor Richard Mattessich described the theory behind the software spreadsheet model, explaining that automated computation could make financial calculations easier. In 1964 Mattessich released the code for his spreadsheet program, written in the Fortran computer programming language to run on mainframe computers. Business users needed to share time on costly mainframes to perform spreadsheet calculations. Large U.S. corporations and government agencies that had the cash to buy a mainframe used Mattessich's spreadsheet software, but smaller businesses in the United States did not have access to electronic spreadsheets and continued to use pen and paper to keep their records.

TWO VISIONS

Microcomputers gained in prominence during the late 1970s, but most technology firms focused on hardware manufacturing. Dan Fylstra wondered if he could start up a software company, and he proposed the concept during a course at Harvard Business School in early 1978. As software companies were new, Fylstra came up with his own business model. Fylstra would serve as a publisher, licensing software packages from independent authors and then distributing these programs to retailers and business clients.

Another Harvard Business school student, Dan Bricklin, struggled with an assignment that required him to calculate the outcome of a corporate acquisition. Bricklin did not know Fylstra in early 1978, although both students had studied computer science at the Massachusetts Institute of Technology (MIT) and enrolled in Harvard Business School. Bricklin needed to perform all of the calculations again, by hand, if one element of his model changed, so he decided to write a software tool that could make these calculations easier. He talked to his professors about his plan, but they were not impressed. They told him that a corporate manager's staff would perform these calculations, so he should just make the calculations by hand to learn how they worked, according to Stephen Levy in *Harper's Magazine* in November 1984. Bricklin decided to write the tool himself anyway.

GATHERING THE TEAM

Fylstra established a software publishing company, Personal Software, Inc., and licensed a few programs from independent software programmers. In the summer of 1978 Fylstra took a trip to Atlantic City, New Jersey, to attend a major software convention called PC-78. While he walked around the PC-78 convention, he met *Byte* editor

Carl Heimers, who told him to speak with Peter Jennings, according to Jennings's own account at his website. Fylstra noticed that Jennings's Microchess game impressed the conference visitors and offered to work with Jennings. Jennings agreed to let Personal Software sell Microchess, and shortly afterward, Jennings merged his own company, Micro-Ware Limited, with Personal Software.

Bricklin spent several months working on his program, but his prototype could not handle detailed calculations. He requested assistance from fellow MIT graduate Bob Frankston, who added more features to the prototype while ensuring that it could still run on a microcomputer. Bricklin showed the upgraded prototype to his professor, who liked the program. The professor knew that Fylstra sold Microchess and other microcomputer software, and told Bricklin to contact Fylstra.

The graphics capabilities of the Apple II impressed Fylstra, and he believed it had the best potential as a platform for a software spreadsheet. Steve Jobs also offered to sell Fylstra an Apple II for a low price if he developed a version of Microchess for the Apple II, according to Tom Hormby for *Low End Mac.* As spreadsheet software allowed an accountant to visualize financial transactions, the programmers considered naming it the Visible Calculator. Spreadsheet software recorded transactions like a pen recorded items in a paper ledger, so the programmers also considered calling it the Electronic Ledger.

In January 1979 Bricklin and Frankston set up their own company, Software Arts Inc., to develop the spreadsheet software. The programmers decided to name the spreadsheet VisiCalc, abbreviating the Visible Calculator term, although they worried that it sounded like a nutritional supplement. Fylstra realized the great potential of business software, and in May of that year, he moved Personal Software to the San Francisco Bay Area of California to work with other rising technology companies. The Software Arts programmers stayed on the East Coast of the United States, which made communications between the two companies more difficult.

Fylstra owed Jennings royalties on his Microchess sales, but Jennings knew that Fylstra needed cash to pay Bricklin and Frankston to finish VisiCalc. Since Jennings was a partner in Personal Software and expected VisiCalc to earn much more money than Microchess, he agreed to wait until VisiCalc was complete before receiving his Microchess royalties.

VISICALC LAUNCH

Personal Software started selling VisiCalc in October 1979, and the spreadsheet software immediately impressed programmers. Bricklin and Frankston had developed a useful business software that worked with the limited memory and processing capabilities of the Apple II. The technical challenges of VisiCalc development did not impress business managers, but they loved the simplicity of the spreadsheet software.

In the first month of its release, Personal Software sold more than 1,000 copies of VisiCalc for US$100 each, greatly boosting the profile, and the profits, of the company. The spreadsheet software also offered major marketing benefits for Steve Jobs. Other PCs that cost less than the Apple II lacked the power to run VisiCalc. With two important applications, VisiCalc and Microchess, the Apple II held a clear advantage over its competitors in 1980. Hornby, for *Low End Mac,* reported that Apple retailers often sold VisiCalc and the Apple II together, making sure that Apple buyers immediately had a powerful software package available when they brought their computer home. VisiCalc convinced many Apple II owners to upgrade their systems, as it needed 32 kilobytes of random access memory (32KB RAM) to run, but the basic Apple II came with 16KB RAM.

According to Jennings, because Personal Software held the rights to both VisiCalc and Microchess, it dominated the PC software market in the early 1980s, reporting higher revenue figures than Microsoft Corporation. The success of the Apple II and VisiCalc convinced IBM Inc. to go ahead with Project Chess, which produced the IBM PC in 1981.

VISIPLOT

Mitch Kapor had studied psychology and meditation, and he continued to search for direction in his life. Although Kapor gained admittance to the MIT Sloan School of Management, business school did not excite him, and he decided to write software on his Apple II instead. After Kapor left Sloan, he saw a VisiCalc demonstration, and he came up with a plan to help business owners get more use out of VisiCalc. The Personal Software founders had rushed to complete VisiCalc, so they did not include some advanced graphics features. Kapor created a graphics software package, VisiPlot, for Personal Software. The graphics package used the spreadsheets that VisiCalc produced to create graphs and charts, helping business owners visualize their financial calculations.

Personal Software, like its competitors, had little experience with software royalty contracts. Fylstra signed a contract with Kapor that granted Kapor a third of the revenue from VisiPlot and a second software package, Visitrend, which was an extremely generous share. VisiPlot and Visitrend quickly gained customers, as they were obvious upgrades for VisiCalc users. These programs were much more lucrative than the Personal Software founders expected, and soon Kapor was earning US$100,000 a month in royalties, according to *The History of Computing Project.*

In 1981 Personal Software itself earned US$12 million, boosted by its Microchess sales, so it could afford to buy out Kapor. Kapor negotiated a buyout deal for US$1.2 million for his rights to collect VisiPlot and Visitrend royalties. Kapor worked for another company for a few months afterward, but he quickly became restless again and decided to make a new spreadsheet package that improved on the capabilities of both programs.

FOUNDING LOTUS

Kapor recruited a colleague who had also attended MIT, Jonathan Sachs, and hired a few more programmers. Kapor remembered his meditation studies fondly, so he decided to name his software company Lotus Development Corporation. With eight employees, the Lotus team started work on their integrated spreadsheet package, Lotus 1-2-3. This name showed software buyers that the Lotus software suite contained three packages, so it was better than owning both VisiPlot and VisiCalc.

A word processor was an obvious addition to a business software suite, and the original design for Lotus 1-2-3 included a word processor. According to *I Programmer*, after Kapor saw an office software package, Context MBA, that suffered from many bugs because of its word processor, he decided to replace the word processor with a database package. Kapor did not really want to program a word processor anyway because it was a major technical challenge for his team.

Without the word processor, the Lotus team developed Lotus 1-2-3 quickly, and it reached the market in January 1983. Business managers were immediately impressed by the graphics capabilities of Lotus 1-2-3. Although VisiCalc and VisiPlot offered great performance for Apple II programs, Lotus 1-2-3 took advantage of the superior processing power of the IBM PC. The Lotus 1-2-3 package not only boosted sales for Lotus, it convinced business managers to purchase the IBM PC instead of Apple microcomputers.

VISI ON

Fylstra realized that a spreadsheet package was not enough to make PCs truly easy to use. With a graphical desktop environment, users could switch between multiple programs they were using to view information and use the mouse instead of the cursor to select spreadsheet cells, and they would not need to remember complex command line arguments. Xerox Corporation had introduced the graphical user interface concept with the Xerox Star in 1981, and Fylstra wanted to bring desktop graphics to Apple and IBM microcomputers.

Fylstra made development of a graphical desktop the top priority of Personal Software, even changing the name of the company to VisiCorp. VisiCorp released its graphical desktop environment, Visi On, in late 1983.

Visi On impressed business managers, but the hardware requirements of the desktop prevented it from gaining wide acceptance. Lotus 1-2-3, and many programs at the time, could run from a floppy disk, but an IBM PC owner needed to purchase a hard drive to install the Visi On desktop environment. Many IBM PC owners did not own hard drives in 1983, because a hard drive added thousands of U.S .dollars to the cost of a PC.

VISICORP VERSUS SOFTWARE ARTS

Fylstra created Visi On without help from the Software Arts programmers, Bricklin and Frankston. When VisiCorp released Visi On, Software Arts had an obligation under its contract with VisiCorp to release improvements for the VisiCalc package, but the programmers realized that the Visi On package would reduce the sales of their VisiCalc software. Software Arts was still on the East Coast of the United States, so the two companies could not easily negotiate with each other.

According to Ed Esber, who worked at VisiCorp at the time, when Fylstra heard a rumor that Software Arts was going to sue his firm to prevent him from selling Visi On, he responded by filing a lawsuit against Software Arts for failing to update VisiCalc. Throughout 1984 Software Arts and VisiCorp fought each other in court and placed advertisements condemning each other in newspapers and other publications. The controversy convinced many software retailers to carry Lotus 1-2-3 instead of VisiCalc, and distracted VisiCorp leadership during a critical period in 1984. The battle severely weakened both companies. After Bricklin spoke with Kapor in 1985, Lotus bought the VisiCalc technology from Bricklin, preventing another company from using VisiCalc against Lotus in the future, according to *I Programmer*.

LICENSING AGREEMENTS

VisiCorp introduced innovative software concepts before Microsoft and Apple, but it could not convert its advantages into long-term strengths because it did not control the products it sold. Fylstra gave up a large amount of potential income while he had to pay royalties, but canceling the contracts created two new competitors. Kapor was able to found Lotus with the money he received from Fylstra, while Software Arts sold Fylstra's best-selling product after the contract was gone.

BIBLIOGRAPHY

Ditlea, Steve. "The Birth of an Industry." *Inc.,* January 1, 1982. Accessed February 9, 2012. http://www.inc.com/magazine/19820101/2315.html.

Esber, Edward. "Visicorp History." EdEsber.com, 2011. Accessed February 9, 2012. http://edesber.com/visicorp-history/.

Hormby, Tom. "VisiCalc and the Rise of the Apple II." *Low End*

Mac, September 25, 2006. Accessed February 9, 2012. http://lowendmac.com/orchard/06/visicalc-origin-bricklin.html.

Jennings, Peter. "VisiCalc – The Early Days." *Benlo Park.* Accessed February 9, 2012. http://www.benlo.com/visicalc/index.html.

Levy, Steven. "A Spreadsheet Way of Knowledge." *Harper's Magazine,* November 1984. Accessed February 9, 2012. https://files.nyu.edu/ap70/public/levyss.htm.

Lopiccola, Phil, and Rachel Wrege. "Visicorp's VisiOn." *Popular Computing,* 1983. Accessed February 9, 2012. http://www.guidebookgallery.org/articles/visicorpsvision.

"Mitch Kapor and Lotus 1-2-3." *I-Programmer,* October 24, 2009. Accessed February 9, 2012. http://www.i-programmer.info/history/people/403-mitch-kapor.html.

"Mitch Kapor Schneider." *The History of Computing Project,* December 2, 2006. Accessed February 9, 2012. http://www.thocp.net/biographies/kapor_schneider_mitch.htm.

Power, D. J. "A Brief History of Spreadsheets." *DSSResources.com,* August 30, 2004. Accessed February 9, 2012. http://dssresources.com/history/sshistory.html.

Wal-Mart Uses Private Satellite Network as Technological Edge

When Wal-Mart Stores, Inc., the largest retailer in the United States, launched its private satellite network in 1988, it proved to be more than a dominant discount department store. The retailer also placed itself on the cutting edge of technology. The integrated satellite communication system relayed voice and data transmissions from the company's headquarters in Bentonville, Arkansas, to more than 1,200 of its stores and distribution centers. Inaugurated in January 1988 by Sam Walton, the company's cofounder, and David Glass, who was Wal-mart's president at the time, the private satellite network would prove to be one of the smartest forward steps Walton would take as the head of Wal-Mart.

A RETAIL GIANT IN ARKANSAS

Born on March 29, 1918, Samuel Walton grew up during the Great Depression in the 1930s. Exhibiting signs of ambition and entrepreneurialism at an early age, Walton sold newspapers and milk to help his family meet their basic living expenses during the Depression. After graduating from the University of Missouri in 1940, Walton entered the U.S. Army in 1942. His younger brother, James L. Walton (born in 1921) attended Wentworth Military Academy; he served in the armed forces during World War II as a U.S. Navy pilot. After the Walton brothers left the military, using US$5,000 Sam had saved while he was in the army and another US$20,000 he borrowed from his father-in-law, they opened their first Walton's Five and Dime store in Bentonville, Arkansas. The year was 1951; the brothers opened the store under the Ben Franklin discount store franchise brand.

It was not long before Sam Walton realized that by selling products at lower prices than area competitors did,

he could attract new customers, many of them former shoppers of local established department stores. Walton also made sure his store stocked a wide variety of goods. Both of these practices would become hallmarks of his success. In 1954, he opened a Ben Franklin discount store in a shopping center in Ruskin Heights, Missouri. The store did well, causing Walton to open a second store in a shopping center in Arkansas. However, the second store located in a shopping center did not perform as well as the first. Walton abandoned the idea of operating stores out of shopping centers and concentrated his efforts, once again, on separate retail stores. In an effort to gain more customers and open more Ben Franklin franchises, Walton approached Ben Franklin management nearly 10 years after he opened his store and requested that they allow him to lower prices further. This request was denied.

Rather than simply walking away from the retail business, Sam and James Walton opened their first Wal-Mart discount store in Rogers, Arkansas, in 1962, officially naming the store Wal-Mart Discount City. Although Sam selected Willard Walker, the manager of a TG&Y store in Tulsa, Oklahoma, to manage the first Wal-Mart, he visited the store in person once a week, reviewing the profits and losses. Walton also investigated other people's stores to find out the prices of their goods, always striving to ensure Wal-Mart had the lowest prices in town. He placed his stores in centralized locations in small towns. About his business practices, Sam Walton was quoted by Mohan P. Chandran, in his article, "Wal-Mart's Supply Chain Management Practices," as saying, "When we arrived in these small towns offering low prices every day, customer satisfaction guaranteed, and hours that were realistic for the way people wanted to shop, we passed right by that old variety store competition, with its 45 percent mark ups, limited selection and limited hours."

Another practice that Sam Walton instituted at Wal-Mart during the early years was requiring store managers to complete "Best Yesterday" forms. Managers provided information on the ledgers that helped Walton to track each store's daily performance against its performance on the same day of the previous year. In the Tuck School of Business at Dartmouth article, "Wal-Mart Stores, Inc.," Walton was quoted as saying, "We were really trying to become the very best operators—the most professional managers that we could. . .I have always had the soul of an operator, someone who wants to make things work well, then better, then the best they possibly can."

Sam Walton also centralized cash registers at his stores, moving cash registers from locations midway through his stores toward the front of the stores, allowing cashiers to ring up customer purchases as customers neared the exit doors.

Walton's cost-cutting efforts and focus on growing individual Wal-Mart retail stores was successful. By 1969, the Walton brothers had opened an additional 17 Wal-Mart stores, and in 1970 Wal-Mart went public. At the close of the year the retailer posted US$44 million in annual revenues. Seven years later, Wal-Mart started to expand by acquisition, buying 16 Mohr-Value stores and the Hutchenson Shoe Company. In addition to selling household goods and hardware, Wal-Mart also started selling jewelry and opened a pharmacy and auto-motive service center. By 1979 nearly 17 years after Sam and his brother James opened the first Wal-Mart, there were 276 Wal-Mart stores located in 11 states across the United States. Sales at the company had also ballooned to US$1.25 billion.

Seeking new ways to grow his business, Sam Walton opened the first Sam's Wholesale Club, a discount grocery store that allowed customers to yield savings over regular grocery store prices, especially if they bought products in bulk. Customers had to pay a membership fee to shop at the wholesale stores. While Walton concentrated on adding more Sam's Wholesale Clubs to his business, he also began thinking about how he was going to connect communications between the Wal-Mart retail stores, Sam's Wholesale Clubs, distribution centers, and the company's headquarters.

HISTORIC SATELLITE

In 1985 Wal-Mart contracted with Hughes Network Systems, LLC, a satellite and wireless services provider, to supply it with equipment such as a nine-meter antenna dish for its headquarters and 1.8 meter antenna dishes for its retail stores and distribution centers. Headquarters, referred to as the "hub station," was also equipped with

a control unit, video, telephone exchange, and transmitting and receiving equipment. The "hub station" alone cost US$1 million to set up. It cost between US$2,800 and US$3,500 per store to set up the smaller systems and US$50,000 a month to lease the satellite services. Despite these prices, the private satellite network allowed Wal-Mart to control communications costs. It also allowed managers at its individual stores to lower the amount of unsold inventory on hand. Rather than cut prices or shipments on low-selling products across the board at each of its stores, Wal-Mart could now manage price markdowns and the amount of packages ordered per location.

The satellite network also allowed Wal-Mart to communicate with its suppliers using computers. For example, the Procter & Gamble Company (P&G), one of Wal-Mart's major suppliers, was contracted to maintain the inventory for its stores. When products were low at certain stores, managers used an automated reordering system to request additional products. As reported by Chandran, "The computer system at Wal-Mart stores identified an item which was low in stock and sent a signal to P&G. The system then sent a re-supply order to the nearest P&G factory through a satellite communication system. P&G then delivered the item either to the Wal-Mart distribution center or directly to the concerned stores." Chandran continued, "This collaboration between Wal-Mart and P&G was a win-win proposition for both because Wal-Mart could monitor its stock levels in the stores constantly and also identify the items that were moving fast. P&G could also lower its costs and pass on some of the savings to Wal-Mart due to better coordination."

Employees used handheld computers that were linked to terminals located in the stores. Through the use of the handheld computers and terminals, employees and managers could track deliveries and in-store inventory. They could also track the volume of merchandise at nearby distribution centers. Furthermore, using an algorithm system (a set of rules used in calculations), Wal-Mart was able to forecast the amount of products it would need at each of its stores and distribution centers.

After supplies were delivered to individual stores and unloaded, inventory communication systems were updated. To ensure communications from stores and distribution centers to headquarters were delivered in an orderly fashion, communications were staggered into Wal-Mart's Satellite Business System (SBS) 4 satellite, a Ku-band satellite system. This was done to avoid creating short bursts of massive transmissions. The company's smaller individual store antennas, also referred to as "personal earth stations," were installed by National Communications Services, an information technology telecommunications services company. The satellite dishes were placed on steel poles above individual store roofs, facing the orbiting SBS system.

In addition to saving cost, allowing store managers to identify products that needed to have prices lowered due to stagnant sales, and enabling the Wal-Mart home office to track firm-wide sales and inventory levels, the private satellite network also improved communications for credit card authorizations. These transmissions were sent across digital data management systems at 56 kilobits per second. Using a telephone, the data would have been transmitted as slowly as 12 to 24 kilobits per second. Additionally, the satellite network allowed Wal-Mart to receive updates from its individual stores and distribution centers as many as 12 times a day rather than the twice daily updates it would have received had it continued to receive updates using telephones.

The private satellite network allowed Wal-Mart to cut its telephone costs by nearly 20 percent. It also allowed the company to receive quicker and more accurate updates from the drivers who manned Wal-Mart's nearly 3,500 company-owned trucks. Shipments could be ordered and relayed to drivers so that new products could be delivered and stocked on store shelves within two days of the date orders were placed. Describing the benefits of the private satellite network system after it was first developed, Sam Walton said, as reported by Chandran, "I can walk in the satellite room, where our technicians sit in front of the computer screens talking on the phone to any stores that might be having a problem with the system, and just looking over their shoulders for a minute or two will tell me a lot about how a particular day is going." He continued, "On the screen, I can see the total of the day's bank credit sales adding up as they occur. If we have something really important or urgent to communicate to the stores and distribution centers, I, or any other Wal-Mart executive can walk back to our TV studio and get on that satellite transmission and get it right out there."

The same year that Wal-Mart rolled out its private satellite network, it also opened its first supercenter (which was designed with a supermarket) in Washington, Missouri. The company would go on to add supermarkets to many of its other stores over the coming years. In 1990 Wal-Mart opened stores in Pennsylvania, California, Nevada, North Dakota, South Dakota, and Utah. It also became the largest retailer in the United States, recording annual revenues of US$32 billion. An additional 25 Sam's Clubs were opened in various locations across the United States.

By 1991 Wal-Mart had spent nearly US$4 billion on its network. Additionally, approximately 10 million transactions were recorded on the system each day in 1991. In October 2001 Wal-Mart contracted with Atlas Commerce, Inc., a provider of advanced software for supply chain electronic hubs, to upgrade its private satellite network through the Internet.

LARGEST RETAILER IN THE UNITED STATES

Early in 1992 President George H. W. Bush awarded Sam Walton the Medal of Freedom, the highest honor a civilian can be awarded. The award ceremony was held at Wal-Mart's Bentonville, Arkansas, headquarters. Weeks later, on April 15, 1992, at the age of 74, Sam Walton died. His son, S. Robson Walton, succeeded him as chairman of the board. Later that same year, Wal-Mart expanded its operations to international markets, opening stores in Puerto Rico. By 1995 Wal-Mart had stores operating in all 50 U.S. states. It also opened stores in Hong Kong, Argentina, and Brazil.

In 2011 sales were US$422 billion. Wal-Mart's main advantages continued to be its size and low prices. Furthermore, as stated by Emek Basker in the *Journal of Economic Perspectives,* "Technology and scale are at the core of Wal-Mart's advantage over its rivals." Basker continued, " Wal-Mart's technological edge is in its logistics, distribution, and inventory control." It was Wal-Mart's technology, including its private satellite network, that allowed it to grow and outperform its competitors, something Sam Walton might have envisioned during the early years when he started having store managers complete daily "Best Yesterday" forms.

BIBLIOGRAPHY

Basker, Emek. "The Causes and Consequences of Wal-Mart's Growth." *Journal of Economic Perspectives,* Summer 2007. Accessed February 15, 2012. http://pubs.aeaweb.org/doi /pdfplus/10.1257/jep.21.3.177.

Boyle, Matthew. " Wal-Mart Moves Upmarket." *Bloomberg Businessweek,* June 3, 2009. Accessed February 15, 2012. http://www.businessweek.com/magazine/content/09_24 /b4135000941856.htm.

Chandran, P. Mohan. "Wal-Mart's Supply Chain Management Practices." Hyderabad, India: ICFAI Center for Management Research, 2003. Accessed February 15, 2012. http:// mohanchandran.files.wordpress.com/2008/01/wal-mart.pdf.

Healy, Carole. "Wal-Mart Stores, Inc." In *International Directory of Company Histories,* edited by Tina Grant and Miranda Ferrara. Vol. 63, 427–432. Detroit: St. James Press, 2004. Gale Virtual Reference Library (GALE|CX3429000111). Accessed February 15, 2012. http://go.galegroup.com/ps/i.do ?id=GALE%7CCX3429000111&v=2.1&u=gale&it=r&p=G VRL&sw=w.

Heuy, John. "Discounting Dynamo: Sam Walton." *TIME,* December 7, 1998. Accessed February 15, 2012. http://www .time.com/time/magazine/article/0,9171,989791,00.html.

Hopkins, Jim. "Wal-Mart's Influence Grows." *USA Today,* January 29, 2003. Accessed February 15, 2012. http://www .usatoday.com/money/industries/retail/2003-01-28 -walmartnation_x.htm.

Lichtenstein, Nelson. "Wal-Mart: Template for 21st Century Capitalism." *New Labor Forum* 14, no. 1 (2005): 21–30. Accessed February 15, 2012. http://www.uschinalaborex change.org/docs/Wal-Mart%20Template%20for%20

21st%20Century%20Capitalism.pdf.

Markowitz, Arthur. "Wal-Mart Launches World's Largest Private Satellite Communication System." *CBS Interactive,* February 1, 1988. Accessed February 15, 2012. http://findarticles .com/p/articles/mi_m3092/is_n3_v27/ai_6333369.

Ranade, Sudhanshu. "Satellite Adds Speed to Wal-Mart." *Hindu Business Line,* July 17, 2005. Accessed February 15, 2012. http://www.thehindubusinessline.in/2005/07/17/stories /2005071700141600.htm.

"Wal-Mart Satellite Communication." *Emerging Technologies* (blog), October 1, 2007. Accessed February 15, 2012. http:// emergingtechnologiesis.blogspot.com/2007/10/wal-mart -satellite-communication-system.html.

"Wal-Mart Stores, Inc." Hanover, NH: Tuck School of Business at Dartmouth. William F. Achtmeyer Center for Global Leadership. Accessed February 15, 2012. http://mba.tuck .dartmouth.edu/pdf/2002-2-0013.pdf.

Wal-Mart Stores, Inc. "Sam Walton, Our Founder." Bentonville, AR. Accessed February 15, 2012. http://walmartstores.com /AboutUs/9502.aspx.

Walt Disney's Vision of Family-friendly Theme Parks

Amusement parks operated by the Walt Disney Company exemplify the importance of customer service. By satisfying customers' demands, Disney gained a reputation for recovering quickly when mishaps occurred at its parks. Disney's customer service approach was so effective that it became legendary among business executives, and helped the company earn revenue by teaching corporate and government clients to provide better service to their customers.

ESTABLISHING THE BRAND

Founder Walter Elias "Walt" Disney wanted to raise his movie studio employees' morale during the Great Depression of the 1930s, so he came up with the idea of building an amusement park for them in the Los Angeles, California, area. After additional thought, he decided to create a park for the public as well. Walt Disney was disgusted by the seedy appearance of other carnivals and fairs, and he wanted to set up his own park to provide an alternative. Unlike many carnival operators, Disney had other media properties to consider. The park needed to represent the family-friendly Disney brand and promote the images of Mickey Mouse, Donald Duck, and other famous Disney cartoon characters.

PLANNING THE PARK

Carnivals and fairs often sell alcoholic beverages. This complicates management of the park, as a drunken visitor may sustain an injury on a ride or harass or annoy other guests. Walt Disney decided not to offer beer and other alcoholic beverages in the park. Although Disney gave up the alcohol concession revenue his park would have earned, restricting access to alcoholic beverages helped the park promote its family-friendly image.

Walt Disney also disliked the vending arrangements that other carnivals offered. As a carnival received revenue from every food stand, a fair could boast hundreds of vendors, each of which sold its own food, promoted its meals vigorously, and created its own waste. Disney decided to prohibit individual vendors from offering products such as hot dogs, and only served food at a few official locations that the park could conveniently manage. This decision helped Disney limit the trash and litter inside the park.

Walt Disney faced disapproval from investors and local authorities for his new project. Burbank, California's city managers shared his view of other fairs and carnivals and refused to grant permission for the park within Burbank's city limits. Bankers and amusement park operators believed that Disney's park would not bring in enough revenue, so Disney also faced problems financing the park. Disney hired surveyors from Stanford University to find a new location for the park. The park needed to be in the local region, close to a freeway. The surveyors found a suitable plot of land in Anaheim, California, where city authorities approved the Disneyland plans. A 160-acre orange grove provided the site for the park, according to JustDisney.com. Disney kept a great deal of control over the layout of the park, rejecting several of the plans that his subordinates suggested. JustDisney reported that Walt Disney personally designed one attraction, Tom Sawyer's Island, to ensure that it matched his vision.

THE GRAND OPENING

Disney raised the money he needed to build the park from the American Broadcasting Company (ABC) network by creating a show about Disneyland while it was under construction. Since this show was popular with television audiences, the park attracted hordes of visitors when it opened in 1955. According to "Disneyland Timeline," the grand opening boasted a television audience of 90 million, nearly the entire national television audience in the 1950s. Customers held high expectations for the new park and the launch included celebrity guests.

However, Disneyland experienced major customer service failures during its opening day. Fresh, and sticky, asphalt covered the park's walkways, causing some guests to trip and fall and breaking the high heels of female guests. People created fake Disneyland tickets, climbed the fences, and gained unauthorized access by other means, so the park received many more visitors than its rides could handle. The park had planned for 6,000 visitors but received nearly 30,000.

There was a litany of other problems. The rides quickly broke down, disappointing the guests. Guests who complained to ride attendants and security guards found these employees rude and unhelpful. The weather was much hotter than usual for Southern California and water fountains lacked water, a shortage due to a plumbers' strike.

ADDRESSING CONCERNS

The company reorganized the ticketing system to make paying for rides more convenient for guests. Instead of having a customer purchase an individual ticket at each ride booth, tickets were organized into classes, so a C ticket entitled a customer to go on any class C ride. This meant that the concession booths at the front could handle all of the ticket sales, reducing wait times for rides.

When Walt Disney addressed the performance of the fountains, he used this problem as an opportunity to improve the theme of each attraction. Fountains and other amenities were redesigned to fit the decor of each area of the park. This meant that they were not only functional but did not detract from the immersion experience that these themes created. In addition, Disney handled the complaints about his employees by setting up a training system, which he termed Disney University, that taught employees how to properly serve guests. In its early years, the physical presence of Disney University consisted of a small trailer in Anaheim, California.

Disney looked to his movie studio to develop the job application and training process for his Disneyland employees. Every applicant faced a casting call in which they demonstrated their skills in front of other Disney staff. Every park employee went through the casting call process and Disney University training, ensuring that all employees understood their responsibility to entertain the park's guests, no matter what job they performed in the park.

PACIFIC OCEAN PARK

The television network CBS noticed the success of Disneyland and formed a partnership with the horse racing organization, Hollywood Turf Club, to create a competing attraction, Pacific Ocean Park, in Santa Monica, California. Although Disney addressed many of the problems about which his guests complained, the ticketing system remained a customer service weakness. Disneyland sold its guests ticket books that contained a few tickets for each ride tier. Customers who used their C tickets to visit the most popular attractions would quickly be left with tickets for A and B rides that lacked the attractive features of the C rides. This issue worsened after Disneyland introduced the D and E tiers.

The Pacific Ocean Park amusement park addressed the ticketing issue by offering access to every ride for a single admission fee. This ensured that customers could go on their favorite rides without worrying about whether they had tickets left. Pacific Ocean Park also competed on cost with Disneyland. A guest paid US$1 to get into Disneyland, and the basic ticket book cost US$3.50 in 1959, according to Werner Weiss for *Yesterland*. In 1958, Pacific Ocean Park charged an entry fee of US$0.90, offering a less expensive alternative, reported Lisa Newton for *Travelin' Local*. The company used the name of the theme park to promote its pricing structure, coining the slogan "Pay One Price." Los Angeles, California, residents could use the city's mass transit services to reach the park in nearby Santa Monica, California.

In the first day Pacific Ocean Park was open, it achieved almost as much popularity as Disneyland's first day, attracting 20,000 visitors. After six months, more than a million guests had visited the park. Pacific Ocean Park did not retain its attractiveness, however, as it suffered from customer service issues of its own. The park appeared less exclusive than Disneyland, and troublemakers faced fewer challenges in gaining entry. Although cheap fun served as the main draw for its customers, the park faced high maintenance costs, as the salty air and ocean spray of coastal Santa Monica, California eroded the metal machinery of its rides.

FREEDOMLAND

Competitors in New York introduced their own park, Freedomland U.S.A. in Bronx, New York, in 1960, with assistance from some of the contractors who built Disneyland. The United States provided the shape for this park, which was split into five regions: New York, Chicago, San Francisco, the Southwest, and Satellite Land, which represented the Southeast. According to "Disneyland Timeline," Freedomland hosted 60,000 visitors during its first day, June 19, 1960.

Freedomland suffered from two customer service weaknesses that eventually shut down the park. The Walt

Disney Company took great care to ensure that guests could reach Disneyland by constructing it next to Interstate 5 in Orange County. In contrast, visitors could not easily travel to Freedomland, since it could not be directly accessed via the New York City Subway system. In addition, since it was U.S. history themed, its attractions tended to be more educational than thrilling. The 1964 World's Fair provided a more entertaining alternative for many New Yorkers, and the park shut down, although some of its rides continued to entertain guests at other amusement parks. The Walt Disney company introduced its own attractions at the World's Fair, giving its managers evidence that a Disney park could draw crowds on the East Coast of the United States, even if competitors like Freedomland struggled.

DISNEY WORLD

The Walt Disney Company expanded its operations to Florida in 1971 when it established Disney World. Disney World continued to rely on the customer service innovations that made Disneyland successful, including attention to detail, casting calls, and Disney University. Disney World also addressed a flaw in the original design of Disneyland. Walt Disney had not realized how many hotel guests the park could attract, and hotels filled the area around Disneyland. Even worse, many of the hotels and restaurants did not share Disney's family-friendly vision, and parts of the area surrounding Anaheim, California, resembled the sketchy and dangerous fair and carnival atmosphere that had preceded Disneyland.

Instead of building a stand-alone park, Disney World was designed as a resort town. Disney World offered themed hotels and entertainment options to guests who stayed overnight in the area, ensuring that the entire vacation experience remained family friendly. Disney World gained the additional revenue from hotel room rentals, restaurants, and other purchases its guests made in the area. Although building a resort town required a larger capital investment than the construction of an amusement park alone, Disneyland provided additional income that supported the project.

CORPORATE TRAINING

The success of Disney World attracted business executives who were interested in learning the company's customer service secrets. Tom Peters, a management expert, wrote *In Search of Excellence* in 1982, which emphasized the customer service strengths Disney possessed. In response to requests from these executives, Disney developed corporate development programs for students from other enterprises at Disney University. Courses taught the Disney approach to management, customer service,

employee orientation, and leadership. The programs promoted Disney's brand while bringing in additional earnings.

TOKYO DISNEY

The Walt Disney Company expanded its parks overseas in 1983 with the creation of Tokyo Disneyland, in Tokyo, Japan. Unlike its parks in California and Florida, Disney left many of the management responsibilities to the Oriental Land Company, which it did not own. The Japanese managers kept many of the original concepts from the Anaheim, California, Disneyland in place for their park, including the rides and the characters. Disney offered to adapt its park to Japanese tastes, but the Japanese managers preferred to stay close to the U.S. approach, which helped differentiate Tokyo Disneyland from other Japanese amusement parks. Tokyo Disneyland surpassed the U.S. parks in customer service and sanitation, and retained its popularity with Japanese visitors.

EURO DISNEY

Disney began its Euro Disney project with great hopes, but the project did not go as smoothly as other ventures. Managers decided to construct the park in Paris, France, instead of Barcelona, Spain, as French authorities promoted France's infrastructure advantages. French citizens, many of whom already felt exposed to excessive U.S. cultural influences, were not as enthusiastic. Although Disney surveyed the market and found few established theme parks, it failed to recognize the draw of European festivals, museums, and landmarks, which offered alternative entertainment and education possibilities.

Walt Disney had designed his family-friendly policies for U.S. amusement park visitors, and the ban on alcohol sales inside the park bolstered the park's attraction in Anaheim, California, but it served as a deterrent to French visitors, many of whom were angry that the Paris, France, park, which opened in 1992, did not offer wine and other beverages. The company did agree to sell alcoholic drinks outside the park to meet these concerns. However, restaurants outside the park in Paris, France, offered better food at lower prices, and general admission prices were also high. Disney's conservative grooming standards offended French employees, who believed that the company made unreasonable requests. For example, as Robert M. Grant noted in "Euro Disney: From Dream to Nightmare, 1987–94," facial hair and long hair was banned, and female employees were allowed to wear only modest makeup and limited jewelry. French labor unions complained, according to Grant, that the strict policies amounted to "an attack on individual freedom."

THE DISNEY APPROACH

The Walt Disney Company developed a customer service strategy that changed the popular perception of an amusement park from a nuisance to an attraction that cities eagerly competed to obtain. Attention to detail especially benefited Disney, as any flaw could detract from the immersion that its parks offered. The customer service approach helped the company find innovative solutions that solved problems for its customers and provided new sources of revenue, such as designing Disney World to include hotels. The idea of creating Disney University to teach this approach helped ensure that Disney could continue to provide the same level of service when it opened new parks.

BIBLIOGRAPHY

Bennett, Brian. "A Brief History of the Disney Parks." *Mouse Planet.* Accessed January 6, 2012. http://www.mouseplanet.com/dtp/archive/other/history.htm.

"Disneyland Timeline." California State University, Stanislaus, 2007. Accessed January 6, 2012. http://www.csus.edu/indiv/s/shawg/articles/facilities/disneyland_timeline.html.

"Disneyland's History." Just Disney.com. Accessed January 6, 2012. http://www.justdisney.com/disneyland/history.html.

Gonzalez, David. "Celebrating the Short, Sweet Ride of Freedomland." *City Room* (blog), *New York Times,* June 19, 2010. Accessed January 6, 2012. http://cityroom.blogs.nytimes.com/2010/06/19/celebrating-the-short-sweet-ride-of-freedomland/.

Grant, Robert M. "Euro Disney: From Dream to Nightmare, 1987–94." From chap. 15 in *Contemporary Strategy Analysis.* 7th ed. Chichester, West Sussex, UK: John Wiley & Sons, 2010. Accessed January 6, 2012. http://www.blackwellpublishing.com/grant/docs/14EuroDisney.pdf.

Newton, Lisa. "Santa Monica's Pacific Ocean Park." *Travelin' Local,* May 27, 2011. Accessed January 6, 2012. http://www.travelinlocal.com/santa-monics-pacific-ocean-park/.

Paton, Scott Madison. "Service Quality, Disney Style." *Quality Digest,* January 1997. Accessed January 6, 2012. http://www.qualitydigest.com/jan97/disney.html.

Weiss, Werner. "The Birth of the 'E' Ticket at Disneyland." *Yesterland,* July 9, 2009. Accessed January 6, 2012. http://www.yesterland.com/eticket.html.

Williams Lee. "History of the Disney University." *Disneyland's World Famous Dr. Lee!* (blog), April 13, 2011. Accessed January 6, 2012. http://drleeclub33.blogspot.com/2011/04/history-of-disney-university.html.

WD-40: Lubricant, Rust, and Corrosion Inhibitor

■

In 1953 Norm Larsen, a Rocket Chemical Company, Inc. (Rocket Chemical), employee, set out to create a product that would prevent missile covers from corroding by repelling water. Little did he know that the product, WD-40, meant to treat equipment for General Dynamics Corporation and the National Aeronautics and Space Administration (NASA), would find its way around the world, helping millions of people keep a variety of household appliances functioning properly. Over time, WD-40 would become known as much for its beneficial uses as for the persistence its creators demonstrated when they refused to give up on the first versions of WD-40, a product that became familiar to consumers as much for its name as for the bright blue and yellow can in which it was sold.

SOUTHERN CALIFORNIA AND WD-40

Born in 1923 in Chicago, Illinois, Norman Bernard Larsen was a self-taught industrial chemist. He only had a high school diploma and gathered much of what he learned about chemistry from reading books. From his early years, Larsen was inspired to create products that would make people's lives easier. After he moved west to California, he founded Rocket Chemical. Rocket Chemical was located in Southern California, the area where the aerospace industry was booming in the 1950s. In fact, many employees in the aerospace industry worked in one of the large industrial plants, some of them belonging to the military, in Southern California. In addition to Rocket Chemical, North American Aviation, Lockheed Corporation, McDonnell Douglas Corporation, General Dynamics Corporation, Convair, and Hughes Aircraft Company were

a few of the businesses operating in Southern California's aerospace industry at the time.

Of those companies, Rocket Chemical was one of the smallest, having been started in 1952 by Norm Larsen and three investors. Some of the factors that attracted people who worked in the aerospace industry to the area were the mild climate, numerous military installations, and the miles of open space, the latter providing enough room to build large military plants to house missiles and aircraft. The weather, it turned out, although mild due to Southern California's close proximity to the Pacific Ocean, caused aerospace equipment to rust and corrode. Rocket Chemical, based in San Diego, California, planned to create corrosion control products and sell them to large firms such as Convair and General Dynamics.

A SEEMINGLY SIMPLE PRODUCT

Norm Larsen and his Rocket Chemical colleagues set out to create a rust-prevention solvent and degreaser. They worked in a small laboratory, mixing and testing one series of chemical compounds after another. It took 40 attempts before Larsen and his team were able to create a product that not only degreased military missiles and airplanes but also prevented corrosion and rust in the damp Southern California climate. Larsen called the newly created product "WD-40," which stood for "water displacement perfected on the 40th try." To keep the ingredients in WD-40 a trade secret, Larsen decided not to patent the product.

The first major firm Rocket Chemical landed a contract with was Convair, an aircraft manufacturer. The company would later go on to develop rockets and spacecraft. When Rocket Chemical closed the deal with Convair, the manufacturer was working on building the Atlas missile, the first intercontinental ballistic missile designed in the United States. Other aircraft Convair used the Rocket Chemical product on included the B-36 Bomber, F-106 Delta Dart, and the F-102 Delta Dagger.

The WD-40 product worked so well, several Convair employees started sneaking the product out of the Convair plant, taking it home, and using it on personal equipment. Several years after developing WD-40, Larsen contracted to have the chemical placed in aerosol cans. His reasoning was that if WD-40 was produced in aerosol cans, consumers (as had the Convair employees) might find uses for the product at home.

Five years after he developed WD-40, Larsen released the product for general consumer usage in 1958. WD-40 was first sold in sporting goods and hardware stores in San Diego, California. It was available in plain black and gold aerosol cans designed with the words "WD-40, Displaces Moisture, Another Fine Product of the Rocket Chemical Co., Inc." printed across the front of the cans. Rocket Chemical hired several salespeople to market the product to store owners. Early U.S. customers used WD-40 to clean tar off bicycles and cars, clean tools, and to lubricate lawnmowers and other household equipment and appliances. Sales of WD-40 spiked early. By 1960 company employees were selling an average of 45 cases of the corrosion preventer and degreaser a week.

Hurricane Carla, a category five tropical cyclone, came ashore on the Gulf Coast in 1961. By the time the hurricane landed, particularly along Texas and Florida shores, it had been downgraded to a category four cyclone. Even so, it caused more than US$2 billion in damages. The storm also claimed dozens of lives, flooded automobiles, and flattened homes. As the storm subsided, Rocket Chemical received truckloads of orders for WD-40 for hurricane victims, who used WD-40 to recondition their water-damaged automobiles, outdoor equipment, and household appliances. These large truckload orders were the biggest shipments Rocket Chemical had made up to that point.

Consumer sales in the United States of WD-40 increased significantly following Hurricane Carla. Companies in the Texas offshore oil industry used WD-40 on their fleet motors to get their equipment up and running again. Four years after Hurricane Carla came ashore, Rocket Chemical stopped developing and selling other products and focused all its efforts on WD-40. In 1962 WD-40 was used as a protective coating on *Friendship VII*. This was the spacecraft in which John Glenn orbited the earth on February 20, 1962, the first U.S. citizen to do so.

WD-40 would be used several years later during another government-initiated project. This initiative would garner even more headlines than John Glenn's space orbit. As U.S. troops fought in the Vietnam War, WD-40 was used on their firearms, working to keep rifles and handguns in good condition. Relatives, friends, and concerned citizens who sent care packages to the troops in Vietnam often included cans of WD-40 in the packages. As reported in the WD-40 2003 Annual Report, one soldier wrote, "WD-40 saved my life." He continued, "If I hadn't sprayed it on to lubricate my gun, I'd be dead now."

CONTINUED GROWTH

In 1969 WD-40 brought John Barry, formerly with 3M, on board as its president and chief executive officer. In addition to bolstering the company's marketing efforts, Barry changed the company's name from Rocket Chemical Company to WD-40 Company. Barry also changed the product packaging, changing the color of the aerosol cans from black and gold to blue and yellow. Barry sold WD-40 to grocery stores, since he knew consumers often bought products on impulse. His marketing efforts paid off. Douglas Martin, in his 2009 *New York Times* article, "John S. Barry, Main Force Behind WD-40, Dies at 84," quoted Barry as saying, "We may appear to be a manufacturing company . . . but in fact we are a marketing company."

Also in 1969 WD-40 Company broke the US$1 million product sales mark. Four years later, in 1973, WD-40 Company went public. On opening day, the price of WD-40 Company reached as high as US$34 per share. According to the WD-40 Company official website, by this time, the WD-40 product had become known as "the can with a thousand uses." The product had been used by consumers for at least 2,000 different applications. One customer, a bus driver living in Asia, used WD-40 to remove a python from underneath his bus. Police officers also once used WD-40 to remove a burglar who had gotten stuck in an air-conditioning vent. Other uses for WD-40 were chronicled in the *Reader's Digest* article, "Wow, Look What WD-40 Can Do!" Some of the additional uses mentioned included renewing the color and vibrancy of faded plastic furniture. This was done by spraying WD-40 on the faded furniture material and wiping the sprayed area clean. In addition to cleaning barbecue grills and degreasing lawnmowers, WD-40 was also used to prevent snow from sticking to windows.

People who sprayed WD-40 under the eaves of their homes discovered that doing so kept wasps from building nests there. WD-40 was also used to clean dead bugs off automobile grilles, remove stuck or jammed automobile spark plugs, and revive spark plugs. Some of the product's other uses included winter-proofing shoes and boots by preventing and removing water stains from the footwear. Additionally, fishing lures and boats that were sprayed with WD-40 were also waterproofed and kept from corroding.

Despite its many beneficial uses, WD-40 was also linked to lawsuits involving plaintiffs who claimed they were injured while using the product. For example, the *Baltimore Sun* reported in 1996 that "Leon Fields was squirting WD-40 under his Winnebago camper to stop corrosion, one of the advertised '1,000 uses' for the spray lubricant, when the can touched a live wire and another piece of metal and burst into a fiery ball of oil and propane." Fields, a 58-year-old math teacher, received burns over 24 percent of his body. For his injuries, Fields was awarded US\$5 million in damages from WD-40 Company. The article also noted, "In November 1988, Dan Horton of Ocean Springs, Miss., was lubricating a wall fan with WD-40 when the can touched a live wire. The container burst into flames, burning Horton's 18-month-old daughter, Lauren."

Other incidents of WD-40 exploding when the aerosol can came in contact with live wires were also reported. For example, the *Baltimore Sun* reported that "In April 1994, Toni McLane of Yreka, Calif., was using WD-40 to quiet a squeak in a dryer when the can touched a live switch. It blew up, burning her face and arms." In response to receiving notice of the injuries, in 1996, WD-40 Company updated its warning label, alerting consumers to the fact that the aerosol cans could explode and catch fire if they came into contact with live wires or battery terminals. The WD-40 Company also switched from using propane to using carbon dioxide to create a safer product.

Another change that the company made to WD-40 in 2003 was to design a "big blast" can. The cans were designed with a wide-area spray nozzle to allow the product to be easily sprayed across large surfaces. Two years later, in 2005, the company introduced the WD-40 Smart Straw, a can designed with a permanently attached red straw. The redesign was done to satisfy customers who complained of losing the attachable straw. A year later, in 2006, the WD-40 Company launched its WD-40 Fan Club. Before the end of 2006, 100,000 people from around the world had joined the fan club.

In the early 2010s the company had yet to reveal the ingredients that made up WD-40. It continued to avoid patenting its top-selling product in order to keep the ingredients secret. However, on its official website, the company stated that WD-40 did not contain silicone, water, wax, kerosene, graphite or chloroflurocarbons (CFCs).

WD-40 LOOKING FORWARD, ITS PRIMARY PRODUCT DOMINATING THE MARKET

In the article "Birth of an Icon: The Story of WD-40," in *Today's Machining World,* WD-40 Company's marketing chief, Tim Lesmeister, said, "There is one guy who is part of WD-40 who gets up every morning and makes the brew." When discussing the product's secret ingredients, he continued, "We have three locations (in Sydney, London and San Diego) that make the secret sauce, but primarily it is made in the same warehouse in San Diego that has been there for many years. He does have a back-up or two, but even the CEO doesn't have anything to do with making it. In fact, almost no one here knows whether it is something really complicated or really simple."

For 2011 WD-40 Company reported US\$336 million in product sales. Furthermore, WD-40 Company planned to roll out five new products across the United States and Europe in 2012. The company was also starting to see an increase in sales of its WD-40 specialist products, a series of rust release penetrant, long-lasting lubricant, and long-term corrosion inhibitor products. The products were sold at home improvement stores, auto supply shops, and hardware stores. By 2012 the product Norm Larsen developed in 1953 had made WD-40 Company one of the few businesses that established itself as a household name while creating only one primary product.

BIBLIOGRAPHY

"Birth of an Icon: The Story of WD-40." *Today's Machining World,* July 2011. Accessed February 14, 2012. http://www.todaysmachiningworld.com/birth-of-an-icon-the-story-of-wd-40 .

Buchanan, Leigh. "Obituary: The Genius of John S. Barry." *Inc.,* October 1, 2009. Accessed February 14, 2012. http://www.inc.com/magazine/20091001/obituary-the-genius-of-john-s-barry.html .

Di Justo, Patrick. "What's Inside WD-40? Superlube's Secret Sauce." *Wired,* April 20, 2009. Accessed February 14, 2012. http://www.wired.com/science/discoveries/magazine/17-05/st_whatsinside .

Martin, Douglas. "John S. Barry, Main Force Behind WD-40, Dies at 84." *New York Times,* July 22, 2009. Accessed February 14, 2012. http://www.nytimes.com/2009/07/22/business/22barry1.html?ref=wd40company.

Mazloom, Martin. "A Real Space-Age Potion." The History Channel, April 1, 2010. Accessed February 14, 2012. http://www.thehistorychannelclub.com/articles/articletype/articleview/articleid/365/a-real-space-age-potion.

Newman, Andrew. "Which Grease for a Squeaky Wheel?" *New York Times,* April 20, 2010. Accessed February 14, 2012. http://www.nytimes.com/2010/04/21/business/media/21adco.html?ref=wd40company .

"Propane in WD-40 Gives Rise to Lawsuits: Lubricant's Maker Faulted in Explosions." *Baltimore Sun,* October 14, 1996. Accessed February 14, 2012. http://articles.baltimoresun.com/1996-10-14/business/1996288113_1_wd-40-touched-live-wire.

Skibola, Nicole. "Leadership Lessons from WD-40's CEO, Garry Ridge." *Forbes,* June 27, 2011. Accessed February 14, 2012. http://www.forbes.com/sites/csr/2011/06/27/leadership-lessons-from-wd-40s-ceo-garry-ridge.

"WD-40 Company." In *International Directory of Company Histories,* edited by Jay P. Pederson. Vol. 87, 455–460.

Detroit: St. James Press, 2007. Gale Virtual Reference Library (GALE| CX2690300102). Accessed March 2, 2012. http://go.galegroup.com/ps/i.do?id=GALE%7CCX2690300102&v=2.1&u=gale&it=r&p=GVRL&sw=w.

WD-40 Company. "About Us." San Diego, CA. Accessed February 14, 2012. http://www.wd40.com/about-us/history.

———. "WD-40 Company: An Invention. 2003 Annual Report." Accessed February 14, 2012. http://media.corporate-ir.net/media_files/NSD/WDFC/reports/wd40_2003/WD40_AR2003.pdf .

"WD-40 Company Reports First Quarter Sales and Earnings." *Reuters,* January 9, 2012. Accessed February 14, 2012. http://www.reuters.com/article/2012/01/09/idUS190095+09-Jan-2012+PRN20120109 .

"Wow, Look What WD-40 Can Do!" *Reader's Digest.* Accessed February 14, 2012. http://www.rd.com/home/wow-look-what-wd40-can-do.

Whole Foods Market, Inc.: Natural Foods Supermarket Success

Whole Foods Market, Inc., the national natural foods supermarket chain, has experienced remarkable growth since its first store opened in Austin, Texas, in 1980. By the end of 2010 the company had 299 stores across the United States, inspiring fierce loyalty in some U.S. consumers and a negative response in others. This spectrum of feeling is partially because Whole Foods has not been afraid to incorporate new and unique ideas in many aspects of its business model, and not all of these ideas have worked or been well received. However, Whole Foods is a company unafraid to take risks.

AUSTIN ORIGINS

Whole Foods founders John Mackey, Renee Lawson Hardy, Craig Weller, and Mark Skiles demonstrated their creativity and instinct for business in the early days of the company's history. Before the four banded together to open Whole Foods, they were two pairs of partners operating two natural food stores in Austin, Texas. Mackey, 25 years old, and Hardy, 21 years old, had borrowed US$45,000 from family members and friends to open a natural food store they called SaferWay. The name poked fun at the traditional grocery stores operating in Austin at the time, SafeWay. Using all the resources they had at their disposal, they stored large quantities of food in their apartment. When the landlord discovered this misuse of the property, they were evicted. The two then decided to live at their store, using the hose on their Hobart dishwasher to shower.

Meanwhile, Weller and Skiles were operating Clarksville Natural Grocery store. All four founders felt the time had come to launch a natural foods supermarket. At the time, there were very few supermarket-style natural food stores in the United States. The vast majority of natural foods stores were small boutique stores where selection could be limited due to the lack of shelf and freezer space. At the time, many health food stores operated using the cooperative, or co-op, business model. In co-ops, customers pay a membership fee, which typically provides them with certain benefits such as a discount on products. Some stores also offer members the ability to receive an even bigger discount if they volunteer to work at the store on occasion. Members are considered part owners, and the stores operate almost like nonprofits. The Whole Foods' founders, however, were not interested in the co-op model. While they were interested in providing the public with healthful food choices, they were also interested in creating profit for the company.

The first Whole Foods Market opened in Austin, Texas, on September 20, 1980. It had 10,500 square feet of space and a staff of 19 people. Unfortunately, a flood hit the Austin area in 1981 and most of the store was destroyed. Whole Foods was not insured, but customers and neighbors helped the four owners clean up the debris and repair the damage. Flexible creditors gave the company enough time to regain its financial footing.

EXPANSION AND ACQUISITIONS

Whole Foods growth strategy since its inception has been to buy other stores. Expansion did not begin in earnest until 1984, when Whole Foods opened locations in Houston and Dallas, Texas, and New Orleans, Louisiana. In 1989 the company opened its Palo Alto, California, store. During the 1990s, the company acquired Wellspring Grocery of

North Carolina, Bread & Circus of Massachusetts and Rhode Island, Mrs. Gooch's Natural Foods Markets of Los Angeles, Bread of Life of Northern California, and Fresh Fields Markets on the East Coast and in the Midwest.

This trend continued over the years. While the company opened its own locations, it also purchased other natural food stores. By the early 21st century, there were few chains that came close to Whole Foods in number of stores and coverage in the United States. The company's biggest competitor was Wild Oats, which by 2007 had 110 stores to Whole Foods' 191.

WHOLE FOODS' INNOVATIVE POLICIES

Despite the more traditional means of growing, Whole Foods could not have successfully maintained these stores or continued to grow without the mission-driven rather than profit-driven philosophy developed by founder and CEO John Mackey. Although the company also works toward increasing profits, its mission-driven philosophy is incorporated in its value statement. Mackey felt it was important for the company and its employees to feel that they were doing more than working for a company: they were giving consumers the opportunity to live a healthier lifestyle. To promote this idea, the company developed seven primary goals, each designed to please one of Whole Foods' groups of stakeholders. These goals (according to the Whole Foods corporate website as of 2011) are as follows:

- Sell the highest quality natural and organic products.
- Satisfy and delight customers.
- Support team members' happiness and excellence.
- Create wealth through profits and growth.
- Care about local communities and the environment.
- Create win-win partnerships with suppliers.
- Promote stakeholders' health by providing healthy eating education.

At the top of the list is selling high-quality natural products, which Whole Foods accomplishes by ensuring that none of its products contains artificial preservatives, colors, flavors, sweeteners, or hydrogenated fats. Although this definition of "natural," is not a universally accepted one, for many people it is a good first step away from overly processed foods. Whole Foods also seeks out and buys local, organic produce and buys its meat products from producers that treat the livestock humanely. These are all claims that no other large supermarket chain can make.

The real draw for many customers is that Whole Foods is a master of display. Ensuring that customers have an enjoyable shopping experience is not only one of the company's core values, it also helps to sell the food. A lot of effort is put into arranging and displaying the foods so that they are at their eye-appealing best. Another tactic the company uses is to have a wider selection of produce and products. Most mainstream grocery stores will not carry 20 or more varieties of apples, as they simply do not have the space. In contrast, Whole Foods might arrange an entire wall of apples with varying colors designed to please the eye.

While it can seem to traditional business people that Whole Foods' values may be somewhat in conflict with each other, Mackey disagrees. He believes that any company can and should pursue profits and a higher purpose at the same time. He told Nick Paumgarten for the *New Yorker,* "We're trying to do good. And we're trying to make money. The more money we make, the more good we can do."

In fact, the business model that Whole Foods has developed has been designed to give employees more autonomy and allow for employee creativity. The store is separated into districts, which operate almost like separate businesses. While there are overarching values, goals, and standards that each store needs to adhere to, store managers and teams are fully responsible for meeting those goals, and their customers' needs, in a customized way. This decentralization means that local stores can tailor operations to meet the local consumers' needs.

Whole Foods has also allowed employees to vote for the candidates they want to become new team members, rather than having a manager make the final selection. Employees have a say in how their area is designed, and how it is stocked, as long as it meets with the overall values and goals of the company. Whole Foods executives have also been transparent about the company's financial information, publishing the salaries of top executives and managers.

In 2007, Whole Foods launched a loan program for its suppliers, another first of its kind in the grocery supermarket industry. The company granted loans between US$1,000 and US$100,000 to companies that grow produce, raise livestock, and manufacture other food products that the company sells in its stores locally. Start-ups are limited to a maximum loan of US$25,000. The loan operates the same as traditional ones secured from a bank. Collateral is required, and the loan recipient makes payments with interest (between 5 percent and 9 percent in 2011). The supplier is required to provide a viable business plan proving that the company has the cash flow to repay the loan. The goal of the program is to encourage small local businesses to prosper and compete. As of 2011, some of the businesses that had received the loans included organic vegetable farmers, a heritage turkey grower, a nutritional protein bar maker, and a maker of body care products.

Another unique aspect of the company is the fact that it does not charge slotting fees to major manufacturers. Since the late 1990s, large grocery store chains began charging companies a fee to put a new product on their shelf. They claim that this helps them absorb the loss if the new product does not sell. These fees are called slotting fees. The practice of charging slotting fees has been controversial, and it has also been investigated by the U.S. Federal Trade Commission (FTC). Small and independent manufacturers have complained to the FTC that the fees put them at a disadvantage because they cannot afford to pay these costs, which can average $25,000 per new product. In addition, they claim that these fees result in a reduction of the variety of products from which U.S. consumers can choose. While these charges were under investigation in the early 2010s, slotting fees continue to be paid. Whole Foods, on the other hand, does not charge slotting fees, and it decides whether to place a product on its shelf based on whether it fits the description of natural, organic, and humanely produced, and if there is a demand for it.

CONTROVERSIES AND A MERGER

Despite the fact that the company is considered innovative, profitable, and successful, it has received its share of criticism. One example is its definition of natural. Although Whole Foods posts a list of ingredients it deems unacceptable in any of the products it markets or sells, the list does not include recombinant bovine growth hormone, a synthetic hormone used by dairy farmers to increase milk production. Another criticism is that Whole Foods caters to an "elite" or wealthy clientele because its products are too expensive for most U.S. consumers to buy. Whole Foods has worked to overcome this criticism by offering its own product line (365 Everyday Value Products) and publishing *The Whole Deal,* a bimonthly newsletter that contains coupons and money-saving ideas.

In February 2007 executives at both Whole Foods and Wild Oats announced that they were merging. The FTC questioned the merger, arguing that it violated antitrust laws. The FTC claimed that the two chains were the only competitors in their niche market and that their merger would have a negative impact on consumer choice, leading to higher prices and reduced levels of service. However, Judge Paul L. Friedman of Federal District Court in Washington, D.C., ruled in favor of the merger in August 2007 and the deal went through.

After 2007 Whole Foods and Mackey retrenched, refocusing on what made the store successful in the past: providing the freshest natural foods. In 2011 Whole Foods launched its "Health Starts Here" initiative, a program designed to educate consumers and help them make healthful food choices. Mackey stated that he would like the company to have a positive impact on the health of the nation. Like most of its other innovative programs, this one fosters its mission, while it also has the potential to increase profits.

BIBLIOGRAPHY

Apple, Lauri. "Whole Foods Union-Busting?" *Austin Chronicle,* December 20, 2002. Accessed January 15, 2012. http://www.austinchronicle.com/news/2002-12-20/115313/.

Harkinson, Josh. "Are Starbucks and Whole Foods Union Busters?" *Mother Jones,* April 6, 2009. Accessed January 15, 2012. http://motherjones.com/politics/2009/04/are-starbucks-and-whole-foods-union-busting.

Paumgarten, Nick. "Food Fighter: Does Whole Foods CEO Know What's Best for You?" *New Yorker,* January 4, 2010. Accessed January 15, 2012. http://www.newyorker.com/reporting/2010/01/04/100104fa_fact_paumgarten.

Whole Foods Market. "2010 Annual Report." Austin, TX, 2011. Accessed January 15, 2012. http://www.wholefoodsmarket.com/company/pdfs/ar10.pdf.

———. "Company History." Austin, TX. Accessed January 15, 2012. http://www.wholefoodsmarket.com/company/history.php.

"Whole Foods, Whole People, Whole Planet." Cleveland, OH: World Inquiry, Case Western Reserve Case Study, June 3, 2005. Accessed January 15, 2012. http://worldinquiry.case.edu/bankInnovationView.cfm?idArchive=304.

Wi-Fi Devices Benefit
from Industry Standardization

Wi-Fi is one of the top success stories of the technology industry. The term Wi-Fi typically refers to the technology that allows computers and other electronic devices to exchange data over a wireless network. Over the course of its short history, Wi-Fi journeyed from a well-kept secret to an enterprise networking solution, and, in the early 2010s, to worldwide popularity as a wireless connection to the Internet from home or "hotspot." In a single decade, Wi-Fi emerged from the unknown to become a household word.

In many places, Wi-Fi became the preferred method to connect to the Internet and local networks. Homes used Wi-Fi to maximize the number of devices that could be online at one time. Coffee shops, hotels, and airports provided Wi-Fi connectivity to patrons and travelers. Offices and schools provided Wi-Fi access to computer networks and user accounts. According to the Wi-Fi Alliance, a trade association, 300 million Wi-Fi-enabled units were shipped in the United States in 2007. In 2011 that number increased to 750 million. It was estimated that the number of Wi-Fi units shipped would be 1.2 billion in 2013 and that the use of Wi-Fi enabled devices would continue to climb throughout the 2010s.

Wi-Fi's success was not only due to it becoming the preferred method to connect to the Internet. There were several other accomplishments that contributed to Wi-Fi's worldwide acceptance. For instance, regulators and industry leaders worked together and overcame differences to develop a standard. Wi-Fi was the first radio frequency application that could be used without a license from the government. Having almost every computer sold come with built-in Wi-Fi shined as one of Wi-Fi's major accomplishments.

Even with all this success, Wi-Fi is subject to the same life-cycle challenges as all new products and technologies: development, expansion, maturity, and decline. What makes Wi-Fi unique in comparison to other technologies has nothing to do with the product life cycle, how the technology was developed, or who developed it. Wi-Fi's uniqueness comes from being the first technology developed with the support of the U.S. federal government.

TECHNOLOGY RESEARCH AND GOVERNMENT

Governments have a responsibility to maintain economic growth and social development. One way to stimulate economic growth is to encourage research and development in the private sector. Economic growth begins with research and development activities by corporations. New technologies and products that can enhance a consumer's quality of life create a desire and demand for these technologies. This demand creates business opportunities to keep the economic cycle rolling. The Carter administration (1977–1981) viewed deregulation as one way to create new opportunities. Positive results had been achieved in the airline, trucking, and railroad industries. Another federal agency that researched the feasibility for potential deregulation projects was the U.S. Federal Communications Commission (FCC).

The event that sparked the invention of Wi-Fi occurred on May 9, 1985, when the FCC adopted the Report and Order authorizing the license-exempt allocation and assignment of specified spread spectrum wideband frequencies. These radio frequencies were originally used by military applications but were found to have the potential for civil applications. In his report, "Spread Spectrum Systems with Commercial Applications," Robert Dixon explained the potential application of spread spectrum in global positioning systems, personal communications, vehicle location systems, and local area networks (LANs). The advantages of using these frequencies included the short range of the frequencies, resistance to interference, and difficulty intercepting the signal. Deregulation allowed these radio frequency bands to be used by communications applications that used spread spectrum technology.

However, it would take more than deregulation to boost the development of spread spectrum technology in the public sector. It required the cooperation of regulators and industry leaders to create an industry standard. Before the development of a wireless standard, several wireless equipment providers developed proprietary equipment that would work on their proprietary LANs. The problem with this arrangement was that equipment from one vendor was not compatible with equipment from another vendor.

Spread spectrum needed a champion to promote its application in the public sector. NCR Corporation saw access to a license-exempt radio frequency spectrum as a novel method to network cash registers and point-of-sale terminals using wireless technology. In 1988 NCR took the lead in developing an open standard for wireless LANs. NCR and Bell Labs approached the Institute of Electrical and Electronics Engineers (IEEE), and the 802.11 (the numeric designation for a specific set of standards) committee was formed. Other vendors began to see the benefits of adopting a standard and believed consumers would try a new technology if they could be assured of compatibility between product lines.

Even though having a wireless alternative to a wired infrastructure was appealing, a basic specification would not be accepted until 1997. It took technology vendors more than a decade to agree on definitions because of the diversity of the communications industry. Conflicts developed during the standard development process. These problems stemmed from opposition to the allocation of a license-exempt spectrum for radio communication and the uncertainty that the technology could be produced cost effectively. Despite these concerns, as soon as 802.11 was published, vendors began adapting their products to comply with and use this new standard.

WI-FI AND THE INTERNET

While most vendors were busy building Wi-Fi equipment for the business and enterprise markets, Apple, Inc., was busy exploring the consumer market for this new technology. To test this new market, Apple struck a deal with Lucent Technologies to manufacture a Wi-Fi adapter for Apple's laptop computers. In 1999 Apple introduced the AirPort as an option on the iBook computer.

Sales of Apple's new networking product caught the eye of other computer manufacturers who quickly followed suit. A variety of new Wi-Fi-compatible products began showing up in the consumer market. Soon after the introduction of the iBook, Intel Corporation added Wi-Fi capability into the Centrino chipset. This move proved to be very profitable for Intel. A survey by International Data Corporation showed that by 2003, the Centrino chip had been installed in 42 percent of notebook computers sold worldwide. In the 2010s virtually every notebook computer sold had Wi-Fi connectivity.

While Wi-Fi was taking hold in the consumer market, high-speed broadband Internet also became available to the home consumer. Wi-Fi made it easy to connect several computers and other devices to a single broadband link through Wi-Fi devices. Wi-Fi entered the consumer market as a home networking solution and 10 years later its main use was still for home networking.

WI-FI AND THE 21ST CENTURY

For Wi-Fi to maintain its lead in the technology industry, it must continually grow with the wants and needs of consumers. The challenge for Wi-Fi in the early 2010s has been to grow beyond the home consumer market. Past growth in the Wi-Fi market has been from the sale of Wi-Fi- enabled devices. The future holds many opportunities for providers of Wi-Fi services.

One Wi-Fi service that has found a niche with consumers is the Wi-Fi hotspot. Wi-Fi has moved into public places such as coffee shops, hotels, restaurants, and airports. These Wi-Fi hotspots make the Internet accessible to anyone no matter where they are or what device they are using. People can check their e-mail while grabbing a cup of coffee, share a business presentation while waiting for an airplane, or search for a hotel while having dinner. It is estimated that in 2003 there were 24,000 hotspots worldwide. In 2011 there were an estimated 1.5 million hotspots, and a report published by Informa Telecoms and Media projected worldwide hotspots to increase to 5.8 million by 2015.

One reason for this significant increase in hotspots is the growth of mobile data traffic. According to a November 9, 2011, *Computerworld,* article called "Number of Wi-Fi Hotspots to Quadruple by 2015," data traffic for 2G, 3G, and 4G networks will increase 10-fold by 2016. To handle this data traffic, cellular carriers must rely on a number of technologies, including Wi-Fi. It is projected that 750 million Wi-Fi-enabled cellular phones will be sold in 2013. The growth of e-book readers with Wi-Fi capability is another contributor to increased mobile data traffic. In 2009, 3 percent of e-book readers had Wi-Fi. By 2014 that number is projected to increase to 88 percent.

In support of its earlier deregulation efforts, the FCC has made changes to the rules that will allow for hybrids of the Wi-Fi technology and a new breed of standards. These Wi-Fi spin-offs may have many applications that could provide advantages over other existing wireless technologies. An extended version of Wi-Fi, called 802.16, is intended to be a wide range wireless networking solution with a faster data transfer rate. Another change on the Wi-Fi front is 802.15.3 which can provide high-capacity networking for home entertainment systems and consumes less power than Wi-Fi. The ZigBee specification includes a group of high-level communication protocols using lower-power digital radios and operates low-rate wireless personal area networks to control light switches, lamps, and electronic devices.

WHAT DOES THE FUTURE HOLD?

For Wi-Fi to maintain its hold on the market, it must keep evolving, expanding, and changing. The future success of Wi-Fi will be found in the continued interest of industry and government to work together and allow the evolution of the Wi-Fi standard. The history of Wi-Fi's development shows just how far wireless technologies can progress when government and industry work together.

Past actions by the FCC show a continued commitment on the part of the U.S. federal government and government agencies to continually seek out opportunities to open new technologies for development, innovation, and entrepreneurship. For example, in the early 2010s the FCC was looking at opening up airwaves that were assigned to television broadcasters but were not being used. Industry groups also showed a willingness to adopt these new opportunities and to develop standards that prove to be healthy for the efficient and profitable operation of business.

Businesses and industry also showed an eagerness to venture into new product areas and to develop new products. Consumers appeared willing and ready to accept these new technologies. A newcomer to the Wi-Fi generation is the automobile industry. OnStar Corporation, which provides services for motor vehicle operators, showed the industry that profits could be earned from selling Wi-Fi devices and from providing a service through that device.

More and more automobile manufacturers are including Wi-Fi capability in their cars.

Wi-Fi shows great potential in developing nations and may become a driving economic force. Since Wi-Fi was adopted so quickly and the demand for Wi-Fi devices is high, the price of Wi-Fi equipment has been pushed down to affordable levels. This has made it realistic to use off-the-shelf equipment to build wireless networks. In addition, the ability to transmit data over unlicensed, wireless networks makes it feasible to integrate technology into remote areas and areas with difficult geographic access.

BIBLIOGRAPHY

"173 Million Wi-Fi Direct-Enabled Devices to Ship in 2011." *Cell Phone Digest,* April 20, 2011. Accessed February 11, 2012. http://www.cellphonedigest.net/news/2011/04/173 _million_wifi_directenabled.php.

"Case History: A Brief History of Wi-Fi." *The Economist,* June 10, 2004. Accessed February 11, 2012. http://www.economist .com/node/2724397.

Chou, Charles, and Steve Shen. "Centrino Notebooks to Capture 42% of Global Market in 2003." *DigiTimes,* November 20, 2003. Accessed February 11, 2012. http://www.digitimes .com/news/a20031120A2003.html.

"Early Civil Spread Spectrum History." Washington, DC: Marcus Spectrum Solutions LLC, 2011. Accessed February 11, 2012. http://www.marcus-spectrum.com/page4/SSHist.html.

Lemstra, Wolter, et al. The Innovation Journey of Wi-Fi: The Road to Global Success. New York: Cambridge University Press, 2011.

"Motor City Meets Silicon Valley: Automotive Wi-Fi Chipset Revenue to Eclipse $100 Million by 2015." Scottdale, AZ: In-Stat, November 22, 2010. Accessed February 11, 2012. http://www.instat.com/newmk.asp?ID=2926&Sourc eID=00000652000000000000.

Ricknas, Mikael. "Number of Wi-Fi Hotspots to Quadruple by 2015." *Computerworld,* November 9, 2011. Accessed February 11, 2012. http://www.computerworld.com/s/article/9221672 /Number_of_Wi_Fi_hotspots_to_quadruple_by_2015.

Rubin, Ross. The Splint and Sprint of Wi-Fi. *ABC News,* January 26, 2012. Accessed Febaruary 29, 2012. http://abcnews.go .com/Technology/TechOnDeck/splint-sprint-wi-fi/story?id =15431301#.TzhXsMUyn9V.

Shilov, Anton. "Wi-Fi-Enabled Devices to Exceed 1.9 Billion Units by 2014 – Analysts." *Xbit Laboratories,* July 28, 2010. Accessed February 11, 2012. http://www.xbitlabs.com/news /networking/display/20100728234532_Wi_Fi_Enabled _Devices_to_Exceed_1_9_Billion_Units_by_2014_Analysts .html.

Wikipedia

Wikipedia is an online encyclopedia that allows users to generate content for the encyclopedia. The system facilitates the development of articles through which anyone may write about new topics or edit existing articles. Contributors do not need any credentials whatsoever to make changes to the site. Although skeptics argue about the accuracy of the articles, no one can dispute the success of the model. Established in 2001 as a side project for a sister site, Wikipedia generated content at an incredible pace. Still gaining momentum in 2011 as a fundamental resource on the Internet, the online encyclopedia was consistently ranked in the top 10 most visited sites in the world, according to Alexa Internet, Inc. The English Wikipedia alone included over 3.8 million articles and printing it out would produce the equivalent of roughly 1,600 volumes of the *Encyclopedia Britannica.*

Prior to Wikipedia's success, few believed that a team of voluntary contributors could write and edit an encyclopedia's content, much less curate a useful, informative, and largely objective viewpoint. Even the organization's founder, Jimmy Wales, described Wikipedia to the *Guardian* as a "completely insane idea." It was so insane, in fact, that Wales can claim little responsibility for the innovation, which came about due to sheer desperation as much as genius.

By the time Wales began his venture into online encyclopedias, posting information for free had become a trend. In 1999, two years before Wikipedia's debut, the *Encyclopedia Britannica* announced that its 32 print volumes would be published online. This decision was a drastic move for the company, which was beginning to face severe concerns over increasing competition from the Internet. The then 231-year-old publication had become

famous for its door-to-door sales and the innumerable volumes of print that were proudly displayed in homes across the United States and the United Kingdom. Entering the online market with a downgrade in price from the hefty US$1,250 print edition to Britannica.com's free membership (although premium services came with a price) marked the transition to a different era.

Another basic ingredient came from the open-source movement, which had become a major online trend in the 1990s. Linux, a personal computer operating system, was offered for free beginning in the middle of the decade. The only major competition facing Microsoft Windows, Linux was soon downloadable via a number of portals that were accessible across the globe. More importantly, the software was unencrypted, allowing programmers to see and suggest revisions to the code. Against expectations, thousands of programmers volunteered useful contributions by the end of the decade. Seven million people used Linux, a user-base that grew by 40 percent in 1997. According to Amy Harmon of the *New York Times,* "proponents say open source could harness the collective wisdom of the world's best software designers for social good, undermine the Microsoft Corporation's Windows monopoly, and propagate an operating system that does not crash." The positive sentiments surrounding the free model helped the operating system gain momentum, and open-source systems were demonstrated to have the potential for success.

The advent of wikis as a website format also played an integral role, as the name, Wikipedia, may suggest. In 1995, Howard "Ward" Cunningham launched the first website that used a wiki system. Called WikiWikiWeb after the Hawaiian word for "quick," the site granted users free rein to add material and edit the team's work.

Cunningham created WikiWikiWeb as an addendum to the Portland Pattern Repository, a forum for computer languages. Wikis enabled users to perform complex operations with website content easily, without relying on any prior knowledge of hypertext markup language (HTML) or software code. Wikipedia was a bold innovation, but it was a synthesis of preexisting technology, trends, and cultural expectations.

JIMMY WALES, FROM NUPEDIA TO WIKIPEDIA

Before he had the resources to devote to a venture as improbable as Wikipedia, Jimmy Dolan Wales, or "Jimbo," as he is known, was a futures and options trader for Chicago Options Associates. He was exceptionally well qualified for the profession, amassing a small fortune by the time he was age 30. Unsatisfied with mere number crunching, he transitioned to a career as an entrepreneur in 1996 when he launched an online search portal, Bomis.com, which became infamous for the "Bomis Babe Report," which covered attractive females ranging from celebrities to adult entertainment stars.

Wales's first online encyclopedia attempt was called Nupedia. Begun in 2000, Nupedia implemented a system of production that was similar to its competitors. Started in March as a private enterprise, Nupedia was to post articles written by experts, free of charge. Although requirements were slightly flexible, contributors who were known authors or held doctorate degrees in the field were given heavy preference. In order to publish on the site, prospective writers were required to submit résumés for approval. Articles were then sent through a seven-step, peer-review gauntlet before being accepted for online publication.

Despite Nupedia's for-profit classification, the business quickly proved to be a financial nightmare. Wales dispensed over US$250,000 in the first year, during which time less than 12 articles were completed. Stymied by the inefficiencies of his own system, Wales knew that the company required a shift in tactics in order to start producing articles. To expedite the encyclopedia's progress and dilute the cost of production, Wales and his chief editor, Lawrence Sanger, looked elsewhere for sources of inspiration. Sanger suggested applying wiki technology as a way to generate content for Nupedia and help the new site in its initial stages. Having paid an increasing amount of interest to the open-source movement in the four years prior, Wales saw the potential in the idea. With almost nothing to lose in terms of costs, Wales approved and launched the side project, Wikipedia, in January 2001.

Wikis allowed any user to post, flag, or change site content with a series of simple commands. New entries could be created easily and detailed instructions were posted on the site so that anyone could learn how to begin producing articles. The guidelines for content were also designed to be easy to follow. There were three main tenets, including requiring writing that took a neutral position. As an encyclopedia, it was the site's stated function to provide unbiased material, and the other two principles broke down neutrality into its key components, from a user's perspective. One explicit rule strictly prohibited original research, which prevented users from using Wikipedia as a personal outlet. In order for content to remain on the site, it needed to regurgitate information that was already published. The third tenet went further to thwart opinionated content. In a self-descriptive entry on verifiability, the site defines its criterion for inclusion: "The threshold for inclusion in Wikipedia is verifiability, not truth—whether readers can check that material in Wikipedia has already been published by a reliable source, not whether editors think it is true."

THE LARGEST ENCYCLOPEDIA ON EARTH

Within months of Wikipedia's launch it became clear that the website was more effective than Nupedia. It was less costly to maintain and it immediately outpaced its predecessor. By 2002 Wikipedia had produced 19,700 articles and the output was accelerating. One year later, when it contained 96,500 entries, Nupedia counted 24. Moreover, Wikipedia created a community of writers who edited, debated, and built buzz around the endeavor. As the site continued to grow at an astonishing pace, Wales created the Wikimedia Foundation, which spearheaded fund-raising and began other wiki projects, such as Wikiquote, Wikisource, Wikimedia Commons, Wikiversity, Wikispecies, Wikinews, and Meta-Wiki. The last of these was a site devoted to strategizing future Wiki projects and was, like all other wiki sites, developed by the user base.

Excited by the site's success, Wales continued to engage with the extensive community of Wikipedians. Within four years of its inception, the website had gathered hundreds of thousands of contributors. Around 200 of these treated the site like a full-time job, and 2,000 members each added over 100 edits every month. Of the other contributors, 10,000 made five or more edits in the same time period. Disavowing pretensions to grandeur within this community, Wales signed his communications affectionately with his nickname, "Jimbo." For someone whose organization had produced one million articles by early 2006, at a rate of 1,251 articles per day, Wales' behavior showed that the entrepreneur learned as much from his organization as its contributors learned from him. As of 2011 the founder's own Wikipedia user page read: "You can edit this page! Really, you can! Please feel free to do so. Make an edit . . . I like to keep it a certain way, but the thing is, I trust you." He took the same approach with the website itself, allowing it to expand according to user suggestions and interests. For example, 50 encyclopedias sprang up in additional languages and were producing their own content on Wikipedia by early 2004.

Over the first decade of the 21st century Wikipedia outstripped all other encyclopedias. From a quantitative standpoint, no other organization could match the information giant. By comparison, *Encyclopedia Britannica* reported roughly 100,000 articles in its collection in 2011. In the same year, Wikipedia claimed 3.8 million articles in the English version alone. Due to the enormity of the site, many of these articles claimed top spots on search engine results pages, expanding the online presence and fame of the organization to rival some of the world's most prominent enterprises.

DEBATING THE CREDIBILITY OF WIKIPEDIA

Toward the end of the first decade of the 21st century and beyond, article generation flagged. The number of total editors actually dropped by roughly 1,500 in 2009 and fewer articles were added on a daily basis. In 2011 Wikipedia editors estimated that if the deceleration continued, the site's content would stabilize at a total of 4.4 million articles. Wales attributed this trend to a natural maturation process. He argued that as Wikipedia expanded to its broadest scope, growth of its user base would come to a halt.

One problem Wikipedia has had to deal with is vandalism, in which false information is deliberately added to a Wikipedia entry. In December 2009 Wikipedia implemented a new process, called "flagged revisions," which affected entries that were the most consistent targets for vandals. The editing process was changed for these particular entries, which included celebrities and political figures. Instead of proposed edits taking effect immediately, they were held in queue for a trusted Wikipedian to look at. Muckraking and other biased postings were rejected. The change in Wikipedia policy was widely criticized for making the site less open to editing by anyone.

Vandalism continued to be a pressing issue for the online encyclopedia. Although the sheer quantity of content that Wikipedia managed to produce impressed the media and public, scholars and other skeptics questioned the quality of the content and refrained from using the resource. A 2010 study conducted by researchers at the University of California at Irvine demonstrated that approximately 75 percent of entries were high quality. Although this figure was impressive, given that articles could be edited by anyone, serious researchers could not use the resource. Wales and other Wikipedians ventured a number of possible solutions to this main problem. The site used an entry rating system, in which featured articles

had to be approved by official editors. Eighty-six percent of featured articles were considered to be of high quality by the Irvine study.

However, the democratic system did produce certain advantages over the traditional competition. In order to save time and money, professionally written encyclopedias adopted a number of rules, some of which prevented good and useful information from being published. In an interview with David Weinberger, author of "Everything is Miscellaneous: The Power of the New Digital Disorder," for *Wired* in May 2007, Wales pointed out: "A too ruthless consistency really tries to chop through the messiness of the world in a way that may not make a lot of sense." Prior to Wikipedia, rule-making ability was doled out, exclusively, to individuals with professional training and significant experience who made decisions for everybody. On Wikipedia, arguments were conducted on a case-by-case basis. This allowed for nuanced positions to be developed. For instance, rather than mandating that blogs be avoided as sources, users were free to cite whatever content they wished. If a blog was cited, then authors and editors could discuss the validity of the source afterward. Experts in a field sometimes publish their opinions and results of their studies on their personal blog, and in many of these cases a good argument could be presented for the inclusion of the material. Traditional encyclopedias did not share the same flexibility. However, although Wikipedia's democratic process for content creation was clearly powerful and useful, there was still a question of whether it could be used for rigorous scholarship.

THE NEXT GENERATION OF WIKIS

Wikipedia made information readily available, but its impact reached beyond that. Before it was three years old, the online encyclopedia succeeded in popularizing online collaboration, with all the power and inherent messiness of the wiki template. The Wikimedia Foundation itself created a number of offshoots, with varying levels of success. Fan clubs, scholars, and businesses alike started their own wikis. As early as 2004, one could explore and contribute to the Tolkien Wiki, TrekWiki, Tourbus Wiki, among others. Likewise, wikis were constructed for video games, allowing users to explore secrets collaboratively or find solutions when stumped by a particular game level or area. Businesses used wikis both internally (as a working tool), externally (to increase their online presence), or in some combination of the two. Wikileaks, a site that published comments and leaked documents that allege or demonstrate misconduct, became one of the most controversial wiki sites in the early 2010s. It became a powerful tool for the cause of transparency in government, but major financial institutions such as Bank of America,

Visa, Mastercard, and PayPal, forbid online donations to it.

Whether or not Wikipedia can resolve its quality assurance problems, it has left an indelible stamp on the Internet. In the decade since its inception in 2001, the project has demonstrated the incredible power that wikis can bring to online communities everywhere.

BIBLIOGRAPHY

Alexa Internet, Inc. "Wikipedia.org." San Francisco, CA, 2011. Accessed December 6, 2011. http://www.alexa.com/siteinfo /wikipedia.org.

Barnett, Emma. "Jimmy Wales Interview: Wikipedia Is Focusing on Accuracy." *Telegraph,* November 17, 2009. Accessed January 12, 2012. http://www.telegraph.co.uk/technology /wikipedia/6589487/Jimmy-Wales-interview-Wikipedia-is -focusing-on-accuracy.html.

"Britannica Goes Online, Free." *Wired,* October 19, 1999. Accessed December 6, 2011. http://www.wired.com/techbiz /media/news/1999/10/31992.

Encyclopedia Britannica. "About Our Store." Chicago, 2011. http://store.britannica.com/pages/about-us. Accessed January 11, 2012.

Harmon, Amy. "For Sale: Free Software; Backers of Linux Say System Is Basis for Revolutionizing Computer Business." *New York Times,* September 28, 1998. Accessed December 6, 2011. http://www.nytimes.com/1998/09/28/business/for-sale-free -software-backers-linux-say-system-basis-for-revolutionizing .html?src=pm.

Hof, Rob. "Wikis' Winning Ways." *Bloomberg Businessweek,* June 7, 2004. Accessed December 6, 2011. http://www.business week.com/magazine/content/04_23/b3886141.htm.

Javanmardi, Sara, and Cristina Lopes. "Statistical Measure of Quality in Wikipedia." Paper Presented at the Workshop on Social Media Analytics, Washington D.C., July 25, 2010. Accessed December 6, 2011. http://snap.stanford.edu /soma2010/papers/soma2010_18.pdf.

Tweeney, Dylan. "Wikipedia Is Just the Start: An Interview with Jimmy Wales." *Wired,* May 29, 2007. Accessed December 6, 2011. http://www.wired.com/epicenter/2007/05/wikipedia _is_ju.

"User: Jimbo Wales." *Wikipedia.* San Francisco, CA: Wikimedia Foundation, Inc. Accessed December 6, 2011. http://en .wikipedia.org/wiki/User:Jimbo_Wales.

Waldman, Simon. "Who Knows?" *Guardian,* October 25, 2004. Accessed December 6, 2011. http://www.guardian.co.uk /technology/2004/oct/26/g2.onlinesupplement.

"Wikimedia Foundation, Inc." *International Directory of Company Histories.* Farmington Hills, MI: The Gale Group, Inc., 2010. Accessed December 6, 2011. http://www.answers .com/topic/wikimedia-foundation.

"Wikipedia: Administrators." *Wikipedia.* San Francisco, CA: Wikimedia Foundation, Inc., 2011. Accessed December 6, 2011. http://en.wikipedia.org/wiki/Wikipedia:Administrators.

"Wikipedia: Five Pillars." *Wikipedia.* San Francisco, CA: Wikimedia Foundation, Inc., 2011. Accessed December 6, 2011. http://en.wikipedia.org/wiki/Wikipedia:Five_pillars.

"Wikipedia: Good Articles." *Wikipedia.* San Francisco, CA: Wikimedia Foundation, Inc., 2011. Accessed December 6, 2011. http://en.wikipedia.org/wiki/Wikipedia:Good_articles.

"Wikipedia: Neutral Point of View." *Wikipedia.* San Francisco, CA: Wikimedia Foundation, Inc., 2011. Accessed December 6, 2011. http://en.wikipedia.org/wiki/Wikipedia:Neutral _point_of_view.

"Wikipedia: No Original Research." *Wikipedia.* San Francisco, CA: Wikimedia Foundation, Inc., 2011. Accessed December 6, 2011. http://en.wikipedia.org/wiki/Wikipedia:No _original_research.

"Wikipedia: Size of Wikipedia." *Wikipedia.* San Francisco, CA: Wikimedia Foundation, Inc., 2011. Accessed December 6, 2011. http://en.wikipedia.org/wiki/Wikipedia:Size_of _Wikipedia.

"Wikipedia: Verifiability." *Wikipedia.* San Francisco, CA: Wikimedia Foundation, Inc., 2011. Accessed January 11, 2012. http://en.wikipedia.org/wiki/Wikipedia:Verifiability.

Xerox Corporation: Document Management Products and Services

Xerox Corporation (Xerox) is one example of a business that strives to operate in accordance with a strategic plan (a thorough mission statement, a list of realistic and attainable goals, and clearly defined objectives for tasks to help the business attain its goals and fulfill its mission). Strategic plans can help an organization stay focused in order to achieve goals, but these plans are not foolproof. Through 100 years of good and bad strategic planning, Xerox has consistently emerged as an industry leader, and the Xerox Copier has played a major role in this success. According to Xerox's 2010 annual report, revenues in document technology products (copiers, printers, multifunction devices, and related supplies) accounted for US$10.3 billion of Xerox's total revenue of US$21.6 billion in 2010.

Xerox has had a long history in the document technology industry. The company was founded in 1906 and produced photographic paper and equipment. It expanded into the manufacture of photocopiers, and in the 2010s has produced a full line of document products and services designed to save consumers and businesses time and money. Xerox evolved in the photocopying industry and offered more than just photocopy paper and black-and-white copy machines. The company has remained an industry leader by introducing a colorful mix of printers, digital printing presses, scanners, and fax machines. The company also offers document management services such as consulting, imaging, content management, and document outsourcing services.

As stated at the Xerox website, the company's mission is to be the leader in document technologies, products, and services that improve work processes and business results. Xerox has stayed on this path and followed its mission, which has allowed the business to operate successfully and maintain its lead over other copier manufacturers. Maintaining this lead required Xerox to take risks and invest capital in research and development projects that would create new copier, document reproduction, and document storage technologies. Aided by some key acquisitions, Xerox maintained its lead in the copier industry because of its introduction of desktop copying in 1963, laser printing in 1969, and color copying in 1973.

BEFORE COPIERS

The Xerox Corporation started out in 1906 as the Haloid Company. When Haloid entered the photography paper business, it did not offer much of a competitive threat to then industry leader, Eastman Kodak Company. It was not long before Haloid was sold, in 1912, to businessman Gilbert E. Mosher. Its founders remained to run the day-to-day business while the new owner broadened the company's reach by opening sales offices in Chicago, Illinois; Boston, Massachusetts; and New York, New York. To further increase the company's market share, the board of directors decided to develop a new photocopy paper. It took until 1933 to develop this new paper, but it proved to be Haloid's salvation from the Great Depression. The next year, Haloid's sales were close to US$1 million. This put Haloid in an excellent position during World War II, when the U.S. military needed high-quality photographic paper to use for reconnaissance purposes. Supplying photographic paper to the military gave the company an advantage when, after the war, new competitors began entering the photographic paper market. It also put Haloid in a position to look for opportunities to develop new products.

In 1935 Haloid ventured into new markets and purchased the Rectigraph Company, a photocopy machine manufacturer. It required capital funding, which was financed by a public stock offering in 1936, to pay for this acquisition. Haloid did not stop there. This was just the beginning of the company's journey into the document reproduction equipment business. An opportunity that popped onto the horizon was a process called xerography. Xerography, invented in 1938 by Chester Carlson, used electricity to transfer images from one piece of paper to another. In 1944 Battelle Memorial Institute, a nonprofit organization, signed a royalty-sharing agreement with Carlson and developed commercial applications for xerography. In 1947 Haloid approached Battelle about producing a machine that could take advantage of this new process. The xerographic copier became an idea that Haloid could bring to fruition.

Haloid's XeroX Copier (the initial spelling of Xerox) debuted in 1949. On first look, the investment Haloid made in the copier appeared to be a mistake. The copier was difficult to use, created a mess, and frequently made errors. However, it was not a complete loss. The copier could be salvaged and sold as a method of making masters for offset printing, a form of printing in which is first transferred (offset) to a plate before being placed on the printable surface. In spite of a failed first attempt at the xerographic copier, Haloid was able to recuperate its investment and make a profit. The company did not give up on the xerographic process and invested its profits in the next generation of xerographic copiers.

For the next decade, Haloid made short strides with xerography and photocopying machines. Haloid licensed the xerography patents to competitors RCA Corporation, IBM, Inc., and General Electric Company. A new Xerox factory and Xerox copier showrooms were built. Three new photography papers were introduced. An agreement was reached with overseas affiliate Rank Xerox to build a factory and distribution system in Europe. In 1958, Haloid changed its name to Haloid Xerox, and then just Xerox three years later. The company's future now depended on its ability to build a demand and a market for xerography products and services.

In 1959 Xerox introduced the Xerox 914 copier. It was an automatic plain paper copier, the first of its kind. Xerox's limited advertising budget could have hindered sales of the Xerox 914. Creative thinking led Xerox to use some inventive techniques to target business owners, such as lease arrangements to make the copiers affordable. The Xerox 914 exceeded expectations and became quite successful. The enormous growth in revenue allowed Xerox to invest in the growing copier market and to acquire other businesses along the way. Xerox grew to be one of the 100 largest corporations in the United States by the end of the 1960s.

STRAYING OFF THE PATH

In the 1970s Xerox began to diversify. With enormous growth during the previous decade and capital to invest in the company, Xerox started to venture into new markets and industries. As a spin-off of its copier business, Xerox decided to develop the paperless office concept. This led to the purchase of several small computer companies and the opening of the Xerox Palo Alto Research Center (PARC) in 1970. However, Xerox's foray into the computer industry was not successful. Investments in computer firms lost money. Xerox took the lead in developing technologies but encountered problems creating and marketing products based on those technologies. Xerox's computer division and copier division competed for company resources and did not communicate with each other. Xerox also moved into the financial services industry and purchased insurance companies and brokerage firms.

With so many distractions, Xerox was unable to fully concentrate on its copier business. Even though a significant amount of money was spent on copier research and development, new products were not appearing on the market. Xerox showed signs of losing its edge as the leading supplier of copiers and began feeling the effects of its first real competition since it entered the copier market. In 1970 IBM introduced its first office copier. Soon after, Kodak, Ricoh Company, Ltd, and Canon, Inc., appeared on the scene. The competition did more than just follow Xerox into the copier market; some used Xerox's marketing techniques and offered leasing options. Others worked furiously to improve on the copier and offered copiers that were less expensive and more reliable. Consequently, Xerox lost market share. In 1974 Xerox had 85 percent of the worldwide market for plain paper copiers. By 1985 its market share had dropped to 40 percent. Even with this loss of market share, from 1970 to 1980, revenues increased from US$1.6 billion to US$8 billion respectively.

GETTING BACK ON TRACK

In the 1980s it was time for the company to refocus and determine ways to regain the competitive lead it once held. A corporate reorganization seemed to be a solution, and changes were initiated. Xerox adopted some of the quality-control techniques used by its competitors, developed a line of low-end copiers, released several new products, and reduced manufacturing costs. These moves all helped to regain market share.

Some of the new product releases made during the 1980s proved to be a success. In 1982 Xerox introduced the 10-Series copier, which used a microprocessor to operate the copier and to perform different tasks on various types of paper. The 10-Series copier allowed Xerox to utilize technology developed at PARC. Xerox also released laser printers to the market and quickly built a US$1 billion business, although it had spent US$3 billion in research and development.

In the 1980s and 1990s Xerox made a number of changes such as discontinuing business units, selling their insurance and financial services businesses, laying off employees, and creating a new marketing organization. These changes provided Xerox with the boost it needed to gain competitiveness, and Xerox slowly rose back toward the top. In 1989 Xerox received the Malcolm Baldrige National Quality Award. Once again the industry leader, Xerox foresaw the market moving from offset printing to digital printing and copying. Xerox expanded on its line of copiers and developed a series of desktop laser printers, digital color copiers, and multifunction facsimile-copier-telephone machines.

Xerox had evolved into "The Document Company." The switch from analog-based equipment to digital document processing products and the addition of color copying were both fortuitous moves. The company also saw a market for copiers and printers for the small office and home office. From 1995 to 1997 analog copiers saw no revenue growth, but revenues for digital products reached US$6.7 billion by 1997. During this time, there was a 46 percent increase in revenues from color printers and copiers. Xerox kept producing new products, releasing 80 of them in 1997, which was double the number released in 1996.

At the beginning of 2000 Xerox was again in line with its corporate mission. The company had completed its reorganization and regained its place as the leader in the photocopy and document management market. Xerox introduced printers that used solid ink technology. Solid inks produced brilliant quality prints using nontoxic inks at a cost savings. Twenty-eight new products were introduced in 2002 and 2003, with most being digital and color copiers and multifunction devices. New document-related services were also offered by Xerox.

THE FUTURE LOOKS BRIGHT ONCE AGAIN

Xerox, with a history that has spanned over 100 years, was a shining example of how much success could be achieved when a strong mission statement was developed and consistently followed. As long as Xerox developed products and services that met the goals and objectives of its mission, the company maintained its lead position in the industry. When it ventured into areas outside its mission, the company lost standing in the industry.

BIBLIOGRAPHY

Lewis, Scott M., Mary McNulty, and David L. Salamie. "Xerox Corporation." In *International Directory of Company Histories,* edited by Jay P. Pederson. Vol. 69, 374–380. Detroit: St. James Press, 2005. Gale Virtual Reference Library (GALE|CX3429600112). Accessed March 2, 2012. http://go.galegroup.com/ps/i.do?id=GALE%7CCX3429600112&v=2.1&u=itsbtrial&it=r&p=GVRL&sw=w.

Terran, Ed. "Brief History of the Xerox Company." Mfpcopier.com. Accessed February 14, 2012. http://www.mfpcopier.com/blog/printer-copiers/brief-history-of-the-xerox-company.

Xerox Corporation. "Xerox 2010 Annual Report: Operations Review of Segment Revenue and Operating Profit." Norwalk, CT. Accessed February 14, 2012. http://www.xerox.com/annual-report-2010/financial-analysis/operations.html.

———. "Xerox History: Interactive Timeline." Norwalk, CT. Accessed February 14, 2012. http://www.xerox.com/about-xerox/company-history/enus.html.

Index

OWENS COMMUNITY COLLEGE
P.O. Box 10,000
Toledo, OH 43699-1947